DEMCO

A Critical & Exegetical Commentary
on the Book of Amos

A Critical & Exegetical Commentary on the Book of Amos

THE TEXT OF THE REVISED VERSION

EDITED WITH

INTRODUCTION, NOTES & EXCURSUSES

BY

RICHARD S. CRIPPS, M.A., B.D.

St John's College, Cambridge

WITH A FOREWORD

BY

R. H. KENNETT, D.D.

Sometime Regius Professor of Hebrew in the University of Cambridge

LONDON

S·P·C·K

1969

First published 1929
Second edition 1955
Reprinted 1960, 1969

SBN 281 00346 7

Reprinted offset in Great Britain by
The Camelot Press Ltd., London and Southampton

UXORI CARISSIMAE
MEORUM LABORUM
ADIUTRICI

PUBLISHER'S NOTE

After a lifetime of service to Old Testament studies, the Reverend R. S. Cripps died while the second edition of his book was still in proof. The Reverend D. M. G. Stalker added to the help he had already given to Mr. Cripps by seeing the book through the final stages of its production.

CONTENTS

FOREWORD

Within the past fifty years a great change has gradually come about in the study of the Old Testament. Whereas the attention of students was formerly directed almost exclusively to the narrative portions of the Hebrew Scriptures, and the study of Old Testament History (so called) consisted, to a great extent, of the unedifying committing to memory of lists of names such as those of the kings of Israel and Judah, and of unrelated incidents, the centre of gravity of the Old Testament, so to speak, has now shifted to the Prophets. The Prophetical books, of which a generation ago little more than the mere names were generally known—apart from passages made familiar by such works as Handel's *Messiah*—are now commonly recognised as of primary importance for the right understanding of that development of religion in Israel which culminated in the New Testament. For detailed study in this connection the book of Amos is peculiarly suitable, not only because Amos himself was one of the earliest of the Prophets whose teaching has been preserved in separate books, but also because the book which bears his name is well adapted for consecutive reading, and *in the main* presents fewer difficulties of interpretation than some of the other Prophetical books.

Problems there are, however, connected with this book, some which it presents in common with other pre-exilic Prophetic literature, such, for example, as the relation of the canonical Prophets to what may be called the established religion of their time and to earlier prophets such as Elijah and Elisha; and some connected with its literary recension after the time of the Prophet whose name it bears. In the following work readers of the Old Testament will be enabled to gain a knowledge of the nature of such problems, clearly stated, as they are, by an enthusiastic and experienced teacher; and by not a few it will be reckoned an advantage that they should be analysed and dealt with by a scholar whom no one acquainted with Old Testament scholarship will for a moment accuse of reckless or unconsidered theorising.

For a complete understanding of any one book of the Prophets—so far as a complete understanding is possible in view of the fragmentary character of most of the extant Prophetic literature, and of the unsatisfactory condition of the Hebrew text—a comprehensive study of *all* the Prophetic books is essential; but for every one interested in Theology specialisation must, at least to some extent, precede correlation; and for this special study Mr Cripps' book should prove extremely useful.

ROBERT H. KENNETT

1929

PREFACE TO THE FIRST EDITION

Amos is one of the most important Prophets, if not *the* most important, of the Old Testament. He has found many excellent commentators, the works of some of whom will doubtless outlive the youngest theological student of the present generation. It is a fact, however, that in the investigation of the Prophetic books, and indeed of the Old Testament generally, much fresh ground has been broken since there appeared such editions as those of Professor (now Principal) Sir G. A. Smith (in 1896, 2nd edn 1928), Professor S. R. Driver (1897), Professor R. F. Harper (1905) and E. A. Edghill (1913). Upon the Continent, during the present century, a large number[1] of commentaries on Amos or on the Minor Prophets as a whole have been published; and the useful work of Nowack has been enriched by two revisions. Moreover, the rise of the Eschatological theory of prophecy, whatever view may be taken of its ultimate place, has called for a further examination of the book of Amos. And there are other problems which have come to the fore recently, *e.g.* those connected with the characteristics of prophetic inspiration—ecstasy, audition, vision—and with the institution of sacrifice. For such reasons it would appear that the time has come—if it is not already overdue—for the publication in English of a new commentary on the great Prophet. The present edition is an attempt to supply what seems to be needed. In it the author has endeavoured to apply afresh the principles of textual, literary and historical criticism, and to bring to bear upon the exegesis such aids as are afforded by the study of archaeology, and of the prophetic and didactic literatures[2] of ancient peoples other than Israel. Hence it is hoped by the writer that technical students, ministers of religion and others will find in the commentary not only a

---

[1] See Bibliography, p. 106.
[2] Some of this literature is made available to English readers for the first time.

considerable amount of fresh exegesis but a good deal of new material not to be met with in the work of his predecessors.

A few words upon the plan of the commentary may not be out of place. (i) It was felt that, although the English Revised Version is now well-nigh fifty years old, for practical purposes it was the only text upon which a commentary could usefully be based. The notes, however, indicate how frequently it has been necessary both (1) to depart from the Hebrew Massoretic text which lay behind this version, and, (2) to translate otherwise than did those great scholars of a generation ago. (ii) The footnotes at the bottom of the pages contain not merely many of the references to authorities quoted, but also certain citations in ancient or modern languages, and points of more detailed criticisms, etc., which otherwise would interrupt the course of the exposition. (iii) By furnishing additional notes at the end of the book it has been possible to deal more fully with several matters. These more advanced comments upon the text, having their own headings, are self-contained and can be used alone. (iv) The four excursuses represent an attempt to deal with problems of considerable significance, which either necessarily arise in an ultimate interpretation of the message of Amos, or which proceed from a discussion of the text itself. As a result of this plan there would seem to be an advantage to those readers who do not possess much technical knowledge, or who do not wish to enter into the subject in detail.[1]

It will be seen that, in the citation of Semitic terms and phrases, for the most part the practice of transliteration has been adopted. This use appears to be increasing in popularity in learned works, both in German and in English. The scheme employed in the present volume is shewn on p. 109. It is hoped that the readings and renderings of the Targum upon Amos may be of help especially to students who are beginning to work at the Aramaic "paraphrase".

---

[1] By neglecting the footnotes, the additional notes, and the excursuses, theological students and those with but limited time at their disposal should be able to acquire a working knowledge of the book of Amos by using the main body of the notes, together with the earlier portion of the Introduction.

In the study of the Amos-volume there are both great questions and comparatively insignificant details upon which scholars hold entirely differing opinions. The present writer, so far as it has been practicable within the limitations of space, has endeavoured to be fair to views other than his own. Furthermore, dogmatism, being alien to the spirit of pure scholarship, is to be avoided; and in the existing condition of our knowledge it is repeatedly necessary for a commentator to qualify his statements. This very qualification by means of such terms as "probably" and "possibly" may be regarded by some readers as a defect. But, at times when absolute certainty is not attainable, the use of these adverbs becomes imperative. The dictum attributed to the late Lord Morley is sound: "there is a 'perhaps' that comes not of vagueness, but of a desire for greater precision".[1] And in more senses than one Joseph Butler's saying is true, "To *us*, probability is the very guide of life".

In case this commentary is read by any to whom the modern outlook and methods of treatment are more or less unfamiliar, a word may be permitted upon the general position which, for want of a less ambiguous description, is styled "critical". Criticism concerns the true form of the text, its authorship and also its meaning to the men who first heard or read the message. It must be obvious that the processes of *textual*, *literary* and, in the widest sense, *historical* criticism, are absolutely essential for the solution of difficulties raised by a book, such as Amos, which was written fully twenty-six centuries ago. Especially important is the problem of theological outlook. The religious conceptions of the New Testament must not be forced into the Old Testament. In one sense misleading (particularly in the first clause) is the phrase associated with the name of St Augustine, *in Vetere (Testamento) Novum latet, in Novo Vetus patet*.[2] Furthermore, with

---

[1] Also (as experience in the lecture-room suggests) there is a still further use of "perhaps", in introducing a topic mainly for the provoking of thought.

[2] No apology is necessary for quoting the passage in its popular form. The actual words occur in a subordinate clause, "although both the New Testament lies hidden in the Old, and the Old is made clear in the New" (*quanquam et in Vetere Novum lateat, et in Novo Vetus pateat*).—*Quaest. in Hept.* LXXIII.

all the marvellous greatness of the Old Testament it cannot be said too strongly in the interests of twentieth-century ethical religion that not a little of the Israelite system "had its day" with the people for whom the teacher's message was first designed. To much in the conceptions within the pages of the Old Testament the words of Tennyson may be applied:

> Our little systems have their day;
> They have their day and cease to be:
> They are but broken lights of thee,
> And thou, O Lord, art more than they.

But also, surely, Holy Scripture contains something besides what can be treated by means of grammar, dictionary, history and comparative religion.[1]

It is the desire of the writer of this commentary that it may not only contribute somewhat further towards the discriminating study of the immortal poet-preacher, but also in so doing advance the knowledge of and reverence for the God Whom we, inheritors of twenty Christian centuries, worship. May God Who, by His Spirit, 'spake through the prophets', by the same Spirit give us a right judgment in all things. To those who desire the blessings of true religion the Bible is (even as it was portrayed to Christian in *The Pilgrim's Progress*) 'the best of books'. To analyse one of its incomparable volumes, placing it in its true historical setting in the past, should lead both to a greater apprehension of truth for to-day and to guidance for conduct even in the future. He who was, in a sense, the first of the prophets still proclaims 'SEEK THE LORD, AND YE SHALL LIVE'.

The writer desires to express his gratitude to Professor Kennett and Dr S. A. Cook, both of whom formerly were his teachers. Dr Kennett has kindly contributed an Introductory Note and has made a number of most useful suggestions. Dr Cook has generously read the greater part of the proof, giving much valuable help by criticisms and suggestions in

---

[1] Though the commentary is essentially a critical one, occasionally there will be found brief comments of a religious or ethical character after the method of Pusey's great work.

matters both archaeological and general. The writer is extremely indebted to his friend the Rev. Thos. R. Browne, B.D., Rector of Earl Soham, Suffolk, Examining Chaplain to the Bishop of St Edmundsbury and Ipswich, who has given the greatest possible assistance by reading helpfully a large part of the proof, by verifying many Biblical citations, including all the references to the Ancient Versions, and by undertaking the arduous task of compiling the indexes. He wishes to acknowledge the kindness of Dr Alan Gardiner, the Egyptologist, Dr J. K. Fotheringham, of the University Observatory, Oxford, Dr J. T. MacCurdy, Lecturer in Psychotherapy at Cambridge, and of his revered friend, Dr A. Lukyn Williams of Jesus College, the Rabbinical scholar, who have read certain parts of the proof and have given specialised criticism thereon. He also wishes to thank his friend and former pupil, the Rev. A. M. Ramsey, of Magdalene College, for reading carefully in one form or another a considerable amount of the book, and for checking a proportion of the Biblical references. To these and others who have helped in various ways the writer's cordial thanks are due. Responsibility, however, for statements made and conclusions arrived at rests with the author alone.

Thanks are due to the Delegates of the Clarendon Press, Oxford, and the Syndics of the Cambridge University Press, for leave to print the text of the Revised Version. The author desires also to express his appreciation of the kindness and courtesy of Dr W. K. Lowther Clarke, Editorial Secretary to the S.P.C.K., and of the skill and accuracy of the readers and staff of the Cambridge University Press.

R. S. CRIPPS

HORNINGSEY VICARAGE, CAMBRIDGE

7 June 1929

PREFACE TO THE SECOND EDITION

The issue of a second edition provides the author with the opportunity of expressing his appreciation of the reception given to this Commentary by reviewers and readers. By means of this new extended preface an attempt has been made to indicate the progress in the study of Amos since the commentary was first published. References to recent work are given, and in many cases quotations are set out. In addition, it has been found possible to incorporate a few alterations in the text of the commentary itself within the limitations of the photographic method employed. On page xl will be found a bibliography of commentaries upon Amos (with dates) which have appeared since the original edition. Much has been written upon the prophets during the last twenty or thirty years by British, American and Continental scholars. There has been an increasing output by Scandinavian writers. For convenience, this Preface is divided into sections, and accordingly no additional entries are necessary in the Indexes. For general abbreviations see p. 108.

I desire to express my sincere thanks to the Reverend D. M. G. Stalker, B.D., Lecturer in Biblical Studies in the University of Edinburgh, for valuable research in German, Scandinavian and Dutch writers in connection with Sections II and IV and especially Section III in the composition of which he has had a large share. I am also most grateful for the help Mr. Stalker has given in seeing this Edition through the press.

I. ARCHAEOLOGY AND THE BOOK OF AMOS

(i) **Excavations in Samaria.** Reference was made in the Commentary (p. 159) to the Harvard Expedition (1908–1910) to the city of Samaria. The British archaeologist, J. W. Crowfoot, led a further expedition there in 1931 to 1935.

This was sponsored by Harvard University, the Hebrew University in Jerusalem, the Palestine Exploration Fund, the British Academy, and the British School of Archaeology in Jerusalem. Several of the discoveries of this 'Joint Expedition' are of interest to the student of the book of Amos.

(a) Though no investigation of the walls of Samaria was made, the excavations revealed the strength of the palace or citadel area. This was defended by a wall, built in the period of Omri and Ahab, and repaired probably in that of Jeroboam II. It was constructed of regularly bonded stonework, with stones often three feet in length, in the form of casemates, giving an overall width of 32 feet.[1] These discoveries seem to suggest a reason why the capture of Samaria (predicted by the prophet Amos) should have occupied, according to the account in 2 Kings, no less than three years. (2 Ki. xvii. 1–6; see Am. iv. 1–3, vi. 1, 11.) (b) The Joint Expedition found some inscribed potsherds ('ostraca') dating from about half a century before Amos. Like those discovered by the Harvard Expedition they confirm that, in spite of the known prevalence of the cult of Baal and of foreign gods, Jehovah was worshipped in Samaria. One ostracon was read by E. L. Sukenik as 'dedicated to *Yah*'. The personal names '(Blessed be) Ahaz*iah*,' and '*Yo*-yesha' (a parallel form of the name Isaiah), containing the Divine Name were inscribed on others.[2]

(c) An outstanding find was that of hundreds of fragments of beautifully carved ivory work "some probably fallen from couches or thrones, many, in all probability, from wall incrustations".[3] The designs are of Egyptian style and the

---

[1] Examples can be seen in *Samaria-Sebaste I—The Buildings at Samaria* by J. W. Crowfoot, Kathleen Kenyon and the late E. L. Sukenik (1942), plates xii–xxxiv generally.

[2] See *Palestine Exploration Fund Quarterly Statement*, Oct. 1933, p. 203, and Jan. 1936, pp. 36, 37.

[3] *Samaria-Sebaste II—Early Ivories from Samaria*, by J. W. Crowfoot, Grace Crowfoot and E. L. Sukenik (1938), p. 2 and plates i–xxv. (It may be added here that a third volume of *Samaria-Sebaste* is in active preparation, dealing with pottery and potsherds as well as Greek and Latin inscriptions and coins found by the Joint Expedition.)

workmanship magnificent, probably Phoenician. Among the carved emblems are the infant Horus, the sphinx, lotus, palms, animals and human beings. Often the ivory is decorated with gold leaf or with coloured insets, including lapis-lazuli. Incidentally, it may be mentioned that many pieces are inscribed (on the reverse) with letters of the early Hebrew alphabet. Perhaps this was to assist the workmen in fitting them into frames. Amos (in vi. 4) speaks of divans at Samaria inlaid with ivory, and (in iii. 15) of houses at Beth-el decorated with ivory. Some excellent examples of the finds were on view for a time at the headquarters of the Palestine Exploration Fund, Hinde Street, London.[1] The date assigned to these ivory inlays by the Crowfoot expedition is the ninth century. The reason, partly, for this was the unearthing by F. Thureau-Dangin of similar ivories near Carchemish on the Euphrates; on the débris of a wooden bed captured from Damascus was an inscription giving the name of Hazael who, it seemed probable, was the king referred to in 2 Ki. viii. 8–13 who came to the throne of Damascus in 842 B.C.[2] A suggestion by A. F. Albright, however, is that the greater number belong to the eighth century—the century of Amos.[3]

(ii) **Excavations at Ras Shamra.** These now famous excavations began in 1928 and there have been a dozen or more diggings since then. There have been revealed the civilisation and the religious beliefs and practices of the north Syrian (Phoenician) land of Ugarit. The capital city of Ras Shamra lies half a mile inland from the Mediterranean facing towards Cyprus. The period covered is from 1800 B.C. to 1200 B.C. and later. The god of Ugarit was Aleyn Baal ("the mighty Baal"); his temple and that of Dagon have been unearthed, together with an altar of burnt-offering. The god Hadad, already familiar to us, was their war-god, and

---

[1] The expedition's total finds are housed in the Palestine Archaeological Museum, Jerusalem (Jordan) and the Fogg Art Museum, Cambridge, Mass.; and a small collection of fragments can be seen in the University of London Institute of Archaeology.

[2] Crowfoot, *Early Ivories*, pp. 5, 6.

[3] *The Archaeology of Palestine* (Penguin), p. 129 and plate 24.

incense was offered to the god El. The houses were well-appointed, and the art of writing was advanced, including the use of an alphabetic script. We understand afresh the difficulties Israel would encounter in trying to maintain a pure worship of their one God, Jehovah, in a land so nearly adjoining Ugarit. Although, of course, no light is shed directly upon life within Palestine itself and in the time of Amos, a wonderful picture has been presented to us of native social and religious life. It is hardly to be doubted that the conditions against which Amos lifted up his voice in Beth-el and Samaria were to some extent of the pattern revealed by the finds in Ras Shamra. For the bearing of the texts upon the study of Hebrew poetry, see below, pp. xxxvif. Many have written upon Ras Shamra, but the work of the excavator provides the best aut!.ority.[1]

(iii) **Alphabetic Writing.** A note upon Tyre (Commentary, pp. 281, 282, on Am. i. 9) refers to Alan Gardiner's thesis concerning the common parent of Phoenician and Greek being akin to the alphabet of Serābît. The ultimate origin of the proto-Semitic alphabet is still (1954) a matter of controversy. The finds on various sites of Palestine, including Lachish, Gezer and Shechem, and of Phoenicia, tend to complicate the problem rather than to solve it. While it is usually agreed that practically all existing alphabets descended from a Semitic source, who can tell what future research may yield regarding the nationality of the inventors? Were they Semites from Serābît—or Phoenicians, Canaanites or even Hebrews of the Patriarchal age? For discussions, see D. Diringer, *Antiquity* (1943), pp. 77ff., *The Alphabet* (3rd reprint, 1952), pp. 195ff, R. O. Faulkner (following Gardiner), *Antiquity* (1943), p. 207, W. F. Albright, *Bulletin of American Schools of Oriental Research* (*B.A.S.O.R.*), February and April, 1948 and his *Archaeology of Palestine*, pp. 189–195.

---

[1] C. F. A. Schaeffer, *Ugaritica*, Paris, 1939 and 1949. A useful little book is J. W. Jack's *Ras Shamra Tablets*, 1935. G. R. Driver has prepared a *Text and Translation of the Ras Shamra Tablets*, the issue of which is expected before long.

II. THE DATE OF THE PROPHESYING OF AMOS[1]

From about the year 1890 the date of the prophecy was generally placed within the period 765–750 B.C. In view of the biographical passage, Am. vii, 10–17, it was during the reign of Jeroboam II, whose death has been set by some indeed as early as 747 B.C.,[2] but by others as much as three or four years later.[3] In his Commentary the present writer placed Amos after 745 B.C. in order to allow for the rise of the great Tiglath-pileser III, who usurped the throne of Assyria in 745 B.C., and for some progress in his conquests. Since 1929 what may be styled the orthodox view has had its supporters, among them the late Aage Bentzen[4], who sets the date of Amos' activity as approximately 760–750 B.C., because he feels that the book seems to reflect materially prosperous conditions in the history of the Northern Kingdom (vi. 13 *etc.*), and J. M. Powis Smith,[5] who gives the date as "about 750". J. Morgenstern has argued at length for the year 751 B.C.[6]

On the other hand, the late W. L. Wardle shewed in 1936 a leaning in favour of a date after 750 B.C. "The chief development in the study of Amos has been the attempt by R. S. Cripps to revise the accepted date of the preaching of that prophet", and, while Wardle did not accept all the details of the present writer's argument, he stated that there was force in the main contention that the preaching of

---

[1] *Cf.* Comm., pp. 34–41.

[2] Oesterley and Robinson, *History of Israel* I (1932), p. 463, give 747 B.C.; M. Noth, *Geschichte Israels* (1950), pp. 216, 217, has 747–746 B.C.

[3] J. A. Bewer, *The Book of the XII Prophets*—I, p. 10, gives 744 B.C.; Adolphe Lods, *Histoire de la Littérature hébraïque et juive* (1950), p. 231, has 743 B.C.

[4] A. Bentzen, *Introduction to the O.T.* (Eng. Transl. 1949), p. 140.

[5] *The Prophets and their Times* (ed. Irwin, 1940), p. 57.

[6] *Amos Studies* (1941), pp. 127–179. Space does not permit any full discussion of this author's argument. The passages which he cites are 1 Ki. xii. 31–33, xiii. 1–11, 2 Ki. xv. 3–5, 2 Chron. xxvi. 16–21, Zech. xiv. 4, 5, Josephus *Ant.* IX. x. 4 and the Targum on Isa. xxviii. 21 ("For just as the mountains shook when the glory of the Lord revealed itself in the days of king Uzziah"). For a criticism of the hypothesis, see A. Neher, *Amos*, pp. 31–33.

Amos should be brought down to 743 B.C., because the
prophecy is most naturally interpreted against the background of an imminent Assyrian invasion.[1] Norman Snaith
fixes the message at 745–744 B.C. He agreed (in 1946) that
the date should be as late as possible and "certainly after
the rise of the Assyrian usurper".[2] In 1953, in his *Mercy
and Sacrifice, a Study in the Book of Hosea* (pp. 14, 15), Snaith
argues for a late dating of Amos, and expresses his opinion,
"It may well be that the Rabbis were right in their belief
that Hosea was the first of these eighth-century prophets".
The late Adolphe Lods, while admitting that too little is
known of the details and of the chronology of the events of
this period to make possible the fixing of the precise date
of Amos' short appearance in the Northern Kingdom,
declares, "The fact that Amos threatens Israel with deportation indicates perhaps that Tiglath-pileser III had already
ascended the Assyrian throne (745); it is this sovereign who
systematically employs the displacement of entire populations in his conquests".[3] Accordingly, Lods would date
Amos within the *second* half of Jeroboam's long reign,
760–743, and possibly 745–743. The present writer does not
overlook the problems, and indeed the obscurity, connected
with the ultimate chronology of the period around the death
of Jeroboam II, but the accepted chronology does not
interfere with his primary argument as to the dating of

---

[1] *Supplement to Peake's Commentary*, p. 13.

[2] *Notes on the Hebrew Text of the Book of Amos*, II, pp. 8, 9.

[3] Lods, *Op. cit.*, p. 231. *Cf.* also *Les Prophètes d'Israel*, p. 90 (1935); Eng.
transl., p. 80. It is to be noted that as long ago as 1886 the Dutch scholar
H. Zeydner, commenting on Am. viii. 3, definitely connected the prophecy of
Amos with the rise of Tiglath-pileser III. He remarked on the unsuitability of
festival rejoicing (alluded to in this passage) in view of the political thunder-
storm following the elevation of Tiglath-pileser to the throne in 745 B.C. Jeroboam was dead by 742. "Amos' appearance", he argued, "thus falls between
745 and 742 B.C., presumably in the late summer of 744, *cf.* Am. viii. 2."
Bijdragen (on Am. iii. 3) tot de tekstcritiek op het O.T.—*Theol. Stud.* 1886,
pp. 205, 206 and n. 1. In 1894 this thesis was followed up by J. J. P. Valeton
in his commentary, *Amos en Hosea*, of which a German translation by K.
Echtern cht appeared four years later. Valeton declared, "It is not improbable
that the appearance of Tiglath-pileser was for Amos the thing in which he heard
God's voice calling, and was the occasion of his prophetic activity" (pp. 10–12).

Amos. Unless and until further light is shed on the chronology, he sees no sufficient reason to depart from his dating of 742–741, or at earliest 744–743, that is, within Jeroboam's lifetime and after the rise of Tiglath-pileser III, the same monarch whose career so profoundly influenced the prophesying of Hosea and Isaiah.

Connected with the date of the prophecy is the duration and scene of Amos' work. Morgenstern is of the opinion that he made one appearance—lasting at the most half an hour—at Beth-el.[1] On the other hand there has been an increasing emphasis laid upon the possibility of what might be called a tour of North Israel before Amos was driven from Beth-el. Lods, for example, points out that Amos addresses the leaders of Samaria (iv. 1–3), announces to the capital the dissolution of its ramparts and its palaces (iii. 11) and threatens its nobles (vi. 1). In speaking of Beth-el, he says "Come", not "Go" (iv. 4). Likewise Amaziah's language in vii. 10 ("Amos hath conspired") implies that Amos spoke more than just a *single* discourse at Beth-el.[2] The same applies to Gilgal. In any event, however, his ministry in North Israel can hardly have lasted more than a year.

III. LITERARY PROBLEMS

Because of the existence of historical evidence the date of the action of Amos, at any rate within a score of years, has been determined, and is agreed by all. However, the problem of when and how the "book of Amos" (quite apart from certain additions) took shape is today more in debate, as the following review will shew.

i. The edition of 1929 assumed the then prevailing belief (that of *e.g.* Marti, Driver) that probably either Amos himself or an amanuensis or a hearer was the one who committed the prophecies to writing.

ii. Already, however, a view was beginning to be suggested

---

[1] *Op. cit.*, p. 177.
[2] Lods, *Histoire etc.*, p. 231 *ad init.*

(see p. 66 *ad init.*, p. 65 n. 2) that, while pieces in the 1st person may have been put into writing by the Prophet (*e.g.* the Visions), other passages, especially those which speak of him in the 3rd person (*e.g.* the Amaziah incident) were due to other hands. Finally, the whole was edited into what is now the Book of Amos.

iii. Since that time there have been developments. (*a*) There has been a tendency to premise, for reasons of varying validity, that in every case Amos' utterances were brief, and in some cases very brief.[1] These short oracles have been arranged according to a definite scheme. Chapters iii, iv and v all begin with 'Hear this word', while the other two large divisions i, ii and vii, viii have an equally obvious plan (i. 3–5, 6–8 *etc.*, vii. 1, 4, 7, viii. 1). A reason for this hypothesis is to account for certain dislocations of passages and cases of abruptness in the text. For examples of such, see the Commentary[2]. As a result of this view there is now less inclination to explain these roughnesses as being due to copyists' errors creeping into a completed text. Moreover, the tendency is to find more dislocations and examples of abruptness than formerly.

(*b*) Another tendency of more recent study has been to think that in the final arranging of the book the Prophet's own share was somewhat less than was formerly supposed. Weiser, for instance, believes that only the original sketch of his visions (vii. 1–9, viii. 1–3, ix. 1–4) comes from Amos himself. Debarred from re-entering the Northern Kingdom (*cf.* vii. 10ff.) he made a draft in writing of his basic experience and the proclamation of the earthquake and sent it there. Later this vision-document was united with a collection of the Prophet's oracles which had been made, and which existed separately for a time.[3] The

---

[1] In *The Book of Amos in Colloquial English* (1921) by T. H. Robinson, and in *Notes on the Hebrew Text of Amos*, Part II (1946) by Snaith, the text is set out, not in chapters but in short sections. See also Weiser, *Amos* (1929), esp. p. 8, and Robinson's *Die XII kleinen Propheten*, I, Handbuch zum A.T. (1938), p. 71.

[2] Notes on 'surely', iii. 7 (p. 156), on 'be they better', vi. 2 (p. 204 *ad fin*) and on vi. 11 occurring after verse 10 (p. 211, n. 1).

[3] *Das Buch der XII kleinen Propheten*, I, Das A.T. Deutsch, Teilband 24 (1949), pp. 112 f.; *cf.* his *Einleitung in das A.T.* (1949), pp. 181 f.

position of Otto Eissfeldt is somewhat different. As the book lies before us, he says, it gives on the one hand the impression of a good and conscious ordering, but on the other it shews traces of a still better ordering which is now disturbed. As an instance he suggests the occurrence of the narrative portion vii. 10–17 in the middle of an account of visions. ('Thus he shewed *me*'.) This Eissfeldt seeks to explain by saying that the account of the visions must go back to Amos himself; and further that the presence of an 'I-form' in v. 1 ('this word which I take up') makes it likely that we should derive, if not the whole of i–vi, at least parts of it, from the Prophet's own writing or dictation. But the final ordering of the whole does not go back to Amos, since what appear to be disorders are unlikely to be due to the Prophet. Eissfeldt holds, however, that there is no reason to doubt the genuineness of the utterances contained in the book, or at least the preponderant majority of them; their pregnant diction and fixed rhythmic form preserved them as they had been spoken.[1]

It should be remembered, however, that such opinions do not command universal agreement. Neher, for example, in his Commentary, believes that Amos wrote the book, and R. Gordon similarly attributes everything except ix. 13–15 to the Prophet.[2] E. Sellin,[3] too, holds that all the original material of the book undoubtedly goes back to the Prophet himself. The origin of the book he conceives thus. Amos' experiences in the North were the subject of lively interest and talk in Jerusalem. People waited for the fulfilment of the word of doom. For a time nothing happened. But two years after came a great earthquake. Through it Amos suddenly became a famous man, for was not what he had proclaimed in i. 2, ii. 13 and ix. 1 beginning to be fulfilled? So people went to Tekoa and compelled the Prophet to set down all his words in writing, that they might remain preserved for all generations. Sellin, like most other scholars,

---

[1] *Einleitung in das A.T.* (1934), pp. 441 ff.

[2] *Harvard Theological Review* (*H.T.R.*), 33 (1940), pp. 239–251 (quoted in R. H. Pfeiffer, *Introduction to the O.T.*, p. 583).

[3] *Das XII Prophetenbuch*, 2nd /3rd edn., pp. 187 ff.

believes that there have been certain expansions and additions (*e.g.* iii. 7, viii. 8 *etc.*) and that the actual order of the delivery of the utterances is unknown. But he maintains that the book, taken as a whole, is to be regarded as a writing coming from Amos himself.

iv. A quite different approach to the composition of the prophetic books has been made during the period under review by what is generally called the Uppsala school. Its writers hold that, in making our judgment as to how a book like Amos arrived at its present form, we have to reckon with 'oral tradition'. By this is meant that there was a period, short or long, during which the prophetic utterances did not exist in written form, but were preserved and handed on by word of mouth, especially in the circles of the prophet's disciples.[1] Such *oral* transmission, it is claimed, was the normal procedure in the East, and parallels are cited from Arabic literature.[2] The interval, it is held, between the spoken and the written explains the structure of the books as we have them now. For during it the single oracles came to be grouped together orally. The groups are known as 'complexes'. What is meant is that oracles having the same or similar structure, or the same beginning, or the same or kindred subject-matter, and so on, came together into collections. These collections were then transmitted orally entire. (See next paragraph concerning Amos.) The final

---

[1] The thesis was first put forward in 1935 by H. S. Nyberg, *Studien zum Hoseabuche.* For summaries of the positions of the Uppsala school, see C. R. North, *Expository Times, vol.* lxi, 10 (July 1950), pp. 292–296, and G. W. Anderson, *H.T.R., vol.* xliii, 4 (Oct. 1950), pp. 239–256.

[2] *Cf.* H. Birkeland, *Zum hebräischen Traditionswesen*, Oslo (1938), pp. 7–13. For a vigorous criticism of Birkeland, see G. Widengren, *Literary and Psychological Aspects of the Hebrew Prophets*, Uppsala and Leipzig (1948), pp. 11–56. For general discussion and criticism of the Uppsala school, see J. van der Ploeg, *Revue Biblique, vol.* liv (1947), pp. 5–41 (in French) and Eissfeldt in *The O.T. and Modern Study*, pp. 115–161. For a plea for moderation see pp. 159, 160, where, in a summary, Eissfeldt, accepting the processes of oral transmission, utters this warning: "but it is as certain that from an early period, fixed written forms were usual, and that the prophets that gave their names to our books themselves began the writing down of their own sayings, and that this may apply to many more sayings than is generally agreed today. The view that right down into post-exilic times only oral transmission need seriously be considered is certainly to be rejected".

editing of the books was then little more than an arranging
of these already existing complexes. The writers of the
Uppsala or Scandinavian school are not agreed amongst
themselves as to how far it might be necessary to rule out
our former ideas of *literary* transmission. Some, as for
example Ivan Engnell,[1] go to the extreme of believing that
very little was fixed in written form until after the Exile,
two centuries after Amos; but others, as S. Mowinckel[2] and
G. Widengren, take the view that literary transmission and
oral transmission went side by side for a period. It is of
interest to note that both Nyberg and Engnell stress that
the oral transmitters were faithful in their handling of the
material and made little change.

As an indication of the Scandinavian school's view of the
composition of the book of Amos, the following points from
the work of Michelet, Mowinckel and Messel may be cited.[3]
Amos himself spoke in short utterances and was responsible
for the grouping of these into complexes. Then, in the period
of oral transmission, each complex would gather to itself matter which had associations with it. For example, viii. 4–10
attached itself to the fourth vision, and vii. 10ff. to vii. 9,
in each case because of similarity of subject. Again, at iii. 1
starts a group of oracles beginning with the word 'Hear';
together with these in oral tradition came a few oracles also
beginning with an imperative, iv. 4, 'Come', v. 4, 'Seek'—
and so on. The transmitters of the tradition who finally
put the complexes together needed only to find the most
reasonable order for them. Chapters i and ii made a natural
beginning, because the unit gave expression to the pronouncement which Amos' successors regarded as his main
thought and activity, namely, that he had foretold doom over
the whole people. The placing of the oracles beginning
'Hear' before those beginning 'Woe' was natural. The visions
were put last, because in the earthquake the people saw
the fulfilment of Amos' words of doom. The final form of the

---

[1] *Gamla Testamentet, En traditionshistorisk inledning*, i, Stockholm (1945).

[2] *Prophecy and Tradition*, Oslo (1946); see esp. pp. 34, 66.

[3] *Det Gamle Testamente*, iii *De Senere Profeter*, Oslo (1944), pp. 618–622.

tradition was arrived at only a few years after Amos, the occasion for making this collection being the fall of Samaria in 722 B.C.

While the Scandinavian school is playing an increasingly important role in O.T. scholarship, its views on the part taken by 'oral tradition' in the composition of the prophetic books are by no means universally, or even generally, accepted. The majority probably of non-Scandinavian scholars would still agree with van der Ploeg[1] who, after a careful examination of the 'oral' hypothesis, concludes that, while prophetic oracles could have existed for some years in oral tradition before they were put into writing, it is not possible to prove with certainty that a prophet's work was brought together into a single volume only after his death. Van der Ploeg also makes the further valuable point that the fact that the prophetic utterances were not just human sermons but were regarded as *words of God*, makes it *a priori* very improbable that they were transmitted orally from generation to generation without people taking the trouble to put them into writing.

IV. SACRIFICES AND THE SACRIFICIAL CULT IN THE PROPHETS WITH SPECIAL REFERENCE TO AMOS

Various aspects of this subject are discussed in the notes on Am. iv. 4, v. 21–26 and in Excursuses III and IV. The general conclusion presented (see pp. 295 *ad fin*, 296) is that the prophets, including Amos, upbraided their hearers for offering sacrifices[2] in ways and with intentions displeasing to Jehovah. At the time of writing the commentary the view most popular amongst scholars followed the lines of Marti, Hölscher and Kennett, *viz.* that the great prophets were opposed to the institution of sacrifice itself. Since then, however, while this view has had its supporters, the general

---

[1] *Op. cit.*, p. 41.
[2] The word is used in a comprehensive sense. See Commentary, p. 195.

trend of opinion has inclined to the interpretation maintained in the commentary. The subject is obviously one of
importance; let us therefore review briefly what has been
written concerning the position of Amos in particular, and
the eighth-century prophets in general, finally drawing some
conclusions.

i. Those who consider that Amos desired the entire
abolition of the sacrificial system include the following.
Weiser expresses himself thus: "It is not idolatry, not a false
cult, not cultic over-zeal, . . . not abuse of the cult that
Amos wants to attack, but the legitimate cult of Yahweh
itself." Amos objected to the shouting by the people of
their songs and prayers at the sanctuary; these were signs
only of their importunity. The fact was that the God of
Amos was of a different character from the God whom the
masses thus worshipped.[1] W. A. L. Elmslie, in *How came
our Faith?* (1948), considers the question: "Did Amos really
wish that the ritual worship of his time should be swept
away, leaving—a blank?" Elmslie declares that Amos
would have answered his contemporaries that he meant
exactly as he said, and that, if *we* could see now what he
beheld then, we would have had no doubt but that to end
sacrifice "was the first step towards hope of discovering
spiritually sensible ways and means of adoring Him who
must be worshipped in spirit and in truth".[2] In 1949 Bewer
interprets the view of Amos as being that righteousness was
God's "sole requirement". (*The Book of the XII Prophets, I*,
p. 16.) In a study of Amos published in 1951, V. Maag of
Zürich uses the following contention to uphold his view that
Amos was against the cult *in toto*. As Amos saw the state of
affairs in his day, the luxury within Israel had spread to the
centres of worship; the priests were eating up the people's
choicest things (Am. vi. 4ff); the very sanctuaries were thus
contributing to the impoverishment of those who were
weak. The sacrifices had nothing to do with the con-

---

[1] *Prophetie des Amos* (1929), p. 318. Similarly in *Die XII kleinen Propheten*
I (1949), p. 150, "Amos rejects the whole cult".
[2] Pp. 260–262.

sciousness of sin. Jehovah neither commanded nor wished for sacrifice.[1]

ii. Among those who take the opposite view, *viz.* that the eighth-century prophets did not desire the abolition of the system (the fault lying not with it but with the worshippers) are the following. The late Adam C. Welch in 1936 wrote: "The judgment that the prophets were unanimous in their attitude towards the cult, and that they agreed in condemning it *per se*, does not do justice to the facts. Men like . . . Elijah, who said he had been very jealous for the LORD because the children of Israel had thrown down the Yahweh altars, were certainly not opposed to the cult on principle . . . As for the oracles of the later prophets, . . . that their common view was one which condemned the cult *in toto* can only be proved from isolated passages pressed beyond the terms of a just exegesis".[2] Sven Herner, of Lund, in *Atonement and Forgiveness*, explains Am. v. 25 by saying that Amos was a "self-taught", uneducated shepherd who, unlike Hosea, had not sufficient knowledge about the period of the wilderness wandering, including the legal enactments. (*Hosea's* condemnation was probably not of sacrifices but of the sacrifices of his godless compatriots.) The hard judgment which *Isaiah* makes upon the sacrifices of his countrymen is of a piece with what he says of God not listening to the prayers of those who are impenitent. Thus, Herner does not think the eighth-century prophets were essentially against the cult.[3] The late Wheeler Robinson's view was that "the prophets' criticism of contemporary sacrifices was not necessarily intended to do away with them altogether, but was more probably intended to check the abuse of them, by which they became the substitutes for, instead of the accompaniments, expressions and encouragements of, true piety and right conduct".[4] H. H. Rowley has con-

[1] *Text, Wortschatz etc.*, pp. 221–227, including n. 10. *Cf.* L. Köhler, in *e.g.* *Theologie des A.T.*, edn. 1953, p. 185.

[2] *Prophet and Priest in Old Israel*, pp. 17, 18.

[3] Herner wrote his book, *Sühne und Vergebung in Israel*, in 1942 (see pp. 30 ff.).

[4] *Redemption and Revelation* (1942), p. 250. Four years later Wheeler Robinson in *Inspiration and Revelation in the O.T.*, p. 226, touched on the vital

sistently denied the view that the prophets, including Amos, were absolutely opposed to sacrifice: "We may find that when the pre-exilic prophets denounced sacrifice, it was not sacrifice as such that they condemned, but the particular sacrifices that their fellows offered, and that they declared them futile because they were invalidated by the spirit of the offerers, and by the life out of which they sprang and to which they led."[1] He says that prophet and priest were not *ex hypothesi* opposed to each other: "The over-sharpening of antitheses, that was in vogue some years ago, is less common today, and there is a greater readiness to recognize an affinity between priest and prophet without ignoring the difference of emphasis and function that marked their work or their message".[2] The late B. D. Eerdmans held that the prophets generally did not object to sacrifice . . . Hosea prophesied that (as a calamity) Israel should abide a long time without sacrifice; this notwithstanding his own famous words in vi. 6.[3] The present writer has always held that chs. iv and v contain nothing to indicate that Amos was

point: "It is difficult to conceive how these prophets would have devised a worship wholly without sacrifices".

[1] "The Unity of the O.T.", *Bulletin of the John Rylands Library*, Manchester (1945), xxix, p. 339.

[2] "The Meaning of Sacrifice", *B.J.R.L.* (1950), xxxiii, p. 89. To illustrate this it may be recalled that (a) Nathan and Zadok were united in an enterprise, (b) together 'the priests and the prophets' were requested to save Jeremiah from death on his delivering God's message in the court of the temple, and (c) after the Return prophet and priest certainly were not in opposite camps. Mowinckel in *Psalmenstudien* has argued for the existence in the Jerusalem sanctuary, even in the time of the monarchy, of a prophetic personnel in connection with the composition and singing of Psalms. Readers desirous of pursuing the question of 'cultic prophets' as a sanctuary institution should see A. R. Johnson's *The Cultic Prophet in Ancient Israel* (1944), and for another point of view, A. Haldar's *Associations of Cult Prophets among the Ancient Semites* (1945). Making use of a Ras Shamra text, the latter would interpret (p. 79, n. 5) the term *nôqēdh* in Am. i. 1 (as indeed does E. Hammershaimb in his Commentary), as 'keeper of the temple herd'. *Cf.* also Haldar's *Studies in the Book of Nahum* (1946), pp. 110, 152 and especially 155 ff. For a succinct and balanced statement upon the subject see N. W. Porteous in *Expository Times*, Oct. 1950. Whatever part some prophets (men, surely, not of the stature of the great canonical prophets) may, or may not, have played in conjunction with Hebrew priests of the sanctuary, evidence produced hitherto fails to convince us that their functions could have extended to assisting in the offering of sacrifices.

[3] *Religion of Israel*, Eng. Transl. (1947), pp. 140 ff.

against sacrifice as such—the one and only verse in the book calling for discussion being ch. v. 25: "Did ye bring unto me sacrifices in the wilderness?' This verse E. Würthwein would eliminate from Amos' genuine words; what the prophet said amounts to no more than "The time when Jehovah received sacrifices from Israel is now over. The relation which obtained between God and man in sacrifice ritual is now done away with, for in place of this relationship Jehovah is now bringing judgment upon Israel" (v. 27).[1] Neher sees in the prophets no attack on the sacrificial system. In his work, *Amos* (1950), he views Amos as the opponent of superstition, formalism and hypocrisy. Commenting on iii. 14, 15, he declares that the altars will perish in the general catastrophe, not because they are objects of the cult, but because in them is shewn the *religious* guilt of the people in the same way as the houses reveal the *social* guilt and the dynasty the *political*.[2] He goes on to cite K. Cramer: "It is impossible to admit that Amos would have been in principle against the cult, on the contrary, he would wish to protect and to purify it".[3]

To sum up. Those writers who take the view that Amos was radically opposed to the sacrificial system and that he desired its complete end do not appear to furnish sufficient religious and moral grounds for the adoption of a proposition so far-reaching. Perhaps their strongest argument is that the cult itself was based on an inadequate view of Jehovah and His requirements. Some of them begin with references to the faults of the worshippers in Amos' time and then pass to the conclusion that Amos desired to abolish the cult itself. Again and again, however, it seems that the issue is thought to turn simply upon Am. v. 25. But for this verse, perhaps the idea would never have arisen that Amos, Hosea, Isaiah and Micah were radically opposed to sacrifice. Herner speaks

---

[1] *Theologische Literaturzeitung* (1947), lxxii, pp. 143 ff.

[2] P. 91. The present writer would compare Jeremiah's prediction of the fall of the temple (Jer. vii. 14 ff.) and of Jerusalem itself (vii. 20). So the parallel passage xxvi. 6 ff. "this house . . . this city".

[3] Cramer, *Amos* (1930), pp. 113 ff.

of a country tradition that the wilderness knew no sacrifice.
Such an idea must have sprung from the obvious fact that
in Israel's desert wanderings no extensive sacrifices and gifts
were possible. In the ancient world sacrifice was a universal,
necessary religious rite. No special revelation from God
imparted the principle to Israel. A glance at the verse in the
Hebrew shews it to be not in the same rhythm as that of
the various verses beside it, and that, at least as the M.T.
stands, it is hardly different from prose. Würthwein would
deny that the words proceeded from Amos at all. This
suggestion seems unnecessary; it is simpler to believe that
the words are out of their original context and that in any
case they were spoken partly playfully, with the meaning
"After all, there could not have been sacrifices in the wilderness, could there? Would it matter so vitally if, the sanctuaries today being what they are, there were no sacrifices
now?" In other words, an *obiter dictum* has been given the
authority of an actual pronouncement. The fact is that until
the Exile and the age of synagogues came there simply was
no way for the Hebrews to engage in public worship other
than by attendance at the shrine (at which, indeed, the
earliest laws of the Pentateuch required every Israelite to
appear). If the prophet had brought about the abolition of
sacrifice, surely there might have been a real possibility of a
spiritual vacuum being created—and who knows what might
not have happened to such faith as the people did possess?
Rather, would not Amos have appealed to priests and people
to reorganise the accepted method of public worship, substituting for the worship of the cult, confession and repentance? Of this there is no sign.

Amos said as the words of Jehovah, "I hate, I despise your
sanctuary festivals". If in these days a preacher were to say,
"Your public worship gives no pleasure to God, your lives
are out of accord with your professions and your prayers
take too much for granted", would his words be rightly
interpreted to mean that God wished the church doors to
be closed for ever?

3

V. TRANSLATION: HEBREW POETRY

(i) **Some notes on Translation and Text.** (*a*) Am. i. 9, 10 "The brotherly covenant" (*b^erîth 'aḥîm*): see Comm. pp. 127, 128. Neher, who emphasises the importance of the Jewish conception of God's covenant with Noah (Gen. ix. 1–7), maintains that this 'covenant of brothers' is something much wider than any specific agreement between two nations. Even before Jehovah's choice of Israel all nations were called upon to respect human personality. Indeed, God's covenant with Noah and his descendants required that men should regard one another as brothers. The 'Noachide' law embodied the principle of humanitarian ethics and this Tyre had not 'remembered'.[1] The same writer, it may here be added, traces Amos' principle of universalism to the primeval Noachide covenant, by which God's name had been 'called over' all nations[2] (Am. ix. 12). (*b*) Am. ii. 13 "Behold, I will press you in your place", *etc.* Sellin in his first edition rightly connected the M.T. with an Arabic root *'āqa* although he was wrong in saying that it meant 'the crackling noise of the threshing-waggon passing over straw'. In his second/ third edition (1929), however, he translated the word as in the present Commentary, p. 148 n. 1, 'to hinder', as Gesenius-Buhl (under the root *'ûq*). Further, he now renders the noun, not 'threshing-waggon' but 'threshing-wheel' (*cf.* Isa. xxviii. 27, 28), translating "I shall cause it to halt (or stop) under you as the threshing-wheel that is full of (*i.e.* choked up with) sheaves". It thus becomes a metaphor of the consternation which causes a complete paralysis—the result of terror emanating from God. Sellin cites Wetzstein in *Z.A.W.* 1883, pp. 278f. It is possible that Sellin's final solution is the correct one. (*c*) Another crux is in iii. 12: "In the corner of a couch, and on silken cushions of a bed" (R.V.). See Comm. pp. 162 and 291. Suggestion (2) on p. 291 is upheld in Sellin's second/third edition; *i.e.* the

---

[1] Neher, *Amos*, pp. 52, 65, 66.
[2] *Op. cit.*, p. 144.

word translated 'silken cushions' does not in fact mean any
kind of article or material but, as A.V., the city of *Damascus*
itself. He transposes the words 'Damascus' and 'bed'
translating "in a bed of Damascus"[1], and takes it as an early
gloss upon the foregoing words "in the corner of a couch"
(so Köhler). When the time came that the connection of
Damascus with divans of ivory was forgotten, the Massoretes thought they would change the word 'Damascus'
into an incomprehensible word ('*d^emesheq*'). In the present
writer's opinion this reconstruction is much to be preferred
to trying to translate the M.T. as it stands. Otherwise
Driver's emendation seems the best, "*at the upper end of* a
couch" (*J.T.S.* July 1938, p. 262) or, less simply, "*on the
frame of*" (in *Studies in O.T. Prophecy*, Robinson Festschrift,
1950, p. 69). (*d*) Am. vi. 10: "When a man's uncle . . . even
he that burneth him" (*dôdhô 'ûm^esar^ephô*). Is the second
term a mere gloss upon the first? As the note in the Comm.,
p. 211, mentions, the Hebrews did not normally burn their
dead, but in any case the Hebrew seems to call for comment
even though no solution can be found. One suggestion is
that of Driver (see *J.T.S.* article referred to above) who
connects *m^esārēph* with the Arabic *silph*, 'brother-in-law'.
(There is also an Arabic *salaph* meaning 'ancestor, grand-
father'). The interchange of *l* and *r* does not present an
insuperable difficulty but, after all, the M.T. *m'sārēph*, a
participle indicating action, does not seem very natural to
express a family relationship. The origin of the suggestion
comes from a Jewish *tradition* (*viz.* the commentaries of
Rashi and Qimhi) that *m^esārēph* means '*ahî 'immô*, 'mother's
brother'. (See Sellin *in loc.*) As in classical Hebrew so in
Rabbinic the root *sāraph* (which is spelt always with a *sîn*
not a *sāmekh* as M.T.) means, of course, 'to burn'. Maag
pp. 164–167 defines 'his burner' as a relative (next-of-kin)
who offers up the sacrifice for the dead as a duty. He traces
the word to a pre-Semitic custom in Palestine (3rd and 4th

---

[1] See Crowfoot, *Early Ivories*, p. 6 *ad init.* ("inventory of beds and stools of
ivory from the palace" of Damascus). *Cf.* above, Section I, pp. xviii, xix and
Maag, *Wortschatz*, pp. 17, 18, 140–142 (esp. p. 141 *med*), and refs.

millenia B.C.) 'to burn the dead body' and he sees in *m'sārēph* an old Canaanism—'my *m'sārēph*' meaning in Canaanite times 'he who will bury me one day'. In Israelite times the letter *sīn* was changed to *sāmekh*, so that (Maag claims) *m'sārēph* comes to mean 'next of kin', a ἅπαξ λεγόμενον, and is genuine in the present passage. For another suggestion, see J. Reider, *H.U.C.A.* xxiv, 1952/3, p. 96.

(ii) **Hebrew Poetry.** Reference was made in the Introduction to the Commentary to the close similarity between Hebrew poetic form and that of the Babylonian texts. deciphered in the early part of the twentieth century.[1] Further interest in Hebrew parallelism and rhythm has been stimulated by the discovery of a wealth of poetic texts at Ras Shamra (Ugarit) and at Mari. An example from Ras Shamra is

> Let him overturn the throne of thy royalty:
> Let him break the sceptre of thy sovereignty.[2]

Moreover, it is not only temple songs which fall into poetry, but also declamatory statements exhibit parallelism and metre. Such material from outside Israel confirms our confidence in the principles of Hebrew poetic form which have been familiar to British scholars since Bishop Lowth published his thesis in 1753.[3] In this, moreover, Lowth pointed out that not Psalms and Proverbs only but all the *Prophets* are for the most part in poetry. Further, in his *Commentary on Isaiah* he used poetic form as one of the bases of the emendation of the M.T.[4] In this he gave a lead to all future scholarly work on the Prophets.

As regards the book of Amos, the text upon the whole is well preserved. In such places, however, as the M.T. presents difficulties in sense, grammatical structure or rhythm, emendations are recorded in the present Commentary (see references on p. 34 and elsewhere, also 1 (c)

---

[1] P. 32, n. 4.   [2] C. Virolleaud, I AB, VI, 28, 29.

[3] *De Sacrâ Poesi Hebraeorum Praelectiones Academicae.*

[4] A discussion of Lowth's principles and, in particular, of several of his Isaiah emendations may be seen in the author's "Two British Interpreters of the O.T." (*B.J.R.L.* xxxv, March 1953, pp. 386–397, *etc.* and offprint).

above). These, or almost all of these, have been confirmed by such a recent writer on Amos as Maag. On the side of caution in not using extravagantly the principle of Hebrew poetic form in revising the M.T., an observation concerning Ugaritic poetry is useful. To quote A. M. Honeyman, "The occurrence of different (poetic) forms according to no discernible pattern should be a warning to critics not to treat Biblical poems too cavalierly on account of such freedom of structure".[1] For further consideration of Hebrew poetry in the light of the Ugaritic and Babylonian, see W. F. Albright, art. "The Psalm of Habakkuk" in *Studies in O.T. Prophecy*, 1950. For a general article upon Hebrew metre (though not specifically from the book of Amos) the reader is referred to Joiachim Begrich, *Zur hebräischen Metrik, T.R.*, Neue Folge 4 (1932), pp. 67–90 and references.

VI. EXEGESIS AND APPLICATION

The Prophets knew what they intended their words to mean. In the course of time, however, the circumstances and the original meaning of the message would often be overlooked. Down the ages some readers only (Jews and Christians) would seek to recapture this foundation meaning, that is to say, were interested in pure 'exegesis'. Until one or two centuries ago there had been a tendency to suppose that a prophet might be speaking about events, practices or doctrines of the age of the reader, whensoever that might be. An instance of this is provided by the Scroll of Habakkuk discovered near the Dead Sea in 1947. The text of Habakkuk i and ii is divided into sections, after each of which a commentary is added. The writer had no notion of true exegesis. The setting of the delivery of the prophecy, in Judah say ten years before Jerusalem's first capture by

[1] Article, 'Semitic Epigraphy', in the volume *The O.T. and Modern Study*, p. 281. For the general reliability of the Hebrew text of the O.T., *cf.* Winton Thomas in ch. viii of the same work: 'The reputation of the M.T. stands deservedly high; for the serious study of the O.T. it must, in spite of its imperfections, constitute the proper starting point' (p. 243).

Nebuchadnezzar in 597 B.C., is entirely ignored by this commentator. The text has "For, lo, I raise up the Chaldeans" (i. 6). The author calls the enemy "Kittim" (a sufficiently vague term, but one never applied to the Babylonians); and the circumstances which he describes, so far as the text can be understood, are utterly remote from those of the prophet's time—whether they were, as scholars have variously suggested, the ninth century A.D. or the second century A.D. or even as early as the first century B.C. There is, however, a good intention behind this allegorising commentator. He does seek, though perversely, to make the original message come home to his own generation.

It is hoped that the objective study of the book of Amos is assisted by the present commentary. Its aim, however, goes further; and it is hardly an over-statement to say that more and more real scholars of the O.T. of the present generation have been giving themselves to add to their pure exegesis— theology and to their interpretation—application. "The supreme business of the Biblical theologian is to ensure that the Bible should be seen not as man's witness to himself but as his witness to God",[1] while Köhler devotes several pages to a discussion of Cramer's *Theological Interpretation of Amos*. Characterising the commentary as a theological understanding of Amos, Köhler says, "The What of the message is more important than the When, Where, and through Whom".[2] Most strikingly was a similar conviction expressed by the great Cambridge Semitic scholar, Stanley Cook, who brought his life-work to its consummation with *The O.T., A Re-interpretation* (1936) and *The "Truth" of the Bible* (1938). In *The "Truth" of the Bible*, speaking of the prophets, he appeals for attention to the theology of the O.T. Indeed, he says that we must go back and grasp the spirit of the Bible to discover the cause of the failure of our present reforming schemes. For the idea of God has not its

---

[1] N. W. Porteous, "Semantics and O.T. Theology", in *Oudtestamentische Studien*, 1950. The reader is referred also to the same writer's article on "O.T. Theology" (in *The O.T. and Modern Study*, pp. 311–345).

[2] *Amos-Forschungen von 1917 bis 1932, T.R.*, 1932, pp. 105–212.

roots in the social order *but in the cosmic*.[1] In the former book
he reminds us that "the better we understand the prophets,
the clearer will be our outlook on both the past and the
future".[2] The O.T. contains facts; it contains also a revelation of God and a revelation of His will.

Few men of the past generation have made this depart-
ment of O.T. study so much their own as Wheeler Robinson.
In his *Inspiration and Revelation in the O.T.* he reminds us
that such revelation is not so much a series of propositions
about God as a disclosure of God Himself.[3] The two elements
in the Bible are reflected in the title of the book of essays
edited by him in 1938, *Record and Revelation*. It is not
always easy to draw the line between theology and ethics,
but one thing concerning the book of Amos deserves stress-
ing; when all has been said about the Prophet's passion for
social righteousness, the analysis of his book cannot end
there. It was God who was interested in the oppressed, in
and outside Israel. It was God who shewed Amos what was
His will. To omit this element in the psychology of Amos is
to degrade him from being one of the loftiest and loveliest of
the many messengers of God. At the end of a list of social
evils in Amos' day "which persist as long as human selfishness
prevails" a recent writer adds the significant words "deter-
ioration of religion".[4]   And Amos holds out no hope for an
irreligious society.

Is not the plight of the world today due to *"a famine, not
a famine of bread, nor a thirst for water, but of hearing the
word of the LORD?"*[5] It is not due to a lack of God-sent
messengers, but to the *total indifference* of men and women
to the living word of the living God which is proclaimed in
the churches and which could be read and assimilated by all.

HEAR YE THIS WORD[6]

[1] P. 154.
[2] *Cf.* p. 167.
[3] P. 281.
[4] Bewer, *Book of the XII Prophets* I, p. 17.
[5] Am. viii. 11. Or 'words'; but see notes on vv. 11 and 12, Commentary, p.
251.
[6] Am. iii. 1, iv. 1, v. 1.

COMMENTARIES ON AMOS SINCE 1929[1]

A. Weiser: *Die Prophetie des Amos* (Beihefte für Z.A.W.), 1929.[2]

E. Sellin: *Das Zwölfprophetenbuch*, 2nd and 3rd edn., 1929.

K. Cramer: *Amos, Versuch einer theologischen Interpretation*, 1930.

J. Morgenstern: *Amos Studies*, Hebrew Union College Annual, 1936–1940. Published in one volume 1941.[3]

T. H. Robinson: *Die XII kleinen Propheten*, I, Handbuch zum A.T., 1938 (first published in 1936).

N. H. Snaith: *Notes on the Hebrew Text of Amos*. Pt. I, 1945, Pt. II, 1946.

E. Hammershaimb: *Amos*, 1946.

S. M. Lehrman: *Amos*, Soncino Press, 1948.

A. Weiser, *Das Buch der XII kleinen Propheten*, I, A. T. Deutsch, Teilband 24, 1949.

J. A. Bewer, *Book of the XII Prophets*, vol. I, 1949.

A. Neher: *Amos: Contribution à l'Etude du Prophétisme*, 1950.

V. Maag: *Text, Wortschatz und Begriffswelt des Buches Amos*, 1951.

L. Köhler, *Amos Forschungen von 1917 bis 1932*, T.R., Neue Folge, 1932.

W. Rudolph, Gott und Mensch bei Amos in *Imago Dei* (ed. Krüger), 1932.

[1] Supplementary to the Bibliography on pp. 105–7.

[2] Published after Sellin's 2nd/3rd edn. and after the present commentary (1st edn.) and commenting upon both (pp. 325–331).

[3] The pagination of the 1941 volume is that to which reference is made in this Preface.

SYNOPSIS OF THE BOOK OF AMOS

PART I

Ch. i. 1. SUPERSCRIPTION

Ch. i. 2. INTRODUCTION

Chs. i. 3–ii. 16. "ORACLES" AGAINST THE NATIONS AND AGAINST ISRAEL: OR TRANSGRESSIONS AND THEIR VISITATION

    (a) i. 3–5. Judgment upon Aram ('Syria')

    (b) i. 6–8. Judgment upon Philistia

    (c) i. 9, 10. Judgment upon Phoenicia

    (d) i. 11, 12. Judgment upon Edom

    (e) i. 13–15. Judgment upon Ammon

    (f) ii. 1–3. Judgment upon Moab

    (g) ii. 4, 5. Judgment upon Judah

    (h) ii. 6–16. Judgment upon Israel

PART II

Chs. iii–vi. IMPASSIONED DISCOURSES OF AMOS: THE COMING JUDGMENT

    (a) iii. 1–6. The Coming Disaster is the work of Jehovah

    (b) iii. 7, 8. Amos justifies his appearance as a Preacher

    (c) iii. 9–15. The Transgressions of Samaria, and the Sentence

    (d) iv. 1–3. Kine of Bashan: Samaria's Women

    (e) iv. 4–13. Displeasing Worship at the Shrines. Jehovah's Chastisements have failed

    (f) v. 1–17. Lack of Morality leads to Ruin

    (g) v. 18–27. Judgment upon the Nation, whose Worship is a Mockery

    (h) vi. The Downfall of the Nobles of Judah and of Israel proclaimed

PART III

INTRODUCTION

I. A SUMMARY OF THE HISTORY OF THE KINGDOM OF ISRAEL UP TO THE ERA OF AMOS

UNDER the rule of Saul, David, and Solomon, the Twelve Tribes of Israel formed a united kingdom. On Solomon's death (c. 932 B.C.), however, ancient rivalries re-appeared and the realm was split in two, and that permanently. Whilst the southern portion, 'Judah', continued to be ruled over by the descendants of David, the northern country, 'Ephraim', consisting of ten tribes, had kings of its own of varying, or at times even of no, dynasty. In the prophets' ideal the descendants of Jacob formed one people still (cf. 1 Ki. xviii. 31); but in actual fact there were two nations, each exhibiting differences in outlook and in life. They were sometimes at war (e.g. 2 Ki. xvi. 5), not seldom in alliance (1 Ki. xxii. 4), but always more or less foreigners to one another. The Northern Tribes seem to have had a less pure worship than the Southern; yet it was they, and not Judah, who succeeded in retaining the title 'Israel'. It is probable that it was to this Northern Kingdom principally that Amos preached.

Any account of the political history of the Ten Tribes would not be alone concerned with their relationship to Judah in the south. Adjacent to Israelitish territory on the north-east lay various Aramaean peoples, the principal and nearest branch of whom (generally known as 'Syria') had its capital at Damascus. From the time of king David's (temporary) subduing of Damascus (2 Sam. viii. 6) until the capitulation of that city to the Assyrians in 732 B.C. (2 Ki. xvi. 9), the military story of Northern Israel tells mostly of their dealings with Syria. Between the reign of Jeroboam I and the fall of the house of Omri, Israel's fortunes were at least variable; but the first two reigns of the next dynasty were a time of most intense suffering at the hands of the Syrians. In Jehu's days (c. 841–814 B.C.) 'Jehovah', according to 2 Ki. x. 32 (M.T.), 'began to cut Israel short'. Hazael devastated the Trans-Jordanic province (cf. 2 Ki. x. 32, 33), committing, apparently, horrible atrocities (2 Ki. viii. 12, cf. Am. i. 3). Further, Hazael is described in 2 Ki. xiii. 7 as having reduced the fighting forces of Jehoahaz, Jehu's son, to but ten thousand infantry, fifty cavalry and ten chariots; he 'made them like the dust in respect of threshing'. It is clear that the Aramaeans had now overrun Israel's territory west of Jordan. Hazael took even Gath, if not the whole of the Philistine coast (2 Ki. xii. 17, cf. xiii. 22 Lucian's text[1]); and only on recèipt of a payment of money withdrew from the capital of the Southern Kingdom (2 Ki. xii. 18). There is some reason to conjecture that the terrible events recorded in 2 Ki. vi. 24–30 also belong to the time of Jehoahaz.[2]

And now another Semitic[3] country which lay likewise to the north-east of the Aramaeans was gradually strengthening and extending its influence in the west. The Assyrian Empire was incomparably more powerful than any state such as Israel or Aram. In 802 B.C., and once and again, it defeated Damascus. It was probably about the same time that king Zakir[4] of Hamath inflicted severe loss upon Ben-hadad III, the son of Hazael. The weakening of Syria gave Israel its chance. Ben-hadad III, at first a source of distress to Israel, was worsted by Joash, the son of Jehoahaz, in three battles (2 Ki. xiii. 17, 25). Probably this was on the west of the Jordan.[5] Then, under Joash's son Jeroboam II, Israel

---

[1] 'And Hazael had taken the Philistine out of his (Jehoahaz's) hand from the Western Sea even unto Aphek'.

[2] The twelve years' reign of *Jehoram* is short for such extremes of fortune as seem to be assigned to it according to the existing arrangement of the narrative in Kings. Moreover, it is difficult to reconcile 2 Ki. vi. 24 with vi. 23 *b*. On the other hand, the 'Ben-hadad' of *v.* 24 might well be the *third* king of that name, the one mentioned in xiii. 3 *b* as contemporary with Jehoahaz.

[3] The commonly used term 'Semite' (*i.e.*, very approximately, descendant of *Shem*) includes both the Israelites and all the races of the same family of peoples, e.g. Assyrians, Aramaeans, Phoenicians and Canaanites.

[4] See the note on 'Ben-hadad', Am. i. 3. There was no question of Israel itself being attacked by Assyria. During most of the reign of Shalmaneser IV (782–772 B.C.) the Assyrian Empire was occupied with wars against Argistis I, king of Urartu (Ararat) or, more accurately, of Vän. Indeed, under Sarduris II, the son of Argistis, the Vannic Empire reached its farthest limits until that king's defeat by the great Tiglath-pileser (*C.A.H.* III. pp. 176, 377, and *cf.* below, p. 37).

[5] 'Aphek', mentioned in these verses and in Lucian's text of 2 Ki. xiii. 22 (cited in footnote (1) above), is referred to also in 1 Ki. xx. 26 as a base for Aramaean invasions of Israelite territory. *Probably* it is the 'Aphek' of 1 Sam. xxix. 1 in the vale of Esdraelon; or else it was situated in the northern part of the plain of Sharon, *cf.* 1 Sam. iv. 1. (There may, however, have been an Aphek east of the Sea of Galilee, the modern *Fik*. See G. A. Smith, *Hist. Geog.* pp. 427, 459. But this may be left out of consideration here if we regard Joash's victories as being confined to the west of Jordan.)

regained all its lost territory. Further, 2 Ki. xiv. 28 says that
Jeroboam 'recovered Damascus'. In spite of its textual and
exegetical difficulties, this passage is evidence that at least
the southern district of the land of Syria became tributary to
him. Indeed, except for Judah and Edom, the boundaries of
Jeroboam's kingdom could be described (in general terms) as
equal to those of king Solomon's (2 Ki. xiv. 25, cf. 1 Ki. viii.
65). Most probably Moab bowed to Jeroboam's rule;[1] and
possibly even Hamath in the north acknowledged his suzerainty. This brings the history down to the period c. 775–
765 B.C. Meanwhile, in part at any rate contemporary with
Jeroboam II, Azariah (or Uzziah), king of Judah, also enjoyed
signal military success (2 Chron. xxvi. 1–8).

II. SOCIAL, MORAL AND RELIGIOUS LIFE IN ISRAEL, PARTICULARLY NORTH ISRAEL, IN THE TIME OF AMOS

The change of condition from military defeat to complete
victory was succeeded by reconstruction. A temporary, but
very definite, decline in Assyria's fortunes[2] had prevented that
power from following up its victories over Syria by an invasion of Israel. It is true that a short time previously famine
and other disasters had come upon Israel's land (Am. iv. 6–
11); but, none the less, the most significant element in its
political life was its freedom from the Aramaean menace. The
nation had opportunity to renew its commerce; indeed, in
time it became extensively prosperous. This, however, in
turn, led to a number of vices. It is somewhere here that the
figure of Amos the poet-preacher makes its appearance in
history.[3] The facts of Jeroboam's reign given in 2 Ki. xiv.
23–29, and, indeed, what is known from 2 Chron. xxvi. 6–15
of that of his contemporary in Jerusalem, Uzziah-Azariah,

---

[1] See Amos vi. 14, note, p. 305 b. For the relation to Hamath, see p. 305 a.
[2] Cf. p. 4, note 4.
[3] For an examination of the evidence for fixing the date of Amos more exactly,
see pp. 35–41.

are confirmed and amplified by the chapters of the book of Amos.[1]

(i) **Social condition.** The nation was divided very sharply into upper and lower classes. The former consisted of the possessors of the land, and the merchants. From them were supplied the king's counsellors and the administrators of justice. The other stratum of Israelitish society was composed of peasants or labourers.

(ii) **Moral condition.** This was characterised by *luxury and self-indulgence* on the part of the richer element. The book of Amos furnishes details. The dwellings of these men were of 'hewn stone' (Am. v. 11 *b*), and some were ivory-fitted (iii. 15). Not a few were built in the combination of 'summer house' and 'winter house' (iii. 15). Though it would be a mistake to lay too much stress upon the use of a word, yet it is not without significance that the term which Amos employs to denote the dwellings of the upper class is 'palace', or castle (Hebrew *'armôn*).[2] In the houses were couches, often inlaid with 'ivory' (vi. 4*a*), and furnished with 'damask' cushions (iii. 12 *b*). Food might be of choice 'lambs', or of 'calves of the stall' (vi. 4*b*). Wine was drunk by the bowlful (vi. 6*a*), the women being drinkers as much as their husbands (iv. 1). With the choicest of oils the people anointed themselves (vi. 6).

Worse, however, than self-indulgence was *the oppression of the weak by the strong* (iii. 9). They 'trampled upon the poor' (v. 11 *a*). This vice exhibited itself in two special forms. (*a*) There was *commercial dishonesty*. The dealers cheated with measures and money, and what they sold was 'the refuse of the wheat'.[3] (*b*) There was *injustice* in the courts. The judges, by accepting bribes and giving the case against those whom they knew to be guiltless (v. 12), turned 'judgement to worm-

---

[1] As indeed by the chapters of Hosea and Isaiah also. It is obvious from the words of the first great prophets that even if the "religious reformation associated with the reign of Jehu was in fact a reformation in *religion*, neither that king nor any other, nor the pre-Amos prophets, had been able to influence public opinion in great moral questions".

[2] Am. iii. 10 *b*, 11 *b*, vi. 8. In i. 4 the same word is used of the residence of the king of Syria, where see note. Amos does not *necessarily* mean the word to convey a reproach, any more than does Micah (in Mic. v. 5, '*our* palaces').

[3] Ch. viii. 5, 6. The text of the concluding phrase is not quite certain.

wood' and to 'gall' (v. 7, vi. 12). They 'sold the righteous for silver'; and the oppressive creditor delivered into slavery the poor man whose debt was but the value of 'a pair of shoes' (ii. 6, *cf.* viii. 6).

To *immorality*, in the narrower sense of the word, Amos makes, at the most, but one reference (ii. 7).[1]

(iii) **Religious condition.** There is frequent allusion in the books of Kings to the two gold-covered images of young bulls, "symbol of strength, virility and fierceness",[2] which were used at this time in the worship of Jehovah. These sanctuaries at *Beth-el* and at *Dan* are referred to in the chapters of Amos (iv. 4, vii. 13, viii. 14). And there were other shrines (or 'high places')—at *Gilgal* (iv. 4) and *Samaria* (viii. 14); while to *Beer-sheba* (in the south of Judah) pilgrims perhaps went even from the kingdom of North Israel (viii. 14).

The apparatus of a *high place*[3] consisted of an *altar* (Jeroboam I had erected such an altar at Beth-el), a *sacred tree* or an *'ashērāh* (or tree pole), and, in particular, a *maṣṣēbhāh* (translated 'obelisk' in *e.g.* 2 Ki. xvii. 10, R.V. marg.). Though Amos himself does not allude to anything but *altars*, yet the books of Kings, and the writings of the prophets in general, make it apparent that the above adjuncts of worship were used in the service of Jehovah by the kingdom of Ephraim until its fall. Indeed, this is true also of Judah down to the time of Josiah, and even afterwards (*cf.* 1 Ki. xiv. 23, 2 Ki. xxiii, especially *v.* 15—the *'ashērāh* at Beth-el).

There were many sanctuaries of Jehovah, and not one only;[4] and the mode of worship was not always easily distinguishable

---

[1] In this he is like Isaiah, his younger contemporary in Judah, who does not refer to the sin.

[2] S. A. Cook, *C.A.H.* ii. p. 351. Hadad was represented as standing upon a bull. If the 'golden calf' be conceived of as a *heifer*, we must suppose that this was the result of equating Jehovah with the gods of rain and storm. For bull-images discovered on the east of Jordan, see Gressmann, *Bilder*, edn 1, Nos. 138, 139; edn 2, Nos. 352, 353.

[3] For photographs *etc.* taken at Gezer and other ancient sites, see Gressmann, *Bilder*, edn 1, Nos. 1–48; edn 2, Nos. 407–467.

[4] Contrast the law of Deuteronomy limiting to a *single* shrine (Deut. xii. 13, 14). See p. 309. The same code expressly forbade, in connection with Jehovah's worship, both *'ashērāh* and *obelisk* (Deut. xvi. 21, 22); though in Isa. xix. 19 the latter at least is held to be a desirable thing (E.VV. 'pillar').

from the Canaanitish worship of Baal (as Am. ii. 7 alone is
sufficient to prove), yet it was worship of *Jehovah*. Moreover,
from the chapters of Amos it is clear that, at the time of
Jeroboam II and Azariah, nothing could have exceeded the
zeal and thoroughness of Israel in the prosecution of outward acts of religion. The recent victories over neighbouring
nations were interpreted by the people to signify that
Jehovah their God was well pleased with them; whilst famine,
plague, and even earthquake, had done nothing to awaken
them from their moral self-complacency (iv. 4–11). Hence, in
abundance were offered to Him *sacrifices* (iv. 4), *peace-
offerings* (v. 22), *meal-offerings* (v. 22), *thank-offerings* (iv. 5),
freewill-offerings (iv. 5) and *tithes* (iv. 4). The festivals were
celebrated to the sound of lutes ('viols', v. 23, E.VV.), and
other instruments of music (vi. 5). In 1 and 2 Kings not a
little is said about observance by Israel of (a) the worship of
foreign deities, and (b) the Jehovah-Bull cult; yet only incidental in Amos[1] are the references to either the one or the
other—(a) *Sakkûth* and *Kaiwān* (v. 26), *'Ashîmāh* and *Dôdh*
(viii. 14) and, doubtfully, *Bēth-'ēl* (iii. 14); (b) the bull at Dan
(viii. 14). In Amos' view of things, more obnoxious to Jehovah
than any worship of other gods, more essentially pagan than
idolatry and the mode of worship generally at the Jehovah
sanctuaries, was the trust of the people of Israel in *mere* ritual
in the worship of their God.[2] Nay more, their guilt was
aggravated by their disregard of His claims upon their conduct when they returned from the sanctuaries to the affairs
of everyday life (v. 23, 24). Such was the moral and spiritual
condition of the mass of the people to whom Amos preached.
It should never be forgotten, however, that there must have
been some who had preserved higher ideals, probably from

[1] And these may not all belong to the original recension of the book.
[2] This is not to say that there was in actual fact nothing wrong with Israel's
religion. Hosea, and after him Jeremiah, make the Baalim the *source* of Israel's
evil conduct in daily life. But in Am. iii. 14, the reference to the destruction of
altars at Beth-el is but by the way, and seems to prove nothing as to Amos'
teaching upon high place worship as such. (On the other hand, the opposite view
has been held. Cheyne in W. R. Smith, *Prophets*, edn 2, p. 400, writes: "In
Amos iii. 14, the altars of Beth-el appear to be regarded as the chief causes
of Samaria's guilt".)

the time of Moses himself. The Rechabites of Jer. xxxv are an illustration of this in Judah. *Cf.* pp. 296 *med.* and 343, 344.

III. AMOS

(i) **His Importance.** Amos is one of the twelve who have been called "the Minor Prophets". It is worth noting, however, that the term "minor" in this connection does not appear either in the English Bible or in the Hebrew manuscripts. It hardly requires to be stated that the adjective, when associated with the name of Amos, can be used rightly neither of the genius of the Prophet, nor of the quality of his message. It refers to the space occupied by the chapters of the book. (a) Amos is *great*[1] because in point of time he was the earliest of all the prophets whose words form a book of the Bible. Indeed, so far as evidence has survived, he may even be regarded as the first of a new order (see pp. 18–21). (b) He is *great* because he shared with Hosea the distinction of being one of the only two such prophets who preached in the Northern Kingdom.[2] (c) He is *great* because he was of fearless character (Am. vii. 9–17). (d) Above all, his *greatness* lies in his knowledge of divine truth, and in the fresh and forceful way in which he uttered it. Especially remarkable is his teaching concerning the character and the requirements of Israel's God (see pp. 22 ff.). The ministry of Amos, no less than that of St John the Baptist (St Matt. xxi. 25, 26), was not 'from men' but 'from heaven'. If not in his life-time, at least after his death, all have held him 'as a *prophet*'.

(ii) **Tekoa and the 'Wilderness'.** In i. 1 Amos is connected with the easternmost village of Judah. According to 2 Chron. xi. 6 Tekoa was fortified by king Rehoboam (*cf.* also Jer. vi. 1). Tekoa (the modern *Teḳū'a*) stood upon an eminence 2800 ft. above sea level, other lower hills surrounding it. Ten or twelve miles north from Tekoa, probably the Temple

---

[1] It would seem that his 'greatness' was not fully recognised either by the ancient Hebrew or the early Christian. See note on ix. 12, p. 322, footnote.

[2] The 'Book of Jonah' is not a collection of the sayings of the contemporary of Amos mentioned in 2 Ki. xiv. 25. It is a story composed several centuries later.

of Jerusalem was just visible. The inhabitants, gazing east, could catch sight of the Dead Sea a dozen miles distant, and nearly 4000 ft. below them. And beyond this the red mountains of the Tableland of Moab were to be seen.

Amos would move about in the 'Wilderness', or Pasture-land, of Tekoa[1] immediately to the east of Tekoa itself. It was a desolate region, the haunt of wild beasts rather than of man. In this comparatively rocky and waterless land agriculture could not flourish. Probably even grass for sheep and goats was green only in the spring.[2]

(iii) **The name 'Amos'.** (a) The word '$\bar{A}m\hat{o}s$ by derivation might mean 'Burden-bearer';[3] but really the signification of the name is obscure. (b) Possibly the meaning is *passive*, 'Borne [by God]', compare the Phoenician name Eshmun-amos.[4] The name of the father of Isaiah is spelt differently ('Amoz'). Contrary to custom in the prophetic books, the Prophet's parentage does not appear (see *e.g.* Hos. i. 1, Isa. i. 1).

(iv) **The Occupation of Amos.** In the wild region described above, Amos the shepherd lived. From the expression 'among the herdmen' (in i. 1), it is to be concluded that he was not the only sheep-owner or shepherd who moved about this part of the country. Whether he was, or had been, poor, or whether he had always been moderately well-to-do (though living a simple life) cannot be ascertained. At least his time seems to have been his own. Further, the special word for 'herdman' in i. 1 (*nôqēdh*) is entirely consistent with his being of a good social position. In vii. 14 Amos describes himself as of another occupation—apparently parallel to that of shepherd—a 'dresser of sycomore trees', trees growing nearer to the Dead Sea than to the township of Tekoa.[5]

---

[1] For the expression, *cf.* 2 Chron. xx. 20.

[2] See, further, G. A. Smith, *Hist. Geog.* pp. 314, 315; *Book of the Twelve Prophets*, p. 78.

[3] *Cf.* the noun forms *'āmôn* = 'architect', *bāhôn* = 'assayer', *'āshôq* = 'oppressor'.

[4] *I.e.* 'borne by Eshmun'; so also *Ba'al*-amos. If the meaning (b) above be the correct one, 'Amos' is practically a shorter form of the name *Amasiah* of 2 Chron. xvii. 16.

[5] Or else towards the Mediterranean. See 1 Ki. x. 27, and *cf.* the Targum on vii. 14, 'My resting-place (is) in the *Shephelah*'.

(v) The Preparation of the Man for his Prophetic Work.
It has been maintained by Hölscher that Amos, belonging to
the kingdom of Judah as distinct from that of North Israel,
may have had some connection with an old reform movement
such as perhaps had been in existence in the Southern Kingdom from the reign of Joash (2 Ki. xi. 4–19), or even that of
Asa.[1] The conjecture is a useful one, but even so, Amos' particular occupation and immediate surroundings might seem
unlikely soil from which should spring so great a prophet of
God. Indeed the history of Amos the master-shepherd is
hardly less remarkable in its own way than that of the shepherd boy of Beth-lehem five miles north of Tekoa, who, 250
years before, became king of a State feared by many peoples.
However, as we look more closely, it is apparent that, in the
providence of God, Amos' life was in many respects actually
a most valuable preparation for the great spiritual work to
which he was to be called. Later did not also Jeremiah of
Anathoth and John the Baptist draw inspiration from the
same wilderness of Judah? (a) The shepherd's simple existence
as a dweller in tent or hut, with his fare of water, milk, and
sycomore fruit, made him realise more clearly the various
vices of the city (enumerated above, p. 6). (b) By his experiences with the 'lion', the 'bear' and the 'serpent' (v. 19,
iii. 12) all unconsciously he was accustoming himself to be
able later to face danger bravely when he did God's work
(vii. 10–17). (c) His desert life was to supply him with the
symbols and metaphors of which he made such lavish use in
his discourses (iii. 3–5, iii. 12, v. 19). (d) The forces of nature—
manifest in the winds, thunder and earthquake—and perhaps
the stars by night in the clear desert sky, seemed to speak to him
of Jehovah and His greatness.[2] (e) It was here in the wilder-
ness-land, or not far from it, that Amos beheld certain sights,
which, through the Spirit of God, became to his spirit 'visions'
—*the grass and the locusts* (vii. 1), the desert *fire*, or *drought* (vii.
4), *the basket of summer fruit* (viii. 1, 2). Indeed, not improbably

---

[1] 1 Ki. xv. 11–15. See, further, the note on ii. 4, p. 138.
[2] Chs. i. 2, viii. 8, iv. 13, v. 8; but see notes on authorship of these two last
passages.

his call eventually came directly by means of these very objects of his environment (see below, pp. 98, 101). (*f*) To sell the wool of his sheep, Amos had to leave the wilderness of Tekoa and to visit the towns of Judah and of North Israel and (we may believe) of neighbouring countries also. These journeys would give him a knowledge of Israelite town life as it was, and of the ways and the history of foreign peoples, such as is so fully reflected in the contents of his nine brief chapters.

It was after such preparation that Jehovah's call was heard. Cornill has said, "Amos is one of the most wonderful and inexplicable phenomena in the history of the human spirit". Whether or not he came in the wake of a reforming movement in Judah, as suggested above, from a natural standpoint Amos the prophet, to be sure, cannot be explained. The Spirit of God, however, had been preparing His servant, partly by means of, partly in spite of, his wilderness and town circumstances. The sheep-breeder felt that it was Jehovah Himself Who said to him, 'Go, prophesy' (vii. 15).

Further, it may well be that, when the Shepherd-Preacher gave forth to Israel the ideas which gradually had come to him, he was assisted even in the utterance of them by the Spirit of God who (as Christians believe) 'spake by the prophets'.

(vi) **The Scene and the Scope of his Preaching.** 'The LORD said unto me, Go, prophesy unto my people Israel'. These words, in their context in the historical section vii. 10–17, indicate that Amos conceived that at least an essential part of his mission lay with the Northern Kingdom. It is commonly supposed that throughout verses 7–17 the term 'Israel' is used in the sense of 'the Ten Tribes'. The particular spot at which the visions of chs. vii–ix were described by Amos appears to have been at, or close to, the sanctuary of Beth-el (vii. 13, ix. 1). Other sermons of which we have extracts were delivered at Samaria (iii. 9, 12, iv. 1, vi. 1, and *cf.* vi. 6). During this visit to the kingdom of Ephraim, doubtless Amos preached at various centres, *e.g.* at Gilgal (iv. 4, v. 5), where pilgrims or traders could be found gathered together.

However, though parts of the book of Amos furnish us with

oracles delivered exclusively in Northern Israel, yet it would seem a thing incredible that the Prophet should neither have preached in Judah, nor have intended his words to have reference to that kingdom.[1] Of all men the Prophet of justice could not have denounced the faults of *ten* tribes and at the same time been blind to those of *two*; still less could he have visualised so clearly, as it seems, the fall of the Northern Kingdom and of all the surrounding peoples, and yet fondly have imagined to himself that his own kingdom of Judah would escape. Moreover, in the prophetic outlook, Israel was one[2]. Indeed, there are a great number of discourses which, wherever they were *uttered*, appear to be intended to *apply* to both kingdoms. It may be said that as a rule Amos has in mind the whole nation.

The present writer finds himself in general agreement with the position of Buttenwieser that the oracles of ii. 6–16, iii. 1–8, vii and viii, ix. 1–8 *a* (and indeed of iv. 4–12, v. 1– vi. 14) are so worded as to render it probable that they were meant to apply, at least in the main, to both kingdoms.[3] Nor is it at all certain that in Am. vii. 7–17 the term Israel is used in the sense of 'the Northern Kingdom'.[4] At the least it would seem that Amos must have desired that the roll of his sayings—if compiled within his life-time—should serve as some warning also to his own people of Judah. Certainly the volume as it now stands confirms this view, *cf*. iii. 1 (upon which see note), 'against you, O children of Israel, against *the whole family* . . .', and vi. 1, where 'Zion' is expressly addressed. The frequent reference to 'Jacob' (in vi. 8, vii. 2, 5, viii. 7), and in particular that to 'the house of Jacob' in iii. 13, ix. 8, cannot well have applied to every tribe *except*

[1] Is the position of Ezekiel somewhat analogous, with his two audiences?

[2] *Cf.* the attitude of the Judaean Jeremiah towards *Northern* Israel, Jer. xxxi. 1–6.

[3] *Cf.* the notes on the oracle against Judah (p. 285); 'children of Israel', iii. 1 (p. 150); 'house of Jacob', iii. 13, ix. 8 (pp. 163, 265); 'Isaac', vii. 9 (p. 226). The words of Edghill (*Amos*, p. 92) are to the point: "Though his ministry was mainly confined to the Northern Kingdom, his indictment was directed to the whole house of Israel". Buttenwieser, *Prophets*, pp. 232–236, goes so far as to claim that only in iii. 9–iv. 3, v. 6, 15, vi. 6, 13, vii. 9 *b* is the Prophet addressing Northern Israel specifically.

[4] See note on pp. 236, 237.

Judah. There are reasons, however, for supposing that at this time North Israel stood in need of the message rather more than did the Southern Kingdom.

IV. PROPHECY IN ISRAEL

Amos was a preacher of a particular type. The appropriateness of the description 'preacher' has even been denied. Amos was a *prophet*. The use of the term 'prophet' in the O.T., however, requires explanation. Moreover, from a brief study of the history of the institution which is known as 'prophecy' it is possible to appreciate the special place of Amos. If in the course of time the Israelite system became unique among religions, it was, more than for any other reason, because of its prophets. And, surely, no higher tribute could be paid to the greatness of the O.T. prophets as a whole than the application of the title in the N.T. narrative to our Divine Saviour Himself. One man, who knew Jesus Christ well, felt it to be an apt description of Him to say: 'Jesus of Nazareth, *which was a prophet*'.[1] Some prophets of the O.T. were reputed to have wrought miracles, but all true ones had been revealers to their generation of Jehovah's character and will. As the priests represented man in the presence of the Deity, so the prophets were God's spokesmen to mankind.

Several stages, however, are discernible in the long history of prophetism in Israel. To apply the words of St Paul used in another connection,[2] 'That is not first which is spiritual, but that which is natural; then that which is spiritual'. Probably the earliest descriptions of prophecy amongst the Hebrews are those which come in the stories of how the proverb arose, 'Is Saul also among the prophets?' There would not appear to us to be anything very highly spiritual in such 'prophesying' as would be uttered by 'a band of prophets...with a psaltery, and a timbrel, and a pipe, and a harp, before them' (1 Sam. x. 5–13).[3] Primitive also is the 'prophesying' of Saul

---

[1] St Lu. xxiv. 19; *cf.* also vii. 16, 39, xiii. 33, 34, St Mark vi. 4, 15, viii. 28, *etc.*   [2] 1 Cor. xv. 46.

[3] The primitive prophetic ecstasy of 1 Sam. x. 10 finds a certain parallel in the gift of *tongues* of 1 Cor. xiv. 1–28, Ac. x. 46, xix. 6; a phenomenon, moreover,

in the presence of Samuel, when Saul 'lay down naked all that day and all that night: *wherefore* they say, Is Saul also among the prophets?' (1 Sam. xix. 24). For such a mental and physical condition, which is induced by music, and is infectious and which leads to excited, uncontrolled actions, the most appropriate phrase would seem to be *wild ecstasy*. Now, the Hebrew verb 'to *prophesy*' does actually signify (in one of its grammatical *voices*) 'to be in a frenzy'. In 1 Sam. xviii. 10,[1] 'he (Saul) *prophesied* in the midst of the house' means (as R.V. marg. correctly renders) Saul 'raved'. A more extreme form of this religious enthusiasm is to be met with in the narrative of the 450 prophets of the Phoenician Baal who danced (*cf.* R.V. marg. 'limped') about their altar—'*cut themselves...with knives...*' and '*prophesied* until the time of the offering of the evening oblation' (1 Ki. xviii. 25–29). Not entirely dissimilar is the behaviour of Elijah himself in running twenty or twenty-five miles, 'the hand of Jehovah' being 'on him' (xviii. 46).

From such evidence from the O.T. two deductions would seem to be clear: (1) that 'prophecy' of a kind was not peculiar to the Israelite religion;[2] (2) that, taken as a whole, the earliest 'prophecy', even among the Israelites, was of a

manifest to-day in less educated Christian communities in India (see a discussion by L. E. Browne, *Acts*, pp. 34–37). It may also be compared with the ecstasy of the Montanists of the 2nd cent. A.D. (Eusebius, *Hist. Eccl.* v. xvii. 2). It would appear to be even more comparable to the ecstasy of the holy man of the East to-day such as is characterised by incoherent speech and bodily contortions and which not seldom ends with the ecstatic lapsing into unconsciousness. "The Indian practice of inhaling and exhaling the breath was known to the Sūfīs of the ninth century and was much used afterwards. Among the Dervish Orders music, singing, and dancing are favourite means of inducing the state of trance called 'passing-away' (*fanā*), which...is the climax and *raison d'être* of the method" (Nicholson, *Mystics of Islam*, p. 48).

[1] M.T. Verses 10 and 11 are absent from the LXX.

[2] There is not sufficient evidence at present to draw the conclusion that prophecy was a *universal* Semitic institution. It is a fact that no direct proof exists that it flourished among the Canaanites. "We know nothing of Canaanite prophets", says Prof. Peake (*Roots of Heb. Prophecy and Jewish Apocalyptic*, p. 5). There were seers at *Hamath*. A story has come down of an oracle delivered through a man in a religious frenzy in *Byblos* in the 11th cent. B.C., *i.e.* about contemporary with Saul (Breasted, *Ancient Records of Egypt*, IV. §§ 570 ff.). But this again, like the prophesying of 1 Ki. xviii. 25 ff., is connected with Phoenician Baal worship. There were prophets and prophetesses of a sort in Assyria and Babylon. See below, pp. 42–54.

somewhat low *ecstatic* kind.[1] Indeed, it cannot be too strongly
emphasised that the Hebrew word which we know in the
English O.T. as *prophet* (through the LXX προφήτης)[2] had
within it, philologically, no suggestion of prophesying in the
sense of forecasting events;[3] but that it meant, according to
its etymology, *frenzied ecstatic*.[4] In this connection it may be
said that it is probable that in the earlier stages of Hebrew
religion all psychological abnormalities, without any distinction, were attributed to the direct action of the spirit of
Jehovah upon the man concerned.[5]

Not only were there prophets, but we read much in the
earlier period of the monarchy of *sons of the prophets*. These com-
panies of men were useful in fostering the worship of Jehovah;
but their prophetic gift was of a less spiritual order than was
the inspiration of such men as *e.g.* Elijah, prophets whom
perhaps they considered their head.[6] Each one could be called

---

[1] The 'seer' also possessed peculiar psychological powers. *Cf.* note on Am. vii. 12.

[2] And yet the prefix *pro* of the Greek word *prophētēs* would naturally signify
'forth', rather than 'beforehand'; *cf.*, exactly, with the verb προφέρω, in St Lu.
vi. 45, 'out of the good treasure of his heart bringeth *forth* that which is good';
so also with προάγω in Ac. xii. 6, xvi. 30. The same view as to the force
of *pro* in *prophētēs* is advocated by Erich Fascher, ΠΡΟΦΗΤΗΣ (Giessen,
1927). He demonstrates that *prophētēs* in Classical Greek signifies *one who
proclaims*; and, further, that the term is never employed by itself to mean
one who predicts. For the predictive element in prophecy, *cf.* below, p. 21, and
footnote 1.

[3] How all-absorbing to generations of Christians before our own day was the
purely predictive element in prophecy may be seen from a perusal of such a
work as that by the learned and devout Samuel Lee, successively Professor of
Arabic and Regius Professor of Hebrew in the University of Cambridge. His
Inquiry into the nature, progress, and end of prophecy (509 pp.) is concerned almost
entirely with supposed forecasts in Daniel and Revelation. The prophetic
doctrine of social righteousness is not so much as mentioned.

[4] The truth of this statement remains unaffected if the Hebrew word for
prophet (*nābhî*) is held, as *e.g.* in the *Oxford Heb. Lexicon*, to be derived from a lost
Hebrew root meaning *to utter*. It is to be noted that in actual fact the predicting
of events soon became a characteristic of prophecy. It is more apparent from
Amos onwards (*cf.* Skinner, *Proph. and Rel.* p. 4).
Alternatively, another meaning of the word *nābhî* is suggested by the Babylonian name Nebo or Nabu. *Cf.* S. A. Cook in *C.A.H.* III. p. 459: "The prophet
is not his own master: his name recalls the god Nebo, the divine herald, the
intermediary later identified with Mercury". Nabu is the scribe in the assembly
of the gods. An oracle of the reign of Esarhaddon ends with the words, "I am
Nabu, the lord of the writing-reed". See Introd. p. 43.

[5] See 1 Sam. xvi. 14, 15, 23.

[6] But see the note on vii. 14, 'sons of the prophets', pp. 233 and 313, 314.

a 'prophet' (compare together 2 Ki. ix. 1 and ix. 4). Further, it needs to be added that many Jehovah-prophets were hardly worthy of the name; cf. Jehoshaphat's question after listening to such: 'Is there not here a prophet of the LORD besides?'[1] By comparison, some prophets might almost be called 'false'[2] (cf. also later, Jer. xxiii. 9–40 and, of prophetesses, Ezek. xiii. 17–23).

However, prophecy, from being a phenomenon which to some extent Israel shared with her neighbours, was, in the providence of God, to become in the course of generations a more and more spiritual vehicle for the communication of the Divine will to the Hebrew nation and so to the world. This required time. In the four or five centuries from the Exodus to the generation before the fall of Samaria the names of only three or four great prophets stand out. *Moses* himself may well be called a prophet,[3] and for his age one of an exceptionally high order. Probably *Samuel* was an important prophet, though there are two very different descriptions of him within the book which bears his name. *Elijah* undoubtedly was a great prophet; and at a time of crisis he

---

[1] 1 Ki. xxii. 7 (A.V.). The age of Ahab seems to have been one of great prophetic activity. In 1 Ki. ch. xviii alone reference is made to four classes of prophets—(1) Elijah, representing the true succession of religion, perhaps deriving its theology ultimately from Moses himself; (2) 'the prophets of Jehovah' (xviii. 4), *i.e.* the sons of the prophets; (3) the 400 'prophets of the *Asherah*' (also Jehovah prophets, but to some extent with the ideals and practices of the Phoenician religion, xviii. 19 *b*); (4) the 450 'prophets of Baal'. These last, it is stated, were slain by command of Elijah (xviii. 40).

No attempt has been made in the above brief sketch to analyse the usages and meanings of the phrase 'man of God'. It is applied to Moses (Deut. xxxiii. 1), to Samuel the seer (1 Sam. ix. 6–10), to Elijah (1 Ki. xvii. 18, 24, 2 Ki. i. 9–13), and to Elisha (2 Ki. iv. 7–9, *etc.*); not to mention prophets of much less distinction and merit (1 Sam. ii. 27, 1 Ki. xii. 22, xx. 28). The passage Judg. xiii. 6, 8 seems to shew that the expression could be used of a divine messenger generally (= 'angel of God', xiii. 3, 9). For *prophetesses*, *cf.* pp. 42, 43, and 2 Ki. xxii. 14, *etc.*

[2] The actual expression 'false prophet' occurs nowhere in the O.T., though the phrase 'prophesy falsely' (or 'falsehood') is found in Jer. v. 31; *cf.* xiv. 14, xxiii. 32. For 'false prophet' see *Test. Judah*, xxi. 9; St Matt. vii. 15, *etc.*; *Didache*, xi. 5, *etc.*

[3] "Moses is to all intents and purposes a prophet" (Driver, *Exodus*, p. lxix). So he was regarded by Hosea (xii. 13) and by the writer of Deut. (xviii. 15 and xxxiv. 10). He and his work possessed, apparently, such exceptional elements, and, furthermore, so little really is known of his methods, that he cannot well be included in the history of prophetic origins.

played a noble part as the accredited representative of
Jehovah (1 Ki. xviii); and in his witness for the principle of
justice between man and man he boldly faced the king alone
(1 Ki. xxi). Even Elijah, however, the most wonderful
prophet before Amos, except perhaps Moses himself, did not
go about preaching righteousness; still less did he endeavour
to produce a general reformation of Israelite religion. *Elisha*
in his long ministry does not appear in the pages of 2 Kings
to be at all so significant in the history of Hebrew religion as
Elijah.[1] The fewness of great names makes us realise how
mediocre most prophets must have been during this period.[2]

V. AMOS AND THE NEW ORDER OF PROPHECY

Then comes Amos. If hitherto one prophet had stood out as
being greater than another, it is true that, so far as is known
to us, none like Amos had yet arisen. Indeed, though without
doubt it is possible to over-emphasise the distinction between
Amos and those before him, it seems not too much to say that
with Amos, "the old order changeth yielding place to new".
Let us examine this. (a) Although Amos can see visions,[3]
yet evidence is entirely absent that the primitive or lower
kind of *ecstasy*, which was the distinguishing feature of earlier
'prophecy', was part of Amos' equipment.[4] We do not read

[1] Elisha, even after he left the plough at the bidding of Elijah, seems to have
been only his servant (2 Ki. iii. 11 *b*). Nor did he ever receive, as is commonly
supposed, double the prophetic gift of Elijah. He merely had, as it were, the
status of the first-born son; at most he became in some sense the *successor* of the
older prophet (2 Ki. ii. 9; *cf.* Deut. xxi. 17). Elisha's chief title to fame lay in
his action on behalf of the nation against its foes. He was the 'chariots of Israel
and the horsemen thereof' (2 Ki. xiii. 14). But, as Barton says, the higher
religion of Israel owes nothing to him.

[2] Other prophets before Amos include Nathan, Gad (David's 'seer'), Ahijah
of Shiloh, Shemaiah (1 Ki. xii. 22), Azariah the son of Oded (2 Chron. xv. 1),
Hanani the 'seer' (2 Chron. xvi. 7), Jehu the son of (probably another) Hanani
(1 Ki. xvi. 1), Micaiah the son of Imlah.

[3] See, further, pp. 83–101.

[4] *Cf.* also Hölscher, who draws the sharpest distinction between old and new
prophecy in this very respect. "In all this, the words of Amos stand out as
ecstatic speech—but what a distance from the older prophetic ecstasy! No
stammered, half-intelligible sounds, but distinct announcement of divine truths.
All external expedients, dance and music, which in the guilds of the prophets
were still practised, all exaggerated behaviour has disappeared before manifest

of such men as Amos and Isaiah having any characteristic
manner (as with Eldad and Medad, Num. xi. 24–29) suggesting inspiration; being accompanied by a band of musicians;
or even requiring—like Elisha—a minstrel either to calm
their righteous anger or to produce conditions favourable for
obtaining a Divine message.[1] Amos was fearless, as were
many before him; but no one would call him a 'mad fellow',
as happened with one of 'the sons of the prophets' sent by
Elisha to anoint Jehu (2 Ki. ix. 1, 4, 11). If prophets in the
line begun by Amos received at times, in an abnormal state,
their message, or their first 'call', the 'ecstasy' seems to have
been almost entirely of a high order, having its analogy somewhat in that of the Christian mystic; it is difficult to understand how it could be compared with that which is common in
a primitive religion.[2] Nor does there seem to be sufficient evidence to conclude that their messages were *delivered* in ecstasy.

(*b*) Samuel the 'seer'[3] may have possessed curious knowledge, Elijah and Elisha the prophets probably were powerful
in wondrous deeds, but men whose line Amos is to inaugurate
are mighty in thought and word. 'John did no miracle';[4]
and this is characteristic of most of the greater prophets of the
Old Testament. Men such as Amos *speak*—and they do not
come forward and utter a mere sentence or two, as did
Elijah.[5] They declare to their generation predictions, warnings

spiritualisation" (*Profeten*, p. 197). It is quite true that occasionally the
adversaries of the great prophets deliberately confused them with common
ecstatics: see Am. vii. 14, 16 *b*, Mic. ii. 6 (*lit.* 'foam not').

For the opposite contention, see T. H. Robinson, *Prophecy and the Prophets*,
pp. 43–45. S. A. Cook also gives a greater recognition of such elements in all prophecy (*C.A.H.* III. ch. xx). "The prophets were Semites, supreme examples of the
ancient Semitic mentality; and we misunderstand them and their influence if
we separate them too rigorously from the lower and cruder phenomena of their
day" (p. 460).

[1] 2 Ki. iii. 15, which moreover perhaps describes Elisha's habit, *lit.* 'Now it
would come to pass that, when a minstrel played, the hand of Jehovah came
upon him'.

[2] And so far as information is available it must be held that men like
Jeremiah had communion with God through the most natural methods of
confession and prayer. Jer. xi. 20, xx. 12, *etc.*

[3] 1 Sam. ix. 9. See Am. vii. 12 (note).   [4] St John x. 41.

[5] 1 Ki. xvii. 1. A further point may be added: the great prophets did not
take sides with the king as did *e.g.* Elisha, Jonah (2 Ki. xiv. 25) and the four
hundred 'prophets of the LORD' in 1 Ki. xxii. 6.

or at times encouragements, with some amount of detail. In short, they deliver discourses. These impassioned poetic oracles are held to be so important that they, or at least parts of them, are committed to writing, at times by hearers or disciples, at times by themselves. Thus the words of these men, however written down, form separate books of the Bible. These are the *literary*, or (better) the *Canonical*, Prophets.

The difference between Amos and earlier prophets is a clear one, apart from the question of the exact interpretation to be put upon his disclaimer in vii. 14.[1] The Hebrew text reads, 'No prophet [am] I, nor one of the sons of the prophets'. These words were not uttered because he lacked consciousness of a Divine revelation to himself—quite the reverse; but spiritual prophets like Nathan, Elijah, and Micaiah the son of Imlah had been comparatively rare; the word 'prophet' was, to say the least, ambiguous in meaning.

Amos denied being a prophet of the sort which Amaziah had in mind. The passage in its context serves to remind us of one or two further well-known points of difference between Amos and at least the majority of the prophets before his time.

(c) He was not a king-maker as were Ahijah the prophet of Shiloh, Elisha (1 Ki. xi. 29–31, 2 Ki. ix. 1–3), and Samuel in the case of both Saul and David.[2] Even if Amos predicted the collapse of the dynasty of Jeroboam II, the court priest Amaziah need not have feared that Amos, as on one occasion Elisha, had in mind to promote *another* dynasty (Am. vii. 9).

(d) Again, Baal prophets had lived on the bounty of their supporters (1 Ki. xviii. 19); and the example of Samuel shews that it was customary for those who inquired of Jehovah's 'seer' to give him a fee.[3] Amaziah told Amos to depart from Beth-el to 'Judah, and there eat bread' (*i.e.* probably, earn

---

[1] See further, pp. 311, 312.

[2] However, it would be misleading to compare such pre-Amos prophets to 'Warwick the king-maker'; for there was always a moral reason prompting their action.

[3] 1 Sam. ix. 8: 'Behold, I have in my hand the fourth part of a shekel of silver: that will I give to the man of God, to tell us our way'. *Cf.* 1 Ki. xiv. 3.

his living), 'and prophesy there'. It seems to be in view of such characteristics of prophecy that the retort is made, 'I am *not* a prophet'.

And yet, notwithstanding all this, Amos *was* a prophet; and other such prophets were to follow. In Northern Israel very soon will arise a Hosea; there will be an Isaiah, a Micah and a Jeremiah in Judah. Each will be a prophet in a noble sense of the term, *telling forth* God's message to his contemporaries, and enunciating the great principles upon which he conceives that Jehovah acts. The prophet of the type of Amos will predict[1] either punishment for sin, or the possibility of a happy future; but, none the less, his impassioned sermons are directed to the men of his own generation, and his words can, for the most part, be tested almost at once by his hearers (Deut. xviii. 21, 22). Whatever the place assigned to Moses in the making of the religion of Israel—and there are reasons for believing his was a very great part—humanly speaking, his work would not have survived but for the prophets.[2] It was these prophets of Israel's land who secured to the Hebrew religion a place above that of the surrounding nations, and prepared the way for Jesus Christ Himself. It is a tribute to them, and to the magnificence of their work, that He may be compared to them.

But He is greater than they. His deeds were mightier than those of the prophets before Amos, His words truer and more

---

[1] For the predictive element, *cf.* also Peake (*op. cit.* p. 6), Burney, *O.T. Conception of Atonement*, pp. 5, 6. The present writer cannot go quite so far as Skinner, *Proph. and Rel.* p. 4, in the direction of an older conception: "Prediction is no secondary or accidental feature of O.T. prophecy even in its highest manifestations, but a central interest round which all other forms of prophetic activity ranged themselves". See p. 16, *nâbhî.* After all, Deut. xviii. 9–22, which represents Israelite prophecy as displacing in the Hebrew economy pagan soothsaying, was written sufficiently late for a development of interest in the predictive element in prophecy to have taken place in Israel. Moreover, the writer of that famous passage does not appear to be enunciating a formal theory of prophetism, so much as to be delivering an *obiter dictum.*

[2] The Jewish supposition that there was a continuous stream of authoritative teachers between Moses and the prophets is gratuitous, and indeed opposed to the facts of history. "Moses received the Torah from Sinai, and delivered it to Joshua, and Joshua to the elders (Josh. xxiv. 31, Judg. ii. 7), and the elders to the prophets, and the prophets to the men of the Great Synagogue" (*Aboth*, I. 1, transl. Taylor).

permanent than those of Amos and his successors. To us
Christians, it is a fact that Amos and Isaiah, as well as Moses
and Elijah, must on occasion pass behind the cloud. Whenever
the teaching of Jesus Christ is greater and more complete than
theirs, they should vanish out of sight, and we must *hear Him*
(St Mark ix. 7).

VI. THE TEACHING OF AMOS

The teaching of Amos may be most conveniently discussed
under the headings: (i) Amos' Conception of Jehovah;
(ii) Social Righteousness; (iii) Sacrifice; (iv) Jehovah's
Visitation.

(i) *Amos' Conception of Jehovah*

(a) Jehovah is *the God of nature*. From early time Israel's
God was pictured as being attended by earthquake (*e.g.*
Judg. v. 5). Moreover, on occasion He 'rained fire' (Gen. xix.
24, 'J'),[1] caused pestilence (Exod. xii. 29, 'J') or sent drought
(Gen. xli. 27, 28, 'E'). To Amos Jehovah has *all* the forces
of nature, and every natural plague, in His control (iv. 6–11,
viii. 8, ix. 5). He can, moreover, cause an eclipse of the sun
(viii. 9). He has power in heaven and in the underworld, as
well as in the bottom of the sea (ix. 2, 3). But preeminently
Amos' picture is of a Divine sovereignty through nature over
man (ix. 7, 8). Yet it is not at all certain that Amos, like the

---

[1] The hypothesis as to the composition and dating of the Pentateuch assumed
throughout this commentary is that known as the Graf-Wellhausen theory. This
in the opinion of the present writer, is still (taken as a whole) the best working
theory as to how "the five books of Moses" really came into existence—notwithstanding suggestions by Kennett, Hölscher, Eissfeldt, Welch and others to move
dates forward or backward. On the other hand, it should be understood that
Wellhausen's view of the history of Israel is accepted only with modification, and
the documentary theory only as a theory. It may come about that another
hypothesis, even possibly in some respects more in accordance with the traditional
dates, may finally supplant it. The history of the origin of the first five books of the
Bible may well be irrecoverable. One thing seems certain; though it is probable
that Moses played a considerably greater part in Hebrew religion and law than
that which Wellhausen was willing to assign to him, yet it will scarcely be held
again that the Pentateuch, even substantially, came from his age. For the
symbols of the various documents assumed in the Pentateuch by Wellhausen,
see p. 108. Note in particular that 'D' and 'P' belong to the time after Amos.

Second Isaiah, thought of Jehovah as transcendently great above the entire *universe*.[1]

(*b*) Jehovah is *the God, not of Israel only, but of all the world.* For those days this was a remarkable creed. Whether mankind, or any group of men in a prehistoric era, believed in the existence of one God only, can neither be proved nor utterly disproved. In Canaan before Israel entered it, there were many gods, *e.g.* Addu (Hadad) and Baal,[2] as well as several others. In the period after the final entry of the Tribes, the faith of Israel's neighbours was in patron deities or tribal gods, *e.g.* Moab worshipped Chĕmôsh. While each nation recognised the reality of the gods of the peoples surrounding it, it believed that there was one god properly its own. Such theology was (strictly speaking) neither ˙polytheism nor monotheism. A convenient name for it is *heno*theism.[3] That the Hebrews, or at least the mass of the nation, were, before the time of Amos, *heno*theists rather than *mono*theists, seems to be proved by Jephthah's words in Judg. xi. 24, by David's in 1 Sam. xxvi. 19, and possibly by Elijah's in 1 Ki. xviii. 27.[4] Whether *Moses* was an absolute monotheist, or only a henotheist, cannot be stated categorically. He insisted that for Israel there was but one God, *viz.* He who was worshipped by the name Jehovah (Hebrew ? 'Yahweh').[5] In like manner it may be taken as certain that *Samuel, Elijah* and *Elisha* all proclaimed the exclusive right of Jehovah to Israel's homage. He, and neither the Phoenician Baal, nor any other deity, was the God of Israel. However, such an expression as 'Jehovah the God *of Israel*', in the mouth of either the teacher or the people, lent itself to a narrow attitude towards the Deity. His worshippers, in prosperity, patronised Him as though He needed them and their offerings; at all times they thought that

[1] For the 'Doxology' passages, iv. 13, v. 8, 9, ix. 5, 6, are hardly by Amos. See p. 184.

[2] 'The owner', the local deity's title.   [3] Or *monolatry*, the *worship* of one God.

[4] In 1 Sam. xxvi. 19 David does not say that he shared the popular view. The speech of Elijah in 1 Ki. xviii. 27 may be interpreted *either* as admitting Baal's reality (for non-Israelites), *or* as pouring scorn upon the very idea of Baal's existence. Volz, in *Mose* (1907), regards Elijah as a pure monotheist, and so also does Causse in *Les Prophètes d'Israel et les Religions de l'Orient.*

[5] See Excursus I. i (4), pp. 329, 330.

they were entitled to count on their national God to march at
the head of their armies. Further, from what is to be found
expressly stated in the books of Kings, it is impossible for us
to believe that the people as a whole had a high conception
of Jehovah.

There was need for a purer idea of God. This Amos goes
a long way in supplying. Though Israel is Jehovah's people
(Am. vii. 8), Amos avoids entirely the use of the phrase 'God
of Israel'.[1] Jehovah is a much greater God than the people
think. He controls all nations. And He has no favourites;
according to Amos the relationship between God and Israel
involves national responsibility, not national comfort (iii. 2).
In truth, Jehovah's interests extend far beyond the narrow
boundaries of Palestine. The Prophet actually declares, 'Are
ye not as the sons of the Kushites unto me, O sons of Israel?
says Jehovah'; and he maintains that Jehovah was behind
the ancient movements of the Philistines and of the Aramaeans (ix. 7). It does not fall to Amos, in so many words, to
deny the existence of other gods as two centuries later the
great Prophet of the Exile denied such existence;[2] but, none
the less, his teaching *logically* implies that there is no God in
all the world but Jehovah.

(c) Jehovah is *righteous*. God is righteous, just, moral; for
these are the qualities which He demands both from Israel
and from the peoples around (chs. i and ii). It is this truth
(taken for granted by us to-day) which distinguished Jehovah
from the gods of all other nations. It is only consistent with
the facts to say that the God whom Amos preaches is *more*
than a God of nature or even a God of all nations; He is a God
concerned above everything with righteousness.[3]

---

[1] Once in these nine chapters Amos speaks of 'thy God', but in no happy
sense (iv. 12).

[2] Isaiah xliii. 10, xliv. 6, 8, xlv. 6, *etc.*, xlvi. 9.

[3] See p. 26. The words of F. D. Maurice are applicable to Amos: "The theology
of the prophets [*i.e.* their conception of God's character] was the ground of all their
human morality. Every perception of what man is and what he ought to do must
rest upon some perception of what God is and of what He does....To lay down
rules how a man should govern himself and others without declaring how God
governs, was in their minds a vanity, nay an impossibility" (*Prophets and Kings
of the O.T.* 1853, pp. 437, 438). It may well be also that Amos derived his doctrine

Before leaving this subject it may be remarked that caution is necessary in estimating the extent to which Amos' conception of Jehovah was new. Noble ideas of God may have been, and probably were, kept alive by a few in Israel down the centuries from Elijah or even from Moses. It is possible that in more than one matter sufficient notice has not always been taken of the general *tone* of the book of Amos. We feel, as we hear Amos speak, that the Prophet is telling the people what at least some of them have heard before.[1]

Whether old or new, the Prophet's conception of God is not perfect. One of the mistakes which the Christian Church has made, issuing in damage impossible to calculate, has been to standardise as eternal and ultimate truth that which was but a stage[2]—however lofty—in the slow process of its revelation and discovery. A first principle in the modern study of the O.T. is to realise that all O.T. teaching was given primarily to generations of people of varying immature degrees of religious, moral and mental equipment. Another point is that the teachers themselves were learners in God's school. Hosea, while emphasising judgment to come, no less than did Amos, depicts much more adequately than does his fellow prophet[3] the milder attributes of God: 'How shall I give thee up, Ephraim?...I am God and not man' (Hos. xi. 8, 9). Indeed, Hosea can preach a gospel of love and of redemption. If any picture of God found within the O.T. had been perfect,[4] then one of the reasons for the appearing of Jesus would have become unnecessary. The only complete and final revelation of

of pure monotheism from the same fundamental conception that Jehovah is righteous, as perhaps Isaiah did from a sense of Jehovah's holiness (Isa. ch. vi).

[1] *Cf.* the apt words of Dr Wardle in arguing for an early date for monotheism in Israel: "They [the prophets] certainly on the whole do not speak as if they had recently made the discovery that there was but one God" (*Isr. and Bab.* p. 114).

[2] And it is obvious that we have no right to expect in any one prophet an all-round, balanced, statement of truth upon any subject. A prophet's thought was so often the result of a direct reaction from *certain specific obstacles* existing in the minds or habits of the men to whom he was speaking.

[3] *Cf.* note on Am. vii. 2, 'O Lord God, forgive, I beseech thee'. It is a mistake to suppose that Amos' conception of God was *entirely* as of One stern, just and great.

[4] The reader may perhaps be referred to the notes upon iii. 6, v. 27, pp. 289, 290, 302.

God, we believe, comes through Jesus Christ: '*the only begotten Son*, who is in the bosom of the Father, *He* hath declared Him' (St John i. 18).

A less important point is that Amos, for all his noble contribution to the conception of God, did not avoid using anthropomorphic speech, even if he were capable of rising above such *ideas*. In v. 21 Jehovah is said to refuse to 'smell' (Hebrew) the people's offerings. Thrice He is described, in the language of men, as taking an oath (iv. 2, vi. 8, viii. 7). The proportion of such crudities seems to be larger in Amos than in the other great prophets.

(ii) *Social Righteousness*

Amos came forth as a champion of civic and commercial righteousness[1] and, in general, of the duty of man to his brother man. Hammurabi king of Babylon,[2] *c.* 1700 B.C., had been a promoter of civic justice. Amos, however, went farther than considering oppression and injustice to be breaches of a law. With the Hebrew Prophet oppression was *sin against a righteous God*. In this respect Amos was able to build upon the work of Moses, who may well have taught that righteousness was a part of a true worship of Jehovah. In Jehovah's name Nathan had denounced the king[3] for the sin of robbery, and Elijah had proclaimed God's wrath at the unjust treatment which Naboth received from the hands of Ahab and Jezebel (1 Ki. xxi. 17–24). Almost certainly Amos was not the first in Israel to preach ethical religion; but, in a conspicuous degree, and in language of magnificent forcefulness, he laid stress upon this requirement of Jehovah:[4] 'Seek the LORD, and ye shall live....Seek good, and not evil, that ye may live.... Hate the evil, and love the good' (v. 6, 14, 15).

---

[1] For the meaning of the word 'righteousness' (as distinct from *e.g.* 'holiness'), *cf.* note on Am. v. 7.

[2] *Cf.* note on Am. iii. 9, p. 160. The accepted dating (in 1954) for Hammurabi is 18th–17th century B.C. See W. F. Albright in *O.T. and Modern Study*, p. 34.

[3] The proposition of Gressmann (*Alt. Proph.* edn 2, p. 156) that this story (2 Sam. xi. 27 *b*–xii. 15 *a*) is of the nature of unhistorical folklore, will hardly, it may be supposed, command general acceptance.

[4] See notes on 'righteousness' (v. 7), 'sin' (v. 12) and 'transgression' (i. 3).

(iii) *Sacrifice*

To the Semitic mind worship and sacrifice were joined together indissolubly. "Prayer was my practice, sacrificing my law".[1] In Israel and in Judah there were many well-worn stories current[2] and also legal enactments in force[3] bearing upon sacrifice. Indeed, most of the Israelites, exactly like the neighbouring nations, were actually thinking that *all* that their patron Deity required was sacrifice (*cf.* above, p. 8). It was from this idea of God's requirements that the soul of Amos revolted. He felt that the performance of the outward acts of religion without morality was positively displeasing to Jehovah; in fact it only increased the worshippers' guilt. In Am. iv. 4 we read the derisive words, 'Come to Beth-el, and transgress: to Gilgal, and multiply transgression; and bring your sacrifices every morning'. The same teaching is to be seen in the other prophets of Amos' line.

But in his hatred of the abuse of sacrifice, Amos has another point to make; and here especially his view was either daringly fresh, or at least entirely out of accord with the general religious convictions of his day. In spite of the traditions of the past, unwritten and written, Amos in v. 25 says, as the words of Jehovah, 'Did ye bring unto me sacrifices and offerings in the wilderness forty years, O house of Israel?'[4] In the original the question is so put that it admits of but one answer—'No'. Now with Amos, as with other early canonical prophets, the nation's political and spiritual history began at the Exodus (*cf.* Am. ii. 9, 10). In the eyes of a contemporary prophet at least, the wilderness[5] was, as it were, Israel's honeymoon with Jehovah. Yet the words of Amos seem to imply that, at least for the greater part of that time of Israel's intimate relation with her God, sacrifices and offerings were not made. The conclusion to which the Prophet's words were meant to lead was: They cannot be necessary *now*. If Amos

---

[1] So the Babylonian king Tâbi-utul-Bêl.
[2] *E.g.* Gen. iv. 4 'J', xii. 8 'J', xiii. 4 'J', xxi. 33 'J', xxii. 2 'E'.
[3] *E.g.* Exod. xx. 24 'E', xxxiv. 25 'J'.
[4] For various interpretations of this passage, see pp. 338-340.
[5] Interpreting Hos. ii. 15 picturesquely but reverently.

intended this (and the context of the passage renders it impossible to doubt that, whether rightly or wrongly, he *did*), he was but foreshadowing what Jeremiah was to declare in language more sweeping—but not till a century and a half later: 'I spake not unto your fathers, nor commanded them in the day that I brought them out of the land of Egypt, concerning burnt offerings or sacrifices'.[1] Amos says that not ritual-slaughterings, nor gifts at the sanctuary, are what God seeks, but righteousness in daily life. The Prophet works out this theme in one of the most exalted passages of the O.T. (v. 21-27). Consistent, moreover, with Amos' view of sacrifice, is his contemplation without misgivings of the overthrow of the places where sacrifice was wont to be offered.[2]

(iv) *Jehovah's 'Visitation'*[3]

Amos held that above all Jehovah was a God of righteousness; he also stated that He could and would punish the nations around Israel for their transgressions of the law of righteousness. To Israel this last idea might indeed be a welcome announcement; but that Jehovah would do the same to *them*, and on account of moral faults, was an unpleasant truth. And Amos says that Jehovah not only is about to

---

[1] The whole passage, Jer. vii. 21-23, is illuminating: *cf.* also Jer. vi. 20.

[2] See iii. 14 *b*, vii. 9, ix. 1, 2, and the note on iv. 4, pp. 295, 296.

[3] It is convenient to treat this subject after the last three, although the view taken in this commentary is that probably it was the *pressure of Assyria* that forced on Amos the question of God's speedy retribution upon Israel's sin. He saw on the horizon Israel's conquerors. The Prophet, and the people also, when the time came, would interpret the disaster as a proof of Jehovah's displeasure. Amos, however, would differ from the majority of his contemporaries in holding that this displeasure was in no way to be connected with ritual faults, but that it was on account of national moral corruption. On the other hand, some scholars, conspicuously Hölscher, hold that the primary thought in the Prophet's mind was not Assyria, but rather the wickedness of Israel: "The motive of his prophecy was not the Assyrian peril, though he was aware of it, but an ethical postulate". Punishment of some sort, soon or late, *must come*. War and captivity are but one form—and by no means the main form—of such chastisement. The view of Professor Peake is worthy of consideration here: "It is not unlikely that both causes were at work [in the mind of Amos], the psychical sensitiveness to atmospheric change, the moral postulate that sin so flagrant as Israel's demanded exemplary chastisement. And keen political foresight should be taken into account" (*The People and the Book*, p. 266). See, further, p. 302 of this commentary.

'visit' them thus (iii. 2); but that 'the *end* is come upon My
people Israel; I will not forgive them further'.[1] This was perhaps the most original part of his message. Israel as a nation
would be annihilated. They had thought that they were
necessary to Jehovah, His 'inheritance', just as Moab was
the 'portion' of Chemosh; but the teaching of Amos implied
that God is content if *righteousness* is vindicated, even though
such vindication should leave none to worship Him. Incidentally, we see that even if, after all, some Israelites should survive,
no one in Israel will be able to hold the belief in a mere tribal
Deity. Amos breaks up this dogma for all time. To quote the
words of Hölscher: "In that Jehovah exposes His people to
annihilation, the idea of a national god is dissolved".[2]
Further, it is worth observing that when Assyria should
conquer Israel it would seem to the majority of the people
like a triumph against Israel's national God. For that age, the
one escape from such a conclusion, theologically, lay in such
a position as that of Amos, *viz.* that Jehovah the God of many
nations was using Assyria as His instrument.[3] Amos' teaching,
as has been said before (like much in the earliest books of the
O.T. revelation), is not final for all time, but rather the highest
truth comprehensible to the minds of the people of his day.

What form, if the Book of Amos be allowed to speak for
itself, will the visitation take?[4] (1) First and foremost,

---

[1] Am. viii. 2. It may be that only slowly did Amos arrive at the conviction
that Israel was doomed. It is not necessary to suppose that the Prophet's
career was a question of months only. Hosea's ministry covered several reigns.
If Amos was prophesying into the reign of Pekah (even as Winckler, for his own
purposes, dates Amos, *cf.* note on vii. 12, p. 231, footnote 2), he would have time
to observe both the slight effect of his preaching and also the gathering strength
of Assyria. *Cf.* note on vii. 15, 'The LORD took me'.

[2] *Cf.* also G. A. Smith, *XII Prophets*, p. 54. See further the note on the phrase
'Day of the LORD', in v. 18–20, p. 193 of the present commentary.

[3] This is practically the view of Amos. So, more clearly, Isaiah soon after,
Isa. vii. 18, 19 and, especially, x. 5–15.

[4] For the suggestion that the predictions of Amos are essentially a part of a
fixed eschatological scheme—an Assyrian war (and captivity) belonging not to
the forefront but being somewhat incidental—*cf.* pp. 62–64 on *Eschat. and the Book
of Amos.* The view taken above receives support from the emphatic words of
Hölscher that the prophecies of both Amos and Hosea were "pure threatening
predictions. What they predicted was a definite historical catastrophe by Assyria,
and this prediction is no more to be termed eschatological than is that of Cassandra
concerning the fall of Troy" (*Die Ursprünge der jüd. Eschatologie*, 1925, p. 14).

Assyria will overrun Israel. It is true that at the date usually assigned to the preaching of Amos this great empire was not, for the moment, a menace. However, the power recently that chiefly had weakened Israel's neighbour Aram was Assyria. To Shalmaneser III Jehu himself (Jeroboam's great-grand-father) had paid tribute. Though never does the name Assyria actually occur in the nine chapters, the meaning of Amos would seem to be clear enough. In chs. i and ii the nations are to be overthrown in battle; and of the Israelites in particular hardly one man will escape. In iii. 11, 12, 'an adversary' is alluded to somewhat obscurely; but the capital of the Northern Kingdom is mentioned by name, with its castles, as being conquered. In vi. 14 'a nation' is to 'afflict' Israel 'from the entering in of Hamath unto the brook of the Arabah'. Ch. vii. 9 gives details of the coming war. The sanctuaries of Israel will be devastated; and Jeroboam II's dynasty will perish 'with the sword'. And, worst of all, the people are to be removed from Israelite territory (v. 5, vi. 7, vii. 17, ix. 4). They are to go into exile 'beyond Damascus' (v. 27). This is the one *precise* reference to the foe. The only power which could take Israel into exile to the other side of the Aramaean capital was the Assyrian Empire.

(2) But there will be another means of punishment. In Israel's case, the conditions of the conflict will lead, as not seldom in the East, to *plague* (v. 16, 17, see note, vi. 9, 10, viii. 3).

(3) Also, in the Prophet's[1] presentation of coming disaster, there are elements of *natural*, as well as of political, cata-strophe. (a) In viii. 8 an *earthquake* is foretold in vivid lan-guage. It is picturesquely represented as being so severe that

[1] For the explanation that a universal catastrophe provided the background of a pre-prophetic, and indeed prophetic 'eschatology', *cf.* Introd. pp. 56–58. On the other hand, the view that the apocalyptic, or more correctly, *natural*, element is secondary, and indeed only a sort of *filling in* of a prophetic picture of judg-ment, seems to be confirmed by a study of those prophets who without any question prophesied with a definite political event before their eyes. The short oracle on Babylon in Jer. ch. 1 supplies a case in point. The idea of 'the sword' is primary, and dominates the passage (*vv.* 35–37, *cf. v.* 41). But there is, in a subsidiary position, a supernatural drought (*v.* 38), and something comparable to the *over-throw* of Sodom and Gomorrah (*v.* 40). Similarly in Egyptian oracles the political element is primary, not the nature-catastrophes. *Cf.* Introd. pp. 54, 58.

the whole of Palestine will rise and sink again like the Nile
(viii. 8 = ix. 5).[1] According to iv. 11 there had been a seismo-
logical disturbance recently. As referring to an earthquake
some would also explain ii. 13–16 and ix. 1 a (see notes). (b) In
viii. 9 something of the nature of an *eclipse* is foreshadowed.[2]

Thus, whatever the order of the events, and however much
of the programme the Prophet seriously believed in,[3] destruction is foretold by means of war, pestilence and earthquake; and there is to be no escape (ix. 1–4). This is the
'end' (viii. 2). The very purpose of the Shepherd's leaving his
work was to bring this message to Israel (vii. 14, 15). Yet
(theoretically) it is conceivable that Amos prophesied believing, at any rate at first, that his predictions might have
been stultified had the people repented.[4] For, all prediction in the O.T., so far as it contains a divine element,
must have been conditional. 'Seek the LORD, and ye shall
live', cried Amos, as it were giving the people a chance
(v. 5 and *cf.* v. 15 *b*, with notes). However, the mainspring of
Amos' impulse was not a hope of the people's repentance and
reformation. For, in vision, he already had seen Israel 'fallen'
(v. 2). He is a prophet of inevitable (or all but inevitable)
doom, as was Jeremiah in the Southern Kingdom in the time
of king Zedekiah and the Babylonians. However, whilst
Jeremiah was distinguished by a firm faith in an ultimate
regeneration of God's people and their return from exile,

[1] Possibly both these passages are interpolations.

[2] Prof. Micklem (*Proph. and Eschat.* pp. 114, 115) is right in insisting that the
references to such disasters as (2) and (3) are not to be taken as metaphors
consciously used by the Prophet to convey to the people the idea of punishment
by *captivity*. On the other hand, it seems difficult to believe that Amos intended
the eschatological pictures (in some respects popular ideas) to be taken literally.
It may be that sometimes the Prophet is giving us various elements from *visions*
of his by means of which there came to be borne in upon himself *personally* the
terrible truth of the coming calamity of captivity. This is specially the case in
ix. 1–4. See, further, the note on vi. 7.

[3] After all, a prophet need not see a consistent picture in his mind. It will
hardly be denied that no man foretold *exile* more definitely than did Jeremiah in
the case of Judah. Yet, in Jer. xvi. 16, that prophet says emphatically 'both great
and small shall die in this *land*; they shall not be buried'. Moreover, he predicted other catastrophes, *viz.* famine and wild beasts at the same time as war
and captivity (xv. 2, 3).

[4] But did Amos believe that they would repent? *Cf.* Introd. pp. 69 and
70.

Amos could, as a fact, see only the extinction of Israel, even as Aram and Moab must disappear. Ch. ix. 8 c–15 is an appendix of a later age.[1]

What did Amos expect would happen when Samaria should fall? Some scholars think that he based his hope still upon Judah;[2] unless, indeed, his message of doom was intended to apply almost equally to both kingdoms. Probably he had no programme for the more distant future, only a magnificent trust in the permanence of Jehovah and righteousness.[3]

VII. A SUMMARY OF THE PRINCIPLES OF HEBREW POETRY, WITH SPECIAL REFERENCE TO THE POETRY OF AMOS

The work of the great prophets of Israel did not consist in writing philosophy in long sentences, but in speaking upon very practical matters with considerable conciseness. For the most part their language falls into poetry. Many scholars regard the poetry of the prophets as the natural outcome of an elevated (or even 'ecstatic') condition of mind. There may be truth in this view. On the other hand, the prophets may consciously have chosen the medium of poetry for conveying their message, because by it their teaching would be presented forcefully at the time of its utterance, and, moreover, it could be retained the more easily in the hearers' memory.

Poems always suffer much by translation, but, upon the whole, those of the ancient Hebrews lose less than do those composed in modern languages. The chief distinctive features of Hebrew[4] poetry should be mentioned:

---

[1] Introd. pp. 67–77.   [2] So Hölscher; but see on iii. 1.

[3] Cf. Marti, 'Der Prophet Amos und seine Bedeutung', Dodekapropheton.

[4] Hebrew poetry has close affinities with both (1) Babylonian and (2) Egyptian. (1) Parallelism and strophic arrangement with a refrain occur in the Tell el-Amarna Tablets (see C.A.H. II. p. 338 and G. R. Driver in Psalmists, pp. 114–117). (2) Examples of parallelism in Egyptian poems may be seen in the citations on pp. 286, 287, 308. For fuller treatment of the extremely important subject of Hebrew poetry the reader may be referred to G. A. Smith (Schweich Lectures, 1910), G. B. Gray (The Forms of Hebrew Poetry), Duhm (The Twelve Prophets (translation Duff, pp. 21–27)), and the article "Poetry" by K. Budde in H.D.B. IV. pp. 3 ff. The question of Rhythm is discussed by T. H. Robinson in

(i) The most easily recognised characteristic is *Parallelism*, *e.g.* in Am. iv. 4 (R.V.):

(a) Cóme to Béth-el, and transgréss; | (b) to Gílgal, and múltiply
transgréssion;
(c) And bríng your sácrifices every mórning, | (d) and your títhes every
thrée dáys.

In line 1, clause (b) is parallel in meaning to clause (a); similarly (d) to (c). Other good examples would be i. 2, i. 4, iii. 3–8, v. 23, 24, viii. 10.[1]

(ii) *Rhythm*. (A) In the case above (Am. iv. 4) each half-line, or *stichos*, in Hebrew has three 'beats', or stressed syllables. This example is the (extremely common) *trimeter*.[2] See *e.g.* Am. i. 2–5, iv. 4, 5, v. 14, 15 a. (B) Another, and more clearly marked, rhythm is *qînâh* or elegiac measure, *e.g.* Am. v. 2:

(a) Hath fállen no móre to ríse | (b) vírgin Ísrael:
(c) Is cast dówn upón her lánd | (d) nóne raísing her.

In *qînâh* the second part of each line fills out the meaning of the first,[3] and (in its most characteristic form) has but two beats as against three in the first. The *whole* line is thus a *pentameter*. This is the rhythm of the book of Lamentations. It can also be used when the subject is not elegy, as in Am. ii. 8, iii. 2–6. (C) The *tetrameter*, with its *four* 'beats' in each half-line, is usually (though not invariably, *e.g.* Am. ii. 4) the result of the juxtaposition of *di-meters*, or stichoi consisting of two beats: so Am. ii. 7 b, iv. 1, ix. 12 b. And there are less common verse-forms. In passages in the book of Amos where the rhythm is very clearly marked, reference to the metre frequently will be made in the commentary.

(iii) Lines are sometimes grouped into distinct *Strophes*. Not seldom these divisions are marked by the poet himself by means of recurring introductory formulae or closing *refrains*,

his metrically arranged text of *Amos*, pp. 4–6, and by H. Schmidt in *Amos*, pp. 110–140. The poetry of Amos has been investigated by (amongst others) Harper (1897–1904), Löhr, Sievers, Condamin (all in 1901), and Baumann (1903).

[1] The poetic *parallelism* of the prophets is exhibited conveniently to the eye in such an edition as that of Woods and Powell.

[2] The term *trimeter*, as also *pentameter*, is applied even by Josephus to ancient Hebrew poetry, *Antt.* VII. xii. 3.

[3] Buchanan Gray terms this "echoing rhythm" (*Isaiah*, p. lxiii).

e.g. in Am. chs. i and ii the several strophes are introduced by
'Thus saith Jehovah: For three transgressions of...punish-
ment thereof'. A striking instance of the refrain, finishing
each of five strophes of a poem, occurs in Am. iv. 6, 8, 9,
10, 11, 'Yet have ye not returned unto me, it is an oracle of
Jehovah'.

All the prophetic preachers were poets, and Amos (though
his metre is not as regular as *e.g.* the poetry of Isaiah, chs. xl–
lxvi) ranks among the most effective. For the consideration
of Hebrew rhythm in the determination of the true text, as
distinct from additions or corruptions, see the notes on such
passages as Am. ii. 4 (p. 285), iii. 1, 4, 5, iv. 10, v. 26, viii.
9 *b*, ix. 2, 9.

VIII. THE DATE OF THE PREACHING OF AMOS

(i) Whether or not the section, vii. 10–17, is in its true
position in the book, it certainly may be held to be historical.
Consequently, the preaching of Amos may be fixed definitely
as having taken place **during the reign of Jeroboam II**.
The passage opens with the words: 'Then Amaziah, the priest
of Beth-el, sent to Jeroboam..., saying...'. According to
the most accepted chronology, this Jeroboam reigned from
783 B.C. to 745 B.C.[1]

(ii) Ch. vi. 14 suggests the time somewhat more precisely:
'They [*i.e.* the foe] shall afflict you from the entering in of
Hamath unto the brook of the Arabah'. These terms would
not afford an accurate description of the bounds of Israelite
territory in any year from the death of Solomon until after
Jeroboam II's great victories. By what is, probably, "an un-
designed coincidence", almost the very words of Am. vi. 14
are found in the account of Jeroboam's reign in 2 Ki. xiv. 25.
Further, we read in xiv. 28, 'he [Jeroboam II] recovered
Damascus, and Hamath,...for Israel'.[2] Hence Amos must
come **a few years** (though not necessarily very many) **after
783 B.C.**

[1] But see below, (vii), p. 38.
[2] *Cf.* p. 305 *infra.*

(iii) The period within Jeroboam's reign may be further narrowed down. The condition of comparative prosperity, and indeed of luxury, of many in Israel as revealed in the impassioned discourses of Amos, shews that there had been some *years of rest* after the wars with Syria referred to in (ii), above. Considerations (ii) and (iii) bring down the date within Jeroboam's reign to, say, **760 B.C.** at the earliest.

(iv) Agreeing with this date is the allusion, in Am. viii. 9, to a darkening of the sun, 'I will cause the sun to go down at noon, and I will darken the earth in the clear day'. We may regard the prediction of what is, presumably, an eclipse as being suggested by the actual occurrence of one recently. Such a simple and natural reference to an eclipse stands alone in the O.T. As a matter of fact, there is a record upon an Assyrian tablet of a total eclipse of the sun having taken place in 763 B.C.

Consistent with all the above evidence, Sir G. A. Smith gives the date "towards the **middle** of the **eighth century**"; Cheyne "**765–750**"; Canney, "**about 760 B.C.**"; Nowack, "in the **latter half of the reign** of Jeroboam II"; Gressmann and Sellin, "**about 750**".[1]

Is it not, however, a reasonable proposition that wholly inadequate attention has been given to a possibility that the date of Amos should be nearly twenty years later than 760 B.C.?

(v) During the reign of Jeroboam II till 745 B.C., the Assyrian Empire, notwithstanding activity in various directions (even in Syria in the year 765), would appear to have been more or less on the decline. At least the Assyrian kings were comparatively peaceful, and mainly by reason of the might of the Vannic Empire[2], of limited power. However, in the year 745 B.C. the great warrior, Tiglath-pileser III, usurped the throne of Nineveh.[3] Even in his accession year, he shewed his power by a thorough defeat of the Aramaeans of Babylonia and by the organisation of the Assyrian administration in

---

[1] *Cf.* also Peake, "Amos probably began his career several years before... 745" (*People and Book*, p. 266).
[2] *Cf.* p. 4, footnote 4, *supra*.   [3] In the month *'Iyyār* (May).

that region. Thus began Tiglath-pileser, than whose reign
none was destined to be more glorious in the whole of Assyrian
history. Hence the preaching of Amos might well be placed at
745 or 744 B.C.[1] Doubtless in any circumstances an Amos
could have arisen with so definite a message as that which
concerned the destruction, or 'captivity', of Israel at the
hands of a foe from 'beyond Damascus'; but, surely, it is not
as probable that the Prophet would feel the call to proclaim to
Israel this disaster when the military power of the only great
empire 'beyond Damascus' was weak and declining; nor
would this be in accordance with what we know otherwise of
God's way with the prophets.[2] On the other hand, the rise of
a monarch suddenly reviving Assyria's temporarily waning
prestige would exactly furnish the circumstances in which the
call to Amos would appear natural.[3] The exploits of the same
Tiglath-pileser may well have led Isaiah to become a prophet
in Judah about 740 B.C.; by which date also Hosea[4] in North

[1] So Zeydner and Valeton. See p. xxii, n. 3.

[2] Nowack, who keeps to an earlier date (before the rise of Tiglath-pileser)
consistently with this, declares that Amos is independent of political circumstances. By the operation of Jehovah within him he becomes inspired to preach
the downfall of Israel (*Kleine Propheten*, edn 3, pp. 112, 113; edn 2, p. 121).
It is noteworthy that Nowack's chief objection to Zeijdner's dating of Amos is
that Amaziah in ch. vii had not yet heard of Hosea. Against this it must be said
that there is not any necessity to date Hosea earlier than the reign of Jeroboam's
son Zechariah. *Cf.* note 4 below.

[3] The present argument assumes that Amos *did* prophesy the coming of
Assyria, and that it was fundamental in his thinking. For a different point of
view based upon the 'eschatological' theory, see below, pp. 62–64. But even
Sellin, who declares that Amos uses the material to hand from the old *Unheil*
eschatology, admits, "He means the Assyrian, who at the command of
Jehovah will surround the land..." (*Zwölfprophetenbuch*, p. 149).

[4] Either Jeroboam, or his son who reigned but six months and was the last of
the dynasty, must have been living when the words of Hosea in i. 4 were spoken.
How, otherwise, would it be possible to 'avenge the blood of Jezreel', *i.e.* the
blood shed by the founder of the Jehu dynasty? Moreover, the two men, Hosea
and Amos, appeared to posterity to be so nearly contemporary that the Jewish
copyists of the "Book of the Twelve" transcribed Hosea actually *before* Amos.
In the uncial MSS. of the LXX Amos is never separated from Hosea by Joel
(see Swete, *Introd. to LXX*, pp. 201, 202). On the other hand it should be borne
in mind that whilst Amos' ministry may not have lasted much more than a year
(some scholars would make it much less), that of Hosea almost certainly continued through the reigns of Menahem, Pekah and even Hoshea—as the various
allusions to the repeated changes of government policy indicate. The length of
Hosea's ministry accounts for his references to Assyria being more definite
than anything found in Amos (Hos. vii. 11, viii. 9, ix. 3, x. 6).

Israel certainly had begun to prophesy. Similarly in the century following, it was at the moment that the Scythians appeared to be a menace to Judah that both Jeremiah and Zephaniah felt the call to be prophets.

(vi) If the hypothesis is sound, that in the main the figure of Tiglath-pileser provided the moving cause of the prophesying of Amos, a date slightly later than 745–744 B.C., when that king's greatness had become established beyond any doubt, would in the view of the present writer be more probable. The evidence, though of varying value, is cumulative.

In 744 B.C. Tiglath-pileser wasted the lands to the east of Assyria, and sent an expedition into Media. The year 743 B.C. witnessed a triumph of considerable significance. Sarduris, king of Urarṭu,[1] with a wide and threatening alliance in the north and west of Nineveh, was thoroughly worsted, and much spoil was taken. The allies sent in presents and tribute. Tiglath-pileser was able therefore later, in 743, to renew the siege[2] of Arpad in Northern Syria, from which the above military action had compelled him temporarily to withdraw. Thus the entire Syrian country was opened to Assyrian invasion, without the possibility of the interference of the hitherto powerful Urarṭu.[3] Therefore, in the year **743 B.C., or a year or two later**, much more obviously than in 745 B.C., Assyria would appear to be a danger to Israel. Amos, selling the wool of his sheep at Damascus, would hear the stories about Tiglath-pileser, convincing him that a new age in Assyrian history had begun. As yet, however, the politicians of Israel had not realised what was happening. The book of Amos gives a picture of careless, and indeed boastful, rulers (vi. 1, 13). The Syrian nightmare had lasted a century; the reaction of optimism would not die down quickly. It is hardly too much to say that (in contrast to the mind and attitude of the leaders of the people), while Amos' references to the advance of Assyria are somewhat indefinite as compared with those occurring in Isaiah

---

[1] Ararat or Armenia. Rogers' dates are one year later than those given above.

[2] The city was taken in 741. The vassal state of Arpad had become actually a part of the kingdom of Urarṭu.

[3] *Cf.* Rogers, *Hist. of Bab. and Assyria*, II. pp. 113–116.

chs. vii and viii (735 B.C.) and even in Hosea, there are in his utterances a ring of certainty and a note of almost impending doom, which suggest that, in fact, the dread invaders are not far distant.[1] If the refrain of chs. i and ii is to be translated 'I will not turn him back', the invader is already almost on his way.[2] The whole land is to suffer from some 'nation' (vi. 14); and if the *Assyrian* be not in the mind of the Prophet, who is to exile Israel 'beyond Damascus' (v. 27)?

Furthermore, of the several references to approaching captivity made by Amos, that which is contained in the passage vii. 17 is definite and detailed, and the peril is *imminent*.[3] The wife and children of Amaziah himself are to suffer in the capture of Beth-el. Is such a prediction thinkable, except in circumstances in which Assyria had already become a real danger to Israel? Moreover, the prophecy with regard to Amaziah, and, in particular, his wife, might stand some reasonable chance of being accomplished if uttered only twenty years before the fall of Beth-el;[4] but there would be far less probability of its fulfilment[5] if it were a question of *forty* years. Would either person have been alive?

(vii) Probably the main difficulty that could be urged definitely against the date 743 B.C., or slightly later, would be that, according to the most usual reckoning, Jeroboam II's death had occurred in 745 B.C. This obstacle might seem at first sight to be indeed a fatal one; but the death of Jeroboam

---

[1] *Cf.* Kent, *Kings and Prophets of Isr. and Judah*, p. 58. It should be pointed out that though Kent suggests Amos' date to be "probably about 745 B.C.", he gives as the extreme limits, on the one hand, 750, and, on the other, as late as 740.

[2] See note on i. 3, p. 119. H. W. Hogg, in the paper there quoted, rem.rks, "The most natural explanation is that one of the burning questions of the hour was: What is Assyria going to do? Will it, or will it not, come on southwards.... Amos's answer is clear and decided: Yes, the Assyrian will: 'For triple, nay, quadruple, iniquity', srys Yahwè, 'I will not turn him back'".

[3] Even if the oracle may have come down to us in a form adapted to the later actual occurrences at the fall of Beth-el, probably few scholars would regard it as being of the nature of a *vaticinium post eventum*.

[4] This event would take place before the conquerors had begun the three years' siege of the nation's last stronghold, Samaria, *i.e.* about 725 B.C. It may be the capture of Beth-el by Shalmaneser that is referred to in Hos. x. 14, 'as Shalman spoiled Beth-arbel [or, rather, *Beth-el*, emendation Kennett] in the day of battle'.

[5] Including the reference to the fate of his wife.

may be, perhaps in any case *should* be, brought down to
743 B.C.,[1] or even a year or two further.[2] If the year of
Jehu's tribute to Shalmaneser III, 841 B.C., was his *accession
year*, the subtraction of 102 years (*viz.* 28 of Jehu's reign +
17 of Jehoahaz' + 16 of Jehoash's + 41 of Jeroboam's) would
make Jeroboam's death take place in 739 B.C.[3] At any rate,
it may be placed as late as 741 B.C., which would allow three
years, if needed, before the fixed date of the tribute of
Menahem in 738 B.C.;[4] and this is all that matters for the
purposes of ultimate chronology. Thus, the preaching of Amos
could fall just within the reign of Jeroboam II.[5]

(viii) A late dating for Amos may receive a certain amount
of corroboration from the statement in i. 1, 'two years before
the earthquake'.[6] This clause was intended by the editor of the
book to fix the date. The question, however, in the mind of
the modern reader is: But *when* was the earthquake? Now,
earthquakes were common enough on the coast of the
Mediterranean. Only one of exceptional severity could have
been regarded as affording a means of dating Amos' prophecy.
The same verse (i. 1) says that it was in the reign of Uzziah,
i.e. Azariah, king of Judah. Azariah's death may have taken

[1] 743 B.C. is the date given by Dr Peake for the accession of king Zechariah
(*Commentary*, p. 120).

[2] By any computation, the fixing of the year of Jehu's tribute as 841 B.C.,
rather than 842 (see *C.A.H.* III. p. 3), makes it possible to count the year of
Jeroboam's death as one year later than used to be thought.

[3] This suggestion of Dr Kennett's seems to meet the difficulty. Also for the
further argument upon the earthquake (p. 41) the writer is indebted to Professor Kennett, who makes the call of Amos 743–740 B.C.

[4] Menahem's tribute naturally was offered in his *first* year. And in any case
it is quite impossible to allow to the kings from Menahem to Hoshea the length of
reigns assigned to them in 2 Kings. 738 and 722 B.C. are *fixed* dates. Mr
Lanchester in Driver's *Amos* puts Jeroboam's death at 741.

[5] Another objection to the later date for the preaching of Amos might be that
Am. vi. 13 seems to imply that certain victories over Syria were of quite recent
occurrence, whereas if the date of Amos be about 743–741 Jeroboam's great
triumph was now a generation old. The answer to this would be that if the passage
contains place-names, *Lo-debar* and *Karnaim*, it will probably be necessary to see
in vi. 13 an allusion to a *fresh* victory over Syria. See note, p. 304. Am. iv. 10
may provide evidence of some military action on the part of Syria since Jeroboam's first triumph: 'Your young men have I slain with the sword...yet have
ye not returned unto me'.

[6] Other references to an earthquake occur in ii. 13–16 (possibly), viii. 8
(= ix. 5), ix. 1.

place about 749 B.C. But probably it was later than this; indeed there is reason to believe that it did not occur before 740 or 739 B.C.[1] Now, if the statement of Josephus[2] can be trusted that

[1] This is following (against, indeed, Winckler, Hommel, and many other scholars) what may be, after all, the simplest explanation of the appearance in an inscription of the name *Azriyâ'û* of *Yâûdî* as the chief of a coalition with Northern Syrian states in 739 B.C. See *C.O.T.* (*W.*), I. pp. 209–212. That Azariah, though a leper, should, when the alliance was formed, still be technically the head of the Judaean kingdom, would seem to the present writer to be less unlikely than the coincidence of two monarchs named Azariah (the name apparently signifying in each case 'whom *Jehovah* has helped') reigning respectively in Yâûdî, interpreted as *Ya'di* in N. Syria (*cf.* the Zenjirli inscriptions) and *Judah*, at so nearly the same period of history. Moreover, 2 Ki. xiv. 28 ('how he recovered Damascus, and *Hamath*,...to *Judah*'), corrupt though the text be, furnishes some evidence for the existence of relations between *Judah* and *Hamath*. Schrader assumed the identification of Yâûdî and Judah, in *C.O.T.* (*W.*), p. 213; so also George Smith and Rogers. Gray (*Isaiah*, pp. lxx and lxxvi) is prepared to discuss the identification; and S. A. Cook in *C.A.H.* III. p. 378 leaves the question open (but see this writer in *E.B.* art. "Uzziah", § 7). Kennett, *Isaiah*, pp. 9, 10, would account for the alliance of states by the attractive suggestion that it was directed not against Assyria but against *North Israel*: "If the king of Judah was anxious to throw off the yoke of North Israel, the rulers of the Northern Syrian states may well have felt that the same yoke was a menace to them. For Jeroboam II had considerably enlarged his kingdom, of which the northern boundary had finally reached 'the entering in of Hamath'". Then in 739 B.C. Tiglathpileser III would attack the North Syrian states (which were supposed to be under Assyrian suzerainty) for 'faithlessness' in entering into alliance with a foreign power (Judah), which alliance might at any time, strengthened by the aid of Egypt, be directed against himself. It is not improbable indeed that it was as a result of Egyptian influence that Shallum succeeded Jeroboam's own son on the throne of Israel. Nor is it necessary to suppose that Azariah was living at the time of the punitive expedition to which the above inscription refers; but only that he cannot have died very long before. Not too much importance need be attached to the statement in 2 Ki. xv. 33 that Jotham reigned sixteen years, even if the writer intended the figure to cover the period of Jotham's *regency*, which he did *not*.

[2] "He [Uzziah] went into the temple to offer incense to God upon the golden altar.... And when they cried out, that he must go out of the temple,... he was wroth at them.... In the meantime a great earthquake shook the ground, and *a rent was made in the temple*, and the bright rays of the sun shone through it, and fell upon the king's face, insomuch that the leprosy seized upon him immediately. And before the city, *at a place called Eroge* (*i.e.* En-rogel), half the mountain broke off from the rest on the west, and rolled itself four furlongs, and stood still at the east mountain, till the roads, as well as the king's gardens, *were spoiled by the obstruction*. Now, as soon as the priests saw that the king's face was infected with the leprosy, they told him of the calamity he was under, and commanded that he should go out of the city as a polluted person". (*Antt.* Book IX. x. 4.) With regard to the historical value of this passage it may be said that, notwithstanding its extravagancies and its obvious dependence on the prophecy of Zech. xiv. 4, it does not look like a pure invention. The references to 'the temple' and to 'the place called En-rogel' seem to point to some real historical event.

this mighty earthquake was observed at the time of the 'trespass' of Azariah (2 Chron. xxvi. 18–21) it must have occurred near the *close* of his reign.[1] 'Two years before the earthquake' would probably be within the years **745–740 B.C.**

Even if Josephus had no authority for connecting the earthquake with Azariah's trespass, there seems to be evidence, though indeed somewhat slight, that the great earthquake took place about that time, or perhaps at the *very end* of his life. For, apparently, not long after Isaiah had begun his ministry (which was *c.* 740 B.C.) that prophet is found making an allusion to a very severe earthquake with which Jehovah had already smitten the inhabitants of Judah.[2] It is, surely, at least possible that this calamity is no other than that which happened in the reign of Azariah; and the prophet's way of referring to it seems to suggest that it had occurred comparatively *recently*. On this evidence from the book of Isaiah, the earthquake may have been *some months, or more, after* the 'trespass' of Azariah; indeed, in his last year, which we have dated as 740 or 739 B.C. According to this line of reasoning 'two years before the earthquake' would make the date of the ministry of Amos **742 or 741 B.C.**

(ix) By 741 B.C. Tiglath-pileser had added to his fame by bringing to a successful conclusion the siege of Arpad; and it has been shewn above that there is no fundamental reason against holding that the year did not fall within 'the days of Jeroboam the son of Joash, king of Israel'.

For the circumstances of the *writing* of the book of Amos, see pp. 65, 66.

---

[1] Not, as Josephus says, at the *beginning*.
[2] Isa. v. 25, 'He hath stretched forth his hand against them, and hath smitten them, and the hills did tremble, and their carcases were as refuse in the midst of the streets'. Isa. vi. 4 *a* might be evidence that this earthquake occurred actually at the time of the call of Isaiah.

IX. PROPHECY IN ASSYRIA AND IN EGYPT

It has been said above[1] that prophecy, especially of an ecstatic nature, was known in Phoenicia and in ancient Israel before the rise of the great prophets. Of recent years, the attention of Biblical students has been directed to examples of prophecy (more or less predictive) from both *Assyria* and *Egypt*. It has been maintained, moreover, by certain scholars that the general scheme of, and many elements in, Hebrew prophecy were in some way derived from either the Babylonian or the Egyptian form.

The reader may find it helpful to see some at least of the material collected together. This will be shewn, with a discussion under each heading (1) Assyria, (2) Egypt. The question of the existence of what may be termed an "eschatological scheme", possibly in Babylon, more certainly in Egypt, has been the subject of considerable study, especially in the presumed relation to it of an Israelite Eschatology. The student may like to bear this fact in mind in reading this section: though the subject of Eschatology will receive more attention in the next section of this Introduction.

(1)

There are ASSYRIAN and BABYLONIAN documents[2] of a prophetic character, or with prophetic affinities. In some of these the seer foretells victory and prosperity to the king (Esar-haddon, 681–668 B.C.).

(I) The following are the words of a prophetess speaking in the name of the goddess Ishtar:

Esar-haddon, king of the Lands, be not afraid!...I am Ishtar of Arbela,[3] who thy enemies will annihilate before thy feet...I will give them (to thee). I, Ishtar of Arbela, will go before thee and behind thee. Fear not! (Remain) thou in joys (?)!...From the mouth of Ishtarlatashiat, of Arbela.

[1] Pp. 14, 15.
[2] Conveniently collected in Gressmann's *Texte*, edn 1927, pp. 281–284, from which the above summaries are made. Some of the material is also to be found in Meissner, *Babylonien und Assyrien*, II. ch. xviii, especially pp. 281, 282.
[3] The Ishtar of *Arbela* was considered more definitely a war goddess than her namesake of *Nineveh*. See, in *E.B.*, L. W. King's art. "Assyria", § 9.

(II) Another is an oracle on behalf of the same king, ending with the words:

I am Nabu,[1] the lord of the writing-reed, honour me.—From the mouth of Baia of Arbela.

(III) A third begins:

I am Ishtar of Arbela, O Esar-haddon king of Assyria...long days, eternal years, will I grant to Esar-haddon, my king!

(IV) Another oracle of the same reign from a "prophetess (?) of the king" contains such expressions as:

The kingdom is thine (?), the power is thine....Prosperity to Esar-haddon....Ishtar of Arbela has taken the field.

(V) There is a collection of oracles purporting to predict reigns of Assyrian kings, some ideally prosperous, others disastrous in the extreme. The first runs:

A prince will arise, eighteen years will he (hold) regal (sway). The land wil' dwell secure; the heart of the land will be joyful; men will (enjoy) plenty....The Deity of cattle and the Deity of wheat will create in the land plenty. Rain showers and floods will be there, the men of the land will enjoy a feast. The prince, however, will in a rising be killed with the sword.

Another foretells revolution in the land of Assyria, owing to the rise of an upstart king, and declares that during his reign there will be a mighty famine. While yet another predicts that, after what appears to be an earthquake, towns will become ruins, and revolution and destruction will take place; "the land of Amurru will slay the prince with the sword".

Prophecies numbered I–IV have their analogy in the utterance of the court prophets of 1 Ki. xxii who said, 'Go up and prosper'. The prophesying of Elisha may be compared in 2 Ki. iii. 17, 18, and in xiii. 14–19, and of Jonah in xiv. 25. In early Israel 'Deborah, a prophetess', was useful to the warrior Barak (Judg. iv. 4–9). Clearly, however, there can be no comparison between the Assyrian prophecies and the characteristic pronouncements of Amos, Isaiah or Jeremiah.[2]

---

[1] Cf. the Hebrew word nābhî, 'prophet'. For Nabû, cf. p. 16, note 4, of this Introduction.

[2] But Winckler would bring down the great prophets of Israel to such a level. Cf. above, p. 29, footnote 1, and see Wardle, Israel and Babylon, pp. 102, 103.

Of course, the oracles of the court prophets of Israel would be "in the name of Jehovah", as those of the Assyrian prophets and prophetesses were "in the name of Ishtar", etc.

Prophecies grouped under (V) are of *either* weal *or* woe. Perhaps it may be said here that, in contrast to the Egyptian oracles to be cited below, it cannot easily be argued that they suggest any scheme[1] such as that of an age of disaster being followed by an ideal era of bliss. Some of the predictions are interesting in connection with those prophets of Israel who foretold political and natural disasters, and also plenty and prosperity. However, 'earthquake', 'destruction', 'slaughter', *etc.*, are ideas likely to recur in any nation's prophetic literature without question of borrowing.

Prof. G. R. Driver, rejecting in the main the hypothesis that the Hebrew Psalter depends on Babylonian *psalms*,[2] says: "Illustration is not proof". A theory of Israelite dependence, at least on the part of its great prophets, on Babylonian *prophecy* would seem to be, upon the evidence, even less warrantable. So far as there may be any connection, it might be through early Babylonian culture in Canaan at the Tell el-Amarna age, passed on by the Canaanites to the Hebrews. So the lesser and the 'false' prophets of Israel might have acquired such affinities as present themselves.

The Assyro-Babylonian literature is, however, useful as illustration, *cf.* notes on i. 3 (for the *Ira myth*), ii. 6, iii. 7, v. 12, 17, ix. 13, 14.

(2)

The relevant evidence gathered from EGYPTIAN sources is considerably fuller; and more definite characteristics are observable in it.

(I) *The Prophecy of Neferrohu.* This purports to be by a lector-priest, 'a wise man of the East', brought in to amuse king Snofru (*c.* 2950 B.C.). Neferrohu, on asking whether he should speak of the past or of the future, is told to speak of the future; and what he utters is committed to writing. Since the prophecy ends with a panegyric of Amenemhet I, of the XIIth Dynasty, called therein Ameny, it is to be assigned to

---

[1] *Cf.* below, p. 45 and p. 55.
[2] In *The Psalmists*, edited by Prof. Simpson, p. 175.

his reign, *c.* 2000 B.C.[1] The following extracts from Prof. Sir Alan Gardiner's translation seem best to illustrate the O.T. prophets. Somewhat over three-quarters of the way through the oracle, after a description of a period of *disaster*, without introduction commences a prophecy of *weal*. These two natural divisions of the subject are shewn below under (1) and (2).

(1) Up, my heart, and bewail this land whence thou art sprung.... Behold, princes hold sway in the land, things made are as though they had never been made.... The land is utterly perished, and nought remains.... Perished is this land...; none speaks, none acts.... The sun is veiled and shines not in the sight of men.... I will speak of what is before me. I prophesy not that which is not yet come. The river is dry, (even the river) of Egypt.... All good things are passed away.... I show thee the land upside down; happened that which never (yet) had happened. Men shall take weapons of warfare; the land lives in uproar.... All good things have departed.... Men take a man's possessions from him; they are given to him who is a stranger. I show thee the possessor as one needy, while the stranger is satisfied.... The land is minished, its rulers are multiplied. Lacking is any rich in his produce. Little is the corn, great the corn-measure;... Rê removes himself from men. (If) he shines, it is (but) an hour(?). None knoweth that midday is there; his shadow is not discerned.... I show thee the land upside down.... (2) There is a King shall come from the South, whose name is Ameny, son of a Nubian woman, a child of Chen-khon. He shall receive the White Crown; he shall assume the Red Crown; he shall unite the Two Powerful Ones.[2]... The people of his time shall rejoice, (this) man of noble birth shall make his name for ever and ever. Those who turn to mischief, who devise rebellion shall subdue their mouthings through fear of him. The Asiatics shall fall by his sword, the Libyans shall fall before his flame, and the rebels before his wrath, and the froward before his majesty. ... And Right shall come into its place, and Iniquity be cast forth. He will rejoice who shall behold and who shall serve the King. And he that is prudent shall pour to me libation when he sees fulfilled what I have spoken.

[1] The prophecy is preserved best in the hieratic papyrus, *Pap. Petersburg,* 1116 B *recto,* of the XVIIIth Dynasty, 1580–1350 B.C., published by Golenischeff. Parts of the work also exist in other forms, notably on the Cairo Tablet, translated by Ranke in Gressmann's *Texte,* edn 1909, pp. 204–206; edn 1926, pp. 46–48. The opening lines are to be found also on a limestone tablet in the museum of Liverpool. The whole is available in English in the translation of Dr Alan Gardiner, *J.E.A.* (1914), I. pp. 100–106. A translation of Neferrohu is also contained in Erman, *Die Literatur der Aegypter,* rendered into English by A. M. Blackman, 1927. It will be noted that in the following pages no reference is made to Egyptian 'oracles' in a wider sense of the term, such as is used by *e.g.* Blackman in his article in *J.E.A.* XII. pp. 176 ff.

[2] *I.e.* the two diadems of the two divisions of Egypt.

(II) *The Lamb Prophecy*. This fragment of Demotic papyrus[1] was written in the 34th year of the Emperor Augustus (*i.e.* 7 or 8 A.D.). The prophecy is represented as being delivered by a lamb in the reign of king Bokchoris (*c.* 720 B.C.). It likewise divides itself (though not very definitely) into two parts: (1) The first concerns the coming misery of Egypt, to last 900 years: "They (the enemy) will take the sanctuaries of the gods of Egypt for themselves to Nineveh into the region of the Amor". (2) The second describes the recovery of the spoil by the Egyptians, and the restoration of good fortune: "they find the (plundered) sanctuaries of the gods of Egypt (again)". The lamb is afterwards ordered by the king to be given divine honours in the Temple. It is to be regretted that the fragment is very incomplete, and that its meaning is not perfectly clear.

(III) More material is to be found in *The Potter*. The oracle is represented in the text as a prophecy in the presence of king Amenophis (= Amenhotep of the XVIIIth Egyptian Dynasty). This *Greek* papyrus of the 3rd cent. A.D. goes back to an Egyptian source.[2] According to the document, the potter broke off in the middle of a word, and the king, though distressed at the prediction, assigned to him honour and comfort. (1) The MS. is defective at the beginning, but clearly the first part of the prophecy from the outset is concerned with a time of misery.

...The hated king of Syria will besiege it...it will later be laid waste... only few (?) of Egypt's inhabitants will remain over....

(2) The rest of the text is almost complete, and predicts at considerable length the reversal of the defeat, the return to Egypt of captured sacred objects, and the advent of a good king:

...when the powerful king of Heliopolis appears, gracious for 55 years, the giver of the good, installed by the great goddess Isis, so that the sur-

---

[1] Now in the Rainer collection in Vienna, as also is the *Potter* papyrus. The quotations furnished from the *Lamb* and the *Potter* Prophecies are from Ranke's German transl. in Gressmann, *Texte*, edn 2, pp. 48–50; edn 1, pp. 206–209.

[2] But not earlier than the 4th cent. B.C.

vivors wish that those who had died before might rise again that they might take part in the good.

Nature will once more be kindly.

...Thereupon (will also) summer again take its proper course, and well-ordered will the...winds be....For in the time of the typhoon the sun was darkened. It will (however) shine again, after it has brought to light the punishment of the wicked and the distress of the Girdlewearers.[1] And Egypt—

(IV) *The Admonitions of the Wise Ipuwer*[2] should be mentioned last because the work is probably not a prediction at all. The poems were claimed in 1903 by H. O. Lange of Copenhagen to be genuine prophecy,[3] both of coming misfortunes and of the advent of a Messianic king. However, six years later, Dr Gardiner, in his edition, *The Admonitions of an Egyptian Sage*, advanced cogent reasons for believing that the words were addressed to the 'slumbering pilot' himself, in whose reign the disasters enunciated in the form of predictions were actually occurring.[4] Though Erman suggested a point of view differing somewhat from Gardiner's (based on variations in rendering, and in treatment of the defective portions of the text) yet the net result would seem to be not essentially different. The poems emanate from the period which *followed* the fate of the country as 'predicted' by Ipuwer. "No one will doubt", says Erman, "that historical events are mirrored therein; the details are so correct that no poet could have imagined them".[5]

In 1906 Eduard Meyer[6] claimed that the essential elements of Hebrew prophecy were to be found in that of Egypt; that the great prophets of the Israelite nation were working on a

[1] The term, in this oracle, denotes strangers who had invaded Egypt.
[2] The *Apu* of Meyer in *Israeliten u. ihre Nachbarstämme*, p. 451. The (extremely imperfect) papyrus, now in Leyden, dates from about 1300 B.C. The poems were composed not later than c. 1900 B.C.
[3] As is indicated by the title assigned by Lange, "*Prophezeiungen eines ägypt. Weisen*". [4] Pp. 7, 8.
[5] "Die Mahnworte eines ägyptischen Propheten", *Sitzungsberichte der Preussischen Akad. der Wissenschaften*, 1919, XLII. p. 813. The subject will be alluded to again (p. 52, below). A translation of Ipuwer is to be found also in Erman-Blackman, pp. 92–108, and a summary in Breasted, *Development of Rel. and Thought in Anc. Egypt*, pp. 204 ff. [6] *Op. cit.* pp. 451–453.

fixed scheme; and that they were using stock material which they found ready to hand in Egyptian prophecy. Meyer maintained that the form of the Israelite and the Egyptian prophecies was in essential features absolutely identical, thus: "(1) First a time of heavy visitation, of destruction of the political power, of the laying waste of the land and of its shrines: then (2) the glory of the Messianic kingdom under the righteous king beloved of the gods, from the old legitimate stock, to whom all peoples become subject". The Hebrew prophets' own contribution (he maintained) consisted only in applying the material to the circumstances of their times, and in assigning an ethical-religious reason for the Divine judgment. A notable feature of Meyer's position was his theory that the Egyptian prophecies contained definite *Messianic* prediction. Hugo Gressmann[1] classifies (and with general correctness) the leading features of Egyptian prophecy as: (1) Close connection between prophecy and folklore; (2) Combination of threat and promise; (3) Patriotic-political aim; and (4) Dynastic interest. (Associated with this last comes the Messianic element.) He considers that such prophecy may have been common in the Near East[2] generally; and he argues for the direct dependence of Hebrew prophecy upon foreign.

Obviously the problem presented is sufficiently important to deserve careful consideration. There can be no doubt that points of resemblance exist between Hebrew prophecy and that of Egypt. To take Gressmann's classification in order. (1) In our narratives of the pre-Amos prophets of Israel prophetic utterances are embedded in history and folklore. Elijah and Elisha are instances of this. (2) In the great prophets there are predictions both of weal and woe. (3) and (4) The political and dynastic interest is very marked in early Israelite prophetism.[3] In Isaiah and Micah occur predictions, of quasi-Messianic

---

[1] *J.T.S.* April 1926.

[2] Points (3) and (4) were noticeable in Assyro-Babylonian prophecy also. See, above, p. 43.

[3] See above, pp. 20 (c), 43. And a (refined) political interest remains a feature of the work of even the great prophets. Dynastic interest is to be seen in Zech. vi. 12.

significance, concerning a good king to come. It is clear that a detailed comparison between Israelite and foreign prophecies must throw light upon the significance of some of the *phraseology*, at least, of the Old Testament. The modern commentary on the prophets can no longer ignore such evidence as will help to put Hebrew prophecy in its right perspective internationally, as well as in its national historical setting. In the notes upon the following passages in the book of Amos, reference is made to material from Egyptian prophetic and philosophic sources: ii. 6, iii. 14, iv. 3, v. 2, vii. 3, viii. 9, ix. 11 and ix. 13.[1] If further discoveries from Egypt (or from the Euphrates valley), and fuller investigation into the actual historical circumstances of the first production of such prophecies, should make it indisputable that Hebrew prophecy is definitely dependent upon Egyptian (or Assyrian, or both), the phenomenon would be not different from that perhaps presented by the Hebrew books of Proverbs and Psalms.[2] A part of the earliest work in the modern study of the O.T. was to demonstrate a certain conscious dependence of at least one of the sources of Genesis upon the Babylonian literature of folklore and legend, conspicuously in the stories of the Creation and of the Flood. But, as with the compiler of Genesis, so also it would be claimed that "the vigorous originality of the *prophets* enables them to transmute all foreign elements into their own spirit".[3] Moreover no Christian need hesitate to admit that the Spirit of God was at work in Egyptian and Babylonian Psalmists, Sages (and if it be so) Prophets, and not only in those of Israel.

On the other hand, there are difficulties in the way of accepting an hypothesis of Hebrew indebtedness to Egypt in the matter of prophecy; and, moreover, it would seem easy to exaggerate the amount and degree of similarity in the two types of prophecy. (1) To take the first point. Egyptian influence could conceivably have been felt upon Israelite

---

[1] Pp. 286 and 287, 164, 167, footnote, 179, footnote, 308, 247, footnote 2, 272, footnote 1 and 320, 323.

[2] It is not denied that the element of predictiveness differentiates *prophecy* from Psalms and philosophy. On the character and degree of such in Egyptian oracles, see below, pp. 52, 53. [3] Gressmann, *J.T.S. ibid.*

religion and institutions from the Tell el-Amarna age up to the end of the Egyptian partial occupation of Palestine under Rameses III,[1] and, of course, by means of the Israelite sojourn in the Delta. Yet, actually, it is possible to take the view that there are few or no traces in the O.T. of any early Egyptian influence that are indisputable. Very much in accordance with the facts are the words of Hölscher (arguing emphatically against an Egyptian origin for the Hebrew prophetic form, and claiming that the ideas of 'doom' and 'happiness' found in the Hebrew prophets do not need to come from a mythological or literary scheme): "the Egyptian influence on ancient Israel in general is slender to vanishing point...; their ideas and customs nowhere reveal traces of Egyptian influence".[2] If there had been an early dependence

---

[1] See note on "Philistines", Am. i. 6–8, p. 123.

[2] *Profeten*, 1914, p. 459, and see below, pp. 53, 54. It is not, however, maintained that Egypt with other nations could have offered no contribution to *e.g.* the early poetical mythical ideas in Israel. It has often been observed how slight was the importance which the early Hebrews attached to a doctrine of an after life, as contrasted with the Egyptians. If Israelite prophecy was dependent on Egyptian sources, why did it not recognise a value in the Egyptian belief in the world to come? All the great prophets of Israel were enthusiasts for civic justice, yet not one strengthened his appeal by a reference to the great eternal tribune, after the manner of the Egyptian sage quoted below, p. 287 (5). Unquestionably the publication (by Budge in 1924) of *The Teaching of Amen-em-ope* has again brought before us the problem, in the form of a literary connection of at least portions of the Hebrew book of Proverbs with Egyptian material, or of the existence of a common source for both. It is possible that such borrowing, if it took place, occurred in the pre-exilic period. On the other hand, the book of Proverbs, as it stands, is a production of the 4th or 3rd cent. B.C.; and any Hebrew borrowing from Egyptian sources may belong to this date. Alternatively, it has been held that the sage of Egypt depended upon *the Hebrew book of Proverbs* (Oesterley, *The Wisdom of Egypt and the O.T.* S.P.C.K. 1927. *Cf.* Blackman in *The Psalmists*, pp. 196, 197). The full text of Amen-em-ope (Amenophis) with notes is edited by Griffith in *J.E.A.* XII. 1926, pp. 191–231; which is followed in the same volume by an article by D. C. Simpson on the comparison between the *Teaching* and the Hebrew book of Proverbs. One by Gressmann on this subject is to be found in *Z.A.W.* 1924, pp. 272 ff. Citations from the *Teaching* are made in the present commentary, pp. 287 and 244, n. 3 (on ii. 6, viii. 5). It seems to be a fact that with all the *possibilities* of Egyptian influence upon its insignificant neighbour Israel over long periods of its history through personal contact, little influence is discernible. The Hebrew language was written in *Phoenician* script; it contained *Aramaisms* and *Arabisms*; yet from Egypt it borrowed very few *Egyptianisms* (*e.g.* Moses, Hophni, Phinehas, *y*^{e}*ōr*, *āhú*). As regards *prophecy*, though the *magicians* of Egypt are alluded to by the Hebrews with awe and respect (Gen. xli. 8, 24, *etc.*; in Exod. vii. 11 and viii. 7 they are able to do as Moses; they are inferior in ix. 11 only), yet if they did use the prophecies of Egypt the existence of Egyptian

upon Egypt, it would seem strange that the lower form of prophecy in Israel, called 'false', contained no threat.[1] The higher order, at least until the Captivity, consists far more of threat than of promise.

(2) In the second place, obvious as are the resemblances between Hebrew and Egyptian prophecy, the *differences* are not less remarkable. (*a*) The Egyptian uniform scheme of threat and promise, fairly sharply divided, finds no parallel in Hebrew prophecy except in the volumes of Amos, Micah and Zephaniah in their present shape, and perhaps in Hosea and Joel.[2] Meyer believed the Epilogue to the book of Amos to be the genuine work of the Prophet, apparently because the book exhibits the Egyptian 'scheme' of Misery and Bliss. But considerations of language and of historical allusions leave little doubt that the great *promise* passage at the end of Amos is the addition of a generation at least 200 years after Amos' time.[3] The concluding portions of the books of Micah and Zephaniah are additions also. What is characteristic of the Hebrew prophets is a different phenomenon, *viz.* the interspersing of promises of hope, at intervals, upon a background of threat. (*b*) Further, the circumstances

prophets is passed over without so much as one mention in all the pages of the O.T. References to Egyptian sacred scribes (ἱερογραμματεῖς), skilful in foretelling future events, occur in Josephus (*Antt.* II. ix. 3, 10) in connection with the birth of Moses.

[1] *Cf.* Sellin, *Introd. to O.T.* p. 170. See also Peake, *Roots of Hebrew Prophecy and Jewish Apocalyptic.* Dr Peake sums up: "It will be clear then that we cannot with any confidence assert the derivation of the prophetic eschatology from an Egyptian source" (p. 14).

[2] And there are signs that within Isaiah and Jeremiah some groups of oracles were made (? by the collectors) to end upon a joyful note. Isa. chs. xi and xii form a happy conclusion. Chs. xxviii–xxxv appear to have been arranged "in a rising series of promises of happiness". Jer. xii. 14–17 and Jer. ch. xvii each forms a happy conclusion to their respective groups of oracles. But it is easy to note the opposite phenomenon. See T. H. Robinson, "Die prophetischen Bücher im Lichte neuer Entdeckungen", in *Z.A.W.* 1927, Heft 1/2, p. 8, *ad init.*

The books of Micah and Hosea, unlike Amos, have hopeful passages *intermingled* with the judgments, as well as at the end. Some Canonical Prophets (conspicuously Nahum, Habakkuk, Obadiah and the Second Isaiah) foretell only good to Israel. How is this fact to be accounted for if the Hebrew prophets worked on a fixed scheme?

[3] It is possible to hold that the very late editor who added such promise passages was under the influence of the Egyptian scheme; but that is quite another matter. For this view, see Robinson, *op. cit.* p. 8 *ad fin.*

of composition of the Egyptian oracles are almost an unknown quantity, in contrast to the very great deal that has been discovered as to the history and methods of prophetism in Israel. For example, while probably it is fair to argue that the normal scheme of Egyptian 'prophecy' was first *Threat*, then *Promise*, we cannot presume that any one of the oracles which have come down to us is, even substantially, as originally uttered by the sage.[1] They are, for the most part, too full of precise detail to be genuine predictions from beginning to end. Are we to suppose that in Egypt alone of all the nations of antiquity the phenomenon of *vaticinium post eventum* was unknown? Meyer and Lange regarded the *Admonitions of Ipuwer* as predictive. Gardiner, however, it has been said above,[2] proved—conclusively it would seem—that Ipuwer was, in the main, a spectator, and not a predictor, of the miseries of Egypt;[3] and that the *Admonitions* were not actually composed until two dynasties later than that of the king supposed to be addressed. Thus the predictive element in Ipuwer is confined practically tó an expectation of *a happy future*. Of the promise concerning a coming king, this Egyptologist holds the opinion that it is not Messianic at all, but refers rather to "the god Rê, the supreme ruler of the world".[4] He continues, "at all events it seems now to be clear that whichever hypothesis scholars may choose [that is, the historical or the predictive], there is too much uncertainty about the matter for it to be made the basis of any far-reaching conclusions as to the influence of Egyptian upon Hebrew literature". Such an opinion of Professor Gardiner's would

[1] It is obvious that doubts must hang about the question in the case of those oracles which are preserved only on papyri as late as the Christian era (the *Lamb* and the *Potter*).

[2] P. 47.

[3] *Admonitions*, pp. 7, 8, 111. *Cf.* this scholar again in *J.E.A.* i. p. 100.

[4] *Admon.* pp. 13–15. The words of Gressmann himself are very true: "We have as yet no specimen of Messianic prophecy (Egyptian) in the strict sense of the word, which does not apply to an historic king"; *i.e.* that which has come down to us is *post eventum* prophecy. It would seem reasonable to suppose that what the Egyptian prophets expressed was no more than that national adversity would issue eventually in prosperity under a good king. This kind of prediction is really natural enough, and it is not confined to the literatures of Egypt and Israel.

seem to convey a warning against holding the other Egyptian 'prophecies' to be actually predictive.

As regards the Prophecy of Neferrohu, while Gardiner styles it 'predictive',[1] he places the composition of the oracle in, or later than, the reign of the good king named therein (Ameny or Amenemhet) who is destined to usher in the return of Egypt's fortune.[2] This is only logical. Otherwise, the proportion of supernatural element in a prophecy in Egypt would be altogether in excess of what Biblical scholars would allow that the God of Israel would think fit to provide in *canonical* prophecy. And *Neferrohu* seems to be the strongest example of an Egyptian oracle of a predictive character.[3]

Similarly, Ranke, writing of the *Oracle of the Potter*, admits the presence of interpolations from the Hellenic age in an original Egyptian work of the period of the New Kingdom.[4]

The *Lamb* prophecy is so fragmentary and brief as to contribute little evidence.

(3) The following further points of difference between Hebrew and Egyptian prophecy should be noted: (*a*) There is the important feature that in Egyptian oracles the moral note, though sometimes struck, always remains low and scarcely audible. It is a fact that, in the outlines of coming bliss, righteousness and ethical religion[5] find almost no part. Indeed the general conceptions of God and man in the two literatures move upon entirely different levels. The Egyptian prophecies were delivered in a perfectly natural manner and with no ecstasy of any type.[6] This is very different from, at least early, prophetism in Israel.[7] (*b*) Though the Egyptian oracles

---

[1] *J.E.A.* I. p. 100. [2] *Ibid.* I. p. 106.

[3] *Cf.* Sellin (*Introd. to O.T.* p. 100), "if at all".

[4] In Gressmann's *Texte*, edn 2, p. 49; edn 1, p. 208.

[5] So Gressmann, *J.T.S. ibid.* p. 245. The (occasional) allusions to 'right' and 'iniquity' are hardly more than *political.* Contrast, in the O.T. canon, such passages as Isa. ix. 7 *b.*

[6] Hölscher (*Profeten*, p. 131), on the basis of Herodotus II. 61 and later classical writers, argues that ecstasy was not native in Egypt, but was introduced from Asia only as a result of later syncretising of religions.

[7] Since writing the above, the author has seen that this difference is noted also by Dr T. H. Robinson; who likewise adopts the view that the Egyptian prophecies are essentially not predictive: "In nearly all the Egyptian prophecies which tradition has preserved the pretension [to prediction] is false"; *op. cit.* p. 6, *ad init.*

announce the spoliation of Egypt by foreigners, yet there are
none foretelling *exile*. It is hardly necessary to point out
how significant in this respect is the contrast with the great
prophets of Israel. (*c*) The Egyptian prophecies confine themselves to the fate of Egypt. Israel's great prophets, however,
declare God's judgment not only on their hearers, but on
nations neighbouring upon Palestine, and even at a distance.[1] A lesser point is that, whilst the Egyptian sage is
honoured notwithstanding the unwelcome nature of much
of his pronouncement,[2] the prophet of Israel, if his message
contains unpalatable items, is banished from the realm, or
runs the risk of losing his life.

To sum up. It seems improbable, almost impossible, that
the great prophets of Israel consciously worked, as Meyer held,
with Egyptian material. It is, if anything, even less likely
that the earlier *nᵉbhî'îm*, and the 'false' prophets, knew the
Egyptian prophecies. Where similarity exists between the
work of the great Hebrew prophets and the Egyptian oracles,
the similarity is that of form rather than of content. That
there may have been a certain amount of, as it were, *unconscious* indebtedness from contact in an early age is not an
idea improbable in itself. On the whole, however, it would
seem that the evidence, general and detailed, decidedly
inclines against such a proposition. As to how much, or how
little, Israel's early religious thought may have been influenced by contact with Egypt is an unsolved problem. One
point is clear. We know, even now, very little about Egyptian
prophecy; whereas we really do know a very great deal about
Hebrew prophecy. In the history of Israel's life it took a
foremost place. Under the Divine Providence it was prophecy
that made the Hebrew religion unique among ancient religions. The German eschatological school has rendered at
least this service (no slight one):—it has enabled us to
appreciate the distinction, the *unique* greatness, of the prophets of Israel.

---

[1] Gunkel likewise, in denying connection, notices the absence from the
Egyptian prophecies of the cosmic and universal elements to be met with in
several of the great Hebrew prophets.

[2] *Cf.* above, the *Lamb*, and the *Potter* (p. 46).

X. ESCHATOLOGY

(1)

ESCHATOLOGY IN ANCIENT ISRAEL

Eschatology, literally, *a theory of the Last Things*, may be defined as a belief in a supernatural change in the present order, which is to come about either in the distant future or soon. Eschatological ideas, strictly speaking, involve the end up of the world; and that, out of the coming misery, perhaps world chaos, an era of blessedness will arise. Such notions may be held in varying degrees. But eschatology must concern a coming age; and it is presumed that the conceptions are not held merely occasionally, and by a few, but (to a greater or less extent) form the background of a nation's outlook.

Was early Israel[1] profoundly under the influence of definite eschatological beliefs? Gunkel and others maintain that it was. The most notable hypothesis is that which has come to be associated chiefly with the name of the lamented Hugo Gressmann. This scholar held that there was a general *Semitic* eschatology. He was inclined to connect the ultimate origin of such belief with the ancient Babylonian time computation founded upon the then supposed course of the sun around the earth, a course completed and again renewed every so many centuries or millenniums of years.[2] Thus eventually, says Gressmann, expectations of future Woe and Weal (in German, *Unheil* and *Heil*) have their roots probably in nature and mythology. The Disaster element in eschatology is, he suggests, a mitigated representation of a return to chaos, *i.e.* the destruction of the world, with its inhabitants, excepting only those fortunate ones who might be spared—in the case of Hebrew eschatology, the Israelite nation itself. Similarly, the Happiness element is the re-appearance of the golden age

---

[1] For a treatment of the subject, more especially from the period 200 B.C. onwards, when undoubtedly eschatology influenced Jewish thought, the reader may be referred to the article "Eschatology" by Charles, in *E.B.* II. columns 1353–65.

[2] *Der Ursprung der isr.-jüd. Eschatologie*, 1905, pp. 167, 168; but *cf.* also p. 247, footnote.

of primitive time, with the government of the new God-king.[1]
The German professor believed that such a *world*-eschatology,
originating outside the people of Israel, was afterwards
appropriated by them, but limited primarily to their own
nation. This eschatology was the foundation upon which
the great prophets worked. The stages in the history of its
development would be (*a*) foreign, *universal*, (*b*) Israelite,
national, (*c*) prophetic, *refined*. In this last form the main
divisions of Woe and Weal remain, but the earlier, popular,
mythical elements tend to vanish. What takes their place is
ethical truth. On account of its sins Israel, so far from alone
escaping the catastrophe, will be carried away in the vortex.
The world-wide character of the disaster, though still recognised by the prophets, is much effaced. Gressmann, after
writing his brilliant thesis,[2] became strengthened in his belief
in a foreign source for Israelite eschatology. The *Unheil* and
Heil scheme[3] he attributed chiefly to Egypt; but not to Egypt
alone, for he believed such eschatology to have been current
in the Near East generally.

There are grave difficulties, however, in the view that the
Hebrew nation, before the Exile, was to any great extent
under the influence of a formal eschatology. It may be
allowed that in ancient Israel there were beliefs that certain
evils must come to pass—war, plague, earthquake—and that
one day something of the happy conditions of the Eden age[4]
would return, possibly under a coming deliverer-king. But
of this we know nothing definite, certainly not sufficient to
enable us to conclude that an eschatological scheme dominated
Israelite thought.

(*a*) In particular, it is hardly too much to say that the
eschatological conception of a destruction and renewal of the
world is nowhere to be found reflected in the O.T. In a short

---

[1] It is noteworthy that, in later Jewish and Rabbinical theology, the theory
of an age of Woe to precede and usher in the Messianic era of Bliss was developed
independently. The technical term was *hebhᵉlē hammāshîaḥ; cf.* the ὠδῖνες of
St Matt. xxiv. 8, St Mark xiii. 8.

[2] *Eschatologie* referred to above, extending over nearly 400 pages.

[3] *Cf.* preceding section, p. 48.

[4] Isa. xi. 6–9 may be evidence for such, though the passage is probably a *late*
one. So Am. ix. 13; see note, p. 323.

INTRODUCTION 57

space it is impossible to do justice to the whole of Gressmann's
argument. The following points may be referred to briefly.
He uses the prophecy of Zephaniah[1] as an argument to shew
that in ancient Israel there was the belief in a 'world-catastrophe'.[2] But the Prophet, surely, is speaking primarily of
a general *Scythian invasion*—invasion of Judah and the
Philistines, Ammon, Moab, Ethiopia, and Nineveh. The incursion does not issue in world-destruction; indeed it is difficult
to see what connection any war could have with a return to
primeval chaos. The 'fire' of Jehovah's jealousy (Zeph. i. 18,
iii. 8) is, strictly, not a fire at all; there is no conflagration.
Moreover, when the invasion has passed, things are to go on
very much the same as before, except that Ethiopia and Judah
will serve God better (Zeph. iii. 10, 13). Even the (late)
passages, Isa. xxxiv. 4–10, lxv. 17, lxvi. 22,[3] do not certainly
imply, much less plainly declare, an *annihilation* of the universe. Nor is the reference to the darkening of the sun in
Am. viii. 9, which Gressmann uses,[4] at all necessarily concerned with the world as such; for *vv.* 10–13 refer to Palestine,
and the preceding section, *vv.* 1–8, to the sins of *Israel*. The
passage Hag. ii. 6, 7,[5] belonging to two centuries after the time
of Amos, may not be used to illustrate a belief in world-catastrophe as existing before the time of Amos. And what it does
seem to shew. is that phrases about the 'world' and 'all
nations' are employed freely by the Hebrew prophets purely
from a national, isolated, point of view. 'The desirable things
of all nations shall come...' *to this house*. Everything is for
Israel's benefit. And so in Zech. ch. xiv, especially *vv.* 4–7,[6]

---

[1] He translates *'ădhāmāh* in Zeph. i. 2, not 'ground', or 'land' as E.VV., but
'earth'. In view of Am. iii. 2, Isa. xxiv. 21, such a translation is not impossible.
But it is unlikely. The expression *p'ne hā'ădhāmāh* could not be quoted in support
of it, for it signifies 'face of the *ground*'. In Zeph. iii. 8, where the word is *'ereṣ*,
no cosmic catastrophe is contemplated, only widespread war. In i. 18 the context
favours rendering *'ereṣ* by 'land'.

[2] *Eschatologie*, pp. 50, 145, 146, 230.　　　　[3] *Ibid.* pp. 27, 28, 220.
[4] *Ibid.* pp. 25, 142, 147.　　　　　　　　　　[5] *Ibid.* p. 12.
[6] *Ibid.* pp. 221, 227, *etc.* Isa. xiii appears at first sight to deal with a cosmic
catastrophe in 'the day of the LORD' (*vv.* 6, 10, 12–14); but, as the oracle
proceeds, it is manifest that its subject is solely the destruction of *Babylon* by
the Medes: 'Behold, I will stir up the Medes *against them*' (*v.* 17). Hence the E.VV.
are probably correct in rendering *hā'āreṣ* in *vv.* 9 and 14 by 'land'.

there is no real *world*-catastrophe. From first to last every thing is transacted in Judah, including the feast of tabernacles for 'all nations'. (*b*) Moreover, if a cosmic eschatology is not native in Israel, it is hardly too much to assert that still less is it contained clearly in *Egyptian* sources.[1] The scheme in the prophecies of Egypt, of two periods sharply contrasted, first Misery, then Bliss, upon which considerable stress is laid by some, is not eschatological, but (bearing in mind the circumstances of the composition of these oracles) would seem sufficiently explained as psychologically obvious. It cannot be emphasised too strongly that the Egyptian prophecies say nothing of the destruction of the universe, or even of the world. Those things which the country holds as precious will depart, and nature will be against her:

> The sun is veiled...the river is dry.[2]

The Egyptian hope of an era of Bliss refers merely, as Hölscher says, to the restoration of happy political conditions in Egypt.[3]

---

[1] See the examination of the evidence on pp. 52, 54 above.

[2] *Cf.* the quotation from *Neferrohu* on p. 45 and *The Potter* on p. 46.

[3] As the references to the "king...from the South" (*Neferrohu*, p. 45) and "the king of Heliopolis" (*The Potter*, p. 46) are sufficient to shew. This feature has some counterpart in the so-called 'Messianic' Fourth Eclogue of Virgil, which rests not so much on eschatology as on dynastic interest. Virgil may have been (in more than one sense of the term) a prophet; but none the less we cannot fail to recognise predominantly, in the author of the Fourth Eclogue, a court poet uttering extravagant eulogies upon the line of Julius and Augustus.

> "From high heaven descends
> The firstborn child of promise....
> The age of iron in his time shall cease
> And golden generations fill the world.
>
> *   *   *   *   * . *
>
> The treacherous snake and deadly herb shall die,
> And Syrian spikenard blow on every bank.
>
> *   *   *   *   *   *   *   *
>
> Then behold
> Another Tiphys take the helm and steer
> Another Argo, manned by chosen souls
> Seeking the golden, undiscovered East.
>
> *   *   *   *   *   *   *   *
>
> Come then, dear child of gods, Jove's mighty heir,
> Begin thy high career; the hour is sounding".

(Transl. by R. S. Conway in *Virgil's Messianic Eclogue*, 1907.)

The child born proved to be no future emperor, but a girl (Julia).

As to prophetic details in the Egyptian and Israelite prophecies, it may be

Certain it is that the Egyptian scheme, if scheme it be, is not one of *world*-eschatology; hence it seems extremely difficult to suppose Egypt to be the source of an Israelite eschatology. It has not been proved that eschatological ideas in any way lay behind *Babylonian* prophecy.[1] And precarious is the contention of Sellin that there was in pre-Amos Israel an influential, popular, and prophetic eschatology of Weal and Woe *indigenous* to the soil. Thus we arrive at Professor Peake's position: "When all is said, it must still be regarded as very questionable whether there was in early Israel any developed eschatology at all".[2]

(2)

ESCHATOLOGY AND THE BOOK OF AMOS

The question of the existence of a defined eschatology moulding ancient Israelite thought has a bearing upon certain points in the interpretation and criticism of the book of Amos. (a) What is implied in the expression the 'day of the LORD', in Am. v. 18? (b) What is the relation of the Assyrian[3] peril to a general Woe eschatology? (c) Must not the concluding *happy* verses of the book (ix. 11–15) be regarded as an essential part of the work as a whole?

(a) The Day of the LORD

In the notes upon v. 18 the expression in the mouth of the people, 'Jehovah's day', is interpreted to mean God's day of victorious battle. The Prophet's new signification for the

pointed out that they are not very similar. Nor are they of such a kind as would not naturally suggest themselves to a prophet of any nation quite independently. For some discussion of the idea of a Redeemer-Messiah, see above, pp. 48, 52.

[1] *Cf.* Wardle, *Israel and Babylon*, p. 104. To prove the existence of a Babylonian eschatology if would be necessary to shew that the predictions of war fitted into a theory of a coming catastrophe in *nature*. The examples cited on pp. 42, 43, above, cannot possibly be so classed. Hardly more convincing on this point is the instance of the *Ira myth* quoted on p. 117, footnote 2, which in any case, standing alone, is not evidence that Babylonian thought was dominated by eschatological ideas. [2] *Roots of Hebrew Prophecy*, p. 14.

[3] *Cf.* Introd. "Visitation", pp. 30, 31.

phrase, it is there maintained, consists in a reference to the
coming *defeat* of Israel, through the advent of Assyria. Prof.
Gressmann, commenting on the passage,[1] follows a sound
tradition of exegesis when he argues that in the context the
repetition of the expression 'day of Jehovah' indicates that
the Prophet is endeavouring to refute a popularly held conception of 'Jehovah's day'. He quotes the words of Wellhausen. They longed for "the great crisis which would bring
in with one blow the new glorious era, without their requiring
to move a finger".

On the other hand, it is less easy to follow him when he
maintains that 'the day of the LORD',[2] or 'that day' signifies
for the most part, even in the *Prophets* (as also in his opinion
it does in the minds of the *people* who 'desire it'), the dawn of
the golden age, the return of Paradise, and the quintessence of
light, happiness and bliss.[3] Also Gressmann maintains that the
expression 'the day of the LORD' may be employed to include
the disaster[4] which is to precede the golden age. He believes
that, at one stage in the development of eschatological thought
in Israel, '*days* of Jehovah' of many varieties were conceived
—exhibiting themselves in several ways, as Jehovah appeared in earthquake, storm, lightning, fire, war, *etc.* Finally,
these came to be summed together in the conception of His
epiphany in '*the* Day of Jehovah'. It is to this catastrophe-
element that the prophet Amos, he suggests, is here referring:
'You long for the end of the world, because you believe destruction will strike only the heathen, and spare you! No,
disaster threatens you also, and you first of all'.

[1] *Alt. Proph.* edn 2, p. 348; edn 1, p. 347; and see *Eschatologie*, pp. 151, 152.
[2] For the 'day of the LORD' in a happy sense in canonical prophecy, see the references to Joel, Ezek. and Obad., given in the note on Am. v. 18. *Cf.* on ix. 11, 'that day' (and 'those days'), p. 270.
[3] In fact, the kind of conception associated with the term 'millennium'. For this theory of two periods yet to come—*Unheil* and *Heil*, see above, pp. 55, 56. The 'Day' is supposed to be made up of these together.
[4] Perhaps Ezek. vii. 10, 12 supplies an instance of this. *Cf.* the whole context, *vv.* 5–27; and see Am. viii. 8–10. But is there not a danger in assuming a technical meaning, whether of good or evil, to be attached to the term 'day' and 'days' where no such meaning may be present? The word is so very common in all languages. See such passages as Isa. lviii. 5 (*lit.* 'a day of acceptableness to Jehovah'), Gen. xxxv. 3, Jer. xviii. 17.

It cannot be denied that such an explanation, if it were the only one possible, would commend itself as very effective, but an obvious difficulty lies in the amount of *hypothesis* upon which the exegesis is based. Furthermore, Professor Gressmann builds upon this very passage (Am. v. 18) to yield one piece of evidence for the *thesis* that a definite, widely accepted, eschatology was current in early Israel. The general observation may be made that at present we possess no sufficient information of the prevalence of a cosmic eschatology in ancient *Israel*. It would seem that the quantity of really eschatological belief existing in ancient *Egypt and Babylon* has been somewhat exaggerated, quite apart from the question whether such belief penetrated into Israelite thought. From the evidence (such as is collected in the preceding section of this Introduction), one is led to suppose that there was no contemplation in Egypt or Babylon of *either* a coming world-catastrophe[1] *or* any perfect conditions in nature such as are associated with the thought of a golden age to come and the return of Paradise.

It is also a very significant fact that in the literatures of these countries there appears to be no example of the use of the word 'day' in any eschatological sense. Moreover, it is difficult to prove that in the pre-exilic prophets of Israel the expression 'day of Jehovah' implies the belief in any developed eschatology among *their own countrymen*.[2]

---

[1] *Cf.* p. 54 '(c).

[2] Hölscher, who does not accept an eschatological explanation of the popular desire for 'the day of the LORD', offers his own interpretation of Am. v. 18. This, though hardly more convincing, may be quoted here in so far as it seems to support the theory (see note on p. 193) that the expression 'the day of the LORD' can be used for the manifestation of the Deity in the destruction of a man's foes. In Hos. ii. 13 (Heb. v. 15) 'the days of the Baalim' may mean, not the period during which the Baalim held sway, but their festival days—as mentioned in v. 11 (Heb. v. 13)—'wherein she [Israel] used to make offering to them'; *cf.* the rendering in R.V. marg. Hölscher (*Eschatologie*, p. 13), using the analogy of 'Baal's day' = Baal's festival day, and comparing 'this is the day which Jehovah hath made' (Ps. cxviii. 24), and Neh. viii. 9, holds that '*Jehovah's* day' is an expression almost equivalent to Jehovah's *feast-day*—*i.e.* it is a cult term. He relies more, however, upon the occurrence of the expression in Babylonian private prayers. In one such prayer a man appeals to the *Fire-god*

(b) The Assyrian Peril in relation to
an Eschatology of Woe

In predicting Jehovah's visitation upon Israel, (a) is Amos moved chiefly by a consciousness of danger from Assyria: or (b) is he working, as it were, mechanically, upon the foundation of a generally accepted eschatological principle of coming disaster in nature as well as in national politics? The latter is the view taken by Gressmann: "In the background of the prophetical threats, stands the belief in a world-catastrophe. Heaven and earth must disappear, the order of the kosmos must pass away, men and animals must be annihilated. In a word, that chaos must return which once reigned in the first beginning of all things".[1] He cites Jer. iv. 23 ff. But that passage is particularly exalted poetry. Another reference, Isa. xxviii. 14 ff., is of local application, and would seem to carry no weight at all. Lastly he refers to Isa. ii. 10 ff., a passage which supplies better evidence: it is, moreover, against the wizards and witches whom he supposes to have been the cause of his affliction:

> "To thee I appeal like Shamash the judge,
> Judge my cause, pronounce my verdict,
> Restrain the wizard and the witch,
> Devour mine enemies, tear in pieces mine evil foes,
> May *thy terrible day* reach them."

Similarly also there is the conjuration:

> "O strong fire-god, *fearful day*,
> *   *   *   *   *   *
> May thy *terrible day* break upon them."

This scholar sees in the expression 'fearful day' a technical term *in Babylonian cult language* for the epiphany of the god for the rescue of the sick man by the destruction of his foes, probably by means of storm. In Israel the phrase 'Jehovah's day' (according to this view) stood for the healing epiphany of God as looked for through the cult. He believes, therefore, that Amos borrowed the phrase 'Jehovah's day' from the *devotional* language of his fellow-countrymen. It would seem, however, that in the Babylonian passages the term, though occurring in prayers, need have no necessary connection with the cult or with private devotions. It is a day of the deity's action, and its use is consistent with the interpretation generally claimed for 'the day of Jehovah' in Am. v. 18, *viz.* a divine manifestation to deliver by means of smiting (the national) *foes*. The reason for alluding to Hölscher's explanation is that it supplies an exegesis of Am. v. 18 without any reference to eschatology.

[1] *Alt. Proph.* edn 1, pp. 327, 328.

professedly a description of a 'day' which God will 'have' (*v.* 12, R.V. marg.). Again, however, the allusion is not to the universe, but to the land of Palestine. Certainly 'high mountains' are involved (*v.* 14), but such language is frequently used in describing theophanies in the past *happy* history of Jehovah's people,[1] and in prophecy the word 'mountain' is patient of the metaphorical sense of 'immovable obstacle' (Zech. iv. 7).

According to the eschatological view, invasion by a foreign foe (which to Amos, though he does not clearly say so, is probably Assyria) is merely *one* of the coming disasters; and it is looked for only as forming a part of a more or less fixed eschatological scheme.[2] Indeed, the tendency of such interpretation of the book of Amos is to minimise the amount of reference by the Prophet to Assyria, by bringing into prominence the other elements—earthquake, pestilence, famine, drought, and natural disasters generally.[3]

Sellin, who believes that Israel was profoundly influenced by a native *Israelite* eschatology, holds that political calculation, or insight into danger arising from a world-power, was never the root cause of Amos' announcements of judgment; because the above-mentioned means of national annihilation have no connection with Assyria. Parallel to the instruments of destruction through nature this scholar places the *Divine Sword*,[4] which to Amos without doubt means the Assyrian, who, at Jehovah's command, will destroy or carry captive both Israel and the peoples round about.

It is manifest that any theory which would account for the enumeration by Amos of so many natural punishments—plague, earthquake, *etc.*—would be valuable. Undoubtedly there has been a tendency to overlook these, or at any rate to regard them as meaningless dressing: inasmuch as, unlike the Assyrian threat, they, for the most part, were not actually

---

[1] Exod. xix. 18, Judg. v. 5, Hab. iii. 6.

[2] In point of fact, however, it is significant that, so far as the present writer has been able to discover, there is no instance of *exile* in any oracle of Babylon or Egypt. *Cf.* above, p. 54 *ad init.*

[3] See Introd. "Visitation", pp. 30, 31. *Cf.* notes on ii. 13–16, v. 27, vi. 14.

[4] See, further, the notes on vii. 9 (p. 310) and ix. 4.

executed. But is there sufficient evidence that there was any
doctrine generally held, involving the destruction of either
the universe, or even the land of Palestine only? It is a fact
that captivity is not writ large upon every page of Amos. None
the less, in reading Amos it is difficult in the extreme to escape
the conviction that the Prophet has pre-eminently in mind
the destruction of the people and their buildings by war, and,
further, the exile of such few of the population as escape.
That Assyria is not mentioned by name in Amos, scarcely
tells against this. The evidence of eschatology is too slender
to compel the laying aside of the view which makes Assyria
the main judgment ever before Amos' mind, and which
perhaps alone led him to leave his sheep in the wilderness.

(c) Is the passage ix. 11–15 essential to the Prophecy of Amos?

It has already been said that, if there was a fixed scheme
of eschatology (whether derived from foreign sources or
indigenous) embracing the two elements—first 'Woe' then
'Weal', sharply divided—this would supply an à priori reason
for holding ix. 11–15 to be an integral part of the prophecy of
Amos. See Introd. p. 70. It is significant, however, that
even Gressmann came to feel[1] that the arguments against the
authenticity of the Epilogue were stronger than those which
even he with his eschatological theory could offer in its
favour.

It would seem to the general student of the O.T. that the
case for the genuineness of the concluding verses of the book
falls to the ground unless it can be proved that all prophets of
Israel were irrevocably under the thrall of a popular Weal-
eschatology. The fact is that, except for this passage in dispute, there is no evidence that Amos was influenced by an
eschatology of ultimate Bliss; whereas the book itself supplies much to demonstrate his belief in the nation's doom.[2]

---

[1] See below, p. 77.
[2] For Sellin's view see Introd. on ix. 11–15 (p. 70 ad init.).

XI. LITERARY PROBLEMS [See also Preface II.]

I. Did the 'book of Amos' come from the *pen* of the Prophet? (1) In the first place, it must be conceded that although writing was in use in Palestine[1] in the 8th cent. B.C., it would not of necessity be a common art—any more than it was in a large part of England in the 18th cent. A.D. There is a presumption that Amos the shepherd would not know how to write. We have seen that he was *par excellence* a poet-preacher with a spoken message to the men of his own time. (2) It might be held, therefore, that the document owes its origin to the memory of one—a ready writer—who became interested in his message.[2] Moreover, from time to time the vocabulary of the book shews signs of being 'spoken', rather than purely 'literary' Hebrew.[3] (3) On the other hand, however, the several parts of the volume are not disjointed, as might be expected if they were the notes, so to speak, of a listener or disciple. In general terms, we are inclined to say that the book exhibits such internal coherence as rather

---

[1] The *Moabite Stone*, inscribed c. 850 B.C. in the land of Israel's neighbour, is the work of a professional (on behalf of Mesha the king). So also probably is the *Siloam* inscription. It is difficult to see what motive the writer of the *Gezer* inscription (8th–6th cent.) could have had in carving it *if*, as is sometimes suggested, he were a working farmer. See note on vii. 2.

[2] In this connection it might be significant that Amos is spoken of in the *third person* in vii. 10–17. *Cf.* also what is said in the notes as to the fragmentary nature of such a passage as iii. 1–6 (p. 156). If Amos did not succeed at the time in getting any number of adherents to his spiritual message, the stimulus to *write down* what could be remembered of his words might come twenty or twenty-five years later, when the destruction of the sanctuaries by Assyria proved that his claim was no false one (*cf.* Deut. xviii. 21, 22). It is not impossible that the *logia* of the prophets were usually preserved in the first instance *orally*.

[3] Are traces of Aramaisms to be so classed? In vi. 3 and viii. 9 *l⁶* occurs for '*ēth*; vi. 4 and 7, the participle (*s⁶rūḥîm*) has a Syriac use; in vi. 10 *samekh* occurs for *sîn*. For various reasons Amos himself may not have been the writer of the book. So far as the *New* Testament canon is concerned, as Dr Kennett reminds us, the Greatest of all the Prophets never penned a line, or even signed an epistle. This scholar suggests the further comparison that, as it is probable that our Lord's sayings ('Q') were committed to writing before His earliest surviving biography was written (St Mark), so with Amos the biographical section, vii. 10–17, may have been written later than the remainder of the book. *Cf.* further, *Isaiah*, pp. 5–8.

The admission that the book was not written necessarily in Amos' own lifetime, but at a period soon after the fulfilment of his predictions, does away with all difficulty arising out of the historical situation implied in, *e.g.*, v. 26, viii. 14.

to suggest that, if it did not come from the preacher's own
hand, he wrote it by means of a disciple amanuensis. The case
of Jeremiah, though a century and a half later, would (up
to a point) supply us with a parallel.[1] The 'I sections' of
Amos, *i.e.* vii. 1–9, viii. 1–3, ix. 1–4, appearing without any
introductory setting, seem to be indeed autobiographic, rather
than the work of a listener. And if Amos may be considered
responsible for writing this part, there would seem to be no
difficulty in the way of accepting—as *e.g.* do Marti and
Cornill—his composition of the book as a whole.[2] The
matter must be left open.

II. The next question presents itself: Is the book of Amos
substantially the document which left the hand of the first
writer, whether listener, disciple, amanuensis, or Amos himself? Probably it is. Truly, here and there occur verses which
from one cause or another came to be added subsequent to the
time of the original author, *e.g.* i. 1, 2, 11, 12; ii. 4, 5; vi. 2.
Also, for strong reasons, the three (doxology) passages (iv. 13;
v. 8, 9; ix. 5, 6) and especially the 'Epilogue' (ix. 8 *b* (or 11)–
15) appear to most modern scholars to be additions. (See,
further, the notes on the above passages, and, for the Epilogue, the next section of this Introduction.) It is indisputable
that in books like *Kings* and *Jeremiah*, even after they had
been translated into Greek, alterations were deliberately
introduced in the Hebrew text. The book of Amos, however,
was one of the first parts of the O.T. to be written, and the
presumed additions to its text were made before the age of

---

[1] Jer. xxxvi. 4; *cf.* also Isa. xxx. 8, and, possibly, viii. 16. It is noteworthy,
however, that (in the words of Dr Kennett) "it was only after Jeremiah had been
preaching for more than twenty years that he made any attempt to commit his
words to writing; it is probable that he would not have done so even then, had
it not been for his desire to make his preaching known at court" (*Isaiah*, p. 6).
Nor is there any evidence that either Isaiah or Jeremiah dictated *all* the genuine
oracles contained in the books bearing their names.

[2] We should like to believe that whatever the manner of their composition
the nine short chapters of the book (which could be read aloud in an hour)
represent only *portions* of Amos' public utterances. Such a compression is to be
met with in the N.T. The passage St Lu. iii. 7–14 stands for one whole sermon of
the Baptist, including practical applications of the discourse. The conversation
of our Saviour and Nicodemus would, judging by St John iii. 2–15, have occupied
but two minutes. A postscript to the Fourth Gospel states that 'even the world
itself would not contain the books' necessary to tell of all the *works* of Jesus.

the LXX. For a somewhat elaborate hypothesis as to the composition of the book, see Harper, pp. cxxx–cxxxvi.

XII. THE PROBLEM OF THE AMOS ORIGIN OF THE EPILOGUE

The question whether the passage Am. ix. 11–15 (indeed, 8 c–15) represents the genuine teaching[1] of the Prophet Amos, or is a later addition to the book, is one of considerable importance to those who wish to recover the actual message to his contemporaries of the great Prophet from Tekoa. There are grave, and (in the opinion of the present writer) insuperable, difficulties in holding the view that the book is an entire unity. Of recent years, however, the traditional belief in the Amos origin of vv. 8 c–15 has been championed by a number of critics, mainly (though not entirely) upon grounds of the presumed existence in ancient Israel of a scheme of prophetic eschatology, either native or derived from foreign sources. The principal objections to attributing the verses to Amos may be classified as seven in number. They are by no means of equal value.

I. As regards vv. 8 c–10, the idea of a separation between the righteous and sinners implied in v. 8 c, and perhaps in both vv. 9 and 10, is alien to the thought of Amos. The following points concern in the main vv. 11–15.

II. A promise of restoration such as is outlined in vv. 11–15 is quite incongruous after the threat of absolute destruction which is characteristic of the main body of the prophecy of Amos.

III. The reference to *Judah* and the dynasty of David in v. 11 is not what would be expected from Amos.

IV. Verses 11–15 are an anti-climax contrasting with the main prophecy since they contain no ethical element.

V. Linguistic considerations tell against the disputed verses being by the same author as the body of the book.

[1] The word 'teaching' is used above, because, after all, no part of the book may have been written down, or even dictated, by Amos.

VI. The historical background implied is not that of
Amos' time.

VII. The undoubted occurrence in other prophets of the
phenomenon of an *added* happy ending creates a suspicion
that the concluding verses of the book of Amos are not
authentic.

These objections must now be elaborated in some detail,[1]
along with the corresponding counter-arguments, *i.e.* those
supporting the authenticity of the verses.[2] The present writer's
opinion will be indicated briefly in each case.[3] The reader will
probably like to have some of the discussion presented in the
very words of the various scholars interested in the problem.

I. As regards *vv.* 8 c–10, the idea of a separation between
the righteous and sinners implied in *v.* 8 c, and perhaps in
both verses 9 and 10, is alien to the thought of Amos.

(1) It is argued that in the book "Amos everywhere holds
the entire nation answerable, although his anger attacks the
lordly rather than the humble".[4] "In the punishment which
will overtake the nation, there will be no distinction between
just and unjust" (Edghill). Now, here in ix. 8 c–10 (or at least
in *v.* 8 c, 'saving that I will not utterly destroy the house of
Jacob, saith the LORD'), *separation* is suggested between the
good and evil such as is, indeed, characteristic of the theology
of a later age.[5]

(2) On the other side, it is emphatically denied (*e.g.* by
Sellin) that Amos pictured a *universal* ruin in Israel. His
prophecies concern the fall of the kingdom and of the cult,
and nowhere has "he calculated that the whole people would
be annihilated once and for all, but he has, on the other hand,
spoken quite clearly of the possibility of the salvation of
a remnant (Am. v. 3, 15)".

---

[1] Exhibited throughout under the figure (1).
[2] Exhibited throughout under the figure (2).
[3] Exhibited throughout under the figure (3).
[4] Gressmann, *Alt. Proph.* edn 2.
[5] The verses 8 c–10 (sometimes styled 'the bridge') are discussed in detail
in the notes. (1) The clause in *v.* 8 c surely must be an addition to the genuine
text of Amos. (2) *V.* 9, which speaks of Jehovah's 'sifting', would seem at first

(3) The result of these opposing arguments may indeed appear, in the last resort, to be inconclusive, but, everything considered, if *vv.* 8 c–10 must be taken together,[1] the result seems to turn against a connection with Amos. It is impossible to prove that Amos ever believed that in fact there would be any righteous, or repentant, for God to save.[2] At the least the statement of ix. 8 c, 'saving that I will not utterly destroy the house of Jacob', must be an addition to the true text.

II. A promise of restoration such as is outlined in *vv.* 11–15 is quite incongruous after the threat of absolute destruction[3] which is characteristic of the main body of the prophecy of Amos.

(1) It is very doubtful whether Amos *expected* that his hearers would repent; moreover, the actual terms of his preaching seem to exclude the idea that amendment (if conceivable) would make any real difference to the on-coming catastrophe. Israel is doomed (v. 27, vi. 14). 'The end has come'. This is only what he had from the first seen in visions (viii. 2).

(2) (a) To this it is replied that all true prophecy must be conditional, as Jer. xviii. 7–10 expressly states, and as the book of Jonah illustrates; and that, indeed, two offers of salvation occur (in Am. v. 4, 14). (b) Further, it has been claimed that, in any case, the combination of promise following *threat* is of the genius, so to speak, of Hebrew sight to suggest a separation between Israelites and Israelites, whatever be the kind of sieve (small- or large-meshed) contemplated. However, if, as appears probable, the whole emphasis is on the *punishment*, the reference might be, without discrimination, to the 'house of Israel', the 'sinful kingdom' of *v.* 8 *a*, and so the verse be genuine. (3) *V.* 10 may, or may not, imply a distinction in judgment—according to whether the Hebrew is to be translated '*all* the sinners *of my* people' or '*my entire* sinful nation'. Amongst modern scholars Volz and Nowack count both *v.* 9 and *v.* 10 to be genuine. With this view the present writer finds himself in agreement.

[1] But see the preceding footnote.

[2] See the notes on v. 2, 15. The latter verse may, indeed, be an actual interpolation into the true text.

[3] This is not to say that prophets of woe cannot intersperse promises of happiness. Cf. p. 51. In point of fact most of the great prophets did so. *E.g.* contrast Mic. iv. 1–4, v. 2 with iii. 12; and Jer. xxx. 1–3, xxxi. 31 ff. with iv. 23–31. In Jer. xlviii. 47 and xlix. 6, 39, the restoration after captivity of Moab, Ammon and Elam is predicted. The literary difficulty (II) arises in part because of Amos' special message.

prophecy as of that of Egyptian oracles. It was maintained by Ed. Meyer and by Gressmann that such a happy element in Amos was to be expected. In the words of the latter scholar, "On the world-catastrophe must necessarily follow world-renewal".[1] Sellin urges the necessity of the prediction of weal (regarding it as a principle of native Israelite prophetic eschatology). He speaks of "the age of happiness which follows judgment as naturally[2] as day follows night".

(3) The position is, again, inconclusive. (a) It may be conceded that a preaching of absolute destruction is scarcely conceivable, and that it is perhaps unfair to tie down Amos too severely to such a message. It is one thing to call people to 'seek Jehovah', all the while hardly daring to hope that they will respond, but quite another matter to hold a definite dogma that they will not 'seek' Him. And, even if Amos normally was under this sad conviction, to be inconsistent is only human. (Ch. ix. 7 is well-nigh incompatible with iii. 2 a, yet both were uttered by Amos.) Opinions will differ as to how completely the Preacher, in a matter of this kind, could have contradicted his own language. (b) On the other hand, as regards the argument from supposed current eschatological conceptions, two questions may be asked: (i) Was there in Israel a prevalent eschatology embracing periods of (first) woe and (then) weal? (ii) Even if there were, would Amos have been a victim to it in such fashion as is presented in the book in its present shape? (i) The Egyptian oracles are, strictly speaking, not eschatological at all, but merely political. And in any case it does not appear that the Egyptian oracles had any influence upon the great Israelite prophets (cf. Introd. pp. 51–54). As regards the question of a native Israelite eschatology, it is difficult to find compelling or reliable evidence for the existence in early Israel of any definite set scheme of (1) misery, (2) bliss. (ii) But whatever view is taken as to the prevalence of a belief in a set eschatological scheme, it is hard to believe that Amos, of all men, would feel himself tied to any Israelite,[3] or

---

[1] See reference in the note on 'tabernacle of David', p. 320, and pp. 55, 56, above, in this commentary.

[2] "Selbstverständlich", Zwölfprophetenbuch, p. 150.

[3] Compare G. A. Smith in 1896: "We have the impressive and incommensur-

generally Semitic (*popular* or *prophetic*), notions prevalent
before his time; that is, unless he very clearly links the promise
to moral character in the same manner as he has already brought
threat into connection with transgression. We find it well-
nigh impossible to imagine that Amos expected that a golden
age must dawn automatically upon Jehovah's people (even
upon the tribe of Judah alone). What is missing from the
Epilogue is just the very thing which we should look for in
it if it owed its origin to the great moralist Amos; *viz.* some
statement, however brief, that the future of happiness described in the disputed verses was essentially bound up with
God's ethical government of the world.[1] In the words of
Cornill,[2] written in this connection:

> What is won by the acceptance [of the prophecies of salvation]? and at
> what price? Won is an earlier date for a few prophetic passages than the
> critical school is willing to concede, but the price paid is that we have to
> break the back-bone of the prophets, to reduce them to weaklings who had
> not the courage to think their thoughts through to the end and draw from
> them the necessary consequences, but who, when their own people are in
> question, blunt the edge of their threats and "let milk and honey flow from
> the cup of wrath of Yahweh" (Wellhausen).

III. The reference to Judah and the dynasty of David in
v. 11 is not what would be expected from Amos.

(1) It has been felt that the introduction of a promise of
happiness to the Southern Kingdom is not probable from a
prophet whose main interest, at least, seems to have been with
the Ten Tribes; whereas, at some period after one or both
kingdoms had *fallen*, the hope for Judah and for the remains
of North Israel is comprehensible. Jeremiah, it appears, after
the destruction of Samaria, thought that the descendants of
those who had survived the fall would be pleased to be
'brought to *Zion*' (Jer. iii. 14). With Ezekiel the ultimate

able facts... *that this change to hope comes suddenly, without preparation and
without statement of reasons*, at the very end of a book whose characteristics are
not only a final and absolute sentence of ruin upon the people, and an outlook of
unrelieved darkness, but *scornful discouragement of every popular vision of a
prosperous future*...". (The italics are the present writer's.)

[1] *Cf.* Micklem, *Prophecy and Eschat.* p. 109. Of this more is said under IV
below. The material blessings promised at the close of *Hosea* and in the second
part of the book of *Joel* are definitely associated with national regeneration
(Hos. xiv. 1–4, 8, Joel ii. 28–32).

[2] *Cf.* McFadyen in *The People and the Book*, p. 211.

union of the two kingdoms under Davidic rule became a conviction (Ezek. xxxvii. 16–28). It is hardly too much to say that for Amos before 721 B.C. to have proclaimed the substance of ix. 11 within the jurisdiction of the Ten Tribes would have involved him in a charge of sedition. Certainly it could not have suggested comfort to those who were proud of their non-dependence upon Jerusalem.

(2) This whole difficulty is lessened if it be admitted that Amos generally included Judah within the scope of his message.[1] Further, even Hosea, a Northerner, prophesied that the 'children of Israel' after affliction 'shall return and seek the LORD their God, and *David* their king' (Hos. iii. 5). Sellin has defended the authenticity of the Epilogue by attempting to shew that the significance of the promise of blessing to Judah lies in its being a *threat* spoken to Amaziah, the priest of the principal North Israelite sanctuary.[2]

(3) To sum up this part of the controversy: once again it is inconclusive. If Amos wrote the Epilogue, or any part of it, possibly it was on some occasion subsequent[3] to his preaching, and when he was in Judah. He may have thought that he saw signs of reformation. It would thus be not an addition by a scribe or editor, but an interpolation or insertion by the original writer.

With regard to Sellin's specious hypothesis that *vv.* 11–15 constitute a threat, the arguments which he advances seem to be counterbalanced by the difficulties which the proposition leaves still unsolved.

IV. Verses 11–15 are an anti-climax contrasting with the main prophecy since they contain no ethical element.

(1) Verses 11–15 exhibit a bad anti-climax. Amos was above all things an enthusiast for ethics. Here, however, neither does repentance usher in the new era, nor is righteousness a characteristic of it.[4] In place of moral and spiritual features characteristic of the genuine Amos, come political and material. Amos' preaching may have contained a happy

---

[1] See pp. 12, 13, above.   [2] See the note on '*thy* God' in ix. 15 (pp. 323, 324).
[3] *Cf.* Sellin (*A.T.-liche Proph.*) in 1912; F. C. Burkitt, S.P.C.K. *Comm.* p. 423 *a.*
[4] *Cf.* what was said in summing up argument II (p. 71 *ad init.*).

element,[1] but would *he* have uttered *vv.* 13–15? It was Sir G. A. Smith who in 1896 put this contention finely:

All these prospects of the future restoration of Israel are absolutely without a moral feature. They speak of return from captivity, of political restoration, of supremacy over the Gentiles, and of a revived nature....Such hopes are...legitimate to a people who were long separated from their... land....But they are not natural to a prophet like Amos....Imagine him describing the consummation of his people's history, without mentioning one of those moral triumphs to rally his people to which his whole passion and energy had been devoted. To me it is impossible to hear the voice that cried *Let justice roll on like waters and righteousness like a perennial stream,* in a peroration which is content to tell of mountains dripping with must and of a people satisfied with vineyards and gardens.

(2) No counter-argument has been produced.

(3) This difficulty in the way of the Amos authorship would seem to be almost insuperable.

V. Linguistic considerations tell against the disputed verses being by the same author as the body of the book.

(1) The following words or usages[2] suggest, more or less, the exilic or post-exilic age—*hărîsāh* ('ruin'), and *y*ᵉ*mē 'ôlām* ('days of old'), in *v.* 11; *'āsîs* ('sweet wine'), *mûg*, in *Hithpô'lēl* voice ('melt'), in *v.* 13; *shûbh sh*ᵉ*bhûth* ('bring again the captivity'), in *v.* 14; *'Elôhekhā* ('thy God') in consolatory sense, in *v.* 15.

In the text of the Epilogue, moreover, there is a far greater proportion of *scriptiones plenae* than elsewhere in the book: *e.g.* in *yippôl* (in *v.* 9), *Dāwîdh* (in *v.* 11), *ḥôrēsh* and *qôṣēr* (in *v.* 13).

(2) G. A. Smith, though an advocate of a later date for the section, goes so far as to affirm that nothing in the language of the verses precludes their being by Amos.[3] It may even be argued that the expression 'behold, the days come' (in *v.* 13) is distinctively of the Amos vocabulary. With regard to the form of the text, Sellin maintains (p. 223):

The *scriptio plena* (which we so often meet with here,...above all in *Dāwîdh*) can prove nothing, because this ending, on account of the significance

---

[1] Conceivably even, as Dr. Cook suggests, an original happy *ending* has been replaced by the present one.

[2] These points are dealt with more fully in the several notes in the commentary.
[3] *Op cit.* p. 194.

which it gained for the later community, must have been touched up more frequently in the MSS. than the rest of the book would be. And especially the *Dāwidh* could easily come to the pen of a scribe who had just read vi. 5.

(3) As with many arguments and counter-arguments based upon language, though nothing is *proved* as to a late date, the evidence is of value when taken with other considerations. Sellin's contention might be more convincing if it could be shewn that it was customary for the Epilogue of Amos to be copied as a separate document. The question of language does tell against the Amos origin of the Epilogue.

VI. The historical background implied is not that of Amos' time.

(1) The situation indicated in the concluding verses is that *Judah* has now been taken captive by the Babylonians. It is reasonable for Jeremiah (in xxxiii. 6, 7, 12) to prophesy ultimate restoration for a land which was already well-nigh a desolation; and so with Ezekiel (in xxxvi. 33–36). On the other hand, there is little evidence (apart from perhaps Am. iv. 10, 11) that at the time of Amos Israel (both Northern and Southern) was anything but, upon the whole, well inhabited and prosperous. The expression 'waste cities' (in ix. 14), if used in Jeroboam's reign, is hardly intelligible. Again, Amos has in prospect only one nation, Assyria, as the administrator of Divine justice upon Israel. In ix. 9, however, there is a reference to 'the house of Israel' being shaken 'among *all* the nations'. Such an idea seems to reflect the facts as they came to be in a considerably later age. Nor is there much point in the people being told that they will not be exiled 'any more' (*v.* 15), when as yet the exile has not taken place once. Furthermore it is difficult to believe that, at a time when David's dynasty was *standing*,[1] men were bidden to look for the restoration of his 'fallen hut', the closing up of 'the breaches thereof', the raising up of 'his ruins' and its rebuilding 'as in the days of old' (*v.* 11). In other words, in the Epilogue, the

---

[1] Doubtless Amos the prophet did as a matter of fact picture Judah's collapse as being equally imminent as that of the Northern Kingdom, but even so the laboured succession of phrases applied to David's dynasty in *v.* 11 *b* is far from natural until such time as the ruin of the house was seen and known by all men.

viewpoint is shifted; and the problem becomes similar to that of the authorship of Isaiah, chs. xl ff.

(2) Against this, it can be said that the words 'among all the nations' are themselves a later addition.[1] It is also claimed (with less reason) that the expressions referring to the *dynasty* and to the *land* are capable of a meaning and implication consistent with a pre-exilic date. See, further, the notes on the crucial expressions 'fallen', 'breaches', 'build', 'of old' (in *v*. 11); 'remnant of Edom' (in *v*. 12); 'bring again the captivity', 'waste cities' (in *v*. 14). Some scholars translate 'fall*ing* tent', or consider that the idea is of a dynasty *about* to fall.

König (*Geschichte der A.-T. Rel.* 1924, pp. 343, 344) holds that the happy prospect for Judah is pictured by Amos as destined to follow *almost immediately* upon the execution of the judgment on North Israel. Sellin appears to believe that 'falling tent' is a fit description of "the dynasty, which, in spite of some intermittent success in the days of Uzziah, did, when compared to what it had been in David's and Solomon's time, resemble such" (*Zwölfprophetenbuch*, p. 225).

(3) To sum up. This argument against the emanation of the passage from the historical situation of Amos' day would seem, even taken alone, to be sufficiently strong.

VII. The undoubted occurrence in other prophets of the phenomenon of an *added* happy ending creates a suspicion that the concluding verses of the book of Amos are not authentic.

(1) There appears to have been a softening-down by a later hand of the messages of judgment[2] in other pre-exilic prophets. So Mic. vii. 7–20; Zeph. iii. 14–20. Many critics have felt that the last chapter of Hosea is an addition.[3] To the volume of Isaiah, chs. xl–lxvi were added long after the age of the prophet Isaiah. Not entirely dissimilar is the

---

[1] See the note, pp. 265, 266.

[2] In fact, this is so with all those pre-exilic prophecies of judgment which would otherwise have ended upon the sad note. Zeph. iii. 8–13 may possibly be genuine.

[3] Not to mention other portions. Nowack and certain scholars would regard the second half of the (very late) book of Joel as having been the work of someone other than the predictor of the locust plague.

phenomenon of the (probable) re-editing of Ecclesiastes by
someone not satisfied with the theology of the book as it stood;
and it is to be compared with the adding of the first three
(happy) verses of Ezra to the books of Chronicles, which, as
originally composed, had concluded the Hebrew Bible upon
a sad note.[1]
   (2) Defence of the authenticity of Mic. vii. 7–20, Zeph. iii.
14–20 has been attempted by certain scholars.
   (3) Unquestionably the fact that additions have been made
to at least some other prophetical writings is a further reason
for doubting the Amos authorship of ix. 11–15.

   To sum up the entire position: whereas several of the above
arguments against the Amos authorship are of less force than
others, and one or more are perhaps of no force at all, yet
taken as a whole the case against the Amos origin of the
verses would appear to be almost irresistible; and, on the
other hand, there is no compelling argument in *favour* of the
authenticity of the passage. Our doubts are further confirmed by the *abruptness* (which every reader must feel) of the
transition in the chapter from *darkness* to *light*.
   Finally, the attitude upon this question taken up by different scholars is of interest. When Pusey, in 1861, compiled
his commentary, he found no difficulty in writing: "Amos, as
the prophets were taught to do, sums up his prophecy of woe
with this one full promise of overflowing good". Amongst
critics who, since his day, have regarded the Epilogue as
contradictory to the message of Amos (rather than as a
'summing up'), or as exhibiting an imperfect promise (more
than a 'full' one of 'overflowing good'); or who for other
reasons have denied its Amos origin; there may be mentioned:
Wellhausen (1892), G. A. Smith (1896), Nowack (1897),[2]
Marti (1904), Harper (1905), Duhm (1911), Riessler (1911),
Ehrlich (*Randglossen*, 1912), Edghill (1913), Canney (1920),
T. H. Robinson (1923).[3] To these must also be added Gress-

---

[1] 2 Chron. xxxvi. 22, 23 = Ezra i. 1–3. See Elmslie on Chronicles.
[2] *Kl. Propheten*, and *cf.* edn 2, p. 174 and edn 3, p. 170, "Wir haben hier
kein echtes Wort des Amos.".
[3] *Prophecy and the Prophets*, p. 71; *cf. Z.A.W.* 1927, Heft 1/2, pp. 7–9.

mann, who, though he had argued for the Amos authorship in 1910 (*Älteste Geschichtsschreibung u. Prophetie Israels*), rejected it in 1921 (2nd edn of same work). Similarly, Cornill changed his opinion (*Einleitung*, 1912).

The names of modern scholars who have defended the view (or assumed it) that the Epilogue is from the same hand as the rest of the prophecy may be given (more completely) as follows: von Orelli (1888), Mitchell (1893), Driver (1897), Valeton (1898), van Hoonacker (1908), Hans Schmidt (1917), Köhler (1917), Ed. Meyer (1906[1]), Sellin (1922). König in *Geschichte der A.-T. Rel.* edn 1924, defends the passage, though in the edition of 1912 he had argued against it. Meinhold (*Zur isr. Religionsgeschichte*, 1903) maintains that there is a possibility of the passage containing a genuine *nucleus*.

A negative is seldom satisfying. If, then, the concluding portion of the book has no connection with the Prophet Amos, may we conjecture in what circumstances the verses were written? (1) The prophecy of ix. 8 c–15 would be suitable if uttered to the exiles in Babylon (or among a section of the community in *Judah* who had not been transported) at about the period of Isa. xl–xlviii (c. 540 B.C.), and when the memory of Edom's action in 586 B.C. was still fresh. (2) But perhaps *vv.* 11, 14 and 15[2] rather suggest that the writer of the passage was a contemporary of Haggai and Zechariah, *i.e. c.* 520–518 B.C. The reference to Edom in *v.* 12 may imply a date prior to the desolation of that land alluded to as an accomplished fact in Mal. i. 2–4, c. 460 B.C.[3] Or (3) he may have belonged to some subsequent[4] period of discouragement before the Seleucid age, such as is known to have recurred again and again. The message of a patriotic, optimistic preacher or writer would always be "A new and a bright future is before you".

---

[1] *Die Israeliten und ihre Nachbarstämme*, p. 543, and note.

[2] With their reference both to the revival of the house of David and to the re-population of Judah without fear of a *further* captivity.

[3] The date of the expulsion of the Edomites from their mountains is uncertain. All that is known is that it had occurred by 312 B.C.

[4] For the reference is to 'the remnant of Edom and all the nations', not to Edom only.

XIII. THE SIGNIFICANCE OF THE PHRASE
'THUS SAITH (OR SAID) JEHOVAH'[1]

There is, however, a question more fundamental than that
of the human authorship[2] of certain portions of the book of
Amos, or, indeed, of the whole nine chapters. A greater
problem is presented by the fact that in the prophets (and
particularly in Amos) we meet with much which seems to be
represented as the words of God Himself. The startling phrase
'Thus saith Jehovah' (or 'Thus hath Jehovah said') is of constant occurrence in the book of Amos; and the expression 'it
is an oracle of the LORD' is to be found in the present text
twenty-one times.[3] What this phenomenon does and does not
imply is, obviously, a matter of extreme practical importance.

(i) It may be stated at the outset that a certain amount of
this apparent definiteness is due merely to the limitations
of the Hebrew language. In pure Hebrew, *oratio obliqua* is
almost unknown. Therefore, such a phrase in modern speech
as *God said that He would destroy* becomes in Hebrew *God
said: "I will destroy"*. Thus a passage by a Hebrew reporter
meant to be understood as giving the contents, or even the
substance only, of God's words must, for no other reason than
the necessity of Hebrew idiom, be cast in the first person. It
is obvious, therefore, that there is a risk of our reading into
such utterances a precision of meaning not always intended
by the Prophet himself.

(ii) Again, not seldom in Hebrew the very term 'said' is
used when a Western tongue would have employed some word
expressing *thought* and not speech at all.[4] From the phrase,
in Exod. iii. 3, 'Moses said, I will turn aside now', we are not to

---

[1] In the expressions, 'Thus saith Jehovah' and (at the close of a passage)
'saith Jehovah', the verb is almost always in the perfect tense ('āmar). The
rendering of E.VV. 'saith' probably means 'he has said and still says'. However, the view is not unlikely that the perfect tense is used with special reference
to the time of the audition, 'Thus God *said*' (to me).

[2] Referred to in the two preceding sections of this Introd.

[3] See on ii. 11. The term is *nᵉ'ŭm*, not '*āmar*.

[4] See R. H. Kennett, *In Our Tongues*, p. 21.

suppose that Moses *spoke*. So also in 2 Ki. v. 11, the R.V. rightly has 'Behold, I *thought*, He will surely come out to me', whereas the Hebrew is 'Behold, I said *etc.*'[1] As to how far and when this usage may apply to the phrase 'Thus saith (or said) Jehovah', there is room for divergence of opinion. This much, however, may safely be claimed. Not seldom, when a prophet utters the words 'thus saith Jehovah', his meaning might be expressed in a modern way, 'It is my profound conviction that such and such is God's thought (or will or purpose)'.

(iii) Readers of the Talmud will be aware of the fact that, years after the O.T. was completed, the Rabbis, notwithstanding their very real reverence for God, composed stories in which they put into His mouth words which must have been of their own invention. The formula is: *The Holy One, blessed be He, said* ——. This seems to shew that the Hebrews in the East in times past did not make the clear distinction which we should draw to-day between words which, it might be believed, God actually uttered, and words which were only considered to be *worthy* of God. It may well be a fact that Israelites of all ancient times were apt to be somewhat indefinite in their ideas of what was spoken by God. They did not always draw a hard and fast line between God's words and man's,[2] and the psychology of the vision state tended further to blur the distinction; *cf.* vii. 3, 6, 8, 9, viii. 2, ix. 1–4.

(iv) This view is confirmed by the comparative study of religion. In almost all ages and quarters it has been believed that gods speak, and that by using the right means it is possible to hear their voice. Oracles made available the sayings of the gods. "*Chemosh said unto me*, Go take Nebo against Israel", wrote Mesha on the Moabite Stone at the time of Elijah or Elisha. The king, or in the first instance the seer, had a conviction that the national god desired, or encouraged,

---

[1] And see, amongst numerous other examples, Gen. xx. 11 (*lit.* 'Because I *said*'), Ruth iv. 4 *a* (*lit.* 'I *said* I will disclose it') and Am. ix. 10.

[2] The LXX translators allowed themselves at times considerable freedom in omitting, inserting and transposing the prophetic formula—'saith Jehovah'.

a certain act. With the Semites, 'God said' (or 'saith') was
a current phrase for expressing what was understood to be the
will of their Deity.

(v) The above considerations seem to warrant the conclusion that, when using such expressions as 'Thus saith
Jehovah', the prophetic writer did not of necessity mean
that he was reporting the very words of God. It may also be
argued that in some instances he cannot have been giving even
His *thoughts*. If we judge by what from the loftiest parts of
the O.T. and the N.T. we know about God, there are certain
suggestions and acts attributed in the O.T. to Him which from
their nature are unlikely to have been His. An example of
this is supplied by the advice attributed to God in 1 Sam. xvi. 2,
'Take an heifer with thee'. This, being only a *half truth*, is not
in accordance with a high standard of morality. Or again
phrases in Am. iv. 10, vii. 17 would, we can be sure, have been
expressed more delicately if they had been sayings or thoughts
of God. Instances might be multiplied; *e.g.* 1 Sam. xv. 2—
(note *the reason* given)—2 Sam. xii. 8, 11 *b*.[1]

(vi) There remains, however, a vast amount of material in
the great Canonical Prophets which (the present writer believes)
is something more than human. Obviously no voice proceeded
from heaven to their outward ears.[2] But the true prophets
were capable of receiving Divine communications. Sometimes
this was by means of an 'abnormal' psychological condition of

---

[1] If once the principle be accepted that such—reverent—discrimination is
legitimate on our part, many moral, 'anthropomorphic' and also historical difficulties in the prophets will vanish. For example, if in the book of Amos a certain
thing seems to be predicted by the mouth of God, which as a matter of fact did
not afterwards occur, we are not involved in the problem of any words of *God*
being unverified (*e.g.* in Am. viii. 8, 'rise up wholly like the river'). Similarly
with two mutually contradictory pronouncements attributed to God, at least
one must be merely the writer's supposition, and not an actual statement by
God. The subject of sacrifice supplies such an instance. Contrast the *denial* of
Jer. vii. 22 with the positive *commands* in passages like Levit. i. 1 ff., vi. 8, 9.
Some may feel it to be a distinct loss that—in view of the points mentioned
in (i) to (iv)—the prophets cannot always be regarded as uttering the very
words of God Himself. But, surely, we have not to discuss the kind of revelation
which we should like to have found in the O.T., but that which in fact God has
given. Moreover, the gains to ethical religion suggested by (v) are of such a
nature, and so numerous, that their worth cannot easily be calculated.

[2] 1 Sam. iii. 8 *b* shews that the Divine Voice was audible to none save the
prophet himself.

noble ecstasy[1] in which there was *audition* or *vision*, or both. At other times (probably more often), in experiences, perfectly natural[2] as far as they were concerned, they had promptings and thoughts which came from God, addressed to their will and conscious intelligence, of which they could in truth declare 'Thus Jehovah said'.[3] In this connection significant experiences may be quoted from the history of Isaiah. 'The LORD of Hosts revealed himself *in mine ears*', the prophet declares (in xxii. 14). And again, this calm and practically-minded man exclaims, with reference to the irresistible power with which the revelation from without seemed to come to him, 'The LORD *spake* thus to me *with a strong hand*' (viii. 11, R.V. marg., Hebrew 'with strength of hand'). Perhaps, in Am. iii. 7, 8, Amos refers to such an audition as this, 'He revealeth this secret unto his servants the prophets...the Lord GOD hath spoken, who can but prophesy?' And these abnormal conditions may have been not uncommon with the prophets.

The revelation, howsoever received, they spoke out in human language, for the most part in sober reasoned utterances. The

---

[1] *Cf.* Skinner, *Proph. and Rel.* pp. 194, 220; also pp. 10–12. The phenomenon of *vision* is discussed in the next section of this Introduction. It is *possible* that the expression 'Thus Jehovah shewed me' (in vision) is strictly parallel to the phrase under discussion 'Thus Jehovah said'.

[2] What else is the meaning of Num. xii. 6–8, especially 'With him will I speak mouth to mouth'? (*v.* 8). To be distinguished, though not entirely dissimilar, is such an experience as that of Fox the Quaker in 1651. He believed he was commanded by God to go to Lichfield—"As soon as I was within the city, the word of the Lord came to me again, saying, 'Cry, Woe to the bloody city of Lichfield'". (This was when he seemed to see the city full of blood.) Elsewhere Fox recounts a dispute with Anglican clergy when he asked them "whether any of them could say he ever had the word of the Lord to go and speak to such or such a people? None of them durst say he had, but one of them burst out into a passion, and said he could speak his experiences as well as I. I told him experience was one thing, but to receive and go with a message, and to have a word from the Lord, as the prophets and apostles had and did, and as I had done to them, this was another thing. And therefore I put it to them again, could any of them say he had ever had a command or word from the Lord immediately at any time? but none of them could say so". (Parker, *Fox's Journal*, pp. 57, 90.) Instances of auditions of various kinds might be multiplied indefinitely. For an account of a remarkable one in connection with modern missionary enterprise, see Stanley Jones, *The Christ of the Indian Road*, 1925, pp. 29–31.

[3] Whatever the explanation of the phenomenon, it is obvious that the prophets make a claim to inspiration different from that of, *e.g.*, the scribe who compiled Proverbs. However sound and lofty the teaching of the latter may be, he does not feel that he has the right to say, 'Thus saith the LORD'.

words heard by the people were not always the very sayings of God, if for no other reason than that they passed through the prophets' own consciousness, and of course it was not possible for these men to rise entirely above its limitations. But the great prophets were true 'men of God', mediators between God and His world. God was communicating His will unto Israel as unto no other nation. As through neither Greek philosopher nor poet He *spoke in the prophets*.[1] And it is a fact that the religious man to-day, opening the pages of the prophets, with and without 'Thus saith the LORD', and reading with spiritual discrimination, can hear the very words of God to his soul.[2] The religious consciousness of every age *reacts* to such words, and they are found to be from above. They are life-giving because, in essence, they are from God Himself. In Amos can be seen at least the germ of some of the great ideas taught by Jesus Christ.[3] Moreover, when Amos delivered the message, for example, that Jehovah was more pleased with sound morality than with 'religious' ritual of any kind, he was uttering (to the minds of the majority of his hearers) a paradox. Now, however, the principle has become so obvious a commonplace to modern readers of Amos that they may have difficulty in appreciating how striking, if

[1] Ep. Heb. i. 1. *Cf.* Gore, *Belief in God*, pp. 105 *ad fin.*, 106, 107: "The message which Ezekiel and St Paul delivered was a message addressed to their will and conscious intelligence, and by their will and conscious intelligence received and delivered. I see, therefore, no evidence at all making it plausible to suggest that what presented itself to them was really—though they mistook its nature—their unconscious mind. Whence did the unconscious mind get this astonishing series of messages? It does not lie within the compass of the materials out of which, as far as we can judge, it is and must be formed. In other words, it seems infinitely more probable that it was 'a downrush from the super-conscious' —the voice of the Spirit of God, as the prophets themselves so imperiously insist. ...As to the psychological method of the divine communication, we may be as ignorant as we generally are of the psychological conditions under which artists and poets and mystics attain their intuitions. But of the source of the communications, as coming really and directly from God, I dare to feel certain".

[2] This is so notwithstanding the fact that these great men were raised up, in the first instance, for their own generation, and their message was suited to circumstances of their age. St Paul never thought that summaries of his speeches, and letters written under his dictation, would be read by us to-day. Am. vii. 15 indicates the limits of Amos' ministry as he conceived it—*viz.* a ministry 'unto Israel'.

[3] See the notes on such passages as ii. 7 (p. 141), iii. 8 (p. 158), iv. 4 (p. 296), v. 4 (p. 180), ix. 7 (p. 264).

not how new, was his teaching. It is not easy to formulate definitions of 'revelation' and 'inspiration', but surely here is a clear *example* of both. What was to Amos' first hearers paradox, is to his present-day readers axiom. They of whose message this is true made no rash claim when they used the words 'Thus saith the LORD'.

XIV. VISIONS AND THE BOOK OF AMOS[1]

(1)

VISIONS AND PROPHECY. GENERAL CONSIDERATIONS

Many were the means by which the great prophets gained their knowledge of divine truth, and arrived at the various messages—moral, social and political—which they were to deliver to their fellow-countrymen. Much came to them by foresight, by intuition and by calm reflection. This, however, represents but one aspect of the subject. That they both claimed to, and actually did, receive in their mind impressions through abnormal channels can hardly (upon the evidence of the O.T. at least) be disputed. In the prophetic writings are to be found two special methods of experiencing (so it appeared) contact with the Divine, (a) hearing, (b) seeing.

(a) Examples of the audition are given above, on p. 81.

(b) The phenomenon of vision supplies another means of contact between God and the prophet: 'Thus Jehovah caused me to see'. The testimony furnished by the prophetic writings makes it difficult to hold that the descriptions of such visions were, as a rule, merely written up.[2] In the case of Amos especially, they are peculiarly brief, naïf and real. In their spontaneity they contrast with compositions such as the dream-allegory of Bunyan: and perhaps the 'dreams' of

---

[1] The subject of 'vision' seems to demand a somewhat full and wide treatment in view of its importance in the history of religion in ancient and modern times.

[2] So, in contrast to Marti, is the emphatic opinion of Hölscher, *Profeten*, p. 46. However, as with the terminology of audition also, this is not to deny that the terminology of the vision state might at times be used by a true prophet to describe impressions which, as a matter of fact, had come to him otherwise; *cf.* note on 'which he saw' (Am. i. 1).

Zechariah.[1] It would seem, also, to be doing violence to the texts to assert that such visions as those of Amos (at least *all* of them) were actual events, or ordinary everyday sights, and nothing more—to which the prophet gave a symbolic meaning.[2] Yet there is room for a variety of opinions; indeed many views are held upon the subject. To define to ourselves very precisely what happened to the prophets is not possible, if for no other reason than that they themselves would have been unable to express adequately in human language their experience of so exalted a condition as that of psychic vision.[3] Moreover, different beliefs will be held as to how *unique* were the Israelite prophets as the recipients of any revelation from God.[4] None the less, it must be helpful to study prophetic visions[5] in the light of what is known (as authentically as the nature of the case permits) concerning psychopathological and mystical states, and methods of teaching by symbolic vision, in various ages. The following section contains a brief attempt to examine from the point of view of the O.T. and of Religion a problem which presents itself to the thoughtful student of the book of Amos.

A certain point has been suggested with reference to Sundar Singh—the Christian teacher in India and Thibet who com-

---

[1] Not to mention such visions as the great poem of Dante, and the book of Arda Viraf. (This latter Zoroastrian work, purporting to be a vision, goes back at least to the 6th cent. A.D. A quotation is made in the note on Am. viii. 5, p. 244.) Another type of vision is the night dream of certain Mohammedan mystics, *e.g.* of Sha'rānī in the 16th cent. A.D. (*cf.* Prof. R. A. Nicholson in *E.R.E.* iii. p. 735 a). But doubtless these also are worked up when they become literary productions.

[2] See *e.g.* Buttenwieser, *Prophets*, pp. 142, 223; and *cf.* pp. 100, 101 of this commentary.

[3] Furthermore, Hebrew psychology, according to which the mind was conceived of as very distinct from the body, would assist any tendency to hold as abnormal, experiences which we should call normal. *Cf.* Jer. xxxii. 8 b, and see H. Wheeler Robinson, "The Psychology and Metaphysic of 'Thus saith Yahweh'", *Z.A.W.* xli. 1923, pp. 3, 4.   [4] *Cf.* below, p. 96.

[5] Not *all* prophets saw visions. None are recorded of such outstanding characters as Hosea, Micah and Zephaniah. In the same way that many even of the greatest saints of the Church have had no experience of the vision, so the physical and mental constitution of some prophets was doubtless less suited to the vision-state than was that of others. *Cf.* remarks upon "Voices and Visions" in *St Joan* by G. B. Shaw (pp. xiv, xv). On the other hand, though temperament may well be an important factor, the history of psychological experience renders it precarious to hold that it is a *vital* one.

bined with a very practical religious life a remarkable experience of visions. Canon Streeter and Dr Appasamy assert that the Sadhu's claim to have enjoyed a spiritual state which, if not identical with, is at least closely analogous to that of the author of the Apocalypse, is one which would appear to deserve very serious consideration. "If so, it follows that a study of the Sadhu's experience will throw light on the psychological mechanism through and by means of which religious truth was mediated to certain of the Biblical writers".[1] Whatever the similarity with apocalyptists may be, it would seem that the short visions of the *prophets* present an even closer analogy to those of the Sadhu than do the lengthy schemes of the apocalyptists. In the written apocalypses it is impossible to separate the record of ideas which welled up into the seers' minds when in an exalted condition, from that which was a result of conscious literary industry in the normal state.[2] It may be left out of consideration that the seers of the Old and New Testaments ever beheld with their bodily eyes[3] the sight of God Himself 'seated upon a throne'. Neither did a 'saraph' touch a prophet's lips with 'a live coal', nor did God place before other seers 'a seething cauldron' or 'a basket of summer fruit'.[4] To the comparison with the experiences of the Christian Sadhu we shall return more than once.

[1] *The Sadhu*, 1921, p. 114. For another remarkable account of this modern visionary preacher, see *The Gospel of Sadhu Sundar Singh*, by Prof. Friedrich Heiler of Marburg (rendered into English by Olive Wyon).

[2] Elsewhere Streeter and Appasamy include the prophets in a comparison: "We should...argue that exactly the same psychological principles have determined the form, and exactly the same factors of personal character and concentrated devotion account for the value (a value which, we should hold, is not the same in all cases) of the visions recorded in the Bible" *(op. cit. p. 145).*

[3] The stories in the book of Genesis of objective appearances of angels present an entirely different problem, being not history but folklore. Other accounts of visions which suggest objective reality, though such narratives may be essentially historical, yet probably have reference to subjective rather than exterior vision. So we must interpret 1 Sam. xxviii. 7–19. For the occurrence described in this passage to have been real, the following succession of miracles would need to have been wrought by God: (1) Samuel's decaying body restored to his spirit, (2) the body clothed with a coat of the cut which he used to wear in his former life, (3) the prophet brought to converse with the witch in the presence of Saul while unseen by him.

[4] Isa. vi. 1, 6, Jer. i. 13, Am. viii. 1.

One may compare the vision of Amos with, but in some way one must also distinguish it from, the 'second sight' or *trance* condition of the inferior[1] type of prophet, such as is described, in Numb. xxiv. 3, 4, 15, 16, as 'the man whose eye was closed...which seeth the vision of the Almighty,... having his eyes uncovered'. Though it is true, historically, that the phenomenon of spiritual and didactic vision grew out of the lower forms of vision, yet it would be a serious mistake to hold that the great prophets clung to the mechanism of a lesser order.[2] The distinction between the higher and the inferior kinds of prophetic vision may find some illustration in the analysis of mystic vision given by the famous St Theresa. Some "feel certain they see whatever their fancy imagines. If they had ever beheld a genuine vision, they would recognise the deception unmistakably".[3] The best prophetic experience was not the result of mere vivid imagination. The relation between the visions of the *n'bhî'îm*, or lower order, and those of the greater prophets will come up again for consideration.[4]

Nathanael Micklem, in a brief but suggestive study of the subject in *Prophecy and Eschatology*, draws this distinction: while conceding that the visions of the prophets who are styled 'true' are not less the work of the imagination than are the visions of those usually called 'false', he sees the special characteristic of the former in their always being the expression of "the result of profound meditation into *the meaning and order of the actual world*—in other words, they are not mere fancies; they are interpretations" (p. 44). In the same direction is the view of Skinner.[5] "The *meaning* of the vision passes into the prophet's thinking, and becomes the nucleus of a comprehensive view of God and the world....And the

---

[1] *Cf.* note on 'O thou seer', Am. vii. 12, p. 230.

[2] Amos himself supplies a case in point. His words in vii. 14 almost imply that he felt uneasy in assuming the title of *nābhî* (vii. 14) because of its inferior associations. Would he, then, have recounted five *visions*, if his experience was no different from that of the lower seer and *nābhî*?

[3] *Interior Castle* (or *Mansions*), vi. ix. 6; Zimmerman, edn 3, p. 240.

[4] Pp. 93 *ad init.*, 94. The tendency of modern scholarship is to emphasise the difference of their *content* rather than of their essential *form*. *Cf.* Skinner, *Proph. and Rel.* pp. 194 *ad fin.*, 195.

[5] *Op. cit.* pp. 220 and 221.

substance of the prophet's revelation is not the mere vision or audition itself but the truth which it has evoked or symbolised in his mind".

(2)

THE BEST TYPE OF PROPHETIC VISION AND ITS ANALOGIES

What was the experience of prophets such as Isaiah, Amos, Jeremiah and Ezekiel,[1] when in the vision state?

It would appear that not with their bodily eyes, but with interior sight, even the eyes of the soul[2] or the spirit, these men saw various scenes or objects, and they apprehended certain truths. God was always present to them in such spiritual visions, and upon Him the prophets' higher faculties were focused in contemplation. When we are considering prophetic vision, it would seem reasonable that Isaiah's wonderful experience should be kept in mind. The phenomenon described in Isa. ch. vi exhibits the important spiritual elements of 'seeing' God, of realising personal sinfulness, of hearing the Divine voice, and of giving oneself in surrender to the call for service. This, at least, corresponds to a high mystical

---

[1] The reference is not to all of Ezekiel's trance experiences, real as they probably were (cf. Lofthouse, *Ezek.* pp. 94, 95), but to visions such as those concerning a revived Israel (xxxvii. 1–14) and the bestowal of God's grace (xlvii. 1–12).

[2] "The eyes of the soul", says the Christian mystic Angela of Foligno, "do behold a spiritual and not a bodily presence" (*Book of Visions and Instructions*, Engl. transl. 1880, p. 24). It does not seem necessary to go into the question of what is technically named by the mediaeval and scholastic writers the 'intellectual' vision, as distinct from the 'imaginative'. (i) The 'intellectual' vision is one in which nothing is seen or heard by the eyes and ears. "The impression... is directly imprinted upon the intellect" (Zimmerman, *op. cit.* p. 173). St Theresa asserts that "a person...is conscious that Jesus Christ stands by her side, although she sees Him neither with the eyes of the body nor of the soul" (*Int. Castle*, VI. viii. 2). This is the mode of vision of angels, and of the saints after death. Pratt seems to hold that such visions are not altogether unreasonable psychologically (*Religious Consciousness*, p. 404, n. 21); and G. C. Joyce considers that this experience helps us to understand certain types of O.T. vision, *e.g.* some of Ezekiel's visions (*Inspiration of Prophecy*, p. 113). (ii) St Thomas Aquinas says: "The name of prophet is more properly applied to those who see by imaginary vision. And yet the more excellent prophecy is that which is conveyed by intellectual vision". (*Summa*, II. ii, Q. 174, art. 2, reply obj. 3. Dominican transl. 1922.) St Thomas classes the prophetic visions generally as (according to scholastic philosophy) 'imaginary' (II. ii, Q. 174, art. 3, cf. Q. 175, art. 3, reply obj. 4).

experience far removed from that of the prophets of *early* Israel.[1] In the inaugural vision of the great prophet of faith, God is central, as God, or at least Christ, usually is in the visions of the Christian mystics.[2] Is it to be supposed that only to saints of the Christian dispensation, or solely at man's 'mortal hour' (as with St Stephen), a vision is 'accorded'? With Amos the vision of God Himself, though not so fundamental in the picture before his spiritual eye, is yet quite essential.[3] To the man's inner sight God is present: in his inner ear God speaks. The Presence of whom the shepherd is aware day by day in ordinary life seems to be brought even nearer in 'vision'. May it not be that it is not to the primitive prophets or *n^{e}bhi'im* so much as to the best types of mystics in all the Christian communities,[4] that one must turn for a comparison, if it is desired to understand the vision experience of the great seers of Israel?[5] Like the mystics, Amos finds that earnest prayer comes to him readily: 'O Lord GOD, forgive, I beseech thee' (Am. vii. 2, 5). And moreover—more important in the present argument—he receives an irresistible

[1] *Cf.* above, p. 15.

[2] Since suggesting the above, the writer has noticed Joyce's reference to this vision. He concludes a noble summary of it with these words: "Surely this is a vision such as in all ages saints have been privileged to behold" (*op. cit.* p. 95). The reader may be referred also to Hamilton, *The People of God*, I. pp. 152–160. For the vision of God in non-Christian religions, *cf.* Prof. R. A. Nicholson, *The Mystics of Islam*, p. 7: "When the gnostic's spiritual eye is opened, his bodily eye is shut: he sees nothing but God". In the words of Prof. E. G. Browne: "The Sūfī was a saint before he became a seer. This view is supported not only by the history of those to whom a later age has given the name of Sūfī, but by the history of mysticism in general. How readily devotion passes into contemplation, and contemplation into vision and ecstasy, is seen not only here, but amongst the German mystics of the fourteenth century, the saints of the Romish Church, and the quietists of France". ("Sufiism" in *Religious Systems of the World*, p. 317.)

[3] In the first, second and fourth visions God is not so central as in those of the Plumbline and of the Sanctuary. It is clear, however, that in all alike Amos was conscious, in an abnormal way, of the Divine presence, though not (as with Isaiah in ch. vi and with the mystics often) in such a manner that he gives himself up to contemplation and communion.

[4] And, it may be, in the higher forms of certain non-Christian religions; *e.g.* (in the words of Nicholson, *op. cit.* p. 59), "The whole of Sūfism rests on the belief that...ecstasy affords the only means by which the soul can directly communicate and become united with God".

[5] It is recorded of Jesus Christ, who on His human side has been described as the Greatest of the mystics, that 'he *saw* the heavens rent asunder, and the Spirit as a dove descending upon him' (St Mark i. 10). On another occasion He 'was beholding Satan as lightning fallen from heaven' (St Lu. x. 18).

conviction that his request will be granted: 'It [the punishment] shall not be, saith the LORD' (vii. 3, 6). Again, in the vision state[1] the Prophet seems to learn direct from God what is ultimately to happen to the people, for whom both God and he have a solicitous care (vii. 8, 9; viii. 2, ᵔ; ix. 1–4). Possibly a mystic experience is alluded to when he declares that God unveils 'His secret counsel [Hebrew, *sôdh*] to His servants the prophets'. Jeremiah maintains that the true prophet, as distinct from the false, has actually stood in 'Jehovah's council [also *sôdh*] of heaven'.[2]

It is not to be expected that the prophets should always be able to distinguish between the two species of seeing—the natural and the inner. The Christian mystics, however (to whom visions came much more frequently than was, apparently, the case with the prophets of the O.T.), for the most part clearly differentiate between the two. "When I come back to my body", says Sundar Singh, "I find a great difference between what I have seen in ecstasy and what I here see bodily with my eyes".[3]

The *reality* to the mind of what (presumably) is seen in vision is emphasised by St Theresa, who describes it as not a mere "picture...like a painting; Christ appears as a living Person Who sometimes speaks and reveals deep mysteries". Yet "the image is seen by the interior sight alone".[4] Similarly

---

[1] The 'vision state', while not a technical expression, seems to be a convenient one by which to describe the Prophet's experience. 'Ecstasy', though a Biblical term (ἔκστασις, Ac. x. 10, xi. 5, xii. 17) is in some ways liable to be misleading. Indeed the word 'ecstasy' is employed with reference to conditions widely different, as, on the one hand, the highest spiritual communion with God including 'rapture'; and, on the other, the mental state of a maniac. In classical usage the adjective ἐκστατικός may mean 'out of one's senses', 'distraught'. For an interesting discussion upon the distinction between true ecstasy and physical and mental disorders, see Poulain, *Graces of Interior Prayer*, transl. Yorke Smith, pp. 257–263.

[2] Concerning this claim of Jeremiah, Dr Skinner asks: "Does this...denote a visionary experience, like the sublime scene described by Micaiah in 1 Ki. xxii. 19–22, or a spiritual condition removed from every trace of ecstasy?" (*op. cit.* p. 194).

[3] *The Sadhu* (by Streeter and Appasamy), p. 136; *cf.* p. 117: "in heaven I see not with bodily but with spiritual eyes".

[4] *Op. cit.* VI. ix. 2, 3. Indeed the reality of such 'vision' and 'rapture' can hardly be doubted. *Cf.* the full description which Theresa gives in, *e.g.*, VI. viii. 2.

it was with that philanthropist of the eighteenth century, John Woolman the Quaker. He gives this account of a vision of his—

> It was yet dark,...and as I opened mine eyes I saw a light in my chamber ...near its centre the most radiant....As I lay still...words were spoken to my inward ear....They were not the effect of thought...but as the language of the Holy One....The words were, CERTAIN EVIDENCE OF DIVINE TRUTH. They were again repeated in the same manner, and then the light disappeared.[1]

Some characteristics of the vision state, as it seems to have come upon the great prophets of Israel, may briefly be referred to, and a comparison may be suggested with mystical experience generally. The paragraphs numbered (2), (4) and (5) shew points of contact of the Canonical Prophets with the greater mystics, rather than with that form of prophecy out of which higher prophecy grew.

(1) As with dreams,[2] so with visions there often is a natural sight, or the memory of a real occurrence in ordinary life, which forms the starting-point or groundwork of, or which supplies the material for, the psychic.[3] It would seem probable that a prophet's visions took their rise from the close scrutiny of some *natural* sight, or from the memory of an actual occurrence. These physical elements from the world of sense provide the *material* for the vision which is to be seen by the inner eye. In the instance of Isaiah's temple vision the Prophet saw, not only God, but also the *altar, tongs, coals,* and *thresholds* of the temple. Even so Amos' five visions started from the literal sight of (a) a brood of locusts, (b) severely parched land, (c) a workman with a plumbline, (d) a basket of fruit, (e) a religious service attended by Israelite worshippers.

Though the parallel is not perfect in all respects, yet an

---

[1] *Journal IV* (*ad init.*), quoted by H. Wheeler Robinson, *op. cit.* p. 9.

[2] The comparison between the prophets' visions and our dreams is in some respects useful (*cf.* Professor Hans Schmidt, *Amos*, p. 14). It must not, however, be overlooked that a characteristic of such visions as those of Amos is that they come while the seer is *awake*—a fact which would seem to add to their value; so St Thomas Aquinas, *op. cit.* II. ii, Q. 174, art. 3.

[3] Compare 2 Ki. vi. 17 b with v. 15. See Aquinas, *op. cit.* Q. 173, art. 3, reply obj. 4: "This [the prophets'] abstraction...is due to some well-ordered cause".

analogy appears to be provided by the experience of mystics.[1] It is easy to understand how the type of vision seen by Juliana of Norwich and St Francis of Assisi sometimes arose out of the act of gazing on the crucifix.[2] Similarly, at the service of the Mass, in the Roman Church, some have had a vision of Christ during the consecration of the sacred elements. In a measure analogous is such a phenomenon as that recounted by Miss Carmichael, a missionary in India. She was looking from her verandah at a piece of ground in the distance, when, as she says, "the word came as clearly as ever I had known it, 'Ask for that piece of land'". In response to her protest, 'But, Lord, we do not want it', again the word came 'Ask'.... "There was no escape from that strange urging as of another will than mine". The field was bought, its purchase-money being provided for by special unexpected gifts.[3] The fact seems to be that in visions like those of Amos 'normal' sense perception and 'abnormal' psychological condition flow the one into the other; although it is difficult for the modern scholar, in looking into the text in which is recounted the Prophet's life, to decide always where is the point of transition. The expression 'Thus Jehovah causes me to see' may apply *either* to the object as seen by his bodily eyes, *or* to the vision which followed the scrutiny of that object. And probably the seer himself, as it has been said above, would not invariably be able to distinguish between the normal and the abnormal.[4]

(2) The visions of Amos are not purely contemplative. They are a means of his apprehending, or being confirmed in, truth. The lesson which Ezekiel learned from the vision of the

[1] The trance condition which comes to the *yogis* of Buddhism and other religions takes its rise from an extreme and special form of natural seeing, *viz.* concentration (*samādhi*) of the mind on a particular object. *Cf.* E. J. Thomas, *The Life of Buddha*, pp. 180–183. By such concentration the mind "becomes more and more intently fixed, and passes through certain psychical phases as the sphere of consciousness becomes narrowed and intensified, and at the same time shut off from outside influences" (*op. cit.* p. 180). Some such process may, or may not, have played a part with Amos.

[2] Underhill, *Mysticism*, pp. 218, 435; *Revelations of Divine Love*, ch. III. Juliana lived 1342–1442 A.D.

[3] *Nor Scrip*, ch. VI, alluded to, in another connection, by Miss Willink, *Prophetic Consciousness*, p. 101 (a suggestive study in the comparison of the O.T. prophetic experience with that of the Christian mystics).

[4] *Cf.* Hölscher, *Profeten*, pp. 45, 48; Skinner, *op. cit.* p. 31.

Dry Bones (ch. xxxvii) may have been to him a veritable *revelation*. Certainly the story of this symbolic sight ranks amongst the finest descriptive literature in the O.T. Didactic, for the most part, were the visions which came to St Benedict, Heinrich Suso[1] and St Gertrude.[2] The visions of Amos, in their didactic aspect, may find illustration in such a circumstance as that which Juliana of Norwich relates concerning herself: "He shewed me a little thing, the quantity of a hazel nut lying in my hand;...I looked thereupon and thought 'What may this be?' and I was answered...'It is all that is made. ...It lasts and ever shall, for God loves it'". Juliana's narrative goes on with a long exposition of the teaching of the vision.[3]

(3) If, as is probable, the first four visions of Amos came to him, not when he was engaged in devotion, but while he was in the open country, this would only be parallel to the experience of other of God's children in different ages. St Catherine of Siena appears to have had her first vision when she was walking. Fox saw the city of Lichfield full of blood, as he was entering it to preach.[4] It is related of Sundar that once while under a tree he fell into ecstasy—indeed he was stung by hornets, without knowing it until he had come out of the ecstatic condition.[5]

[1] A Dominican of Swabia (fl. *c.* 1296-1365 A.D.). Engl. translations of his autobiography were published in 1865 and 1913.

[2] St Gertrude (1256-1303 A.D.), *Life and Revelations* (Engl. transl. 1865). Moreover, the vision of a *yogi* may have doctrinal and practical value. "With divine purified vision he sees evil doers being reborn in hell, and the virtuous in heaven, just as a man in a palace may see persons entering and coming out of a house". E. J. Thomas, *op. cit.* p. 183 (*ad init.*).

[3] *Comfortable Words*, ch. IV. Miss Underhill has a striking remark upon the "philosophy of vision", in connection with what one may call its *didactic* value. Writing of Dante's *Paradiso*, XXX. 61-81, she says: "Since this dream is directly representative of truth, and initiates the visionary into the atmosphere of the Eternal, it may well claim precedence over that prosaic and perpetual vision which we call the 'real world'" (*Mysticism*, p. 344).

As an instance of a vision which served to confirm the visionary in the truth of his previous convictions, the story of St Thomas Aquinas himself may be cited. In what is called a "corporal and open" vision, one from the state of the blessed gave the Angelic Doctor great satisfaction in acknowledging the truth of St Thomas' opinions on the subject of the next life as expressed in the *Summa*. See *Acta Sanctorum*, 7 Mart. p. 674 *a*.   [4] See p. 81, footnote 2.

[5] *The Sadhu*, p. 134. Here a lapse of normal consciousness is implied.

(4) The narrative of Amos is against any idea that he *drew upon himself* the ecstatic state. Needless to say, this is in general[1] true of all real visionaries. To quote one example: the same Indian mystic sharply distinguishes his condition from self-hypnotism, as indeed from any form of hallucination. Speaking of his ecstasy, he says, "I never try to get into it".[2] On the other hand, from what is known of the lower forms of ecstasy in the East to-day, and from the express statement that the Baal prophets deliberately worked themselves up into a frenzy,[3] it is obvious that in nothing does the higher prophecy differ from that of the primitive *n*ᵉ*bhî'îm* more than in this very respect.

(5) It is held by not a few scholars that the visions of Amos constituted his 'call'[4] to lay aside his ordinary work, to which call he definitely alludes on two occasions: 'The Lord GOD hath spoken, who can but prophesy?'; and 'the LORD took me...and said Go, prophesy' (iii. 8 *b*, vii. 15). If such a view is correct, it is easy to find parallels to the receiving of a call by means of a vision. In the story of mystical experience in all religions, nothing is commoner than for *conversion* and *vocation* to be accompanied by either *audition* or *vision*.[5] What happened with St Francis on St Matthew's day is a case in point. St Paul himself is a supreme example. The circumstances in which the religious teacher, Sundar Singh, became a Christian, are recounted somewhat as follows: In the room where Sundar was praying he saw a great light. Then, as he prayed and looked into the light, he beheld the form of the Lord whom he had been insulting a few days before. He was convinced that this was no vision of his own imagination; and, on hearing a voice saying, "How long will you persecute me?"

---

[1] The words "in general" are used because the high spiritual experiences of the Asiatic *yogis*, which are accompanied by trance, might be said to be induced by a definite *process*. See S. N. Dasgupta, *Hindu Mysticism*, pp. 74–78; A. Tillyard, *Spiritual Exercises*, p. 56 (S.P.C.K.). With the Mohammedan *Sūfî*, ecstasy may, or may not, be induced *deliberately*. *Cf.* pp. 147–150; Nicholson, *op. cit.* p. 48.

[2] *The Sadhu*, p. 136.

[3] 1 Ki. xviii. 26 *b*, 28. *Cf.* Introd. pp. 14, 15 and footnote 3.

[4] *Cf.* p. 101, below.

[5] In the case of Mohammedan *Sūfîs*, *cf.* Tillyard, *op. cit.* pp. 115–121.

he had the thought, "Jesus Christ is not dead but living and it must be He Himself". When he arose from his knees the vision had disappeared.[1]

It is a difficult question, but one of some importance: Wherein does the vision of the great prophets *differ* from (A) that of the false prophets, and (B) that of the Christian mystics? Probably the answer which psychology would give is that all three examples are, so far as any scientific test is concerned, alike in essential character, being, indeed, ultimately subjective. And to this many O.T. scholars might in a measure assent. Thus, in the words of the late Prof. Skinner:[2] "The prophetic vision is undoubtedly a creation of the sub-conscious mind, working uncontrolled by voluntary reflexion, and producing subjective images which have something of the vividness and reality of actual sense perception".

But when all is said, and much could be said from such a point of view, is it not also a fact that the true Divine order is ever ready *to break through into* the world, if men will only suffer it to break through into their hearts?[3]

(A) The nature, or *form*, of the vision which comes to the Witch of Endor,[4] St Theresa and Isaiah, may be psychologically the same. The last two persons, however, are examples of those who live ever 'aware' of the presence and goodness of God. To such He can reveal Himself. That pioneer of religious psychologists, the late Prof. Wm James, seems to have held that the sub-conscious state in man, which plays so important a part in visions, was open to the direct influence of God.[5] And so, it may be suggested, there comes to be a difference in the *content* of the visions of the two types of prophets.[6] Moreover, teaching both new and (at least for their age)

---

[1] *The Sadhu*, pp. 6 and 7; and the biography by Mrs Parker of the London Mission, Travancore.

[2] *Op. cit.* p. 10. Is this the view of W. R. Smith, *Prophets*, edn 2, pp. 220, 221?

[3] *Cf.* Willink, *op. cit.* pp. 111 and 112. And *cf.* what A. Tillyard says of the Mohammedan *Sūfīs*, *op. cit.* p. 152. See Skinner as quoted on pp. 96, 97.

[4] Quoted as representative of the subjective vision of the lower kind, including that of the 'false prophets'. [5] *Varieties of Relig. Exp.* pp. 511, 512.

[6] No importance can attach to a vision merely because it is a vision. Streeter, writing of Sundar's psychical experiences, uses these words: "The visions are of value...because they are *the Sadhu's* visions" (*op. cit.* p. 144). And it is impossible to over-emphasise the importance of establishing the reality and authenticity of any vision (*cf.* Poulain, *op. cit.* chs. XXI, XXII). Similarly, with the Canonical

true may be vouchsafed to some rather than to others. The prophetic and highest mystic vision thus stands somehow in a class alone. To express this contention differently, the problem raised by the phenomenon of the best type of vision seems to be not *purely* a psychological one, in so far as it involves something more (we believe) than naked mental processes.

The weighty sentences of the modern psychologist Professor J. B. Pratt seem applicable to this matter:

May it, then, perhaps be that the mystics are the seers of our world, and that whenever they open the eyes of their souls, the Eternal Light pours in; and that though we blind ones learnedly describe, generalize, and explain their experience by regular psychological laws which take account only of the psycho-physical organism, still the light is really there and the mystic apprehends it directly,[1] even as he says? This question is not for psychological discussion.... Nothing that [the psychology of religion] can say should prevent the religious man...from seeing in his own spiritual experiences the genuine influence of a living God.[2]

Our interest, as religious people of the 20th cent. A.D., attaches not to the similarity, so far as it may have existed, between the experiences of the lower Israelite ecstatic[3] and that of great prophets and saints, but to the dissimilarity between them.

(B) If the vision of the early ecstatic may from a religious aspect be classified in a category by itself, is it possible for us to

Prophets, it has been said: "The differentiating characteristics are to be sought and found, not in the peculiar circumstances of the vision, but in the contents of the message thereby conveyed" (Joyce, *op. cit.* p. 97, and *cf.* G. A. Cooke in Edghill's *Amos*, p. xvii). See also Povah, *New Psychology and Hebrew Prophets*: "He [Micaiah] distinguishes, not merely between degrees of true inspiration, but between true and false inspiration. His message to his fellow-countrymen is that not all 'inspiration' is true; that there are, not only true prophets, but also false prophets" (p. 99). And again on p. 97: "'JE' failed to distinguish between what we call the genuine inspiration of God, and what we call the mere outcropping of the unconscious".

[1] Perhaps the words of Miss Underhill may be quoted in this connection: "In this [the *imaginary* vision], the imagery seized upon by the subliminal powers, *or placed before the mind by that Somewhat Other* of which the mystic is always conscious over against himself, is at once so vivid...and so perfectly expresses its apprehensions of God, that it is not always recognized as symbolic in kind". (*Op. cit.* p. 345. The italics are the present writer's.)

[2] *Religious Consciousness*, p. 458. Ch. xviii on "The Ecstasy" and ch. xix on "The Mystic Life" are worthy of special study in connection with the subject.

[3] After all it is a fact that very little is known concerning pre-canonical vision in Israel.

proceed a step farther, and to endeavour to differentiate between the *prophetic* and the *mystic* visionaries (each at their best), even as, indeed, it has been generally felt that there is a difference? Surely it is possible. Of course, it would be absurd to suppose that either vision or audition, even in the higher type of prophets, was *ipso facto* infallible. It is a matter of positive gain to religion to admit fully that in the visions of the Biblical seers there is much that should be interpreted as arising out of their limited ideas, and as conditioned by their (in some respects) comparatively primitive minds. Often the ultimate value of any vision exists *in spite of* those elements which it has derived from the previous conscious state of the seer. These necessary component parts are only the material; it is the structure that is of value. A broad distinction is evident. To speak generally, it may be said that the mystics, for the most part, had their visions to their own uplifting, spiritual enjoyment and personal benefit.[1] With the prophets it is quite the reverse. Amos may have seen his visions as an Israelite, a desert-dwelling shepherd, but he was destined to *use* them as a teacher, a preacher of social righteousness. That which such prophets saw in vision was of historical and ethical importance to their fellows. It had a national value. The certainty of the doom from Assyria, which the contemporaries of Amos were slow to perceive, was brought, or confirmed, to Amos in vision. Problems which were exercising the minds of prophets and people received through vision a solution, even though, in some cases, it was only a partial or temporary one. It was because of the special content of the vision that they were forced to go out and say: 'Thus hath Jehovah caused me to see'. Theirs was *Canonical* vision. The words of the late Dr Skinner seem to have a bearing upon this point:[2] [When one considers the ancient Israelite nation and how] "spiritual intercourse could be maintained between a moral personality...and a nation

[1] No one would doubt the sincerity of *e.g.* that truly remarkable Christian mystic St Theresa, nor the value of the work which she did with her disciples, but do not the lengthy accounts which she gave of her vision experiences present a contrast with the simplicity and brevity of the Canonical Prophet?

[2] *Op. cit.* p. 8.

...it is evident that the only possible channel of such intercourse was a succession of men of God, conversant with the purpose and character of Yahweh, standing as mediators between Him and His people". Because there is a God who desires well for His creatures, it would seem not unreasonable to suppose that He neither leaves them entirely to think out their own gospel, nor is content with stimulating the processes of certain minds working in a healthy direction. It would appear that the vision state is peculiarly suited to such stimulation, and intensification, of all that is best in a prophet's beliefs and inner desires concerning God and the service of mankind. But, more than this, the condition of psychic vision (so it would seem) provides a vehicle for God to communicate a revelation to His prophet. This message the seer will then in sober, albeit sometimes impassioned, speech tell to his fellows. What is beheld in vision is told naturally.

The present subject is not one upon which it would be wise to dogmatise. But this much can be said. The minds of the great prophets were (at least for those times) singularly under the control of God. The words of Joyce may be quoted: "However much subjectivity there was in the form which the vision assumed, it does not, therefore, become the mere product of human imagination and destitute accordingly of authority. To those who profess their belief in a Spirit who 'spake by the prophets', it is clothed with the dignity of a revelation".[1] The visions of the great prophets (if we bear in mind the limitations imposed by the period in which these men lived) take precedence over the visions of other saints. In both, we believe, is God; but *by comparison* those of the prophets are (like 'the baptism of John') from heaven rather than from men. It comes not within the province of Psychology to say this, but may not Religion say it? At least canonical vision is the highest type.

[1] *Op. cit.* p. 96. *Cf.* Bp. Gore, in *Belief in God*, p. 107, cited above, p. 82: "As to the psychological method of the divine communication...." And perhaps the words of Prof. Kennett (in another connection) may be quoted: "The Old Testament is not a compendium of moral rules, but a record of God's revelation to Israel. That revelation is unique...because the revelation of God to Israel, regarded as a whole, possesses a unity and a completeness not found elsewhere". (*The People and the Book*, edited by Prof. Peake, pp. 395, 396.)

(3)

The Five Visions of Amos

Having in mind the foregoing principles, or at least some of them, we may tentatively suggest the following as an account of the visions of the Prophęt in relation to his life.

As dreams, and not seldom mystical experiences, arise out of some actual event or natural occurrence, so the visions of Amos came.[1]

(I) Ch. vii. 1–3. One day in spring, Amos the shepherd, passing through the country, noticed a brood of young locusts devouring crops. He thereupon prayed to God (either in the usual way, or already transported into a condition of higher ecstasy): 'May this pest not spread over the whole land; O Lord Yahweh, remit, for the nation is not strong enough to bear it'. In the vision state he received an assurance, as from the mouth of Jehovah, that his intercession had availed. When Amos returned to himself, he found the danger already past.

(II) Ch. vii. 4–6. Again, perhaps some weeks after, Amos was noticing the effect of a very severe drought. Then, in the vision state, he saw that which lay behind the catastrophe. The huge subterranean mass of water which was supposed to be the source of supply for the springs was dried up as by fire, and this fire was about to consume the solid land of Palestine itself. Again the Prophet interceded, and he received a further assurance that this visitation also should cease.

(III) Ch. vii. 7–9. Later, Amos happened to be watching a workman testing a wall with a plumbline.[2] Soon the Prophet's mind passed into phantasy. The workman became Jehovah Himself; the wall, about to be broken up because of its faulty condition, was Israel. Amos tried to intercede, but there was no opportunity; for the dread word came from his God: 'Pardon is past, the sword[3] is coming against Israel'.

---

[1] Cf. p. 90, supra.   [2] But see also p. 225, especially footnote 1.

[3] If the view is right that Assyria provided the moving cause of Amos' becoming a prophet, the enemy in this and the fourth vision is no other than Assyria ever

(IV) Ch. viii. 1–3. In the summer (or, possibly, early autumn), he was observing a basket of fruit, perhaps of his own gathering. Presently in vision he was asked by Jehovah, 'What seest thou?' On replying, 'A basket of summer fruit' (in Hebrew, *qayiṣ*), the significance of the object seemed to be revealed to him by the Deity Himself: 'The end [in Hebrew, *qēṣ*] is come upon my people Israel; pardon is past.[1] Indeed, the songs of the temple-singers will be howlings, on account of the dead bodies which shall be cast forth'. To his inner eye, perhaps the basket of fruit itself had become a mass of ruins and corpses, around which the singing-women moved uttering wailing cries.

The four visions probably came to Amos at intervals during several months—from the appearance of locust larvae in spring to the time of the gathering of late summer fruit. Yet, almost certainly, they should be interpreted together. If so, they indicate *either* how there came to[2] the Prophet the belief that Israel was doomed, *or*, how he was confirmed in such a conviction already held by him. Twice Jehovah forgives, but that stage is past. He will not forgive them any further.

It may be that, at this point, Amos began his public work, conceivably, as some scholars think, making these visions the subject of his first prophetic utterances. On the other hand, the present sequence of chapters would seem, upon the whole, better to represent the order of his discourses.[3] However this may be, if vii. 10–17 is rightly placed, Amos narrated these three, or four, visions at Beth-el (perhaps at the autumn feast of Ingathering); and thereupon was driven away on account of his dire message.

---

in the Prophet's thoughts. On the other hand, some scholars hold that above all things a sense of Israel's sinfulness weighed upon the shepherd's mind, and that this, not Assyria, provided the background for the visions. Possibly it was during the weeks between the first two, and the third and fourth, visions, that Assyria began to loom before Amos. In either case, it is probable that, at any rate, Visions III, IV and V did not precede, but followed Amos' belief that Israel was doomed.

[1] *Cf.* notes *ad loc.*

[2] If so, they suggest the line along which the Prophet's mind moved until he came to the conviction that Israel must perish.

[3] See p. 217.

(V) The vision of ch. ix. 1–4 came to Amos later, and in different circumstances. While at one of the sanctuaries, at Beth-el or elsewhere, the Prophet was contemplating the shrine, its priests and the worshippers, and, lo, (again in psychic vision) he beheld the majestic figure of *Adonai*, the Lord of all; he then began to hear His judgment on Israel, as He bade someone (either a supernatural agent of His—perhaps the angel of earthquake—or else the Assyrian) to smash the pillar capitals, making the building shake to its foundations. The worshippers were to perish in the ruins. At all events, to the last one they must die. For nothing would save those who sought to escape, whether to Sheol, or to heaven, or to the top of Carmel, or to the bottom of the sea. Even any who supposed that they would be safe in captivity would be destroyed. Amos seems to say in the text that he heard words of Jehovah to the above effect; but it may be that we should understand that with his interior sight he *saw* the terrible scene which one day was indeed to happen to Israel.[1]

Two problems demand brief comment.

(A) (1) In interpreting the visions, the principle used above is that generally held,[2] *viz.* that, when Amos says, 'Thus Jehovah caused me to see', it is with reference to an object seen with his natural eyes, concentration upon which became the starting-point of a psycho-pathological condition. (2) The words 'caused me to see' may, however, apply to each 'vision' entire as described in the book of Amos, the object seen in nature being reproduced also to Amos' inner eye. In the vision of the plumbline and the basket the actual sight may have been some weeks before. This is, practically, Hans Schmidt's position.[3] (3) There is also the opinion held by some[4] that a distinction should be drawn between the first

---

[1] For detailed notes upon the five visions, the reader is referred to the commentary.

[2] It is put forcibly by Hölscher in *Profeten*, p. 198 a. But this scholar is of the opinion that the abnormal consists *only* of "the divine word with which the visions finish".

[3] *Amos*, p. 14.   [4] *E.g.*, by Buttenwieser, *op. cit.* p. 223.

37239

two and the last three visions.[1] According to this interpretation, there was *nothing* psycho-pathological in the 'visions' of the locusts and of the drought; but these were entirely events in the external world—the very events, indeed, which are recorded in iv. 9 ('palmer-worm'), iv. 6–8 ('drought').

(B) Is there a relation between these visions, or any of them, and the call of Amos to be a prophet?[2] (1) Hölscher suggests that it was the receiving, in the first two visions, of the conviction that his prayers were to be *answered*, that led Amos to ask himself whether he was not destined to be God's servant, to call his contemporaries to repentance.[3] (2) Lofthouse and others, taking the four visions as an essential unity, argue that it was through their message of doom that Amos the shepherd was called or 'taken' (*cf.* vii. 15) to be a prophet.[4] This latter theory is exceedingly attractive, and receives confirmation from the fact that Amos certainly had a call.[5] With Isaiah, Jeremiah and Ezekiel, we possess narratives of prophetic calls which shew that the conviction of vocation came by means of, or *was accompanied by*, a vision. (3) If (as the present writer holds) the pressure of Assyria was the main cause of Amos' first thoughts, at least, of Divine judgment on Israel, and also, probably, of his own mission,[6] then the visions furnished a 'call' only in a secondary sense. Possibly they brought to a point and to a definite conclusion questionings and fears which had been slowly forming in the shepherd's mind, or they confirmed a conviction already upon him that God was to punish Israel through Assyria. Truly the word had gone forth that Assyria was coming[7] (vii. 7–9; viii. 1–3). So it was that Jehovah spoke to Amos and 'took' him.

---

[1] Other scholars maintain that viii. 1–3 narrates an incident, not a psychical vision; see note, *ad loc.*

[2] *Cf.* p. 93 above.   [3] Hölscher, *op. cit.* p. 195 *ad fin.*

[4] Lofthouse, *Expositor*, July 1922. *Cf.* Nowack, edn 1922, p. 154; Harper, *Amos*, p. cviii; following Meinhold, *Studien zur isr. Rel.* p. 39; H. P. Smith, *O.T. History*, p. 211. So Canney in Peake's *Commentary*, p. 547 a, and *cf.* H. Schmidt, *op. cit.* p. 22.   [5] So Am. iii. 8 b, vii. 15.   [6] *Cf.* pp. 35–37.

[7] If comparison may be made with the call of Jeremiah (narrated in Jer. i. 4–10) no one doubts that, somehow, it was the religious problem raised by the Scythians moving south that supplied the cause of his becoming a prophet. Yet, if Jer. i. 13, 14 is rightly placed, we must believe that a vision at about the same time as his call presented to the young man's mind the conviction, or, rather, supported

XV. THE FULFILMENT OF THE POLITICAL PREDICTIONS OF AMOS

From approximately 760 B.C. (or possibly, shortly before 740 B.C.; see pp. 34 ff.) Amos foretold (i) the captivity of Syria (i. 3–5) and (ii) the ravaging of Israel by a foreign foe, and its exile 'beyond Damascus' (v. 27). These predictions were fulfilled.

(i) In 735 B.C. Syria and North Israel together attacked Ahaz, king of Judah, apparently to force him into an alliance against the now threatening power of Assyria. On the appeal of Ahaz to Assyria itself to help him against his two neighbours, Tiglath-pileser III in the year 733 overran and deported the northern and eastern parts[1] of the kingdom of North Israel. Also, after devastating the country around Damascus, he received the capitulation of that city in 732 B.C., carrying into captivity much of the population.[2] Thus the kingdom of Damascus was destroyed, not for centuries to b' revived.

(ii) Less than a dozen years after Tiglath-pileser's incursion into the northern portion of North Israel, referred to above, Central Palestine was overrun by his successor Shalmaneser V, and Samaria itself was besieged. In 722 B.C. the city fell into the hands of his son Sargon; and some 27,000 inhabitants were deported. The territory of North Israel was incorporated into the Assyrian Empire.[3] Although certain foreign tribes who had been brought to Palestine learned to worship Israel's God, and although sufficient of the Israelite stock remained[4] in the country for Israelite identity

such a conviction already formed, that a foreign nation was (as it appeared) moving against Palestine.

[1] This is according to 2 Ki. xv. 29. Tiglath-pileser's own description is obviously an exaggeration: "The land Beth-Omri...the whole of its inhabitants (and their property) I carried away to Assyria"—*C.O.T.* (*W.*), I. p. 251.

[2] 2 Ki. xvi. 9. *Cf. C.O.T.* (*W.*), I. pp. 250, 254.

[3] *C.O.T.* (*W.*), I. 262–266.

[4] It is a nice problem as to what proportion of Israelites were never exiled. The fact that two, or even three, importations of foreigners into their territory were possible, is consistent with but a bare majority of Israelites having been left

to be maintained, the nation as an independent one under a king had ceased. Conceivably Amos himself lived to see the downfall of the Ephraimite Kingdom;[1] particularly is this possible, if his preaching may be assigned to so late a date as *c.* 740 B.C. In any case, probably Hosea (who during the years of North Israel's rapid decline reiterated the warning given by Amos in the last days of its prosperity) witnessed the fulfilment of the prophecy: 'the virgin daughter of Israel is fallen; she shall no more rise' (Am. v. 2).

Judah suffered severely at the hands of Assyria under Sennacherib (*cf.* 2 Ki. xviii. 13; Isa. i. 8, 9); but the kingdom survived until its destruction by the *successors* of Assyria in world empire.

XVI. LATER INFLUENCE OF THE BOOK OF AMOS

The teaching of Amos' younger contemporary *Hosea* had points of contact with that of Amos. It is even more manifest that a good deal of the distinctive message of Amos was known to *Isaiah*. Without any doubt the genius of *Jeremiah* and *Zephaniah* owed much to the book of Amos. *Ezekiel*, in composing his great section upon the foreign nations (chs. xxv–xxxii), must have been influenced by the work of Amos in i. 3–ii. 3. The *visions* of *Zechariah* (Zech. i. 7–vi. 8) shew a general resemblance to those in Amos vii–ix. Three times he alludes to the threats and the moral exhortations of 'the former prophets'.[2] Much of the ethical teaching of *Proverbs* is to be traced ultimately to the influence of such writings as Amos, more particularly the section of Prov. x. 1–xxii. 16.

Express citations from the text are as follows: (i) Possibly Joel iii. 16 is a quotation of Am. i. 2 (but see p. 115). (ii) Tobit ii. 6 = Am. viii. 10, 'I (Tobit) remembered the prophecy of

behind by the Assyrians. The immigrants came both from cities (2 Ki. xvii. 24) and the desert, *cf.* Sargon's inscription of 715 B.C., *C.O.T.* (*W.*), I. p. 269. See also Ezra iv. 2, 9 (Asshurbanipal).

[1] Though it has been held that, had Amos actually survived the fulfilment of his predictions, the wording of them would not have been left as vague as it is.

[2] Zech. i. 4–6 *a*, vii. 7, 12. In particular the correspondence of Zech. vii. 9 with Am. v. 24 is to be observed. See notes on v. 18, 25.

Amos, as he said, Your feasts shall be turned into mourning, and all your mirth into lamentation' (see note, p. 249, on the Greek). (iii) In the N.T. two references only are made to the book: both are citations in Acts, and in neither case is Amos named. Acts vii. 42 b, 43 = Am. v. 25–27 a; and Acts xv. 16–18 a = Am. ix. 11, 12.

BIBLIOGRAPHY

The following are the chief commentaries and a short selection of the general works consulted in the preparation of the present commentary. The Bibliography is chronologically arranged.

I. AMOS: COMMENTARIES AND TEXTS

(a) British and American

ABBREVIATIONS

E. B. Pusey: *Minor Prophets*, 1861.

Mit.   H. G. Mitchell: *Amos, an Essay in Exegesis*, 1893; 2nd edn, 1900.

XII Prophets   G. A. Smith: *The Book of the Twelve Prophets* (vol. I) (Expositor's Bible), 1896. The references are to this edition and not that of 1928.

Driver   S. R. Driver: *Joel and Amos* (Camb. Bible), 1897; revised by H. C. O. Lanchester, 1915. This latter edn is referred to as "Driver".

W. O. E. Oesterley: *Studies in the Greek and Latin Versions of the Book of Amos*, 1902.

R. F. Horton: *The Minor Prophets*, I (Century Bible), 1903.

W. R. Harper: *Amos and Hosea* (International Critical Commentary), 1905.

J. C. H. How: *Joel and Amos* (Smaller Camb. Bible), 1910.

J. E. McFadyen: *A Cry for Justice: A Study in Amos*, 1912.

Edgh.   E. A. Edghill and G. A. Cooke: *Amos* (Westminster Commentary), 1913.

A. Lukyn Williams: *Joel and Amos* (The Minor Prophets Unfolded), 1918.

M. A. Canney: *Amos* (in Peake's Commentary), 1920.

Amos   T. H. Robinson: *The Book of Amos* (in National Adult School Union series of translations), 1921.

Amos: Heb. Text   T. H. Robinson: *The Book of Amos*, Hebrew Text, 1923.

(b) Foreign

Orelli   von Orelli (of Basel): *Die zwölf kleinen Propheten*, 1888 (translated, 1893); 3rd edn, 1908.

Wellh.   J. Wellhausen (of Marburg): *Die kleinen Propheten*, 1892.

ABBREVIATIONS

Now.
: W. Nowack (of. Strassburg): *Die kleinen Propheten,* 1897; 3rd edn, 1922. The 3rd edn is cited as "Nowack" or "Now."

Marti
: K. Marti (of Bern): *Dodekapropheton,* 1904.
: J. Meinhold (of Bonn): *Amos, the Prophet.* Hebrew and Greek texts critically edited (in Lietzmann's Texts), 1906.

Hoonacker
: A. van Hoonacker (of Louvain): *Les Douze Petits Prophètes,* 1908.
: B. Duhm (of Basle): (1) *Die zwölf Propheten: in den Versmassen der Urschrift,* 1910. *The Twelve Prophets:* a Version in the Various Poetical Measures of the Original Writings. Authorised translation by A. Duff, 1912. (2) *Anmerkungen,* 1911.

Gressm. (*Ält. Proph.*)
: H. Gressmann (of Berlin): *Die älteste Geschichtsschreibung und Prophetie Israels* (Part II of *Die Schriften des A.T. in Auswahl*), 1st edn, 1910; 2nd edn, 1921. The 1921 edition is cited as "Gressmann" or "Gressm."
: P. Riessler (of Tübingen): *Die kleinen Propheten,* 1911.
: Hans Schmidt (of Tübingen): *Der Prophet Amos,* 1917.
: L. Köhler (of Zürich): *Amos,* 1917.
: E. Sellin (of Berlin): *Das Zwölfprophetenbuch,* 1922.

II. SOME GENERAL WORKS

C.O.T. (*W.*)
: E. Schrader: *Cuneiform Inscriptions and the O.T.* Translated by O. C. Whitehouse, 1885.

Prophets
: W. Robertson Smith: *The Prophets of Israel,* 1882; edited by Cheyne, 1895.

Semites
: —— *Lectures on the Religion of the Semites,* 1889; 2nd edn, 1894. The 3rd edn (1927), containing 200 pages of additional notes by S. A. Cook, preserves the pagination of the 2nd edn, which is now out of print.

O.T.J.C.
: —— *The O.T. in the Jewish Church,* 2nd edn, 1892.

L.O.T.
: S. R. Driver: *Literature of the O.T.* 1891; 9th edn, 1913.

Hist. Geog.
: G. A. Smith: *The Historical Geography of the Holy Land,* 13th edn, 1906.

N.S.I.
: G. A. Cooke: *North Semitic Inscriptions,* 1903.

Rel. sémitiq.
: M.-J. Lagrange: *Études sur les Religions sémitiques,* 1903.

Eschatologie
: H. Gressmann: *Der Ursprung der israelitisch-jüdischen Eschatologie,* 1905.

Texte, Bilder
: —— *Altorientalische Texte u. Bilder zum A.T.* 1909; 2nd edn, 1927.
: R. H. Kennett: *In Our Tongues,* 1907.

Isaiah
: —— *The Composition of the Book of Isaiah,* Schweich Lectures, 1910.
: Woods and Powell: *The Hebrew Prophets* (I), 1909.

BIBLIOGRAPHY 107

ABBREVIATIONS

Rel. of Isr.	A. C. Welch: *The Religion of Israel under the Kingdom,* 1912.
Profeten	G. Hölscher (of Göttingen): *Die Profeten,* 1914.
Prophets	M. Buttenwieser: *Prophets of Israel,* 1914.
Proph. and Rel.	J. Skinner: *Prophecy and Religion,* 1922.
Isr. and Bab.	W. L. Wardle: *Israel and Babylon,* 1925.
Rel.	R. Kittel: *The Religion of the People of Israel.* Translated by R. C. Micklem, 1925.
Proph. and Eschat.	N. Micklem: *Prophecy and Eschatology,* 1926.
C.A.H.	*Cambridge Ancient History.*
H.D.B.	Articles in Hastings' *Dictionary of the Bible.*
E.R.E.	Articles in Hastings' *Encyclopaedia of Religion and Ethics.*
E.B.	Articles in *Encyclopaedia Biblica.*
J.E.	Articles in *The Jewish Encyclopaedia.*
J.T.S.	Articles in *The Journal of Theological Studies.*
Expositor	Articles in *The Expositor.*
J.E.A.	Articles in *The Journal of Egyptian Archaeology.*
P.E.F. Qrly St	Articles in *The Palestine Exploration Fund Quarterly Statement.*
Z.A.W.	Articles in *Zeitschrift für die alttestamentliche Wissenschaft.*
Ges.-K. *or* G.-K.	Gesenius' *Hebrew Grammar,* as edited by Kautzsch and translated by Cowley.
Dav. Syn.	A. B. Davidson: *Hebrew Syntax.*
Oxf. Heb. Lex.	Brown, Driver, Briggs: *Hebrew and Eng. Lexicon.*

LIST OF ABBREVIATIONS
NOT APPEARING ON THE PREVIOUS PAGES

O.T.: Old Testament.

N.T.: New Testament.

'J': the Judaean 'Jahvist' (presumed) source of the Pentateuch, c. 850 B.C.[1]

'E': the Ephraimite 'Elohist' (presumed) source of the Pentateuch, c. 750 B.C.[1]

'D': the 'Deuteronomic' (presumed) source of the Pentateuch, shortly before 621 B.C.[1]

'P': the 'Priestly' (presumed) source of the Pentateuch, the second half of the Exile[1]—or, more probably, the middle of the 5th cent. B.C.

MSS.: manuscripts.

Heb.: Hebrew.

M.T.: Massoretic Text, *i.e.* the text according to the mediaeval copies from which our Hebrew Bibles are printed.

LXX: the Septuagint, or principal Greek Version of the O.T., begun in the 3rd cent. B.C.

Targ.: the Targum, or Aramaic Translation of the O.T., written in the first centuries of the Christian era.

Vulg.: the Vulgate or Latin Translation made by Jerome, c. 400 A.D., based on a text similar to the M.T.

Pesh.: Peshîṭtâ, or Syriac Version. A Jewish Translation based on a text similar to the M.T., but sometimes shewing knowledge of the LXX.

A.V.: the 'Authorised' Version, 1611.

R.V.: the 'Revised' Version, 1884.

E.VV.: the above English Versions (*i.e.* where the two agree).

marg. *or* m.: margin.

ch.: chapter.

v., *vv.*: verse, verses.

a: first half of a verse, or of a page.

b: second half of a verse, or of a page.

c: the last part of a long verse.

ad init.: towards the beginning of a page, or paragraph (of a work cited).

ad fin.: towards the end.

ff. or *et seq.*: and following.

c.: about.

lit.: literal, or literally.

Introd.: the Introduction to this commentary.

n.: note.

ad loc.: on the passage cited.

op. cit.: in the work cited.

† against references indicates 'all passages cited'.

[2] (against the name of a work, placed above the line): second edition.

---

[1] These dates are Cornill's. Of course they are very tentative, those of the sources 'D' and 'P' in particular. He assigns 'E', perhaps rightly, to Jeroboam's reign.

SCHEME OF TRANSLITERATION OF HEBREW LETTERS

א	' (*spiritus lenis*)		מ	*m*
ב	*b, bh*		נ	*n*
ג	*g, gh*		ס	*s*
ד	*d, dh*		ע	' (*spiritus asper*)
ה	*h*		פ	*p, ph*
ו	*w*, or (if vocalic) *û*[1], *ô*[1]		צ	*ṣ*
ז	*z*		ק	*q*, at times *ḳ*
ח	*ḥ*		ר	*r*
ט	*ṭ*		שׂ	*s*
י	*y*, or (if vocalic) *î*[1]		שׁ	*sh*
כ	*k, kh*		ת	*t, th*
ל	*l*			

VOWEL-POINTS

־	*a*		ֱ	*ĕ*
ָ	*â*[1] or *ā*[2]		ֻ	*u*
ֲ	*ă*		ֻ	*û*[1]
ִ	*i*		ָ	*o*
ִי	*î*[1]		וֹ	*ô*[1], *ō*[2]
ֶ	*e*		ֳ	*ŏ*
ֵ	*ê*[1] or *ē*[2]		ְ (*sh^ewa*)	*^e*

---

[1] 'Pure', or 'diphthongal', long.
[2] 'Tone' long.

CHRONOLOGICAL TABLE

Kings outside Israel are shewn in italics

B.C.

c. 1025	Accession of SAUL. The prophet Samuel.
c. 1010	Accession of DAVID. The prophet Nathan.
970	Accession of SOLOMON.
932	Disruption of the kingdom.
875–850	The prophet Elijah.
853[1]	Battle of Qarqar.
850–800	The prophet Elisha.
841[1]	JEHU paid tribute to *Shalmaneser III*.[2]
816	Accession of JEHOAHAZ. Israel suffered at the hands of *Hazael* in these two reigns.
803	Damascus suffered defeat from Assyria.
c. 800	Damascus defeated by *Zakir, king of Hamath*.
800	Accession of JEHOASH. Three victories over *Ben-hadad III*.
790 (or 779)–739 (or 738)	AZARIAH, or UZZIAH, reigned over Judah.
783–743 (or 741)	JEROBOAM II reigned over North Israel.
782–744	Assyria weakened by the Vannic Empire.
c. 760	Amos, according to the view commonly held.
745–727	*Tiglath-pileser III*,[3] *king of Assyria*.
743	Defeat of Sarduris by Tiglath-pileser.
744–741	Amos' year of activity within these dates. (See Introd. p. 41, also Preface II, pp. xxi ff).
c. 740	Isaiah began to prophesy in Judah.
738	MENAHEM paid tribute to *Tiglath-pileser*.
733	First deportation of North Israel.
732	Fall of Damascus.
724–722	*Shalmaneser V*[4] besieged Samaria.
722	Samaria captured by *Sargon*.
586	Jerusalem captured by *Nebuchadnezzar, king of Babylon*.
c. 540	The preaching of the Great Prophet of the Exile. (? The "doxology" sections added to the book of Amos about this time.)
516	The returned exiles of Judah finished the Second Temple. (? Addition of the "Epilogue" to Amos about this time or later.)

---

[1] These fixed dates as given above are one year later than used to be thought. *Cf.* also *C.A.H.* III. p. 3, note 1 (citing E. Forrer, *Chronologie*, 1916).

[2] Formerly styled "II".

[3] This Tiglath-pileser is now found to be the *third* (not the *fourth*) and is so styled throughout the commentary.

[4] Formerly styled "IV"

TEXT AND COMMENTARY

AMOS

I. 1 The words of Amos, who was among the herdmen of
Tekoa, which he saw concerning Israel in the days of

PART I, CHAPTERS I, II

I. 1. SUPERSCRIPTION

1. The first verse is, as it were, the title-page of the Book. It supplies
(1) the name of the *author* (or, some would say, of the *hero*), (2) his *calling*
in life, (3) the *contents* of the volume ('the words...which he saw concerning
Israel'), and (4) the *date* of the delivery of the discourses. Probably this
verse, like Hos. i. 1 and Isa. i. 1, is the work of an early editor.[1] Conceivably
the same hand drew together the "Minor Prophets" into one collection,
styled in Hebrew, "The Book of the Twelve". See Ecclus. xlix. 10.

Amos. See Introd. pp. 9, 10.

who was among the herdmen. In Hebrew *nôqᵉdhîm*. Though 'herds'
in the E.VV. = 'cattle', not 'sheep', 'herdmen' here is intended to signify
'shepherds'. The Arabic *naqad* is used of sheep of a particular breed with
short legs, and producing good wool.

among. It is not a question of many shepherds living together: Amos
was one of the several sheep-breeders who each made use of the wilderness of
Tekoa. See, further, vii. 14, note. Kimhi finds in the Hebrew phrase nothing
disparaging to Amos, but rather a suggestion of greatness. This is in accordance with Jewish tradition generally. *Cf.* the Targum rendering of
vii. 14, which represents that it was by choice that Amos adopted a life
of hardship: 'because of the guilt of my people I (am) afflicting my soul'
(*i.e.* leading a peasant life). The chief arguments that he was of mean
extraction are to be derived from the facts (1) that he was a 'dresser of
sycomore trees'; and (2) that his father's name is omitted. The prophet
Micah's parentage is not given in Mic. i. 1, and not improbably that prophet
was a son of the people.

of Tekoa. See Introd. p. 9. The expression does not *necessarily* imply
that Amos was a native, or even an inhabitant, of Tekoa itself. The township was in Judah. Kimhi somehow locates it in the tribe of *Asher*, doubtless because it was thought appropriate that the Prophet should be of North
Israelite birth.

he saw. The title 'seer' is applied to Amos by Amaziah the priest in
vii. 12, where see note. The older prophets, especially, were so styled (*cf.*
1 Sam. ix. 9, Mic. iii. 6, 7). Within the book of Amos are five *visions*

---

[1] In the N.T. St Paul did not commence his letters with such headings as
"The Epistle of Paul the Apostle to the Romans": and St Mk i. 1 may be but
a late title to the Second Gospel.

Uzziah king of Judah, and in the days of Jeroboam the son
of Joash king of Israel, two years before the earthquake.

(vii. 1–ix. 4); but in the present verse the term 'saw' is probably intended
to cover also "auditions", and, generally, any other method of learning
the Divine will. So Mic. i. 1: 'The *word* of Jehovah that came to Micah...
which he saw'.[1]

Israel. Perhaps = the North Israelite Kingdom, as in the latter half
of the verse. However, it may well be used in the sense of *all* Israel; for
the verse introduces a volume which, in its present form at least, includes
specific references to Judah (ii. 4, 5, vi. 1, ix. 11–15).[2]

in the days of Uzziah. The prowess of king Uzziah (Hebrew = 'Jehovah
is my strength') must have been considerable, although the chief evidence
concerning the reign is late (2 Chron. xxvi. 1–15). 'Uzziah' is referred to in
the prophets also in Isa. vi. 1, Zech. xiv. 5. Almost certainly he is the
'Azariah' (Hebrew = 'Jehovah has helped me') of 2 Ki. xv. 1–7 (*cf.* 2 Ki. xv.
13, 30, 32, 34, 'Uzziah' M.T. but not LXX[3]); and possibly it is he who is
mentioned on two Assyrian inscriptions as *Azriyā'u* of *Yāūdi*. See Introd.
p. 40, footnote 1. Uzziah's reign was from *c.* 790 to *c.* 739 B.C.; there is
uncertainty about the latter date owing to the ambiguity of the Biblical
statements dealing with the fact that his son Jotham was regent during
the latter part of Uzziah's life, when he was a leper. See Skinner, *Kings,*
pp. 42–45, 447, 448.

Jeroboam the son of Joash. For a summary of the reign of this king,
see 2 Ki. xiv. 23–29, and Introd. p. 5. Jeroboam II's reign is generally
thought to have been from *c.* 783 to 745 or 743 B.C. The immense success
which this king achieved is reflected in Am. vi. 13, 14. The name Jeroboam
(almost certainly referring to the Second) has been found upon a seal
shewing a lion, and bearing the inscription in the old Hebrew characters,
'To Shema', servant of Jeroboam'.[4] Though the chronological statements
made in 2 Ki. xiv. 23, xv. 1 are difficult, it may be taken that the reigns of
Uzziah and Jeroboam, if not approximately co-extensive, at least (as this
verse implies) overlapped each other by a considerable number of years.

two years before the earthquake. *General* allusions to earthquakes
are not infrequent in the O.T. This is, however, the only particular one
mentioned, and, doubtless, the reference did at one time help to date the
preaching of Amos. For a suggestion by which it may so assist the student
to-day, see Introd. pp. 39–41. Possibly the same disturbance is referred

---

[1] *Cf.* also Hab. i. 1. Very similarly the Hebrew of Isa. xxx. 10 *b* runs, 'which
say...to the *seers,* See not for us right things, speak unto us smooth things,
see deceits'. *Cf.* further, Introd. pp. 83–101, "Visions". Just possible as a
rendering would be: 'The words of Amos...*who saw* (visions) concerning...'.

[2] Upon the question as to whether the audience of the Prophet was Northern
Israel only, see Introd. pp. 12–14.

[3] LXX of *v.* 34 has 'Uzziah' (MS. A 'Azariah').

[4] See Handcock, *Archaeology of the Holy Land,* pp. 173, 174; Gressmann,
Bilder, edn 1909, p. 103, No. 197; edn 1926, No. 578.

2 And he said, The LORD shall roar from Zion, and utter

to again in iv. 11 *or* viii. 8, 9; and *cf.* ix. 1. In ch. viii an eclipse seems
to be predicted as an accompaniment. The phrase 'the earthquake in the
days of Uzziah' occurs in Zech. xiv. 5; but it may be hardly more than
a borrowing from this verse.[1]

I. 2. INTRODUCTION

2. And he said, The LORD shall roar.... 'He' = Amos. Not improbably *v.* 2 should be regarded as another editorial addition. It is a "preface",
so to speak, giving a *résumé* of what Amos 'said' throughout the book:
viz. that Jehovah was speaking in judgment. So Jer. i. 10–14 prepares
the reader for the fact that Jeremiah has a message of destruction. Likewise, Ezekiel in his inaugural vision already sees the glory of Jehovah
depart from the sanctuary (Ezek. iii. 12). Similarly in Isaiah's first vision
(or at least the record of it) his message is represented as one of all but
hopeless doom (Isa. vi. 10–13). In this verse, and indeed in the opening
passage *vv.* 3–5, the poetic *parallelism* and the *rhythm* (trimeter[2]) are well
marked.

The phrase **The LORD shall roar from Zion, and utter his voice
from Jerusalem** occurs also in the fourth-century prophet Joel (Joel
iii. 16, in Heb. iv. 16). Some scholars (*e.g.* van Hoonacker) hold that Joel is
dependent on the present passage of Amos. More probably, however, Joel
has been *used* by the editor of Amos.[3] Am. ix. 13 *b* seems to be dependent
on Joel iii. 18 (in Heb. iv. 18) rather than *vice versâ*. The reference to
'shepherds' and 'pastures' would make the words an apt addition to the
prophecies of Amos the shepherd.

The LORD. See Excursus I. pp. 327–330.

shall roar. (1) Probably the significance of this verse is that Jehovah's
judgment will soon come, and will *consist of*, or be *accompanied by*, both
storm and thunder. This is the meaning of Joel iii. 16, and *cf.* Jer. xxv. 30.
So Wellhausen, Sellin. (2) Less likely is it that Jehovah is here compared
(as He is in iii. 8) to a lion about to spring, Jehovah's *words* of judgment
being symbolised by the preliminary 'roar' of the lion. According to this
latter view the Hebrew verbs should probably be rendered by *present* tenses;
and the book of Amos would be an account of what God is already 'roaring'
or saying.

from Zion. (1) It may be that 'Zion' is used poetically as a mere synonym
for 'Jerusalem' of the next half-line. From here trouble will issue. Or (2) the
writer may be representing God's *words* as proceeding from the *temple* of
Zion, 'the place' (according to Deuteronomy) 'which the LORD shall choose
to put his name there'.

utter his voice. 'Voice of God' is the Hebrew equivalent of 'thunder'.
Cf. Ps. xviii. 13, 'The LORD also thundered in the heavens, the Most High

---

[1] See, however, Josephus, *Antiquities*, IX. x. 4, quoted on p. 40, footnote 2.
[2] See, above, p. 33.   [3] So Volz, Marti, Harper.

his voice from Jerusalem; and the pastures of the shepherds
shall mourn, and the top of Carmel shall wither.

uttered his voice'. So Job xxxvii. 4, 5, 'when his voice is heard', following
v. 3 ('lightning'); and in the well-known passage, Ps. xxix. 3–9.[1]
   from Jerusalem. Mentioned again in ii. 5. This familiar place-name
dates back as far as *c.* 1400 B.C. in the form *Uru-salim* (in the Tell el-
Amarna Tablets). In Gen. xiv. 18 it is called 'Salem': and by whatever
name it was known it certainly existed as an important settlement at least
as early as the time of Abraham. It is not impossible that the name of
Jerusalem, impregnated as it is with spiritual associations belonging to the
worship of the only true God, is connected ultimately with a sun-god,
Shalman.[2] From the time of the capture of Jebus (2 Sam. v. 6–9) Jerusalem
had been the capital, first of the united kingdom under David and Solomon,
then of 'Judah' under their descendants. Moreover, the Temple gave it a
special prestige, which fact probably presented a real problem to the
founder of the Northern Kingdom (1 Ki. xii. 26, 27). On the other hand, it
cannot have been held in such unique veneration at the time of Amos as
it was later when the books of Kings came to be compiled.[3] None the less,
the shepherd may have drawn inspiration, as Isaiah did but a few years
later, from the chief and royal shrine of the house of Judah (*cf.* Isa. vi. 1 *b*).
   the pastures of the shepherds shall mourn. A highly poetical phrase.
The havoc which Jehovah's thunder produces is represented as making
the 'pastures' (around Tekoa) 'mourn' with consternation and grief.
The grass *dries up* (*cf.* the parallel 'shȧll wither'). See Jer. xii. 4, 11,
xxiii. 10.   **pastures.** These are the meadows which normally spring with
grass (Joel ii. 22) and where at night, according to Ps. xxiii. 2, the sheep
lie down. Less probable is the A.V. rendering (following that of the
Targum) 'habitations', which the R.V. relegates to the margin.
   Carmel: *lit.* = 'garden-land' (*cf.* Isa. xvi. 10, Jer. ii. 7, 2 Ki. xix. 23,
where the word is used as a common noun). The mountain ridge of Carmel,
west of the vale of Esdraelon, must have been one of the most fertile parts
of Palestine. Even to-day it is abundant in woods, flowers, and the cultivated vine.[4] Thus the passage indicates the serious degree of desolation
coming. *Cf.* Nah. i. 4, 'Bashan languisheth, and Carmel'; so Isa. xxxiii. 9,
Jer. l. 19.

---

   [1] Notwithstanding the dissemination of natural science, the belief that thunder
is God speaking (*cf.* St John xii. 29) has been slow to die out. Unfortunately
the idea is not a harmless one, for it is scarcely compatible with belief in the
love and gentleness of God as revealed in His Son.
   [2] *C.A.H.* ii. p. 396.
   [3] *Cf.* the note on 'high places', pp. 308, 309.
   [4] See on ix. 3, and *cf.* G. A. Smith in *H.D.B.* i. p. 355 *a*.

I. 3–II. 16. "Oracles" against the Nations and against Israel:
or Transgressions and their Visitation

V. 1 announced 'words' which Amos 'saw concerning *Israel*'. Yet with
v. 3 there begins a series of judgments, or "oracles", upon the peoples
surrounding Israel. These prophecies, however, should not be regarded as
having been promulgated in the various countries respectively enumerated.
Rather, they were a means of teaching Jehovah's own people. In the
sermon of chs. i and ii the Prophet would ensure a hearing from the
Israelites (always slow to recognise their guilt) by first stating the crimes
of, and Divine sentences on, their neighbours. The judgment upon the
Israelitish nation at the close (ii. 6–16) forms an effective climax.[1] As she
has broken the same moral laws as others, so she too must be punished.[2]
This is the same if the view is taken that chs. i and ii are not so much a
résumé of one actual discourse of Amos as a finished literary creation,
introductory to the book as a whole. Am. vii, not chs. i and ii, may represent the Prophet's first words.

Considering the smallness and, to a certain degree, aloofness of his nation,
Amos in the opening chapters exhibits a noticeable breadth of view in two
respects: (1) geographically, (2) theologically. (1) His mind moves from
Phoenicia in the north to Moab in the south, from Ammon in the east to
Philistia in the west. But note that almost certainly all the nations mentioned in these two chapters (except the Philistines) are related ethno-
graphically to Israel. (2) Jehovah is supreme not only over Israel, but
over all these peoples,—even over Assyria herself, the instrument of moral
retribution. For "oracles" by other prophets upon foreign nations, see
Isa. xiii–xxiii, Jer. xlvi–xlix, Ezek. xxv–xxxi.

(a) I. 3–5. *Judgment upon Aram* ('*Syria*')

'*Ărām* here, as generally in the O.T. after the 10th cent. B.C., means that
branch of the Aramaean family whose capital was Damascus. This people
was subdued by David, but became independent of Solomon towards the
close of the latter's reign.

The name '*Ărām*, however, was at various times applied to a very wide

---

[1] In his Epistle to the Romans St Paul adopts a somewhat analogous method—
in i. 18–32 enlarging on the sinfulness of the *Gentile* world, in ch. ii bringing home
the guilt of God's own people, the *Jews*.

[2] How different is the O.T. seer from his counterpart in Babylonia. According
to the *Ira myth*, the plague-god is to devastate the entire world, including
Babylonia. A poet saw 'as a vision of the night' a general uprising, "Assyrian
shall slay Assyrian,...one land another,...one house another, one brother
another. And thereupon shall the Akkadian (= N. Babylonians) arise, fell them
all, and cast them all down together"; reaching again to the world empire
(Gressm. *Texte*, 1926, pp. 212 ff.; *cf.* Meissner, *Babylonien*, II. pp. 186, 187).
Amos, on the other hand, prophesying the fall of the nations around Palestine,
predicts the annihilation of his own people also. Moreover the catastrophe
that is coming is a form of Divine *judgment*. In short, the words of the Hebrew
prophet do not originate in blind patriotic impulse.

3 Thus saith the LORD: For three transgressions of

tract of land with its inhabitants. In addition to the above 'Aram of Damascus' (2 Sam. viii. 5), the following regions also are mentioned in the O.T.: (1) *Aram of the Two Rivers* (translated by the LXX *Mesopotamia*), Gen. xxiv. 10; *cf. Paddan-Aram*, Gen. xxv. 20 and Hos. xii. 12: (2) *Aram of Zobah* (2 Sam. viii. 3, x. 6; *cf.* 1 Sam. xiv. 47, where Saul is credited with 'vexing' the kings of Zobah): (3) *Aram of Beth Rehob* (2 Sam. x. 6, 8): and (4) *Aram of Maacah*, east of the sea of Galilee (1 Chron. xix. 6). The ultimate distinction between the Hebrew and the Aramaean is not always a clear one. Not only had Abraham and Isaac Aramaean connections (Gen. xi. 29, xxiv. 15), but both Jacob's wives were of Paddan-Aram (Gen. xxix); and that patriarch himself is described in Deut. xxvi. 5 as 'a wandering Aramaean' (R.V. marg.).[1]

3. Thus saith the LORD. Perhaps, strictly, to be translated 'Thus *has said*'..., or '*said*'.... This phrase, used by all the prophets, may point to some experience wherein they felt that they had received such a word from God. *Cf.* iii. 1: 'Hear this word that the LORD *hath spoken* (Hebrew *dibber*) against you'. See Introd. pp. 78–83.

For three transgressions...punishment thereof. The formula is repeated throughout, in order to introduce the separate "oracles", which form strophes in a poem extending over the two chapters.

three transgressions...yea, for four. The translation (of R.V.) 'yea' is preferable to that of A.V. 'and'. Certainly no special significance attaches to the precise figures 'three', 'four', as might be the case if the book had been written later, when the symbolism of numbers had become important. Rather, the phrase here is intended to suggest a large, but *indefinite*, number. For this free use of consecutive numerals in pairs, *cf.* Job xxxiii. 14, 'God spake *once*, yea *twice*'; and xxxiii. 29, 'Lo, all these things doth God work *twice*, yea *thrice* with a man'; and Prov. vi. 16, xxx. 15, 18; Eccl. xi. 2. Similarly in Am. iv. 8, 'two or three cities'. On the other hand, the same construction as that of Am. i. 3, *etc.*, occurs with literal meaning 'three or four leaves' in Jer. xxxvi. 23.

transgressions. The Hebrew *pesha'* signifies originally 'rebellion'. *Cf.* Isa. xlvi. 8, 'You *rebels*' (Moffatt's transl.). 'Transgression', or 'trespass', in the O.T. may be against (*a*) man (*e.g.* in Gen. l. 17, 1 Sam. xxiv. 11) or (*b*) God. The crimes enumerated in Am. i. 3–ii. 3 do not appear to their perpetrators to be against any God, but only (if the offenders think of such things at all) against the victims. Perhaps in the cases of *Philistia* and *Phoenicia* (i. 6–10), and certainly of *Moab* (ii. 1–3), the sufferers were not Israelites. It is clear from the whole context that Amos regards these acts as 'transgressions' against the moral laws of the God of righteousness (who, as it happens, is the God of Israel). Amos was not the first prophet to insist that sin is not against man alone: *cf.* Nathan's words in 2 Sam.

---

[1] See, further, *C.A.H.* I. p. 234.

Damascus, yea, for four, I will not turn away the punishment
thereof; because they have threshed Gilead with threshing

xii. 9, 'to do that which is evil *in his sight*'. By this teaching does not the
O.T. provide a corrective against a tendency in some modern thinking?

Damascus. In Amos' day an ancient city, see Gen. xiv. 15, xv. 2
(R.V. marg.). 'Damascus' here stands for the country of which it was the
capital. So exactly in Assyrian '*the land of* Dimashka'. *Dimashk* is still
the chief town of modern 'Syria'. Skilfully the Prophet seeks to appeal
to the Israelites by beginning with a denunciation of their greatest foe;
cf. 2 Ki. xii. 17, xiii. 7.

I will not turn away the punishment thereof. The exact meaning
of the M.T. is by no means clear, for the object of the verb is expressed
by a pronoun only—'it'. But *cf.* the expression, hinting at Divine punishment, 'I will *require (it)* of him' (Deut. xviii. 19).[1] Possibly, however, least
difficulty lies in the suggestion of the R.V. marg. 'I will not revoke *my word*'.
Or there may be a direct reference to the Assyrian, "I will not turn him
back'.[2]

they have threshed Gilead. The 'threshing' of corn used to be effected
by 'trampling', or by dragging an instrument over it. In oriental countries
the custom was not uncommon of placing prisoners of war on the ground
like grain, and driving the machine over them (Harper). In 2 Sam. xii. 31
it is stated, according to the M.T., that David put the Ammonites 'under
harrows of iron'.[3] Perhaps, however, Amos is only saying in a graphic way
that the Syrians subdued the Gileadites with the greatest cruelty. Compare
the use of the same metaphor, with reference to this very war, in 2 Ki.
xiii. 7. For diagrams of modern Syrian threshing instruments, see Benzinger,
Heb. Archäologie, p. 209 (a wooden sledge, studded with sharp stones),[4]
and p. 210 (an instrument with sharp cutting *iron wheels*, such as is probably
alluded to by Amos here): also Thomson, *Land and Book*, pp. 539, 540.
It is known from 2 Ki. viii. 12 that the Syrians were capable of committing
great atrocities.

Gilead was, strictly speaking, the land exactly east of the Jordan river,
inhabited by the tribe of Gad and by the southern portion of the eastern
branch of Manasseh. Being nearer Damascus it suffered earlier, and more
severely, than did Israel west of Jordan. See Introd. p. 3. In 2 Ki. x. 32, 33

---

[1] The pronoun object is to be understood. The Hebrew is simply '*ānôkhî
'edhrôsh mē'immô*.

[2] So the late Prof. H. W. Hogg, of Manchester, in a paper entitled, "The
Starting-point of the Religious Message of Amos", *Transactions of the Third In-
ternational Congress for the History of Religions*, 1908, i. pp. 325–327. This scholar
compares the use of the same verb in 2 Ki. xix. 7 R.V. 'Behold...he (*i.e.* the
Assyrian) shall return to his own land' and, in the *Hiph'il* voice, in 2 Ki. xix. 28,
'I will turn thee back by the way by which thou camest'.

[3] But see 1 Chron. xx. 3, and Hoffmann's emendation of the text of 2 Sam.
xii. 31 based upon it in Driver's *Samuel*, pp. 294–297.

[4] This sort may have *iron teeth*. *Cf.* Jastrow, *Targ. Dict.* art. *ḥārbû*, p. 526 a.

instruments of iron: **4** but I will send a fire into the house
of Hazael, and it shall devour the palaces of Ben-hadad.

we read that in the time of Jehu 'Hazael smote...all the land of *Gilead*,
the Gadites, and the Reubenites, and the Manassites...even Gilead and
Bashan'. In this passage, as not improbably in Amos i. 3, the term 'Gilead'
is used to include territory both north and south of Gilead proper (so in
Josh. xxii. 9). But perhaps the first "Gilead" is a dittogram.

4. I will send a fire. The phrase occurs in each oracle except (as it happens)
in the one against 'Israel'. It is borrowed by Hosea (Hos. viii. 14), and
nearly exactly by Jeremiah (Jer. xvii. 27, xxi. 14, *etc.*); but these passages
supply no hint of the precise meaning of the expression. (1) Some find
in it an allusion to 'Jehovah's fire', *cf.* Deut. xxxii. 22; Pss. xviii. 8 (in
Heb. 9), xcvii. 3, Isa. xxx. 27, and see on Am. vii. 4. God Himself, as it were,
lights the flame with His own hand. Sellin compares Gen. xix. 24. "The
day of Jehovah", says Gressmann (*Eschatologie*, p. 49, *cf.* p. 53), "is
already in Amos as also it is in Zephaniah (Zeph. i. 18, iii. 8) a day of fire".
Similarly Adam Welch (*Religion of Israel*, p. 67), insisting that the use of
the expression 'fire' in vii. 4 should guide the interpretation of the word
in chs. i and ii, maintains that the fire which Jehovah lights "can only be
the fire of the world catastrophe". (2) However, the term 'fire' is actually
employed elsewhere by Amos, in a metaphorical sense, for the disaster of
war.[1] In i. 14 'with shouting in the day of battle' immediately follows, and
seems to explain, 'the fire' which Jehovah will kindle. Similarly, fire and
war are associated in ii. 2; and in v. 6 the prophecy of decimation by war
occurring in v. 2, 3 is followed up by 'lest he break out like fire'. It is
probable that throughout the book Amos presumes that Jehovah, in His
war of retribution, uses human agency. (*Cf.* Introd. p. 30.) Furthermore,
whatever Zephaniah meant by 'the fire of Jehovah's jealousy', his prophecy
certainly concerns the Scythian invasion more than anything else. The
suggestion of van Hoonacker upon the present passage is unnecessary, that
the fire which Jehovah sends refers literally to the burning and devastation
which always accompany conquest by a foreign army.

into the house of. In all probability 'house' does not signify 'royal
family' (as it does in 2 Sam. vii. 11, 1 Ki. xiii. 34, *etc.*, and *cf.* note on Am.
vii. 9), in view of the parallel word 'palace' in the next line. Furthermore,
in all the similar verses the scene of the 'fire' is something material
('wall' in i. 7, 10, 14, a country in i. 12, ii. 2, 5).

Hazael...Ben-hadad. The names are perhaps used here to designate
the *kings* of Syria in general. **Hazael** was the founder of a dynasty (2 Ki.
viii. 7-13; *cf.* 1 Ki. xix. 15). His name occurs on the Black Obelisk of
Shalmaneser III as king of Damascus in 841 B.C.

palaces. It is possible that the Hebrew *'armôn* has here (and throughout

---

[1] And *cf.* Isaiah's use with reference to internal anarchy (Isa. ix. 18, 19),
'Wickedness burneth as the fire...the people also are as the fuel of fire'.

**5 And I will break the bar of Damascus, and cut off the in-
habitant from the valley of Aven, and him that holdeth the**

chs. i and ii and in iii. 9) the force of 'citadel' or 'stronghold',[1] as probably
in 1 Ki. xvi. 18, 2 Ki. xv. 25, Hos. viii. 14 b, Prov. xviii. 19 b (R.V. text,
'castle'), Ps. cxxii. 7 (parallel to 'thy wall', or 'rampart'). On the other
hand, the word means an Israelite 'mansion', 'palace'[2] (R.V.) in Am. iii.
10, 11, vi. 8, and it would seem not unreasonable to assign this latter
meaning to it at every occurrence in the book. Furthermore, it is not
likely that there would be several citadels (*plural*) in one town, *e.g.* Gaza,
Rabbah, *etc.*[3] It would appear that Amos popularised the use of this term
for canonical prophecy: *cf.* Isa. xxxii. 14, Jer. vi. 5, *etc.* See, further, on iii. 9.

Ben-hadad. The third king of Syria of that name mentioned in the O.T.
(Ben-hadad I, 1 Ki. xv. 18; Ben-hadad II, 1 Ki. xx. 1; Ben-hadad III,
2 Ki. xiii. 24). He was the son and successor of Hazael.[4] In the O.T. the
syllable *ben-* of Ben-hadad is the Hebrew equivalent of the native Aramaean *bar-* = 'son of'. *Hadad* had been the chief Syrian deity for many
centuries. Doubtless the same god is referred to in 2 Ki. v. 18 under the
name of Rimmon. We learn from the Tell el-Amarna Letters that about
the period of 1400 B.C. Addu (= Adad or Hadad) was well known *west*
of Jordan also.

5. I will break the bar: *i.e.* part of the defence of the city gate. The cities
in Bashan, according to 1 Ki. iv. 13, had 'brazen bars'.

the inhabitant. The use of the singular collectively is very frequent in
Hebrew, and particularly with this word (*e.g.* in Gen. xxxiv. 30). (1) 'Inhabitant' is probably the correct translation, and it is that adopted by
most moderns. (2) However, it is just possible that both here and in *v.* 8
the rendering should be as R.V. marg. 'him that sitteth (*upon the throne*)'.
So Isa. x. 13 (R.V.), Pss. ii. 4, xxii. 3 (R.V. marg.).[5] Certainly the parallel

---

[1] In German, *Burg*—Duhm, Riessler.

[2] In German, *Palast*—Nowack, Sellin.

[3] P. J. Heawood, in *J.T.S.* XIII. pp. 66–73, raises some points which are at
least interesting. LXX renders the term sometimes by 'field' (χώρα), *e.g.* in
Am. iii. 9, 10, 11, sometimes by 'foundation' (θεμέλιον) as in chs. i and ii.
Following this second hint Heawood sees the original meaning of Hebrew *'armón*
to be the 'general outline' or 'ground plan' of a city. But the word is *plural*,
not singular.

[4] The correctness of the name of this third Ben-hadad (doubted by at least
one scholar) was strikingly verified by the publication in 1908 by M. Pognon of
an Aramaean inscription which he discovered. 'Bar-hadad, son of Hazael, king
of Aram' with a number of other kings besieged a certain king Zakir in Hazrek
(the Hadrach of Zech. ix. 1). Zakir, however, through seers and soothsayers,
was promised deliverance by his god. 'Baal of the heavens'. Finally he erected
the monument to celebrate the subduing of Bar-hadad and his fellows. *Cf.*
Introd. p. 4.

[5] And *cf.* Harper and Driver. A quotation from one of the Zenjirli inscriptions, referred to on the next page, is not out of place. The king says, "...for

sceptre from the house of Eden: and the people of Syria
shall go into captivity unto Kir, saith the LORD

clause in *v.* 5 and *v.* 8 supports this: 'him that holdeth the sceptre'. There
may have been a vassal king whose residence was in the valley of Aven.

the valley of Aven. 'Valley' = 'plain', as in the A.V. 'The Plain'
par excellence in territory claimed by Aram would be that lying between
Lebanon and Anti-Lebanon, which in Josh. xi. 17 is referred to as '*the valley
of Lebanon* under mount Hermon'. It is called to-day '*el Beqâ'a* = 'the
Valley'. See Additional Note, p. 281.

him that holdeth the sceptre: *i.e.* the king. The same phrase in the
language of the Aramaeans occurs on a contemporary inscription, one of
three discovered in 1890–91 at, or near, the modern village of Zenjirli in
north-west Syria.[1]

the house of Eden. If *Beth-eden* (R.V. marg.) be the modern '*Ehden*
(Syr. *'Edēn*) 20 miles N.-W. of Baalbek, or *Jubb 'Adīn* 25 miles N.-E. of
Damascus, the clause makes a good parallel to the preceding one.[2]

shall go into captivity. The sentence of judgment is pronounced by
Jehovah (*v.* 3). The instrument of its accomplishment is the same world-
power as will deport Israel also (v. 27, vi. 14). Though Amos (unlike Hosea,
Hos. ix. 3) never mentions the name Assyria, it is difficult to believe that
it ever was far from his thoughts.

unto Kir. According to ix. 7, Kir was the region from which the Aramaeans had migrated. To return now, after so many centuries and as captives, would be a real exile.[3]

---

my own righteousness, (my) lord *made me to sit*" (*i.e.* upon the throne), *Panammu*,
l. 19. Cooke, *N.S.I.* pp. 173, 174.

[1] See Cooke, *N.S.I.* pp. 160, 162.

[2] Alternatively, following Schrader, *C.O.T.* (*W.*), II. pp. 11, 12, is the identification with *Bît Adini* (of the Assyrian inscriptions) on the Euphrates. The statement would thus imply a destruction from extreme west to farthest east. This
Bît Adini is probably the 'Eden' of Ezek. xxvii. 23, 2 Ki. xix. 12. Though, of
course, not situated within Aram of Damascus (if Aramaean at all), it might
have been a kingdom tributary, or allied, to it. *Cf.* Driver, *Amos*, pp. 233–235.
If this identification can be accepted, a further connection with the 'Eden' of
Gen. ii. 8–15 becomes not impossible (though the vowel spelling is not quite the
same). For, in that passage, a garden is imagined *within* the general district
of Eden (Gen. ii. 8, 'eastward *in* Eden'; ii. 10, 'a river went *out of* Eden to water
the garden'). And in Gen. ii. 14 one of the rivers near Eden was the Euphrates.

[3] The locality of Kir is quite uncertain—except that this verse would imply
that it lies (*a*) not very near Damascus, and (*b*) within the bounds of the Assyrian
rule. (1) *Cyrene*, the rendering of both the Targum and Vulgate here and in
ix. 7, is ruled out by (*b*). (2) Perhaps it lay by the river *Kur* in North Armenia.
(3) In Isa. xxii. 6, Kir is mentioned as, apparently, near Elam. In accordance
with (3), a recent suggestion, based on the blood connection between Aramaeans
and Hebrews (see above on Aram), identifies Kir with *el-Muḳayyar*, the Ur of
the Chaldees, the home of the Patriarch of both peoples (*C.A.H.* I. p. 234).

For the fulfilment of this prophecy, see the inscription of Tiglath-pileser III:
"Into the chief gate of his city I entered, his superior commandants alive...
I caused to be crucified; his land I subjugated". Then follow, in a broken
text, details of the captivity.[1] The passage 2 Ki. xvi. 9 confirms Am. i. 5
by the phrase 'carried it captive *to Kir*' (though LXX does not contain
the words 'to Kir'). The reader should perhaps be reminded that in connection with both the Israelite and the neighbouring nations the expression
'carry captive' in a prediction, and certainly in fact, by no means corre-
sponded with complete depopulation. Damascus, situated as it was on
the great caravan route between Egypt and the Euphrates, could not be
entirely extinguished either by slaughter or by slavery.

Damascus became unnecessary only when, after the founding of the
Port of Antioch, ships from Alexandria could unload at the port, and the
merchandise pass east, by the short and direct route, to the Euphrates valley.

(b) I. 6–8. *Judgment upon Philistia*

As Syria on the north-east had been the worst foe of the Israelites during
the preceding 100 years, so at one time the Philistines on the south-west
had been their most troublesome neighbours. This condition of affairs,
described in the books of Judges and Samuel, lasted for a century or more,
until their power was broken by king David, and some of them were made
into his bodyguard, the Pelethites (2 Sam. xv. 18). Notwithstanding what
is said in 1 Sam. xiv. 47, at the death of Saul the Philistines actually held
the eastern gates of the plain of Esdraelon—Beth-shan—as is recounted
in 1 Sam. xxxi. 8–12.

Amos here refers by name to each of the five states in the Philistine
federation—except indeed to Gath, a fact which some scholars seek to explain
by the supposition that it was already destroyed (see note on vi. 2, p. 303).
Apart from the federated cities there were others, *e.g.* Beth-shemesh, Beth-
car, Ziklag, Lydda. The Philistines were a strong immigrant people, coming
from Asia Minor, but some of them, not improbably, *via* Crete. See, further,
the note on ix. 7, 'Caphtor'. Egyptian records speak of the *Peleset*[2] (also
transliterated *Pulesati, Purasati*). After attempting, in a powerful combination with other tribes from the north of the Mediterranean, to obtain
a footing in Egypt in and after 1194 B.C., the Peleset were beaten back by
Ramses III. Eventually they settled on the southern part of the sea-coast
of Palestine in precisely the region in which the 'Philistines' (in Hebrew,
Pᵉlishtîm) appear in Bible history at the period of Samson and Saul a
hundred years after.[3] These immigrants thus represent a colonisation of
the Holy Land later than that of the Israelites.

---

[1] Schrader, *C.O.T.* (*W.*), I. p. 254. See, also, Introd. p. 102.

[2] *Cf.* the terms *Philistine,* and *Pelethite.*

[3] *C.A.H.* II. pp. 173–177. The Philistines, driven off by the Egyptians, continued
in some condition of dependence upon that people, paying them tribute, perhaps
till David's time. This is the relationship which seems to have given rise to the
"genealogy" of Gen. x. 13, 14: 'Mizraim (*i.e.* Egypt) begat Casluhim (whence
went forth the Philistines), and Caphtorim'.

6 Thus saith the LORD: For three transgressions of Gaza, yea, for four, I will not turn away the punishment thereof; because they carried away captive the whole people, to deliver them up to Edom: **7** but I will send a fire on the

The term 'Palestine', derived from *Philistine*, is a reminder till this day of the comparative greatness of these people in the land of their new home. And there is a presumption that this nation, like the others surrounding the Israelites, intermarried with them (*cf.* Judges xiv-xvi) at least in the early period, thus modifying the original Semitic stock.[1]

6. Gaza: now spelt *Gazzeh*, here seems to represent Philistia, just as Damascus in *v.* 3 stands for Syria. Gaza was the southernmost of the cities of the Philistine league, being on the edge of the desert (*cf.* Acts viii. 26). It stood at the great cross roads, and caravan routes passed through it to both Edom and Arabia, and from the Euphrates to Egypt. Gaza figured in the Great War. After the second battle of Gaza, on November 7th, 1917, the conquest of Palestine was swift.

the whole people: *lit.* 'an entire exile' ("abstract" for "concrete"). The expression recurs in *v.* 9 (of Tyre), and *cf.* Jer. xiii. 19. When one people vanquished another it was usual for prisoners to be made slaves; but in this instance the Philistines had been engaging in slave-raiding pure and simple. Whole villages (whether or not of *Judaeans* it is not clear) had been depopulated. With this verse and *v.* 9, *cf.* Joel iii. 4, 6, 'O *Tyre* and Zidon, and all the regions of *Philistia* . . . ; the children also of Judah . . . have ye sold unto the sons of the Grecians'. It is instructive to note in what company 'men-stealers' ($\dot{\alpha}\nu\delta\rho\alpha\pi o\delta\iota\sigma\tau\alpha\iota$) are placed in 1 Tim. i. 10. In view of the tenour of O.T. and N.T. teaching upon the subject, it would appear strange that until well on into the last century citizens of the British Empire should be involved in traffic in slaves.[2]

to Edom. Gaza, by virtue of its geographical position on the caravan route, was able to sell slaves to the Edomites—who in turn probably passed them on to Arabia.

---

[1] For additional information the student may be referred to Sir G. A. Smith's *Historical Geog. of the Holy Land*, ch. ix; Hall in *C.A.H.* II. pp. 275–295; and S. A. Cook, pp. 379–381. Remarkable excavations have taken place at *Beisān* (Beth-shan) under the auspices of the University of Philadelphia. Six Canaanite temples were found, together with interesting cult objects, *e.g.* representations of birds. Beth-shan belonged to the Philistines at the time of Saul, 1 Sam. xxxi. 10. If they did not take it from the Hebrews it had probably been acquired in some way from the *Egyptians*, who possessed the fort under Ramses III; indeed it was in Egyptian hands throughout the period 1313 to 1167 B.C. (*Z.A.W.* 1924, pp. 347, 348). It seems likely that the Philistines used for their own worship the temple of which they had come into possession; and it may well be that this was 'the house of Ashtoreth' (M.T. 'Ashtaroth') into which king Saul's armour was carried as a trophy after the Philistines' victory at Gilboa. See also *P.E.F. Qrly St*, Apr. 1927, esp. p. 77, Apr. 1928, and *Z.A.W.* 1926, Heft 1, pp. 71–75.

[2] See R. Coupland's *Wilberforce—A Narrative*, 1924.

wall of Gaza, and it shall devour the palaces thereof: **8** and
I will cut off the inhabitant from Ashdod, and him that
holdeth the sceptre from Ashkelon; and I will turn mine
hand against Ekron, and the remnant of the Philistines shall
perish, saith the Lord GOD.

7. on the wall. Perhaps translate 'within' (or 'into') 'the wall', as also
in *v.* 10. The R.V. recognises this meaning of the preposition in *v.* 14 ('*in*
the wall of Rabbah'); also in *v.* 4 ('*into* the house of Hazael').

8. Ashdod, the modern *Esdûd*, was twenty-one miles from Gaza, and,
like it, was three miles from the coast, on the trade-route of the Maritime
Plain. If the M.T. of Am. iii. 9 can be trusted against LXX, it seems to
have been a place of very considerable importance, for it is coupled with
'Egypt'. In 1 Sam. v. 1–5 (and 1 Macc. x. 83, 84) a temple of Dagon at
Ashdod is mentioned; though this fish-god, or more probably *corn*-god
(Hebrew *dāgān* = 'corn') was worshipped by others besides Philistines.
'The speech of Ashdod', referred to in Neh. xiii. 24, probably did not differ
very greatly from Hebrew; for the Philistines, though of non-Semitic stock,
after immigration came to adopt, amongst other things, Semitic speech
(*C.A.H.* I. p. 232). 'Ashdod' is mentioned in the N.T. (Acts viii. 40,
Ἄζωτος).

Ashkelon. In modern Arabic '*Askalân*. This city lay midway between
Ashdod and Gaza, but on the coast. Ashkelon, like probably the other
famous Philistine sites, had a history before it became Philistine. Some of
the Tell el-Amarna letters are from the governor of Ashkelon to the king
of Egypt. In *c.* 1220 B.C. the male population was almost exterminated.
The citizens were led away captive by Mineptah, according to the famous
stele of that Pharaoh.[1] Herodotus mentions the existence at Ashkelon of
a temple of Aphrodite, by which probably is meant the Phoenician goddess
'Ashtoreth. In Christian times Ashkelon figured in the story of Richard
and the Crusades. British excavations under Garstang on this site in 1920
and the following years laid bare almost all the strata of the civilisation
of this city. Pottery has been discovered, which is either Greek or Carian
(Caria may have been the Philistines' original home, *cf.* p. 263). A Greek
amphitheatre has been unearthed; also a Senate house (βουλευτήριον), and
a shrine with a statue of Apollo belonging to the Roman period.[2]

Ekron: now the village '*Akîr*, *cf.* LXX Ἀκκαρών. It was twelve miles
north-east of Ashdod, being the northernmost of the Philistine Pentapolis.
It was to 'Baal-zebub, the god of Ekron', that Ahaziah, king of Northern
Israel, sent, thus provoking Elijah's wrath (2 Ki. i).[3]

---

[1] "Led captive is Askelon, seized is Gezer, destroyed is Yenoam: Israel—its
people are few, its seed no longer exists" (Wardle, *Israel and Babylon*, p. 48).

[2] *Cf. P.E.F. Qrly St,* 1924, pp. 24–35.

[3] Through a mistake of Jerome in his translation of the N.T., the name of
the Ekronite deity became an appellation for the devil, Beelzebub displacing
Beelzebu*l*, even in Greek MSS. *Cf.* St Matt. x. 25, R.V. marg.

9 Thus saith the LORD: For three transgressions of Tyre, yea, for four, I will not turn away the punishment thereof;

the remnant of the Philistines. Either (1) proleptically, that portion of them which at first may escape the punishment predicted (*cf.* ix. 12, Jer. viii. 3), the expression containing in itself a threat; or else (2) Philistia as *already* no longer in its former strength. Perhaps Gath was even now in decline (see on vi. 2); but in any case the Philistines were a shadow of what they had been in Saul's time. The Prophet's words mean that the Philistines are to be annihilated. On the word 'remnant' see v. 15, note, and *cf.* iii. 12 (note on 'be rescued').

In 734 B.C. Tiglath-pileser III inflicted a severe defeat upon *Ashkelon* and *Gaza*.[1] In 711 B.C. the inhabitants of *Ashdod* were carried into exile.[2] In 701 B.C. *Ashkelon* and *Ekron* (led by king Padi) joined Sidon and Judah in the revolt of king Hezekiah against Sennacherib, and were defeated.[3] It must be admitted, however, that the Philistines, severely as they suffered, were not overwhelmed in the general catastrophe which Amos pictures. More than a century later Zephaniah is still predicting the extermination of Gaza, Ashkelon, Ashdod and Ekron (Zeph. ii. 4, 5). For two months Gaza withstood the siege of Alexander. The Philistines figure frequently in the history of the Maccabees. Even Jonathan's methods of conducting warfare in 148 B.C. (1 Macc. x. 77–89) did not destroy them. Prophecies of the overthrow of the Philistines occur also in Isa. xi. 14, Jer. xxv. 20, Zeph. ii. 4–7, Ezek. xxv. 15, and even as late as Zech. ix. 5–7 (4th–2nd cent. B.C.). Duhm, with no sufficient reason, assigns the oracle Am. i. 6–8 to the Maccabaean period. To-day this great race as a distinct entity has disappeared.

(c) I. 9, 10. *Judgment upon Phoenicia*

'Tyre' here stands for Phoenicia, the narrow strip of land which included also Acco, Zarephath, Zidon, Gebal (the Greek *Byblos*), and Arvad. As the Aramaeans migrated from 'Kir', so the Phoenicians claimed to have come from the Persian Gulf. In Judg. xviii. 7 the inhabitants of Laish, or Dan, are described as 'dwelling in security, after the manner of *the Sidonians, quiet and secure*'. The mountains behind shut off Phoenicia from the continent of Asia, and its power was almost entirely maritime.

In view of what is now known as to the antiquity of the Phoenicians, Josephus' statement that Tyre was founded as late as about the year 1200 B.C. needs revising. *Gebal* (north of Zidon) is mentioned as a port as far back as the time of Snofru king of Egypt, *c.* 3100 B.C.[4] Possibly Tyre

---

[1] *C.O.T.* (*W.*), I. p. 249.   [2] *C.O.T.* (*W.*), II. pp. 89–94. *Cf.* Isa. xx. 1.

[3] *C.O.T.* (*W.*), I. pp. 285, 286.

[4] In the early history of Phoenicia Gebal was the principal city. For extensive and significant finds upon this site, the student is referred to the full accounts that have appeared from time to time in *Syria: Revue d'Archéologie*, and to the articles by Vincent in the *Revue Biblique* (Apr. 1925) and by the late Hugo Gressmann in *Z.A.W.* 1925, pp. 225–242. From these excavations it would seem that the golden age of Phoenician culture may be carried back to the Middle Egyptian Empire.

because they delivered up the whole people to Edom, and
remembered not the brotherly covenant: **10** but I will send

was a colony from Zidon; but no evidence on this point is to be derived from
Isa. xxiii. 12, where the words 'virgin daughter of Zidon' are addressed to
Zidon, and not to Tyre (of *v.* 8). In the Amarna Letters, Byblus, Tyre and
Zidon are revealed as loyal to Egypt, *c.* 1400 B.C. In these Abimilki, king
of Tyre, speaks of Pharaoh as his 'divine overlord'. About the time of
the Exodus the goddess of Tyre is mentioned in a treaty between Hattushil,
king of the powerful Hittite empire, and Pharaoh Ramses II. The maritime
supremacy, however, of the Phoenicians may not perhaps be earlier than the
12th or 13th cent. B.C.; their predecessors being the Greeks of the Aegean
Sea, the Cretans, and indeed the Egyptians.[1] In all probability, from about
a century before the time of David and Hiram, the Phoenicians were
actually establishing trading centres and perhaps colonies—*e.g.* Utica in
North Africa. They appear in the pages of the O.T., not as warriors but
as that which in fact they came to be, until the days of the Romans, the
supreme sea-traders. Interesting in this connection are the descriptions of
Tyre given in Ezekiel (xxvi. 17, xxvii. 3, 26–29) and in Isaiah (xxiii. 8,
'whose traffickers are the honourable of the earth'). Hiram I, king of
Tyre, supplied Solomon with timber, artists and workmen. A man of the
name of Hiram (or rather, perhaps, *Hûram-ābî*), half-Tyrian, half-Hebrew,
was put in charge of brass work for the Temple, according to 1 Ki. vii. 13,
et seq., 2 Chron. ii. 13 (in Heb. iv. 16). The inhabitants of Phoenicia were, for
the most part, Semitic like the Canaanites and the Hebrews. In relation
to this, the occurrence in the 4th millennium B.C. of the name Gebal, which
is pure Semitic, is significant. And *cf.* the name '*Abi-milki* referred to above.[2]

The Phoenician religion, like that of all Canaan, was nature-worship;
the deities being Baal (*Lord*) or Melqarth, and Ashtarte ('*Ashtôreth* of the
M.T.). Its failure to produce any moral appeal made Elijah fight against
its influence on Israel. For a further note upon the Phoenician language
and the remains, see p. 281. The authenticity of the oracle is briefly discussed on p. 282.

9. and remembered not. The subject of the verb is, of course, Tyre
(not Edom). The English idiom would be 'not remembering...'.

the brotherly covenant: *lit.* 'covenant between brothers' (*cf.* the
Targum and the R.V. marg.). Like the Philistines in *v.* 6, the Phoenicians
had carried on extensive slave-raiding—or, possibly, only slave *commerce*
('delivered up', *v.* 9, instead of the 'carried away captive', *v.* 6). The
crime, however, is declared to have been aggravated by neglect of a
'covenant'. Is a treaty with *Israel* referred to? 1 Ki. v. 1 says, 'Hiram was

---

[1] *Cf. C.A.H.* I. p. 191; II. p. 378.
[2] On the other hand, it is not impossible that the Φοίνικες of Greek tradition
(? = 'purple men', *or* 'introducers of purple') may have been in reality Minoan
Cretans, and not the Semitic inhabitants of what we call 'Phoenicia'. *C.A.H.*
I. p. 178.

a fire on the wall of Tyre, and it shall devour the palaces thereof.

ever a lover of David'; and in *v.* 12 we read (Hiram and Solomon) 'made a league (Hebrew 'covenant') together'. Compare also the expression in ix. 13, 'my brother'. This friendliness was renewed, and strengthened, by Ahab's marriage to the daughter of Ethbaal (1 Ki. xvi. 31). But, from the time of the slaughter of Jezebel by the express order of Jehu, king of Israel,[1] and also the assassination of her daughter Athaliah who had become queen of Judah, nothing is known of any friendly relations on the part of either nation. Nor are such probable. Indeed, to judge impartially, it would appear that after the above-mentioned events Israelites could make no claim to special consideration from Phoenicians. Still, the possibility should not be overlooked that Amos, as a patriotic Hebrew, ignoring the political significance of the Jezebel and Athaliah episodes, thought only of the brotherliness and good understanding which *had* existed, and which just possibly may have been renewed by a treaty or 'covenant' within the memory of the Prophet's contemporaries. The policy of Jeroboam II had distinct points of contact with that of Omri, Ahab's father.

It is not improbable, however, that the incident to which Amos is referring is Tyrian commerce in slaves belonging to some *non-Israelite* tribe, in defiance of a covenant with it. In ii. 1 also, Amos denounces a 'transgression' which in no way affects Israel (Moab's treatment of the king of Edom). From the evidence of Homer it is clear that the Phoenicians were notorious slave-raiders.

Finally, is it just possible that the 'covenant' to which reference is made is one between the brother nations Edom and Judah, and not between Tyre and Ephraim?

The overthrow of Tyre is predicted in Isa. xxiii, Ezek. xxvi–xxviii, Zech. ix. 2–4; *cf.* also Jer. xxv. 22. In 738 B.C. the king of Tyre, Hiram II, together with Menahem of Samaria, gave tribute to Tiglath-pileser III.[2] Tyre does not seem to have suffered severely at the time. At the end of Assyria's history, the name 'Baal of Tyre' occurs on lists of kings, who, apparently, were tributary to Esar-haddon and Asshurbanipal.[3] Later, Tyre capitulated to Nebuchadnezzar of Babylon, after sustaining a thirteen years' siege, from 585 to 573 B.C.[4] Amos' prophecy was not completely fulfilled until 332 B.C., when Alexander the Great took the city after a siege lasting seven months. It is said that on this occasion six thousand were slain, two thousand were crucified, and thirty thousand were sold into slavery. The founding, however, of the port of Alexandria was more

---

[1] The 'J' tradition, usually assigned to this period, is that the Phoenicians were by origin aliens (Gen. x. 15 declares that it was *Canaan* who 'begat Zidon his firstborn').

[2] *C.O.T.* (*W.*), I. p. 245.   [3] *C.O.T.* (*W.*), II. p. 41.

[4] Rogers, *Hist. of Babylonia*, II. p. 337.

11 Thus saith the LORD: For three transgressions of Edom, yea, for four, I will not turn away the punishment thereof;

injurious to Tyre's prosperity than was this event, especially as it was to be followed by the rise of Antioch with its harbour Seleuceia under the Seleucid kings. The city did not receive its final blow until A.D. 1291, when it fell to the Saracens. "Tyre is now content at the close of her career to be a stagnant village in stagnant Turkey" (G. M. Mackie, in *H.D.B.*).

(d) I. 11, 12. *Judgment upon Edom*

The land of Edom lay S. of the Dead Sea, to the E., probably, of the lower *'Arābāh* valley. The Edomites supplanted, at least partially, the more ancient Horites. Like the Israelites, the Edomites traced their ancestry to Abraham and Isaac, but through Esau (or 'Edom', Gen. xxv. 29, 30), Jacob's elder brother. Appropriately, these two peoples are called 'brothers' here, in Numb. xx. 14 (though in each passage Edom's *actions* are represented as unbrotherly in character) and in Deut. xxiii. 7. It is clear from the O.T. that Judahites and Edomites were racially connected. One of the Edomite 'dukes' was named Kenaz (Gen. xxxvi. 11, 40, 42; *cf.* Numb. xxxii. 12, Josh. xiv. 6, 14). Descended from Kenaz were Caleb, one of the twelve 'spies', and his brother, or possibly nephew, Othniel, who with him dispossessed Canaanites in the southern portion of what became 'Judah' (Judg. i. 13, Josh. xv. 16, 17). Similarly the Jerahmeelites, who traced their descent from another brother of Caleb (1 Chron. ii. 34, 42), had moved into Judah from Edom or its vicinity (1 Sam. xxvii. 10, xxx. 29). Whatever the details of the race connection, it is certain that in early history Edom meant more to Judah than was at one time supposed. (*C.A.H.* II. pp. 367, 404; III. pp. 478, 479.)

A late source in 1 Sam. (xiv. 47) states that Saul 'fought against' and 'vexed' Edom, along with Moab, Ammon, Zobah and the Philistines. David[1] conquered Edom (2 Sam. viii. 13, 14, R.V. marg.), probably with the help of his general Joab (Ps. lx, title), and, possibly, with that of Abishai (1 Chron. xviii. 11, 12). At the disruption of the Twelve Tribes, upon Solomon's death, Edom was retained by Judah, as was Moab by North Israel. The prince of Edom appears in 2 Ki. iii. 9 as the vassal of Jehoshaphat; but in the time of the latter's son, Jehoram, the Edomites threw off the Judaean yoke (2 Ki. viii. 20–22). Later, Amaziah 'took Sela (the capital) by war' with a slaughter of ten thousand men (2 Ki. xiv. 7); but, except that it is possible[2] that he gained control of Edom's port Elath, that king does not appear to have reduced Edom, at any rate, permanently. If the statement of 2 Chron. xxv. 12 is correct, Amaziah's behaviour towards ten

---

[1] Sayce conjectured that king David is the 'Baal-hanan' in the list of kings of Edom contained in Gen. xxxvi. 38 ('J'). In 2 Sam. xxi. 19, essentially the same name, El-hanan, is assigned to the victor over Goliath.

[2] The allusion in 2 Ki. xiv. 22 is, to say the least, ambiguous. It is simpler to understand it of Azariah rather than of Amaziah.

because he did pursue his brother with the sword, and did
cast off all pity, and his anger did tear perpetually, and he

thousand Edomite prisoners can be described only as deplorable. It was his
successor (so it seems) Azariah, or Uzziah, who put Judaean colonists in
Elath after further 'restoring' it to Judah (2 Ki. xiv. 22, 2 Chron. xxvi. 2).
At the destruction of Jerusalem in 586 B.C. the Edomites joined with the
attacking Chaldaeans, an unbrotherly action which lived long in Jewish
memory (Obad. vv. 10–15, Ps. cxxxvii. 7, Ezek. xxv. 12–14, 1 Esdr. iv. 45).

In view of the intermingling in earlier times of Edom and Judah, referred
to above, it has been conjectured that Amos' own ancestry was in part
Edomite.[1] Although, for more than one reason, this suggestion may fail
to commend itself to scholars generally, it would help to account for the
dispassionate view of the doom of the descendants of Jacob which, for the
most part, the Prophet is able to take.

As to the religion of the Edomites, while direct evidence does not at
present exist, it would seem at least possible that the two peoples claiming
descent from the patriarch Isaac should be worshippers of the God whose
blessing both their ancestors had sought (Gen. xxvii. 18–40). It was Jehovah who gave mount Seir to Edom (Deut. ii. 5). It may be significant
that nowhere in the O.T. is the religion of Edom condemned; nor is there a
national god of the Edomites referred to corresponding to (e.g.) the Moabites' Chemosh. Indeed, the Hebrew poet declares concerning Jehovah,
'God came from Teman' (Hab. iii. 3). There is reason to suppose that the
site of Sinai, where Jehovah met Israel, was in actual fact close upon the
border of Edom.[2] There is a connection between the book of Job and Edom.

N.T. students will recall the fact that Herod the Great was the son of
Antipater, who was the governor under Jannaeus Alexander of the Edomite
settlement of 'Idumaea' in the south of Judah. Josephus is probably right
in regarding the Herods as of Edomite stock.

11. did cast off all pity. Perhaps translate[3] 'was (or kept) crushing
down all pity'; lit. 'was destroying·(or 'corrupting') his compassions'.

---

[1] Hölscher (Profeten, p. 189) goes so far as to trace the descent of the shepherd
of Tekoa from the Edomite clan Zerah of Gen. xxxvi. 13, which eventually came
to be regarded as Judahite (Gen. xxxviii. 30). For the general thesis he refers
to E. Meyer, Die Israeliten u. ihre Nachbarstämme, p. 435 (ad fin. "Teqoa'").

[2] It may be that the use of Hadad as a proper name among the Edomites
(e.g. in 1 Ki. xi. 14) indicates that the god Hadad was worshipped by them as
he was by the Syrians. This would not, however, necessarily exclude the possibility of the Edomites worshipping Jehovah, for Hadad- (or Addu-) worship
existed also in Palestine before the rise of the cult of Jehovah (see Introd. p. 23).
Certainly in 2 Ki. iii. 12 an Edomite king finds no theological difficulties in the
way of seeking the help of a prophet of Jehovah in military operations within
Edomite territory. As 'Ashur' and 'Gad' are the names both of places and of
deities, so it is possible that to non-Israelites 'Edom', from whom the Edomites
were named, was a god: cf. Obed-edom = servant of Edom (the native of Gath,
2 Sam. vi. 10, 11). Cf. E.B. III. col. 3462.

[3] But not certainly. Of the four clauses in the indictment in v. 11, the first is

kept his wrath for ever: **12** but I will send a fire upon Teman,
and it shall devour the palaces of Bozrah.

his anger did tear perpetually: *i.e.* from generations before the writer's
time there had been hostility; *cf.* Ezek. xxxv. 5. Probably this culminated
in some act of spite or bitterness, when 'he did pursue his brother with the
sword'. But the Hebrew means 'he tore (transitive) his anger': not 'his
anger tore'. Without doubt the M.T. should be emended to agree with that
form which was probably read by the Peshiṭṭa and Vulgate,[1] 'his anger
he guarded (*i.e.* 'cherished') perpetually'. Grammar and poetic parallelism
both suggest this.

Taking this emendation, we see that the conduct of Edom was precisely
opposite to that predicated of Jehovah towards mankind in Ps. ciii. 9,
Jer. iii. 5.

Teman. A district of Edom, probably in the north. In this verse, however, 'Teman' is used almost as a synonym for the whole kingdom: so in
Hab. iii. 3, Obad. *vv.* 8, 9 and Jer. xlix. 20. It appears from Jer. xlix. 7
that Teman was celebrated for wisdom. 'Eliphaz the Temanite' figures
in Job. In Gen. xxxvi. 42 '*duke* Teman' is mentioned with 'duke Kenaz'.

Bozrah for a period may have been Edom's chief city, *if* Sela was
dismantled by Amaziah. As in this passage, so in Isa. xxxiv. 6, lxiii. 1, the
city of Bozrah is singled out to represent Edom. According to Jer. xlviii. 24,
there was another Bozrah in Moab. *Boṣrâh* = "fortified place" (from *bâṣar*,
'to cut off').

For a discussion upon the authenticity of the prophecy against Edom,
see the Additional Note on pp. 282, 283.

With regard to the fulfilment of this "oracle", it should be said that
already, at the close of the ninth century, or at the beginning of the eighth,
Edom had paid tribute to Adad-nirari III of Assyria.[2] It continued to

---

a construction with the infinitive: *lit.* 'on account of his pursuing'. The other
three verbs are, in accordance with Hebrew idiom, finite (*cf.* i. 9, G.-K. § 114 *r*).
In such cases it is the tense of the verb immediately following upon the infinitive
which, as it were, reflects itself upon the infinitive; so *e.g.* in Gen. xxxix. 18,
2 Ki. xviii. 32. Thus, strictly, we should translate 'Because he *was* (always)
pursuing his brother with the sword'. On the other hand, 'he was casting off
all pity' may be but a gloss: and the two *last* sentences seem to refer grammatically to definite actions in the past (*waw consec. impf.*, and *perf.*). Thus the
past may be the tense of the opening clause also, as in E.VV., 'he *did* cast off all
pity'—with allusion to a definite military action in the memory of the writer.

[1] יטר for יטרף. It is probable that the corruption of the Hebrew text existed
already in the MSS. known both to the Targum and LXX translators. The fact
seems to be that they each endeavoured to avoid the literal rendering of a text
which they felt to be awkward. The Targum rendering has 'killing, he killed his
anger for ever', which, though it makes no intelligible sense in the context,
appears to be intended to represent the M.T., 'he tore his anger'.

[2] *C.O.T.* (*W.*), I. p. 180.

13 Thus saith the LORD: For three transgressions of the
children of Ammon, yea, for four, I will not turn away the

be subject to Assyria as long as that empire lasted. By the time Mal. i. 3, 4
was written, the eastern range of mountains (though not necessarily the
inhabitants) of Edom was a 'desolation'. Edom was conquered by the
Nabataean Arabs[1] in the 4th cent. B.C. Probably, though not certainly, it
was the ancient Edomite Sela[2] that, under the name of *Petra*, became the
capital of the powerful state, whose jurisdiction during the reign of Aretas IV
extended to Damascus itself (2 Cor. xi. 32). In the reign of Trajan, however,
the Nabataean kingdom became absorbed into the Roman Empire as
Arabia Petraea.[3]

(e) I. 13–15. *Judgment upon Ammon*

The Ammonite territory lay on the farther side of the Jordan, to the
east of the tribe of Reuben, and separated from Moab on the south by the
river Arnon. The two nations are stated in Gen. xix. 30–38 ('J') to have
been descended from Lot, who according to Gen. xi. 27, 31 ('P') was the
son of Haran, Abraham's brother. These passages reflect a known fact—
that the Ammonites and Moabites (like the Aramaeans) were allied to the
Israelites in ancestry. It is not impossible, however, that 'the children of
Lot' date back to a period anterior to the time of a nephew of Abraham.
The O.T. itself seems to give one or two hints of this.[4]

In the period of the Judges, an attack by the Ammonites upon the Israelites was defeated under the leadership of Jephthah (Judg. xi. 4, 5).

---

[1] *Cf.* Diodorus XIX. 94–100.

[2] *Sela'*. The name occurs always with the definite article (*lit.* 'the Rock');
Judg. i. 36, 2 Ki. xiv. 7, Isa. xvi. 1, xlii. 11. The LXX of the two latter passages
renders πέτρα (edn Swete, without capital letter), though in the two former,
ἡ πέτρα.

[3] A description of the very famous Petra may be found in Lagrange, *Revue
Biblique*, 1897, pp. 208 ff., or in *H.D.B.* art. "Sela". For two inscriptions of
the 1st cent. A.D. found in this city, as well as specimens of others of the same
kingdom, see Euting's *Nabatäische Inschriften*, or G. A. Cooke, *N.S.I.* pp.
214–246. The region for centuries has been a desert rocky waste, inhabited by
only a few nomad Arabs. In contrast, its extraordinarily well-preserved rock-
hewn temples, altar, tombs and theatre are all the more impressive as tokens
of its former religion and civilisation.

[4] (1) In 'P's' genealogical list in Gen. xxxvi. 20, 22, 29 (= 1 Chron. i. 38, 39),
Lôṭān (? = *Lôṭ* of the 'J' narrative) is a tribe of the *aboriginal Horites* of mount
Seir, whom Esau and his clan partially dispossessed. (2) In Numb. xxiv. 17 ('J')
'sons of *tumult*', mentioned in connection with the names Moab and Edom, should
probably be rendered 'sons of *Sheth*', in accordance with the text of the LXX,
etc., and indeed with the parallelism of the Hebrew poem itself (see R.V. marg.).
If so, it is tempting to identify the tribe ancestor Sheth with the S[h]eth who
is represented in Gen. iv. 25, v. 3–8 as a son of Adam and Eve. In any case, the
Ammonites or children of Sheth may perhaps be the *Sutu*, a Bedouin tribe
mentioned along with the Habiru (or Hebrews) in the Tell el-Amarna correspondence, *C.A.H.* I. pp. 234, 235; II. p. 369.

punishment thereof; because they have ripped up the women
with child of Gilead, that they might enlarge their border:
14 but I will kindle a fire in the wall of Rabbah, and it shall
devour the palaces thereof, with shouting in the day of

According to the ancient source preserved in 1 Sam. xi. 1–11 (*cf.* also xii. 12),
it was the oppression of king Nahash of Ammon that gave Saul the farmer
the occasion to take the lead of his countrymen as the first king of Israel.
David with provocation, and after a desire for friendship, fought the
Ammonites (whose king was now Hanun, the son of Nahash), using extreme
severity at the fall of their capital (2 Sam. x. 2, 8, xii. 31[1]). This did not
prevent another son of Nahash being loyal to David during Absalom's
rebellion (2 Sam. xvii. 27). That, but a few years before Amos' oracle,
Uzziah, king of Judah, received tribute from Ammon, is probably quite
accurate history, though our source of information dates from many
centuries after Uzziah's time, 2 Chr. xxvi. 8. It is said also in xxvii. 5 that
Uzziah exacted tribute. These references serve only to shew how slight,
generally, was the hold over Ammon after Solomon's death.

Once only (*viz.* in Jephthah's speech, Judg. xi. 24), the national god of
the Ammonites is named as Chemosh. Elsewhere he is Milcom (1 Ki. xi. 5),
or *Malcam* (Zeph. i. 5, 2 Sam. xii. 30, R.V. marg., E.VV. 'their king').
It is interesting to note that, while in the M.T. of Am. i. 15 the Hebrew
malkam is rightly translated by E.VV. 'their king', the Peshiṭta and Vulgate
translators thought that they saw an appropriate reference to the Ammonite
god 'Malcam', and they rendered it thus in their text.

13. they have ripped up. In the course of the war, the Ammonites had
indulged in a particularly gruesome, though hardly uncommon, eastern
practice: *cf.* Hazael's action in 2 Ki. viii. 12, and the behaviour of Menahem
of Israel in civil war, 2 Ki. xv. 16.

Gilead. See on *v.* 3. The Israelite territory of Gilead lay to the north
and west of Ammon, and was the usual invading ground of the enemy.
V. 3 states that (a century previous to Amos) Gilead had suffered also from
Syria. Possibly Ammon and Syria were allied together in a campaign, as
they had been in David's time (2 Sam. x. 6–19). If so, the action alluded to
in the preceding note was the work of both nations together.

enlarge their border. Add 'merely'. It was a war of aggression, not
of defence: and therefore the guilt was aggravated.

14. in the wall. 'In' is correct: 'within its enclosure'. See note on i. 7.

Rabbah. The chief city, and in fact the only city of Ammon mentioned
in O.T. (2 Sam. xi. 1, xii. 27, 29, Ezek. xxi. 20). From the time of Ptolemy
Philadelphus to the 3rd cent. A.D. it was called *Philadelphia.* Its modern
name is *Amman.* It is the capital of Transjordania.

with shouting in the day of battle. Cf. on ii. 2, 'trumpet'.

---

[1] *If* the M.T. is to be trusted; but *cf.* note above on 'threshed Gilead' (p. 119).

battle, with a tempest in the day of the whirlwind: **15** and their king shall go into captivity, he and his princes together, saith the LORD.

with a tempest in the day of the whirlwind. (1) Some scholars see here a reference to a 'day' of, as it is supposed, Jehovah's epiphany.[1] For the tempest of Jehovah, see Jer. xxiii. 19, Nah. i. 3, and *cf.* Hos. xiii. 15 and perhaps *v.* 2 of the present chapter. In Ps. lxxxiii. 15 (in Heb. 16) God's judgment is in 'tempest' (*sa'ar*) and 'storm' (*sûphâh*), the same Hebrew terms as occur here. Sellin maintains that the expression in Amos "has nothing to do with the Assyrians". (2) On the other hand, it is easy to attach a significance to the word 'day' which was not intended by the O.T. writer. In the clause here the name of Jehovah does not occur:—it is *'the* day' (not *'my* day') 'of whirlwind'. The expression would seem to be accounted for sufficiently if taken as furnishing "a figurative description of the onslaught of the foe: it will level all before it, like a destructive hurricane" (Driver, *ad loc.*). In Isa. v. 28, Prov. i. 27 *sûphâh* is again used in metaphor, and in Isa. xxviii. 2 the Assyrian attack is likened to a 'storm' (*sa'ar*).

The prediction of Amos received its general fulfilment when Ammon became tributary to Tiglath-pileser III, continuing in subjection to Assyria. The nation existed in the time of the Maccabees (1 Macc. v. 30–43); but probably by the 3rd cent. A.D. it had, like Edom and Moab, disappeared.

(f) **II. 1–3.** *Judgment upon Moab*

This brother-nation to Ammon occupied the fruitful 'tableland' (Deut. iii. 10, R.V. marg., in Hebrew *hammîshôr*) due east of the Dead Sea. Already at the time of the Exodus the Moabites seem to have been a flourishing people; though king Balak is pictured as 'sore afraid of' Israel (Numb. xxii. 2–19). In the period of the Judges the neighbouring Israelites 'served Eglon king of Moab eighteen years', the Moabites holding Jericho (Judg. iii. 12–30). During David's outlaw life the king of Moab was friendly to him (1 Sam. xxii. 3, 4). According to Ruth iv. 17–22 David himself was partly of Moabite ancestry—and the whole narrative shews how natural in early times was migration between Palestine and Moab, and intermarriage between the two nations.[2] When, however, David became king of Israel he subjugated the Moabites, putting to death two-thirds of the prisoners taken (2 Sam. viii. 2). Like Ammon, Moab must have recovered

---

[1] *Cf.* Gressmann, *Eschatologie*, pp. 19–30. "Jehovah himself sets fire to the palaces with 'Hurrah' on the day of battle, with tempest in the day of sirocco" (p. 24); and *cf.* Introd. pp. 59, 60.

[2] The severe attitude towards Moab embodied in the legislation of Deut. xxiii. 3–6 (in Heb. 4–7) belongs to a later age. According to this, David, who was of the fourth generation from Ruth the Moabitess, could not, presumably, have entered 'the assembly of the LORD'!

II. 1 Thus saith the LORD: For three transgressions of Moab, yea, for four, I will not turn away the punishment thereof; because he burned the bones of the king of Edom into lime:

its freedom shortly subsequent to the Disruption, for, according to the Moabite Stone, Omri re-conquered Moab. Again it revolted at, or soon after, Ahab's death (2 Ki. iii. 5). To celebrate his victory in that campaign, Mesha the king erected the famous "Moabite Stone" in which he records as a fact that "Israel perished with an everlasting destruction" (l. 7).[1] Jeroboam II freed Israel from such inroads as are mentioned in 2 Ki. xiii. 20. Indeed, it is probable that a re-subjugation of Moab was one of that warrior's successes alluded to generally in 2 Ki. xiv. 25. In Jer. xlviii the destruction of Moab is declared to be imminent. (It is interesting to note that, in this passage and the Moabite Stone together, as many as between forty and fifty cities of Moab are enumerated.)

Of all the ancient monuments hitherto discovered which throw light upon the religion of the Semites, the Stele of Mesha (or the Moabite Stone) is of quite unique significance. No student of the O.T. can afford to be unfamiliar with its text.[2] The languages of Moab and of Israel are shewn therein to have been to all intents and purposes identical; the identity extending even to details (*e.g.* the *waw consecutive*). However, more interesting to the general student are the parallels in idiom, and the similarity of not a little of the religious phraseology. The religion of Moab was a non-ethical worship of Chemosh, or '*Ashtăr-Ch*ᵉ*môsh* (probably the deity designated 'the Baal of Peor' in Numb. xxv. 1–5). Sacrifices were offered on 'altars' with 'altar-hearths' (l. 12, *cf.* Ezek. xliii. 15, 16, Isa. xxix. 1, 2), at 'high places' (ll. 3, 27). Conquered enemies were 'devoted' to Moab's national god (l. 17). Chemosh might, on the one hand, be angry with his land (l. 5), or, on the contrary, he might 'save' the king from his enemies, 'making him to see (his desire) upon all that hated' him (ll. 4 and 7). The stele reflects that which was, and probably always *remained*, Moab's religion. Israel drew away from its neighbours under the spiritual influence of the prophets. In what is indeed a problem not without its difficulties, Christians may well believe that Israel more than, *e.g.*, Moab was inherently fitted for God's ultimate purpose of giving His greatest revelation to the world.

1. he burned the bones of the king of Edom. 'He', *i.e.* the nation, as in i. 11. Who the Edomite king was, and what were the circumstances, are unknown. It is tempting to conjecture that the verse relates to the events of 2 Ki. iii. 4–27. According to this passage an unnamed king of Edom, under Ahaziah of Israel and Jehoshaphat of Judah, was fighting

---

[1] How precisely the story of 2 Chron. xx. 1–30 is to be related to this period is not clear.

[2] A convenient form of text and translation is edited by H. F. B. Compston, S.P.C.K.

2 but I will send a fire upon Moab, and it shall devour the

Mesha, king of Moab. The latter, towards the close of the battle, seems to
have made a special onslaught upon the king of Edom (2 Ki. iii. 26 b,
'to break through unto'). Failing to achieve this, Mesha offered up his
own son to the national deity. Now, if, soon after the withdrawal of the
Israelites, or at a time later, the king of Moab ever captured the king of
Edom, or got hold of his corpse, he may have committed an outrage upon
the body of one who had been his foe in that fearful campaign. Such action
would be in keeping with the general character of Mesha as known from
his stele. However, the crime alluded to in this verse may have been connected with some unknown events much nearer to the Prophet's own time.

Note how, according to Amos, Israel's foe, Edom, shares with her in
the blessings of Jehovah's universal moral rule. "This is the first trace of
international law in history" (Kittel, *Rel.* p. 139).

into lime. The remains had been burnt to 'lime'. For the word, see
Deut. xxvii. 2, 4 (R.V. 'plaister') and Isa. xxxiii. 12. The act took place
either (1) before the body could be buried by the deceased's supporters,
or (2), more probably, at some time later, by ravaging the tomb of the
dead. Contrast the friendly act of burning a body in order to put it out of
the enemy's reach, followed by the burying of the bones (1 Sam. xxxi.
11–13). The Targum of our passage makes the gruesome addition '*and
plaistered* them in the lime (or as lime) on the house'. See vi. 10, note.
There is considerable evidence that to disturb the dead was regarded by
the ancient Semite as a particularly serious offence. It was felt generally
(though not *necessarily* by the prophet Amos) that such action deprived of
repose the spirit of the dead. *Cf.* the inscription on the tomb of Eshmunazar
king of Sidon in the 3rd cent. B.C.:[1] "I adjure every prince and every man
that they open not this resting-place...nor take away the coffin of my
resting-place, nor carry me from this resting-place (and lay me) on a second
resting-place!...For every prince and every man who shall open this
resting-place...may they have no resting-place with the Shades, nor be
buried in a grave". *Cf.* also a 13th cent. B.C. inscription:[2] "(Ippe)sba'al,
son of Aḥiram, king of Gebal, made this sarcophagus for Aḥiram his father,
as his resting-place for ever...". In Jer. viii. 1, 2 the exposure of buried
bodies is to be part of Jehovah's punishment of Judah. A general discussion
as to funeral rites, *etc.*, is to be found in Lagrange, *Religions sémitiques*,
ch. viii.

2. I will send. In this case, particularly appropriate is Amos' formula.
They have burnt, therefore *Jehovah* will burn. Note the poetic parallelism
in the verse. The measure is trimeter.

---

[1] *C.I.S.* I. 3. Deposited at the Louvre; a cast is in the British Museum.
Transl. by Cooke, *N.S.I.* p. 31.

[2] Referred to on p. 281. Text and French translation by Dussaud in *Syria*,
1924, pp. 135–7. In Gressmann, *Texte*, 1926, p. 440, *Ithoba'al* is read.

palaces of Kerioth; and Moab shall die with tumult, with shouting, and with the sound of the trumpet: **3** and I will cut off the judge from the midst thereof, and will slay all the princes thereof with him, saith the LORD.

4 Thus saith the LORD: For three transgressions of Judah, yea, for four, I will not turn away the punishment thereof;

Kerioth. Hebrew '*the* Kerioth', if the text is correct. Kerioth[1] is a city representing the whole state of Moab. Not improbably the town is to be identified with the capital Ar (Isa. xv. 1 a) and Kerioth of the Moabite Stone, l. 13, where there was a sanctuary of Chemosh. It may be also the Kir-hareseth of 2 Ki. iii. 25, a stronghold of the Moabites. The Kerioth to which Judas' family belonged would be in Judah (*Iscariot* signifies 'man of *Kerioth*', according to the usual etymology).

trumpet: *lit.* 'horn'. Shouting and trumpet-blowing by the attacking force are meant; *cf.* i. 14, Numb. x. 6, Josh. vi. 5. See on iii. 6.

3. the judge: *i.e.* the king. With 'the judge...and all the princes thereof' (or rather, 'his princes') *cf.* in i. 15, 'their king...he and his princes'. The 'judge' (Heb. *shôphēṭ*) of the nation, in addition to holding judicial authority in time of peace, was its leader in war. This is illustrated in the book of Judges. The same word, according to Livy, was employed by the Semites of Carthage, in which state there were always *two* "suffetes", corresponding to the Roman *consuls*. Inscriptions shew the use of the term in Marseilles in the 4th cent. B.C. and in other Carthaginian colonies (G. A. Cooke, *N.S.I.* pp. 113, 116).

Tiglath-pileser III records that tribute was paid to him by Sanib, king of Ammon and Salman of Moab...and Kosmalak of Edom.[2] After the captivity of Judah the only reference in Jewish literature certainly implying the existence of the Moabite state, appears to be Isa. xxv. 10;[3] and in that passage Moab's destruction is confidently anticipated.

(g) II. 4, 5. *Judgment upon Judah*

At the revolt of the Ten Tribes upon the death of Solomon, Judah remained loyal to the house of David, who not only had been a native of Bethlehem-Judah, but whose rule for the first seven years had been over Judah only (possibly the southern part of the tribe). When Jeroboam came to be king over the Ten Tribes, Judah with Benjamin formed the kingdom which is styled in this verse and elsewhere 'Judah'. During the first years, the two kingdoms were at war together continually (1 Ki. xiv. 30, xv. 7,

---

[1] Meinhold, who is followed by Nowack, reads, "I will send a fire against *Kir* of Moab, and it will devour its palaces" (see Isa. xv. 1 b).

[2] Schrader, *C.O.T.* (*W.*), I. p. 249.

[3] An oracle of the 4th cent. B.C. Dr Kennett would assign it to Maccabaean times, placing in Moabite territory the Baean of Judas' exploits (1 Macc. v. 4). See *Isaiah*, pp. 67, 68, 70, 74.

because they have rejected the law of the LORD, and have
not kept his statutes, and their lies have caused them to

16-21). Under the Omri dynasty North Israel was able to keep Judah in
somewhat of a condition of vassalage (1 Ki. xxii. 4, 2 Ki. iii. 7). Joash, the
third king of the dynasty of Jehu, dismantled Jerusalem (2 Ki. xiv. 13, 14).
From Solomon's death Israel and Judah were, and remained (while brother
kingdoms), entirely separate.

Religiously and morally there probably was not very much to choose
between the two. Nevertheless, upon the whole, Judah was the better, notwithstanding the fact that it did not have the benefit of the ministry of men
like Elijah. It lay just off great trade-routes, which (as in the case of the
Northern Kingdom) would have been the cause of a certain moral and religious corruption (Hos. vii. 8, 9). Its mountains fostered a hardier race—
of shepherds, not merchants. In Judah, Jehovah was not worshipped under
the form of a young bull, though the charge of idolatry generally is constantly being brought against it in the books of Kings and in Isaiah (as
well as in Am. ii. 4). A significant difference may have lain in the efforts
which, according to the writer of Kings, were made by one Judaean monarch
after another to effect some reform in worship. Asa's reign shews a trace
of this (1 Ki. xv. 11-14). Joash, under the influence of the priests, not only
(like Jehu in North Israel) drove out foreign Baal-worship, but instituted
repairs in Jehovah's temple (2 Ki. xi. 17-20, xii. 4-16). From 2 Ki. xiv. 6
it appears that Amaziah was sufficiently in advance of his age not to allow
the punishment of the *children* of murderers. (Contrast the pronouncement
of the oracle inquired of by David in 2 Sam. xxi. 1, 6, 14.) Uzziah (*or
Azariah*), Amos' own king, appears to have been a pious, as well as an
exceedingly able, monarch. He seems to have married into a priestly
family (2 Ki. xv. 33). Hölscher regards the prophet Amos as deriving no
little of his inspiration from a long and general movement in his own tribe
against the Canaanite cult. This critic carries the idea to the length of seeing
therein the explanation of the fact (as he supposes it to be) that Amos
"directed his prophecies not against Judah but against the Northern
Kingdom" (*Profeten*, p. 192). The verdict against Judah (in contrast to
North Israel) in Jer. iii. 11 is certainly not to be understood as applying
to the general course of the religious history of the two brother kingdoms.
Isaiah, almost contemporary with Amos, pictured the Judaeans as exhibiting the same selfishness and oppression, the same blind trust in ritual, as
did the Northerners.

4. **they have rejected.** The term is employed of God rejecting men,
e.g. in 2 Ki. xvii. 20. It occurs in the sense of 'despise' in Am. v. 21,
Job xix. 18. The passage is somewhat heavy, but it can be scanned as
trimeter.

   the law of the LORD. See Additional Note, p. 284.

   their lies. Hebrew *kᵉzābhîm*, probably means 'idols', symbols of Jehovah;
so LXX, which adds 'which they *made*'. There is no need to suppose the

err, after the which their fathers did walk: 5 but I will send
a fire upon Judah, and it shall devour the palaces of Jerusalem.

6 Thus saith the LORD: For three transgressions of Israel,
yea, for four, I will not turn away the punishment thereof;

reference to be to 'other gods'. The helpful existence of the idols is a
self-deception, or imagination, of the worshippers. Another interpretation
is to make the 'lying' apply, as it were, to the idols themselves, *i.e.* delusion-
gods, or imaginary gods.[1] A parallel to this would be Prov. xxiii. 3, '*de-
ceitful (i.e.* disappointing) meat' (R.V., in Hebrew 'bread of lies'). So the
word *sheqer* (E.VV. 'falsehood') is applied to a molten image in Jer. x. 14,
the expression 'vanities' is used of idols by the prophets, *e.g.* in Jer. viii. 19.
Cf. the use of the word '*âwen* mentioned in the note on Am. i. 5, p. 281.

their fathers. Their forefathers also had 'walked after', *i.e.* worshipped,
idolatrous images of Jehovah.

5. Jerusalem. See note on i. 2. Very similar to the closing words of this
verse is Jer. xvii. 27 *b.* On the authorship of the oracle against Judah, see
Additional Note, pp. 284–286.

Jerusalem, though reduced to straits by Sennacherib, king of Assyria
(*c.* 701 B.C.), did not fall until the time of Nebuchadnezzar of Babylon
(586 B.C.), and many have been its fortunes since that date. It has been
computed that when Allenby took Jerusalem in 1917 it was the twenty-
third[2] fall of the city!

(h) II. 6–16. *Judgment upon Israel*

Whether the section i. 3–ii. 16 was actually spoken in this form, or
assumed it only when it came to be written down, cannot be determined.
There would seem to be no serious objection to holding the former view.
In either case, however, it exhibits a very skilful progression of thought.
The Prophet at last brings the lesson home to the people themselves,
'Israel'. The term 'Israel' implies either (1) according to the present text
of the book of Amos, Northern Israel as distinct from Judah, or (2) if ii. 4, 5
are by a later hand (as is almost certainly the case), the whole Israelite
nation as, ideally, a unit; in this latter sense Amos in *v.* 10 refers to
the commencement in ancient time of Jehovah's relations with Israel.
Judging from the early chapters of Isaiah the items in Amos' indictment
would apply to the Southern Kingdom hardly less than to the Northern.

The Prophet uses the same introductory formula as with the non-Israelite
nations; and the 'transgressions' of the Hebrews (set out, as it were, as
counts in a charge) and the punishment for them, are stated with even

---

[1] So Marti, *Truggötter, Scheingötter.*
[2] See allusion by Abrahams in *Campaigns in Palestine*, p. 48, who shrewdly
adds, "I know not by what arithmetic".

because they have sold the righteous for silver, and the
needy for a pair of shoes: 7 that pant after the dust of the

greater detail. "Israel has sinned as the heathen, very differently, but not
less deeply. For, wild as are the horrors of war, selfishness and sensuality
may turn peace into a curse, and merit a yet more dreadful doom at the
hands of the Judge of all the earth" (Edghill). The list of Israelitish sins
given is doubtless not an exhaustive one—idolatry, *e.g.*, finds no place in it.
In this respect, however, the rest of the book adds little except in detail:
cf. Introd. p. 8. The sins (*vv.* 6–8) may be classified roughly as four in
number: (i) *injustice, v.* 6; (ii) *oppression, v.* 7 *a*; (iii) *immorality, vv.* 7 *b*, 8 *a*;
(iv) *luxury, v.* 8 *b*.

6. they have sold the righteous for silver. In a general sense 'they'
means the nation as a whole. Logically, however, the subject of the sentence is the judges (*cf.* v. 12), or, possibly, the creditors, as in the next
clause. 'The righteous' = the innocent party in a lawsuit, *cf.* v. 12, Deut.
xxv. 1, Isa. v. 23. The judges have been taking bribes from the guilty
parties; and thus, metaphorically speaking, they have 'sold' the righteous.
All the great prophets bring a charge against the public administration of
justice; see *e.g.* Isa. v. 23, Mic. iii. 9–11, Ezek. xxii. 29. The selling of justice
is expressly alluded to in Isa. i. 23, iii. 14. Deuteronomy, a document
also proceeding from the prophetic school, attaches special value to civic
justice, and enlarges upon the subject with considerable detail (*e.g.* Deut.
xvi. 18–20).

the needy for a pair of shoes. Notwithstanding the awkwardness, the
subject now to be understood would seem to be the 'creditors' (and not
the 'judges' of the preceding clause). A man 'sells' (in a literal sense) his
brother Israelite into slavery because he cannot discharge some trifling
debt (*cf.* 2 Ki. iv. 1, Lev. xxv. 39).

For *'ebhyôn*, a 'needy', and perhaps destitute, man as contrasted with
dal (of the next clause), a 'poor' or impoverished man, see J. Kennedy,
Hebrew Synonyms, pp. 83–87. *'Ebhyôn* occurs in v. 12, viii. 4, Ezek. xviii. 12;
dal in iv. 1, v. 11, viii. 6. For references to teaching upon justice in Egyptian
literature, see Additional Note, pp. 286, 287.

a pair of shoes: *i.e.* 'the value of a pair of sandals'; or, as we should
say, 'because he owed a few pence'. This, probably proverbial, illustration
occurs (with the change only of 'sell' into 'buy') also in viii. 6. The LXX
rendering of 1 Sam. xii. 3 seems to be a late echo of Amos' phrase. The
judge in that passage protests: 'Of whose hand have I taken a ransom,
even *a pair of shoes*? Answer against me and I will restore' (*cf.* R.V. marg.).
This can hardly be quoted as an *independent* illustration of the present
passage; for, though the LXX there has the support of Ecclus. xlvi. 19
(Greek and Hebrew), it is doubtful whether the LXX translators obtained
it from any Hebrew text of Samuel (see Driver, *Heb. Text of Sam.*).

7. that pant after the dust of the earth on the head of the poor:
i.e. apparently, 'long even for the dust...'. But for the Hebrew *shô'äphîm*

earth on the head of the poor, and turn aside the way of
the meek: and a man and his father will go unto the *same*

('pant after'), *shāphîm*, a less common word, almost certainly should be
read. In the famous passage, Gen. iii. 15, it is rendered 'bruise'. So translate here: 'Who *tread on to* the dust of the earth *the head* (not '*on* the head')
of the poor'. *Cf.* Vulgate, *Qui conterunt super pulverem terrae capita pau-
perum.* See also the LXX here and in v. 12. *Cf.* also v. 11 *a* (*bûs*), Heb. and
LXX. The verb 'pant' occurs again in M.T. of viii. 4 (E.VV. render 'swallow
up'), where also it should be emended to the word for 'bruise' or 'crush'.
Certainly the grammar and poetry[1] would be much easier with the omission
of the words translated in R.V. 'after the dust of the earth', which may be
a gloss both in the LXX and M.T. (so Wellh. and Nowack). They do not
occur in the text of viii. 4. Thus render simply 'who tread on the head of
the poor'.

Micah uses even stronger metaphors in Mic. iii. 1–3; *cf.* Lam. iii. 34–36
(though the word rendered 'to crush' is not the same, being *lᵉdhakkē*).

poor. See note on viii. 4.

turn aside the way of the meek. The rich pervert the 'way', *i.e.* the
'cause' or 'just judgment' of the poor. For 'meek,' see note on 'poor of
the land' in viii. 4. For the sense of the passage, *cf.* v. 12 *b*, 'that *turn aside*
the needy in the gate from their right'. Clearly the subject of the sentence
here is the *litigant*. Van Hoonacker renders the first portion of the verse,
'They crush the weak upon the dust of the earth at the head of the (public)
way'—(*au carrefour du chemin*, taking 'way' from the succeeding clause
and translating it literally)—'the poor they drive back'.

This passage supplies an illustration of the fact that Amos' moral teaching
was not only a practical message to his own age, but a permanent contribution to ethical truth. Jesus Christ Himself "sets the kingdom of God[2] and
His righteousness above all the riches of the world". In the Sermon on the
Mount He championed the cause of the 'poor in spirit'. Am. ii. 6–8 exem-
plifies the idea that (again in the words of Kittel, *Religion of Israel*, p. 224):
"There is nothing that belonged to Jesus which was not to be found in the
O.T. in some form, in perfection or in its beginnings". It is evidence of the
infinitely slow progress of the triumph of true religion in the world that
in the 20th cent. A.D. such ethical teaching of Amos should still have a
practical, and not rather only an historic, interest.

a man and his father will go unto the *same* maid. Both the complex
subject[3] and the choice of the verb[4] seem somewhat strange in the Hebrew.

---

[1] *Vv.* 6 and 7 *a* with the omission fall into three pairs of perfect trimeters.

[2] *I.e.* the personal and world-wide acknowledgment of the sway of a Deity
who is essentially righteous.

[3] 'Son and father', instead of 'father and son'.

[4] The appropriate word to express intercourse is not *hālakh* 'resort', but *bô'*.
It is interesting to note that Gressmann regards as a later gloss v. 7 *b*, and also
(with Nowack) 'beside every altar' and 'in the house of their God' in *v.* 8.

maid, to profane my holy name: 8 and they lay themselves
down beside every altar upon clothes taken in pledge, and

Translate not 'the same maid' but 'a maid', probably 'the sanctuary maid'.
The charge may be that of general debauchery (Hölscher, Kennett); or
more likely that of immorality *at the shrines*, a widespread feature of Semitic
religion. A good deal turns on whether *v.* 8, with its 'beside every altar',
is part of the same charge. Such practice may have been learnt by the
Israelites from the Canaanites.[1] It is indicative of the low condition of
Hebrew religion in that age. Hosea probably alludes to religious prostitution in Hos. iv. 14*b.* *V.* 7*b* is a good specimen of a quatrain of four dimeters.
    to profane my holy name. On 'holy', see note on iv. 2. Immorality
as a part of the worship of Jehovah 'profanes his *holy* name', in the
ethical sense of the word 'holy'. It is prohibited in Deut. xxiii. 17.
The temple devotee was designated *q^{e}dhēshāh*, '*holy* woman', in the sense
of 'consecrated' to Jehovah. The attempt to abolish the custom from Judah
was perhaps the most important of Josiah's reforms, 2 Ki. xxiii. 7. '*To*
profane', of course, refers to the result or consequence—'*so as to* profane'.
It is, however, represented as the *purpose*. The prophets not seldom so
speak in irony. 'To profane God's holy name' is a frequent expression in
Levit. (xviii. 21, xix. 12, xx. 3, xxii. 32, *etc.*) and in Ezekiel (*e.g.* xxxvi. 20).
In Rabbinical Judaism 'Profanation of the Name' (*Ḥillûl hashshēm*), and
the converse 'Sanctification[2] of the Name' (*Qiddûsh hashshēm*), became
technical terms in connection with an inspiring principle of ethics. 'Profanation of the Name' was nearly unforgiveable; Abrahams, *Pharisaism*,
I. p. 142 *ad fin.* *Cf. Sayings of the Fathers*, IV. 7: "Whoso profanes the
name of Heaven in secret, they punish him openly. The erring is as the
presumptuous, in profanation of the NAME". See *Jew. Encycl.* VII. pp. 484,
485 (Kohler), and Abrahams, *Glory of God*, ch. iii, especially p. 66. And
the first petition of the Christian Prayer is 'Hallowed be Thy name'.

8. lay themselves down...upon clothes. One would suppose that the
Hebrew causative voice (*yaṭṭû*) could hardly have borne the meaning
'lay *themselves* down'. Yet the Targum also translates so. Oort, Sellin
and others, omitting the preposition 'upon' (with a slight improvement
of the metre[3]), render 'and they *spread out* clothes'; but there seems to
be not sufficient evidence for this meaning of the verb. If *v.* 8 is to be
linked in sense closely to *v.* 7, it is clear that the sin is made worse in
that the 'clothes' (Hebrew 'garment', a general term), in which the man
resorts to this worship, are those held back from some poor debtor. According to Exod. xxii. 26, 27 (a law recognised, and probably written down[4],
by this period), the 'cloak' (Hebrew *simlāh*, an outer garment), taken during

---

[1] Its prevalence among the Semites of Cyprus in the 4th cent. B.C. is attested
by the inscription *C.I.S.* i. 86 B.

[2] *Cf.* Isa. xxix. 23, Ezek. xxxvi. 23 *a.*

[3] *Vv.* 8–12 are *qînāh*, very fairly.

[4] Though the Prophet's reference here does not prove this.

in the house of their God they drink the wine of such as
have been fined. **9** Yet destroyed I the Amorite before them,

the day as a pledge, should not be retained after nightfall: 'that is his
only covering...wherein shall he sleep?' For the 'cloak' used on a bed,
see Gen. ix. 23, Deut. xxii. 17. In Ezekiel's catalogue of vices (in Ezek.
xviii. 10–13) one item is 'hath not restored the pledge' (v. 12, cf. v. 7).

the house of their God. Any shrine, e.g. Beth-el and elsewhere (1 Ki.
xii. 31 a), perhaps even Jerusalem, where (so the people imagined) they
were rendering worship acceptable to Jehovah.

their God. He is their God, although they have false ideas of His Being,
His worship, His moral requirements. The R.V. rightly prints 'God' with
a capital letter notwithstanding the ambiguity of the Hebrew, which may
be 'house of their gods'. The A.V. 'their god' presumably means Baal.
Clearly, however, the Prophet is not thinking of the worship of deities other
than Jehovah. The Targum renders 'their errors', i.e. their idols, or, perhaps, false deities. Hosea, Isaiah and, especially, Jeremiah say much against
their countrymen's use of idols, but Amos only in v. 26 and viii. 14, where
see notes.[1]

they drink the wine of such as have been fined. Wine was part of
the sacrificial meal (1 Sam. ix. 12, 13, Deut. xiv. 26). In this case, however,
the text seems to mean that the wine had been bought with money that
had come to the worshipper through securing (presumably unjustly) some
fine from his neighbour. The worship itself was, therefore, an act of gross
hypocrisy. The simplest drink-offering was water, cf. 1 Sam. vii. 6, 2 Sam.
xxiii. 16. Probably the Hebrews learned to use wine for this purpose from
the Canaanites.[2] For drunkenness in Israel, see iv. 1. In v. 8 the measure
has changed to qinâh.

9–16. *God's past goodness, and the impending retribution.* The four charges
are ended. The Prophet now proceeds, in vv. 9–12, to point the contrast
between the people's conduct, and the favour which from the first had
been shewn to them by Jehovah. Finally, Amos will pronounce, in Jehovah's
name, the retribution which must fall (vv. 13–16). Similarly Jeremiah
enlarges upon Judah's long record of infidelity to Jehovah, notwithstanding
His goodness to them in the past (Jer. ii. 2, 3, 6, 7). The idea of Divine
kindness unappreciated leading to Divine punishment is exhibited also in
Isa. v. For other references by Amos to Israel's early history, see iii. 1,
v. 25, ix. 7. The prophet Hosea is much richer in allusions to the past.

9. Yet destroyed I the Amorite before them. Here (and in v. 10 also)
the pronoun is emphatic, '*Yet it was I who* destroyed'—I, whose laws of
human kindness you wilfully ignore; I, whom you mechanically (and foully)
worship. That it was Jehovah who dispossessed the inhabitants in Israel's

---

[1] For the contention that the Deity may have been a Canaanite divinity
Bethel, cf. iii. 14, note.

[2] *Cf.* Gray, *Sacrifice in O.T.* pp. 400, 401 and refs. there given.

whose height was like the height of the cedars, and he was
strong as the oaks; yet I destroyed his fruit from above,
and his roots from beneath. **10** Also I brought you up out of

favour would be accepted as a fact by Israel and its foes alike. To the
modern reader, however, such a proposition raises a serious problem.

the Amorite. The name as used by Amos here and in the next verse
clearly stands in a general way for the peoples displaced by the Hebrews.
Cf. Gen. xv. 16 ('E'), 'The iniquity of the *Amorite* is not yet full'. Amos,
though a Judaean, does not follow the practice of the 'J' literature (of
Judah) in which the inhabitants are, also loosely, styled Canaanites (Gen. x.
18, xii. 6, xxiv. 3, 37, l. 11). The fact is that the Amorites were of an origin
quite different from the Canaanites. According to Numb. xiii. 29 the former
inhabited the highlands, the latter the lowlands: 'The Hittite...and the
Amorite dwell in the mountains; the *Canaanite* dwelleth by the sea, and
along by the side of Jordan'. *Cf.* Deut. i. 19, 20. The victory over Sihon,
king of the Amorites (Numb. xxi. 21–35), is often alluded to in later history.
The *Amurru* were powerful in the district of Lebanon in the time of the
Amarna letters, taking part in an anti-Egyptian movement.[1]

like the height of the cedars. The giants of ancient Palestine are
referred to also in Numb. xiii. 33, Deut. ii. 20, 21.

strong as the oaks. *Cf.* Isa. ii. 13, Zech. xi. 2. The Hebrew here, *'allôn*,
is probably correctly translated 'oak'. The LXX has δρῦς, Vulgate *quercus*.

his fruit from above, and his roots from beneath. Or, as we should
say, "root and branch". In the inscription of Eshmunazar, to which
reference was made on p. 136, a passage occurs which shews that the
phrase used here by Amos was not confined to Hebrew idiom. "May he
have no *root beneath*, or *fruit above*, or any comeliness among the living
under the sun": *cf.* also Job xviii. 16, Isa. xxxvii. 31.

10. Also I brought you up. The abrupt change from the third to the
second *person* makes the appeal more direct. It would seem that chronologically the 'bringing up' must have taken place *before* the conquest referred
to in *v.* 9. Some take *v.* 10 as a later prose insertion, or regard *vv.* 9 and 10
as having been accidentally transposed by a scribe. However, though it
cannot be confidently affirmed that *Amos* has the fact in mind here, it may
be regarded as well-nigh certain that not *all* the Hebrew nation went into
and emerged from Egypt.[2]

---

[1] See *C.A.H.* II. pp. 302–309. Clay (*Amurru, the Home of the Northern Semites*)
advances a theory that the *Amurru* had an empire in Syria and Palestine as
far back as the 5th millennium B.C., and that largely they are the fountain of
Babylonian civilisation. Ezek. xvi. 3 and 45 suggest that there was known to be
a strong Amorite element in the Israelite stock.

[2] At the time of the Amarna Tablets some "Habiru" had *already* established themselves in Canaan. These probably entered not later than 1400 B.C.
(*cf.* Burney, *Judges*, p. cxii). In the words of Wardle (*Israel and Bab.* p. 44),
"We are to find in the Habiru of the Tell el-Amarna Letters one element

the land of Egypt, and led you forty years in the wilderness, to possess the land of the Amorite. **11** And I raised up of your sons for prophets, and of your young men for Nazirites.

and led you forty years in the wilderness: or, '*through* the wilderness'. For the thought of Jehovah caring for them all that time, *cf.* Deut. ii. 7, Jer. ii. 6.

Vv. 9 and 10 point to well-known traditions as to Israel's earlier history, such as had been, or before long would be, embodied in written documents ('J' and 'E'). It is noticeable how Amos here, like Jeremiah a century later, drops no hint of unpleasant relationships between Jehovah and the people in the wilderness such as are rather characteristic of the story in the document 'P', which probably proceeded from a period later than this.[1] The 'forty years' are referred to again in v. 25.

11, 12. The previous two verses enumerated temporal blessings: now the Prophet mentions spiritual ones. *Vv.* 11 and 12 are by some regarded as a later gloss, partly owing to the supposed discrepancy of outlook between *v.* 11 and vii. 14.

11. I raised up of your sons for prophets. Though other Semitic religions (Phoenician, Egyptian, Assyrian[2]) had prophets of a sort, prophetism in Israel, more particularly from the time of Amos himself, was to prove of unique spiritual and moral significance, not to that nation alone but to the world. Between Moses and Amos there had been men of the type of Samuel, Elijah and Micaiah ben-Imlah, and also the class known as the 'sons of the prophets'. Amos possibly includes them all as, at least in a measure, Jehovah's gift to the people.

This verse, and still more iii. 7, 8, shew that even if Amos disclaimed personal connection with the prophets, or most of the prophets, he allowed that they had a value. It would be easy, however, to exaggerate the significance of the reference. After all, Isaiah in one passage mentions 'the prophet' side by side with not only 'the judge' but 'the *diviner*' as the support of Judah, which support Jehovah (presumably as a punishment for the nation's sins) is about to remove (iii. 1–4).

of your young men for Nazirites. The spelling Nazirite is to be preferred to that of A.V. (Nazarite), being more in accordance with the

---

of the people whom we know as the Hebrews: [although] this must be qualified by a recognition of the truth that the Habiru embraced more than the Hebrews" (and see his convenient conspectus of Amarna references to the Habiru, p. 42). At a period later than this first immigration of certain Hebrews (probably of Aramaean stock, see note on 'Aram', i. 3, p. 118) into Palestine, others (generally known as the 'twelve tribes' of Israel, but in reality only some of the twelve) came up, after escaping from Egypt, and joined with their brethren who were already settled in the Holy Land. In course of time the whole became the Israelite nation.

[1] *Cf.* Exod. xvi. 2, Numb. xiv. 2, 27, 29, xvi. 11; and see Carpenter, *Hexateuch*, I. p. 215, 'murmur'.

[2] *Cf.* Introd. pp. 42 ff.

Is it not even thus, O ye children of Israel? saith the LORD.
12 But ye gave the Nazirites wine to drink; and commanded
the prophets, saying, Prophesy not. 13 Behold, I will press

Hebrew, *nāzîr*. The meaning of the verb-root is illustrated in the expression,
applied to erring Israel, '*consecrated* (R.V. marg. 'separated') *themselves* to
Baal' (Hos. ix. 10). It is possible that the Nazirites arose as a protest, or
witness, against Israelite assimilation to Canaanite life. Not seldom also
they appeared at, or just before, a war (for in Israel all wars were 'holy
wars'). In the latter circumstances come the first examples of Nazirites
on record, Samson and Samuel; *cf.* towards the end of Israel's national
history, 1 Macc. iii. 49 (at the advent of Antiochus' army); and perhaps
Josephus, *Jewish War*, II. xv. 1 (the vow of Berenice, sister of Agrippa).
Nazirites may well have been specially numerous during the Syrian conflict
immediately preceding the time of Amos. On Naziriteship, see further, the
Additional Note on pp. 287, 288.

Is it not even thus...saith the LORD. In their present position these
words seem to break into the argument about the 'prophets' and 'Nazirites'.
In any case a parenthesis is not in accordance with Hebrew idiom. The
clause would come with singular effectiveness at the close of the charges
and before the punishment, *i.e.* after *v.* 12. So most commentators.[1]

saith the LORD. Hebrew *nᵉ'ûm Yahweh*, 'it is an oracle of Jehovah'.
It is a somewhat more solemn expression than the usual formula, *'āmar
Yahweh*. It occurs some four hundred times in the Prophets, and in them
almost exclusively. This is the first instance of it in the book of Amos,
where in the M.T. it appears no fewer than twenty-one times; *cf. v.* 16,
iii. 10, 13, 15, *etc.* The LXX omits in vi. 8, 14.

12. But ye gave the Nazirites wine. The people endeavoured to frus-
trate the Nazirites' witness, causing them to go astray (Targum). Not
improbably the luxurious age in which Amos lived is referred to especially,
when the example of the Nazirités would be particularly unacceptable;
cf. iv. 1, vi. 4–6. Perhaps render here 'ye *have given*'.

and commanded the prophets, saying.... Rather, 'and upon the
prophets you have laid a charge, saying...'. The best commentary upon
these words is Amos' own treatment recorded in vii. 12: 'O thou seer, go,
flee thee away...prophesy not again any more at Beth-el'. And possibly
ch. vii comes before ch. ii chronologically. For the similar experience of
a true prophet before Amos' day, see 1 Ki. xxii. 8, 27. 'Thou shalt not
prophesy in the name of the LORD' was said to Jeremiah (Jer. xi. 21).

13–16. *The punishment.* The judgment is in more detail than is the case with
any of the other nations. Contrast the brief stereotyped phrase, 'I will
send a fire...and it shall devour'. Jehovah, against whom Israel had
sinned (*vv.* 6–8) in the face of His goodness and grace (*vv.* 9–11), will Himself

---

[1] For the Hebrew *'aph*, translated 'even', *i.e.* 'indeed', or 'really', *cf.* Gen.
xviii. 13, 23, Job xl. 8.

you in your place, as a cart presseth that is full of sheaves.

now administer the retribution due: and no one will escape. How, exactly, in the revelation of God, Amos came to this conviction, we do not know. One thing is obvious—that though Amos cared for Israel he cared for principles still more. Was the Prophet's conviction of an approaching annihilating judgment (*a*) "an inference from the moral and social conditions in Israel, a certainty resting on the ethical postulate that the righteous Ruler of the world could not suffer such sins to pass unpunished? or was it (*b*) the sensitiveness to approaching change, a presentiment that Yahweh was going to intervene in history...?"[1] In favour of (*a*) might be urged the fact that the Prophet speaks of other punishments besides that from Assyria—earthquake in viii. 8 (= ix. 5), plague in v. 17; and neither in the present passage nor in iii. 11, 12 is the allusion to a foreign foe unmistakable. (*b*) On the other hand, if Amos in Damascus, or elsewhere, had begun to hear rumours of a threatening Assyria, and especially if we may be allowed to date his mission to Israel within the reign of the great Tiglath-pileser III (see Introd. pp. 36–41), a natural explanation is to be found in the actual pressure of Assyria westward. Amos, from the first, saw the disaster ahead, and he interpreted it as Jehovah's way of dealing with Israel's sin. In the Prophet's mind the greatest (though not the *only*) judgment was Assyria; *cf.* v. 27, Introd. pp. 28–32, 102, 103.

13. Behold, I will press *you* in your place, as a cart presseth that is full of sheaves. Jehovah will crush the people down on the ground, "as anything would be, in the path of a laden wagon" (Horton; *cf.* also G. A. Smith). The illustration, however, would seem, even for O.T. times, to be too harsh to put into the mouth of God. The rendering of the A.V. (and R.V. marg.), 'I *am* pressed under you',[2] is not defensible, as the verb is a *causative* (transitive), and not a *passive*, voice. Further, the fact that the root in the original ('*ûq*) appears to be Aramaic, not Hebrew, makes the text at least doubtful; though it does not *prove* it to be corrupt, in view of the existence of other traces of 'Aramaisms' in the book (*cf.* Introd. p. 65, n. 3), indeed sporadically in classical Hebrew generally. (1) An easy emendation is to read, 'Behold, I *let* (the ground) *totter*[3] under you, as the cart *totters* which is full of sheaves'. In the Targum this verb is found in the second half of the clause: 'I will afflict (or press) you in your place, as the cart *totters*'. Punishment by *earthquake* is anticipated in viii. 8 (and *cf.* i. 1), and may well be in the Prophet's mind here. (2) With the same exegesis,

---

[1] Peake, *The People and the Book*, p. 266.
[2] Longfellow refers to this passage in *The Theologian's Tale*, IV:
"Being pressed down somewhat, like a cart with sheaves overladen".
[3] Wellhausen's conjecture, reading the root *pûq* in place of *sûq* twice. So essentially Hitzig. The translation of these scholars, 'under you' (*cf.* also A.V.), is simpler than 'in your place' (R.V.). On the other hand, it is somewhat bold to supply the words, 'the ground', 'I *let* this (as well as Wellhausen), retaining M.T., and translating, 'I will *press (the ground)* under you, as the waggon *presses* (the threshing-floor)'—*Kl. Propheten*, 1922.

14 And flight shall perish from the swift, and the strong

Sellin (retaining M.T. *'ûq*) claims[1] that a form of the Arabic root *'âqa* is
appropriate (*a*) to the crackling noise of the threshing-waggon passing
over straw, and also (*b*) (*cf.* Marti) to the ground making a creaking sound
as it bursts with the earthquake. (For Hebrew *'ăgâlâh*, of a threshing-
sledge or -waggon, *cf.* Isa. xxviii. 27.) After all, there would seem to be
no need to think with Nowack that "*vv.* 14–16 do not fit in any way on to
the threshing-waggon of *v.* 13".[2] The sense is sufficiently clear:—against this
visitation no one can stand; and even arms, which are a protection against
most sudden dangers, are now utterly useless.[3] Gressmann,[4] emending the
text as in (1), and also translating 'threshing-waggon' (declaring that "the
East has no harvest carts"), maintains—and it would seem rightly—that
the picture of a *battle* is standing before Amos' mind. If, however, the
verses following certainly refer to Divine retribution through an *enemy*, it
might be the easiest solution of a very perplexing problem to leave the
Hebrew text unaltered and to attempt, as Hoffmann, to translate it,
following the Arabic *'îq*, 'I will make you to groan[5] in your place as the
threshing-waggon makes (the threshing-floor) to groan'.

14. *Vv.* 14–16 seem to be intended to indicate not so much the nature of
the doom, as its universality and its *unescapableness*; *cf.* v. 18–20, ix. 1–4.
Variety and repetition in words alike emphasise the absolute impossibility
of escape. See on v. 2. In the paraphrase of Harper, "Neither the swift,
nor the strong, nor the hero [mighty], experienced in war, nor the armed
man, skilled in handling the bow, shall find refuge, or be able to assert his
strength, or rescue himself, or stand, when the great calamity shall come".

   flight shall perish. Better, as R.V. marg. and the Targum, 'refuge
(*i.e.* place of flight) shall fail'.

   the strong shall not strengthen his force. This phrase is rather un-

---

[1] Sellin is expanding with variations an explanation given by Marti. However, the verb-form *'ayyaqa*, quoted by the latter scholar, merely means to
'utter a cry' (*'îq*) such as is addressed to animals. It is unlikely that this de-
nominative verb would be known as early as Amos, even in Arabic. In any case,
it is not, as Sellin maintains, a general term covering 'crackling' and 'creaking'.
The simple verb *'âqa* signifies 'to hinder', and this meaning appears to be
reproduced in MS. A of the LXX (*κωλύω*).
   [2] Nowack places the passage ii. 9–13 between *vv.* 2 and 3 of ch. iii.
   [3] *Cf.* 1 Sam. xiv. 15.
   [4] *Alt. Proph.* 1921. In *Eschatologie*, p. 148, however, he took the reference
as being to an earthquake.
   [5] Hoffmann, *Z.A.W.* III. 1883, p. 100. In Ps. lxvi. 11 *mû'âqâh*, R.V. 'sore
burden', may signify 'a load under which one *groans*'. It would seem that in
Am. ii. 13 Aquila, who is followed by Jerome, attached some such meaning to
the root *'ûq* of the M.T. Jerome has *stridebo subter vos, sicut stridet plaustrum*
(Aquila, *τριζήσω...τρίζει*). Hence the Douai, 'I will *screak* under you as *a wain
screaketh* that is laden with hay'. As Hoffmann points out, Aquila has *τρίζει*
again in Ps. lv. 4 (3) where M.T. has the same root *'ûq* (R.V. 'because of the
oppression of the wicked').

shall not strengthen his force, neither shall the mighty deliver himself: **15** neither shall he stand that handleth the bow;
and he that is swift of foot shall not deliver *himself*: neither
shall he that rideth the horse deliver himself: **16** and he that
is courageous among the mighty shall flee away naked in
that day, saith the LORD.

intelligible, or at least ambiguous. Translate (as T. H. Robinson), 'The
strongest will not retain his strength'. The order of the words in the
Hebrew is significant.

the mighty. Hebrew *gibbôr*; *cf. v.* 16. This word, in the plural, is used
in the annals of David's reign (*e.g.* 2 Sam. xx. 7, xxiii. 8–22) as virtually
a technical term for 'picked warriors'. The historians apply it also to such
men as Gideon, Jephthah, Saul and David himself.

15. he that rideth the horse. The Hebrew army was in the main
infantry: 2 Ki. xiii. 7, xviii. 23, 24. Even horses will be of no avail when the
judgment falls.

16. courageous among the mighty: *lit.* '*the strong* (or, possibly, the
strong*est*) in his heart among the great warriors'. The Hebrew is a little
difficult. Two words may have fallen out. The LXX reads 'the strong *will
not find* his heart'. In the O.T. psychology the heart was considered to be
the seat both of intellect and of courage: *cf.* Pss. xxvii. 14, lxxvi. 6, 2 Sam.
xvii. 10.

naked: *i.e.* having flung away, in his attempted flight, arms and armour.
For the non-literal use of words translated 'naked', *cf.* Isa. lviii. 7, Ezek.
xviii. 7, St John xxi. 7, *etc.*

in that day. *Cf.* viii. 3, 9, 10 and Introd. p. 60, footnote 4.

saith the LORD. See on *v.* 11. The phrase was not employed by the
Prophet in his oracles against the other nations in chs. i and ii. Its use
here, therefore, seems to give a greater seriousness to the prophecy of
Israel's doom.

PART II, CHAPTERS III–VI

IMPASSIONED DISCOURSES OF AMOS: THE COMING JUDGMENT

With ch. iii begins the second main division of the book (chs. iii–vi).
In these chapters the subject already introduced in the oracle of ii. 6–16
is treated in more detail—the sins and the coming punishment of Israel.
Some commentators, noting the formula 'Hear ye this word' in iii. 1,
iv. 1[1], v. 1, hold that the section represents the substance of, at the least,
three exhortations by the Prophet.

III. Scholars who suppose that there was a definite audience to chs. i and ii
and that ch. iii (to *v.* 6 or to *v.* 8) is a continuation of the discourse, seek a
connection as follows. Amos' hearers object: (1) How *can* Jehovah allow

---

[1] But see note on iv. 1, p. 165.

III. 1 Hear this word that the LORD hath spoken against you, O children of Israel, against the whole family which I

His nation to be so completely ruined as the shepherd has predicted in the last verses of ch. ii? (2) That they can see no sign of danger. Objection (1) is answered by *v.* 2, 'your iniquities'; (2) by *vv.* 3–8: the signs of the approach of the foe are obvious to all but fools. But see, further, on *vv.* 3–8, p. 153 (3) where another interpretation is suggested.

Next to ch. v, the third chapter of Amos is perhaps the most important in the book.

III. 1–6. THE COMING DISASTER IS THE WORK OF JEHOVAH

1. Hear this word. The messages of all the prophets were *spoken* ones—to their contemporaries; *cf.* Deut. xviii. 18–22. The recording of them, so important to later generations in the providence of God, was, in a sense, secondary.

against. It is possible that the preposition should be translated simply 'concerning'.

you. After the oracles in chs. i and ii, 'you' may have the force of 'you, and not the surrounding peoples only'.

O children of Israel. The Ten Tribes (in the books of Kings, and elsewhere) were known by the title 'Israel', as distinct from the Southern Kingdom which was called 'Judah'. Most critics hold that this is the usage here. However, in these words, the Prophet, even if he is addressing the inhabitants of the Northern Kingdom alone (as is the case in *vv.* 9–15), may be merely styling them, what they actually were, 'descendants of Jacob'. The expression itself does not necessarily single out the population of North Israel. It would seem likely, indeed, that the words definitely cover *all* the 'children of Israel'.

against the whole family. Amos' discourses are in poetry; but it would appear reasonable not to expect poetic structure in the *formulae* introducing such discourses.[1] This is true of the present verse even more than of iv. 1 and v. 1. Most critics declare that the second half ('against the whole...land of Egypt'), or at least the words 'against the whole family', are a later Judaean addition to the original text of the book, as are the similar words 'against this family' in Mic. ii. 3. This may be so; the shortening of the text, however, will not, as is sometimes claimed, produce poetry but only much less cumbersome prose. Probably the greatest reason influencing those critics[2] who omit the words, is that they represent the Prophet as addressing *all* Israel rather than the Northern Tribes only.

However, even if the phrase is an interpolation so as more clearly

---

[1] For prose before a poem, *cf.* Jer. xiv. 1, xvi. 1.
[2] The *sole* reason suggested by, *e.g.*, Sellin.

brought up out of the land of Egypt, saying, **2** You only have
I known of all the families of the earth: therefore I will visit

to cover Judah,[1] there is some reason to believe that Amos did, as a matter
of fact, intend his words to include, and apply to, the Southern Kingdom;
cf. v. 13, 'testify against *the house of Jacob*'.[2] If so, Amos never set his hopes
upon Judah, but, rather, he consigned both kingdoms to a like immediate
destruction. Hostility between the two kingdoms was by no means continuous in their history. Unquestionably it was greatest after the Samaritan
schism.

family. For this use of the word *mishpâḥâh* in the sense of 'nation',
cf. Jer. viii. 3, Mic. ii. 3, besides the well-known passages Gen. xii. 3,
xxviii. 14; so in the next verse also.

which I brought up out of the land of Egypt. See on ii. 10.

2. You only: most emphatic. The Hebrew order is 'Only you'.

have I known. The verb 'know' means (1) 'to be acquainted with',
e.g. in Job xxiv. 16 *b*; (2) 'to have intimate relations with' (in various
senses). So probably here, as in Hos. xiii. 5, Deut. ix. 24 (of Jehovah and
Israel), and especially in Gen. xviii. 19 (of Jehovah and Abraham). Similarly, the complementary idea of 'knowing Jehovah' is of frequent occurrence; *cf.* Jer. xxii. 16, 1 Sam. ii. 12, Hos. v. 4. Jehovah's close relations
with Israel, referred to in the present verse, are explained more fully in
ii. 9–11 *a*. Duhm translates by a present tense according to the idiom
of this verb: 'do I know' (so E.VV. in v. 12). (3) Harper's view is that the
addition of the preposition 'of' (Hebrew 'from') gives the meaning 'to
distinguish from, to choose';[3] but the references furnished do not contain
this preposition (Gen. xviii. 19, Jer. i. 5, Isa. lviii. 3).[4] See, further, Excursus II, "Jehovah's relation to Israel", pp. 334 ff. Not impossibly the
Prophet is echoing, perhaps with a certain irony, a watchword of the
common people, 'Us only has Jehovah known'.

of all the families of the earth. 'Earth' here is in Hebrew *'ădhâmâh*.
(1) Perhaps render 'soil' or 'ground', *cf. v.* 5, so Isa. xxv. 21 *b*. (2) Almost the
only occurrence of the term in the sense of 'world' is in Gen. xii. 3 = xxviii.
14 *b*, with which the present passage may be connected.

therefore: *i.e.* "Because you did not take the moral advantage of My

---

[1] The passage Jer. xxxi. 31 might be an instance of a scribe adding 'and with
the house of Judah' lest the title 'Israel' should not be taken to cover the
Southern Kingdom.

[2] See, further, Introd. p. 13. Similarly also Hosea, though preaching in and
to North Israel ('Ephraim', v. 3, 9, 11, 12, 14, vii. 1, 8, 11), yet definitely em-
braces 'Judah', i. 7, 11, v. 12, vi. 11, viii. 14, xi. 12, xii. 2. Conversely, Micah,
primarily addressing the Southern Kingdom, speaks in iii. 8, 9 to 'Jacob' and
'Israel'.

[3] Gressmann also renders 'I have chosen' (*hab' ich erwählt*).

[4] The Hebrew term always employed for Jehovah's 'choosing' of Israel is
different (*bâḥar*). And even this word was capable of bearing a meaning almost
the equivalent of 'be good to': *cf.* Isa. xiv. 1 (parallel to 'have compassion on').

upon you all your iniquities. **3** Shall two walk together, except

intercourse" (G. A. Smith, p. 144). The usual exegesis, however, of the
verse is: 'You are indeed the people of my special care, but that fact does
not imply that I shall treat you more leniently than I do other nations
who transgress my moral laws (i. 3–ii. 3). The greater your privileges, so
much the more your responsibility'; or, in N.T. language, 'Unto whom
much is given, from him much shall be required'. With God there is no
respect either of persons or of *nations* (*cf.* ix. 7). Such a line of argument
and appeal would be more forcible if the saying had belonged to a period
a century or two later than Amos, when a prophet could build upon the
fact that the people had come to realise that their God Jehovah was in
reality the God of the Universe.

In any case, however, Amos' conclusion is opposite to that which would
naturally arise in the minds of the people. They would have drawn the
inference, 'Therefore *we can always count on* Jehovah'. Kittel says (*Religion*,
p. 135): "For the prophets the people was no longer the special possession
of Yahweh in a merely external and natural sense as the majority supposed, but in the sense of ethical obligation". Early Jewish interpretations of this verse are unsatisfying, *cf.* T.B. *'Aboda Zara* 4 *a*.

I will visit upon you all your iniquities: *i.e.* (as A.V.), 'I will
punish you for all your iniquities'. The Hebrew expression, 'to visit upon',
is a common one in the O.T. (*cf. v.* 14, Exod. xx. 5, Hos. i. 4). Jehovah
'sees', or 'visits', His people (*cf.* ix. 4, 8); and, finding them sinful, retribution follows. See Jer. v. 9, vi. 15, xlix. 8.

On the other hand, the Christian commentator hastens to add that in at
least ten passages in the O.T. Jehovah is said to 'visit' in order to *bless*,
e.g. in Gen. xxi. 1, l. 24, Exod. iv. 31, 1 Sam. ii. 21, Ruth i. 6, Jer. xv. 15
(parallel to 'remember'), Ps. cvi. 4 (*object*, 'with thy deliverance'). The
student of the O.T. should observe that, whilst often Jehovah is described
under the severe limitations of contemporary Semitic thought, yet lofty
and lovable conceptions of Him are to be found in abundance. It is interesting to note that in the N.T. the terms 'visit' and 'visitation' are used
only in a happy sense, *e.g.* St Lu. i. 68, 78, xix. 44, 1 Pet. ii. 12 (probably).

all your iniquities. There is no stress upon the word 'all'. **iniquities.**
The term, though very frequent in O.T., occurs here only in Amos.

3–8. There are three main lines of interpretation of these well-known
verses, of which (3) seems, upon the whole, to be the most probable.
(1) We may take the questions in *vv.* 3–6 and in *v.* 8 as rhetorical ones, all
obviously expecting the answer "No", and treat them as mere *illustrations*
of the principle that there is no *effect* without a *cause*. The climax is reached
in the eighth verse, which explains the presence of the Prophet with his
message. Jehovah is the cause, Amos the effect.[1] This outburst on the
part of Amos might be the result of listeners challenging his right to make

---

[1] *Cf.* G. A. Smith and Driver.

they have agreed?　4 Will a lion roar in the forest, when he

such utterances as are contained in ii. 6–16.　Against this *personal* interpretation must be set the argument that, until *v.* 7, there is nothing whatever
to suggest that the Preacher is talking about himself.　(2) We may give the
questions severally a definite parabolic meaning; making them *not* instances
of cause and effect but references to observable *facts*.　By this explanation
it is not a matter, as in (1), of the Prophet producing his "credentials"
(Mitchell); the argument concerns entirely the relationship of *Jehovah* and
the *nation* Israel.　*Vv.* 3–6 are connected closely with *v.* 2.　It is a fact that
the people are on the verge of being 'visited' by Jehovah.　Assyria is
'roaring' (*vv.* 4, 8); the nation is even now like a bird 'trapped' (*v.* 5).
Cf. what is said on p. 150 as to a supposed connection of thought between
ch. iii and chs. i and ii.　So Harper. (3) Holding *vv.* 2–6 to represent a sermon
complete in itself, we may take the questions, as in interpretation (1), as
rhetorical; without seeking a precise signification in each, except that they
illustrate the principle of cause and effect.　The climax comes not at *v.* 8,
but at *v.* 6 *b*, 'shall evil befall a city, and the LORD hath not done it?'　The
clue is given in *v.* 2.　The Prophet is not calling attention to a danger which
is unnoticed by his hearers; rather he is vigorously proving that the on-
coming disaster is the *direct work of Jehovah*—because of Israel's 'iniquities'.[1]　According to this interpretation *vv.* 7 and 8 are a fragment of a
separate discourse in which the shepherd explains why he has become a
preacher.　To the present writer, such treatment alone solves all the difficulties of this perplexing problem.　*Vv.* 3–6 are in *qînāh* measure[2] but not
vv. 7 and 8.　This exactly suits the variety of subject in the two poems:
(*a*) Israel's downfall at the hands of Jehovah (*vv.* 3–6); (*b*) the Prophet's
defence (*vv.* 7, 8).

3. Shall two walk together...? The Hebrew "tense" expresses custom:
'will (or 'do') two walk together?'　The familiar 'can' of A.V. (*cf. v.* 5,
R.V.), though quite legitimate if it had helped an interpretation of the
verse which was generally satisfactory, is by no means necessary.　**together.** There is no evidence of this word (*yaḥdāw*) having the signification
of 'in accord', as Ehrlich claims.　In the passage Gen. xxii. 8, cited by him,
'together' bears the usual meaning of 'side by side'.

have agreed: *i.e.* 'have made an appointment'.　But see, further, the
Additional Note, p. 288.　Probably the LXX preserves the original text,
'Will two walk together *unless they know one another?*'　This is a general
fact.　Some may interpret the 'two' as being Jehovah and Israel.

4. Will a lion roar...when he hath no prey? The verb perhaps denotes
here the roar of a lion when its prey is within reach (*cf.* Driver).　See

---

[1] *Cf.* Gressmann, *Ält. Proph.* edn 2, p. 339.

[2] This is clearly presented to the eye in Robinson's arrangement of the text.
For a brief discussion of Hebrew poetry, see Introd. to the present volume,
pp. 32 ff.　*Qînāh* measure is not confined in usage to solemn themes, but is more
appropriate to such.

hath no prey? will a young lion cry out of his den, if he have taken nothing? 5 Can a bird fall in a snare upon the earth, where no gin is *set* for him? shall a snare spring up from the ground, and have taken nothing at all? 6 Shall the trumpet

Isa. v. 29 *a*, Ps. civ. 21, Am. iii. 8. Probably the question is but an illustration of the principle of cause and effect. There is a cause either (1) why the Prophet speaks, or, most likely, (2) why the people are to be overthrown. Some see a definite reference to Assyria about to pounce upon Israel. Are the rulers so blind to the facts? The 'roaring of the lion' is a symbol of invasion in Isa. v. 29 *a* quoted above, and Jer. ii. 15; *cf.* Ps. xxii. 13 (in Heb. 14). See also Am. iii. 12. In i. 2 the verb probably refers to the 'roar' of *thunder*.

young lion. A mere synonym for 'lion', employed here to produce poetic parallelism.

cry out of his den: *lit.* 'utter his voice from his lair'. *Possibly* the allusion is to growling over his prey, as he is about to devour it. However, the word for 'out of his den' overweights the half-line, and may be a gloss.[1]

5. Can a bird fall in a snare upon the earth, where no gin is *set* for him? Both the English word 'gin' and the Hebrew which it represents (*môqēsh*) signify a 'trap', whereas the argument of the whole sentence, as it stands, would require the idea of 'bait'; so Driver, as also the Targum. However, the first half-line in the Hebrew ('Can a bird...the earth') seems to contain too many words; and, moreover, the syntax is loose. Preferable, therefore, is the LXX text, which does not contain in it the word translated 'snare' (Hebrew *paḥ*). Probably it was introduced into the Hebrew accidentally by a copyist, who caught sight of the same word standing towards the end of the verse ('shall *a snare* spring up?'); so Marti. *V.* 5 *a* should thus run, 'Can (or, will) a bird fall *upon the earth*, where no gin is (set) for him?'—'gin' meaning, as it should do, 'trap'.[2]—If the Prophet's question contains in itself a *parable*, the trapper or huntsman represents Assyria.

shall a snare spring up from the ground, and have taken nothing at all? The flying up of a part of the net-snare is a sure sign that a bird has been caught. This is an excellent illustration of cause and effect.—Or, if the sentence has a parabolic significance in itself, it carries the idea further than the first half of the verse. The trap (Assyria) has actually caught the bird. The punishment foreshadowed in *v.* 2 is not really improbable. It should be obvious to *all*. Jehovah is speaking clearly to the nation, and all, if they wished, could observe the signs of the times (*cf.* St Matt. xvi. 3). Those who follow such interpretation would find it easier if the late date of

---

[1] Löhr, Nowack, Duhm.

[2] Not a few scholars see in *môqēsh* (as distinct from *paḥ*) a reference, not to a 'trap', but to a kind of simple boomerang as shewn on Egyptian monuments (so Canney, Marti; *cf.* Sellin, Gressmann, 'throwing-club', *Wurfholz*).

be blown in a city, and the people not be afraid? shall evil
befall a city, and the LORD hath not done it? **7** Surely the

Amos were assumed (see Introd. pp. 35 ff.) than if the Prophet were
supposed to be prophesying while Assyria was inactive.

The word translated 'spring up' ('*ālāh*) occurs here only with this
meaning.—The A.V. 'Shall one *take up* a snare...', means 'Will anyone,
after setting a trap, take it away again before it has been successful in
catching something?' But Ps. cii. 25 (Heb.) is not sufficient support for this.

6. Shall the trumpet be blown...the people not be afraid? The
shôphār or 'horn' was, in the main, used in war (ii. 2) and on civic occasions
(1 Ki. i. 34, 39). For religious purposes the straight metal trumpet (Hebrew
hăşôşērāh) was employed, *cf.* 1 Chron. xiii. 8. In the present verse the
secular 'horn' is represented as being sounded within the city announcing
to all inhabitants danger from without (*cf.* Jer. vi. 1, Hos. v. 8). In *vv.* 4, 5
effects are stated as proceeding from causes. *Vv.* 6 and 8 illustrate the same
principle but in the converse form of *causes* producing *effects*. The alarm-
horn blows: normally, the people would tremble. The Prophet's questions
seem now to be of special force. Either (1) people are frightened only
when the horn sounds. Misfortune comes upon a state only if it is produced
by Jehovah, and in the same way Israel's downfall has no other reason than
the anger of God at His people's sin (Gressmann); or (2) it is inconceivable
that an alarm-trumpet be blown and the people go on as if nothing were
happening. Yet so it is in this case: I, the prophet, am unheeded (*cf.*
Harper). The next clause, *v.* 6 *b*, supports interpretation (1).

shall evil befall a city, and the LORD hath not done it? By 'evil',
not moral but physical evil is, of course, meant: and the context suggests
some *big* evil. So 1 Sam. vi. 9, 2 Ki. vi. 33, Jer. i. 14. See, further, the Add.
Note on p. 289. If the Assyrians come, it is because Jehovah has sent
them. You ought to realise this, and learn the lesson of it. *Cf.* also v. 27,
'Therefore will I cause you to go into captivity'.

III. 7, 8. AMOS JUSTIFIES HIS APPEARANCE AS A PREACHER

**7. Surely the Lord GOD will do nothing, but he revealeth his secret
unto his servants the prophets.** Naturally this does not mean that it
is found that in the course of the world's history every great event has
already been 'prophesied'.[1] It declares that "God always gives a warning"
(Kennett): "His prophets fly like His storm-birds ahead of the on-coming

---

[1] The idea so frequently met with in the early generations of Christianity;
see *e.g.* Tertullian, *Apology* (fragment within ch. xix), "For what could furnish
a more powerful defence of their testimony (*i.e.* of the Holy Scriptures) than
the daily checking off and fulfilment of some prophecy by the events of history, when
the disposal of kingdoms, the fall of cities, the destruction of nations, and the
state of the times correspond in every particular with what was foretold a
thousand years before?" (Bindley's transl. p. 62). The clause in italics runs in
the Latin of the MS. Fuldensis: *nisi dispunctio quotidiana saeculi totius.*

Lord GOD will do nothing, but he revealeth his secret unto
disaster" (Wellhausen). So exactly in Ezek. xxxiii. 1–7, where the prophet
is represented as a 'watchman' set by Jehovah (*v.* 7) in order to warn the
people of His coming 'sword'.

Surely. (1) The Hebrew *kî* cannot be translated 'surely' (as A.V. and
R.V. here), as this use is reserved for a solemn asseveration bordering upon
an oath. (2) 'But'[1] is even less possible—with the sense of: But God does
nothing in the way of sending calamity without always revealing its
significance ('His secret purpose') to His prophet, whose duty it is to warn
(*cf.* Harper). (3) The word means 'for'. Edghill suggests a connection
something like: Has not Jehovah done it? Yes, *for* He even tells it to
His prophets. Driver, who likewise feels that it must be 'for', supposes the
reason to be given in the verse *following.*[2] Some scholars[3] declare the verse
to be a gloss,[4] interrupting the argument which is supposed to begin at
v. 3 or *v.* 4, and to culminate at *v.* 8. (4) In view of the difficulties, and of
the diversity of treatment of the passage, the suggestion made above would
seem to deserve consideration, *viz.* that *vv.* 7 and 8 be taken as a separate
fragment—a part of a further discourse of Amos, even as *vv.* 9–15 represent
yet another sermon. Thus in *vv.* 7 and 8 the Prophet justifies his appearance
on the scene. To such a question as "Why did you not stay at home?"
the shepherd replies, in effect, "I could not help it. It is Jehovah Himself
who urges me on". The 'for' would then refer to something going before
which is not contained in the text. The abruptness of the transition from
vv. 2–6 to *v.* 7 is particularly apparent in the Hebrew. Almost perfect
qînāh measure sustained in the six verses changes to rather prosy trimeter
in *v.* 7. *V.* 8 consists of a quatrain of dimeters. See, further, the Additional
Note on p. 290.

the Lord GOD. This expression may be claimed to support, in a measure,
the authenticity of *v.* 7. It is the title of God most characteristic of the
Prophet Amos, and occurs in the very next verse.[5] See Excursus I. p. 333.

---

[1] The use of *kî* in the sense of 'but', after a negative sentence as, *e.g.*, in Deut.
xv. 7, 8 (*lit.* '*for* thou shalt surely open...'), is not really comparable (Ges.-K.
§ 163 *b*).

[2] "I give all these examples of events and occurrences in nature being due
regularly to their proper cause, *for* Jehovah does nothing without communicating His purpose to His prophets, *and when He does so the call to declare it is an
irresistible one* (*v.* 8)" (Driver, *Amos*[2], p. 162). Such a mode of argument, however,
which looks *forward*, does not seem very natural in Hebrew. (The italics are
n t Driver's.)

[3] *E.g.* Duhm, N wack, Hölscher.

[4] A gloss upon *v.* 8 *b*. It is true that *v.* 8 is more like prose than are the other
verses: and, moreover, it has been held that (in contrast to what Amos says in
v. 8 *b*) in vii. 14—the only other reference in this book to prophecy—Amos *disclaims* being a prophet. However, it is easier to style the words a later gloss
than to account for what was in the mind of the glossator in introducing them.

[5] On the other hand, a *glossator* might have been influenced by this occurrence
in *v.* 8.

his servants the prophets. 8 The lion hath roared, who will
not fear? the Lord GOD hath spoken, who can but prophesy?

his secret. So the Targum[1] translates the Hebrew *sôdh. Cf.* Prov. xi. 13
(= xx. 19), 'he that goeth about as a talebearer revealeth *secrets*'. Amos
states that Jehovah has opened to him His secret-*counsel, i.e.* the plans
and purposes (Mitchell) which He has made in the private council of
heaven. The 'secret' is that Assyria is coming. For a further note on the
idea of *sôdh*, see Additional Note, p. 290.

his servants the prophets. This phrase is common in a later generation
(see Jer. vii. 25, 2 Ki. xvii. 13), and it becomes stereotyped in post-Christian
literature, *e.g.* 2 (4) Esdras i. 32, Rev. x. 7; *cf.* also xi. 18, xxii. 6. Moses
was a *prophet* (Deut. xxxiv. 10), and he is styled Jehovah's *servant* in
Deut. xxxiv. 5, Num. xii. 6-8.[2] The LXX of Jonah i. 9 reads, 'I am
servant of Jehovah', in place of the M.T.[3]

8. The lion hath roared. Those who interpret each question separately
see a reference to the Assyrians here as in *v.* 4 where the Hebrew has the
same words. The Prophet seems to say: '*I* hear, why are others so deaf?'
(*cf.* Harper). **lion.** Certainly the 'lion' is not Jehovah, though such a
use of the term would not have struck Amos' hearers as strange. In i. 2
Jehovah's 'roar' is that of thunder, rather than that of a lion, but in
Hos. xi. 10 Jehovah is represented as a lion[4] calling his young to him. The
poetic parallelism of *v.* 8 *b* is not strictly "synonymous parallelism".
Considered as a mere illustration, *v.* 8 *a* introduces *v.* 8 *b*. Causes lead
irresistibly to effects: The Lord Jehovah has spoken to the shepherd's inner
ear: thus he has no alternative but to prophesy. So it was the LORD
'took' Amos (vii. 15; *cf.* note).

who can but prophesy? This idiomatic English brings out well the
sense of the Hebrew, which is *lit.* 'who will not prophesy?' In the words of
Gressmann, "When the lion roars, people become afraid, whether they will
or not. When Jehovah speaks, prophets must prophesy, however much
they may strive against it". Thus, Amos is not only warranted in announcing judgment upon Israel; he is compelled to do so (*cf.* van Hoonacker).
The point is, "Jehovah has spoken to me" (so in vii. 14, 15).[5] Jeremiah
(in Jer. xx. 7-9) recounts the same prophetic experience even more keenly

---

[1] The Targum uses the same Aramaic *râzâ* to render the Hebrew *sêther* in
Ps. xci. 1, and *lât* in 1 Sam. xviii. 22. In Gen. xlix. 6 it again represents
sôdh.

[2] Num. xii. 8, 'with him will I speak mouth to mouth', is to be compared with
the idea of the present verse, 'he revealeth his secret unto his servants'.

[3] *i.e. 'ebhedh Yahweh* for *'ibhrî.*

[4] Semitic deities were commonly depicted as riding upon lions; for illustrations, see Gressmann, *Bilder*, edn 1, Nos. 128, 130, 132; edn 2, Nos. 354-364.

[5] The Targum of the present passage gives a strange meaning to the *Niph'al*
voice *hinnâbhê'*, 'who will not *receive* (the) prophecy?'—apparently referring to
the people rather than to the prophet.

9 Publish ye in the palaces at Ashdod, and in the palaces

felt. Any attempt to give up 'speaking in Jehovah's name' was to Jeremiah simply impossible. *Cf.* Buttenwieser, *Prophets*, p. 9.

With Amos the Divine compulsion is characteristic of prophecy. Balaam, who is represented as a kind of prophet, could speak *only* the word which he believed Jehovah to have 'put in his mouth' (Numb. xxii. 38, xxiv. 12, 13). Ezekiel lived in restraint under Jehovah's 'hand' (see *e.g.* Ezek. iii. 1–3, 16–27). The allegory of the book of Jonah recounts the untoward experiences of a prophet who attempted to evade the Divine impulse. Amos is a true type of the Greatest Prophet, who always said 'I must' ($\delta\epsilon\hat{\iota}$); St Lu. ii. 49, iv. 43, xiii. 33, St John ix. 4, *etc.* *Cf.* also St Paul in 1 Cor. ix. 16.[1] For a different explanation of the passage, see the Additional Note on p. 291.

III. 9–15. THE TRANSGRESSIONS OF SAMARIA (*vv.* 9, 10) AND THE SENTENCE (*vv.* 11–15)

Probably these verses summarise another oracle entirely—addressed to the inhabitants of Samaria (*vv.* 9 and 12) or, possibly, to the pilgrims at Beth-el (*v.* 14). Though, however, the immediate audience was Northern Israelite, yet the Prophet's words were, apparently, intended to have a wider application, *viz.* to the 'house of Jacob' (*v.* 13). It would seem unlikely that in using the name of the patriarch 'Jacob' he would imply *only* North Israel. This exhortation may continue as far as iv. 3.

9. Publish ye in the palaces at Ashdod. The sense of this verse is: 'Let your neighbours and your enemies take a view of, and be witness to, your corruptions'. The word for 'in' ('*al*, 'at', 'over', or, as R.V. marg. 'upon') would more naturally be translated 'concerning', if only it harmonised with the meaning of the end of the verse. The prophet Isaiah (in Isa. i. 2) uses the same appeal to an audience beyond the borders of Jehovah's people, but he widens it considerably, 'Hear, *O heavens*, and give ear, *O earth*'.[2]

---

[1] Two well-known stanzas from F. W. H. Myers' *St Paul* come to mind:

> "Scarcely I catch the words of his revealing,
> Hardly I hear him, dimly understand,
> Only the Power that is within me pealing
> Lives on my lips and beckons to my hand.

> Whoso hath felt the Spirit of the Highest
> Cannot confound nor doubt him nor deny:
> Yea with one voice, O world, tho' thou deniest,
> Stand thou on that side, for on this am I."

[2] With the present verse should be compared Jer. i. 15, 16, a difficult passage, which Adam Welch (*Expositor*, Feb. 1921, pp. 140, 141) is inclined to interpret as referring to nations from the North being called to 'the entering in of the gates of Jerusalem' to be *witnesses* of the idolatry of the inhabitants. So the testimony

in the land of Egypt, and say, Assemble yourselves upon the
mountains of Samaria, and behold what great tumults are
therein, and what oppressions in the midst thereof. **10** For

palaces. See on i. 4. The same word is used for the dwellings of the
rich Israelites in *vv.* 10, 11, of the present chapter. The meaning of 'mansion', rather than 'fort', seems to be supported, not only by a comparison
of *vv.* 10 and 11 with *v.* 15, 'houses', but by the LXX rendering, 'fields',
i.e. 'estates'. Israel's aristocracy is to be judged by its equals.

Ashdod. See on i. 8. Many commentators prefer the LXX reading
'Assyria'. On the other hand, *if* Amos said 'Ashdod', it would not be very
strange that the Greek translators should substitute for a Philistine state
the great world empire, the peer of 'Egypt'.

Egypt. For high ethical teaching upon the subject of *oppression, cf.* the
references collected together on pp. 286, 287.

the mountains of Samaria. The famous heights of Ebal and Gerizim
(Deut. xi. 29, xxvii. 4, 12, Josh. viii. 30, 33) were but five miles from the
city of Samaria; but the phrase is strange. The LXX reading is generally
accepted, 'mountain (*singular*) of Samaria', *i.e.* Samaria itself. *Cf.* further
on in this address iv. 1, and also vi. 1.

Samaria. In Hebrew *Shômᵉrôn, i.e.* probably, 'Watch-tower'. Samaria
'at the head of a fat valley' commanded an extensive view (Isa. xxviii. 1).
This city had been the capital of the Northern Kingdom since the time of
Omri, who according to 1 Ki. xvi. 24 purchased the 'mountain (R.V. 'hill')
of Samaria' from one *Shemer*, and then 'built' (or 'fortified', R.V. marg.) it.
Previous capitals had been Shechem and Tirzah. Samaria fell before Sargon
in 722 B.C. The use familiar to us of the name Samaria for the *province*
arose at a later period than that of Amos. Several potsherds of the time
of Ahab and inscribed with Hebrew were found by the Harvard expedition
when excavating Samaria; see Reisner, Fisher, Lyon (1924).

tumults: *i.e.* (1) 'strife of rich and poor'; or more likely (2) 'arbitrary
deeds of might', *cf.* 2 Chron. xv. 5, E.VV. 'vexations' (the only other occurrence of this Hebrew term in the *plural*). Probably the word should be
translated by a *singular* as an abstract noun; see next note.

oppressions: of the poor by the wealthy, referred to in the next
verse as 'violence and robbery'. The word is not a *participle* as A.V.
'oppressed', but an *abstract* noun.[1] Hence, 'oppression' would seem to be
more accurate than 'oppressions' (concrete acts).

---

against each Israelite capital comes from non-Jehovah worshippers. Such com-
parisons by the prophets do not necessarily imply that they seriously thought that
the religion and morals of the heathen were superior to those of the Israelites.
A somewhat similar thought underlies our Saviour's reference to the Queen of
Sheba and to the Ninevites in St Lu. xi. 29–32.

[1] *'ǎshûqîm*, Job xxxv. 9 (M.T.), Eccl. iv. 1. In Hebrew such substantives are
not infrequently cast in the plural, *cf.* *'iwwᵉᶜîm* = 'perverseness' (Isa. xix. 14);
and especially is this so with words of this particular form, *e.g.* *bᵉḥûrîm* = 'youth'.
Ges.-K. § 124 *d*.

they know not to do right, saith the LORD, who store up
violence and robbery in their palaces. **11** Therefore thus saith
the Lord GOD: An adversary *there shall be,* even round about

To champion the cause of the 'oppressed'[1] is characteristic of Amos, to
an even greater degree than it is of the other Israelite prophets. Such
general teaching went back to Moses—and, indeed, seems to have inspired
the Babylonian Hammurabi himself, who affirms that the gods called him
'to cause justice to prevail in the land, to destroy the wicked and the evil,
to prevent the strong from oppressing the weak'.[2]

10. For they know not to do right: or *'And* they...'. 'They' refers to
the great ones, who inhabit the 'palaces'.

right: the Hebrew word $n^e kh\hat{o}h\bar{a}h$ is of not very common occurrence.
Lit. it means, as an *adjective,* 'straight', or as a *noun,* 'what is straight, in
front'. Hence, 'straightforwardness', 'honesty'; *cf.* Isa. xxvi. 10 ('in a
land of *rectitude*', Cheyne), xxx. 10 ('right', *i.e.* 'true, things').

violence and robbery: *i.e.* the *proceeds* of 'violence and robbery'—
abstract for concrete, result for process.[3] The identical sin, in the Southern
capital, is referred to by Isaiah (Isa. iii. 14), 'The spoil of the poor is in
your houses'. The word rendered 'robbery', *shôd,* occurs in v. 9 (and not
infrequently) in the sense of 'devastation' or 'ruin', rather than as denoting
a *vice.*

11. An adversary...even round about the land. Though the meaning
seems clear, the Hebrew, as also the English translation, is awkward. For
'even round about', $w^e s\hat{o}bh\bar{e}bh$, read a verb-form, $y^e s\hat{o}bh\bar{e}bh$, 'an adversary
will *surround* the land'.[4] The enemy will attack the whole country of
Israel, not merely the town Samaria. In ii. 13–16 it was not certain that

---

[1] A countryman, coming to a city like Samaria, could not be expected to
see in perfect balance the ethical problem which it presented. The student of
Amos sometimes feels that not a little of the shepherd's appeal is the result of
the outburst of a pent-up passion. This must be so, yet, in general, Amos'
estimate of the moral condition of Samaria is confirmed by his contemporary
the North Israelite Hosea (*e.g.* in Hos. vii. 1).

[2] Prologue to the *Code.* For an application to the present day of the ethical
message of Amos, *cf.* McFadyen, *A Cry for Justice,* 1912, and *Expositor* for Jan.
1921, pp. 1–18. Unfortunately, not a few of the public prayers used in connection
with the National Mission of 1916 held in England during the Great War seem
still to be not out of date, "Where we have hoped for wealth without regard for
Thy Word and Law—Where we have asked for nothing but our own success and
enjoyment—Where we have heard the deep sighing of the poor, and have failed
to still their sighing—*Forgive and heal and save*" (*A Litany of National Repentance and Hope,* p. 3, S.P.C.K.).

[3] In accordance with the same method of Hebrew thought, such a term as
'*āwôn,* in v. 2 translated 'iniquity', can be employed to express *punishment,*—
the result of iniquity, *e.g.* Gen. iv. 13, Isa. v. 18. See, further, Kennett, *In Our
Tongues,* pp. 25, 26; *Early Ideals of Righteousness,* pp. 6–8.

[4] So Peshiṭta Version.

the land: and he shall bring down thy strength from thee,
and thy palaces shall be spoiled. **12** Thus saith the LORD:
As the shepherd rescueth out of the mouth of the lion two

a foe was intended; here it is as good as certain. The word for 'adversary',
indeed, might be translated 'adver*sity*' (so Nowack); but the details given
later in the verse, and in *vv.* 14 and 15, do not easily fit in with anything
else but a personal foe. The fall which seems to be predicted here, and is
more vaguely alluded to in *v.* 2, came about as a result of (*a*) internal strife,
and (*b*) Tiglath-pileser III's attack upon the outlying districts of Israel in
733 B.C., followed by Sargon's capture of Samaria in 722 B.C. (see Introd.
pp. 102, 103).

he shall bring down. Hardly to be translated, as Harper, 'he shall
strip (from thee thy strength)'. Probably the passive voice should be read
(*hûradh*), 'shall *be* brought down'; *cf.* Ezek. xxxi. 18, Zech. x. 11.

thy strength. Better, 'thy *strongholds* will be brought down' (Nowack).
Cf. the use of the same word, *'ôz*, in Pss. xxviii. 7, 8, xlvi. 2 (E.VV. 1), lix.
10 (E.VV. 9), and Jer. xvi. 19.

and thy palaces: whose owners have been the worst—in Amos, apparently, the only—moral offenders. In *v.* 11 Israel is addressed directly, and
in the second person *singular*: *cf.* iv. 12.

spoiled: *i.e.* plundered by the 'adversary'.

12. By a simile the Prophet declares ironically that the number of the
voluptuous rich who will escape will be negligible.

As the[1] shepherd rescueth...two legs, or.... For other figures suggested
to the Prophet by his shepherd life, see Introd. p. 11. It was a recognised
principle (embodied in the law in Exod. xxii. 13) that when an animal was
slain by a wild beast the man in whose keeping it had been should preserve
(and if necessary produce) whatever remains he was able to save. It might
be, as here, '(but) two ankles (from the four) or a piece of an ear'. In 1 Sam.
xvii. 34, 35 the shepherd David is represented as, not infrequently,[2] slaying
a lion or a bear attacking sheep, in a region not so very far from the
'wilderness of Tekoa'.   **two legs.** Though by etymology the word for
'legs' should mean the whole leg including above the *bend* of the knee, the
few cases of occurrence of the term in the O.T. suggest rather the mere shank
by the foot, something not worth eating:[3] 'its head with its legs', Exod.

---

[1] The definite article is much more commonly employed in Hebrew than in
English. In the present passage the object is conceived of, either (1) as defined
by the context, *cf.* in v. 19, 'as if a man should flee from *the* lion, and *the* bear
should meet him; and should go into *the* house...*the* wall...*the* serpent...',
and *cf.* ix. 1; or (2) as representative of a *class*; *cf.* in English, '*the* Canaanite',
'*the* Russian'. By a simple extension of this latter idiom Amos writes in iv. 9,
'*the* blasting and *the* mildew...*the* palmerworm'; and see ix. 8.

[2] So the Hebrew tenses.

[3] Duff's Engl. transl. of Duhm, "two bits of bones", would thus represent
the meaning of Amos better than does the German of Duhm (*Schenkelchen*).

legs, or a piece of an ear; so shall the children of Israel be
rescued that sit in Samaria in the corner of a couch, and on
the silken cushions of a bed. **13** Hear ye, and testify against

xii. 9, Lev. iv. 11; 'its inside and its legs', Exod. xxix. 17, Lev. i. 9, 13,
viii. 21, ix. 14.

a piece of an ear. The word 'piece', *lit.* 'fragment', or 'severed piece',
occurs here only. A scrap of an ear would be worthless.

so...be rescued: or 'delivered'; better than A.V. 'taken out', which
is of ambiguous meaning. When the foe comes like a 'lion' against Samaria,
the proportion of inhabitants who escape will be insignificant. Clearly,
the point which Amos is making is that there will be practically no 'rescue'
at all (*cf.* ii. 14–16), not that he is looking forward to a 'remnant' being
preserved. The 'remnant' of v. 15, ix. 8 *b* is quite another thing. *Cf.* notes
ad loc. The *indestructibility* of Israel seems to be a later conception (Jer.
xxxi. 35–37, Ezek. xxxvii. 15–28). Nearly contemporary with Amos, Isaiah
in Judah may have cherished the hope of a happy remnant surviving
judgment in the Southern Kingdom (Isa. i. 9, 27, iv. 2–6, vi. 13; *cf.* 2 Ki.
xix. 30).[1]

sit: *i.e.*, probably, 'recline', as the Assyrian and the Greek custom;
cf. vi. 4, 'lie...stretch themselves'. Canney and some others translate, as
A.V., 'dwell'. The same ambiguity of the Hebrew word is manifested in
i. 5, E.VV. 'inhabitant', R.V. marg. 'him that sitteth'.

in the corner of a couch: or 'divan'. Driver[2] describes the modern
Eastern divan: "A cushioned seat about a yard in width extends along three
sides of the principal room, while a row of richly woven stuffed cushions
lines the wall behind, and forms a support for the back: the seat of honour
is the inmost corner of the divan, opposite the door". In Am. vi. 4 the same
two words for 'couch' and 'bed' occur, but they are translated by R.V.
in the reverse way, 'bed...couch'. There, the 'couch' has ivory inlaid in
its wooden framework.

on the silken cushions of a bed. This is probably not far from the
meaning of a most perplexing Hebrew text: see the Additional Note on
p. 291. Amazing to Amos are the luxury and self-indulgence of the wealthy.
Cf. Introd. p. 6.

13. Hear ye, and testify. Unless this verse introduces a fragment of
another discourse, which seems hardly probable, the 'Hear ye' looks back
to *v.* 9. The Philistine (or, *Assyrian*) and Egyptian grandees, having witnessed the *transgressions*, are now called upon to announce Jehovah's severe
sentence, the gist of which is contained in *vv.* 14 and 15.

---

[1] The famous expression, however, *Shear-yashub* (Isa. vii. 3), which without
any doubt belongs to the earliest period of his ministry, contains, like Amos'
words in the present passage, a threat, not a promise. The significance of the
Hebrew (to say nothing of the context) of x. 21–23 is '*only* a remnant will
(re)turn'. *Cf.* Kennett, *Isaiah*, pp. 10, 11; Kittel, *Rel.* p. 142.

[2] Summarising Van-Lennep, *Bible Lands, etc.* pp. 460, 461.

**the house of Jacob, saith the Lord GOD, the God of hosts,
14 For in the day that I shall visit the transgressions of Israel
upon him, I will also visit the altars of Beth-el, and the horns**

house of Jacob. The expression surely must include all the tribes:
cf. ix. 8.[1] It is interesting how Amos uses names with a tribal meaning;
so 'Joseph' in v. 6, 'Isaac' in vii. 16, as well as 'Israel' in *v.* 14.

the Lord GOD, the God of hosts: *lit.* 'the Lord Yahweh, the God
of the hosts'. This somewhat full title of God occurs here only. On the
use of the word 'hosts' in connection with God, see Excursus I. pp. 330–333.

14. For. Some commentators prefer to separate *v.* 14 from the preceding
verse by a comma only, and to translate '*that* in the day...'; so A.V. The
sense is thus rendered quite well, but the translation 'for' has the advantage
of leaving the Hebrew syntax *simple.*

visit...transgressions...upon him. *Cf. v.* 2, 'visit upon you...
iniquities'.

upon him: *singular* number. The conception of the nation as the unit
is very characteristic of Hebrew thought and idiom. *Cf.* Numb. xx. 18–21
(especially *v.* 19, 'let *me*...pass through on *my* feet').

I will also visit the altars. Not only the people (*vv.* 2 and 12) and
their houses (*v.* 11), but the very altars, dedicated to Jehovah, and in which
they trust, will come within the range of the 'visitation'. The Hebrew is
lit. 'visit *upon*', as in the preceding clause and in *v.* 2. Amos does not seem
to be attacking the worship because it was either schismatic or idolatrous.
See the Additional Note on p. 292, cf. p. 295. The text reads 'altars'[2] (*plural*).
Doubtless an altar existed at Beth-el from early times; another is said to
have been erected by Jeroboam I ('*the* altar', 1 Ki. xii. 32, 33, xiii. 1).
This latter altar is that especially mentioned in 2 Ki. xxiii. 15, 16 as
being demolished eventually by Josiah. It is to be noted that Amos draws
no distinction between them.[3]

Beth-el. See iv. 4, v. 5, 6, vii. 10, 13. Beth-el city lay just within the
territory of Ephraim, being but ten miles north of Jerusalem. Although,
in the context, Samaria is the particular city addressed, or apostrophised
(*vv.* 9, 12), *Beth-el* is now singled out, being the greatest shrine in North
Israel, and the centre of the worship of Jehovah by means of the Golden
Bull (1 Ki. xii. 29). It was a 'royal sanctuary' (vii. 13), even as Samaria
was the political capital. For a further note on 'Beth-el', see p. 293.

---

[1] Driver, in his commentary on ix. 8, while holding that the phrase from its
context refers to the Northern Kingdom alone, yet admits "at most, the
expressions (*house of Jacob, house of Israel*) may be meant in a general sense,
including implicitly Judah" (edn 2, p. 225—the italics are not his).

[2] The *singular*, 'altar', however, is conjectured by Nowack, Robinson, Köhler;
cf. the clause following. In this case the reference would be directly to the
notorious Jeroboam altar.

[3] For photographs of ancient Semitic altars and temples discovered in Palestine and elsewhere, see Gressmann, *Altorientalische Texte und Bilder*; *Bilder*,
Nos. 32–60; edn 2, Nos. 439–467.

of the altar shall be cut off, and fall to the ground. **15** And
I will smite the winter house with the summer house; and the
houses of ivory shall perish, and the great houses shall have
an end, saith the LORD.

the horns of the altar shall be cut off. The 'horns' were the most
sacred part of the apparatus of the altar (Benzinger, *Archäologie*, p. 379).
See, further, the Additional Note, p. 292.

shall be cut off: by, presumably, the victorious foe; *cf.* ix. 1–4. Or
is the allusion to an earthquake? *Cf.* ii. 13, viii. 3, 8.

and fall to the ground. If the thought is that of helplessness, an
illustration could be found in the fate of the image of Dagon in 1 Sam.
v. 3, 4, *etc.* It would be unwise to see a *religious* significance in Amos'
prediction of the fall of the Beth-el sanctuary. The ruin of the shrine is
prophesied, not because of evil done there but, so to speak, *incidentally*,
as it is in the Egyptian prophecies referred to in the Introd. p. 46.[1]

15. the winter house with the summer house. 'With' (Hebrew *'al, lit.*
'upon') = 'in addition to', 'as well as'.[2] (1) The context seems to suggest
two buildings as separate; so Driver, Sellin. The sense is, 'I will smite
winter houses and summer houses alike'. Support for this view is to be
gained, possibly, from the Bar-rekub inscription[3] belonging to the generation of Amos: "I took the house of my father, and made it better than the
house of any of the mighty kings...it was their winter house and it was a
summer house" (*bêth kaiṣâ* = the Heb. *bêth haqqayiṣ* of Amos). The writer
means that one house took the place of two. (Probably the reference is to
a mausoleum.) In Jer. xxxvi. 22 there is an allusion to a winter house of
king Jehoiakim. (2) From Judg. iii. 20 it is clear that within one and the
same building there might be two *departments*,[4] a 'summer parlour', or
better, 'cool upper storey', being suitable for summer use.[5] Some hold
that the words of Amos here mean no more than this.

houses of ivory: of course *decorated* with, not made of, ivory. Targum
well renders, 'inlaid with ivory' (*cf.* vi. 4). Ahab had such a 'house', 1 Ki.
xxii. 39, and *cf.* Ps. xlv. 8. Here, however, it is the nobles who indulge in
a like luxury.

great houses. The word translated 'great' means, when attached to

---

[1] *Cf.* "They will take the sanctuaries of the gods of Egypt for themselves to
Nineveh" (*Lamb Prophecy*); and, again (in a prediction of the happy future),
"The sacred objects carried away thither will again return to Egypt" (*Oracle of
the Potter*).

[2] *Cf.* references given in footnote 2, p. 297 *ad fin.*

[3] Discovered at Zenjirli in North Syria. In G. A. Cooke, *N.S.I.* pp. 180, 181,
the inscription is printed in the Aramaic, with an English translation.

[4] As also a house might be divided so as to comprise the mother's apartment;
cf. Ruth i. 8, Cant. iii. 4.

[5] See also Thomson's *Land and Book*, p. 309.

IV. 1 Hear this word, ye kine of Bashan, that are in the
mountain of Samaria, which oppress the poor, which crush

a *plural* noun, 'many' (*rabbîm*), so R.V. marg.: many houses besides[1]
those of the aristocracy will fall. But this thought seems to produce an
anti-climax. An ingenious emendation of Marti's[2] is to read *bâttê hobhnîm,*
'houses of *ebony*'.

Vv. 13–15 in their sequence are an effective climax. Although the people
of Amos' day were very enthusiastic about the worship of Jehovah at His
shrines, yet their real god was ill-gotten luxuries. Not even the ruin of the
altar of the Beth-el sanctuary (*v.* 14) would move them so much as the
destruction of their mansion property (already mentioned in *v.* 11 *b*).[3] In
v. 15 the Divine sentence closes with an imposing enumeration, 'winter
house, summer house, houses of ivory, houses of ebony' (if this be the
reading).

IV. 1–3. KINE OF BASHAN: SAMARIA'S WOMEN

Notwithstanding the formula *Hear this word* (which may, after all, be
but editorial), *vv.* 1–3 are, not impossibly, part of a poetic discourse delivered
on the same occasion as iii. 9–15; *cf.* the reference to 'Samaria' here and in
iii. 9, 12. So also, in iii. 13 and viii. 4, 'Hear ye' introduces no fresh sermon.[4]
V. 1 (from 'ye kine') consists of three pairs of perfect dimeters.

1. ye kine of Bashan. Owing to the presence of several *masculine*
genders in this verse, some have interpreted this expression as referring
to men, perhaps the judges and nobility.[5] The Targum transla.es as
masculine gender throughout. It is more reasonable, however, to suppose
that *vv.* 1–3 are a *résumé* (however imperfectly preserved) of an exhortation
to the noble women; two other such are found in the O.T., *viz.* in Isa.
iii. 16–iv. 1 and xxxii. 9 *et seq.* These fat 'cows' graze, not in the rich
pastures east of Jordan (*cf.* Mic. vii. 14 and Deut. iii. 19 concerning the
'cattle' of the Eastern Tribes), but 'in the mountain of Samaria'. Nowhere
else in the O.T. are women called cows; the use of this illustration, to
describe the women's lazy and unthinking lives, may be attributed to Amos'
rural experience.

which oppress the poor: *cf.* ii. 6, iii. 9, and v. 12 *b.*

---

[1] So LXX ἕτεροι οἶκοι πολλοί. In vi. 11 the destruction of 'the little house'
as well as of 'the great house' is threatened.

[2] Followed by Nowack, Gressmann, McFadyen, Robinson and others.

[3] *Cf.* 2 (4) Esdr. i. 33, 35, 'Your house is desolate.... Your houses will I give
to a people that shall come'.

[4] It might be supposed that the book of *Micah* should be divided into
(*a*) i. 2–ii. 13, (*b*) iii. 1–v. 15, (*c*) vi. 1–vii. 17, if we were to follow the hint of
'*Hear*, ye peoples' (i. 2), '*Hear*, I pray you' (iii. 1), '*Hear* ye' (vi. 1). This, however, would prove false as regards the second division, which quite obviously
commences at iv. 1, 'But in the latter days'.

[5] Urging 'their lord' the king to join them in intemperance. For the use of
the term 'lord' in the sense of 'king', *cf.* 1 Ki. xii. 27.

the needy, which say unto their lords, Bring, and let us drink.
2 The Lord GOD hath sworn by his holiness, that, lo, the days

crush the needy: *cf.* ii. 7, v. 11 *a*.

which say unto their lords. Of the three terms[1] for 'husband' in
Hebrew this one, *'ādôn*, is of the least frequent occurrence: *cf.* Gen. xviii. 12
(*sing.*), Ps. xlv. 12 (Heb.), Judg. xix. 26 (*plur.* of rank). It reflects the status
of women in pre-Christian civilisation. The close of the verse shews that,
in whatever capacity these wives may have ministered to their husbands,
it was not for the uplift of their lords' personal character. *Cf.* the story of
Jezebel and Ahab in 1 Ki. xxi. 7.

Bring: *scil.* 'the bowls of wine'.

and let us drink. The Hebrew text 'bring *thou*, and let *us* drink' seems
to suggest that each woman urges her husband to drink with her. For
references to self-indulgence in wine,[2] *cf.* vi. 6 (in Zion and Samaria) and
ii. 8. The present verse illustrates the fact that the modern habit of intemperance amongst women may be a sign, not so much of civilisation as of a
revived paganism. *Cf.* Mic. ii. 11, Isa. v. 11, 12, xxviii. 7, 8 (with reference
to the Southern Kingdom), Isa. xxviii. 1 ('Samaria'). On the other hand,
it is obvious that, just as modern sermons may be directed against the moral
faults of but a small proportion of the community, so the denunciations of
the ancient prophets should not be interpreted as carefully composed historical statements upon the condition of the entire population. The present
passage is not evidence that *no* wealthy Samaritan women possessed self-
control.

2. hath sworn by his holiness. This is the only occurrence in Amos
of the noun *qôdhesh*. In the earliest use of the term, 'holiness' meant
separateness. It was therefore, from the Hebrew standpoint, the attribute
par excellence of God. Perhaps here (as in Isa. vi. 3, and in the use of the
adjective in Am. ii. 7) the idea is already passing into that of *moral* holiness,
i.e. separation from sin.

In Am. vi. 8 Jehovah is represented as swearing 'by *Himself*', and in
viii. 7 'by *the pride of Jacob*', each time "provoked by the spectacle of
some crying moral wrong" (Driver). For a further note on anthropomorphisms in Amos, see p. 294.

that. Render 'surely' (the formula introducing an oath); or leave
untranslated, as should be the case in *e.g.* Dan. vi. 13 ('*Daniel, which...*').

the days shall come: or, more simply, 'days are coming'. The expression recurs in viii. 11, ix. 13. It may be that Amos originated its prophetical use as a formula for introducing a calamity or threat. In Jeremiah
it occurs fifteen times (Jer. vii. 32, *etc.*), but in no other prophetic book
except Isa. xxxix. 6.[3] *Cf.* St Mk ii. 20 (ἐλεύσονται δὲ ἡμέραι).

---

[1] The commonest is 'man' (*'îsh*). *Ba'al* (*lit.* 'lord' or 'owner') occurs in Gen.
xx. 3, Deut. xxii. 22, *etc.*

[2] See, further, McFadyen, *Expositor*, Jan. 1921, pp. 3–5.

[3] The occurrences in 1 Sam. ii. 31, 2 Ki. xx. 17 are late.

shall come upon you, that they shall take you away with hooks, and your residue with fish hooks. **3** And ye shall go out at the breaches, every one straight before her; and ye shall cast *yourselves* into Harmon, saith the LORD.

they shall take you away. The Hebrew leaves the (singular) subject indefinite; *scil.* 'the enemy'.

and your residue. (1) The original word, *'aḥărîth*, seems to have almost the same meaning as *sheʾērîth*, translated 'remnant' in i. 8, v. 15, *i.e.* 'what is left of you all', when the enemy has made the attack. So in ix. 1 (R.V. 'the last of them'). (2) The A.V. renders 'posterity', as does R.V. in Dan. xi. 4. *Cf.* Targum here, 'your daughters'. (3) The context and the parallelism might suggest some part of the body—'your *posterior*' (so Duhm)—but there is no lexicographical support for such a translation. *Cf.* Marti, who (making certain changes in the text of *vv.* 2 and 3) renders: 'then they will lift *your noses* with hooks and *your posterior* with harpoons; you shall be swept out as *dung* and *mud* and be cast *down naked*'.

with fish hooks. The two words in this verse for 'hooks' mean originally 'thorns'. The metaphor for the women has passed from 'cows' to 'fish'; *cf.* also Hab. i. 14. The Hebrew mind adapts itself quickly to a change of metaphor (*cf.* Isa. xxviii. 18 *b*).

3. at the breaches: *i.e.* rents made in the city wall by the enemy.[1] *Cf.* on ix. 11.

straight before her: *i.e.*, apparently, not in file. Each will go forward through a 'breach'. In English we should prefer 'straight before *you*'. *Cf.* footnote 1, p. 183.

ye shall cast *yourselves*. The Hebrew (*causative*, or active, voice) cannot be so translated. The alteration of one vowel only would produce 'ye shall *be cast*'. So the ancient versions.

into Harmon. There is no place 'Harmon' known. The Targum renders 'And they shall carry you captive to beyond the mountains of Ḥûrmînî (*i.e. Armenia*, or a part of it). The Hebrew has the definite article, and some (*cf.* A.V.) have endeavoured to see in the expression a common noun—either (1) 'the palace' (*'armôn*), or (2) 'the *harem*' (*cf.* Arabic), of the invading king. Actually, the text must be corrupt.

In such a terrible denunciation as the above the *sternness* of Amos' language must not be thought to imply anything of the nature of satisfaction or pleasure on his part in pronouncing judgment. It is well said that

---

[1] In the *Admonitions of Ipuwer* there is a passage about the distress of rich women of Egypt, during an invasion: "A foreign tribe from abroad has come to Egypt....There are no Egyptians anywhere. Forsooth, gold and lapis lazuli, silver and malachite, carnelian and bronze, stone of Yebhet...are fastened on the necks of female slaves. Good things are in the land. (Yet) the mistresses of houses say: would that we had something to eat....Their limbs are in sad plight by reason of (their) rags..." (Gardiner, *Admonitions*, pp. 30, 31).

4 Come to Beth-el, and transgress; to Gilgal, *and* multiply

Amos is "an incarnate conscience". He is that—no less and no more.
Undoubtedly, however, the more perfect picture of God's attitude to man
is to be found reflected in the words of Hosea. See Introd. p. 25.

From iv. 4 to the end of ch. vi is a section which seems to be complete
in itself.[1] All of the oracles or exhortations within it "vehemently attack
the national worship and the sense of political security which it has en-
gendered" (G. A. Smith, p. 156). The separate oracles are (*a*) iv. 4–13,
(*b*) v. 1–17, (*c*) v. 18–27, (*d*) vi. 1–14.

The section iv. 4–vi. 14 provides a good illustration of the words of
W. R. Smith (*Prophets*[2], p. 125): "The prophecy of Amos appears one of
the best examples of pure Hebrew style...the simplicity of diction...is a
token...of perfect mastery over a language which, though unfit for the
expression of abstract ideas, is unsurpassed as a vehicle of impassioned
speech".

IV. 4–13. DISPLEASING WORSHIP AT THE SHRINES (*vv.* 4, 5)
JEHOVAH'S CHASTISEMENTS HAVE FAILED (*vv.* 6–13)

The outburst against the women of Samaria is ended. The Prophet now
addresses the throngs at a festival at *Beth-el*, or *Gilgal*. He maintains that,
whatever may be the zeal of the people in worship (*vv.* 4, 5), God is not
pleased. Indeed, for some time He has been shewing signs of regarding
His worshippers as sinners in His sight (*vv.* 6–12). The poem opens in
remarkably regular *trimeter*.

4. Come to Beth-el, and transgress. Irony is used by the prophet
Jeremiah in a connection exactly similar (Jer. vii. 21). The common verb,
pâsha', 'to transgress', is found here only in the Book, but the corresponding
noun occurs in chs. i and ii *passim*, iii. 14, v. 12. In the eyes of a righteous
and holy Deity the very 'coming' of the people to their religious service is
'transgression' or 'rebellion'. For 'Beth-el', see note on iii. 14, p. 293.

Gilgal. In Hebrew '*the* Gilgal', or circle (of stones). From Am. v. 5 as
well as Hos. iv. 15, ix. 15, xii. 11 it is apparent that this was an important
'high place' (*cf.* note on vii. 9, p. 308). National sacrifices were offered at
(probably the same) Gilgal in the time of Samuel (1 Sam. xi. 14, 15, xv. 21).
According to Josh. iv. 19, 20, v. 10, x. 15 a city bearing this name was the
Israelite base in the conquest of the land west of the Jordan. This site is
now known as *Tell Jiljûl*, which lies 4½ miles from that river and 1½ miles
from Jericho.

---

[1] Though it is usual to suppose that these three chapters represent sermons
directed against Northern Israel (*cf.* the place names in iv. 4, v. 5, vi. 13 note,
and the reference to 'the house of *Joseph*' in v. 6, 15, vi. 6), they embrace the
Southern Kingdom also ('Beer-sheba', v. 5; 'Zion', vi. 1; 'the excellency of
Jacob', vi. 8; 'house of Israel', v. 6 LXX, and vi. 14).

transgression; and bring your sacrifices every morning, *and*

and **multiply transgression:**[1] *lit.* 'and transgress greatly' (so *Oxf. Heb. Lex.* p. 915). The clause is in strict parallelism with the preceding. Sir G. A. Smith well translates:

> 'Come away to Beth-el and transgress,
> At Gilgal exaggerate your transgression!'

The Hebrew idiom does not signify that sanctuary worship increases the guilt of the people's daily life (though such a thought may not be alien to the Prophet's ideas); but that coming to the sanctuary is another—and a great—act of transgression. A discussion of the reason for Amos' attitude here is to be found in the note on p. 294. For a description of the length to which, among oriental peoples, a belief in the value of sacrifice can extend, see p. 347 *ad fin.* (Excursus IV).

your sacrifices. *Cf.* v. 25. 'Sacrifice' (Hebrew *zebhaḥ*) is a technical term for the *slaughter*[2] of an animal (or as here, for the animal when slaughtered) as an act of religion. In contrast with a burnt offering (v. 22) the beast, after ceremonial slaughter, and cooking at the sanctuary, was partaken of by the offerer and his family. The Deity was conceived of as sharing in the meal; for the blood had been poured out before Him, to disappear into the ground, and the fat of the intestines, which was burned upon the altar, went up in smoke (Ps. l. 13 *b*, Deut. xxxii. 38 *a*). The priest also, in certain circumstances, might lawfully receive a portion (*cf.* 1 Sam. ii. 13-17). The root idea of sacrifice[3] may have been either (*a*) that of a clan *meal*, "the central significance of the rite lying in the act of communion between God and man",[4] or (*b*) all species of sacrifices and offerings may originally have been but various forms of *gifts* to God.[5] In the use of sacrifice, sometimes the idea of *thanksgiving* is prominent; or at other times

---

[1] The English word 'multiply', though it is in accordance with the thought of the Prophet (*cf.* W. Robertson Smith in *Prophets*, edn 2, p. 139, "the multiplication of gifts and offerings is but multiplication of sin"), does not represent the force of the Hebrew construction *harbû liphshôa'*. In Ezra x. 13 the identical Hebrew expression is correctly rendered by R.V. 'we have *greatly transgressed*'; *cf.* 2 Chron. xxxvi. 14. In 2 Ki. xxi. 6 the meaning is 'he did *great* evil'. On the other hand, *quantity* more than *degree* seems to be suggested in Ps. lxxviii. 38, Exod. xxxvi. 5, and perhaps Isa. lv. 7.

[2] Instances of the use of the verb to 'sacrifice', *zābhaḥ* (R.V. 'kill'), of killing an animal for food, occur in 1 Sam. xxviii. 24, 2 Chron. xviii. 2, *etc.* In 1 Ki. xiii. 2, 2 Ki. xxiii. 20 it is employed of the slaughter of priests by king Josiah. The corresponding Greek word θύειν is applied in 1 Macc. vii. 19 to the 'slaying' of deserters, and in St John x. 10 to the act of a thief in 'killing' a sheep. From all these passages it is clear that the root idea of *zābhaḥ* is not *offering*, but *killing*.

[3] Perhaps this subject will always be obscure. "Everyone who reads the O.T. with attention is struck with the fact that the origin and *rationale* of sacrifice are nowhere fully explained" (W. R. Smith, *Semites*[2], p. 3).

[4] W. R. Smith, *Semites*[2], ch. viii. p. 240; see 1 Sam. xx. 6.

[5] See, *e.g.*, G. B. Gray, *Sacrifice in the O.T.* pp. 2, 32, 42, and the notes in the present volume on v. 22-25.

your tithes every three days; 5 and offer a sacrifice of thanksgiving of that which is leavened, and proclaim freewill

that of *placating* God, or of keeping Him in a favourable frame of mind.
It seems extremely doubtful, however, whether *expiation* occupied much
place in the primitive idea of sacrifice.[1] In Israelite religion piacular sacrifice does not seem to have become an important feature until the legislation
of 'P'. It is noteworthy in this connection that sacrifices and offerings were
always made of some *edible* substance. It is interesting to observe the
change in meaning which the word 'sacrifice' has undergone from the
original sense of 'ritual slaughtering', so that it has become possible to
frame such an expression in English as '*self*-sacrifice'.[2]

every morning. The Prophet continues his irony. There was no rule
requiring the people to offer sacrifice more frequently than three times, or
even only once, in the *year* (1 Sam. i. 3).

your tithes every three days. (1) Deut. xxvi. 12 speaks of 'the third
year, which is the year of tithing'. *Cf.* Deut. xiv. 28. Amos carries his
hyperbole to the extent of urging the people to bring their tithes each
'third *day*': so the Targum renders, and G. A. Smith, Harper, *etc.* (2) Wellhausen, in order to avoid this exaggeration, suggested, 'Bring your sacrifices
in the morning, *on the third day* your tithes', and he has been followed by
almost all the foreign commentators. According to this view, Amos is
alluding to a recognised custom at Beth-el or Gilgal of offering sacrifice on
the first day after arrival at the sanctuary, and tithes on the third day.
Outside the verse itself, however, there is no evidence for it.

5. offer a sacrifice of thanksgiving: *lit.* 'burn (or, *send-up-as-sweet-
smoke*) a praise offering'. The Babylonian hero of the Flood, describing
his sacrifice made on safely landing, says, "The gods smelled the savour.
The gods smelled the sweet savour, the gods gathered like flies about him
that offered up the sacrifice" (Gilgamesh Epic, ll. 160–162; *cf.* Gen. viii. 21 *a*).
The Hebrew *tôdhāh* bears, according to its context, the various meanings of
(1) *praise* (Josh. vii. 19), (2) *thanksgiving-song* (Ps. xxvi. 7, Jon. ii. 10 Heb.),
and (3), as here, *thank offering* (a subdivision of the *zebhaḥ*; *cf.* Pss. cvii. 22,
cxvi. 17). When the laws concerning the sanctuary rites came to be
written down in a developed form, *tôdhāh*, very naturally, became a species
of 'peace (or 'thank') offering' (Lev. vii. 12 *a*). See on v. 22 *b*.

of that which is leavened. By usage the term covered not only *yeast-
made bread* but also *honey* as substances easily liable to fermentation.
'Leaven' was forbidden not merely in the late "Priestly" Code (Lev. ii. 11,
vi. 17), but in the 'E' legislation of Exod. xxiii. 18. It seems probable,
however, that Amos here is not so much blaming people for ignoring a known
ritual law (he shews no interest in such matters elsewhere) as alluding to a

---

[1] With this compare the fact that the occurrence of the Hebrew word translated 'atone' (*kipper*, *lit.* 'cover') in connection with sacrifice is confined to
the late codes and Ezekiel.

[2] *Cf.* Kennett, *Sacrifice*, p. 32.

offerings and publish them: for this liketh you, O ye children of Israel, saith the Lord GOD. 6 And I also have given you cleanness of teeth in all your cities, and want of bread in all

"mistaken zeal" (possibly a survival of Baal-worship) in which the worshippers "thought to make their thanksgiving-offerings more acceptable".[1] **proclaim...publish.** "The irony...lies in the prophet's urging the people...to publish far and wide their voluntary gifts, an action which was directly contrary to the spirit of such gifts" (Harper). *Cf.* words, which also may be ironical, spoken by a greater Prophet in St Matt. vi. 2, xxiii. 5 *a*. It is possible that the second expression above, translated 'publish', is an incorrect reading. The Peshiṭta has 'and pay them'.

freewill offerings: Heb. *nⁿdhābhôth*. The same word is used with general application in Hos. xiv. 4 (Heb. 5), 'freely' R.V., *i.e.* 'voluntarily', and in Ps. cx. 3, 'Thy people will be all *ready to volunteer*'. In Exod. xxxv. 29 voluntary gifts are styled *nⁿdhābôth*. In 2 Chron. xxxv. 8 the term is applied to slain animals at the Passover, additional to the offering which was prescribed as *essential*. The term is, of course, quite distinct from *nⁿdhārîm*, '*vow*-offerings' (see, *e.g.*, Lev. vii. 16, Deut. xii. 6, 'your vows and your freewill offerings').

for this liketh you: or, more simply, 'for so you love (to do)'.

6–13. These verses recount that there has been a series of seven[2] Divine chastisements, but in vain: famine, drought, mildew, locusts, plague, battle and earthquake (*vv.* 6–11). Let Israel expect, therefore, a final one (*v.* 12). Before the rise of scientific knowledge, all natural phenomena were apt to be regarded as being the direct and immediate work of the Deity. Disasters were thought to indicate Divine displeasure; *cf.* 1 Sam. xii. 15, 2 Sam. xxi. 1. In such a manner here, the Prophet interprets events in the recent history of Israel. Upon the general problem raised, see notes on iii. 6 (p. 289) and v. 27 (p. 302). This much is permanent in the prophetic outlook: when calamity comes it will, as a matter of fact, always be right for man 'to look well to his ways' and *return to Him*—so that physical evil, howsoever it be caused, may issue in moral good.. After all, God is above *nature*.

6. Universal *famine* in Palestine.

And I also. *Cf.* again, *v.* 7 *init.* These words point a contrast: '*You* like to make all these offerings: *I*, on my side, have sent you famine (*v.* 6) and drought' (*vv.* 7, 8). *Vv.* 6 ff. are no misplaced addition.

cleanness of teeth. This expressive phrase for 'famine' occurs here only.

in all your places. *i.e.* either (1) 'towns' or 'villages', as *e.g.* Judg. ii. 5, parallel to 'cities' in the preceding clause; or (2) 'houses', as frequently in the O.T. (*e.g.* Judg. vii. 7). In either case, the affliction was widespread.

---

[1] Driver. See G. B. Gray, *Sacrifice*, pp. 26, 27, and W. R. Smith, *Semites*³, pp. 220, 221.

[2] Or, if the references to 'locusts' (*v.* 9) and 'battle' (*v.* 10) are interpolations, *five*.

your places: yet have ye not returned unto me, saith the
LORD. 7 And I also have withholden the rain from you, when
there were yet three months to the harvest: and I caused it
to rain upon one city, and caused it not to rain upon another

Van Hoonacker (*XII Prophètes*, p. 192) points out that these verses correct
the picture given in iii. 15 and vi. 4. On the other hand, if the date c. 741
for Amos be accepted, there would be time for these disasters to have fallen
since the prosperity immediately following upon Jeroboam's victories. The
reference in *vv.* 6–10 to famine, drought, locust-ruined crops[1] and battle
should be compared with the visions of vii. 1–9.

yet have ye not returned unto me, saith the LORD. Perhaps
translate as present: 'ye do not return...' So Duhm. This refrain
comes after the mention of five out of the seven plagues, and is very
effective.[2] Some scholars, *e.g.* Mitchell and McFadyen, see in it a sign that
Amos taught Jehovah's *love*: but this does not seem clear. Isaiah closes
similar strophes with 'For all this his anger is not turned away, but his
hand is stretched out still' (Isa. v. 25, ix. 12, 17, 21, x. 4).

returned. This use of the expression 'return' or 'turn' (= Hebrew
shûbh) in a moral sense is common in the prophets, and is, of course, the
ultimate source of its occurrence in the N.T. (*e.g.* in Acts iii. 19). *Teshûbhâh*,
in later Hebrew, is the equivalent of 'repentance'. On the expression
'saith the LORD', see ii. 11, note.

7, 8. Spasmodic *drought*. Chronologically the drought *preceded* the famine
described in *v.* 6, as it was the cause of it. Marti and Nowack regard most
of the passage after 'withholden the rain from you' as an explanatory gloss.
The similar description in viii. 11, 12 may well have led to such an insertion
here.[3] For a graphic account of a drought in the time of Jeremiah, see
Jer. xiv and xv.

7. yet three months to the harvest. The 'latter rain' was counted upon
to fall at the end of February, before the harvest of April–June.

I caused it to rain. For the remainder of the verse and throughout
v. 8, the tense changes to the *imperfect*, or its equivalent. Either (1) it
denotes repeated action, 'I kept causing...', *etc.*, or, more probably, (2) it
vividly portrays the deed in process of developing.[4]

---

[1] In iv. 9, however, the locusts devour *fruits and olives*; in vii. 1, 2 general
crops, probably *cereals* especially.

[2] For the use of the words, 'they have not returned', after the record of a
single Divine chastisement, see Isa. ix. 13, Jer. xv. 19, Hos. vii. 10.

[3] Is there not something to be said for omitting *vv.* 7 and 8 entirely, as Lohr?
Logically they mean the same as *v.* 6, to which, moreover, they come as an
anti-climax.

[4] *Cf.* in Isa. vi. 4, 'the house *began to* fill with smoke' (Kennett, *Tenses*, p. 10).
In neither passage is the reference to the future. And Weiser is right in maintaining (in *Z.A.W.* 1928, pp. 49 ff.), against Sellin, that the tenses of Amos
here cannot be interpreted as English futures.

city: one piece was rained upon, and the piece whereupon it rained not withered. **8** So two or three cities wandered unto one city to drink water, and were not satisfied: yet have ye not returned unto me, saith the LORD. **9** I have smitten you with blasting and mildew: the multitude of your gardens and your vineyards and your fig trees and your olive trees hath the palmerworm devoured: yet have ye not returned unto me, saith the LORD. **10** I have sent among you the pestilence

upon one city. Possibly there is no numerical force here and in the next verse in the term 'one'. The word can be used for 'a', or 'a certain', as *e.g.* in 1 Sam. i. 1, 2 Ki. iv. 1 (and see the list in Burney's *Kings*, p. 209).[1]

whereupon it rained not. Read, as LXX, 'whereupon *I* caused it not to rain'.

8. So two or three cities wandered unto...: *i.e.* the inhabitants of; *lit.* 'And as a consequence two—(yes) three—cities would go staggering to one city'. The verb is not to be translated 'wander', even in Gen. iv. 12, 14 (E.VV. 'vagabond'). See Pss. lix. 15, cvii. 27, Isa. xxiv. 20, and Lam. iv. 14 ('they *totter* as blind men in the streets'). The Targum expressively renders the word both here and at its occurrence in viii. 12, 'they will tire themselves'. On 'two or three', *cf.* note on i. 3, 'three..., yea, for four'.

9. *Blasting and mildew.*

I have smitten you with blasting and mildew. 'The blasting'— the Hebrew has the *definite article*—is caused by the scorching wind, *cf.* Gen. xli. 6, 23, 27; see 1 Ki. viii. 37, 2 Ki. xix. 26. It would very naturally succeed 'drought'. Hag. ii. 17 must be a quotation, or, at least, a reminiscence, of this verse. 'The mildew' is "a blight, in which the ears turn untimely a pale yellow, and have no grain" (Driver). The same word is applied in Jer. xxx. 6 to the colour of human beings in distress ('all faces are turned to *paleness*', R.V.).

Locusts.

the multitude of. The Hebrew text, though apparently it has the support of the Targum, is strange. Read, 'I *have laid waste* your gardens and your vineyards' (*heḥĕrabhtî* in place of *harbôth*).

hath the palmerworm devoured: *i.e.* 'the locust'. The Hebrew term is *gāzām*, *lit.* 'shearer', called so on account of its destructiveness. Render, 'And your fig trees and your olive trees the locust *was eating*'. See on vii. 1. Nowack and Sellin omit the plague of locusts from the present passage. 'Hath...devoured' is, according to Sellin, 'will...devour'.

10. *Plague.*

pestilence: *lit.* 'plague'. Such often follows, or accompanies, war: in

---

[1] If, as Burney suggests, this weak use of the numeral can be a sign of North Israelite vernacular, it is appropriate to the prophet Amos' speech in Beth-el and Gilgal (*v.* 4).

after the manner of Egypt: your young men have I slain
with the sword, and have carried away your horses; and

this case, however, it seems to *precede* it, *cf.* next clause, 'your young men
…sword'. Probably the translation of the E.VV. '*among* you', and not
'*against* you', is quite correct; *cf. v.* 11 *init.* The plague affects some only.

after the manner of Egypt: *lit.* '*in* the *way* of Egypt'. The same phrase
occurs in Isa. x. 24, 26 with reference to Israel's sojourn in that land.
In the present verse, however, it hardly means 'like the smiting of the
first-born in Egypt'; rather, a 'thorough-going Egyptian plague', *i.e. of the
sort that comes* from the Nile delta;[1] *cf.* Deut. xxviii. 27, 60. The clause may
be but a gloss. There are records of plagues in *Assyria*, which probably
ravaged Palestine also, in the years 765, 759 B.C. See, further, Am. v.
17 note, vi. 9, 10, and viii. 8. In Isa. v. 25 there is a similar reference to
plague (or else earthquake). For 'way' in the sense of 'experience' or
'condition', see Gen. xix. 31, xxxi. 35, and *cf.* Prov. vi. 6.

Battle.

The reference must be to the devastating wars of Jehu's and Jehoahaz's
reigns. See Introd. p. 3. It cannot be denied, however, that an allusion
to any slaying with the *sword* seems out of place, and that the Hebrew for
'and have carried away' is difficult. If, however, as would seem reasonable,
v. 10 concerns plague only, then battle would come well as the final catastrophe which lies behind the threat of *v.* 12. Sellin attains simplicity in
the present verse by eliminating the reference to *plague* in the opening part
of the verse, and adapting the text of the remainder of it as indicated below
in the notes upon 'have carried away', 'the stink of', and 'even into your
nostrils'.

young men: not the same word as in ii. 11. The Hebrew term is
lit. '*choice* young men', *i.e.* in the prime of manhood. A township between
the mount of Olives and Jericho went by the name of *Baḥurim*, 'young
men's village' (2 Sam. iii. 16, *etc.*). In modern Hebrew the word comes
to mean, simply, 'young men'.

and have carried away your horses: *lit.* 'together with the captivity
of your horses'—not very probable Hebrew.[2] The simplest course is to
regard the words as a gloss which has crept into the text from the marginal
note of a scribe. The omission of the clause, as indeed that of 'after the

---

[1] Cheyne. The Hebrew might perhaps even be rendered, 'I have sent among
you a plague *by way of* Egypt'.

[2] The difficulty is not with the preposition as such. '*Im* occurs elsewhere in
the sense of 'along with', 'besides', 'and'; but properly it couples two *like words*,
e.g. 'Joshua utterly destroyed them with their cities' (Josh. xi. 21), 'scarlet
with delights' (2 Sam. i. 24), 'the bullocks with the bulls' (Isa. xxxiv. 7), 'both
small *and* great' (Ps. cxv. 13). In the present passage, however, there is no
word in the preceding clause to which 'captivity' is strictly *parallel*. The expression has every appearance of being an afterthought. (For Hebrew '*ēth*,
'with', in the sense of "together with', see Gen. vi. 13, xxxii. 24.)

I have made the stink of your camp to come up even into
your nostrils: yet have ye not returned unto me, saith the
LORD. **11** I have overthrown *some* among you, as when God
overthrew Sodom and Gomorrah, and ye were as a brand
plucked out of the burning: yet have ye not returned unto me,
saith the LORD. **12** Therefore thus will I do unto thee, O

manner of Egypt', would vastly improve the Hebrew rhythm: so Duhm.
Richter conjectures 'with the *beauty* (or *pomp*) of your horses': so Sellin
($s^e bhî$ for M.T. $sh^e bhî$). Ehrlich reads 'with the *best* of' ($t\hat{o}bh\bar{e}$).

I have made the stink of your camp to come up. See Introd. p. 80.
Just possibly, however, we should point the Hebrew differently ($b\bar{a}'\bar{e}sh$,
LXX ἐν πυρί), 'I have consumed (made to go up) your camp(s) *with fire*'.[1]

even into your nostrils. The use of the Hebrew word 'and' in the
sense of 'and *that*' or 'even', is claimed by grammarians to be normal,[2]
but the text in the cases cited is usually suspicious.[3] In the present verse
the conjunction should be omitted, or, better, the whole word, as interfering
with the rhythm (Sellin).

11. *Earthquake.* Cf. i. 1, iii. 13–15, viii. 8, ix. 5.

overthrown *some* among you, as...overthrew. Frequently is the
Hebrew *hāphakh* used of the sudden and complete[4] destruction of Sodom:
Gen. xix. 25, 29, Deut. xxix. 23, Isa. xiii. 19, Jer. xlix. 18. It would seem
that, by the time of the writing of the present verse, the tradition had already
assumed a permanent form. Here only in the book of Amos is Jehovah
styled 'God' absolutely. Elsewhere it is '*thy* God' (iv. 12, ix. 15) or 'God
of *hosts*' (*e.g.* v. 16, 27).

and ye were as a brand plucked out of the burning. Better translate,
'*became* as a brand plucked...', *i.e.* you had the experience of being rescued
at the last moment. The expression was a proverbial one, at least by the
time of Zech. iii. 2, as it has since become in English usage. In Isa. vii. 4
the illustration is used rather in *contempt*.

12. So far the *past*. The lesson not having been learnt hitherto, something
worse is in store for Israel.

Therefore thus will I do unto thee. The 'thus' is, perhaps, deliberately
left indefinite, as in the fearful oath, '*Thus* will God do to me, and thus
will he add...' (1 Ki. ii. 23, *etc.*). The abrupt change in this verse, from
the plural number of the preceding verses to the *singular*, finds many
parallels in the O.T. (especially *e.g.* in the book of Deuteronomy).

---

[1] Van Hoonacker, Sellin.   [2] *E.g.* Dav. *Syn.* § 136 Rem. (c).

[3] *E.g.* Am. iii. 11, 'even round about'; Jer. xv. 13, where the versions have
(simply) 'in all the borders'; Isa. lvii. 11, 'even from of old', where the versions
represent an entirely different reading.

[4] In the present passage only *some* are destroyed, as the preposition b^e indicates (*cf.* Ps. lxxviii. 31, *hārag b^e*); and see the next clause.

Israel: *and* because I will do this unto thee, prepare to meet
thy God, O Israel. **13** For, lo, he that formeth the mountains,

and **because I will do this unto thee, prepare to meet... O Israel.**
Possibly (though not by any means certainly) this is an exegetical gloss
from the margin.[1]

prepare to meet thy God, O Israel. (1) These words (whether
v. 12 *b* is original or a gloss) are generally taken by commentators as a
solemn warning, the spiritual application of the prediction of judgment
upon the nation Israel contained in the first half of the verse and indeed
in *vv.* 6–12 *a.*[2] (2) As a definite exhortation to individuals to repent before
it is too late, the phrase has made a useful moral appeal in all generations.
(3) For yet another interpretation, see the Additional Note on p. 296.

prepare. For the Hebrew *hikkôn* in the sense of 'to prepare', *cf.*
Prov. xxii. 18 ('if they be established', *i.e.* ready), Ezek. xxxviii. 7, and,
in a not dissimilar connection, Exod. xix. 15.[3]

thy God. The context shews that Amos does not employ this expression
in the sense which the people would attach to it; *cf.* Introd. p. 24. The
writer of ix. 15 uses the phrase 'thy God' with an affectionate significance.

13. Some think that the genuine words of Amos end at *v.* 12 *a,* 'Therefore
thus will I do unto thee, O Israel'. Almost all commentators, including the
most recent, regard at least *v.* 13 as an addition to the prophecy. See
Introd. p. 66, and the note on v. 8, 9. In support of an opposite view it
might be urged that this sublime ejaculation or doxology, 'For, lo, what
a great God He is!' adds real point to the prophecy of judgment in *v.* 12 *a.*
See, moreover, what is said under 'treadeth upon the high places'. There
is no predicate in all *v.* 13—a difficulty illustrated by the action of the
Targumist in inserting into the text, 'For, lo, *He is revealing Himself* who
formed...'.

he that formeth the mountains: or, *lit.,* 'who fashions mountains'.
The Hebrew participle may refer to present or past. The same verb is used
in the earlier account of the Divine work given in Gen. ii. 7, 8, 19, the
objects 'formed' being *animals* and *man.* In Isa. xlv. 18 it is *the earth*
that is formed'; *cf.* Jer. x. 16. In the present passage, the LXX reads,
perhaps correctly, instead of 'mountains' (*hārîm*), 'thunder' (*hāra'am*).

---

[1] So Nowack, Hölscher, Sellin. The Targum endeavours to avoid the immediate repetition of the identical words 'I will do unto thee' by expanding them
the second time into a paraphrase, 'Because *thou dost not return to the law which
I was making for thee* (= will do unto thee), adorn thyself to receive the instruction of the law of thy God, O Israel'. For Heb. *'ēqebh kî* instead of the
more usual *'ēqebh 'ăsher,* see 2 Sam. xii. 10.

[2] *Cf.* McFadyen, *Expository Times,* Mar. 1927, pp. 241–243.

[3] In later Hebrew the corresponding substantive (*kawwānāh*) means 'religious
devotion'.

and createth the wind, and declareth unto man what is his
thought, that maketh the morning darkness, and treadeth
upon the high places of the earth; the LORD, the God of hosts,
is his name.

and createth the wind. The term translated 'create' (*bārā'*) "does not
in itself express the idea of *creatio ex nihilo* (though it was probably in usage
often felt to denote this); but it implies the possession of a sovereign trans-
forming, or productive, energy, altogether transcending what is at the
disposal of man" (Driver). It is employed in the loftier account of Divine
activity given in Gen. i. 1, ii. 3, 'P'; and it occurs in the exalted passages
Isa. xl. 28, xliii. 1, 7, xlv. 12, 18, with which Am. iv. 13 should be compared
generally. For the idea of the word, *cf.* Numb. xvi. 30 (Heb.).

wind: perhaps means 'storm'.

and declareth unto man what is his thought. The happenings which
are referred to in the first two clauses of the doxology belong to the *past*.
Now in the last three, the Heb. participles must represent present tenses.
The word *sēaḥ* translated 'thought' occurs here only; but doubtless it has
the same meaning as *sîaḥ* rendered in 1 Sam. i. 16, Job vii. 13, *etc.*, 'com-
plaint', and in Ps. civ. 34 used of the Psalmist's 'meditation'. (1) Hence,
here also, in spite of the context, it would seem most appropriately to refer
to *man's* 'thought'. So Marti, who compares the present passage with
Jer. xi. 20.[1] (2) If, upon the basis of 1 Ki. xviii. 27, it could mean '*God's
musing*', *i.e.* 'purpose' or 'mind' (so G. A. Smith), the best comment
would be Am. iii. 7.[2] In either case, God would 'declare' through His
prophet, though how this was understood to be effected outside Israel
(*cf.* 'declareth unto man', *i.e.* mankind) is not clear. The LXX has the curious
rendering 'His Messiah' (*Meshîḥô*).

that maketh the morning darkness. Jehovah in a moment can
blacken the dawn with His clouds. Though the Hebrew idiom is good, the
LXX reading, 'that maketh dawn *and* darkness', is, perhaps, to be preferred.

and treadeth upon the high places of the earth. The 'high places'
here are, of course, quite different from the 'sanctuaries' of vii. 9. In Isa.
lviii. 14 the expression 'I will make thee to ride upon the high places of the
earth' is used in the sense of God granting *triumph* to Sabbath-observing
Israel. *Cf.* Deut. xxxii. 13. The present passage describes God in His
terrible greatness, conceived of anthropomorphically as striding 'upon'
(or 'on to', or 'over') the hill tops. *Cf.* Job ix. 8, R.V. marg. Perhaps there
is a hint of judgment, as manifestly is the case in Mic. i. 3–6, where God
in His thundercloud 'will...tread upon the high places of the earth'. *Cf.*
v. 12 and i. 2.

---

[1] An example in the prophetic history would be 2 Ki. v. 26 (Elisha and Gehazi).

[2] The Vulgate boldly renders the present passage *et annuntians homini elo-
quium suum*; Douai 'and declareth his word to man'.

V. 1 Hear ye this word which I take up for a lamentation over you, O house of Israel. **2** The virgin of Israel is fallen;

V. 1-17. LACK OF MORALITY LEADS TO RUIN

Quite possibly this extremely interesting chapter represents the continuation of the impassioned exhortation which seems to begin at iv. 4; or it may be that a new discourse, or discourses, commence here. In either case, the Prophet is still addressing the whole nation (*vv.* 1 and 25, 'house of Israel'), though specially North Israel in *v.* 6. In ch. v the nation is warned that its destruction is imminent (*vv.* 1-3). Jehovah wants not mere worship, but religion and morality. Morality (in particular, *justice*) has been conspicuously lacking (*vv.* 4-15). The Prophet repeats that punishment must come (*vv.* 16-27).

1-3. An elegy over Israel's fall.

1. a lamentation. Hebrew *qînāh*, 'dirge', as in viii. 10. The same idea, but not the Hebrew word, occurs in Mic. ii. 4. *V.* 2 is in the elegiac measure (see Introd. p. 33). Examples of *sustained* elegies in the O.T. are exhibited in the book of Lamentations.

over you, O house of Israel. As in iii. 1 Amos addresses *the people* as a whole. Yet obviously, if his words are to lead to a reformation of conduct, *persons* must make the response, particularly in the case of a call to repentance such as is contained in the words, 'Seek the LORD' (*v.* 6); *cf.* Wheeler Robinson, *Religious Ideas of O.T.* p. 89. Amos has a place in the history of the evolution of individual religion from tribalism and nationalism. He prepares the way for the doctrines of personal responsibility for guilt and of God's grace in the individual heart, found apparently for the first time in the O.T. clearly stated in Jer. xxxi. 29-34. This latter conception of religion commonplace to-day was by no means so in ancient systems. See, further, Peake's *Jeremiah* (Century Bible), pp. 43-48.

2. The virgin of Israel: *i.e.* 'the virgin Israel'. Here (for the first time in extant Hebrew literature) the nation as a whole is styled a 'virgin'. With this personification of a nation, *cf.* iv. 12, '*thee*', '*thy* God'. The exact expression is employed by Jeremiah (in Jer. xviii. 13, xxxi. 4, 21), which prophet is the only one to make use of Amos' phrase 'virgin Israel'. In Jer. xxxi. 4 the metaphor of the young woman is developed.[1] The rhythm of *vv.* 2-6 is, appropriately, *qînāh*. Indeed this measure preponderates throughout the chapter, except (for the most part) where trimeter appears.

is fallen: *lit.* 'has fallen', or 'fell'. There can be no reference, however,

---

[1] The somewhat similar expression '*daughter* of Zion' is very frequently used for 'inhabitants of Zion', *e.g.* Isa. i. 8, Jer. iv. 31, *etc.*; and the combination '*virgin* daughter of Zion' occurs in 2 Ki. xix. 21 (= Isa. xxxvii. 22), Lam. ii. 13. But, unlike the term 'virgin', 'daughter' may be used also for the inhabitants of non-Israelite localities, both in and out of Scripture (*e.g.* Isa. xxiii. 10, the *Panammu* inscription, l. 14, 'the *daughters* of the east he brought to the west').

she shall no more rise: she is cast down upon her land; there is none to raise her up. **3** For thus saith the Lord GOD: The city that went forth a thousand shall have an hundred left, and that which went forth an hundred shall have ten left, to the house of Israel.

to the *past*, even to the wars of iv. 10; for the 'fall' is immediately explained in *v.* 3 by means of verbs in the *future* tense, introduced by the phrase, '*For* thus saith the Lord GOD'. To the lively imagination of the Prophet, Israel's coming destruction by Assyria is as good as accomplished. *Cf.* 2 Ki. xix. 21, Jer. xiii. 19.[1]

The intellectual and moral courage of Amos in making the present statement cannot be appreciated unless it is realised that probably no one had ever before said such a thing concerning the nation. The prophecies, therefore, of Jeremiah in the next century concerning Judah's destruction do not present so striking a phenomenon. The later prophets had the words of Amos, and the actual fall of the Northern Kingdom, to guide them.

she is cast down: *lit.* 'has been left', or 'forsaken'. So Isa. xvi. 8, Judg. xv. 19 (Hebrew).

there is none to raise her up. In Hebrew a "circumstantial clause". Translate, 'without anyone raising her up': so *v.* 6 *b*, 'with none to quench it'. It may well be that the Prophet in vivid imagination is picturing only the *possibility* of Israel's irrevocable doom; see on *v.* 4. On the other hand, he usually seems to speak as if he did not expect that the evil would be averted; see v. 27, vi. 14, vii. 8, 9. And note what he says in ii. 14, 15, v. 18–20, ix. 1–4, as to its *unescapableness*.

3. the Lord GOD. See Excursus I. iii. p. 333, 'ĂDÔNAI.

that went forth: *i.e.* as the Targum, '*from which* went forth'.

shall have ten left. Both this and the preceding clauses express literal decimation. The Targum attempts (against the context) to render a happier meaning, 'shall have *as many as* (Aramaic *'adh*) ten'. Amos' message may not have been that every soul in Israel was to perish, but the present passage does not prove that he anticipated a 'remnant' which would be either righteous or repentant. *Cf. v.* 15 and p. 69.

4–7. The Prophet's evidence that Israel deserves the fall which he predicted in *vv.* 1–3. For religion and morality the nation has substituted thoughtless attendance at the shrines.

---

[1] This idiom occurs also in Egyptian prophecy, if such a passage as the following is genuine prediction: "I prophesy not that which is not yet come. The river is dry....Men shall need water for the ships....Perished are those good things (of yore)....The earth is fallen into misery". (*Neferrohu*, transl. Gardiner in *J.E.A.* I. pp. 103, 104.) The rendering in Erman-Blackman, p. 113, is different.

4 For thus saith the LORD unto the house of Israel, Seek ye me, and ye shall live: 5 but seek not Beth-el, nor enter into

4. For. The connection is not easy. Some omit the whole clause until 'Seek ye me'. Otherwise, it seems best to interpret: 'The reason for the defeat just foretold is that you have yet to learn how to seek Jehovah'. It is precarious, however, to go so far as to translate (with Harper), 'thus *said* the LORD', as of a command uttered long ago.

Seek ye me. The common verb *dārash* is used in three senses in connection with religion: (*a*) *to resort to* a sacred place; so in Deut. xii. 5, 'unto his habitation shall ye seek, and thither thou shalt come', and in 2 Chron. i. 5 (concerning the altar at Gibeon); (*b*) *to inquire of, i.e.* consult, *e.g.* in Gen. xxv. 22 (the object being God), 1 Chron. xiii. 3 (object, the ark), and 1 Sam. ix. 9 (of seeking through a prophet), 1 Ki. xxii. 5, 7, 2 Ki. iii. 11; (*c*) *to seek God*, either in true worship (*e.g.* Pss. ix. 10, xxiv. 6, xxxiv. 10), or, generally, in sincere endeavour to please Him, especially by observing His moral law, *e.g.* Isa. ix. 13, lxv. 10, 2 Chron. xv. 2, xxii. 9, Ps. xiv. 2 (quoted in Rom. iii. 11), Ps. cxix. 2 ('that seek him with the whole heart'). In Ps. cxix. 45, 94, the Psalmist 'seeks' God's statutes.

In *vv.* 4–6 Amos makes somewhat of a play upon the two senses of the word, (*c*) and (*a*). And the call to true worship becomes, in effect, a call to repentance. With offerings in their hands all Israel 'seek' to the sanctuaries, but Jehovah meets this with the words, 'seek ye ME'. (So also Hosea appeals for national regeneration in the words, 'Break up your fallow ground: for it is time to *seek* the LORD', Hos. x. 12. In Isa. lv. 6, 7, the prophet declares that by repentance man may 'find' God, who, so far from desiring to stand aloof from His creatures, will at once forgive.[1]) Repentance will shew itself in reformation of morals (Am. v. 7, 10–12, 24). Perhaps, in the Prophet's simple theology, morality *was* repentance (*cf. v.* 14). As regards the true worship of the Deity, the Israelite people had yet to learn that to 'appear before God'[2] was not a physical act accomplished by a movement of the body. Formally to go to the 'place of meeting' may be easy: to meet God is not so simple. Only the pure in heart can see Him; and worship of a *spiritual* God is a matter rather of the *spirit* than of place[3] (St Matt. v. 8, St John iv. 24).

---

[1] *Cf.* also the parable in St Lu. xv. 20, 21, and St Paul in Acts xvii. 27.

[2] The Hebrew expression is *lit.* 'to see God's face'. *Cf.* the Babylonian representations of worshippers in the presence of the Deity, in Gressmann, *Bilder*, Nos. 92, 95, pp. 57, 59; edn 2, Nos. 322, 323.

[3] On the other hand, it is unthinkable that any spiritual prophet would sympathise with the attitude condemned in Heb. x. 25 *a*. For the use of the present passage by Jews when sacrifice had become impossible through the destruction of the Temple by Titus, *cf.* Excursus IV. pp. 343–344. In the Talmud (T.B. *Makkoth* 23 *b*, 24 *a*) the number of the commandments is discussed. According to Moses (*i.e.* the Pentateuch) they are 613, in David (*i.e.* the Psalms) they are 11, in Isaiah 6, in Micah 3. This passage of Amos and Hab. ii. 4 are cited as shewing that all precepts may be comprehended in *one*.

Gilgal, and pass not to Beer-sheba: for Gilgal shall surely go

and ye shall live. The same words recur in *vv.* 6, 14. If the nation
'seeks', it will *continue happily in the land*; *cf.* Gen. xx. 7, 2 Sam. xii. 22.
So the Targum, 'Seek my fear, that ye may be established'. The Prophet
has not in mind a life beyond the grave; nor the spiritual 'life' of St John
v. 40.[1] The strongest appeal to repentance here as always (even in the
New Testament) is made from the point of view of self-interest. (1) The
clause could well express but a theoretical possibility, 'merely a pious
wish', which the Prophet does not anticipate will be realised. This seems
the more reasonable position in view of v. 1-3. The hopeful section, ix. 8 *c*-15
(with, just possibly, v. 15), almost certainly does not represent the teaching
of Amos. The tenor of the exhortations of Amos is, '*Because* you have done
so and so, *therefore* you will be destroyed'.[2] (See, further, Introd. pp. 29, 31.)
So, *e.g.*, Buttenwieser (pp. 212-220), who, moreover, suggests a rearrangement
in the order of the verses. (2) The other view is that, in the words of
G. A. Smith (p. 165): "Judgment is not yet irrevocable. There break forthwith the only two promises which lighten the lowering darkness of the
book....*Seek Me and ye shall live*, and *seek good and ye shall live*". In
support of this, it might be urged that the Hebrew idiom in *vv.* 4 and 6
signifies 'Seek *in order that* ye may', or '*If* ye seek ye shall';[3] *cf.* Gen.
xlii. 18. *V.* 14 is more clearly an exhortation with a definite purpose
(*lᵉma'an tihyû*), and *cf. v.* 16 *b*. Taken thus, *vv.* 4 and 6, contradicting as
they do *vv.* 2, 3 as well as other passages in the book, would supply an
instance of the *conditionalness* of Divine prophecy.[4]

5. Beth-el...Gilgal. For these 'high places', see notes on iii. 14, iv. 4,
and Additional Note, p. 293.

Beer-sheba. The locality was a religious site consecrated by patriarchal
sojournings and worship; *cf.* Gen. xxi. 31-33 (tamarisk tree), xxvi. 23-25
(altar). It lay in the extreme south of the tribe of Judah (1 Ki. xix. 3).
If Amos be not addressing the whole of Israel, his words here and in viii. 14
imply that pilgrimages from the *Northern* Kingdom took place thither;
cf. '*pass* not to'. Except for the two allusions in Amos, and that in 1 Ki.

---

[1] Though for this latter in an O.T. exhortation, perhaps *cf.* Isa. lv. 3; and for
the noun 'life' in a spiritual sense, see Prov. viii. 35, and note the verb 'quicken'
(*Pi'el*), Ps. cxix. 50, 93, *etc.*

[2] Notwithstanding the offer conveyed in *vv.* 4 and 6, Amos contrasts un-
favourably with certain other prophets of doom, who, prophesying with more
obvious regret, interspersed their threats with a greater proportion of promises
and of loving inducements to the sinful nation to return to God, *e.g.* Hos. vi. 1,
4, xi. 8, 9, 14, Jer. vi. 16, viii. 18, ix. 1, Ezek. xxxiv. 11 *b*, *etc. Cf.* also Pace,
Idea of God, pp. 189, 190.

[3] Or, 'If ye were to seek me, ye would live'—a contingency which probably
will not arise.

[4] Undoubtedly it would be easier to believe that Amos entertained the
possibility of Jehovah's sparing Israel on repentance, if the hypothesis be adopted
that a slowly advancing Assyria was hardly, if at all, in the Prophet's thoughts.

into captivity, and Beth-el shall come to nought. **6** Seek the
LORD, and ye shall live; lest he break out like fire in the house

xix. 3, there is no other evidence for Beer-sheba being so important a
shrine; but that is not a reason for doubting (as some do) the authenticity
of the clause and that in viii. 14.[1]

Gilgal shall surely go into captivity. The exile is even more unambiguously foretold in v. 27. In the Hebrew there is an intentional jingle
of sounds (*haggilgāl gālôh yigleh*); *cf.* Hos. xii. 11 (Heb. 12), *Gi*lead and
Gilgal will become heaps (*gallîm*).

shall come to nought. So also the A.V. and the Targum; but the
Hebrew is not quite this. Translate '*āwen* instead of 'nought', either
(a) *wickedness* (especially idolatry, 1 Sam. xv. 23, Hos. xii. 11, and *cf.* Am.
i. 5, note); or, better, (b) its consequence, *trouble*, *e.g.* Jer. iv. 15 (R.V.
'evil'), Hab. iii. 7 (R.V. 'affliction'). The R.V. marg. rendering 'vanity',
though perhaps possible in view of Isa. xli. 29, Zech. x. 2, is not likely in
the present context. But after the bold punning of the first part of the
verse, it is not unnatural to look for something vigorous in this clause.
The original text of Amos may well have read: 'Beth-el (house of *God*) will
become Beth-aven (a house of *trouble*)'. Point would be given to such an
expression from the actual existence of a village with the name of Beth-aven,
east of Beth-el, on the edge of the desert (1 Sam. xiii. 5, xiv. 23). Hosea,
possibly having in mind such a saying of Amos, in irony frequently dubs
Beth-el 'Beth-*aven*' (Hos. iv. 15, v. 8, and, especially, x. 5).

The Prophet, feeling that he has said enough upon this topic, silently
leaves the doom of *Beer-sheba* to the imagination of his hearers. There can
be no question of clemency towards the sanctuary merely because it was
Judaean.

6. lest he break out like fire. For the comparison of Jehovah's visitation
to fire, see i. 4, 7, *etc.* The offer of escape contained in the first clause,
'Seek...shall live', now passes into a threat. Reference to Divine punishment has always been a powerful force in effecting individual conversion.
Not seldom to-day, however, it is wise and right to make use of varied
means to awaken conscience and to lead to repentance and amendment
of life.[2]

break out: *lit.* 'rush' or 'penetrate'. There are signs, however, that
originally the clause ran, 'lest *fire* rush against the house of Joseph'; or
else (with Wellhausen), 'lest *He kindle with* fire the...' (*cf.* the construction
in 2 Sam. xiv. 30, 31).

---

[1] Some scholars believe that in Hos. iv. 15 a place-name has fallen out of the
text; and, upon the evidence of Am. v. 5, viii. 14, Wellhausen and Nowack
read in that passage, 'come not ye unto Gilgal, neither go ye up to Beth-aven,
nor swear *in Beer-sheba* As Jehovah liveth'. There may be an allusion to Beer-
sheba as a prominent 'high place' in 2 Ki. xxiii. 8.

[2] *Cf.* Archbishops' Report, *The Evangelistic Work of the Church*, S.P.C.K.
1918, pp. 12 (end), 13.

of Joseph, and it devour and there be none to quench it in
Beth-el: 7 ye who turn judgement to wormwood, and cast
down righteousness to the earth; 8 *seek him* that maketh the

Joseph. See v. 15, vi. 6. 'Joseph', *i.e.* Ephraim, stands for the Northern
Kingdom.

in Beth-el. For effective parallelism of structure it is preferable to
follow Marti in reading, as LXX, 'in the house of *Israel*' (*cf. v.* 3 end).

7. ye who turn judgement...and cast down righteousness.... The
criticism which maintains that *v.* 7 is hardly a continuation of *vv.* 4–6 seems
unnecessary. The verse provides a striking form of address[1] to the sinful
worshippers, whose sin (oppression), moreover, is described further in
vv. 10 and 11. 'Judgement', which should be fair, has become in the hands
of the nobility a *bitter* thing. The metaphor occurs again in vi. 12 and
is an instance of Amos' desert images. In Deut. xxix. 18 (Heb. 17) it stands
for the bitter fruits of idolatry; in Jer. ix. 15 (Heb. 14) for Jehovah's
chastisements. 'Wormwood' is a Palestinian plant (Hebrew *la'ănāh*;
ἄψινθος, Rev. viii. 11). See also Jer. xxiii. 15, Lam. iii. 15, 19.
Wormwood[2] is a species of the genus *Artemisia*; it is used to-day in some
countries medicinally to reduce fever, also to flavour *absinthe*.

Amos is now upon his favourite theme—justice and righteousness; *cf.*
ii. 6, 7 *a*, note. His message was seed 'cast upon the waters' which returned
'after many days'. The Jews came to have a national instinct for justice,
and it was conceived of as a pre-eminent attribute of their God (Ps. ciii. 6).
The eleventh of the eighteen daily "Benedictions" concludes, "Blessed art
Thou, O Lord, the King, who lovest *righteousness* and *judgment*".[3]

righteousness: *i.e.* here, social righteousness. The same combination
with 'judgement' occurs in *v.* 24 and vi. 12. 'Righteousness' (*ṣᵉdhāqāh* or
ṣedheq) has a quite different history from that of 'holiness' (iv. 2). (1) Originally, in elementary form, it was perhaps a *clan* virtue,[4] corresponding to
'what is *due*'. *Cf.* S. A. Cook's note in W. R. Smith's *Semites³*, pp. 655 ff. Or
(2) the term was a forensic one, taken from the primitive court of justice,
its opposite being 'guilt'. *Cf.* Davidson, *Theology of O.T.* pp. 266, 267;
Wheeler Robinson, *Religious Ideas*, p. 168; and see Am. ii. 6, where 'the
righteous' means the *innocent* party. (3) According to Amos, righteousness

---

[1] The verb 'cast down' in the original is in the third (not the second) person;
but such is in strict accordance with Hebrew idiom (*cf.* Ps. civ. 3–5 following
on *vv.* 1, 2). The LXX has some curious misreadings, '(*The Lord* is) he who makes
judgment *on high*, and has set righteousness in the earth', the verse becoming
part of the doxology of *vv.* 8 and 9.

[2] Concerning it G. E. Post writes (in *H.D.B.* IV. p. 940): "In point of fact,
the excessive dread which the Hebrews had of most bitter substances was
founded not on clinical experience but on prejudice".

[3] Jewish *Daily Prayer Book*, edn Singer, p. 48.

[4] *Cf.* the same root used apparently in the simple sense of 'authorised, or legal,
kinsman' in the Nabataean inscriptions (G. A. Cooke, *N.S.I.* pp. 226, 229, 232).

should be exhibited in just commercial dealings (Am. viii. 5, 6) and in the
execution of social obligations generally. (4) The word degenerated in its
connotation, so that in post-Biblical Hebrew it could be used of mere
external righteousness shewn in 'almsgiving'.[1] Few would agree with
Rendel Harris (*Aḥiqar*, p. 123) that this is the *primitive* sense of the word.

8, 9. The connection in thought between the majestic description of God
in *vv.* 8 and 9, and the passage preceding, appears to be that the two verses
are "intended (like iv. 13) to remind the disobedient Israelites of the power
and majesty of Him, whose will they defy, and whose judgements they
provoke, the Creator and Ruler of the world" (Driver). Whether, however,
this description of the Deity was placed there by the original writer is, for
the following reasons, open to serious question. (1) 'That maketh the
Pleiades...' comes in most abruptly after *v.* 7.[2] To understand, as E.VV.,
'seek him' from *v.* 6 is quite impossible; and it is not too much to say that
it is inconceivable that the writer of the preceding passage would himself
have followed it with *v.* 8. (2) Moreover, *vv.* 8 and 9 actually *interrupt* the
flow of the exhortation contained in *vv.* 6 and 7, and continued in *vv.* 10
and 11. 'Seek the LORD... (*v.* 6), ye who turn judgement to wormwood...
(*v.* 7), O haters of him that reproveth in the gate... (*v.* 10): forasmuch
therefore... (*v.* 11)'. (3) Similar "doxologies" occur in iv. 13 and in ix. 5, 6;
and, while it cannot be said that these destroy an argument, yet like
that in v. 8, 9 they have no syntactical connection with their context.[3]
(4) Although it might conceivably be claimed that these three doxologies
were introduced without due care by the writer of the book *after it was
finished*, yet against such a suggestion is to be set the coincidence that
each of the three passages contains the phrase, 'The LORD (of hosts) is his
name', an expression which the prophet Amos does not use elsewhere.[4]
Furthermore (to quote Sir G. A. Smith, p. 204), "the phrase does not occur
in any other prophet, till we come down to the oracles which compose
Isaiah xl–lxvi. Here it happens thrice—twice in passages dating from the
Exile (xlvii. 4 and liv. 5)—and once in a passage suspected by some to be
of still later date (xlviii. 2). In the book of Jeremiah the phrase is found
eight times; but either in passages already on other grounds judged by
many critics to be later than Jeremiah (x. 16, xxxi. 35, xxxii. 18, l. 34,
li. 19, 57), or where by itself it is probably an intrusion into the text

---

[1] And the term means 'gift' as early as the 5th cent. B.C. *Têma* inscription,
Cooke, pp. 195, 197; and in Arabic. The LXX translates on seventeen occasions
in O.T. by ἐλεημοσύνη (*cf.* McNeile on St Matt. vi. 1).

[2] The Targum found it necessary to add a link: '*They have left off fearing
before* the One who made the Pleiades...'.

[3] A characteristic of the doxological passages is that they are constructed with
participles (any finite verbs being secondary and dependent)—in chs. iv and v with
no grammatical subject. Participles are eminently suited to exalted descriptions of the Deity, *cf.* Job xxvi. 7–9—a passage which probably does lie in its
original context. For an added doxology, see Hos. xiii. 4 (LXX).

[4] Its occurrence in the Hebrew text of v. 27 is a scribal slip. See note
ad loc.

Pleiades and Orion, and turneth the shadow of death into the
(xlvi. 18, xlviii. 15 b)". Lastly, (5) whilst Amos does represent Jehovah as
the God of history, powerful over all nations, and having control over the
elements of nature (see Introd. p. 22), in the "doxology" passages God is
more than this. He is Creator and Lord of the whole scheme of the *Universe.*
This point, indeed, would not necessarily furnish sufficient reason to deny to
Amos the three passages. A more significant fact is that the exalted
descriptions of the Deity contained in the sections under consideration
find no parallel in details in the sacred literature until the exilic chapters of
the book of Isaiah and the (late) book of Job.[1] The conclusion that the
three hymn-like sections have been added to the text of Amos during, or
after, the Exile seems hard to resist. For a defence of the Amos authorship
of the doxologies, see W. R. Smith, *Prophets*, p. 400, edition Cheyne (on
which the editor comments, pp. xv, xvi); König, *Geschichte der A.-T. Rel.*
1924, pp. 342 ff. Kuenen, in maintaining their authenticity, compares the
undoubtedly pre-exilic passages, Mic. i. 2–4, Jer. v. 20–22. But of these it
may at least be said that they are unlike the Amos doxologies in being
deeply embedded in their context (Nowack).[2]

8. that maketh the Pleiades and Orion. maketh: *i.e.* 'made'. 'The
Pleiades' are mentioned also in Job ix. 9 (the passage Job ix. 5–9 should
be compared as a whole), xxxviii. 31, 32, in each case along with 'Orion'.[3]
Aquila renders 'Pleiades' by 'Arcturus'; Hoffmann argues for the identification of the Hebrew term with *Sirius* (the Dog Star). But the word
(*Kîmâh*), probably connected with an Arabic root suggesting a 'herd' (or
'heap'), would well suit the Pleiades, or 'Seven stars' (A.V. rendering here).
In Hebrew the proper name 'Orion' means 'fool': Job ix. 9 alludes to his
'bands'. "It is not improbable that the name preserves an allusion to some
ancient mythological idea, according to which the brilliant and conspicuous
constellation was originally some fool-hardy, heaven-daring rebel,[4] who
was chained to the sky for his impiety". So Driver, who also refers to the
mention of 'Pleiades' and 'Orion' in Homer (*Iliad* xviii. 486–489, xxii.

---

[1] *Cf.* the various references in the notes. The probability of the lateness of
v. 8, 9 is increased if *v.* 9 contains four star-names. See note, p. 297.

[2] On the other hand, that the passages are portions of a once single complete
poem does not seem likely; ix. 6 b is the same as v. 8 b. For a fragment of a
not dissimilar doxology in the text of the N.T., see 1 Tim. iii. 16 (R.V.). This
also, even as the doxologies in the book of Amos, consists of a sentence without
a main verb.

[3] In Isa. xiii. 10 (M.T.) 'the stars of heaven and the constellations thereof'
(R.V.) is, *lit.*, 'the stars of the heavens and their Orions'. The LXX has οἱ γὰρ
ἀστέρες τοῦ οὐρανοῦ καὶ ὁ Ὠρείων. Probably Duhm (followed by Cheyne) is
right in reading 'heaven and its Orions' (omitting 'the stars of'). The Greek
translator of Amos quite mistook the star-names; for 'Pleiades' he has 'everything' (πάντα).

[4] *Cf.* the Targum equivalent in Job ix. 9, *nîphᵉlâ*, *lit.* = 'the giant'. So the
Syriac also. In Greek mythology the star was originally a giant, *Odyssey* v. 121,
xi. 310 ("None but Orion e'er surpassed their height").

morning, and maketh the day dark with night; that calleth
for the waters of the sea, and poureth them out upon the face
of the earth; the LORD is his name; 9 that bringeth sudden
destruction upon the strong, so that destruction cometh upon
the fortress.

26–31; *Odyssey* v. 272–275). For Jehovah's control over the stars in general,
cf. Isa. xl. 26. Such passages exhibit an incalculable advance in thought
beyond *e.g.* Judges v. 20.

and turneth the shadow of death into the morning. 'Turneth'
probably refers to *present* time.

the shadow of death. This is one word in the Hebrew (*ṣalm-ûth*, from a
root signifying 'to be black'). Translate 'deep darkness', as R.V. marg.
Later Jews[1] came to see in the term two words; and the LXX translated
by σκιὰ τοῦ θανάτου (in the present verse by σκιά only) which phrase appears
in the N.T., St Matt. iv. 16, St Lu. i. 79. In this way Ps. xxiii. 4 supplied
the idea of "the Valley of the Shadow of Death" in *Pilgrim's Progress*.

into the morning. The word for 'morning' is not that occurring in
iv. 13. With regularity God changes the pitch darkness of night into the
brightness of early morning.

and maketh the day dark with night: *i.e.* 'and again, at sunset,
brings on the darkness of night'. In iv. 13 *b* the idea was of daylight being
temporarily obscured by the power of Jehovah in a storm; and in viii. 9
the writer has in mind the phenomenon of an eclipse. Neither of these
ideas, however, is likely to be contained in the present sentence, following
as it does upon 'turning deep darkness *into morning*'.

that calleth. This signifies 'who can, if He but wishes, speak and the
waters obey'.

for the waters of the sea. By means of the wind He can drive the
ocean in upon the land: so Job xii. 15; *cf.* Isa. li. 15. If the allusion be to
the Deluge, translate 'Who (once) *called* for...'; but this is improbable.

The whole phrase, 'that calleth for the waters of the sea...is his
name', occurs again in ix. 6. The Targum paraphrases as 'who commands
to assemble *armies* (camps) who are numerous as the waters of the
sea, and scatters them upon the face of the earth'. For the illustration
of Jehovah's might in nature, in the reverse way, see Jer. v. 22 ('by a
perpetual decree that it can*not* pass it'). The point is sometimes made by
those who believe the "doxologies" to originate from Amos that he
exhibits "an innate accord with nature and a preference for images taken
from its province" (Corni!l).

**9. that bringeth sudden destruction upon the strong, so that de-
struction cometh upon the fortress.** Jehovah's government is more
than physical as indicated in *v.* 8; it is moral. His greatness is shewn not

---

[1] Though it is interesting to note that the Targum exhibits the translation
'darkness' (*qᵉbhēl*) and has no word 'death'.

10 They hate him that reproveth in the gate, and they
abhor him that speaketh uprightly. **11** Forasmuch therefore
as ye trample upon the poor, and take exactions from him of

only in the facts, processes and events of nature; He rules also the destinies
of *human* nature, '*causing* destruction *to flash forth*[1] upon the strong and
destruction comes in against the fortress'. The A.V. (under the influence
of the Targum) went astray: 'that *strengtheneth* the *spoiled* against the
strong, so that the *spoiled* shall come against the fortress'. For a further
rendering of the passage, which finds star-names here, see Additional Note,
pp. 297–299.

10. They hate...they abhor. Grammatically the verbs are in the third
person; but, as in *v.* 7 *b* (of which the present verse is probably the immediate continuation), they are best represented in English as second person—
'*Ye* who hate...'. *Vv.* 11, 12 will then follow on smoothly. In *v.* 12*b* itself
the Hebrew is literally 'and *they* turn aside the needy in the gate'.

reproveth in the gate: *i.e.* 'arbitrateth (justly) in the gate'. For
'reprove' in the sense of 'judge', *cf.* Isa. ii. 4, *etc.*; and for the exact phrase,
see Isa. xxix. 21. The 'gateway', or broad space by the gate, is the place
for legal action in *vv.* 12, 15, Ruth iv. 1, 2, 11, *etc.* Or the reference may be
to the Preacher himself. "No honest critic could secure a hearing".[2]

they abhor him that speaketh uprightly. 'Uprightly' is *lit.* 'perfect'
or 'sincere' (Ps. xv. 2). According to the present verse any honest man who
is prepared to speak up for the innocent is 'loathed'. In St Lu. vi. 22
unpopularity in a good cause comes under the blessing of a Greater than
Amos.

11. Retribution from Jehovah.

ye trample upon the poor. Habitually the rich oppress the poor, and
not only in matters which come before the courts. For the metaphor,
cf. ii. 7 (LXX).

and take exactions: *lit.* 'and you *keep taking* enforced gifts',[3] "which

---

[1] *Cf.* R.V. marg. The meaning assigned in R.V. text, 'to bring suddenly', is
impossible as a translation of the Hebrew. Even the rendering 'causing to flash
forth', given above, is obtained only by straining the Hebrew, for the word in
the original (*bālag*) is a *cheerful* term (*cf.* van Hoonacker) not in harmony with
the idea of its grammatical object, 'destruction'. (*a*) The least emendation
would appear to be to read with LXX, '*who divideth*, assigneth' (ὁ διαιρῶν =
Hebrew *hammaphlíg*). (*b*) Further, it would seem reasonable to change the
word *shôdh* ('destruction') *either* in the first *or* in the second half of the verse
into *shebher*, 'ruin', the LXX having two distinct substantives here (συντριμμόν
and ταλαιπωρίαν). (*c*) In place of the Hebrew simple verb translated 'cometh',
the text of LXX, Peshiṭta, Vulgate, is to be preferred, 'who *bringeth*' (*Hiph'il*
voice). The simple result would then be obtained: '*assigning ruin* to the strong,
and bringing in destruction against the fortress'.

[2] T. H. Robinson, *Prophecy and the Prophets*, p. 65.

[3] A certain parallel to such a use of the term *mass'êth* (from *nāsā*, 'to take
away') as applied to a (sacred) 'tax', or 'offering' *required*, is to be found in

wheat: ye have built houses of hewn stone, but ye shall not dwell in them; ye have planted pleasant vineyards, but ye shall not drink the wine thereof. 12 For I know how manifold are your transgressions and how mighty are your sins; ye that afflict the just, that take a bribe, and that turn aside the needy in the gate *from their right*. 13 Therefore he that is prudent shall keep silence in such a time; for it is an evil time.

the poor *fellahin* had to offer to the grasping aristocrats, out of the hard-won produce of their toil" (Driver).

ye have built houses...but ye shall not.... Translate: 'Although ye have built houses...ye will not...'. The punishment is to take the form of spoliation of that which they have made their god. In the time of Solomon, and during the dynasty of Omri, Israel had become builders. The art had revived under the restoration of prosperity during Jeroboam II's reign. For the nobles' houses, *cf.* iii. 15.

hewn stone. Loose stone is a material ready to hand in Palestine for houses, and even for watch-towers. '*Hewn* stone', however, would be procurable only by the wealthy. See, further, *H.D.B.* art. "Stone", iv. p. 618.

but ye shall not drink the wine thereof. This threat is definitely reversed by the 'later voice' of ix. 14.

12. Now Jehovah Himself speaks. Israel merits the judgment threatened in *v.* 11.

how manifold are...how mighty are. This forcible translation, and not that in A.V., is the correct one. Follow R.V. also for the rest of the verse (not 'they', but '*ye*').

transgressions. See on i. 3. **sins.** Hebrew *ḥaṭṭâth*. The root signifies by etymology 'to do wrong', 'to miss the mark' (Judg. xx. 16); and among its earlier usages it is applied to the breaking of a taboo (1 Sam. xiv. 38). With Amos, sins are breaches of an *ethical* code as this whole context (*vv.* 7, 10–12) clearly shews. Unlike the priests both of Israel and of Babylon, the Prophet does not concern himself with ritual or ceremonial faults, such as the eating of unclean food or the omission of a festival. See G. R. Driver in *The Psalmists*, pp. 136, 170: "I know not the sin which I have done, I know not the error which I have committed".

afflict: *i.e.* 'harass'. **the just:** translated in ii. 6 'the righteous', which verse should be compared.

turn aside the needy: *i.e.* as in ii. 7, the 'way' or 'judgment' of the 'meek' man, or member of the poorer class of the community. *Cf.* Mal. iii. 5 (R.V.), 'that turn aside the stranger (from his right)'.

13. Therefore he that is prudent...an evil time. This verse may well

2 Chr. xxiv. 6, 9, Ezek. xx. 40, and probably in the Marseilles Tariff inscr. (l. 1). On the other hand, the term is used of a gift *from* a superior in Gen. xliii. 34, 2 Sam. xi. 8.

14 Seek good, and not evil, that ye may live: and so the LORD, the God of hosts, shall be with you, as ye say. **15** Hate the evil,

be a later apocalyptic gloss (*cf.* Nowack, Hölscher, Sellin). Perhaps the words are introduced from Mic. ii. 3, where their relation to the context is more obvious.

14, 15. A repetition of the exhortation to repentance. The poetic measure is trimeter.

14. Seek good. Rather more than in *vv.* 4 and 6, the message appears to be affirmative and constructive, not merely denunciatory. The same offer is now attached to 'seeking *good*' as was associated with 'seeking *God*'. Zephaniah, in a single verse (Zeph. ii. 3), combines the spiritual and moral appeal, 'Seek ye[1] the LORD...seek righteousness, seek meekness'. In Isa. lviii the prophet urges his hearers to do something better than to 'seek' Jehovah 'daily' in an external religious observance, while they imagine that they are thereby 'drawing near' to Him (*v.* 2): for, the prophet declares, God desires moral virtues such as, indeed, Amos in this chapter is upholding (*vv.* 6, 7). So Mic. vi. 8, 'He hath shewn thee that in which good consists'. All this, however, does not necessarily imply that the great prophets *equated* morality with religion. "Social righteousness is not a substitute for, but an expression of, religion" (Garvie). Surely Amos is but calling attention to the superiority of ethics over empty ritual. *If* he is endeavouring to define religion (in which an integral element is the drawing of the soul nearer to God) we must regard his teaching here, even as in other places, as falling short of ideal truth. The fact was that the moral element in religion had been practically forgotten by the majority of the people, not least by the priesthood itself (Hos. vi. 9). While, however, it is manifest that ethical religion was the warp and woof of prophecy, it is a precarious assumption (though one still finding support) that the eighth-century prophets introduced ethics in Israel (Kittel, *Rel.* p. 136, Engl. transl.).

as ye say. This is correctly a present tense (not perfect as A.V.); so, also, in *v.* 21, 'I *hate*, I *despise*'. In effect Amos' contemporaries say 'Jehovah of hosts is with us', even as the nation does in Ps. xlvi. 7, 11. However, the Prophet here and in *v.* 15 shews that there is a *condition* of God's presence and help, even the 'love' of justice and goodness. For the popular use of the phrase 'Jehovah of hosts', *cf.* Excursus I. pp. 330 ff.

15. Hate the evil, and love the good. These words, almost a converse of *v.* 14 *a*, supply at once an expansion and an interpretation of it. The verb 'to love' in Hebrew, as in English, has a wide range of uses. In Mic. iii. 2 bad people 'hate good and love *evil*'; in Prov. viii. 36 their conduct makes it appear as if they must 'love *death*'. In Am. iv. 5 the Hebrew runs,

---

[1] Hebrew *baqqᵉshû*, not *dirᵉshû*; but the words are practically synonyms: *cf.* Ps. cv. 3, 4, where E.VV. are unable to represent the changes from *baqqēsh* to *dārash* and then again to *baqqēsh*.

and love the good, and establish judgement in the gate: it may be that the LORD, the God of hosts, will be gracious unto the remnant of Joseph. **16** Therefore thus saith the LORD, the

'for this ye *love*'. On the other hand, in Mic. vi. 8 he who would please God 'loves *mercy*'; in Prov. xii. 1 'whoso loveth *correction* loveth *knowledge*'; in Zech. viii. 19 there is an exhortation to 'love *truth and peace*'. The promises, however, in Jer. xxxi. 33, 34, Ezek. xxxvi. 26, 27, seem to shew that it is God's will that man should not 'love' virtue merely in the metaphorical sense of *practising* it, but from a permanent desire and inclination towards it, implanted within the heart. The Targumist of Amos could not rise above the conception, 'Hate *to do* evil, love *to do* good'; *cf.* Isa. i. 16 *b*, 17 *a*. The LXX has the curious turn, 'As ye have said (*v.* 14): *we have hated* the evil things and *we have loved* the good things, restore ye *also* judgment in the gates'.

establish judgement: *lit.* 'set up'; the opposite of 'cast down' (in *v.* 7).

it may be that: *lit.* 'perhaps'. The expression may suggest a hope.

will be gracious unto. For the idea of Jehovah as a merciful God, *cf.* note upon vii. 3, 'the LORD repented'. Illustrations from Egyptian literature of the Deity's readiness to turn aside a threatened or present calamity are given on p. 308.

the remnant of Joseph. (1) In these words 'the (or 'a') remnant' Driver, Sellin, and others have seen something of the idea (without doubt expressed in such prophetic passages as 2 Ki. xix. 30,[1] Mic. iv. 7, v. 6–8, Zeph. iii. 12, 13, Joel ii. 32, and *cf.* also 1 Ki. xix. 18) of a righteous, or repentant, remainder[2] of Israelites saved after, or from, the coming catastrophe. "These two verses are the most hopeful in the book" (Horton). (2) This conception, however, seems entirely inconsistent with the actual outlook of Amos concerning Israel—a people wholly sinful, and therefore entirely doomed; *cf.* iii. 12 (note), viii. 2, and pp. 68, 69 on ix. 8–15. In fact, v. 15 *b* would seem to be an extraordinary mode of expressing the thought, 'Reform, and perhaps Jehovah will remit the punishment as regards those who shall *repent*'. Indeed, it does not appear clearly that the 'remnant', whatever it may be, is a repentant one: the mere handful that escapes in iii. 12 seems to be distinctly of the *worthless* class. More probably, therefore, the sense is: 'Repent, O Israel, so that perhaps the danger threatening the people already diminished in number may even now be averted'. If the writer be Amos, in his estimate, or, at least, in his vision of the near future (*cf. vv.* 2, 3), Israel, though its fortunes had greatly revived under Jeroboam II, is already hardly more than a 'remnant'

---

[1] It is by no means so clear that Isaiah in his *early* ministry contemplated a righteous or repentant remnant. *Shear-jashub* (Isa. vii. 3) seems to mean, '*Only* the fewest will escape'.

[2] Indeed Kautzsch in 1911 said: "Am. v. 14 *et seq.* brings home the question whether perchance the original conclusion of the book of Amos did not contain some consolatory outlook for the remnant of the Northern Kingdom".

God of hosts, the Lord: Wailing shall be in all the broad ways;
and they shall say in all the streets, Alas! alas! and they shall
call the husbandman to mourning, and such as are skilful of

numerically; and it would seem that here he caustically calls it such. So
Micah in Mic. ii. 12. In Ezek. xi. 13 the R.V. translates 'remnant', but in
ix. 8 'residue', which latter is clearly the meaning in both passages. In
Am. i. 8 Amos speaks of the '*remnant* of the Philistines', probably meaning
the nation no longer in its strength. And, after all, the actual condition of
Israel according to iv. 6–11, vii. 1–6 is a rather miserable one.[1]

of Joseph. The use of the name to signify descendants (or 'house',
v. 6) of the patriarch Joseph is not uncommon. *Cf.* vi. 6, Ezek. xxxvii. 19,
Pss. lxxviii. 67, lxxx. 1, lxxxi. 5. The occurrence of 'Israel' for '*sons* of
Israel' is, of course, extraordinarily frequent; *cf.* also 'Jacob' in vi. 8,
vii. 2, 5, viii. 7. Such idiom is possible only because of the fundamental
Semitic conception of the solidarity, and indeed the unity, of the family.

Vv. 16–18 (indeed 16–20) tell of the evil future in store for Israel.

16. Therefore: clearly has no connection with *vv.* 14 and 15, and hardly
any with *v.* 13, but it would follow well upon *v.* 12. As *parentheses* are not
of the genius of Hebrew composition, it would seem that *vv.* 14, 15 and
perhaps *v.* 13 were not intended by the writer to stand where they do
now.

the Lord, the God of hosts, the Lord: an impressive phrase.
"This arrangement of the divine names is unique", though iii. 13 *b* is
somewhat similar. It may be that the LXX and Syriac give the true text
in omitting the final word 'Lord'.[2]

Alas: Hebrew *hô*, a shorter form of the usual *hôî* (*v.* 18, 1 Ki. xiii. 30,
Jer. xxii. 18).

they shall call the husbandman to mourning. That is, from their
farms workmen will be summoned to some general lamentation. The
rendering favoured by not a few, 'the husbandman *shall summon* (*us*) to

---

[1] G. A. Smith (*XII Prophets*, p. 168) and others incline to hold that *vv.* 14
and 15 are a later insertion into the text, made, conceivably, after two-thirds of
the land had been devastated in 733 B.C., and when there certainly was in
Palestine only a 'residue of Joseph'. So Hölscher, who styles the verses a
secondary variant of *vv.* 4–6; similarly Edghill, and as regards *v.* 15, Nowack.
This is an attractive view. The *linguistic* difficulty (see note on 'therefore', *v.* 16)
would be sufficiently met by postulating that *vv.* 14, 15 are out of their right
position. Marti places them between *v.* 6 and *v.* 7. Still, it is almost certain
that great prophecies of judgment were qualified in a later age; and if *vv.* 14, 15
were such an addition to the book of Amos, this fact would account for Israel
being called a 'remnant', and for the lack of cohesion between *v.* 15 and the
passage which now immediately follows it.
[2] Harper emends to 'I will cause (sad) shouting (for) mourning', for '*Adônai*
reading '*arnîn*; *cf.* Lam. ii. 19. But against this, it must be urged that the
normal usage of the verb *rānan*, to 'shout', is of *joyous* shouting.

lamentation to wailing. **17** And in all vineyards shall be
wailing: for I will pass through the midst of thee, saith the

mourning, and professional criers (us) to wailing',[1] does not seem convincing.

The Hebrew terms for 'mourning', 'lamentation' and 'wailing', although
specially appropriate to grief for the *dead*, may also apply to grief at any
great disaster, as *e.g.* in Esth. iv. 3 a, ix. 22 (*'ēbhel*), Mic. i. 8 (*mispēdh*),
Jer. ix. 9 (*neḥî*); *cf.* note on Am. viii. 10. Indeed, they would be appropriate
to a great national *fast*. However, the present passage would seem to refer
to mourning over dead Israelites, and not to lamentation at a catastrophe
as such. See next verse.

and such as are skilful of lamentation to wailing. The paid mourners
will be called also. This would appear to be the sense, and it is supported
by Jer. ix. 17.[2]

17. in all vineyards shall be wailing. *Cf.* Isa. xvi. 10. In the East, in
the days of the Prophet as now also, at the season of grapes there was the
utmost rejoicing. The contrast is striking.

for I will pass through the midst of thee. This rendering is correct,
and not '*when* I pass through...' (Harper). Jehovah's presence will manifest
itself in a very different manner from that conceived of in v. 14. Perhaps
He will come in war (*cf.* v. 27); or possibly the expression 'I will pass
through...' is equivalent to 'I will send *pestilence*', as by the destroying
angel of Exod. xii. 12. Plague used to be considered pre-eminently God's
hand, because there was no human agent (*cf.* especially 2 Sam. xxiv. 14, 15).
For this visitation in Amos, see vi. 8, 10, iv. 10, note.

V. 18–27. JUDGMENT UPON THE NATION, WHOSE WORSHIP IS A MOCKERY

Possibly this exhortation was delivered on a different occasion from
that of v. 1–17.[3]

In *vv.* 18–20, the Prophet makes the surprising statement that the 'Day
of Jehovah' will be an unpleasant event.

---

[1] 'Husbandman' (*'ikkār*) being collective singular subject with plural verb;
cf. i. 3–8, Gen. xxxiv. 24, Judg. ix. 55, xv. 10, and Ges.-Kautzsch, § 145 d.

[2] Though it can be obtained only by *transposing* two words in the text of
Amos (read *'el mispēdh* instead of *mispēdh 'el*). R.V. marg. 'and proclaim wailing
to such as are skilful of lamentation' represents a desperate attempt to render
the M.T. The difficulty in this verse may lie somewhat deep, originating in scribal
dittography. As the text stands, the word 'wailing' occurs no fewer than three
times in a line and a half. If its second occurrence were to be omitted, it becomes
possible to translate the whole clause as 'and the husbandmen will call the skilful
of lamentation to wailing' (Nowack). For information concerning 'mourning
ceremonies', see Driver's Additional Note, *ad loc.*

[3] The two exhortations were placed together in the book not only because of
the common theme of Israel's unworthy *worship* (*vv.* 5, 21–23), but also by the
link of the word *hô*, or *hôî* (v. 16, R.V. 'alas'; v. 18, R.V. 'woe').

LORD. **18** Woe unto you that desire the day of the LORD !

18. Woe unto you that desire the day of the LORD! Here the Prophet
takes up a current conception, or saying, and gives it a new turn of meaning,
following up with his own application. Indeed, he flatly contradicts the
popular idea. For other instances of this method, see iii. 2, v. 4, v. 14.
From the present context of Amos it would appear that in the mouth of
the people the phrase 'the day of the LORD' signified the day distinguished
by His activity—"the day of His judgment, or of His triumph" (G. A.
Smith). Whichever aspect was the more primary one, the expression seems
to have stood for a day or crisis when Jehovah would, as Israel supposed,
champion His nation by working for them a final victory over their adversaries. Instead of this, says Amos in effect, the 'day' will be one of victory
of a great foe over *Israel*. Probably the right view is the one which does
not see in the people's use of the expression a reference to *judgment*.[1] It
would appear likely that to a nation holding generally a henotheistic (rather
than a monotheistic) conception of its God, the 'war-day' would be an
exhibition of their God's *triumph* (His interests and theirs were conceived
of as identical). The idea of judgment (at least of *nations*) would not come
in until the time after Amos had reduced everything to the ethical
principle and also had taught Israel that Jehovah takes cognisance of
men's acts outside Canaan. Not to his contemporaries, though certainly
to Amos and to his great successors, is it a 'day of judgment' upon Israel
and sinful nations wherever found. It is worthy of note how little the Divine
arbitrament figures in any early Hebrew eschatology. In Isa. iii. 13–15
Jehovah stands to judge, but it is to judge Israel (not 'the peoples'); *cf.* LXX.
In the phrase (in Isa. ix. 4) 'the yoke of his burden...thou hast broken as
in *the day* of Midian', the word 'day' is used for the day of Israel's famous
battle[2] with Midian, in which Jehovah gave His people victory. *Cf.* Judg.
iv. 14. Not dissimilarly, the Assyrian appeals to the god of fire, 'May
thy dreadful *day* overtake thy enemies'.

Amos, on the other hand, while by no means denying that Jehovah will
inaugurate a great 'day', points out that all His acts are upon a moral
basis. When He manifests Himself it will be against the sinful, not necessarily the *foreign*, nation. Elsewhere the Prophet declares that Jehovah
has no personal favourites (iii. 2, ix. 7). It is in such *ethical* eschatology, if

---

[1] *Cf.* also W. R. Smith, *Prophets*, pp. 397, 398. Likewise if the background
be that of a popular eschatology the idea of a judgment is not prominent: see
Introd. p. 60.

[2] Or, possibly, Jehovah's 'day' of slaughter. It is likely enough that the
word 'day' contained *in itself* no conception of a day of successful war. In
Meg. Taanith xii 'Nicanor's day' means the day distinguished by the *death* of
the Jews' enemy, Nicanor (*cf.* 1 Macc. vii. 48, 2 Macc. xv. 36). In Assyrian the
word 'day', *ûmu*, can bear the signification of 'storm-day' (Gressmann, p. 143
and references). For the alternative meaning of 'festival day', or 'day of
deliverance', as a *devotional* term, *cf.* Introd. p. 61, footnote 2. The *eschatological*
view is discussed on pp. 59 ff.

wherefore would ye have the day of the LORD? it is darkness,
and not light. **19** As if a man did flee from a lion, and a bear
met him; or went into the house and leaned his hand on the

eschatology it can be termed, that the prophets of Israel shew themselves
superior to the so-called prophets of Egypt and of Babylon. It would
seem that, according to the present context, the form which the 'day',
or activity, will take, ought to be explained as either (a) defeat and
captivity (v. 27), or (b) plague (v. 17), or (c) perhaps earthquake (ii. 16).[1]
The tenor of the book and the use of the term 'day' in Isa. ix. 4 suggest (a).
For later uses of the expression 'day of the LORD', see Additional Note,
pp. 299, 300. The idea of 'judgment' came to figure very definitely.

The rhythm of vv. 18–20 seems to be qînâh, with a few dimeters in the
middle of v. 19.

Woe... The sense is almost 'mistaken, or foolish, are you who...'. This
is well expressed by the next clause, which is perhaps an explanatory gloss
by a later hand: 'wherefore would ye have the day of the LORD?' lit. 'what
good is it to you—the day of Jehovah?'

it is darkness, and not light. The description seems to be suggested
by the thought of a literal 'day'. The day will come, whether or not they
'desire' it: but it will be a 'very dark' day; so v. 20. Similarly speaks
Zephaniah, the "great continuator of Amos' thought",[2] (in Zeph. i. 15 b),
and Joel (in Joel ii. 1, 2). In the present context the 'darkness' is metaphorical. In Am. viii. 9, though there also Jehovah's 'day' may be the
subject, the darkness is literal.

19. As if a man did flee from a lion, and a bear met him. The 'day'
is inescapable: as if the shepherd, endeavouring[3] to avoid a lion, were to
encounter a bear; and, when he at last thinks he is safe in his hut, a serpent
by the wall should attack him. Cf. ii. 14–16, note.

or went into the house. Translate, 'and should come home'; cf. Exod.
ix. 19, 1 Ki. xiii. 7. In the present instance the 'home' is but a shepherd's
hut.

In vv. 21–27 there is a further exposure of cult formalism, concluding
with a definite threat in vv. 26, 27. The statement is made as from Jehovah
Himself. The underlying thought is, "Put not your trust in ritual"
(Mitchell).

Vv. 21–23, taken with iv. 4, 5, render two points abundantly clear.
(1) The popularity of worship in Israel; there was no lack of worshippers

---

[1] Elsewhere in the book of Amos there may be allusions to this 'day of
Jehovah' in such passages as viii. 9, ix. 11, and cf. viii. 11, ix. 13. It would
seem, however, open to question whether, in interpreting the prophetic writings,
we should never allow a non-technical use of the word 'day'. Neither Israel
nor Israel's prophets always wrote 'day' with a capital letter, any more than
we ourselves do.

[2] Welch, Israel under the Kingdom, p. 95.

[3] 'Did flee' in the Hebrew is in the imperfect tense.

wall, and a serpent bit him. **20** Shall not the day of the LORD
be darkness, and not light? even very dark, and no brightness
in it? **21** I hate, I despise your feasts, and I will take no

(iv. 4, v. 5; *cf.* viii. 14, ix. 1). The only sign of a grudging worship occurs
in viii. 5, a passage which may be but prophetic irony. (2) The extent of
ritual already developed. This richness of sacrificial use is confirmed, as
far as Judah is concerned, by the nearly contemporary Isaiah (Isa. i. 11-15).
The references in Amos may be arranged thus:

(1) Animal sacrifices (*zᵉbhāḥîm*),[1] iv. 4, v. 25.

(2) Burnt offerings (*'ôlôth*), v. 22 (but the text is not certain).

(3) Meal offerings (*minḥôth*), v. 22 (though the precise meaning here is
not certain).

(4) Thanksgiving sacrifices (*tôdhôth*), iv. 5.

(5) Voluntary offerings (*nᵉdhābhôth*), iv. 5.

(6) Thank offerings (*shᵉlāmîm*, M.T.), v. 22; E.VV. 'Peace offerings'.

(7) Tithes (*ma'ăsērôth*), iv. 4.

At the festivals were songs and orchestra (v. 23).

21. I hate. *Cf.* Isa. i. 14, 'Your new moons and your appointed feasts
my soul hateth'.

I despise. Rather, 'I reject' or 'refuse'.

your feasts. Hebrew *ḥaggîm*, *lit.* 'your pilgrim festivals'; *cf.* Arabic
'el-ḥaj = 'the pilgrimage'. See Exod. xxiii. 14, 17, Am. viii. 10. In the
O.T., the term is applied to the sanctuary festivals; especially to those of
'Unleavened Cakes', Exod. xxiii. 15 (or 'Passover', Lev. xxiii. 5, 6) and
'Ingathering', Exod. xxiii. 16 (or 'Booths', Lev. xxiii. 34).

I will take no delight in your solemn assemblies:[2] *lit.* 'I will not
smell your solemn assemblies'; *i.e.* as Targum, 'the offering of...'. In
Exod. xxx. 38, Lev. xxvi. 31 also, the verb 'to smell' is followed by the
preposition 'in' or 'at' instead of (as *e.g.* in 1 Sam. xxvi. 19) by the direct
accusative. The smell of burning fat or meat, to Europeans objectionable,
was a pleasant odour to primitive Semites accustomed chiefly to a vege-
tarian diet excepting wild animals slain in hunting.[3] See on Am. iv. 5.
Moreover, by this time *incense* may have been used with the meal offerings
accompanying the burnt offering (Lev. ii. 1, 2). 'I will not smell': on the
possible survival of anthropopathic language, as distinct from essential
ideas, see on iv. 2, p. 294.

---

[1] For detailed discussions of the various forms of sacrifice in use in ancient
Israel and their significance, the reader may be referred to Gray, *Sacrifice in the
O.T.*; Kennett, *Sacrifice*, pp. 6-22; Lagrange, *Religions sémitiques*, ch. vii;
W. R. Smith, *Semites*, edn 3, especially pp. 213-224, 236-243, 269-286, 424-429,
573-574, 577-578.

[2] In connection with the present passage, Isa. xi. 3 is sometimes quoted, 'his
delight (R.V. marg. 'Heb. *scent*') shall be in the fear of the LORD'. The text,
however, is uncertain.

[3] *Cf.* W. R. Smith, *O.T.J.C.*[2] p. 249, and (more fully) *Semites*[3], pp. 222, 223.

delight in your solemn assemblies. **22** Yea, though ye offer
me your burnt offerings and meal offerings, I will not accept

your solemn assemblies. Translate, simply, 'assemblies'; for neither
the word nor the thing suggests the idea of solemnity; the religious assemblies signified were joyous ones; *cf.* the parallel term 'festivals' in the first
part of the verse. Here, as in Joel i. 14, ii. 15, no particular gathering is
alluded to. In later usage, however, the term is applied to a special
'assembly' on the seventh or eighth day of two festivals (Deut. xvi. 8,
Lev. xxv. 36).

22. In the previous verse and in *v.* 5 Amos has declared Jehovah to be
dissatisfied with the people's worship. In this verse and in *v.* 25 the
Prophet seems to single out for particular condemnation their sacrifices
and offerings.

Yea, though ye offer me your burnt offerings and. The rhythm
of *v.* 22 would be greatly improved if this first clause could be treated as
a gloss, the text to read simply, 'with your [meal] offerings I am never
pleased: and upon the thank offerings of your fat beasts I never look'
(Duhm, Marti).

burnt offerings. The Hebrew *'ôlâh* signifies, literally, 'that which *goes
up* (in smoke, to God)'. Sometimes such offerings are designated '*whole*
burnt offerings' (*kâlîl*), *e.g.* in Deut. xxxiii. 10, Ps. li. 21. As they were
consumed upon the altar (1 Ki. xviii. 38), obviously the offerer ate no
portion. The *'ôlâh* was supposed to express devotion, or entire consecration.
The difference between *'ôlôth* and 'sacrifices' is illustrated by the passage
Jer. vii. 21, where the prophet ironically urges the worshippers to convert
'burnt offerings' into 'sacrifices' so that they may 'eat' the 'flesh' of both;
for Jehovah is as little pleased with either. For reference to the burnt
offering consisting of human beings, rather than (as here) of animals, see
Gen. xxii. 2, Judg. xi. 31, 2 Ki. iii. 27, xvi. 3, Jer. xix. 5 and Mic. vi. 7.

meal offerings. The Hebrew word *minḥâh* is used to convey the idea
of (1) a *present* to anyone, (2) *tribute* to a king, and (3) a gift or '*offering*'
(animal or vegetable) *to God*. Instances of (3) are to be found in Gen.
iv. 3–5, 1 Sam. ii. 17, xxvi. 19, 1 Ki. xviii. 29, 36, and so perhaps here and
in *v.* 25. (4) However, it is possible that by the time of Amos the use of
the term had already passed into a fourth and latest stage, *viz.* to signify '*meal
offering*'. So the R.V. translates here and in *v.* 25 in the margin. The
'meal offering' was of grain, or of its products (bread or cakes), and it
accompanied the animal sacrifice. So always in Code 'P', *e.g.* in Lev. ii.
1, 4, 14, xiv. 20, xxiii. 16 (in A.V. '*meat* offering'). Being pre-eminently a
'gift' to the Deity, this offering was either burned upon the altar or assigned
to the priests. As with the *'ôlâh*, the offerer ate no share.

I will not accept them. The verb, which strictly in both Hebrew and
Aramaic means 'to have pleasure in', is frequently used of God's attitude
towards sacrifices (Mic. vi. 7, Ps. li. 18) or towards the offerers of sacrifice
(2 Sam. xxiv. 23, Hos. viii. 13).

them: neither will I regard the peace offerings of your fat
beasts. **23** Take thou away from me the noise of thy songs;
for I will not hear the melody of thy viols. **24** But let judge-

peace offerings of your fat beasts. Here only in the O.T. the M.T.
reads the singular number, 'peace *offering*' (*shelem*). The R.V. rightly
renders it as the plural *sh⁰lāmîm*. (1) Possibly the original purpose of 'peace
offerings' was to provide a means either of *obtaining*, or of *expressing*, peace
(or alliance) with God (*cf.* usual LXX εἰρηνικά). In the latter sense such
offerings would here be appropriate in days of prosperity after Jeroboam's
victories, the worshippers believing that God had recently proved Himself
to be well pleased with them. (2) It seems preferable, however, to connect
the term with the verb *shillēm*, 'to requite a good' or 'to pay';[1] *cf.* Prov.
vii. 14, Ps. cxvi. 14 (E.VV.), 'I will pay my vows'. *Sh⁰lāmîm* were always
z⁰bāḥîm, *i.e.* slaughtered animals eaten in part by the offerer at the social
feast. Not seldom they are associated with burnt offerings, at times of
blessing and rejoicing, as *e.g.* in 2 Sam. vi. 17; and these two classes of
sacrifice are mentioned together as early as the 'E' code (Exod. xx. 24).
Whatever be the derivation of the term, this form of sacrifice, in view of
its usage, may well be designated '*thank* offering', as it is in R.V. marg.

fat beasts. *Cf.* Isa. i. 11, 'I am full of...the fat of *fed beasts*'.

23. Take thou away from me: *lit.* 'from upon me'. The music is a
burden under which Jehovah labours.

noise: Hebrew *hāmôn*. The word does not necessarily imply anything
unpleasant, but the *murmuring* sound of a throng of people; see *e.g.* Isa.
xvii. 12, xxxi. 4, Job xxxix. 7. It is parallel to 'melody' in the second
half of the verse.

thy songs. Of course it is not impossible that some of the 'Psalms'
may have been among these 'songs'; though the liturgical songs of the
Psalter, in their present form, were composed *after* Amos' days. But see,
further, on vi. 5 ('like David'), viii. 3. Gunkel regards all classes of Psalm
composition as dating from the earliest period of Israel's religious life
(see *Die Psalmen*, pp. ix ff. and *Einleitung*). Both here and in viii. 10
the 'songs' are probably sacrificial. It is important, however, to observe
that the word 'song' (*shîr*) has no *necessary* connection with worship.

the melody: Hebrew *zimrāh*, from a root signifying 'to make music in
praise of God'. In Isa. li. 3 it is used of *singing*; but in the present passage
clearly the 'melody' is instrumental; *cf.* Ps. lxxxi. 2, where *zimrāh* (R.V.

---

[1] *Cf.* the Syriac reading in iv. 5: see p. 171. And *cf.* the Vulgate *vota*. It is
interesting to note that in a Carthaginian inscription of the 4th cent. B.C.
found at Marseilles the word *shelem* is used (in the singular as in the M.T. of
Amos) of 'perhaps an ordinary sacrifice' (W. R. Smith, *Semites²*, p. 237, footnote).
The terms *zebhaḥ*, *kālîl* and *minḥāh* also occur, but likewise with a meaning
differing slightly from the O.T. usage, though at the same time shedding light
upon it (G. A. Cooke, *N.S.I.* pp. 112–117).

ment roll down as waters, and righteousness as a mighty
stream. **25** Did ye bring unto me sacrifices and offerings in

'psalm') is parallel with 'timbrel' and 'harp'. From the same root, *mizmôr*
came to be used of the Psalms, all of which were 'accompanied'.

of thy viols: Hebrew *nēbhel*, *i.e.*, probably, 'lyres', or else '(portable)
harps'. For a description of such, the student is referred to a note by
J. G. Wetzstein in Delitzsch's *Isaiah* (2nd and 3rd edns). In Am. vi. 5
the instrument is used in the (?) secular feasts of the wealthy Israelites.

24. But: Hebrew, simply, 'and'. This verse sums up the one indictment
of the chapter—lack of justice (*vv.* 7, 10–12, 15).

roll down. Translate, 'roll *along*'; *cf.* the succeeding clause. The same
passive voice is rendered in Isa. xxxiv. 4, 'roll *together*'. The Targum of the
present passage mistakes the root, and translates weakly, 'let judgment
be *revealed* like waters' (*gālāh*, for *gālal*).

righteousness: or 'justice'; *cf. vv.* 7, 15.

as a mighty stream. 'Mighty' is a false translation. Render, as R.V.
marg. following the Arabic, 'never-failing'; *cf.* Numb. xxiv. 21, '*Perpetual*
is thy dwelling place', and, with reference, as here, to the 'steady flow' of
a river, Deut. xxi. 4, Exod. xiv. 27, and Ps. lxxiv. 15. An ordinary 'stream'
(in Hebrew *naḥal*, Arabic *wādy*) is full after the rains, but in summer it
becomes a mere channel of water, or it may even dry up entirely. Thus
Amos means: 'Let true judgment be constant and not intermittent'. This
is one of Amos' most effective similes drawn from his wilderness life. See
also *vv.* 7, 19.

It is to such ethical teaching as this that Zechariah refers as having been
'sent by (God's) spirit by the hand of the former prophets' (Zech. vii. 12).
He himself echoes it, especially in such a passage as vii. 9, 'Execute true
judgement'.

25. Sacrifices were not offered in the wilderness.

Did ye bring unto me sacrifices and offerings...? This rhetorical
question of course anticipates but one answer, 'No'. (1) There is no
emphasis upon the pronoun 'me', the interrogative particle in the Hebrew
being connected with the object 'sacrifices and offerings'. Hence the interpretation must be set aside '*even* in the wilderness you sacrificed *to other
deities*'. (2) It has been apparent from *vv.* 21–23 (*cf.* iv. 4, 5) that Amos,
like the other great prophets, esteemed daily conduct above sanctuary
duties, sacrifice in particular. The present verse follows this up with a
statement which, at the least, implies that the worship of Jehovah once
went on without sacrifice of any kind; and therefore *a fortiori* sacrifice
cannot be really necessary. See, further, Excursuses III and IV. pp. 338–348.
In Egyptian literature the sentiment of Amos is reflected in the words,
'More acceptable is the nature of one just of heart than the ox of him who
doeth iniquity' (p. 347).

sacrifices. See on iv. 4. In these, the blood and the fat were Jehovah's
portion.

the wilderness forty years, O house of Israel? **26 Yea, ye have borne Siccuth your king and Chiun your images, the star of**

offerings. See *v.* 22. These offerings were His entirely.

in the wilderness forty years. The same allusion to the early history of Israel is made in ii. 10.

26, 27. Taken as they stand in the Hebrew text, these verses together indicate the *punishment* which the people are about to receive for the unsatisfactory conduct, unrepented of, referred to in *vv.* 21–24. In the last resort, they seem to supply an amplification of *vv.* 18–20, explaining the true significance of 'the day of the LORD'. On the other hand, the verses may be a portion of another prophetic oracle. They follow very abruptly upon *v.* 25.

26. Yea, ye have borne Siccuth your king and Chiun your images. (1) Almost certainly the Hebrew should be translated by an English future tense[1] (as in R.V. marg.), 'And you *will* take up Sakkuth, *etc.*' In other words, 'you will bear (*i.e.* be made to carry) your whole pantheon of idols into captivity with you'. In the term 'carry' there is perhaps an ironical reference to processions with religious paraphernalia; *cf.* Isa. xlvi. 1, 7, Jer. x. 5. (2) The translation in the *text* of the R.V. 'ye *have* borne Siccuth', *etc.* is but the survival of that of the A.V., the Revisers hesitating to break away from the traditional interpretation as represented by the Targum, LXX and St Stephen's speech in Acts vii. 42, 43. The Greek version of Am. v. 25, 26 makes the Prophet say that the Israelites did sacrifice in the wilderness— to certain foreign deities.[2]

Siccuth:[3] or, better, *Sakkuth*, the proper name of the war god Adar-Malek ('king')-Saturn, otherwise known as Ninurta ('Nin-ib'). The words

---

[1] According to the idiom of *waw consecutive.* Ges.-K. § 112 *rr* suggests that it is just possible to render as a *frequentative* (referring to the past), *i.e.* 'you used to take up'. A parallel to such a use would be supplied by 1 Sam. xvii. 35. Harper (p. 137), without endeavouring to support his translation, renders by a *present* tense, 'But now ye *lift* up'. Without doubt, the future tense of prophecy, to say nothing of the cohesion of the whole passage, would have been better secured by the use of the simple *imperfect* tense, following an introductory phrase such as 'Behold the days come' (iv. 2) or following the term 'therefore' ('*al kēn* or *lākhēn; cf.* iv. 12, v. 10).

[2] St Stephen's account of the incident of the golden calf contains a rather strange suggestion, *viz.* that it was because of the Israelites bringing a sacrifice unto that idol (Acts vii. 41, 42) that (apparently as a punishment) forthwith in the wilderness God turned and *gave them up* to these acts of star-worship (Acts vii. 43ʹa); for which star-worship they were further to be punished by a Babylonian captivity! Of course, nothing is known of any star-worship in Israel until the later years of the monarchy.

[3] The pointing of the M.T. of both words with the vowels *i–û* (*Sikkûth, Chiûn*) is a fictitious one, being the vocalisation of *shiqqûṣ*, 'abomination', the term of reproach applied by the Jews after Amos' day to heathen deities or their images in general.

your god, which ye made to yourselves. **27** Therefore will

'your king' (1) probably allude to the royal *title* of the god, whose name Adrammelech ('Adar is *king*') occurs in 2 Ki. xvii. 31; or (2) they may refer to the king of *Israel* in king- ("Moloch-") worship. The syncretised worship would thus be of Sakkûth-Melech.[1] (3) The LXX saw a reference to the Ammonite(?) god *Moloch* ('the tabernacle of Moloch')!

Chiun: or, rather, *Kaiwân*, appears to be another name for the same god, with reference especially to the planet Saturn. In an Assyrian text also, the names *Sakkuth* and *Kaiwan* have been found together. The form *Kaiwan* occurs in the Peshitta rendering of this verse.[2]

your images. (1) The plural number is awkward, unless conceivably it is an extension of the use of the plural of divinity, to be rendered into English as 'your (great) image'. (2) Not improbably, another *proper* noun is to be understood—'your Selem'—the Aramaic name of a god (probably Saturn) mentioned in two inscriptions found in Têma in Arabia.[3]

the star of your god. (1) The 'star' may be some representation of the star (Saturn). (2) The translation, 'your star-god', though tempting, and a popular one, would seem to be unsupported by Hebrew grammatical usage.[4] (3) There is much to be said for holding the expression 'the star of your god' to be an explanatory gloss, and perhaps also the words above rendered 'your king', 'your images', thus leaving 'And you will take up Sakkuth and Kaiwan, which you have made to yourselves'. As the verse stands, it makes cumbersome prose, in strong contrast to the trimeter poetry of Amos in the preceding passage. The entire verse is regarded by some scholars as an interpolation into the text of the book of Amos; see the Additional Note on pp. 300 ff.

---

[1] Riessler understands Adrammelech (Adar-meleoh) in 2 Ki. xvii in the same sense.

[2] The view held by Robertson Smith should perhaps be recorded. He maintained (in *Prophets*, edn 2, p. 402) that *Kaiwan* should be taken not as a proper noun, but as signifying a piece of religious apparatus—a *pedestal* or image-stand. Similarly with the other word, this scholar accepted the translation 'tabernacle', *i.e.* portable shrine (as in LXX, Pesh., Vulgate, A.V.) rather than *Sakkuth*. The LXX 'Ραιφάν, or 'Ρεφάν (in Acts vii. 43 Remphan, 'Ρεμφάν) obviously stands for *Kaivân*, but the *K* has become *R* by a very early copyist's slip. The LXX (perhaps correctly) read the words '*Kaiwan* your images' after, not before, 'the star of your god'.

[3] *C.I.S.* II. Nos. 113, 114, ? 5th cent. B.C. The longer inscription of the two is interesting in connection with the present passage, for it represents *Selem* and '*Ashîrâ*, the gods of Têma, as welcoming to their sanctuary the *Selem* of some other place; even as according to the present passage Israel believed it to be legitimate to worship *Kaiwân* and *Sakkûth* as well as Jehovah. In the verse before us, the Israelite cult may have been of *Kaiwân-Selem*; cf. *Sakkûth-Melech*, above.

[4] The idiom for such an expression as 'his weapons of war' in (*e.g.*) Deut. i. 41 is not the same.

I cause you to go into captivity beyond Damascus, saith the
LORD, whose name is the God of hosts.

For allusions to the worship of deities in addition to Jehovah, see note
on viii. 14, and *cf.* that on 'Beth-el' (iii. 14, p. 293). It seems certain that
the service of Jehovah was never really *abandoned* even at the times when
the Hebrew nation may be said, in the language of the prophet, to have
'forsaken' Him (*e.g.* in Jer. ii. 13, v. 19, *etc.*), or to have 'changed their God'
(Jer. ii. 11). Such prophetic language may refer only to the lessening of
the people's attention to Jehovah consequent upon their having admitted
another deity beside Him. Professor Robertson Smith (*Prophets*[2], p. 140),
though not allowing in the present passage a reference to the gods Sakkuth
and Kaiwan, recognised the existence of astral worship in Israel, and at
the time of Amos. He observes: "From the connection it cannot have been
a rival service to that of Jehovah, but probably attached itself in a subordinate way to the offices of His sanctuary".

27. **Therefore will I cause you to go into captivity.** Translate, as
R.V. marg., '*and* I will', *etc.* If *v.* 26 was no part of the original text of the
book, quite possibly neither was *v.* 27; for it connects itself in sense with
v. 26 and not with *v.* 25. Though Amos predicts many catastrophes (*cf.*
Introd. p. 30), yet the captivity threat was one of the characteristics of
Amos' message (vi. 7, 14, vii. 9, 17, ix. 4), and it cannot be denied that
such a prediction couched in brief language makes a singularly impressive
conclusion to the Prophet's address here.

beyond Damascus.[1] Israel will be entirely exiled by Assyria, a power
even greater than Syria who had afflicted them for so long a period and who
had taken a certain number of captives (2 Ki. v. 2). If *vv.* 26, 27 form a
unit, there is an appropriateness in the exile of the people and their heathen
gods to Assyria, the nation from whom they learned to worship such astral
deities. The statement made in this verse is discussed from the point of
view of the present day in the Additional Note on pp. 302, 303.

whose name is the God of hosts. It is quite clear that the expression
'whose name is'[2] belongs to a later age (*cf.* v. 8, p. 184 *ad fin.*); but this
is not so certain concerning the words 'the God of hosts' (Hebrew, 'the
God of *the* hosts').

---

[1] St Stephen in Acts vii. 43 substituted the name 'Babylon' for the 'Damascus'
of the Hebrew and LXX, a strange inexactitude; for Assyria, to which the
Northern Tribes were taken, did not lie 'beyond Babylon', and Judah went to
Babylon itself.

[2] Hebrew *sh^emô*. Driver (*Amos*, edn 1915, p. 121, note) quotes Hos. xii. 6
(E.VV. *v.* 5) in favour of the authenticity of the phrase, but the construction is
not the same.

VI. 1 Woe to them that are at ease in Zion, and to them that are secure in the mountain of Samaria, the notable men

VI. The Downfall of the Nobles of Judah and of Israel proclaimed

Ch. vi, marking the close of the second great section of the book, treats of the same general subject as ch. v, and quite possibly represents what followed immediately in the Prophet's vehement discourse. He is still dealing with the punishment of the people as originally summarised in the smaller oracle in ii. 6–16. The luxury-loving nobles, especially, are addressed (*vv.* 1, 2–6). Perhaps Amos is picturing a sacrificial banquet in their own mansions (*vv.* 4, 5). The 'day of Jehovah', according to the text as it stands, comes through the medium of plague (*vv.* 9, 10) as well as of captivity (*v.* 7, *cf. v.* 14).

1. Woe. As in v. 18, the Hebrew interjection might be more accurately rendered by the English 'Alas!' It is frequent in prophecy (Isa. seventeen times, Hab. five times, Jer. four times, and eight times elsewhere).

that are at ease: or, 'careless'.

in Zion. The problem as to whether the Prophet addressed himself solely to *Northern* Israel is discussed in the Introd. pp. 12, 13. (1) The authenticity of the words 'in Zion' is suspected, or rejected, by Cornill, Marti, Hölscher, and Sellin. The last-named suggests the rather unconvincing emendation 'city' ('*îr* for *Ṣiyyôn*). (2) On the other hand, the genuineness of the passage is not questioned—or it is even upheld—by G. A. Smith (*XII Prophets*, p. 13), Driver, Harper, van Hoonacker, Gressmann, Köhler and others.[1] In the present passage, when originally spoken no less than when first written down, *some* proper noun must have been necessary in parallelism to 'Samaria'; and it seems arbitrary to expunge 'Zion'—with no textual evidence from any source[2]—mainly because 'Joseph' is mentioned in *v.* 6, and on account of a certain theory of the sphere of Amos' prophetic interest. Why should he not, if he wished, when speaking in Samaria couple the name of the Southern capital with that of the Northern? Micah, preaching to Jerusalem, names also Samaria (Mic. i. 5, 6, *cf.* i. 1), and Mic. vi. 16 alludes even to the 'statutes of Omri', king of North Israel.

that are secure in. (1) The expression is closely parallel to 'that are at ease in', earlier in the verse. *Cf.* the use of 'in' with (the *local*) sense of 'upon' in iv. 1. (2) Possibly, however, the A.V. 'and *trust* in', *i.e.* 'rely

---

[1] Duhm and Mitchell support its retention as part of, at least, the *written* text. Nowack in his edition of 1922 emends 'Zion' to 'Gilgal'. Further he omits 'the mountain of Samaria' and reads 'Beth-el' in place of the M.T. 'house of Israel' in *v.* 1 *b*. The latter part of the verse is undoubtedly awkward, but such a reconstruction seems too precarious. Hardly more convincing is the conjecture of Ehrlich, 'those that are at ease *in their pride*'—or, 'on the rock' (Riessler).

[2] LXX and Pesh., which have 'those who *despise* Zion', doubtless intend a paraphrase for Samaria; but none the less their reading attests the presence of 'Zion' in the Hebrew text which they represent.

of the chief of the nations, to whom the house of Israel come!
2 Pass ye unto Calneh, and see; and from thence go ye to

upon', is correct. *Cf. e.g.* Isa. xxx. 12, *'trust in* oppression'. So *Oxf. Heb. Lex.*

the mountain of Samaria. The city was built upon a 'mountain'. See iii. 9, note.

the notable men of the chief of the nations. By 'the chief of the nations' is meant, perhaps quite seriously, Israel (and Judah; *cf. v.* 2, 'these kingdoms'). The same phrase, *rē'shîth gôyîm*, is applied to Amalek in Balaam's oracle of Numb. xxiv. 20.

the notable men: *i.e.* 'appointed' (*lit.* 'pricked off') as the nation's leaders. On the other hand, some would read the *Niph'al participle* in place of the M.T., translating, 'who (*i.e.*, in effect, Israel as a whole)*designate themselves* the chief of the nations'; *cf.* the A.V. 'which are named chief...'. In that case it can be inferred only from the substance of the passage that in reality it is the *rulers* that are being addressed by the Prophet.[1]

to whom the house of Israel come: *i.e.*, as implied by the context, 'come' for *judgment.* Some word, however, seems to be needed to make this clear (*cf.* 2 Sam. xv. 4, Exod. xviii. 16); and, further, it may be questioned whether the verb-tense (*ûbhā'û*) can bear this meaning of '*are in the habit of* coming'. On account of the former difficulty Köhler suggests the rendering, 'who ever come (in the sense of 'make pilgrimage') *to Beth-el*', but the sense would not well agree with the first part of the verse.

the house of Israel. For the expression, see v. 1, 3, 4, ix. 9. In *v.* 14, below, it perhaps refers especially to the Northern Kingdom, but not necessarily in that verse or here. In Jer. v. 15 (where, as here, the Hebrew text has the support of all the Versions) the reference is actually to *Judah* only.

2. Pass ye unto Calneh...your border. (1) Probably the sense of the verse would be expressed by the paraphrase, 'Leaders of the chief of the nations (*v.* 1), consider almost any great and prosperous lands with which Israel and Judah can reasonably be compared (of course excluding Egypt and Assyria). From North to South are any states better than your kingdoms, or greater in extent?' So Targum, W. R. Smith (*Prophets*[2], p. 138), Driver, Duhm. The Preacher's moral (assumed rather than expressed) appears to be, 'Then your failure is the more serious' (*cf.* ii. 9-16). (2) The more popular interpretation is quite opposite. 'Take warning by the *fall* of these great cities, Calneh, Hamath and Gath. Will *you* escape?' According to this, though *vv.* 3 *et seq.* would still follow on *v.* 2 fairly naturally, *v.* 2

---

[1] Torrey's suggestion, '*Make the round of* the foremost nations *and come* (*imperative*) to them! Pass over...', is clever in requiring little change in the Hebrew, and he claims the support of the LXX (ἀπετρύγησαν); but it would appear to be doubtful whether the *qal* voice can be so used (*niqqᵉphû*).

Hamath the great: then go down to Gath of the Philistines:
be they better than these kingdoms? or is their border greater

is generally regarded as an addition to the text of Amos made subsequently
to 720 B.C. (see note on 'Hamath'), or to 711 B.C. (see note on 'Gath').[1]

Calneh. (1) Probably the same as the Assyrian *Kullani* in north-east
Syria, to the north of Aleppo, a city which was conquered by Tiglath-
pileser III in 738 B.C. Apparently it is the Calno of Isa. x. 9, recently fallen
in Isaiah's time (at the hands of Sargon, in 711 B.C.). (2) Calneh in Gen.
x. 10 appears to be quite different (in district of Babylonia). The LXX has
πάντες, mistaking Calneh for Hebrew *kôl*, 'all'.

Hamath. Hamath (the modern *Ḥamā*) lay on the river Orontes to
the north of the Lebanons, 150 miles north of the Israelite city of Dan.
It was the centre of an important kingdom. Toi, or Tou, of Hamath was on
friendly terms with David (2 Sam. viii. 9). The king of Hamath fought side
by side with Ahab of Israel and Ben-hadad of Syria at the battle of Ḳarḳar.
From 2 Ki. xiv. 28, though the text, as it stands, contains obvious errors,
it must be inferred that Hamath was defeated by Jeroboam II. Jeroboam's
pressure upon Hamath, whatever its nature, may have occasioned the
rapprochement between that state and Judah indicated, slightly later, in
the inscription of 738 B.C.—*cf.* Introd. "Date", p. 40, footnote 1. In this
monument Tiglath-pileser III states that he took nineteen districts within
the kingdom of Hamath and carried away more than 30,000 exiles. The
fall of Hamath did not come till 720 B.C., at the hands of Sargon.

Gath. One of the five great cities of Philistia, probably the nearest
one to Hebrew territory (*cf.* 1 Sam. xvii. 52, LXX, R.V. marg.). For the
problem of the relation to the present passage of the fall of Gath, see
the Additional Note, p. 303. With the phrase 'Gath *of the Philistines*'
cf. 'Jordan *of Jericho*' in Numb. xxii. 1, and 'Zion *of the Holy One* of Israel'
in Isa. lx. 14.

be they better...or is their border greater. There comes here a break
in the continuous trimeter rhythm, and also the Hebrew is difficult enough;
but the translation of the E.VV. does not seem impossible (*cf.* Duhm, van
Hoonacker). However, it must be said that most moderns insert the
pronoun 'ye' into this clause, with the reversal of pronominal suffixes[2]
(not really a very simple change, and one without any textual authority),
and so arrive at, 'Are *ye* better than these (foreign) kingdoms: is *your*
border greater than theirs (was)?' In this connection the second of the
above (p. 203) interpretations, for the most part, is adopted, and it is

---

[1] Van Hoonacker stoutly maintains the authenticity of *vv.* 1 and 2, claiming
that they contain no echo of the Assyrian invasions of the close of the eighth
century. "Amos quotes the example of states more ancient than Israel yet
reduced to a condition much inferior". The past does not guarantee the future.
He makes Calneh the well-known old city of Babylonia.

[2] Or, as Köhler, attaching the *min* to the first instead of to the second *gᵉbhûl*,
a simpler way of obtaining the same result.

than your border? **3** Ye that put far away the evil day, and
cause the seat of violence to come near; **4** that lie upon beds
of ivory, and stretch themselves upon their couches, and eat

inferred that *v.* 2, either with or without *v.* 1, is a gloss added after the ruin
of Gath. Undoubtedly 'these kingdoms' would very naturally mean
Calneh, Hamath and Gath; but, as G. A. Smith reminds us, Israel's territory
was much *larger* than Gath's. Taking the former interpretation (*viz.* that
Calneh, Hamath and Gath are *prosperous*) 'these kingdoms' are Judah and
North Israel—the 'Zion' and 'Samaria' of *v.* 1. *Cf.* 'these two nations...',
Ezek. xxxv. 10.

7 The idle leaders of *v.* 1 are more fully addressed. Their luxury and
indifference (*vv.* 2–6) will reap a terrible retribution (*v.* 7).

3. Ye that put far away: more correctly, 'chase away'; *cf.* Job xviii. 18*b*
(Hebrew root, *nādhadh*).

evil day: *lit.* 'day of evil', *i.e.*, here, physical calamity, not 'ethical
evil' as in v. 14. For 'day', *cf.* v. 18.

cause the seat of violence to come near. Note the antithesis to the
preceding clause: well maintained also in the Targum, 'You are going *far*
from the evil day, and are bringing robbery *near* in the house of your
assembly'.　　**seat of violence:** *i.e.* the tribunals in which 'violence' (not
justice) is in authority.[1]　　**violence:** *cf.* v. 12.

Vv. 4–6 *a* enumerate the details of the luxury indulged in.

4. that lie upon beds of ivory. The woodwork of these divans was, as
the Targum expressly translates, '*inlaid with* ivory'. The list of tribute given
by Hezekiah to Sennacherib should be compared: "ivory couches, splendid
seats of ivory, elephant hides, ivory", *C.O.T.* (*W.*), p. 286.

stretch themselves upon their couches. The Hebrew verb *sārah*
occurs again in *v.* 7, *lit.* 'to go free' or 'unrestrained'. In Ezek. xvii. 6
the word is used of a *spreading* vine, and in Exod. xxvi. 12, 13 the noun
and verb are employed of the *overhanging-part* of the curtains 'hanging
over' the tabernacle. Here the verb seems to apply well to the sprawling
idlers. The same two words 'beds' and 'couches' occurred in iii. 12. Micah
denounces similar aristocrats in Judah, 'devising iniquity...upon their
beds' (Mic. ii. 1).

It is difficult to read the description in the Quran of the Mohammedan
Paradise, without being reminded in a general way of this passage in Amos
and also of iii. 12 *b*. "God...shall reward their constancy with Paradise

---

[1] There is, however, no instance elsewhere of a concrete meaning being
attached to the word rendered 'seat' (*shebheth*). 1 Ki. x. 19 hardly supplies an
example, for there the text has the additional word 'the *place* of (sitting)'. On
the other hand, the true abstract sense of 'sitting' would scarcely be possible
in the present Hebrew sentence. Difficulties and obscurities of text occur not
only in *vv.* 1 and 2, but, it may be said, throughout the chapter. The emendation
shēbhet hammas, 'sceptre of the forced levy', is ingenious, but nothing more.
The LXX translators (σαββάτων) pointed it as *shabbāth.* For the 'sitting' of
one in *authority*, *cf.* i. 5, note (on 'inhabitant').

the lambs out of the flock, and the calves out of the midst of
the stall; 5 that sing idle songs to the sound of the viol; that
devise for themselves instruments of music, like David; 6 that

and silken garments, reclining therein on couches;...vessels of silver and
goblets like flagons shall be borne round among them; flagons of silver
whose measure themselves shall mete....Their clothing green silk robes
and rich brocade..." (Surat al-Insan lxxvi. 12–21). "On couches with
linings of brocade shall they. recline, and the fruits of the two gardens
shall be within easy reach..." (Surat ar-Raḥman lv. 54).

lambs...calves: a sign of luxury. In the East to this day there is
comparatively little meat-eating. For 'calves', cf. St Lu. xv. 23.

5. that sing idle songs. The word (pôr*ṭîm*) thus rendered is of quite
uncertain meaning.[1] The root contains in itself no idea of *idleness*. Perhaps
translate, simply, 'chant', as the A.V. Mitchell (followed by Harper)
renders 'twitter' or 'prattle': he considers that the word "indicates the
contempt that Amos felt for the perhaps really not unmusical songs with
which feasts were enlivened". Driver, in an additional note, suggests that
"it is just possible that, it...might be used of those who *extemporized*
poetry over-rapidly, without premeditation, in a hurried flow of unmeaning,
unconsidered words".

to the sound of: *lit.* 'according to the mouth of', 'in accordance with'
(*cf.* Gen. xliii. 7). The word rendered 'viol' is the same as that which occurs
in v. 23. See p. 198.

that devise for themselves: *lit.* 'have devised'. For this meaning of
the verb,[2] *cf.* Exod. xxxi. 4, xxxv. 32, 35.

instruments of music: *lit.* 'implements of song'.[3] So 1 Chron. xv.
16, *etc.* Gressmann denies any reference here to secular drinking songs,
but thinks rather of "sacred songs like the psalms"—and believes that
"Amos knew of David as a psalmist; consequently it is necessary to trace
back the history of the Psalms to David himself" (*The Psalmists*, p. 9).

like David: *i.e.* 'as David *had*'; or, '*just as* David also *used to invent*'.
In the Hebrew the expression 'like David' comes emphatically at the head

---

[1] In Aramaic it signifies 'to break off', and with it is to be connected the term
p*erîṭā*, a small coin.

[2] *Ḥāshabh* usually signifies 'to think', not 'to *invent*', but Mitchell's translation
is hardly tenable—'who think that for them as for David, are instruments of
music' (*Amos*, p. 44). It does not appear right to maintain (with this scholar)
that the sense of this verb should be determined by the fact that the other
verbs in *vv.* 4–6 a seem to be limited to acts *during* the banquet. It is sufficient
if the 'inventing' were *in connection with*, or *in view of*, the feast. Moreover
vv. 3 and 6 *b* do not necessarily refer to what was done at the meal itself.

[3] If this were not a well-established Hebrew phrase, there would be considerable
point in the emendation (Nowack, Gressmann) '*all kinds* of songs' (*kōl* for *k*e*lē*;
cf. also *millê*, 'words of song' (Lohmann, Sellin)), but it would seem legitimate
to doubt whether the verb *ḥāshabh*, applicable to mechanical art, could possibly
be used of the 'composition' of 'songs'. No parallel has been suggested.

drink wine in bowls, and anoint themselves with the chief
ointments; but they are not grieved for the affliction of

of the clause. The Prophet is ironical in comparing, in any respect, these
worthless persons to so famous a man of three centuries previously. In
1 Sam. xvi. 18 David, the minstrel, played the harp, and in 2 Sam. vi. 14, 16
he 'danced and leapt' upon a civic and religious occasion. Does this verse
of Amos help us in determining David's place, if any, in *Psalm* composition?
At the best, not very much. At first sight the context might suggest
David's connection with music of a secular, and even not elevating type;
but, really, the allusion is not *inconsistent* with his being sincerely interested
in sacred music. The minstrel, moreover, in the East *sings* as well as plays:
so he may well have composed *words* of song, as is undisputed (*cf.* 2 Sam.
i. 19–27, iii. 33, 34), and even (in some form) sacred poems such as occur in
2 Sam. xxii and xxiii. 1–7. Probably an early use of the Psalms was in
connection with sanctuary rites[1] and sacrificial feasts. If so, elements in
some Psalms may be even *pre*-Davidic (*cf.* note on 'bowls', *v.* 6). What
should be understood by the phrase 'of (or, 'to') David', at the head of
74 of the 150 Psalms, is another question. Very probably the reference
is to the mode of accompaniment—either tune or musical instrument
—entirely consistent with the M.T. of Amos here.[2]

6. that drink wine in bowls. These 'bowls' are not small vessels;[3] yet
there is hardly foundation for translating 'by the pailful' as do some
scholars. Derived from *zâraq*, 'to toss', the noun carried the idea of a
vessel for *scattering ritually*. *Cf.* Exod. xxxviii. 3 (R.V. 'basons'); Zech.
xiv. 20, 'the bowls before the altar'. Perhaps these ought not to have been
used at the feast of *vv.* 4 and 5. Gressmann, on the other hand, sees here
a fitting reference to the ritual bowl at a *sacrificial* banquet. *Cf.* the reference to 'lambs' and 'calves', *v.* 4 *b*.

the chief ointments: or, more *lit.* 'the best of oils'. The idea may be
either (1) *Jehovah's due*, or simply (2) *the finest procurable* (Mitchell).[4]

but they are not grieved: *lit.* 'they have not made themselves sick'.

---

[1] *Cf.* H. Gunkel, in "The Poetry of the Psalms" (*O.T. Essays*, 1927), pp. 126,
127, *etc.* (briefly) and *Ausgewählte Psalmen*.

[2] Curiously enough, the presence of the word 'like David' in the original text
is, at the least, doubtful. Not only is the manner of its spelling late, but the
poetic structure of the verse is complete without it, and moreover, if it had
been in the Hebrew upon which the LXX translators worked, it is difficult to
see how they could have failed to recognise the name, and should have confused
the clause as they did (ὡς ἑστηκότα ἐλογίσαντο καὶ οὐχ ὡς φεύγοντα). Nowack
and Sellin regard it as a gloss.

[3] Though the presence of the word in Zech. ix. 15 is probably only from a gloss,
the verse reminds us that these bowls were of a fair size.

[4] For the same ambiguity with the word *rê'shîth*, which occurs also in *v.* 1
of this chapter, *cf.* the eighth-century Cyprus inscription: "The governor...gave
this...of *choicest* bronze", or "as *the first fruits of* bronze" (*C.I.S.* I. No. 5); and
see note on p. 281.

Joseph. 7 Therefore now shall they go captive with the first

These selfish leaders of the nation have not given themselves a moment's suffering at the 'breach of Joseph'. The picture drawn by the Prophet is, indeed, a hideous one, and clearly it was taken from real life. The student, however, hardly needs to be reminded that the words of Amos are the bitter rebukes of a reformer, rather than a carefully balanced description of the condition of the nation as by a modern historian sitting in his study chair. For example, how comes it that Amos never once speaks of a fault in the *lower* stratum of society, nor even includes unambiguously the proletariat in his exhortations?[1] Jeremiah is quite different in Judah: *e.g.* Jer. vi. 13, 'from the *least of* them...'; v. 1, 'if ye can find a man, if there be *any* that doeth justly', *v.* 4, 'Surely these are poor'.

for the affliction of Joseph. G. A. Smith sees a reference here to 'moral havoc' to which the rich are indifferent, and he may be right. However, the use of the word (*shēbher*) elsewhere of the nation seems rather to suggest political or social ruin (Isa. **xxx.** 26, Jer. **xiv.** 17, *etc.*, Lam. ii. 11, *etc.*). Hence, we should probably understand a reference either (1) to the damage caused by Tiglath-pileser III, in 734 B.C., or (2) to the disasters enumerated in Am. iv, or, still more probably, (3) to the ruin of the state, the coming of which ought to have been foreseen as necessary because of the nation's sin, or as already a fact upon the political horizon—'the evil day' of *v.* 3 *a*. With the whole passage should be compared Isa. v. 11–13, where the 'work of the LORD' is the coming judgment.

Joseph: see v. 6, 15. The Prophet, speaking in or near Samaria, mentions only Northern Israel.

7. now. (1) The *logical* use of this word in Hebrew is comparatively rare.[2] (2) The usual literal force of 'now', especially as introducing a punishment, occurs in Hos. iv. 16, viii. 8, 13 and Jer. xiv. 10, and is pre-eminently suited to the argument of Amos here. 'Therefore are they to be taken into exile *now*'.

shall they go captive. Grammatically 'they' = the offending nobility of *vv.* 3–6; but it is the *nation* Israel that will now march into exile at the head of exiled peoples.[3] The Prophet, doubtless, thought specially of the offending nobles, as perhaps he expresses more clearly in iii. 11; but Amos, like most O.T. prophets, would not feel any moral difficulty in a whole nation being involved in the meting out of punishment to the guilty within that nation. For processions of captives, see Gressmann, *Bilder* (2nd edition), Nos. 86, 89, and *cf.* 151.

---

[1] The reference in vi. 11 to the destruction of the 'little house' seems to be scarcely more than is involved in the *general* captivity of v. 27.

[2] Examples are 1 Sam. viii. 5, 'Thou art old...*now* make us a king'; 2 Ki. xviii. 20, '*Now* on whom dost thou trust?'; with perhaps the references furnished by Harper (Hos. ii. 10, v. 7). Harper interprets the word in the present passage in this sense. For '*and*-now', see Am. vii. 16, note.

[3] Perhaps there is an ironical reference to Israel's comparative greatness among the states referred to in *vv.* 1, 2. *Rē'shĭth gōyĭm*, 'the chief of the nations', becomes *rō'sh gōlĭm*, 'the first that go captive'.

that go captive, and the revelry of them that stretched themselves shall pass away. 8 The Lord GOD hath sworn by him-

go captive. The taking of captives into exile was a practice not peculiar
to the Assyrians (as the allusions in 2 Ki. v. 2, Am. i. 6, 9 are witness). It
was, however, so much a feature in their conquests that it is hard to suppose
that Amos, in referring (in v. 27, vi. 7, vii. 17, ix. 4) to wholesale captivity,
has not Assyria in mind—and, indeed, is not influenced by consideration
of actual Assyrian movements. *Cf.* Introd. p. 30 and on ii. 13–16, p. 146.

the revelry of them that stretched themselves. The rendering
'revelry' is probably not so accurate as that of 'banquet' (in the A.V.).
The word *marzēaḥ* is used in inscriptions for a clan-feast and a corporation
or council.[1] For 'stretched themselves', *cf. v.* 4.

shall pass away. The feast not merely will come to a close: it will
be forcibly ended by war; *cf.* Dan. v. 1–30. In the three Hebrew words
rendered 'the revelry of them that stretched themselves shall pass away'
there is a powerful assonance[2]—*wᵉsār mirzāḥ sᵉrûḥîm.*

8. The Prophet sums up the position. Jehovah has emphatically affirmed
that He both loathes that of which the nation is proud, and will send
punishment upon her cities.

The Lord GOD. LXX Κύριος (*i.e.* omitting 'Adônai). See on vii. 1.

hath sworn by himself. *Cf.* iv. 2, note, and viii. 7. The exact form of
oath 'by himself' occurs again only in Jer. li. 14 (M.T. but not LXX).
Grammatically, the Hebrew expression is by no means so emphatic as to
justify Duhm's rendering, 'by His very self'.[3] From the nature of the
case, however, it is a very strong one. A 3rd cent. comment upon Exod.
xxxii. 13 in T.B. *Berakhoth* 32a runs: "What means *By Thyself*? R.
Eleazar said—Moses spake before the Holy One, blessed be He: Lord of the
world, if thou hadst sworn to them by heaven and earth, I should say,
since heaven and earth will perish, so too Thine oath will perish; but now
Thou hast sworn to them by Thy great name: as Thy great name lives
and abides for ever and ever, Thy oath also abides for ever and ever".
(In the Midrash *Exodus Rabba* 44 *ad fin.* a similar statement is assigned
to R. Hezekiah, *c.* 240 A.D.) And see Ep. Heb. vi. 13–18.

---

[1] The Aramaic Targum repeats the Hebrew word. (1) In *Aramaic* the
meaning of the term may be '*funeral* feasting' (Dalman). In the only passage
in the O.T., beside the present one, in which the Hebrew term occurs, the
reference is to the cry of *mourning* (Jer. xvi. 5). (2) However, its application to
a happy feast seems to be well established (Cooke, *N.S.I.* pp. 113, 144, 150).
See, further, S. A. Cook in Robertson Smith, *Semites*³, pp. 626, 627.

[2] Another, and even more striking, instance of paronomasia in the prophets
occurs in Isa. v. 7: *mishpāṭ*, 'judgment', *mispāḥ*, 'shedding of blood' (R.V.
marg.), and *ṣᵉdhāqāh*, 'righteousness', *sᵉ'āqāh*, 'a cry'.

[3] Indeed, on the strength of 1 Sam. xviii. 1, 3, xx. 17, and Deut. iv. 9, it may
be said that the Hebrew (*lit.* 'by His soul') means no more than if the simple
pronoun were used, as in the phrase, 'By myself (Hebrew *bî*) have I sworn':
Gen. xxii. 16, Exod. xxxii. 13 (R.V. wrongly, 'by thine *own* self').

self, saith the LORD, the God of hosts: I abhor the excellency
of Jacob, and hate his palaces: therefore will I deliver up the
city with all that is therein.

9 And it shall come to pass, if there remain ten men in one

saith the LORD, the God of hosts. For the Hebrew *neʾúm, lit.* 'it is
an oracle of', see the note on ii. 11. The clause (if rightly in this context
at all) should be placed at the close of *v.* 7; so Wellhausen, Marti, and
others. It is absent from LXX of the present verse and of *v.* 14.

I abhor. The same Hebrew word as occurs in v. 10.[1]

the excellency of Jacob. In such a context as this the Hebrew *gāʾôn*
is better rendered by the more vigorous word 'pride'. So the same word used
in connection with the river Jordan is translated by the R.V. in Jer. xii. 5
(R.V. marg. 'swelling'). The term may be used (1) of "Israel's vain-glorious
temper itself (Isa. ix. 9), or (2) of the objects of which it is proud, its
affluence, material splendour, military efficiency" (Driver). The second
meaning '*object* of pride' seems best to suit at least the present passage
and viii. 7. On the other hand, the rendering 'exaltation', 'excellence',
is appropriate when the term is applied to God (*e.g.* in Exod. xv. 7,
Isa. ii. 10). In any case (Hos. v. 5, vii. 10 notwithstanding) no sinister
meaning need necessarily be intended when the term is employed in connection with Israel. In the present passage 'palaces' supplies a good
parallel to *gāʾôn* if its meaning be 'prestige'. In viii. 7 the Targum paraphrases by '(Jehovah) *who gives greatness to* Jacob'.

and hate his palaces. For the oppression of the mansion dwellers, and
its punishment, *cf.* iii. 10, 11.

therefore will I deliver up. The English 'therefore' (in Hebrew 'and')
is misleading. Handing over to the enemy is, according to the previous
verse because of Israel's *sin*—not on account of Jehovah's hatred. Render,
'*yea* I will give over'.

deliver up. The Hebrew (*sāgar,* in causative voice) is used of Jehovah's
handing over to any chastisement: in Ps. lxxviii. 48, 'hail', in *v.* 50
'plague', *cf.* note on *vv.* 9, 10. But especially it is applied to a city and 'all
that is therein'. The word may suggest war and siege, perhaps followed by
the taking of prisoners. *Cf.* Am. i. 6, 9, Ps. lxxviii. 62, and see *v.* 11 on the
destruction of buildings.

the city. The *article* is not in the Hebrew. The 'city' is neither Zion nor
Samaria in particular. 'City and its contents': population, cattle, goods
are threatened. Some, *e.g.* Sellin, would limit the reference to the capital
of Northern Israel (*cf.* the note on *v.* 1 above, 'in Zion').

Vv. 9 and 10, in their present position, foreshadow plague as heightening
the horrors of war (*vv.* 7, 8). Possibly, however, the two verses (or *vv.* 8–10)

---

[1] In Am. vi. 8, however, the consonants are *tʾb* instead of the usual *tʿb* (perhaps
the result merely of scribal corruption; but *cf.* Wright, *Comp. Gram. Sem.
Langs.* pp. 48, 287).

house, that they shall die. **10** And when a man's uncle shall take him up, even he that burneth him, to bring out the bones

are to be taken as referring to pestilence as a scourge standing alone; *cf.* perhaps v. 17. An epidemic raged in Assyria about 760 B.C.[1]

Notwithstanding possible corruptions within the Hebrew text, the grim scene is so realistic as to suggest that the description comes from an eye-witness of such an event. A household of even ten will be entirely wiped out (*v.* 9). On the death of the ninth the nearest relative left, who has come to dispose of the body, inquires whether there be more than one surviving. The tenth man, speaking from 'an innermost room' (so Nowack) or from 'a corner' (so Köhler), says 'No'. When his turn comes there will be no more to take out: but meanwhile 'Speak softly, lest perhaps uttering the Name of Him who sent the plague, the Name is overheard', and He do even more havoc.

10. uncle. So the Hebrew *dôdh* is translated in 1 Sam. xiv. 50. Perhaps the general term 'kinsman' is better (R.V. marg., *cf.* Targum). In Isa. v. 1 it means 'loved one' or 'friend'; and see note on Am. viii. 14, where possibly the same Hebrew word should be read—in the sense of 'loved one', or 'kinsman (*i.e.* patron)-deity'.

even he that burneth him. Though this may be the sense, it is not an accurate translation, which is 'even (or, 'and') his burner'. The Hebrew suggests some recognised custom *either* (possibly) (1) in times of plague, *or* (2) in connection with the usual funeral rites. (1) Normally the Israelites, and indeed Semites generally, did not burn their dead, the instance in 1 Sam. xxxi. 12 *b* being exceptional. See on ii. 1. Hence, if 'his burner' is to be taken as meaning 'burner of the *body*', the reference can be only to a custom in time of pestilence such as was known also to the ancient Greeks. (2) It is not impossible that 'his burner' has reference to some usage or rite of igniting of spices, *etc.*, at all burials. If so, archaeological evidence of this among the ancient Hebrews has yet to be discovered.[2] Important in this connection are the notices in 2 Chron. xvi. 14, xxi. 19

---

[1] *V.* 11, as Wellhausen pointed out, would follow easily upon *v.* 8; and, as *vv.* 9, 10 seem to stand apart as being in prose, there is a strong presumption that the two verses are not in quite their right place. However, the primitive theology of *v.* 10 prevents the piece from being considered a *late* interpolation.

[2] The Mishnah (before 200 A.D.) contains a reference to the burning (of incense and of valuables) at the death of a *heathen*, but the passage yields no evidence of Jews having any such rite. "...The Wise say, At a death in connection with which burning takes place idolatry occurs, but *when there is no burning* there is no idolatry" (*Aboda Zara*, I. 3, edn Elmslie, pp. 6, 7, whose note compare, p. 23). The later opinion of the Talmud, while disagreeing with the heathen rites accompanying such a ceremony of burning, seems to find no fault with this burning in itself. At the annual festival of the rabbi Simeon ben Yochai, at Meiron in Galilee, burnings of shawls, *etc.* take place to-day (Frazer, *Adonis, Attis, etc.* i. pp. 178, 179, and *P.E.F. Qrly St*, July 1919, pp. 112 ff.

out of the house, and shall say unto him that is in the innermost parts of the house, Is there yet any with thee? and he
shall say, No; then shall he say, Hold thy peace; for we may
not make mention of the name of the LORD.

of 'burnings', which were perhaps offerings to the dead. Both these instances, however, are of *royal* funerals.[1]

the bones. Clearly = 'the body', as perhaps also in ii. 1.

No: *lit.* 'cessation'. The Targum paraphrases well by a verb, 'They-are-
at-an-end' (*sāphû*).

then shall he say: *i.e.* the first speaker (so Duhm). The Hebrew, however (*lit.* '*and* he will say'), suggests a continuance of the words of the
plague-stricken survivor: 'No' (and he will go on to say[2]) 'hold thy peace;
for....'. In the present verse this is a third occurrence of the same expression, 'and he shall say'; perhaps, therefore, it is best to omit it as
having arisen by a form of dittography.

Hold thy peace. The particle (in Hebrew, *has*) occurs also in viii. 3.
Translate, 'hush!' In one passage only (Neh. viii. 11) the word is treated
as a verb, and is inflected.

we may not make mention of the name. The negative is emphatic,
and the syntax impersonal: *lit.* 'there is no mentioning the name'; *i.e.* 'the
name cannot (or, 'must not') be mentioned'. So exactly the Hebrew of
1 Chron. v. 1. (1) G. A. Smith and others hold that the phrase is an
explanatory note supplied by the *writer*.[3] (2) More probably the E.VV. are
right in translating the clause as 'we' (so Duhm, Nowack).

The text of *vv.* 9 and 10 is so difficult that several emendations of it have
been attempted; but none would appear to be convincing.

---

[1] See Benzinger, *Arch.* p. 166, Lagrange, *Rel. sémitiq.* p. 288. The emendation
of Ehrlich, 'his remover' (*mᵉsappᵉrô*; based on Arabic), instead of 'his burner',
lacks support, as Nowack points out, in the Hebrew language. This latter critic
inclines to consider as a possible reading 'his mourner' (*mᵉsappᵉdhô*). The corresponding abstract noun occurs in Am. v. 16, in what is perhaps another 'plague'
passage.

[2] So in 2 Ki. vi. 27 and 28 *a*, that which is clearly a single speech the historian
nevertheless divides by the words 'and the king said unto her'.

[3] A N.T. parallel would be St John iv. 9 *b*, 'For Jews have no dealings with
Samaritans'.

[4] Zeydner (*cf.* also Valeton) reads: "*One who escapes* will be left to bring the
bones out of the house, and he will say unto him that is in the house, Is there
still anyone with thee? And he will say, No; and he will say, *These have done
foolishly* (*hiskîlû 'ēlleh*, *i.e.* these have sinned). Invoke the name of Jehovah".
This is a skilful use of the LXX addition at the close of *v.* 9, 'and the rest will
be left' (καὶ ὑπολειφθήσονται οἱ κατάλοιποι). While, however, Zeydner's conjecture gets over the difficulty of 'even his burner', it ignores the presence in
the M.T. of *dôdhô*, 'his uncle' (which seems to have been known to the LXX
also). A translation 'invoke', 'call upon', rather than 'make mention of', is
supported by the Targum, and also by the sense of the verb in Isa. lxii. 6, and

11 For, behold, the LORD commandeth, and the great house shall be smitten with breaches, and the little house with clefts.

A word may, perhaps, be added concerning the theology of the latter part of *v.* 10. While the Assyrians, and the Semites generally, might believe in a special god of plague, with Israel there was but one God who, it was conceived, was the (immediate) cause of *every* calamity; *cf.* iii. 6. This was an advance theologically.[1] The present verse, however, is unique in the O.T. in the evidence which it furnishes of an appalling degree of popular superstition in ancient Israel, surrounding this belief. If in the course of speech a man should find himself referring by name to Him who has sent the plague, the Deity may do even further damage in the same or in other ways. "The whole of life was believed to be overhung with loose accumulations of Divine anger" (G. A. Smith).

11. For, behold, the LORD commandeth. It would seem that if *vv.* 9 and 10 assumed their present position in the text of Amos through the work of some redactor, then this clause also was added by him to help the connection. With the words which *follow* 'commandeth', the trimeter rhythm of *v.* 8 immediately resumes.[2]

For. The word seems to look back upon *v.* 8 *b.* *V.* 11 shews in what manner and to what degree the ruin will come.

the great house…the little house. *V.* 8 declares that the whole city will be 'delivered up', *cf.* iii. 15. Probably there is no special point intended in the mention here of the small dwelling; for the verse seems to be an

---

(with the same preposition *b^e*) Isa. xlviii. 1, Ps. xx. 7 (xx. 8 in Hebrew). However, these passages seem to suggest conscious and deliberate invocation, as in public worship, and not such as is contemplated in the present context.

Sellin, reading in place of the somewhat awkward *la'ăsher* the word *l^e'ishshāh*, and altering the third 'and he says' into 'and *she* says', obtains the sense: "and if he says *to the woman* in the innermost part of the house, Is there still one with thee? *she* answers, Hush; because we dare not mention Jehovah's name. *And he says, No*". The transference to the very end of the verse of the clause 'And he says, No' is rather bold, and does not seem to yield a correspondingly good result.

[1] Upon the general question of the relation of God to Nature, it may be said that, while the Christian must believe that in some way God is greater than Nature, and that in a sense He is behind it; nevertheless, the survival in Christian countries of the attitude which regarded God and Nature as *identical* is, even to-day, causing harm to Christianity. The progress in scientific medical discovery takes for granted that God is not in the 'plague', any more than He is in the sudden strong wind, the earthquake or the lightning (1 Ki. xix. 11, 12). Of the natives of the Congo Dr Albert Schweitzer writes, "that the diseases have some natural cause never occurs to my patients" (*On the Edge of the Primeval Forest*, p. 35). See iii. 6, note, p. 289.

[2] The question of the metre would seem decisive. Yet Köhler classes together the *four* verses (8–11) as "the finest poetry in the Book of Amos". *V.* 11 he makes to be a continuation of the speech at the close of *v.* 10.

12 Shall horses run upon the rock? will one plow *there* with oxen? that ye have turned judgement into gall, and the fruit

example of the Hebrew idiom known as 'divided parallelism'.[1] The Targum paraphrases 'great kingdom and little kingdom' as referring to North and South Israel respectively. It is true that *bayith* is employed in such a sense extremely frequently both in the O.T.[2] and in the Assyrian inscriptions. It is, however, never so used *absolutely*, and it is difficult to see what could have led Amos to express himself in so cryptic, not to say, ambiguous a fashion.[3]

with breaches. Adverbial accusative: perhaps 'into fragments'.[4]

with clefts. The only other occurrence of this word in the O.T., *viz.* in Isa. xxii. 9 (where R.V. renders 'breaches'), suggests the idea of cracks, or the *act* of causing a break. On the other hand, in the present passage, the sense of 'into *atoms*' or '*bits*' seems to be what is required (Duhm).

12. The End of the State, of which the Prophet has spoken in *vv.* 7, 8 and 11, is only what is to be expected. A condition of affairs is reigning which is so *unreasonable* that it cannot last long.

Shall horses run upon the rock? Translate: 'Can (or, 'do') horses run upon (or, 'up') a crag?' As in the Prophet's questions in iii. 3–5, there appears to be no special point in the selection of the instances, beyond the fact that they are illustrations of preposterous and unreasonable things (Driver). "Only a lunatic would imagine either possible" (Mitchell).

will one plow *there* with oxen? The supplying of the word 'there', solely in order to redeem the M.T. from absurdity, is arbitrary. The emendation, 'will one plow the *sea* with oxen?'[5] is widely accepted.

that ye have turned judgement into gall. Supply 'and yet ye think that the kingdom can continue'. 'Gall' is a misleading translation.[6] Taking the evidence of Deut. xxix. 18, Hos. x. 4 (R.V. 'hemlock'), it is clear that the Hebrew *rô'sh* is some poisonous *plant*. McLean, in *E.B.*, suggests *colocynth*. In Deut. xxxii. 33 the term is applied metaphorically

---

[1] *Cf.* Zech. ix. 17 *b*.

[2] *E.g.* '*house of* Israel' in Am. v. 1, 3, 4, 25, vi. 1, 14.

[3] For a defence of the Targum interpretation, see Wellhausen, Harper and Buttenwieser. This last, in *Prophets*, p. 231, compares 'the two houses of Israel' in Isa. viii. 14.

[4] The Hebrew *r*ᵉ*sîsîm* is ἅπ. λεγ. Praetorius in *Z.A.W.* 1914, p. 44, suggests the emendation *hărîsîm*, a term which occurs in the appendix to the book (ix. 11, 'ruins'), and *cf.* Isa. xlix. 19 (Hebrew *hărîsûth*).

[5] *I.e.* dividing the unlikely plural *b*ᵉ*qārîm*, into *bāqār* (collective) and *yām*. A further clever suggestion, however, of Halévy has received some support: 'Or does the *wild ox* plough *like* the bullock?' *kabbāqār rêm* (=*r*ᵉ*êm*). *Cf.* Job xxxix. 9, 10.

[6] As is also the LXX χολή (='bile') in such a passage as Deut. xxix. 18 (LXX 17). The LXX of Am. vi. 12 paraphrases weakly by 'wrath' (εἰς θυμόν).

of righteousness into wormwood: **13** ye which rejoice in a
thing of nought, which say, Have we not taken to us horns by

to the venom of serpents.[1]   **judgement:** as always in Amos, signifies
'justice' (v. 7, 15, 24).

   the fruit of righteousness. The *effect* of righteousness, or justice,
should have been something good and helpful. Instead, as things are,
there is that which is bitter and injurious—'wormwood'. The use of 'fruit'
to mean 'result' is very frequent in the O.T. *Cf.* Prov. viii. 19, xi. 30,[2]
xviii. 21, Isa. x. 12. It is possible that the word 'fruit' is specially chosen
here because 'wormwood' itself is of the vegetable kingdom.

   wormwood: so in v. 7, also as referring to perverted justice.

13. ye which rejoice in a thing of nought. The people's leaders are
represented as in the act of congratulating themselves,[3] either (1) upon
recent victories over Syria, or (2) upon the material prosperity which had
succeeded thereafter. The Prophet discourages this exuberance of spirits.
As a matter of fact their sins (*v.* 12 *b*) are soon to bring their happiness to
a summary end through the interposition of a greater power than Syria
(*v.* 14). Hence the object of their rejoicing is 'a thing of nought'.[4] But see
next note.

   Have we not taken to us horns...?: *lit.* 'a pair of horns'. (1) The
'horn' was an emblem of strength, especially as *pushing back* an enemy:
so in Deut. xxxiii. 17, 'His horns are the horns of the wild ox: with them
he shall push the peoples'. *Cf.* Jer. xlviii. 25 (where the 'horn' is parallel
in metaphor to the 'arm' of the warrior) and Ps. lxxv. 5. (2) However, it
would seem somewhat tautologous in the present passage to say, 'Have
we not by our *strength*[5] taken (or, 'gained') *strength*?' And there is, surely,
a difficulty in supposing that victory over so persistent a foe as Syria could
have been designated, even from the Prophet's point of view, a mere 'thing
of nought'. Hence there is much to be said for the modern rendering
(notwithstanding the fact that it does not appear among the ancient
versions), 'which rejoice in *Lo-debar*, which say, Have we not taken[6] to
us *Karnaim* by our own strength?' There was a city Lo-debar (or *Lo-dābār*)
in Gilead, probably near Mahanaim[7] (2 Sam. ix. 4, xvii. 27, Josh. xiii. 26);
and a Karnaim in the same region, rather more to the north, is mentioned

---

[1] So, in the Targum here, the corresponding Aramaic word *rē'sh* is used: 'ye
have turned judgement into the poison *of evil serpents*'.

[2] Where 'fruit of *righteousness*' should probably be read, following LXX.

[3] Present participle, in the Hebrew.

[4] Or in Hebrew 'a not-thing'. So in Deut. xxxii. 21, 'a not-god...a not-
people', and in Isa. xxxi. 8, 'a not-man'.

[5] Even the Targum translator seems to have felt this, paraphrasing 'horns'
into 'herds' or 'possessions'.

[6] For the use of *lāqaḥ* of capturing a city, *cf.* Numb. xxi. 25, Deut. iii. 14,
Josh. xi. 19, 1 Sam. vii. 14, 2 Sam. viii. 1. The characteristic word, however, for
this is *lākhadh* (more than fifty times in O.T.).

[7] See Driver, *Samuel*, p. 286.

our own strength? 14 For, behold, I will raise up against you
a nation, O house of Israel, saith the LORD, the God of hosts;
and they shall afflict you from the entering in of Hamath unto
the brook of the Arabah.

in 1 Macc. v. 26, 43, 44 (probably the Ashtaroth-Karnaim[1] of Gen. xiv. 5).
See, further, the Additional Note on p. 304.

14. The punishment threatened (in *v.* 11) and justified by the Prophet
(in *vv.* 12, 13) will come; *for* Jehovah will send a nation against Israel.

For, behold, I will raise up against you a nation: *lit.* 'I (am)
raising up...'. 'Behold', coupled with the Hebrew *present participle*, is a
frequent idiom in prophetic literature used to express imminent punishment.
So also in vii. 8, *lit.* 'behold I (am) setting'. With this somewhat vague
reference to 'a nation', *cf.* Isa. v. 26, also of the coming of Assyria (read
gôi, 'nation', *sing.*). Jer. v. 15 (concerning the *Scythians*) seems to be based
upon Am. vi. 14 and this passage in Isaiah. 'For' is the correct translation,
and not 'yea', 'surely', 'but', or 'therefore', all of which have been suggested.

of hosts: *lit.* 'of *the* hosts', as in iii. 13, ix. 5; elsewhere in Amos, as
normally in the O.T., there is no article (iv. 13, v. 14, 15, 16, 27, vi. 8).
The text of iii. 13 is suspicious, and that of ix. 5 very much so. Moreover
in the present passage the whole clause, 'saith the LORD, the God of hosts',
so breaks up the Hebrew sentence as to make it almost impossible for us
to believe the clause to be original.

and they shall afflict you. The Hebrew verb *lāḥaṣ* signifies *lit.* to
'squeeze' or 'press';[2] *cf.* 2 Ki. vi. 32, '*thrust* him *back* with the door' (R.V.
marg.). Perhaps the English 'harass' expresses best the meaning as in
2 Ki. xiii. 4, 22 (where R.V. has 'oppress'). There is no idea within the word
of captivity. The passage produces a slight bathos after v. 26, 27 (if these
latter verses are by Amos).

from the entering in of Hamath. For 'Hamath', see on *v.* 2. In
Numb. xxxiv. 8 and Judg. iii. 3, 'the entering in of Hamath' represents the
northern boundary of Israel. The writer of 1 Ki. viii. 65 uses the phrase,
'from the entering in of Hamath unto the brook of *Egypt*', to describe the
extreme limits of Solomon's kingdom. For a discussion of the geographical
reference, see the Additional Note on p. 304. It would seem reasonable that
the reference is to the spot where Hamathite territory begins.

unto the brook of the Arabah. This expression is of even more uncertain reference than the foregoing, and it occurs here only. The boundary
referred to may be at the northern end of the Dead Sea, or part of the way
down, or, most probably, at the southern extremity; see, further, the
Additional Note on p. 305.

---

[1] The place-name had been derived from the goddess worshipped there—
'*Ashtoreth of the two horns*. For a representation of an idol 4½ inches long,
exhibiting *Astarte* with two rams' *horns*, found at *Gezer*, see Gressmann, *Bilder*,
p. 83, fig. 152; edn 2, Tafel cxix. fig. 285; *cf.* R. A. S. Macalister, *Gezer*, ii. p. 420.
[2] And so the Targum translates it here (*deḥaq*).

the Arabah: *i.e.* waterless *waste; cf.* Isa. xxxiii. 9, xxxv. 1, li. 3. This was the name given to (1) the depression of the Jordan valley, at least the wider and more desolate part of it lying between Jericho and the Dead Sea (Josh. viii. 14, 20 *b*, 1 Sam. xxiii. 24, 2 Sam. ii. 29, 2 Ki. xxv. 4), and also to (2) the 'desert' west of that inland lake. To-day (3) the broad plain between the Dead Sea and the Gulf of Akabah is called *Wady el-'Arâbah*. 'The Arabah' here is either (1) or (3).

So closes the second great section of the book (chs. iii–vi). Social outrages and the blotting out of any true conception of God are to bring the nation to sore distress (vi. 14), to decimation (v. 2, 3), and even to captivity (v. 26, 27, vi. 7) and to other evils (v. 16–20, vi. 9, 10). Or it may be, rather, that Amos thus *interprets* the significance of evils which are present, or which he believes to be imminent.

It is held by some critics that the prose passage vii. 10–17 which interrupts the narrative of the visions may have stood originally at the close of this section of the book. The reference to 'captivity' in vii. 11 does not arise out of vii. 1–9.

PART III, CHAPTERS VII–IX

vii–ix. 10. Visions and Exhortations

There would seem to be good reason for taking the sequence of the chapters of the book of Amos as they stand, as representing the order in which the Prophet's discourses were delivered:[1] (1) Ch. vii. 1–9 presupposes what is said in iv. 4–11. (2) It is evident that chs. vii–ix represent in other respects a climax to the message and argument of chs. i–vi. In chs. iii–vi there was advanced, at least hypothetically, the possibility (by repentance) of averting the catastrophe, v. 5, 14: now the Prophet extends no such hope. Hitherto the disasters forecast may have been conditional: now the doom predicted is absolute, 'The end is come', viii. 2. Indeed, escape is entirely cut off, ix. 1–4. Though such a conviction may have dated from his call, yet he withheld the uttering of it until his own experience of the reception of his message confirmed it. (3) Moreover, if the section vii. 10–17 is rightly[2] placed within the book it becomes easier to understand the chief priest's animosity towards Amos, inasmuch as he has already delivered his utterances against the cult (iii. 14, iv. 4, v. 5–25). On the other hand, the view has obtained much acceptance that not only did the four visions of chs. vii and viii come to the Prophet at the very beginning; but that, fresh from seeing 'them, he narrated them at Beth-el, continuing his prophetic work through the sermons, abstracts of which are contained in the earlier chapters. Chs. i. 3–ii. 16 may thus follow chs. vii and viii. If Am. vii contains a narrative which corresponds to the call of Amos, such a placing finds a parallel in the account of the call of Isaiah having come down to

---

[1] See note on i. 3 ff. on p. 117. So G. A. Smith, *XII Prophets*, p. 107.
[2] But see Addl. Note on *v.* 10, pp. 310, 311.

VII. 1 Thus the Lord GOD shewed me: and, behold, he

us as ch. vi rather than at the beginning of the book of Isaiah. Moreover
the prophecies of Jeremiah are, as they stand, notoriously out of their
historical, and even written, order.

Ch. vii. 1–9 recounts three visions. The discussion in the Introduction on
the phenomenon of 'visions' (pp. 83–101), and particularly the analysis
of the visions of Amos, should be read before the following notes.

The passages vii. 1–9, viii. 1, 2, ix. 1 supply the only instances in the
book of composition in the *first person*: 'thus the Lord GOD shewed me'.
They have been called the "I sections". These may have been written down
by Amos himself, even if some other composed the volume as it stands.[1]
It is noticeable throughout the narrative how calm and truly unemotional
the Prophet is. He had received his visions in some "abnormal" condition;
but he was in no ecstasy when he recounted them.

VII. 1–3. THE FIRST VISION: THE LOCUSTS

The shepherd and fruit-gatherer, Amos, observing some locusts one day,
enters into a vision experience and receives the conviction that this plague
will pass.

1. the Lord GOD. In Hebrew, 'O, Master, Yahweh'. It is at least possible
that the first name has been copied into the text after being but a marginal
note indicating what is to be read aloud in place of the sacred Name of
Yahweh. So in *vv.* 4 *a*, *b*, 5, 6, vi. 8 more certainly, and (MS. Q) viii. 1, 3, in
each of which LXX has but one κύριος. In vii. 1 AQ have Κύριος, B has
Κύριος ὁ θεός.

shewed me. So *vv.* 4 and 7, and viii. 1. Translate, 'caused me to see'.[2]
(1) It might seem that in such passages the expression implies that God
produced something entirely new. (2) Probably, however, no more is
meant, in the first instance, than that Amos' attention was attracted to
the scene or object in question. It seems likely that on 'seeing' the thing,
he thereupon fell into the vision state,[3] in which he was under the Divine
influence. When he returned to himself, he realised that it had been Jehovah's
will for him to observe closely the field and the locusts. In that sense it
was God who had 'made him to see' them. *Cf.* viii. 1, and Jer. xxiv. 1–5.[4]
(3) On the other hand the prophet Zechariah employs the expressions 'see',

---

[1] *Cf.* Introd. p. 65, footnote 2. The story of Isaiah's vision in ch. vi begins, '*I* saw
the Lord'. This is followed immediately in ch. vii by a piece of prophetic history
in the *third* person. A large portion of the book of Jeremiah is in the first person,
and not only such visions as are described in i. 11–14 and 24.

[2] So also all modern German versions, *liess mich sehen* (or, *schauen*): as against
Luther's *zeigte mir ein Gesicht* and LXX ἔδειξέν μοι.

[3] Some deny that, at least with regard to vii. 1–6, there was any 'vision'
at all, but that Amos' experience consisted in being present when events in the
external world, *viz.* visitations by locusts and drought, were taking place (*cf.*
Buttenwieser, p. 223).

[4] In ix. 1 Amos uses the simple voice of the verb, 'I saw'.

formed locusts in the beginning of the shooting up of the latter
growth; and, lo, it was the latter growth after the king's

and 'make to see', of wholly visionary[1] 'seeing'; Zech. i. 8, 18 (= Heb. ii. 1),
i. 20 (=Heb. ii. 3), *etc.* In the present passage also the meaning *may* be,
'presented to me in vision', making the sight of the locusts, as well as all
that followed, something seen by the inner eye. So H. Schmidt.

he formed locusts: *lit.* '(him) forming . . .'. The same verb (*yâṣar*) is used
in the account of Jehovah's work in Gen. ii. 7, 18, 19, and in Am. iv. 13.
The Hebrew participle, however, unlike the corresponding word 'called'
in the vision of *v.* 4, has no subject. It would seem that the Hebrew consonants should in reality be read as a substantive, *yēṣer*, the clause then
being translated, 'and behold *a formation of* locusts'.[2]

locusts. The locust pest had been ravaging the crops. To the ancients,
God was the direct cause of all natural phenomena. The Hebrew word
rendered 'locusts' is *gôbhai*, one of many different expressions for the
locust. Driver[3] holds that perhaps the term "denotes in particular locusts
in the 'larva'-stage, when they were first hatched", but as voracious as
at any stage. If so the event would be in May or June. In iv. 9 another
word is used (*gāzām*); and Amos here may have in mind the very same
visitation as is referred to in that passage.

For locusts as a pest, see Joel i. 4–20, Rev. ix. 3. In the description of
the like plague of Egypt (Exod. x. 12–19, 'JE'), the Hebrew word used
is '*arbeh* (? *lit.* 'swarmer').

the latter growth. In Hebrew *leqesh*, referring probably to the late
spring[4] crops generally, *e.g.* corn. The word is connected etymologically
with that for 'spring-rain' (*malqôsh*, Joel ii. 23, *etc.*, E.VV. 'latter rain').
If 'latter growth' is taken in the sense of second *mowing* of *hay* (so the
Syriac) the point is not essentially different—the locusts appeared at a
critical moment, *viz.* at the very 'beginning' of the period in question when
the growth was tender.[5]

---

[1] *Cf.* iv. 1, 'as a man that is wakened out of his *sleep*'.

[2] *Cf.* G. A. Smith, Nowack, Sellin, *etc.* So LXX understood it—'offspring (or,
'brood') of locusts', ἐπιγονὴ ἀκρίδων, and the Targum, 'creation'. This evidence
of the Versions seems sufficient to warrant the reading *yēṣer* here. Though the
term is generally employed for what is formed in *the mind* (English 'purpose'
or 'imagination', *e.g.* Gen. vi. 5) yet its use in reference to material things formed
is not without parallel—Isa. xxix. 15 (of the potter's work), Ps. ciii. 14 (= formation, 'frame', E.VV.), and, if the reading is correct, Hab. ii. 18 (of an idol).

[3] There is a good discussion on the Biblical terms for locusts in Driver's *Joel
and Amos*, 1915, pp. 84–93; and see Thomson, *The Land and the Book*, pp. 296–298.

[4] In the Gezer agricultural inscription in Hebrew (assigned by G. B. Gray
to the same century as Amos) 'the month of sowing' is followed by the month
of *leqesh* or 'late *sowing*' (apparently February: see Driver, *Samuel*, pp. vii, viii).

[5] The word *leqesh* is not free from difficulty, and perhaps the conjecture may
be hazarded that in both places where it occurs in the text there stood originally
yereq or *yârâq*, 'green vegetation' of any kind, parallel to '*ēsebh* in the next verse
(the words come together in Gen. i. 30, 2 Ki. xix. 26).

mowings. 2 And it came to pass that when they made an end
of eating the grass of the land, then I said, O Lord GOD, for-

and, lo, it was the latter growth after the king's mowings. This
explanatory clause is possibly an addition to the text. (1) Some critics,
who consider the reference is to 'grass', quote a conjecture of Robertson
Smith's, that the 'king's mowings' were "a tribute in kind levied on the
spring herbage, to feed the horses of the king, *cf.* 1 Ki. xviii. 5. Similarly
the Romans in Syria levied a tax on pasture-land in the month Nisan for
the food of their horses " (*Semites*³, p. 246, note). It would seem incredible,
however, that a king would require the whole of a first mowing. The
tithing of *sown* crops as tribute is referred to in 1 Sam. viii. 15. (2) The
word translated 'mowings' would, according to usage, more naturally
signify sheep-*shearing*, *cf.* Deut. xviii. 4. In the place of 'latter growth'
(in its second occurrence in the verse) it is probable that another expression
for 'locust' should be read, as in the LXX ($\beta\rho o\hat{v}\chi o s$ = the Hebrew *yēleq*,
cf. Nah. iii. 16). If so, perhaps render, 'And behold they became fully-
developed-young-locusts after (the time of) the royal sheep-shearing'.[1]
(3) The clause in the LXX is interesting, 'and behold one locust was *king
Gog*',[2] the translators interpreting the references to locusts as an allusion
to mythological armies.

2. And it came to pass. Possibly translate, 'And it was coming to pass'.
The Prophet graphically describes the very moment of his intercession.[3]
By the 'land' perhaps is meant simply the 'soil' or 'ground' at a particular
spot, and not the 'country' of Palestine. See 1 Sam. v. 4, Gen. i. 11, 12.

the grass: in Hebrew '*ēsebh*. This general term is capable in usage of
including (*e.g.* Gen. ii. 5, Exod. ix. 22) and of excluding (*e.g.* Gen. i. 11, 12,
29, 30, iii. 18) grass, the proper Hebrew for which is *deshe*'. At all events,
the reference may, or may not, be to the same growth as in *v.* 1.

then I said. Some writers describe Amos as being a 'stern moralist'.
His patriotism, however, was deep and sincere. These verses seem to
indicate a tender (and truly lovable) personality such as we associate
especially with that other great prophet of doom, Jeremiah (Jer. viii. 21, 22,
ix. 1). Ezekiel, too, can be very stern under 'Jehovah's hand', but his

---

[1] Or, 'royal *reaping*'. Possibly the scene in the vision has changed. The year
has moved on. The larvae have developed into locusts with wings; the sprouting
crops have become ripe; but just when they should have been reaped, these
locusts destroy them. *Cf.* Schmidt, p. 14.

[2] For *leqesh* they read *yēleq*, for '*aḥar*, '*eḥādh*, and for *gizzē*, *gōg*. Gressmann
(*Eschatologie*, p. 1) is actually inclined to prefer the LXX here to the M.T.
As Joel adorns the 'Northern Army' of locusts with mythical characteristics of
the class of Gog-Magog prophecy, so Amos (according to the LXX) says that
the locust plague is king Gog. For 'Gog', see Ezek. xxxviii and xxxix, Rev.
xx. 8.

[3] The Hebrew, however, is difficult, and an attractive emendation is, 'and
it came to pass *as they were making an end of* (*wayᵉhî-hû mᵉkhalleh*) eating the
vegetation of the land'.

give, I beseech thee: how shall Jacob stand? for he is small.

book at times shews another side to his character, *e.g.* in Ezek. iii. 14, 15.
With each prophet, the severity of his message provides no criterion as to
all his personal emotions. For other intercessors in the O.T., see Jer. xiv. 7–
xv. 18, especially xv. 1, and Dan. ix. 16–19.[1]

O Lord God, forgive, I beseech thee. Judging from this passage,
a feature of such visions as those of Amos is that the Prophet retained a
rational consciousness:[2] Amos could intercede. Isaiah, in the very midst of
his vision, was overcome with feelings of guilt, and he expressed to God his
readiness to respond to the Divine call (Isa. vi. 5–8). We should be wrong
if we supposed that such thoughts and words differ in no manner from
those which come to people nowadays in their dreams. The brevity and sober
reality[3] of Amos', Isaiah's and Jeremiah's (Jer. i. 11–13) speech when in the
vision state, seem most readily explained if such psychological condition has
not suppressed the visionary's full normal faculties. On the other hand,
probably, we are not to suppose that the Prophet made any utterance aloud.
The verse does not provide evidence (though it was almost certainly a fact)
that there was a *heightening* and intensification of his natural faculties.

forgive. In the O.T. not seldom the conception of forgiveness is only
that of the remission of the penalty of sin (*e.g.* in 2 Sam. xii. 13), or of the
averting of a threatened natural disaster (Ps. ciii. 3). This is specially the
case when a *nation* is concerned. It seems probable that Amos interceded
before the locusts had done much damage upon Israel's territory. His
prayer thus amounted to a petition that the pest should pass away. Similarly he prays in the next vision, without any ambiguity, 'cease'. In later
Hebrew theology we find a more developed consciousness of guilt (in an
individual) as a thing in itself, with a corresponding power to appreciate
the *sentiment* of forgiveness, and restored fellowship with God (*cf.* Ps. li.
1–17). In the prophets God's 'forgiveness' or 'pardon' is referred to in
Isa. lv. 7, Jer. xxxi. 34, xxxiii. 8, xxxvi. 3, l. 20 (*sâlah*), Mic. vii. 18 (*nâsâ*').

how shall Jacob stand? The Hebrew is peculiar:[4] '*As who,* will (or,
'can') Jacob stand?' *i.e.* 'in what state?'

Jacob. It is hard to understand how some critics have seen in the
employment of this word a sign that Amos was thinking only of the
Northern Tribes; and particularly so if the scene of the 'vision' was
Judaean territory. *Cf.* Introd. p. 11 (*e*).

---

[1] The Targum expands Amos' prayer, and seems to assume the standpoint of
later history: '*Receive my supplication,* O Yahweh God, forgive now the sins
of *the remnant of* the house of Jacob: who will stand and pray concerning their
sins for they *are scattered* (in captivity)?' So exactly in *v.* 5.

[2] As with the Witch of Endor, who both feared and spoke (1 Sam. xxviii. 12,
13) when in a psychic state.

[3] In this respect the great prophets appear to present the greatest possible
contrast to those ecstatic *nᵉbhî'îm* who were transported beyond self-control
(1 Sam. xix. 24, and *cf.* x. 5, 6, 9).

[4] Isa. li. 19 *b* can hardly be quoted as a parallel. The Versions there suffice to
shew that the Hebrew text is incorrect.

3 The Lord repented concerning this: It shall not be, saith the Lord.

4 Thus the Lord God shewed me: and, behold, the Lord God called to contend by fire; and it devoured the great deep,

stand. The Hebrew word (*lit.* 'arise', so A.V. here but misleadingly) occurs with the same meaning of 'maintain oneself' or 'continue' in Josh. vii. 12, 13, 1 Sam. xiii. 14.

for he is small. Here the Prophet takes a well-balanced view of Israel. Contrast vi. 2. Absolute consistency of thought has probably never been a characteristic of man: it is not to-day. Some have seen a reference to a specially weak condition of the nation owing to previous wars and chastisements. But upon the whole Israel and Judah were just now more prosperous than perhaps for centuries previously.

3. The Lord repented. In his vision the shepherd's prayer is answered. For the use, in connection with God, of the Hebrew word *niḥam*, 'repent', and for instances of Divine mercy in other literature, see the Additional Note on pp. 306–308. Though in a sense it is extremely 'anthropopathic', at least it shews a lovable side of the Divine character.

VII. 4–6. THE SECOND VISION: THE DROUGHT

Amos, contemplating the withered vegetation, found himself in the vision state. As with the former plague, its full force was stayed in answer to the Prophet's intercession. For a visitation of drought, *cf.* i. 2 ('wither'), iv. 6–8, and Jer. xiv. Such is pictured as caused by 'fire' in Joel i. 19, 20 and perhaps in Isa. ix. 18.

4. the Lord God called to contend by fire. The Hebrew reads, 'was calling', *i.e.*, probably, 'was *commanding*, to contend by fire'. The words would be addressed to the Divine agent as in Gen. xix. 15, 22, 2 Sam. xxiv. 16, 17, 2 Ki. xix. 35, and possibly Am. ix. 1. For 'call' in the sense of 'command', *cf.* v. 8, ix. 6. 'Contend', with the meaning of 'commence a lawsuit', is a not uncommon metaphor in connection with Divine justice (Hos. iv. 1, Mic. vi. 2), but the sense required here of 'execute the sentence' which follows the lawsuit, *i.e.* 'punish',[1] is without parallel. The simple emendation (Nowack, Riessler, *etc.*), 'was calling[2] *a flame of fire*' (*lahabh 'êsh*), should perhaps be adopted. The 'fire of God' may come from the sun, or supernaturally. It could be mediated through the phenomenon of lightning (2 Ki. i. 12). According to Isa. xxv. 11 Jehovah has

---

[1] So the LXX, and *cf.* the Targum, '*to judge* with fire'.

[2] Other suggestions, which leave untouched the word 'contend', are: to read (1) 'was *meeting*' (from root *qārāh*, as in Deut. xxv. 18), but the verb *qārāh* requires an accusative, at least to bear this meaning; and (2) 'was drawing near (*qārēbh*) to contend by fire'.

and would have eaten up the land. 5 Then said I, O Lord

fire[1] to consume His enemies. In the magnitude of its action—over (1) 'the
deep', and (2) 'the land'—this 'flame of fire' must have been a more
wonderful spectacle than that of the 'burning' bush at the call of another
shepherd, Moses (Exod. iii. 2). In contrast with the present passage, in
i. 4, etc. Jehovah's 'fire' seems to be a metaphor for battle or destruction;
but see note there.

and it devoured the great deep: or, possibly, read, as Nowack, 'that it
should devour'. The 'deep', in Hebrew $t^eh\hat{o}m$, is the mass of water below
the flat earth, from which issue upwards springs and river sources (cf.
Gen. vii. 11) as also perhaps the ocean itself. To the agriculturist 'the
blessings of the deep which coucheth beneath' the earth were as important
as those of the rain from heaven (Gen. xlix. 25, Deut. xxxiii. 13).

According to the Babylonian legend, Tiamat (in Hebrew $T^eh\hat{o}m$) was a
deity (salt-water god) whom Marduk split in two halves at the creation;
cf. also Gen. i. 7 ('the firmament, and divided the waters'). There can be
little doubt but that in the present passage the Prophet is explaining
that the heat is so terrific that it actually dries up the subterranean[2] storehouse of waters. The expression 'great deep' occurs in Gen. vii. 11 and in
Isa. li. 10.

and would have eaten up the land. It appeared to Amos that the
next step would have been the literal burning up of the solid land[3] itself
in a great conflagration. It is the land of Palestine, the 'portion' (R.V.
marg.) assigned by Jehovah to Israel (cf. Mic. ii. 4); so Targum. A.V. 'a
portion' is quite wrong. The metaphorical use of the verb 'eat' of a fire
devouring, destroying, is familiar in most languages.

---

[1] Gressmann supposes that here what the Prophet sees in imagination is
Jehovah's fire in a pipe or column, from which it is poured out over the 'great
deep'. He compares the illustration of such a pipe, representing Hadad's
lightning, found in the temple of Anu-Hadad in Assyria (*Bilder*[2], No. 327).

[2] Hölscher (*Profeten*, p. 195, cf. p. 47) seems to think that $T^eh\hat{o}m$ can be used
of Jehovah's ocean in heaven from which rain normally would pour forth. A fire
up in the sky is about to pass from swallowing up this to consuming the earth.
Apart, however, from the fact that there is no parallel in the O.T. for this use
of $T^eh\hat{o}m$, it is doubtful (Job xxxviii. 37 b notwithstanding) if the Hebrews regarded ordinary rain as issuing from such 'waters above the firmament'. Others
have taken the reference to be to the Jordan valley or to the Dead Sea. But the
figurative use of 'the deep' as applied to the Great Sea in Jonah ii. 5 (Hebrew 6),
or to a gigantic and mysterious river like the Nile in Ezek. xxxi. 4, seems
scarcely applicable; for hardly anything is impossible with this word if its poetic
setting happens to be in a sufficiently exalted strain (Ps. xlii. 8).

[3] By 'land' (Hebrew $h\bar{e}leq$) 'cultivated land' may be meant; cf. 2 Ki. ix.
10, 36. So Nowack. Cf. also the use of $helq\bar{a}h$ in Am. iv. 7, 'the piece whereupon
it rained not, withered'. But agricultural ground as such, through lack of
moisture, would have perished before, not after, the 'great deep' had been
entirely 'consumed'.

Gᴏᴅ, cease, I beseech thee: how shall Jacob stand? for he is small. **6** The Lᴏʀᴅ repented concerning this: This also shall not be, saith the Lord Gᴏᴅ.

7 Thus he shewed me: and, behold, the Lord stood beside

It will be noted that in this 'vision' the common sight, from the contemplation of which the Prophet passed into the vision state, was in all probability *the withered herbage*, the result of a drought. There can have been no objective sight of the great *tᵉhôm*, nor hardly of such a fire as could 'devour' it.

5. cease: or, 'desist', from the 'contending' or punishing. The parallel expression in *v.* 2 was 'forgive', or 'remit'.

6. also. A further prayer was heard; and thus the second, and more severe, visitation was stayed in its course. Hölscher regards the shepherd's experience of receiving these answers to his prayer for his people as suggesting to him his mission. "Is it true that God has destined him to be His servant? Shall he go, and himself call back his sinful contemporaries?" (*Profeten*, p. 195). But see Introd. p. 101 (3). To bring about the call of one of God's messengers doubtless many influences combine. It may be noted that, though the threatened famine of *vv.* 1 and 4 was averted, another kind of 'hunger' is predicted for Israel in viii. 11–13.

VII. 7–9. Tʜᴇ Tʜɪʀᴅ Vɪsɪᴏɴ: Tʜᴇ Pʟᴜᴍʙʟɪɴᴇ

Gone is the day of Jehovah's passing-by of the Nation's transgression. If the scenery of the desert by Tekoa seems to have been the starting-point for the first two and the fourth visions, it must have been in Tekoa itself that the shepherd observed (if the Hebrew is so) a man examining a wall with a plumbline. Then the vision came to him and lo! Jehovah was testing Israel. The plummet represented Jehovah's standard of righteous conduct required from His people (*cf.* Isa. xxviii. 17). Obviously the 'vision' was only to the Prophet's inner sight. 'No man hath seen God at any time'. (*Cf.* Introd. p. 87.) For the Heb. word rendered 'plumbline', see below.

7. he shewed me. The LXX and Vulgate rightly supply the subject, 'the Lord', the text thus corresponding more to that of the formula which introduces the other visions of chs. vii and viii.

the Lord stood. Better, as the LXX, 'one stood'. The sight is that of a workman.

stood. So ix. 1. Translate, '(was) standing', or, better, 'and, behold one *stationed*', *i.e.* for a particular purpose. *Cf.* Gen. xxiv. 13, 43, Prov. viii. 2.

beside. This is correct, as in ix. 1, though the Hebrew preposition more usually means 'upon' (so R.V. marg. and A.V.). For *'al* = 'beside', especially with verbs of standing, *cf.* Gen. xviii. 2, 8, xl. 1, *etc.* In the famous passage Gen. xxviii. 13 the sense is ambiguous.

a wall made by a plumbline, with a plumbline in his hand.
8 And the LORD said unto me, Amos, what seest thou? And
I said, A plumbline. Then said the Lord, Behold, I will set a
plumbline in the midst of my people Israel; I will not again

a wall made by a plumbline. Read simply 'a wall'. The Heb. seems
to be, 'a wall *of* plumbline', which, if it could mean anything at all, must
signify 'a wall *true* to the plumbline'—and this is just what the context
denies to have been the case. Almost certainly the word 'plumbline' (Heb.
'ănākh) has crept in here by the scribal error of dittography. It is in the
next phrase rightly, and altogether three times in two verses. But the
Versions read as the M.T.[1]

with a plumbline in his hand. It was a sufficiently odd incident which
Amos witnessed; for when a wall is bad enough for it to be necessary that
it should be pulled down, no plummet would be required to indicate this
face. Indeed the plumbline (at least, we to-day should suppose) suggests
more naturally construction than destruction.[2] Or does *'ănākh* signify in
reality 'iron', in the sense of 'sword' or 'war-hammer'? (*cf.* Condamin,
Rev. Bib. 1900, esp. pp. 591–594).

8. And the LORD said unto me. The common sight of a builder has
already passed into a vision—of God Himself who, as He measures Israel,
speaks to Amos. For the question and answer in a genuine vision, *cf.*
viii. 2, Jer. i. 11, 13.

Such are common in dreams (*e.g.* in Zech. v. 2). In their visions God
speaks to Amos, Jeremiah and Ezekiel, calling the first two by name, and
Ezekiel 'son of man'.

Behold, I will set a plumbline. Jehovah was about to test Israel;
for the 'wall' signified, apparently, His 'people'.

my people Israel. See *v.* 15, viii. 2, *cf.* ix. 10. In such passages the use

---

[1] The Targum paraphrased the clause: 'Jehovah was ready by a wall of
judgment, and before Him was judgment'. LXX, Pesh. may be right with 'wall
of *adamant*, with adamant in His hand'. ἀδάμας occurs here only in the LXX.
Stephanus (*Thesaurus*) renders 'plumbline', but the word means *tough iron*.
Stephanus, however, quotes from a scholiast, Τὸ φῶς αὐτοῦ καὶ τὸ σκότος ἐμέρισε
ἀδάμαντι, rendering: "He divided his light and darkness with an adamant:
as though with an adamantine wall". Does the LXX translator of Amos suggest
(and correctly?) that God is about to shut off, or attack, His people as by a
rampart of iron? The Vulgate and with it the Douai version have departed
far from the meaning of the text: 'a plaistered wall, and in his hand a mason's
trowel'. Following on this, the Vulgate renders *'ăbhar lᵉ* (at the end of the next
verse), 'I will not *plaister* them *over* any more' (*superinducere eum*).

[2] So perhaps in Isa. xxviii. 17 *a*, where Jehovah is represented as about to
build upon a foundation (*v.* 16), using 'righteousness' as a 'plummet' (Hebrew
mishqóleth). On the other hand, the image of the plummet occurs twice elsewhere in the O.T. in connection with demolition, *viz.* in 2 Ki. xxi. 13 and
Isa. xxxiv. 11 (Hebrew 'stones'). Compare also the symbol of the *measuring-
line* in these two passages and in Lam. ii. 8. The particular word translated
'plumbline' in the verses of Amos occurs nowhere else (= a metal of some sort).

pass by them any more: **9** and the high places of Isaac shall
be desolate, and the sanctuaries of Israel shall be laid waste;

of this expression seems only to add point to the *threat*; *cf.* in iv. 12, 'thy
God'. However, in the appendix to the book both phrases are used in the
comforting sense (ix. 14, 15).

I will not again pass by them any more. The day of remission has
gone. The Hebrew expression, 'to pass by *for them*' ('*ābhar lᵉ*) = 'to forgive,
remit the punishment of (people)', occurs elsewhere only in viii. 2; but with
the preposition 'by', 'over' ('*al*) and the noun 'transgression', in Mic. vii. 18,[1]
Prov. xix. 11. It is noticeable that in this and the next vision Amos had
no opportunity to intercede for a remission of the threatened punishment.[2]
Yet whatever may be said as to God's relation to peoples, His attitude towards individuals is 'ever to have mercy and to forgive'. According to the
N.T. no person need despair of Divine pardon, as such, whether or not there
be a remission of natural penalties in this life.

9. high places. In Hebrew *bāmôth*. This is the only occurrence in the
book of Amos of a very common technical term for the hill-top shrine.[3]
Names of specific 'high places' occur, however, in iii. 14, iv. 4, v. 5, viii. 14—
Beth-el, Gilgal, Beer-sheba, Samaria and Dan. A 'high place' (1 Ki. xiv. 23)
might be close to, when not *in*, a city; and probably it could be an artificial
mound when there was not a hill available; *cf.* 2 Ki. xvii. 9–11. The shrine
at Jerusalem is not in the O.T. designated a 'high place' though there would
not seem to be any reason why it should not have been described by this
name, at least in the earlier days of the monarchy. See Additional Note,
pp. 308 ff.

of Isaac. The *national* use of the name 'Isaac' occurs only in Amos,
viz. here and in *v.* 16 below. Strictly speaking, the term should be applicable
to 'Edom' (*i.e.* the line of Esau) at least as much as to 'Israel' (*i.e.* the
descendants of Jacob); and it is not impossible that Amos is here referring
to both the 'brother' peoples. *Cf.* on i. 11, p. 129. Furthermore, it seems
difficult to suppose that the kingdom of *Judah* is excluded, more particularly as the Judaean high place Beer-sheba, referred to by Amos in
v. 5, viii. 14, was traditionally associated with the patriarch 'Isaac'.

the sanctuaries. Parallel to, and practically synonymous with, 'high
places'. Probably by the 'sanctuary' some sort of building is meant;
whereas a 'high place' might be entirely open to heaven. In 1 Ki. xiii. 32
reference is made to 'all *the houses of*[4] the high places which are in the cities
of Samaria'.

---

[1] 'Passeth by the transgression of the remnant of his heritage'. In the
Hebrew text the words *lishᵉʾērîth naḥălāthô* are dependent upon '*al-pesha*', not
upon the verb. They are a non-metrical gloss.

[2] *Cf.* Jer. xi. 14, xiv. 11; and in Jer. v. 7 Jehovah is represented as Himself
saying concerning Jerusalem, 'How can I pardon thee?' (Hebrew *sālaḥ; cf.* note
on 'forgive', Am. vii. 2).

[3] In iv. 13 the term is merely geographical.

[4] For this expression, *cf.* possibly l. 27 of the Moabite Stone.

and I will rise against the house of Jeroboam with the
sword.

I will rise up against the house of Jeroboam with the sword.
For 'house' in the sense of 'family' or descendants, *cf.* Gen. xviii. 19,
Deut. xxv. 9 *b.* The word is probably used here in the sense of 'dynasty',
as in 1 Ki. xii. 19, Jer. xxi. 12, Ps. cxxii. 5, *etc.*, and so in Assyrian in-
scriptions, *Bît Ḥumri*, 'house of Omri', and on the Moabite Stone, l. 7,
'I saw (my desire) upon him [Ahab] *and upon his house*'.

From Hos. i. 4 it appears that Amos' contemporary began his public
ministry in the same way with a prophecy of doom upon Jeroboam II's
line, 'the house of Jehu'. In that passage, the defeat of Israel seems to
be secondary (i. 5). The exact point of Amos vii. 8, 9 is not clear. *Either*
(1) the Prophet may be representing the destruction of 'the house of
Jeroboam' as the climax of the Divine judgment upon Israel. Amos finds
no fault with the king's personal life or religion, or with his administration.[1]
Or, (2) the general sense perhaps is, rather, that North Israel's reigning
dynasty will come to an end because there will be no nation to be ruled
over. Its fate is but an *incident* in the general havoc wrought by Jehovah's
'sword' (*cf. v.* 17).

As a matter of history, Jeroboam's line finished with the assassination
of his son Zechariah after a six months' rule, and fifteen to twenty years
before the 'sanctuaries' of the Northern Kingdom were, temporarily, 'laid
waste' by Assyria. Perhaps it would be strange if so far-seeing a person
as Amos should never have had suspicions of the coming internal civil strife
which was to characterise the last years of the Northern Kingdom (ii. 14,
iii. 11). It is noticeable that, if vii. 10–17 may be taken as being rightly
placed, then Amos is speaking at Beth-el. It is natural, therefore, that he
should mention in particular the fall of Jeroboam's house. On the other
hand, the significance neither of this vision (vii. 9, 'Isaac'), nor of the next
(viii. 2), was limited to the Northern Tribes. For an Additional Note on
the expression 'with the sword', see p. 310.

VII. 10–17. An Historical Incident

This is in pure prose, interrupting the (partly prose, partly poetic) account
of the visions, and relates to an incident which took place between Amos
and the chief priest of the Beth-el sanctuary. The passage is valuable both
as affording a sidelight upon the history and the character of Amos, and in
fixing the prophecy within a particular reign. It bears clear signs of being
a true account of actual facts. The peculiarity of its being the only part of
the book in which the Prophet is referred to in the *third person* seems to
point to the conclusion that, whoever may or may not have been the author

---

[1] *Unlike* the Egyptian sage Ipuwer, who accuses the reigning king of being
the cause of his country's misfortunes. "There is no pilot in their moment.
Where is he to-day? Is he sleeping? Behold his power is not seen". (Alan
Gardiner, *Admonitions*, p. 14; Erman-Blackman, p. 106.)

10 Then Amaziah the priest of Beth-el sent to Jeroboam

of the book as a whole, these verses are the work not of the pen of Amos,
but of a disciple of his or of an eyewitness of the incident.[1] The phenomenon
of a (considerable) biographical section within the book of Jeremiah is to
be compared (Jer. xxxvii–xliv). Upon the question as to whether the
historical incident is rightly placed at this point, see the Additional Note
on p. 310.

The conflict between Amaziah the priest and Amos the prophet is no
isolated phenomenon in religious history. The narrative provides an illustration of the attitude too often adopted by the leaders of a close-sealed
institutional religion towards those in whose spirit God's free Spirit is
working. So, also, *Jeremiah* seems to have realised from the first that he
would have the priesthood against him (Jer. i. 18). It was 'Pashhur, the
son of Immer the priest, who was chief officer in the house of the LORD'
who had him put in the stocks in the public gateway (Jer. xx. 1, 2). '*Jesus
of Nazareth*, which was a prophet', met His death at the hands of the
priesthood who in particular derived satisfaction from seeing Him upon
the cross (St Mk xv. 31). It was the high priest who 'commanded them
that stood by' to smite *St Paul* 'on the mouth' (Ac. xxiii. 2). And in
Christian history, from a benighted priesthood have come some of the
bitterest opponents of new learning and heaven-shed light. On the other
hand, not seldom the situation, at least in part, arises from the error of
ignorance. Had Amaziah had opportunity to hear Amos pray (Am. vii. 2 *b*,
5 *b*) he might not have so misrepresented him. *Cf.* Ac. iii. 17.

10. Then. The Hebrew is simply 'and' (*waw consecutive* and the imperfect
tense). If the section is in its right position, it would seem that at this
point in the shepherd's address, the priest felt that he could contain himself
no longer. *V.* 9 *a* touched him closely. *Cf.* also the Prophet's references to
the cult in ii. 8, iii. 14, iv. 4, 5, v. 21–25, vi. 4 *b*, 5.

Amaziah. Nothing is known of this person apart from the context.

the priest of Beth-el. For 'Beth-el', see on iii. 14. No doubt there
was one chief priest[2] over the Beth-el sanctuary. He would be an important
official, especially in his own eyes; he had royal support. Whatever may
have been the social standing of Amos, the conflict was that of 'a dwarf
facing a giant'. It is interesting to compare the position of men like Amos
and Jeremiah with that of such prophets as Elisha. That prophet seems to
have occupied a position of honour in the king's councils, if not in the royal
court itself (2 Ki. vi. 9, 21, xiii. 14–19).

Jeroboam. The second king of this name: by no means an insignificant
monarch. See on i. 1.

---

[1] *Cf.* Introd. p. 65.
[2] When the Hebrew *kōhēn* signifies 'chief priest' the Targum generally renders
by *rabbā*, 'great one'. So here and *e.g.* Gen. xli. 45 (*cf.* Buxtorf, *Lex. Talm.*
col. 2174 *fin.*).

king of Israel, saying, Amos hath conspired against thee in
the midst of the house of Israel: the land is not able to bear
all his words. **11** For thus Amos saith, Jeroboam shall die by
the sword, and Israel shall surely be led away captive out of

Israel. The word is here used, as in the books of Kings, to denote the
Northern Tribes of Israel. For, of course, Amos' use of the word Israel in
vv. 8 and 9 had *included* the Northern Kingdom.

Amos hath conspired. The Prophet's reference to Jeroboam seems to
have caused Amaziah to fear a conspiracy against the reigning house. *Cf.*
the alarm of the elders of the city in 1 Sam. xvi. 1-4. The priest may have
thought of the action of Elisha outside his own country (2 Ki. viii. 10 *b*-13).
In reality Amaziah's apprehension was particularly unreasonable, for was it
likely that Amos would have desired to place a king upon the throne over
a land all of whose high places and sanctuaries were to be ruined? There
was a clear difference between Amos' purpose and the attitude of several
of the earlier prophets. They predicted or took part in the fall of particular
royal houses as such. (*Cf.* 1 Sam. xvi. 1-5, 1 Ki. xi. 29-39, xiv. 10-12,
xxi. 19-24, 2 Ki. ix. 1-3.) He is the first to foretell the doom of *Israel*.

Amos. It is surprising that, apart from its presence in these verses within
the book and in the title verse, the name of Amos does not occur in the
Bible. But see Tobit ii. 6. In St Lu. iii. 25, 'Amos the son of Nahum' was
a Judaean of long-past Captivity times.

in the midst of the house of Israel: 'in the midst', where, of course,
his utterances would have the most serious effect. It is not easy to parallel,
in plain prose, the use of the phrase, 'house of Israel'. The prophets
(including Amos himself eight times[1]) employ the expression in exalted
style.[2]

the land is not able to bear. 'The land' should probably be translated,
'the *earth*'. 'To bear' is a good equivalent of the Hebrew, which signifies
lit. 'to contain'. So Targum, 'support (or, 'endure') all his words'. *Cf.*
Jer. x. 10 and Joel ii. 11 ('abide', R.V.).—The idea is quite different in
St John xxi. 25.—The thought is somewhat similar to that of Ac. xvii. 6 *b*.
Possibly there is an intentional paronomasia in the priest's sentence (*lô-
thûkhal hā'āreṣ lᵉhākhîl 'eth-kol-dᵉbhārāw*).

11. saith. Hebrew *'āmar*. Perhaps we should render 'said', or, 'has said'.
The same tense is used in the expression, 'Thus saith Jehovah' (see Introd.
p. 81).

Jeroboam shall die by the sword. The priest makes the incidental
into the *main* statement. Moreover, what Amos had said referred to '*the
house of* Jeroboam' (*v.* 9).

shall surely be led away captive. Translate, 'and as for Israel, he

---

[1] Am. v. 1, 3, 4, 25, vi. 1, 14, vii. 16, ix. 9.
[2] An obvious emendation would be 'in the midst of Beth-*el*', instead of Beth-
Israel as some scholars suggest in vi. 1.

his land. **12** Also Amaziah said unto Amos, O thou seer, go,

will certainly be taken into exile from upon his land'. This is not expressed
in vii. 7–9, but it is said categorically in v. 5, 27, vi. 7.

12. Also Amaziah said.... This was either because the king thought it
wise to ignore the message sent, or before the priest had even allowed time
for Jeroboam to act. The latter is the more probable, for in the Hebrew the
verb follows immediately upon *v.* 11, '*and said* Amaziah'.

O thou seer. Hebrew *ḥôzeh*. 1 Sam. ix. 9 explains in reference to Samuel
that (at the late period at which the book of Samuel was compiled) 'he
that is now called a Prophet was beforetime called a Seer' (*rô'eh*, a synonym).[1]
Possibly seers, as such, died out as the prophets (*nebhî'îm*) added 'seeing'
to the characteristics of their work. The 'seeing' was of at least two kinds,
which perhaps we should do well to distinguish carefully. (1) That which
partakes of the nature of practical and useful 'second sight' (*cf.* 1 Sam.
ix. 6–10); in this connection the association with 'diviners',[2] of 'seers' in
Mic. iii. 7, and of 'prophets' in Isa. iii. 2, and (in an evil sense) in Jer.
xxvii. 9, xxix. 18, should be noted. With these may be compared also the
existence of seers outside Israel. In the Zakir inscription (l. 12), slightly
earlier than Amos, the king of Hamath says, "The Lord of the heavens
(sent word) to me by the hand of *seers*, and by the hand of men expert in
numbers". (2) Visions which were more connected with God and spiritual
truth; it would appear that it is in this latter sense that the editor of
Amos describes the Prophet in i. 1. Perhaps here Amaziah has in mind the
'visions' which Amos, according to the context, has been narrating.

It is noteworthy that though Amaziah addresses Amos as 'seer', Amos
(in *v.* 14) argues upon the word 'prophet', as if they were identical terms.
In Isa. xxix. 10 *ḥôzîm* are mentioned with 'prophets', and in xxx. 10 with
rô'îm, in both places in a good sense. See note on i. 1. Possibly, notwithstanding what is said in 1 Sam. ix. 9, the term survived in the *second*
meaning.

---

[1] Isa. xxx. 10 seems to shew that no distinction can be made between *ḥôzîm*
and *rô'îm*.

[2] Hebrew *qôsemîm* in both places. This particular expression etymologically,
and perhaps strictly in usage, has reference to obtaining an oracle by a *lot*;
cf. Driver on Deut. xviii. 11. However, the term can be used quite generally;
and in connection with Mic. iii. 7 quoted above it may be noted that in at least
one passage in the O.T. it must refer to what we call 'second sight'. In 1 Sam.
xxviii. 8 we read '*Divine* (Hebrew *qāsam*) unto me by the familiar spirit',
and then in *v.* 13, 'What *seest* thou?...I *see* a god coming up out of the earth'.
Throughout the narrative, though Saul and the supposed Samuel converse,
there is no hint that anyone but the diviner herself had any *vision* of Samuel.
On the other hand it would not be right to limit the comparison of early prophecy
or seer-ship to such second sight as afterwards came to be regarded as ille-
gitimate. (In Deut. xviii. 10 *b*, 11, 18–22 the best Hebrew prophecy is mentioned in contrast with all forms of augury and witchcraft. Obviously this
contrast is present to the writer of the story of the Witch of Endor.)

flee thee away into the land of Judah, and there eat bread,
and prophesy there: **13** but prophesy not again any more at

12. go, flee thee away into the land of Judah. Irritated as Amaziah is,
in the expression 'flee thee away' he speaks (at least in appearance) words
of friendly counsel (van Hoonacker). The Hebrew *bārah* signifies 'to go
through, or away, to hasten'. See Skinner on Isa. xlviii. 20, in which passage
Israel leaves Babylon not in fear but 'with a voice of singing'.[1]

into the land of Judah. Amos was known, or recognised, to be from
the South. In the expression, 'the land of Judah', there does not seem to
be any contrast implied between 'Judah' and the 'Israel' of *v.* 9 as
kingdoms. All that the priest says is geographical: 'But *in Beth-el* (emphatic)
thou shalt not prophesy again any more' (*v.* 13).

and there eat bread. The expression, 'to eat the fruit of', is used of a
man's enjoying the results of his toil (Am. ix. 14, 2 Ki. xix. 29); but here
only in the O.T. does 'to eat bread' signify 'to earn one's living'. The
priest's words, 'eat there thy bread and there prophesy', clearly shew that
he regarded Amos as a professional prophet, and perhaps an insincere one
at that. "Worldly men always think that those whose profession is religion
make *a gain of godliness.* 'He is paid for it', they say. 'Whose bread I eat,
his song I sing'".[2] Samuel the seer appears to have divined for a fee
(1 Sam. ix. 8); but from Mic. iii. 11 it is evident that such a practice was
discredited by the eighth-century prophets. *Cf.* Introd. p. 20. Prophesying 'for handfuls of barley, and for pieces of bread' was a feature
of the female prophets, the opponents of Ezekiel (Ezek. xiii. 17–23, especially *v.* 19).

and prophesy there. Some translate, 'and there *play the prophet*', as
if there was something scornful in Amaziah's use of the term. But it is
the ordinary word,[3] occurring again in *v.* 15 *b.* Between the priesthood and
the lower order of prophecy as such (to which Amaziah believed Amos to
belong), there was no quarrel; Jer. v. 31, R.V. marg., 'priests bear rule at
their hands'.

13. but prophesy not again any more at Beth-el: *lit.* 'but at Beth-el
thou shalt not add to prophesy further'. The prohibition is emphatic and
absolute. With the utterance may be compared that which the prophet
Jeremiah's fellow-villagers said to him, 'Thou shalt not prophesy in the
name of the LORD' (Jer. xi. 21).

---

[1] In Jonah i. 2, 10 another prophet is represented as 'fleeing' for safety from
Jehovah Himself.

[2] Pusey, quoting the proverb, *Wess Brod ich ess', dess Lied ich sing.* Winckler
finds in this narrative an illustration of his thesis that the prophets of Israel
resembled their counterparts in Assyria in being, first and foremost, politicians
of their king. Amos (whom this scholar places in the reign of *Pekah*), the Judaean,
is represented as sent by king Ahaz of Judah to incite the people of Northern
Israel against their king, in connection with such circumstances as are recounted
in Isa. vii. 1, 2. *Geschichte Isr.* i. pp. 78–113; *cf.* Wardle, *Isr. and Babylon,* p. 105.

[3] *hinnābhē', Niph'al* voice.

Beth-el: for it is the king's sanctuary, and it is a royal house.
14 Then answered Amos, and said to Amaziah, I was no

for it is the king's sanctuary. In Hebrew, 'a (or, 'the') sanctuary
of a king'. However the R.V. gives the sense.

and it is a royal house. (1) The R.V. obviously takes the Hebrew to
mean 'house of sovereignty' (or, 'royalty'). For such adjectival use of the
same noun, see Josh. x. 2, 2 Ki. xi. 1. In Beth-el not only were situated
the headquarters of the national religion, but also a *palace* of the king. In
this sense, *cf.* the expression, 'an house for his kingdom', in 2 Chron. ii. 1
(Hebrew i. 18). (2) Royal residences of the Northern Kingdom, however,
are known to have existed (since the abandonment of Tirzah) only at
Samaria (1 Ki. xvi. 24) and at Jezreel (xxi. 1).[1] Not improbably the
expression 'royal house' would be more correctly rendered, 'house of
kingdom', with the meaning of 'national shrine'. For the use of 'house'
(*bêth*) in the sense of 'temple', *cf.* 1 Ki. vi. 2, 3, vii. 50, 2 Chron. xxix. 3,
and (of heathen shrines) Judg. ix. 4, 1 Sam. v. 5, *etc.* So van Hoonacker,
Köhler. Driver translates, 'it is a national temple'. (3) May it not be
that the reference is, literally, to neither palace nor shrine? In Dan. iv. 30
(in the Aramaic, 27) a similar expression (*bêth malkhû*)[2] clearly does not
mean 'palace' as such, but royal[3] *city* (possibly as containing the palace).
This use of 'house' is paralleled in Hebrew in Neh. ii. 3, 'the city, the *place*
of my fathers' sepulchres' (so E.VV.; the Hebrew is 'house of'). The A.V.
rendering of Amos, 'king's court', would represent this meaning fairly.
In Assyrian *Bît Ḥumri* ('*house* of Omri') is applied to the whole land, or
realm, of Israel.

14, 15. Paraphrase: 'No prophet (such as you have in mind) am I: certainly not one of the roving bands of prophets. (This is how it happened:)
I am really a sheep-owner and sycomore-gatherer, and Jehovah, and none
else, called me from my work with the flock, telling me unmistakably to
go out and prophesy to His nation Israel. (So a prophet, in a better sense,
certainly I am:) hear more', *viz. vv.* 16, 17.

14. I was no prophet. (1) This translation means in the context, 'I was
not originally a prophet..., but I was a herdman..., until Jehovah took
me'. This, of course, makes intelligible sense, and the rendering, 'I *was*',

---

[1] No little obscurity hangs over the locality of the royal palaces. The evidence
belongs to the period of Ahab. 1 Ki. xxii. 38 *a*, as it stands, suggests that the
Naboth episode concerned a palace at *Samaria*. According to xxi. 1, 2, a house
was at *Jezreel* (whether or not 'which was in Jezreel' be omitted with LXX).
If Am. vii. 13 *b* refers to a palace at all at Beth-el, perhaps it was Ahab's 'house
of ivory' alluded to in 1 Ki. xxii. 39. His fame as a builder is reflected in LXX
(cod. A) of Jer. xxii. 15, 'Shalt thou reign because thou competest *with Ahab*?'
(*cf.* Jer. xxii. 13, 14).

[2] The same as occurs in the Targum rendering of the present passage, *bêth
malkhûthā*.

[3] In Dan. v. 20 the same noun is used, '*royal throne*'.

prophet, neither was I a prophet's son; but I was an herdman,

is maintained by, amongst other scholars, W. Riedel.[1] Amos states clearly
how he came to utter his prophecy. (2) However, as a matter of fact, there
is in the original no word for 'was' corresponding to any of the three
occurrences of it in the E.VV. here. It is right that some part of the verb
'to be' should be supplied in English; but the insertion of the *present* tense
'I am' (as R.V. marg.) is alone in accordance with Hebrew usage.[2] Precisely
the same Hebrew is translated by the R.V. in Zech. xiii. 5, 'I *am* no prophet'.

See the Addl. Note on pp. 311–313 for a discussion as to why, and in what
sense, one of the greatest of O.T. prophets should make the protestation,
'I am no prophet'. Probably he is only dissociating himself from the less
spiritual and the less worthy prophets of the past and, perhaps especially,
of his own day.

neither was I a prophet's son. There can be no doubt that the R.V.
marg. 'neither am I one of the sons of the prophets' represents better the
meaning. Yet even the rendering, 'one of *the sons of* the prophets', is an
instance of the fact that a translation which is literal may yet be misleading. In 'sons of the prophets', even as in the Hebrew idioms, 'sons of
Belial' (= 'worthless men'), 'sons of the bridechamber'[3] (= 'guests at a
wedding'), there is no suggestion of physical descent.[4] In Ezra ii. 42 the
expression, 'the children of the porters' (or door-keepers), refers to courses,
or, perhaps, corporations.[5] Hence the expression, 'Neither am I one of
the sons of the prophets', refers probably to individual members of small
'bands'[6] of prophets. Such 'sons of the prophets' are alluded to expressly
for the first time in 1 Ki. xx. 35, and by the simple name 'prophets' in
1 Sam. x. 5. They may have been a common sight at the Beth-el sanctuary
when Amos was speaking as they were a few generations before (2 Ki. ii. 3).
Whether or not Amos absolutely disclaimed being a prophet, most certainly
he was not one of 'the sons of the prophets'. For an Additional Note on
this expression, see p. 313.

Quite distinct is St Peter's application of the phrase (in Ac. iii. 25) to
his own hearers. After referring to *Moses'* promise of a prophet (made in

---

[1] *A.T. Untersuchungen*, I. 1902.

[2] Because, for 'I was' the Hebrew *hāyîthî* would be required.

[3] οἱ υἱοὶ τοῦ νυμφῶνος (St Mk ii. 19, St Matt. ix. 15, St Lu. v. 34), an obvious
Semitism. It is interesting that the exact phrase *bᵉnê ḥuppāh* can be found in
later Hebrew, *e.g.* in the Tosephta of *Berakhoth*, II. 10: "The groomsmen and
all *the marriage guests* are free from the Prayer, and from the phylacteries, the
whole seven days" (Lukyn Williams' transl., S.P.C.K. p. 20).

[4] In 1 Sam. x. 12, 'And who is their father?' is a sufficiently obscure phrase,
but it seems to mean merely, 'such men are of no good descent or family'.

[5] *Cf.* Kennett, *In Our Tongues*, p. 49.

[6] It is noteworthy, however, that the actual term 'band', frequently used in
modern discussions of the subject, is very rare in such a connection in O.T. Its
only occurrences are 1 Sam. x. 5, 10 (Hebrew *ḥebhel*, *lit.* 'cord') and xix. 20
(where the M.T. contains the obscure word *lahăqāh*, for which perhaps *qᵉhillāh*
should be read with the LXX, but see G. R. Driver in *J.T.S.* July 1928, p. 394).

and a dresser of sycomore trees : **15** and the LORD took me from

Deut. xviii. 15), and to 'all the prophets from Samuel and them that followed after', he exclaims, 'Ye are the *sons* of the prophets, and of the covenant which God made'.

herdman. (1) The Hebrew text is *bôqēr*, which signifies '*cattle*-tender'. (2) According, however, to i. 1 Amos was a *nôqēdh*, *i.e.* either a shepherd of, or (more properly) an owner of, a particular breed of *sheep*. (The E.VV. have the same word, 'herdmen', as here.) The term *nôqēdh* is of a true Semitic root, found in Arabic and Assyrian. In 2 Ki. iii. 4, king Mesha of Moab is described as a *nôqēdh*; probably also the word should be read upon the Moabite Stone (l. 31), 'I led there the *shepherds of* the sheep of the land'.[1] On the other hand, the Hebrew text, which in the present verse is translated 'herdman', occurs nowhere else; implies a different thing; is contradicted by the occurrence of the word 'flock' in the very next verse;[2] and its presence can be explained as being due to a form of scribal corruption of specially frequent occurrence.

If the text is emended to agree[3] with i. 1, then the belief (as old as Jerome at least) that Amos was a poor man becomes uncertain. For the term *nôqēdh* applied to Amos may mean somewhat the same as it does when used of Mesha—*viz.* sheep-owner. None the less, the next words, 'a dresser of sycomore trees', and the tenor of the book shew that he lived a simple life. The usual word for 'shepherd' occurs in Am. i. 2 *b* (*rô'eh*).

and a dresser of sycomore trees. The timber of this tree is referred to in Isa. ix. 9. The sycomore (*Ficus sycomorus* L.) yielded a small fruit, of a somewhat insipid taste, and which resembled in shape the fig.[4] The trees grew only at an altitude warmer than that of Tekoa; either farther east[5] towards Jericho (St Lu. xix. 1, 4), or else towards the Maritime Plain on the west (1 Ki. x. 27, 1 Chron. xxvii. 28), in which latter locality sycomores were particularly abundant. To one of these districts Amos must have gone from the region of Tekoa at certain times of the year. The word translated

---

[1] It is interesting that the LXX entirely failed to recognise in Am. i. 1 the word for 'shepherd'. This was because, as is shewn by their transliteration (ἐν Ἀκκαρείμ), the Hebrew text on which they worked had suffered the corruption of *dāleth* into *rēsh*. In the present verse they translate 'goatherd' (αἰπόλος).

[2] The Hebrew *ṣôn* which follows in *v.* 15, though it can cover goats as well as sheep, and may be used (metaphorically) even of human beings, not once is applied to cattle. On the other hand, the Hebrew word *rô'eh* (which usually means 'shepherd') *can* be used of the tending of cattle (Gen. xiii. 7, *cf.* xlvi. 32, 34), and this (slightly ambiguous) word is never applied to Amos.

[3] Critics who regard the phrase in i. 1 as a later addition to the text of Amos recognise that it was based upon vii. 14 before the corruption of *nôqēdh* had taken place.

[4] It is to be distinguished from the 'sycamine' (the LXX mistaken rendering). This latter is the 'mulberry' (St Lu. xvii. 10).

[5] The nearness of the wilderness of Tekoa (where Amos wandered) to En-gedi on the very edge of the Dead Sea is illustrated by the narrative of 2 Chron. xx. 2 and 20. Sycomores grow in Egypt, and a sacred sycomore is figured on the walls of the temple of Thotmes III at Karnak.

following the flock, and the LORD said unto me, Go, prophesy

'dresser' (*bôlēs*) is a participle of a verb derived from a Semitic root which
in Arabic signifies a species of fig, and in Ethiopic can be applied to both
the fig and the very similar sycomore. The Hebrew thus denotes someone
who has to do with 'figs' (or, in the present case, with 'sycomores'). A
peculiar characteristic of the occupation is indicated by the LXX version
κνίζων ('scraping'), and Theodotion's χαράσσων ('nipping'). So Vulgate:
a *pincher* of sycomores.[1] The fig of the sycomore suffers from an insect,
the *Sycophaga crassipes*, which has to be released by the incising of the fruit.[2]
Prof. G. Henslow, F.L.S., in *J. R. Hort. Soc.* 1902, pp. 128 ff., shews
illustrations of figs uncut and cut open and the instruments used.[3] After
the scraping process, when the fruit had ripened, Amos picked[4] it not only
for his own purposes, but also, doubtless, for sale. Several crops were possible
in the course of the year. Clearly Amos refers to his work with the sycomores as a definite occupation in life in addition to that of 'shepherd'.

15. and the LORD took me. What distinguished Amos from the typical
court- or false-prophet and from members of the prophetic guilds was that
he had heard, as it were, the voice of God within his heart, saying, 'Go'.
Doubtless those in prophetic frenzy imagined, and it was commonly believed
concerning them, that they too heard Jehovah's voice. In reality, however, they were but victims of infectious emotion (1 Sam. x. 10, xix. 20–24).
On the other hand, different from the history of Amos was that of Jeremiah
(Jer. i. 5) and of the servant of Jehovah (Isa. xlix. 1, 5); both of whom,
so it appeared, were designated God's servants before their birth.

The choice of the word 'took', and preceded by '*and* Jehovah' (not
'but'), seems to suggest a permanent, not a temporary, commission. 'I have
relinquished a remunerative occupation for the very purpose of doing what
I am doing'.

and the LORD said unto me. In meeting the priest's prohibition the
shepherd emphasises his Divine commission by repeating the word
'Jehovah'. Perhaps translate, 'It was the LORD who said unto me...'.
It is possible that Amos is expressing also the idea that he 'must obey God
rather than man' (Ac. v. 29). Rackham on this latter passage quotes
Sophocles' *Antigone*, 453–456:

> "Nor did I deem thy edicts strong enough,
> That thou, a mortal man, should'st overpass
> The unwritten laws of God that know not change".

And *cf.* 1 Macc. ii. 22.

---

[1] 'Non sum propheta, et non sum filius prophetae: sed armentarius
(reading M.T.) ego sum, *vellicans sycomoros*'.

[2] Not impossibly Amos employed labour on this operation, unless the view
be held that he was essentially of most humble circumstances.

[3] See also Cheyne in W. R. Smith's *Prophets*[2], p. 396. There are references in
Theophrastus, Dioscorides and Pliny to the existence in antiquity of this practice.

[4] So the A.V. translation, 'gatherer'. For an interesting account of the sycomore, see van Lennep, *Bible Lands*, pp. 145, 146.

unto my people Israel. **16** Now therefore hear thou the word

Go: *i.e.* from his flock. Even so, a few years later, Isaiah will feel that he hears God say, 'who will *go* for us?'; and after offering himself, he believes that God says, '*Go*, and tell this people...' (Isa. vi. 8, 9). Perhaps Amos is giving the terms of the commission which *followed* his 'call'; or, possibly, the sense is, 'Jehovah took me (*i.e.* called me) *with the words* "Go, prophesy"'.

The story of Amos, whatever may have been his social position, and whether his mission was of considerable duration or but a temporary one, supplies one of the countless instances of God's Spirit calling and using ordinary human beings for His great purposes. Amos may have felt the call during some peculiar psychological experience—see Introd. p. 93, § (5); but he had pondered on the coming of Assyria against Israel, and he must have been deeply influenced by the sight of the sin of his compatriots. 'Would that *all* the Lord's people were prophets'. Such, in modern times, need not wait to see the heavens opened (Ezek. i. 1). The existence of a God of love and the presence in every land of sin and its consequences constitute the call. Men and women to-day at their work may hear it; and though (as with Amos) it is within their power to say 'no', many will answer 'yes' (*cf.* Am. iii. 8). God has said, 'Go'.

> "So with the Lord: he takes and he refuses,
>   Finds him ambassadors whom men deny,
> Wise ones nor mighty for his saints he chooses,
>   No, such as John or Gideon or I".[1]

The quality and the degree of inspiration may not be as with the prophets of old, but, after all, neither were *they* always infallible.

prophesy unto. So Ezek. xxxvi. 1, xxxvii. 9. In the next verse the priest calls the act of Amos 'prophesying against'. (1) However, it is possible that the correctness of the reading 'unto' in this verse will not be questioned in so far as the view is taken that God raised up Amos like some other of His prophets not only to destroy but to build (Jer. i. 10), to call to repentance as well as to announce doom (Am. v. 5 and i. 2). (2) None the less, it is likely that in *v.* 15 the true reading is 'against',[2] as in *v.* 16 (Marti).

my people Israel. See on *v.* 8. (1) The phrase, in the present verse at least, is usually regarded as pointing an antithesis with 'Judah', whence Amos had come. And this is possible. Undoubtedly Amos would be regarded as a foreigner. (2) On the other hand, the very expression, '*my*

---

[1] Myers, *St Paul*.

[2] The phrase, 'prophesy against' ('*al*), is used of the utterance of Jehovah's prophets fourteen times elsewhere, and probably there should be added to these some seven occurrences in Jeremiah and Ezekiel where the M.T. should be changed to '*al*. The expression *hinnābhē 'el* may be said to occur in the O.T. scarcely more than twice (as above, Ezek. xxxvi. 1, and especially xxxvii. 9, 'prophesy unto the wind'). The confusion of '*el* and '*al* is one of the commonest cases of textual corruption.

of the LORD: Thou sayest, Prophesy not against Israel, and
drop not *thy word* against the house of Isaac; **17** therefore thus
saith the LORD: Thy wife shall be an harlot in the city, and thy

people', seems to forbid such a limitation. Amos declares that he has heard
the call to prophesy to *Jehovah's people*: 'The terms of my commission
include all Israel'. Doubtless Amos sees special reason for devoting a larger
proportion of his time among the Northern Tribes; but he will not be
moved on from Beth-el or from *wheresoever* he may be during his preaching
tour until he has delivered his message at that spot. There can be little
doubt that, if the question of the scene of Amos' preaching could have been
decided by the study of the discourses in the book, no one would have
presumed that he preached only in the Northern Kingdom. In any event,
it may fairly be claimed that this verse does not in reality make the view
untenable that Amos' ministry covered both kingdoms. See, further,
Introd. pp. 12, 13.

16, 17. Amos not only does not cease his prophesying as charged by the
priest in *vv.* 12, 13, but he actually repeats what he has said about captivity;
in the prophecy of doom, boldly substituting for 'the house of Jeroboam',
Amaziah and his family.

16. Now therefore: *lit.* 'and-now'. The expression used in this logical
sense is not uncommon; *cf.* Gen. iii. 22, iv. 11, *etc.* It denotes the drawing
of a practical conclusion. Less usual is the simple 'now' (*cf.* Am. vi. 7).

Thou sayest. Better, 'thou art saying'.

drop not *thy word* **against.** The same Hebrew expression *nāṭaph*,
'drip', occurs in its more *literal* sense in ix. 13. The passage, Mic. ii. 6,
supplies an instructive parallel to its use in Am. vii. 16. Of the prophet's
audience of luxurious oppressors it is there said, '"Drip not"—they drip—
"Ye[1] shall not drip of these things"'; *cf.* Mic. ii. 11. So Amos was not the only
prophet to be confused with the common ecstatic, whose words might be
described as *bubbling* or *flowing* from the mouth. On the other hand, it
needs to be taken into account in interpreting the above passages that a
word which expresses historically very definite associations may come to
be used[2] quite generally.[3]

17. Thy wife shall be an harlot in the city. Perhaps render, 'Thy wife
will be outraged in the city'. When a town was captured a usual occurrence

---

[1] Emending to the second *person*. Duhm translates, 'They foam at me, saying,
Give up your foaming! You should not foam about such things'.

[2] An illustration of this is perhaps to be found in Ezek. xx. 45 (in Heb. xxi. 1),
xxi. 2. 'Son of man...cause thy word *to drip* towards (or, 'against') the south,
and prophesy towards the forest'. *Cf.* xxi. 1 (in Heb. xxi. 6). In Job xxix. 22 it is
used without reference to ecstatic, or, indeed, any kind of prophetic utterance.
In Mic. ii. 6 the term is used of the *ordinary Israelite* as well as of the prophet.
Another word ('*āraph*) is rendered 'drop' in Deut. xxxii. 2, xxxiii. 28.

[3] The Targum of Am. vii. 16 renders simply, 'Prophesy not against (*or*
concerning) Israel, and *teach* not against the house of Isaac'.

sons and thy daughters shall fall by the sword, and thy land
shall be divided by line; and thou thyself shalt die in a land
that is unclean, and Israel shall surely be led away captive
out of his land.

was that women were brutally treated by the conquerors. For a discussion
of the sense of the Hebrew phrase, see the Additional Note on p. 314.

and thy sons and thy daughters shall fall by the sword. The phrase
(as also 'thy wife', in the preceding clause) is very emphatic. Yet the
passage is not to be regarded as an example of the supposed sending by
God of suffering upon children for the sins of a parent.—Of course Amos
would have endorsed this principle, as did the prophet Nathan (2 Sam.
xii. 14 b); for the time of Jeremiah and Ezekiel[1] had not yet come.—(1) It
is possible to interpret the passage as just a simple statement of details
which would have occurred at the capture of their city Beth-el,[2] whatever
Amaziah's behaviour had been towards Amos. (2) On the other hand, some
scholars take it as a *personal* oracle, comparing Isa. xxii. 15 ff.; and in
this connection it is noteworthy that the reference to the priest's household
corresponds to that made to the king's—'the *house* (*i.e.* the family) of
Jeroboam', Am. vii. 9.

thy land shall be divided. Not improbably the meaning is that the
priest's estate will be handed over to immigrants introduced by the conqueror. See 2 Ki. xvii. 24; and *cf.* Israel's lament in Mic. ii. 4 b: 'My people's
estate is measured off! How they take it away from me! To the rebels our
fields *are allotted*' (transl. G. A. Smith). In Jer. vi. 12, 'houses', 'fields'
and 'wives' all change hands as a result of the enemy's victory.

by line: *i.e.* by measuring line. The Targum renders, very freely, 'by
lot'.

and thou thyself shalt die. The pronoun is emphatic.

in a land that is unclean. This is but a narrow Hebrew way of saying
'in a foreign country'. Even the food eaten by captives outside Palestine
was regarded as 'unclean'. *Cf.* Hos. ix. 3 (Assyria), Ezek. iv. 13 (Babylon).
In early days it was a common belief amongst the Israelites that it was
impossible for them to worship Jehovah in a foreign land (1 Sam. xxvi. 19).
Jehovah was supposed to reside only in Israel, and therefore all other
countries were 'unclean'. It was not until the Gospel age that the Hebrew
nation knew that it is right to call neither any land nor, still less, any man,
common (*i.e.* defiled) and unclean (Ac. x. 14, 15, xi. 9–12 a).

and Israel shall surely be led away captive out of his land. This
is a reiteration of the Prophet's prediction, in the very words[3] ascribed to
him in *v.* 11. *Cf.*, moreover, v. 5. Though Amos did not actually mention

---

[1] See Jer. xxxi. 30, Ezek. xviii. 2–4.

[2] The fall of Beth-el is implied elsewhere, iii. 14, v. 27.

[3] The metre suggests that the words 'out of his land' are not really genuine
in *v.* 17.

Amaziah as being involved in the capture of Beth-el, he certainly implied it. How otherwise was he to die in a foreign country?

The *boldness* of Amos in facing the king's representative is nearly, if not quite, as striking as the attitude of Elijah to Ahab (1 Ki. xviii. 18, 19, xxi. 20–24), and that attributed to Elisha before the two kings (2 Ki. iii. 13). The prophet of God, convinced of his call and commission, will bear his witness, will stand his ground and will not fear what man can do unto him.

> "Truth, crushed to earth, shall rise again,
> The eternal years of God are hers,
> But Error wounded, writhes in pain,
> And dies among his worshippers".[1]

Ch. viii, as it stands, consists of (1) a vision (*vv.* 1–3), succeeded by (2) prophetic denunciation (*vv.* 4–6) and announcement of doom (*vv.* 7–14).

VIII. 1–3. THE FOURTH VISION: THE BASKET OF SUMMER FRUIT

It may be that as soon as Amos had seen this vision he began his prophetic work.

If vii. 10–17 is in its right context, we must suppose that Amaziah succeeded in preventing the Prophet from telling the story of the fourth vision at the same time as the third. On the other hand, the recital of this vision on that occasion would seem nece: ary to the completeness of the Prophet's denunciatory message. For, twi e Jehovah can forgive Israel: but twice He cannot (vii. 8, viii. 2). See, further, Introd. p. 99. Some critics picture *vv.* 1, 2 (or 1–3) as representing the last words of Amos at Beth-el.

1–3. 'The end is come'. It appears that one day the attention of Amos was taken by a basket of summer fruit, which possibly had been gathered by himself. In Hebrew the term for 'summer fruit' is *qayiṣ*. To the Prophet's mind (which had passed into a state of abnormal vision) came the thought of a word of like sound, but not connected etymologically, *viz. qēṣ*, 'END!' Jeremiah in i. 11, 12 similarly, from contemplating an almond tree (Hebrew *shāqēdh*), was led to believe that Jehovah was 'watching' (Hebrew *shôqēdh*) over His edict to perform it. The Hebrew mind was deeply susceptible to the paronomasia or pun. See, *e.g.*, Mic. i. 14 (*'akhzābh*), Ezek. xxv. 16. The famous passage, 2 Ki. xviii. 4, *may* be another case in point.

It is almost certain that *vv.* 1–3 are to be regarded as referring to an actual psychical vision. This is suggested (1) by the presence in the book of four *other* visions to which this passage bears relation, (2) by the Prophet, according to the narrative, feeling himself to be interrogated, and thereupon replying, (3) by the descriptions of other like prophetic experiences, *e.g.* in Jer. xxiv, especially *vv.* 1, 3 (the two baskets of figs).

On the other hand, a second possibility should not be entirely excluded. Conceivably the narrative of the basket of fruit does not describe an actual

---

[1] William Cullen Bryant, *The Battle Field* (†1878).

VIII. 1 Thus the Lord GOD shewed me: and behold, a basket of summer fruit. **2** And he said, Amos, what seest thou? And I said, A basket of summer fruit. Then said the LORD unto me, The end is come upon my people Israel; I will

vision, but rather is a pictorial or literary representation of the Prophet's *thoughts* upon contemplating a natural sight, which suggested a perhaps obvious, but certainly very effective paronomasia.[1]

1. Thus the Lord GOD shewed me. See note on vii. 1. The story of each of Amos' visions is given in the *first* person.

a basket of summer fruit: *i.e.* of late summer fruit[2] (*e.g.* figs or olives); *cf.* 2 Sam. xvi. 1, 2, Jer. xl. 10, 12. The common meaning of *qayiṣ* is 'summer' (Am. iii. 15, Gen. viii. 22). A few interpreters see in the choice of the word a reference to the conclusion of the agricultural year (*cf.* Jer. viii. 20). "There would be association of ideas as well as similarity in sound. The late ripe fruit proclaimed the fall of the year; the fall of the year brought before the prophet's mind the fall of Israel. *Cf.* Matt. xiii. 39, Joel iii. (in Heb. iv.) 13, Rev. xiv. 14–20" (Edghill). But such exegesis seems doubtful. Gressmann, boldly doing away with the word 'end', translates the next verse, "*Autumn* has come upon my people Israel".[3] The term translated 'basket', *kᵉlûbh*, occurs only once elsewhere in O.T. (of a *cage* of birds, Jer. v. 27; as also in the Amarna Letters).

2. And he said. Amos believed that he heard Jehovah speaking, for He was ever beside him in his visions (*cf.* vii. 3, 6, 8, ix. 1–4). In the present passage, at least, that which he heard would be described in modern language as 'another voice within him'.

The end is come: *i.e.* 'the end' of the nation. So in Lam. iv. 18 of the Southern Kingdom. In Gen. vi. 13 ('P'), 'the *end* of *all flesh* comes in

---

[1] According to this latter interpretation it must be supposed that the Prophet, in telling the story, emphasised the fact that *God's purpose* lay behind his noticing the basket that day. 'God shewed me' would signify 'God *meant me to* see it'. It would seem most probable that what is represented in Jer. xiii. 1–11 as occurring as a result of *conversation* between Jehovah and Jeremiah is to be interpreted as an ordinary event in which the Prophet came later to realise Jehovah's leading.

[2] In the last (the seventh) line of the (imperfect) agricultural calendar-inscription of Gezer (see p. 219, footnote 4) are the words *YRḤ QṢ*, 'month of summer fruit', referring to July or August. The spelling, it may be noted, in the inscription is *exactly* that of the word for 'end' in the text.

[3] It has been suggested that this vision of Amos was recounted at the Beth-el autumn feast (Exod. xxiii. 16, xxxiv. 22). This festival was held in September or, in the Northern Kingdom, a month later (1 Ki. xii. 33). The pilgrim festivals are directly mentioned in *v.* 10. If the offering, or eating, of *fruit* was an element in the worship (*cf.* Deut. xxvi. 2, 10, 11), the lesson of Amos would be all the more impressive. Comparable would be our Saviour's reference to 'water' at the same feast, on most days of which a water libation was made (St John vii. 37–39).

not again pass by them any more. 3 And the songs of the
temple shall be howlings in that day, saith the Lord GOD: the
dead bodies shall be many; in every place shall they cast them
forth with silence.

(same Heb.) before' God.[1] Amos' whole teaching implied that righteousness
is more permanent than man. Even if it should mean that Jehovah's people
were to be annihilated, righteousness must be vindicated.[2]

my people Israel. For notes on the rest of the verse see on vii. 8.

3. If *v.* 3 be related to *vv.* 1 and 2, it would seem that in his vision Amos
watched the basket change into a deserted 'palace' of 'dead bodies'.
Amongst the latter, 'women-singers' (now 'wailing') were conspicuous;
and finally there fell a dread 'silence'.[3]

the songs of the temple: *i.e.* at the Beth-el sanctuary. But perhaps
hēkhāl should here be rendered 'palace', as sometimes in the O.T. (*e.g.*
1 Ki. xxi. 1, 2 Ki. xx. 18) and usually in Assyrian. The word, however, is
not the same as is translated *elsewhere* in Amos as 'palace' (or 'fortress'),
viz. i. 4, vi. 8, *etc.* For 'songs' should probably be read 'singing women':
so Duhm, Nowack, Marti. Difficult Hebrew is then simplified into 'palace-
singers will howl'.[4]

shall be howlings. The Hebrew is, 'shall howl'. It is obvious that
'songs' cannot be the subject of this verb (*cf.* above).

in that day: *viz.* the one implied in *v.* 2. The expression is sometimes
used (as possibly here) as a synonym for 'the day of Jehovah'; *cf.* note
on v. 18, and Introd. p. 60 and footnote 4.

the dead bodies. A similar threat occurs in Jer. ix. 22 (in Heb. 21),
xvi. 4, and, with more gruesomeness, in Jer. viii. 2.

shall they cast them forth with silence. 'They' is impersonal, and
the tense is prophetic *perfect.* The original is extraordinarily abrupt, perhaps
too much so for it to be the original—'a multitude of corpses in every place:

---

[1] In *later* Hebrew 'end' is employed as a technical eschatological term;
Dan. viii. 17, 19, xii. 4.

[2] Sophocles, *Phil.* 1444, may perhaps be compared: "Whether men live or die
righteousness lives". Immanuel Kant wrote: "If righteousness should perish
it would not be worth while for men to live on the earth". In vii. 7–9 judgment
is *threatening* Israel: now it has 'come'.

[3] Harper would transpose *v.* 3 to follow *v.* 9 as the order *v.* 9, *v.* 3 and then
v. 10 produces a very good sequence; moreover, the exact words, 'in that day
saith the Lord GOD', occur in *v.* 9 also (*cf.* 'day' in *v.* 10 *b*). On the other hand,
as to the phrase 'saith the Lord GOD' in *vv.* 3 and 9, it is possible that in *v.* 3 it
is an accidental scribal addition *derived from v.* 9. Certainly if the words are
omitted, *vv.* 2 *b* and 3 approximate slightly more to poetic form. So Robinson.
Nowack puts most of *v.* 3 after *v.* 14.

[4] Less probable is it that an obscure architectural term has suffered corruption
(*sedhērōth*), 'Temple panels (or, 'planks', 1 Ki. vi. 9, R.V.) will howl'; *cf.* Riedel,
following LXX φατνωματα here (and 1 Ki. vi. MS. A).

4 Hear this, O ye that would swallow up the needy, and

he (who[1] casts them forth) casts them (forth in) silence'.[2] Duhm places the
present verse, with vii. 9, after the plague passage vi. 8–11. So essentially
Gressmann. For another allusion to pestilence, see v. 17. Harper sees in
the present verse a reference only to 'indiscriminate *slaughter*', *i.e.* war.
It is true that *v.* 3 contains no very clear allusion to battle, but the theme
of the third vision (vii. 9) was the near approach of the 'sword'; and with
that vision the present one seems to be closely connected in thought.
Perhaps plague is here but a secondary feature of the judgment, following
as a consequence of siege conditions.

VIII. 4–14. THE SINS, AND PUNISHMENT, OF ISRAEL

This is the old theme. It is possible to regard the passage as representing
substantially the Prophet's *exhortation* based upon his vision of *vv.* 1–3,
uttered at Beth-el where he, presumably, had stood his ground. But there
is less homogeneity within these verses than at first appears. It is true that
the reference to 'that day' and the 'bitter day' of *vv.* 9 and 10 follows well
upon *v.* 3. However, the phrases, 'Behold the days come' in *v.* 11, and
'In that day' in *v.* 13, suggest fragments placed in their present context
by an editor. There may, indeed, here be six distinct *logia* of Amos assembled
by the editor, or editors, without reference to any particular occasion during
Amos' mission: (1) An utterance against unscrupulous corn-sellers—*vv.* 4–7.
(2) (?) A later apocalyptic *logion* duplicated from ix. 5—*v.* 8. (3) A threat
of a darkening of the sun to be followed by bitter mourning—*vv.* 9, 10.
(4) A threat of famine of 'the words of Jehovah'—*vv.* 11, 12. (5) A threat
of literal famine—*v.* 13. (6) A denunciation of the cult—*v.* 14. Whether
the chapter as a whole be a unity or not, certain verses seem to be of the
nature of interpolations into the text, *viz. v.* 6 (possibly), *v.* 8 (probably),
and either *vv.* 11 and 12[3] or else *v.* 13.

4. Hear this. *Cf.* iii. 1, iv. 1, v. 1. It is not possible to say whether it
was intended by the writer (or editor) that this formula should introduce
the remaining two chapters of the book, or whether it should apply to but
a few verses, *e.g. vv.* 4–6 upon *the sins of the trading community.* Ch. ix
would seem to be an entirely separate discourse based upon the fifth vision.

O ye that would swallow up. Read,[4] 'O ye that *crush* the needy'. The
Hebrew text as it stands (*lit.* 'ye that pant the needy') is out of the question. See the note on the fuller form of the saying given in ii. 7, where also
the LXX supports the same change being made in the M.T.

---

[1] Sellin makes the (unnamable) *Plague-Deity* the subject of the verb 'casts
forth'.

[2] Possibly the last word should be rendered, as in vi. 10, '(saying) Hold thy
peace'; *cf.* Zech. ii. 13 (in Heb. ii. 17).

[3] Or *vv.* 11 *b* and 12 *b*.

[4] As probably the LXX, ἐκτρίβοντες. The Targum 'despise' is also against
the M.T.

cause the poor of the land to fail, 5 saying, When will the new
moon be gone, that we may sell corn? and the sabbath, that
we may set forth wheat? making the ephah small, and the

cause the poor of the land to fail. Behind the word 'poor' of E.VV.
here stand in the Hebrew two alternative readings: (a) that of the Hebrew
text, 'humble', 'meek', (b) that of its margin, 'poor'. The reading 'meek'
savours of the late Psalms concerning *religious* persecution (*e.g.* Ps. cxlvii. 6
and Zeph. ii. 3), but it occurs again in Am. ii. 7 ('the way of the *meek*'),
and it may not yet have acquired its later ethico-religious significance.[1]
Note in *vv.* 4–6 the accumulation of vices: (i) crushing of the needy,
(ii) killing, or oppression, of the 'poor', (iii) impatience over the festivals, as
interrupting, (iv) dishonest commerce (*v.* 5), (v) sale of human beings (*v.* 6).
    If the chapter is in substance a unity, doubtless the traders are to be
taken as representing the *nation*; *cf. v.* 14.
    5. saying. The prophets delight to place ironically in the mouths of those
whom they denounce speeches which are in reality their own. *Vv.* 5 and 6
form such an imaginary speech; *cf.* Isa. xxviii. 15.
    the new moon. This religious festival is mentioned by other eighth-
century prophets (Isa. i. 13, 14, Hos. ii. 11); but in the Pentateuch it is
taken into account only in 'P' (twice, *viz.* Numb. x. 10, xxviii. 11–15).[2] As
to the mode of observance in Israel of 'the new moon', (1) to a certain extent
Numb. xxviii. 11–15 and Ezek. xlvi. 2 *b*, 3 confirm that which is implied in
the present verse, *viz.* that upon the new moon, even as upon the sabbath,
there was cessation of work; (2) also it seems a fair inference from 1 Sam.
xx. 5, 34 that, at least in early times, 'the new moon' was celebrated with
a household feast.
    and the sabbath. The present reference, and probably 2 Ki. iv. 23,
supply evidence outside the legislation that even in pre-exilic times ordinary
work stopped on the sabbath. This law was in the early code 'J' (Exod.
xxxiv. 21), 'Six days shalt thou work, but on the seventh day thou shalt
desist; (even) in plowing time and in harvest thou shalt *desist*'; and in the
other, probably early, legislation of 'E' in Exod. xxiii. 12. *Cf.* Exod.
xx. 8–11, Deut. v. 12–15. For an Additional Note on the *prophetic* interest
in the sabbath and upon the ultimate *origin* of the institution, see p. 315.
    set forth wheat: *i.e.* 'display' for sale; or, possibly, 'take out' from the
storehouse or sacks. The Hebrew is *lit.* '*open* wheat'.
    making the ephah small, and the shekel great. With the ancient
Hebrews *both* measuring *and* weighing appear to have been necessary in a

---

[1] The *syntax* of the half-verse is not easy, though it can be defended; see
Driver's *Tenses*, § 206. Moreover it is perhaps suspicious that the same root
'cause to fail' comes also in the next verse ('sabbath'). The verb is used in the
sense of 'exterminate' in Hos. i. 4 and elsewhere; but the LXX of the present
passage, 'who *oppress* the poor', suggests a different Hebrew word from that of
the M.T. Nowack reads as the LXX.   [2] See Gray, *Numbers*, p. 410.

shekel great, and dealing falsely with balances of deceit;
6 that we may buy the poor for silver, and the needy for a

commercial transaction. In the present instance the 'ephah' measure by
which the dishonest traders *sold* was smaller than the standard: the 'shekel'
weight by which they *weighed in*[1] the money from those who bought the
wares was deliberately made heavier than the normal shekel. The 'ephah'
was equal to about 8 gallons. The silver 'shekel' was probably 160 grains.
Dishonesty with weights and measures is condemned in such passages as
Deut. xxv. 13–15, Prov. xx. 10, 23.[2] Moreover, Jehovah's interest in commercial honesty is declared in Prov. xvi. 11.[3]

dealing falsely with balances of deceit. This is more correctly,
'making crooked (or, 'falsifying') balances of deception'.[4] 'Balances of
deception' is the Hebrew for 'balances which *effect* deception'. For the
vice here condemned, *cf.* Hos. xii. 7 (in Hebrew xii. 8), Mic. vi. 10, 11,
Prov. xi. 1, xx. 23. The sin of deceit in general is referred to in Jer. ix. 6, 8
(in Hebrew ix. 5, 7). Sins of covetousness are condemned not seldom by
the prophets, *e.g.* in Mic. ii. 2, Jer. vi. 13, viii. 10, xxii. 17.

**6. that we may buy the poor for silver, and the needy for a pair of
shoes.** This clause may be but a (later) editorial repetition from ii. 6,
where see note. Here, 'to *buy the poor*' takes the place of 'they (probably,
the judges) have *sold the righteous*', in the earlier passage. In the present
verse the dishonest traders value human life so slightly that they proceed
to the length of 'buying' to themselves 'for money'—*i.e.* they take in

---

[1] *Cf.* Gen. xxiii. 16.
[2] So also it is in *The Teaching of Amenophis* (XVI. xvii. 18, 19):
> "Tamper not with the scales, nor falsify the *kite*-weights,
> Nor diminish the fractions of the corn-measure".

With the present verse might also be compared the allusion to punishment in
the Zoroastrian 'vision' of the other world: "This is the soul of that wicked man
who, in the world, kept no true bushel, nor gallon, nor weight, nor measure of
length; he mixed water with wine, and put dust into grain, and sold them to
the people at a high price; and stole and extorted something from the good"
(ch. xxvii of the Book of Arda Viraf). Though the MSS. are of a later date, the
book containing his visions belongs undoubtedly to the Sassanian times, perhaps
as early as the 5th or 6th cent. A.D. (*cf.* revised edn by M. Haug, 1872,
p. lxxiii).

[3] *Cf.* also the reference to the action of the deity in the *Teaching* (XVI. xvii.
22, xviii. 1–4): "The *Ape* sitteth by the balance,
> His heart being the plummet.
> Where is a god so great as *Thoth*,
> He that discovered these things, to make them?
> Fashion not for thyself deficient *kite*-weights".

The quotations from Amenophis (Amen-em-ope) are from Griffith, *J.E.A.* XII.
p. 214. For the first, *cf.* also Oesterley, *Wisdom of Egypt*, etc. p. 48.

[4] Or else 'distorting', 'tampering with': root *'āwāh; cf.* Isa. xxiv. 1.

pair of shoes, and sell the refuse of the wheat. **7** The LORD
hath sworn by the excellency of Jacob, Surely I will never
forget any of their works. **8** Shall not the land tremble for

discharge of a debt—a man, or one of his family, sometimes even when the
sum owed is a mere trifle ('a pair of shoes').[1]

and sell the refuse of the wheat: *lit.* 'and sweepings (Duhm) of grain
we will sell'.[2] These words would follow after the *preceding* verse more
easily than upon the (perhaps interpolated) earlier part of *v.* 6. As the
text stands, however, the charge of selling to the poor more or less
worthless grain is of the nature of a climax to the Prophet's very lengthy
indictment against these evil merchants.

7. The LORD hath sworn by the excellency of Jacob. Jehovah will
visit the sins enumerated in *vv.* 4–6. For the Divine oath, *cf.* iv. 2, vi. 8.
The object by which it is sworn, *viz.* 'Israel's prestige' (or 'self-confident
arrogance', *cf.* Hos. v. 5, vii. 10), is alluded to also in vi. 8 (where see note).
The interpretation which would make 'Pride of Israel' a synonym for
Jehovah Himself lies open to serious objections. Quite different is the
Hebrew of Gen. xlix. 24 and 1 Sam. xv. 29. For 'Jacob' in the sense of the
nation Israel, *c.f.* vi. 8, vii. 2, 5, ix. 8.

Surely I will never forget. This means, 'I will requite', or 'punish'.
The only parallel in the O.T., however, for the idiom seems to be Ps. x. 11.
The phraseology of Ps. lxxiv. 19 comes near. For the idea, *cf.* Am. iii. 2
and Jer. v. 9, 29, ix. 8, 9.

any. As an equivalent of the Hebrew the E.VV. rendering is, unquestionably, preferable to that of some moderns, 'all' (*cf.* Gen. ii. 5, iii. 1, Ps.
cxliii. 2).

of their works. Marti and others follow the LXX in reading 'of
your works'. In *vv.* 4–6 the traders are singled out, but *v.* 7 seems to shew
that their sins are mentioned only as illustrations of the sins of the *nation*;
to whom for the latter half of the chapter the discourse is addressed. There
is, surely, eternal truth in the Prophet's words here. While it goes without
saying that it is contrary to God's nature to be arbitrary, vindictive, or
subject to moods, it is a universal instinct that a principle of Divine justice
should be allowed play when man cruelly illtreats his brother man. Moreover, the prophets of the O.T. must be right in representing all sin as sin
against *God. Cf.* on i. 3, 'transgressions'. This is not inconsistent with
Divine forgiveness, upon the individual's repentance and amendment
(St Lu. iii. 7–9, xv. 20, 21, xix. 8, 10).

---

[1] Instead of 'for a pair of shoes', the Targum has the weak paraphrase, 'in
order to become rich'.

[2] The word *mappāl* (? = 'fallings') appears to be good Hebrew, though occurring nowhere else in the O.T. with the meaning required in the present context;
the Targum saw no difficulty at all. The sense of the verb root in Job xii. 3,
xiii. 2 may perhaps be compared ('I am not *inferior to* you'; *lit.* 'I am not *falling*
in comparison with you').

this, and every one mourn that dwelleth therein? yea, it shall

8–14. The threat of punishment contained in the last words of *v.* 7 is, apparently, now expanded in detail to fill most of the remainder of the chapter. The whole nation is involved. *V.* 8 refers to *earthquake, v.* 9 *to an eclipse, v.* 10 to *mourning* (for some reason following the eclipse).

9. Shall not the land tremble: *i.e.* 'quake' or 'quiver; *cf.* 1 Sam. xiv. 14, 15, Pss. xviii. 8 (E.VV. 7), lxxvii. 17, 19 (16, 18). For a threat of earthquake, ii. 13–16 and ix. 1 should be compared (see notes). (1) In these passages the disturbance is probably local; so here. The 'land' is that of the sinning Israelites. In *vv.* 10–14 it is only Israel that is concerned. (2) But in *v.* 9 *b,* the same word, '*ereṣ,* may be rendered (as by E.VV.) 'earth' (*i.e.* the world), rather than 'land', and some would translate it so in the present verse too. Gressmann sees in this part of the book the eschatology of a *world*-catastrophe such as some scholars suppose to have existed in Egyptian oracles.[1] In any case, however, it is significant that Amos confines himself to the effect of such a catastrophe upon a tract of land very carefully defined (*v.* 12). The fulfilment of the prediction may be alluded to in i. 1.

for this. These words, in the Hebrew, are so placed as to be very emphatic. Some interpret 'this' as the *oath* of *v.* 7 (= 'in fulfilment of my oath'). 'This' can, however, mean 'all this evil' (*cf. vv.* 4–6). The remainder of the verse comes again almost verbatim in ix. 5 *b.* It is probable that one of the passages is directly dependent upon the other.[2] Such apocalyptic ideas as the verse exhibits may be a sign of a later date than the time of Amos (Praetorius). But see Introd. pp. 55, 56. For Jehovah's manifestation in earthquake, *cf.* Judg. v. 4, 5, Hab. iii. 6, Zech. xiv. 4, 5.

mourn. See i. 2, and on *v.* 10 below.

it shall rise up wholly like the River. . .the River of Egypt. A perplexing simile; for the rising and fall of a river, especially the annual inundation of the Nile, would be very gradual, as opposed to the short rapid movements of an earthquake.[3]

---

[1] *Die älteste Geschichtsschreibung und Prophetie Isr.* pp. 327, 356, edn 1 only.

[2] There is reason to believe ix. 5, 6 to be an addition to the original work; if so, the present verse, *if already in existence,* would be the source of ix. 5. But the words may not be genuine Amos in either place; and, if this is the case, viii. 8 should be regarded as a still later addition *drawn from* ix. 5. So Elhorst, Praetorius, Riessler. The fact that the text of viii. 8 is more unintelligible than that of ix. 5 lends support to the view that viii. 8 is a secondary passage. Nowack, Sellin consider *v.* 8 as a whole is unsuitable as succeeding *v.* 7. 'Their works' (*v.* 7 *b*) should be followed by 'for these', not 'for this'. Gressmann inserts viii. 8 between ix. 5 *a* and ix. 6, as supplying the true text in place of the existing ix. 5 *b* in the late "doxology".

[3] The M.T. (in this verse, but not in ix. 5) for the first occurrence of the word 'River' has by error 'like light'. Perhaps the scribe's eye caught the word at the close of *v.* 9. Praetorius (*Z.A.W.* 1915, p. 24) proposed to read, 'It will come to an end even as nothing, all of it'. In place of the M.T. 'like the River all of it', Riessler, followed by Canney, would read, 'like the Double River', *i.e.* the Euphrates and Tigris (*cf.* the Babylonian *Killalân*). This would make

rise up wholly like the River; and it shall be troubled and sink again, like the River of Egypt. **9** And it shall come to pass in that day, saith the Lord GOD, that I will cause the sun

it shall be troubled. Probably the Hebrew word so translated has crept into the text by accident.[1] It is absent from ix. 5.

and sink again. So the Hebrew is "read" in accordance with the text of ix. 5. The Hebrew "written" text of this word in the present verse has no meaning. In a description of an earthquake in Isa. xxiv. 19, 20, the ground falls *below* normal level and does not return to it again.

the River of Egypt. The Hebrew virtually means 'the *Nile* of Egypt'. The A.V. rendering 'flood' (twice in this verse) is too general. The Targum paraphrase here and in ix. 5 is instructive as shewing the Jewish belief that *captivity* lay behind even the apocalyptic element in the book of Amos. 'And there will go up against it (*i.e.* Palestine) a king with his camps which are great like the River, and he will cover the whole of it and drive out its inhabitants and it will sink down like the River of Egypt'.

9, 10. Earthquake is succeeded by a *darkening of the sun* (*v.* 9). This latter event is a signal for terrific *wailing* (*v.* 10), perhaps a mourning for those who die either (*a*) in the dark 'day of Jehovah', or (*b*) in the slaughter ushered in by the prodigy of the eclipse.

9. And it shall come to pass in that day...I will darken the earth in the clear day. For the expression, 'in that day', *cf.* viii. 3. The whole verse could equally well (*a*) come after *v.* 8, or (*b*) follow directly upon *v.* 7 (if *v.* 8 be regarded as an insertion in the text). Or 'in that day' might be a connecting link by which an *editor* added to an earlier text *v.* 9, or *vv.* 9 and 10. For this last use of the phrase, 'in that day', *cf.* ix. 11, Isa. xix. 16, 18, 19, 23, 24. If *v.* 8 be regarded as being in its right place, there is a certain majestic climax in the succession upon the same 'day' of wonders (*a*) terrestrial, (*b*) celestial. *V.* 9, however, may well be the genuine work of Amos, and is regarded by most scholars as such. The threat is brief and contrasts with the greater elaboration of the apocalyptic predictions of Joel (in Joel ii. 10, ii. 30, 31 (in Hebrew iii. 3, 4), iii. 15 (Heb. iv. 15)), 'Isaiah' (in Isa. xiii. 9–11), and 'Zechariah' (in Zech. xiv. 6, 7).[2] It

---

good parallelism with 'like the River of Egypt' in the second clause, but the Hebrew term for 'River' is used almost exclusively for the Nile. (Dan. xii. 5–7 is exceptional.)

[1] Nor can it mean 'be troubled', *i.e.* 'heave' or 'be tossed'. Isa. lvii. 20 is a doubtful parallel, for the text is not very certain. The Hebrew word signifies 'be driven away', or 'cast out' (*cf.* Jon. ii. 5, E.VV. 4) and is really not at all suitable to the present context.

[2] It is worthy of note that prophecies of the temporary withdrawal of the sun's light are met with outside the O.T. In the *Prophecy of Neferrohu* of *c.* 2000 B.C., it is said: "The sun is veiled and shines not in the sight of men.... Rê removes himself from men. (If) he shines, it is (but) an hour. None knoweth that midday is there" (*J.E.A.* I. p. 104; *cf.* the *Oracle of the Potter*). It is probably with such a passage as this in mind that Gressmann comments upon

to go down at noon, and I will darken the earth in the clear
day. **10** And I will turn your feasts into mourning, and all

is interesting to note that *darkening of the sun* is coupled with *earthquake*
(as in the present text of Amos) in the first and last of the above references;
and *cf.* St Matt. xxvii. 51, St Lu. xxiii. 44. Some of the prophetic descriptions may be but expansions in metaphorical language of Amos'
anticipation of 'the day of Jehovah' which, he had declared, would be
'darkness and not light' (v. 18 *b*, 20 *b*); *cf.* Zeph. i. 15 *b*. In this way
Mitchell would interpret even the present verse. In Jer. xv. 9, 'her sun is
gone down' is an extreme instance of the metaphor of the sun.

An eclipse, for to such the reference in Amos seems definitely to be, was
regarded by the ancients as a species of disaster; and the verse following
tells of the effect upon the people of the one here threatened. Even to-day,
in spite of mathematical astronomy, there seems a certain uncanniness in
the deepening of the darkness, the alarm of the animals, *etc.*, during an
eclipse. For the bearing of the present verse upon the date of the prophecy
of Amos, see the Additional Note on p. 316, and Introd. p. 35 (iv).

I will darken the earth. Perhaps read, simply, 'I will cause darkness'.[1]
If the reference in the verse is to an eclipse it may be pointed out that such
an event could not cause darkness in *all* parts of the world. This perhaps is
hypercriticism. (1) At any rate, with the adoption of the above reading such
an objection disappears. (2) Or, quite probably, '*ereṣ* here means not 'earth',
but 'land' (of Palestine), as in the verse preceding.

in the clear day. The Hebrew seems to be rightly rendered by most
scholars 'in the (or, 'a') light day'.[2]

10. I will turn your feasts into mourning. The *ḥag* was the pilgrimage
festival connected with the agricultural year (see on v. 21), and was,
characteristically, a joyous event; *cf.* the very parallel allusion in Hos. ii. 11.
The phrase '*to rejoice before* Jehovah' is with great frequency attached to
references to the observance of the sacrificial harvest feasts, *e.g.* in Deut.
xii. 12, 18, xiv. 26, *etc.*, and *cf.* Isa. ix. 3 (in Heb. *v.* 2). Harper's suggestion,
mentioned above (p. 241, footnote 3), of placing *v.* 3 between *vv.* 9 and 10

Am. viii. 9 that, like the Israelites, the Egyptians also depicted the coming woe
partly with the colours of a *political*, partly with those of a *natural*, catastrophe.
See Introd. pp. 56, 57.

[1] This is with the omission of *lā'āreṣ* ('the earth') as a gloss (*a*) interfering
with the rhythm, and (*b*) containing an Aramaism found in Hebrew almost
entirely in books of late date. So Praetorius. *l*ᵉ as the sign of the *accusative*
occurs also in vi. 3 and is found in Aramaic in Ezra vii. 25, Dan. ii. 10, *etc.* (*cf.*
Marti, *Bib. Aramäische Gram.* § 108); in Heb. in Ps. cxvi. 16, 1 Chron. xxii. 19,
xxix. 20, *etc.* (Ges.-K. § 117 *n*).

[2] The idiom by which a noun in the genitive takes the place of an adjective
is familiar in most languages, but is peculiarly characteristic of Hebrew, *e.g.*
'temple of holiness' = 'holy temple'. Thus, *Oxf. Heb. Lex.* explains 'a day of
light' as 'a clear sunshiny day'. It is parallel to 'noon' in the former part of
the verse. LXX misunderstood (ἐν ἡμέρᾳ τὸ φῶς).

your songs into lamentation; and I will bring up sackcloth
upon all loins, and baldness upon every head; and I will make

has the great merit of making it unnecessary to seek a connection in
thought between *v.* 10 and *v.* 9. For **mourning**, see note on 'baldness',
below.

and all your songs into lamentation. For 'songs', *cf. v.* 3*a*. In v. 23*a*
they are, as here, accompaniments of sacrifice. The same word, *qînâh*,[1]
occurs in v. 1 (but not in v. 16). The use of the term is not confined to
funeral elegies. The first two clauses of this verse are quoted as 'Amòs'
in Tob. ii. 6.[2]

and I will bring up sackcloth upon: *i.e.* 'I will *place*', '*clothe*', or, as
the Peshiṭṭa paraphrases, 'I will *gird*'. For the Hebrew idiom, *cf.* Lev.
xix. 19, Ezek. xliv. 17 (*lit.* 'come up upon'). (1) The use of haircloth in
mourning is commonly alluded to in the O.T., *e.g.* in 2 Sam. iii. 31, 2 Ki.
vi. 30, Ps. xxx. 11. (2) In Jon. iii. 6–8 it is a sign of *repentance*. It is not
impossible that it is so here. According to Joel ii. 1, 12, 13, weeping,
mourning, rending of the heart, and *turning to Jehovah* are appropriate on
Jehovah's 'day'.

baldness. To create baldness with the razor was a funeral rite;[3] *cf.*
Lev. xxi. 5, Deut. xiv. 1, Mic. i. 16. In Isa. xxii. 12, as in the present context
of Amos, artificial baldness is coupled with girding with *sackcloth* on the
occasion of a national disaster, perhaps with no reference to mourning for
dead people.

It does not seem possible to determine certainly whether in the present
passage the reference is primarily to grief (1) at the advent of Jehovah's
dark 'day' (*v.* 9), or (2) at *deaths* (in some way not stated here) resulting
from that 'day', or (3) at the eclipse. The accumulation of terms particularly
suited to mourning over the dead, and the comparison 'as the mourning
for an only son', might suggest actual deaths. But obviously the darkening
of the sun mentioned in *v.* 9 could not in itself have caused mortality.

I will make it. 'It' refers to that occasion generally.[4] *Cf.* Robinson:
"*It-will be as bad as* if every man had lost his only child".

---

[1] On *qînâh* measure, see Introd. p. 33 (ii). The poetic structure of this verse
is not in *qînâh* measure, but (like *v.* 9) in trimeter.

[2] The variations from the LXX in Tobit are slight, and may be due to the
author quoting from memory. 'Your feasts *shall be turned*' represents 'I will
turn' (LXX and Hebrew); Tobit has 'mirths' for the Hebrew 'songs' (LXX
'odes'). Such divergence would be consistent with the book of Amos not
having been translated into Greek by the period when the Tobit Greek text came
into existence (? 1st cent. B.C.).

[3] In 2 Ki. ii. 23 the 'baldness' of Elisha may have been a sign of mourning for
Elijah; *cf.* Job i. 20, Isa. iii. 24, Ezek. vii. 18. The Targ. of the present verse
(*mᵉraṭ*) hardly means 'plucking off (the hair)', *cf.* Ezra ix. 3. For funeral customs,
see Lagrange, *Rel. sémitiq.* pp. 277, 278.

[4] Ges.-K. § 135 *p* compares with the indefinite 'it' in Gen. xv. 6, 1 Ki. xi. 12,
etc. Sellin, however, would follow the LXX, and would understand the words
'it' and 'thereof' to refer directly to the expression 'day'.

it as the mourning for an only son, and the end thereof as a
bitter day.

11 Behold, the days come, saith the Lord GOD, that I will
send a famine in the land, not a famine of bread, nor a thirst

as the mourning for an only son. The same example of the very
greatest misfortune is instanced in Jer. vi. 26 (as an illustration of a national
calamity). In Zech. xii. 10 *b* the reference is to the actual mourning over
one slain. In our passage the weeping is not for Tammuz, or Adonis (Ezek.
viii. 14); "no wailing for a dead god who was to come to life again, could
match the agony of bereavement felt for one's own son irretrievably lost,
with no brothers to mitigate the sense of utter desolation, to perpetuate the
family, or to perform the last offices for the parent" (Peake's *Jeremiah*).

and the end thereof as a bitter day. The 'end' (Hebrew *'aḥărîth, cf.*
Deut. xi. 12) remains as bad as the beginning. For 'bitterness' in the sense
of 'wretchedness', see 1 Sam. i. 10, Job iii. 20. The same metaphor is applied
to bereavement in Ruth i. 20 and Zech. xii. 10. For 'Jehovah's day',
if indeed the word 'day' is used in *v.* 9 *a* in a technical sense as a great
calamity, see v. 18 *b*–20.

11, 12. A threat of famine of Jehovah's 'word'. The people in their dire
distress (*cf. v.* 10) will stagger anywhere in the vain search for the counsel
of a prophet. *Possibly* also in the wider sense the verse includes the thirst
of the semi-repentant people seeking at last the knowledge of God's will
in order that now they may obey it.

11. Behold, the days come. For the phrase, *cf.* iv. 2, ix. 13.

**a famine in the land, not a famine of bread, nor a thirst for water,
but of hearing.** Translate, probably, '...not a famine of bread, nor a
drought of water, but of hearing', rather than 'not a *hunger for* bread nor
a *thirst for* water, but *for* hearing'. For 'thirst' in the sense of 'drought',
cf. Deut. xxviii. 48, Neh. ix. 15, 2 Chron. xxxii. 11. This dearth is to be
unlike the others referred to in the book, *e.g.* in iv. 6–8.[1]

Marti, Nowack and Sellin would make *vv.* 11 *b* and 12 *b* a later gloss
which sought to explain a literal thirst as figurative. If the latter parts of
the two verses (or, as Riessler and others would urge, the entire verses)

---

[1] The thought of Am. viii. 11 finds illustration in, though it goes beyond,
Mic. iii. 5–7, where the darkness of the 'day' will consist in there being no
vision or divination in the professional prophets who have been regarded as
Jehovah's mouthpiece. The threat contained in Am. viii. 11, so far as it might
be interpreted as applying to the withdrawal of *spiritual* guidance, could be
compared with Prov. i. 24–28. The N.T., however, tells us that *God* does not
thus retaliate. It may be a solemn fact that if a nation persistently ignores
God's law, by a natural process it separates itself from Divine truth and
guidance. When it seeks Him it may not find Him (Hos. v. 6). Yet, as regards
the individual at least, it seems right to believe that counsel and help from
God are always available upon the appeal of a repentant and trustful soul
(St Lu. xxiii. 40–43).

for water, but of hearing the words of the LORD. **12** And they
shall wander from sea to sea, and from the north even to the
east; they shall run to and fro to seek the word of the LORD,

be omitted, then *v.* 13, which takes account only of literal thirst, does not
clash with the thought which precedes.

With the metaphor of a 'famine' of Jehovah's word, Prov. ix. 5 should
perhaps be compared, where personified Wisdom speaks of her teaching
as 'bread' and 'wine'.

words of the LORD. Most probably the *singular* number should be
read,[1] as in *v.* 12. Undoubtedly if 'words' (*plural*) be the correct text, the
passage lends itself to a wider, and more spiritual, application than when
the *singular* is read.

12. they shall wander. The same root is used in iv. 8 of thirsty people
staggering from city to city in search of literal water.

from sea to sea: *i.e.* from the Dead Sea to the Mediterranean, or,
in the words of Joel ii. 20, 'the *eastern*' to 'the *western* sea'.[2] The phrase
is again applied to the full breadth of Israelite territory in Zech. ix. 10,
Ps. lxxii. 8.

from the north even to the east. In place of 'east' we look, rather,
for *south*. Van Hoonacker suspects an early corruption in the text.

they shall run to and fro. Hebrew *shôṭ*. Not *speed* so much as,
perhaps, eagerness, or uncertainty,[3] appears to be consistent with the
verb, 'wander', preceding. The Massoretes, by the placing of the accent,
have arbitrarily destroyed parallelism and rhythm. Read, rather, 'From
north to east will they move eagerly to seek the word of Jehovah'.

to seek the word of the LORD. The exact phrase in Hebrew occurs
in this passage only. The verb *biqqēsh*, 'seek', is used here as *dārash* is
frequently, of endeavouring to obtain a Divine oracle.[4] For 'the (a) word of
the LORD' in the sense of Divine counsel or help in a crisis, mediated through
His prophet, *cf.* 2 Ki. iii. 12, Jer. xxxvii. 17. The Targum in this verse
renders without justification 'word' as 'teaching'. König[5] holds that
vv. 11 and 12 "point to a time of ethico-religious renewal, and consequently

[1] So the Versions including Targ. (some MSS.) and some Heb. MSS. According to
the *Oxf. Heb. Lex. dābhār* (*singular*), in the sense of 'a divine communication in
the form of commandments, prophecy and words of help to Jehovah's people, (is)
used 394 times'. The *plural* for words of God appears to occur only sixty times,
half of which (thirty-one) are in Jeremiah; otherwise (in prophets) in Isa. xxxi. 2,
Mic. ii. 7, and in the late Ezek. and Zech. (5 times each).

[2] For the (Mediterranean) 'Sea' as a point of the compass, *cf.* Gen. xii. 8
('Beth-el on the *west*', E.VV.), xiii. 14 ('westward'), *etc.*

[3] *Cf.* Jer. v. 1, 2 Chron. xvi. 9, Zech. iv. 10. In Dan. xii. 4 some translate the
same verb, *shôṭ*, '*wander* to and fro'. On the other hand, that the verb "seems
always to denote rapid motion, and especially motion hither and thither", is
maintained by Bevan on Dan. xii. 4.

[4] See the note on v. 4, p. 180, under meaning (*b*).

[5] *Geschichte der A.T. Rel.* edn 1924, p. 343, note.

and shall not find it. **13** In that day shall the fair virgins and
the young men faint for thirst. **14** They that swear by the sin

to a salvation epoch". Such an interpretation would be more convincing
if the text contained any mention of the people's *repentance*.

and shall not find it. For an instance of such failure to obtain an
oracular response, see 1 Sam. xxviii. 6. *Cf.* also Ezek. vii. 26, 'They shall
seek a vision of the prophet; but the law shall perish from the priest, and
counsel from the ancients'.

13. The verse speaks of the exhaustion of the flower of the Israelite nation
through *bodily* thirst.

If *vv.* 11 and 12 entire are in their correct context (and there is no compelling reason against holding such to be the case) it seems clear that *v.* 13
is a fragment, doubtless authentic, placed next to them by an editor on account
of the word 'thirst', and perhaps moreover because the phrase 'in that day'[1]
had already occurred in *v.* 9. It would appear arbitrary to seek harmony by
making the 'thirst' in the *present* verse a figurative one as it certainly is
in *vv.* 11 and 12 (van Hoonacker). *V.* 13 cannot be taken as either a consequence of, or a climax upon, *vv.* 11 and 12.[2]

shall the fair virgins and the young men faint for thirst. An
a fortiori statement. In Isa. xl. 31 there is an allusion to the fainting 'even'
of 'youths'. For the special mention of young men and young women
(in a prosperous era), *cf.* Zech. ix. 17. For the misery in which young
children are involved during the siege and fall of a city, see Lam. ii. 11, 12, 19.
Doubtless the reference in the present context is to distress brought by a
foe, *cf.* vii. 17, viii. 3; it can have no connection with the form of punishment given in *v.* 9. The Targum upon the verse makes the reference definitely to the nation as a whole: 'In that day *the assembly of Israel* shall
wander about (*cf.* Targ. of *v.* 12 *a*), who are *like* fair virgins...and they will
be smitten and prostrated with thirst'.

faint. The same verb is used of Jonah's exhaustion from the sun's rays
(Jon. iv. 8). The verb occurs with similar meaning but in another grammatical voice in Isa. li. 20.

14: supplies an impressive ending to this chapter of denunciation and
threatening. The people—idolatrous and almost polytheistic—will fall for
ever. Jehovah is worshipped at Dan as a bull; whereas at Samaria a
goddess '*Ashîmā* is invoked, and perhaps yet another god *Dôdh* at Beer-
sheba. The syntax, however, is not simple. The rendering, 'They that
swear...even they shall fall' (E.VV.) can *hardly* be obtained from the

---

[1] *Cf.* note on catchwords, p. 290, **Surely....**

[2] Lohr, Duhm, Robinson omit 'for thirst' from the close of *v.* 13. This to a
certain extent helps the metre, and makes it *possible* for the reference to be to
the physical exhaustion of the staggering seekers after a Divine revelation in
vv. 11, 12. The verse, however, would end somewhat abruptly without the word
'for-thirst'. Indeed without it the poetic balance of the line is weakened.

of Samaria, and say, As thy God, O Dan, liveth; and, As the

present text. Moreover, the construction of the verse seems to involve close
sequence with some sentence preceding. Duhm and Gressmann connect
v. 14, as it stands, with *v.* 13. The latter scholar renders:

> (*v.* 13 *b*) "...the fair maidens and the young men faint for thirst,
> (*v* 14)   who swear by *Ashima* of Samaria
>   and say: 'as truly as thy God lives, Dan!'
>   and 'as truly as thy *Dod* lives, Beer-sheba!'
>   They fall, and rise not again".

It may be felt, however, that '(they) that swear...liveth' would follow
better upon *vv.* 11, 12, than upon (the added?) *v.* 13: for it is the nation
as a whole, not only its adolescents, who are the sinners. Some hold that
the verse, all except the last line, is by a hand later than Amos' time; *cf.*
Additional Note, p. 318 *ad fin.*

They that swear. It is the worship, not the *swearing* as such, to which
the Prophet objects. Later, in Judah, Jeremiah *hopes* that the people
will yet 'swear, As the LORD liveth...' (Jer. iv. 2). Such oaths are enjoined
(Deut. vi. 13, x. 20), provided only they are not perjury (Exod. xx. 7).
In our Saviour's time, oaths 'by' God and 'by' various objects were very
frequent among the Jews, and He appears to have forbidden oaths entirely
(St Matt. v. 33–37).

by the sin of Samaria. Probably we should read (with very slight
emendation of the M.T.), 'by *Ashîmâ* (a goddess) of Samaria'. For a discussion of the phrase, see the Additional Note on p. 316.

Samaria. (1) If the reading '*sin* of Samaria' be original, the allusion
must be to the Jehovah Bull at Beth-el. It is true that Samaria was
distant from Beth-el twenty-five miles, even as the crow flies.[1] A similar
reference to 'Samaria', when the city Beth-el really must be meant, occurs
in Hos. viii. 6, 'the calf of Samaria'.[2] Possibly, however, such passages
are to be explained as implying that Amos and Hosea are delivering their
denunciations in the political capital itself. (2) On the other hand, if, as
seems almost certain, '*Ashîmâ* should be substituted for 'sin' in the present
Hebrew text (though the allusion *might* be to the Beth-el sanctuary) no
difficulty stands in the way of the reference being to the city of 'Samaria',
as the text says.[3]

As thy God, O Dan, liveth. (1) This rendering well represents what
the writer meant—'as surely as thy God (is) alive'. So in Deut. xxxii. 40,

---

[1] Not till later than Amos' time was a whole region designated geographically
by the name 'Samaria'.

[2] Nowack makes 'Samaria', the capital, stand in Hos. viii. 6 for Israel
(*cf.* Hos. vii. 1, x. 5, 7, xiii. 6, in Hebrew xiv. 1); as in Amos the names Joseph,
Jacob and Isaac mean the nation.

[3] It is worthy of note that several shrines became popular in Israel in spite of
the fact that, unlike Beth-el and Beer-sheba, they could not boast of patriarchal
traditions; *e.g.* Dan in the next clause, and Gilgal in iv. 4. See on vii. 9, p. 309 *ad fin.*

way of Beer-sheba liveth; even they shall fall, and never rise
up again.

'as I (am) alive for ever'. (2) The Massoretes, however (without foundation
in grammar) always seek to make a distinction between an oath by Jehovah
and one otherwise, by pointing the latter to read 'by the life of...';[1] cf.
1 Sam. xx. 3, xxv. 26. The present passage they handle in this fashion, '*by
the life of* thy deity, O Dan', from the standpoint that a Bull-image cult
could not have been worship of the true God at all.[2]

thy God, O Dan. The *preceding* clause indeed appears to contain a
reference to a deity at Samaria other than Jehovah, and likewise perhaps
that *following* ('*Dôdh* of Beer-sheba'). The 'God' of 'Dan', however, must
be Israel's national God and no other (as worshipped under the form of a
golden bull at Dan). With the phrase, '*thy* God, O Dan', cf. the expression,
'the God *of Beth-el*' in Gen. xxxv. 7 (R.V. marg.). According to 1 Ki.
xii. 29, 30 there was erected to Jehovah at Dan, even as at Beth-el, a
golden bull. Before this there had already existed in the locality a Jehovah-
shrine of some sort with sacred paraphernalia.[3] The Prophet's allusion in
the present passage to the calf-cult may be indirect, but it is none the less
an expression of his contempt for such worship. Dan was situated in the
north of Israelite territory near mount Hermon and the source of the
Jordan. Its ancient name *Laish* (Judg. xviii. 7, 14, *etc.*) is applied to it,
poetically, as late as Isa. x. 30.

As the way of Beer-sheba liveth. Again the text should probably
be slightly emended, so as to read, 'as thy *Dôdh* (a deity) liveth', or, perhaps
better, 'as thy *tutelary deity* (*i.e.* Jehovah) liveth'. See the Additional Note
on pp. 317 ff.

Beer-sheba. With regard to the localities mentioned in *v.* 14, the
simplest explanation of the reference to 'Beer-sheba' (of the tribe of Judah)
is that Amos did not limit his utterances to Northern Israel, but included
the Southern Kingdom within the scope of his message. See on v. 5. The
whole land is involved in Divine judgment, even from 'Dan' to 'Beer-
sheba',[4] not to say 'Samaria', the capital of the principal kingdom. Why
does *Beth-el* escape mention here? The answer is not easy. The difficulty
was seen by Wellhausen who (before the reading '*Ashîmā* was brought
forward) conjectured that, in place of the puzzling 'sin of Samaria', there
stood originally 'the God of Beth-el'.

even they shall fall. It is better to put a full-stop at 'liveth', and
to translate, '*And* they will fall and no more recover'. The grammatical

---

[1] Whereas the Hebrew word, even though pointed as *ḥē*, does not mean 'the
life of'. The Hebrew for 'the life of' (with the single exception of the late passage,
Dan. xii. 7) is always *ḥayyē*. Ges.-K. § 93 *aa*, and note.

[2] *Cf.* the Targum, 'as *the worship* which is in Dan stands, and as *the religious
observances* (*nîmôsîn*, *lit.* 'laws') of Beer-sheba stand'.

[3] See Judg. xviii. 14, and the LXX of 2 Sam. xx. 18 which contains the words
'and at Dan' after 'they shall surely ask counsel at Abel'.

[4] *Cf.* the proverbial phrase occurring *e.g.* in Judg. xx. 1, 2 Sam. xvii. 11.

IX. 1 I saw the Lord standing beside the altar: and ne said, Smite the chapiters, that the thresholds may shake: and

subject is still the same as in *v.* 13 (or, better, in *v.* 12). Nowack, Marti and Sellin transpose the final two clauses of the verse to the *beginning*, so as to read, '*They* will fall...*who* swear...liveth'. Sellin makes the chapter end impressively with the words, taken from *v.* 11, 'saith the Lord Jehovah'. From the point of view of metre, they could be spared better from *v.* 3, the first line of which in M.T. is overloaded.

and never rise up again: the meaning of *v.* 2 *b* (*cf.* v. 2).

IX. 1–4. THE FIFTH VISION: THE LORD BY THE ALTAR

The people, assembled at the high place for worship, will be slain by the fall of the building. Not a person will escape death by one means or another. This, the fifth vision in the book, probably came to Amos while he was at one of the shrines—most likely, though not certainly, that at Beth-el. See on vii. 10–17. For a further note on this vision, see Introd. p. 100.

1. I saw the Lord standing. 'No man hath seen God at any time' (St John i. 18): and the vision state in a man cannot make a spirit visible as 'standing' or in any other posture (St John iv. 24). For instances of the Prophet's anthropomorphism in his conception of God, see p. 294. The Targum paraphrases, 'I saw *the glory* (*y͏ᵉqārā*) of Jehovah *go up from the cherub and* dwell upon the altar'. In the present passage what Amos 'sees' is a vision not only of God, but of God's *punishment*. The word for 'Lord' is '*Adônai*, the Lord of all; so also in the famous vision of Isa. vi. 1.

beside the altar. This is probably the correct translation; though 'above', 'over' (Driver), or 'upon' (R.V. marg. and A.V.) is not impossible; *cf.* on vii. 7.   **the altar:** usually interpreted as the Beth-el altar either (1) as defined by vii. 10–17, or (2) because Beth-el was the leading sanctuary in Northern Israel. Neither of these reasons, however, would seem quite conclusive. In truth 'the altar' might be at almost any sanctuary in either kingdom.[1]

The occasion was perhaps the autumn feast (Hölscher). As in Amos' other visions, the contemplation of a physical object (here temple-furniture apparently) is the starting-point for a condition of 'vision'. *Cf.* Introd. p. 90.

Smite. The Lord addresses an *agent* (as in the story of 2 Sam. xxiv. 16), certainly not the Seer.[2] *Cf.* vi. 11 ('commandeth') and Isa. lvii. 14. The

---

[1] The *article* can be used in Hebrew when applied to an object rendered definite merely by the circumstances of the story (Dav. *Synt.* § 21 (*d*) and (*e*)). So in the N.T. '*the* bushel...*the* stand...*the* house' (St Matt. v. 15). With 'the altar' here, *cf.* also 'city' in vi. 8, even without article.

[2] Perhaps, however, in place of the *imperative* there should be read, '*I* will smite', '*akkeh*; *cf.* later in the verse, 'I will slay'. Praetorius, supposing the M.T. *hakh hakkaphtôr* to have arisen from a scribal *haplography*, reads *hakkēh* (infin. absol.) *hakkaphtôr* with the same meaning, 'I will smite the chapiter'.

break them in pieces on the head of all of them; and I will slay the last of them with the sword: there shall not one of them flee away, and there shall not one of them escape.

'smiting' might be by an upheaval (sounds of which the Prophet heard before the vision came upon him). So Nowack and Sellin who, moreover, following Volz actually emend the M.T. $b^e rôsh$, 'on the head of', to $b^e ra'ash$, 'with an earthquake'; see i. 1 and *cf.* on ii. 13. Possibly the whole passage, '*Smite...for good*' (*vv.* 1–4) is not so much a declaration by 'the Lord', as a description of what Amos in vision actually saw *occurring*.

the chapiters: *i.e.*, apparently, the *capitals* upon the pillars which held up the roof of the shrine. The noun in the Hebrew is *collective* singular. The rendering of the A.V. 'lintel of the door' is misleading. For the same sense of 'capital', *cf.* Zeph. ii. 14.[1]

the thresholds. At the shock of the blow the very 'thresholds' of the building will 'quiver'.[2]

break them in pieces. 'Them' refers to the capitals, of course, not the sills. Perhaps read, '*I* will break...'. The verb $bâsa'$, however, is not easy to parallel in this sense at all, unless possibly in Job xxvii. 8 (*cf.* R.V. marg.) and Joel ii. 8 *fin.* Normally it is used with reference to gaining by greedy violence.[3] One emendation of the text is 'in wrath'; *cf.* Hab. iii. 12 ($b^e za'am$).

on the head of all of them. The fragments of the capitals fall upon the priests and the worshippers. Doubtless the scene included the fall of the roof, as well as the ruin of the 'altar'; *cf.* note on iii. 14. With Am. ix. 1 the description of the fall of the Dagon shrine recounted in Judg. xvi may be compared (see especially *vv.* 23, 25, 29, 30). **all of them.** The *comprehensiveness* of Jehovah's judgment is a feature of Amos' outlook; *cf.* iii. 12.

I will slay the last of them: *i.e.* what is left of them. In iv. 2 the same Hebrew ('$ah\check{a}r\hat{i}th$) is rendered 'residue'. Those who escape death when the sanctuary falls will be pursued by the 'sword'.

there shall not one of them flee away...escape. The R.V. (not R.V. marg.) very fairly renders the idiomatic Hebrew, which literally is, 'The fleer to them (*i.e.* of their company) will not flee (successfully); and the escaper to them will not escape'.[4] The *inescapableness* of the doom is characteristic of Amos' prophecy (*cf.* ii. 14–16, v. 18–20).

---

[1] In Exod. xxv. 31 the word ($kapht\hat{o}r$) is applied to the spherical *knob* (E.VV. 'knop') of a lampstand. The LXX in the present passage read, by mistake, 'mercy-seat' ($\iota\lambda\alpha\sigma\tau\acute{\eta}\rho\iota\sigma\nu$, *i.e.* Hebrew $kapp\hat{o}reth$); and there is the reading of MSS. A and Q of the LXX, 'smite upon *the altar*' (the same by which the Lord is seen stationed).

[2] Van Hoonacker reads in place of $sipp\hat{\imath}m$, the term $sipp\hat{u}n$, 'ceiling' (1 Ki. vi. 15); but it is not a great improvement.

[3] *Cf.* the Vulgate here, *avaritia.* Moreover the very form is suspicious, $b^e s\check{a}'am$ (for —'$\check{e}m$). In Gen. xlviii. 9 $q\hat{a}hem$ (for —$\hat{e}m$) is explainable, for by $maqq\check{e}ph$ the word has lost its accent.

[4] *Cf.* Ges.-K. *Gram.* § 144 *e.*

2 Though they dig into hell, thence shall mine hand take

(1) In *vv.* 2–4 we still seem to have the story of the vision of *v.* 1. It is of the essence of visions and dreams that fantastic and non-logical elements should present themselves. The description of the seer's vision at Patmos on the Lord's day is quite *unthinkable* (Rev. i. 12–16). In the present instance it is impossible for readers of Amos to picture the way in which the scene of *e.g. v.* 4 is connected naturally with that of *v.* 1 *a.* In the words of Micklem (*Prophecy and Eschat.* p. 117): "How can the bewildered and terrified worshippers at Beth-el make good their escape by 'going into captivity'?...This is poetry and vision, not narrative prose and not conscious metaphor. From the point of view of psychology, this is dream language, dream symbolism". (2) Some interpreters, by giving insufficient consideration to this aspect of the case, have regarded the vision as closing half-way through *v.* 1, with a new oracle beginning at 'and I will slay the last of them with the sword'. There is no point at which the Hebrew text can be so divided.

In *vv.* 2–4 Jehovah's power is shewn to extend to 'hell', 'heaven', 'Carmel', the 'sea' and 'captivity'.

2. Though they dig into hell...and...climb up to heaven. The thought is hardly that of the audacity of the enemies of a deity bursting into hell or climbing into heaven; though Gressmann makes this comparison, referring to the myth of the Babylonian *Adapa*.[1] **hell.** The Hebrew word *sheʾôl* is translated variously in R.V. 'hell', 'the pit', 'the grave', and possesses no English equivalent. In the opposite direction to heaven, *sheʾôl* was the subterranean dwelling-place of the spirits of the dead. To it they 'went down'. (Isa. v. 14, and *cf.* 1 Sam. xxviii. 11–14), and from it there was no return (Job x. 21). It was a 'land' of the deepest darkness (Job x. 22). The conception of *sheʾôl* was derived by the Hebrews from Babylon.[2] The Tell el-Amarna Letters are evidence for considerable contact between that land and Western Asia at a comparatively early date. Such passages as Gen. xxxvii. 35, xlii. 38, xliv. 29, 31, Numb. xvi. 30, 33 (post-Mosaic) give the impression that every Hebrew is familiar with the idea of *sheʾôl*. The most detailed picture is that of Isa. xiv. 9–20, a highly poetical exilic passage, which is probably directly influenced (at least in some measure) by the contemporary foreign conception (*cf.* Kittel, *Religion*, p. 105). Popularly it was believed that in *sheʾôl* men were cut off not only from the

---

[1] *Alt. Proph.* edn 2, p. 326 *fin.* For the text, see his *Texte*, edn 1, pp. 34–38; edn 2, pp. 143–146.

[2] In Babylonian *arallû* (a word which possibly should be read in Ezek. xxviii. 10 in place of M.T. *'ārēlîm*, 'uncircumcised'; *cf.* Hermann, Hommel). The existence of an Assyrian word, *shuʾâlu*, is not quite certain. It is not clear whether the term *sheʾôl* is to be derived (conceivably) from a root *s-h-l*, hence = 'deep-sinking' (Vollers), or from *shâʾal* with the sense of 'hollow place', or from *shâʾal*, 'to ask', meaning 'place of inquiry, whence oracles can be obtained'. See *H.D.B.* v. p. 668 (*b*); Jastrow, *Rel. Bab. and Assyr.* pp. 558 ff.; Jeremias, *Bab.-Assyr. Vorstellungen vom Leben nach dem Tode*, esp. pp. 109 ff.

them; and though they climb up to heaven, thence will I bring them down. 3 And though they hide themselves in the

world (Job vii. 9 and 10) but from Jehovah also (Isa. xxxviii. 18). However, in the religion of the prophets *she'ôl* had no significance.[1] Whatever may have been said or thought in former times, Amos, in the present passage, claims that Jehovah is *Lord* of *she'ôl*; hence, even *she'ôl* is useless as a hiding-place from Amos' God. Though the expression employed here, 'to *dig* into *she'ôl*', appears to be unique, it finds illustration in Numb. xvi. 30–32 where certain people '*go down* alive into *she'ôl*' because of the ground 'cleaving asunder' and 'the earth opening her mouth'.

and...climb up to heaven. Dr S. A. Cook, in *C.A.H.* ii. p. 338, quotes from the Tell el-Amarna Letters: "If we go up into heaven, or if we descend into the earth, yet is our head in thine hands". *Vv.* 2–4 should be compared with Ps. cxxxix. 7–12, perhaps written under the influence of this passage; note especially the antithesis of *heaven* and *she'ôl*, followed by the reference to the *sea*. In the Psalm, however, the thought is of God's omnipresence, not as here of the impossibility of eluding Divine retribution. The O.T. could teach the happy, as well as the severe, side of God's presence; *cf.* Gen. xvi. 13, 14, Ps. lxxiii. 23, and the note upon *v.* 4, below.

thence...thence. The occurrences of the word in this verse, in *v.* 3 *b* and in *v.* 4, are probably the result of dittography, destroying, as they do, the trimeter rhythm.[2] To the modern reader *v.* 3 appears somewhat of an anti-climax to *v.* 2. To the ancients, however, '*she'ôl*' and 'heaven' were not conceived of as far removed from the earth.

3. the top of Carmel. The same phrase (*rôsh hakkarmel*) occurs in i. 2, but in the present context the reference is to the *isolation* and *inaccessibility* of the place. The forest of the modern *Kurmul* is extremely dense; and, moreover, the limestone abounds in caves, not to mention tombs (of the Bronze and of the early Iron Age). The 'top' itself is at a considerable height—nearly 1800 feet[3] above the Mediterranean Sea. Carmel being the last hiding-place in the land, the fugitive will now have no other refuge but in the sea which lies at its base. For the 'solitariness' of Carmel, *cf.* Mic. vii. 14.[4]

though they be hid from my sight. Better translate the *Niph'al* voice 'hide themselves' (reflexive). Two verbs are employed in this verse with virtually the same meaning—*ḥābhā*, 'withdraw' (in *v.* 3 *a*), and *sāthar*,

---

[1] Marti, *Rel. des A.T.* p. 62, Eng. transl. p. 180.

[2] Almost certainly also, for the same reason, 'from my sight' (*v.* 3) should be omitted.

[3] Within Israelite territory Carmel is rivalled in height only by mount Tabor rising 1843 feet, at the other end of the valley of Esdraelon.

[4] A description of excavations among the tombs of mount Carmel at 300 feet above sea-level, conducted by Guy and Fitzgerald in 1922, is to be found in *Bulletin* No. 5 of the Brit. Sch. of Archaeol. in Jerusalem.

top of Carmel, I will search and take them out thence; and
though they be hid from my sight in the bottom of the sea,
thence will I command the serpent, and he shall bite them.
4 And though they go into captivity before their enemies,
thence will I command the sword, and it shall slay them:

'cover' (here).[1] The latter verb occurs in Jer. xxiii. 24, a good parallel to
the present passage.

the bottom. The same word is used also of a *floor* (of the Tabernacle),
e.g. in Numb. v. 17.

the serpent. (1) "The virulence of the venom of sea-serpents is equal
to that of the *most* pernicious land-serpents'ᴸ (Pusey, quoting *Zoological
Transactions*, ii. pp. 303–309). (2) As, however, *hydrophidae* are unknown in
the Mediterranean Sea, "the reference is more probably to an imaginary
monster, supposed by the Hebrews to have its home at the bottom of the
ocean" (Driver). Gressmann identifies it with the dragon *Tᵉhôm* (in
Babylonian *T'iamat*). Moreover, it may be added, amongst the ancients the
belief existed that the serpent was supernatural.[2] It is rarely wise, however,
to interpret Hebrew imagery, and particularly prophetic imagery, too
literally; Jer. v. 6 supplies a case in point. (3) The allegorising of the Targum
upon *v.* 3 is consistent with its interpretation of Amos elsewhere,[3] 'And if
they should think to hide themselves on the top of the great fortresses,
thence will I command searchers and they will search them out; and if they
hide from before my Word in *the islands of* the sea, thence will I command
the peoples *who are strong like* the serpent, and they shall slay them'. But
this is not exegesis. Upon the whole, explanation (2) above is the one to
be preferred.

he shall bite them. *Cf.* v. 19.

4. Even in exile the Israelites will be cut off.

they go into captivity: Hebrew *shᵉbhî*. This is the old theme of the
Prophet (*cf.* Introd. p. 30), although previously the term used in the
Hebrew has been *gôlāh*, 'exile' (v. 5, vii. 17, and the verb *gālāh*, v. 27, vi. 7).
It is clear that the vision at the sanctuary concerns more than the group
of worshippers; it is intended to indicate the fate of the entire nation:
cf. vi. 7, where 'they'—strictly speaking, the nobles previously referred to—
comes to mean the people as a whole.

thence will I command the sword. For an *abstract*, but as it were
personified, use of the term 'sword', *cf.* Ezek. xiv. 17, where it is apostrophised, 'Sword, go through the land', and Jer. xlvii. 6, 'How long will

---

[1] See J. Kennedy, *Heb. Synonyms*, pp. 71–74, 77–80.
[2] A bronze image of a serpent has been found at Gezer, which appears to have
been an object of worship. Gressmann, *Bilder*, edn 1, p. 95, No. 177; edn 2,
No. 398. For an ancient Egyptian hymn to the Royal Serpent, see Erman,
Literature of the Anc. Egyptians, transl. Blackman, pp. 12, 13. Some Israelites
may have pictured Jehovah Himself as a serpent (2 Ki. xviii. 4).
[3] See note on viii. 8 = ix. 5, 'the River of Egypt'.

and I will set mine eyes upon them for evil, and not for
good.

it be ere thou be quiet?'[1] It is obvious from its context that Am. ix. 4
contains a pictorial threat, rather than a definite and serious prediction.
For, as a matter of fact, exile, not death, was to be the consummation of
Jehovah's punishment of Israel.

and it shall slay them: seems to take up the expression (from *v.* 1),
'I will slay the last of them with the sword'.

I will set mine eyes upon them. Elsewhere this phrase (*sîm 'ēnaim 'al*)
is used only of looking upon, or watching over, people for their benefit,
Jer. xxiv. 6, xxxix. 12 (Hebrew), Gen. xliv. 21.[2] In the present passage
God is represented as being compelled, because of the sins of Israel, to act
in a manner contrary to that which He would desire and they would expect
('for evil and not for good'). The attitude is indeed very different from His
'making his face to shine upon' and 'lifting up his countenance upon'
Israel, as in the benediction of Numb. vi. 25, 26.

Vv. 1–4 shew Amos to be virtually a monotheist as, still more so, do
vv. 7 and 8. *Cf.* Introd. p. 24. From what is implied here by Amos it is
but a short step to the conception of Isa. vi. 3 *b* ('All the earth belongs to
Him'). Undoubtedly Am. ix. 1–4 points in the direction of the later belief
in Yahweh's *omniscience* and *almightiness*.

IX. 5–10. CONCLUDING WORDS. (COMPOSITE PASSAGE)[3]

5, 6. The third of the 'doxology' passages of the book. (1) Many scholars
have held that these two verses follow upon *vv.* 1–4 sufficiently naturally.
"Such a terrible announcement of judgment might seem to need confirmation: Amos therefore pauses, to describe, in two majestic verses, the
power of the God who has been provoked, and who thus threatens His
vengeance: all great movements in nature are due to Him (*v.* 5); He sits
on high and can control the elements (*v.* 6)"—Driver. (2) But it has been

---

[1] In Ezek. xxi. 3 (in Heb. *v.* 8) the 'sword of Jehovah' *may* be hypostasised as
an independent power in itself; but the passage might well be referring anthropomorphically to Jehovah as a man of war unsheathing His own sword, and it
has the appearance of poetry rather than of mythology. See, further, note on
vii. 9, p. 310.

[2] In Ps. xxxiv. 15 (in Heb. 16) 'the *eyes* of the LORD are *unto* (or, 'towards',
Heb. *'el*) righteous men'; whereas according to *v.* 16, 'the face of the LORD is
against (Heb. *b^e*) the doers of evil'. In Exod. xiv. 24 Jehovah '*looked forth* upon
the host of the Egyptians...and discomfited them'; and see Am. ix. 8.

[3] The literary criticism of these verses is complex, as will appear from the
notes.

    (*a*) *Vv.* 5, 6 are not genuine Amos.

    (*b*) *Vv.* 7, 8 *a, b*, possibly *v.* 9 and more likely *v.* 10 are genuine.

    (*c*) *V.* 8 *c* is almost certainly a later addition.

Many critics would make the passage *vv.* 8 *c*–10 a bridge added to join the
"Epilogue" (*vv.* 11–15) to the body of the book.

5 For the Lord, the GOD of hosts, *is* he that toucheth the
land and it melteth, and all that dwell therein shall mourn;
and it shall rise up wholly like the River; and shall sink again,
like the River of Egypt; **6** *it is* he that buildeth his chambers

said in the notes on v. 8, 9, that there are serious difficulties in the way
of regarding the doxology as being the work of the author of the book of
Amos. (i) The verses do not form a grammatical sentence: 'And the Lord
Jehovah of the hosts who touches the earth...Jehovah (is) his name'.
Moreover, they not only do not cohere syntactically with the verses
preceding and following, but they actually interrupt the thought (for
v. 7 is connected logically with *v.* 4). (ii) Though examples of Jehovah's
command over *nature* (*v.* 5) are found in Amos (iv. 6–11, vii. 1, 4, and even
in ix. 3) yet such a conception as *v.* 6 presents of a transcendental pre-
eminence of Jehovah above the entire universe is hard to parallel before the
later parts of the O.T., when indeed the vastness of creation was better
realised than it was in the age of Amos; *e.g.* Gen. i, Ps. xc. 2, and especially,
Isa. xl. 12, 22, xlii. 5, xlv. 12, 18, li. 13 *a*. *Cf.* also the references furnished
in the notes below upon such words as 'chambers', 'vault', *etc.* (iii) Further,
the latter half of *v.* 6 occurs also as *v.* 8 *b*, and the second part of *v.* 5 is
found in viii. 8 *b*—though, upon the whole, it would seem likely that viii. 8 *b*
depends upon the present passage rather than *vice versâ*, p. 246, footnote 2.

5. For the Lord: or, 'But (or, 'Now') the Lord'.

the GOD of hosts. The Hebrew is 'Jehovah of *the* hosts', a phrase never
used by the writer of the book itself. See p. 332 *ad init.*

he that toucheth the land. Jehovah's 'touching' of the land, or
earth, is in the phenomenon of *lightning* in Pss. civ. 32 *b*, cxliv. 5. The effect
of the fire of lightning might well be described poetically as a 'melting'
of the earth; *cf.* Ps. xlvi. 6, where Jehovah's thunder (the accompaniment of
lightning) 'melts' the earth. Perhaps, however, the reference in the present
passage is to *earthquake*[1] (*cf.* viii. 8 and ix. 1).

shall mourn: not in fear, but in grief at the havoc wrought.

it shall rise up...River of Egypt. For notes on the latter part of the
verse, see upon viii. 8.

6. he that buildeth his chambers in the heaven. '*Upper* chambers'[2]
is the correct reading and translation; *cf.* Ps. civ. 3, 13. For Jehovah's
throne in the heavens, see Ps. ciii. 19 *a*, and *cf.* Pss. cxiii. 3, 4 (in Heb.
4, 5), cxv. 3, 16.

---

[1] In this case 'melts' would probably mean 'quakes' (Duhm, Mitchell, Sellin).
Cf. the Targum, and LXX καὶ σαλεύων αὐτήν.

[2] The M.T., by an error of dittography as ancient as the Versions, has what is
probably a quite different, though not altogether inappropriate, word, *lit.* 'his
step(s)' or 'stair(s)'. So LXX ἀνάβασιν αὐτοῦ; *cf.* Tertullian, *adv. Marc.* IV. 34,
ascensum suum; Vulgate, *ascensionem suam.* Driver and van Hoonacker do
not regard it as impossible to render the M.T. unchanged as '*upper* chambers'.

in the heaven, and hath founded his vault upon the earth; he
that calleth for the waters of the sea and poureth them out
upon the face of the earth; the LORD is his name. 7 Are ye not
as the children of the Ethiopians unto me, O children of Israel?

and hath founded his vault upon the earth. In Exod. xii. 22 the Heb.
word rendered 'vault', *'ăguddāh* (from *'āgadh*, 'to bind'), is used of a *bunch*[1]
of hyssop. Here it seems that the 'heavens' are 'bound' or fitted into a solid
vault, the ends of which are upon the 'earth': so in Job xxii. 14 (Hebrew
ḥûg). Job xxvi. 11 also should be compared. The 'vault'[2] is the same as
the *firmamentum* of Gen. i. 6–14. Pillars to the *earth* are alluded to in
Job ix. 6, a passage which has affinities with Am. ix. 5, 6.

he that calleth for the waters of the sea...his name. The remainder
of the verse is identical with the second part of v. 8; upon which see notes.

7 ff. The vision ended at *v.* 4, but in *v.* 7 the line of thought is continued.
In *vv.* 1–4 Jehovah was pictured as ordering the slaughter of the sinful
nation as represented by the worshippers at the shrine. It is not unreasonable for the Deity to slay them, for Israel *as* Israel is nothing to
Him—as the people are reminded in *v.* 7. In iii. 2 Jehovah had said, 'You
only have I known...', therefore I will visit upon you all your iniquities';
in the present passage He declares that from the first He has been interested
in, and has directed the movements of, other nations besides the Hebrews.
It is the *sinful* kingdom, whatsoever it be, that He must 'destroy' (*v.* 8 *a, b*).
Israel, therefore, will die by the sword (*v.* 10).

**7. Are ye not as the children of the Ethiopians unto me, O children
of Israel?** The Ethiopians of the O.T. (or 'Kushites') inhabited the Nile
valley, from Syene southwards (Ezek. xxix. 10). They may be singled out
in the present context (1) as (conceivably) despised for their dark colour
(Jer. xiii. 23), or (2) as frequently being sold as slaves, or (3), much more
probably, merely as a nation remote from Yahweh's people, Israel. The
Kushites are often mentioned in the Bible, *e.g.* 2 Sam. xviii. 21 (R.V.),
Jer. xxxviii. 7–12, Isa. xviii. It must not be argued from Gen. ii. 13, x. 8,

---

[1] *Cf.* Vulg. here, '*fasciculum suum* super terram fundavit'; see also Vulg. of
St Matt. xiii. 30.

[2] The A.V. translation in Am. ix. 6, 'troop', depends upon the use of the
term (in 2 Sam. ii. 25) with reference to a band of warriors. The sense of a 'group
of men' is assigned to the word in the present passage in *Pirqe Aboth*, III. 9:
"When ten sit and are occupied in words of Torah the Shekinah is among them,
for it is said, God standeth in the congregation of the mighty...And whence
even three? Because it is said: and hath founded his troop upon the earth
(Am. ix. 6)"; translation by Taylor, who furnishes the Rabbinical explanation
of why a 'troop' should consist of *three*. The MSS. of the passage of *Aboth* vary;
cf. the Hebrew Daily Prayer Book, p. 192, and Strack. The Targum renders
Am. ix. 6, 'the assembly (or, 'congregation', Aram. *kᵉnishtā*) upon the earth
he prepares'.

saith the LORD. Have not I brought up Israel out of the land
of Egypt, and the Philistines from Caphtor, and the Syrians

that they were Asiatics. The Jewish Targum obscures the clause entirely,
but it cannot alter the universalism of the remainder of the verse.[1]
   O children of Israel. The use, in the context, of the term 'Israel'
appears to be totally against the thesis that Amos addressed in his preaching
only ten tribes.
   Have not I brought up Israel. For the purposes of argument this fact
is admitted by the Prophet in ii. 10 also. The force of the question as a
whole is, '*Though* I have brought up Israel...*have not I also* brought up
the Philistines...?' Amos delights in rhetorical questions; *cf.* iii. 3–8, vi. 12.
   the Philistines from Caphtor. The place 'Caphtor' is mentioned in
Jer. xlvii. 4, and the inhabitants in Gen. x. 14 and Deut. ii. 23. Since the
middle of last century it has been usual to identify 'Caphtor' with Crete,
and the equation is approximately correct.[2] Conceivably, however, the
use of the term covered in addition other adjacent islands, and, indeed,
that part of the mainland of Asia which was nearest. For, from the
evidence of armour, headdress, *etc.*, it appears now to be established
beyond doubt that the *original* home of the Philistine was not the
island of Crete, but the neighbourhood of Caria and Lycia in Asia.
Perhaps LXX and Symmachus preserved a tradition which was very near
the truth when they rendered 'Caphtor' in Am. ix. 7 as 'Cappadocia'.[3] If
the supposition that Caphtor is Crete, and Crete only, must be adhered to,
we shall then have to make one of the following suppositions. (1) Some
Philistines from the Asiatic coast did inhabit a part of Crete for a period
before migration to 'Palestine'; this is the more probable. (2) The term
'Philistines' here must be limited (arbitrarily it would seem) to the *Krethi*,[4]
who, strictly, were not Philistines ('Pulesati'), but were their close allies.
See, further, the note on i. 6–8, and Hall in *C.A.H.* II. pp. 286, 287.[5] In
Am. i. 6–8 the Prophet predicted the ultimate extinction of the Philistines.
   and the Syrians from Kir. For 'Syrians', see note on i. 3–5; and for
'Kir', on i. 5.
   With the teaching of Amos here, Isa. xix. 23–25 should be compared,
where the prophet contemplates Israel as 'third' with its two great enemies

---

[1] An interpretation of Ehrlich may perhaps be mentioned, according to which
the similarity between Israelites and Ethiopians is to be found in Israel's
treatment of Jehovah, 'Are ye not (in your behaviour) to me like Kushites?'
But apart from nothing being known as to any pre-eminent wickedness of
Kushites, the form of the Hebrew sentence is barely capable of such a translation.

[2] *Cf.* Hall, in *People and Book*, p. 27: "We must still hold that Keftiu was
primarily Crete, and so was Kaphtor, which was the same word and land".

[3] *Cf.* Targum, Ϗαππότᵉϗαιᾱ.

[4] The 'Cherethites' of 1 Sam. xxx. 14, 2 Sam. viii. 18, *etc.* They are mentioned
as *distinct* from the 'Pelethites' (= Pulesati).

[5] There is a Hebrew word *kaphtôr* which means 'crown' or 'capital' of a
pillar (Am. ix. 1), but its connection with the proper name is quite obscure.

from Kir? **8** Behold, the eyes of the Lord GOD are upon the
sinful kingdom, and I will destroy it from off the face of the

Egypt and Assyria, 'a blessing in the midst of the earth', Egypt styled
'my people', and Assyria 'the work of my hands'.

Already in chs. i and ii Amos had declared Jehovah's sway to be over
nations other than Israel; in v. 18 he had spoken of 'Yahweh's day' as an
event not to be desired by Israel. But in ix. 7, in enunciating the complementary truth of Jehovah's *friendly interest* in Israel's enemies, the high-water
mark of inspiration in the book is reached; and, not least so, because the
Prophet's utterance must have appeared to his contemporaries as amazing
and almost incomprehensible. See, further, Excursus II. Both Amos and
Jesus Christ transcend the bounds of the Hebrew nation; the preaching of
Amos in this verse prepares the way for that of the N.T. Teacher. "Nothing
was further from Him than an emphasis upon exclusive nationalism".[1]
In Amos we seem to see already the glimmering of the greater light of the
universality of the fatherhood of God and of the proclamation of salvation
to the whole world.

8 *a, b.* **the eyes of the Lord GOD are upon.** *Cf. v.* 4, 'I will set mine eyes
upon'; also iii. 2, 'therefore I will *visit*'. 'Upon' should perhaps be 'against'
as in the R.V. of Ps. xxxiv. 16 referred to on p. 260, footnote 2. The first two
clauses of *v.* 8 would seem to be closely connected in thought with *v.* 7.

the sinful kingdom. Two interpretations are possible. (1) The article
'the' is used to limit the reference to Israel. So Harper and Duhm, '*this*
sin-filled state'. Already in iii. 9-15, Amos had maintained that 'the house
of Jacob', 'Israel', was more guilty than its neighbours, Ashdod (LXX
Assyria) and Egypt. (The present passage should not be interpreted as
implying a contrast between the kingdoms of North Israel and *Judah*.[2]
If by 'the sinful kingdom' be meant the Ten Tribes in contradistinction to
Judah as a supposed *holy* kingdom, the entire verse cannot be by Amos
who condemns equally both kingdoms, iii. 1 *et seq.*, vi. 1.)[3] (2) More probably, the Hebrew article is 'generic', referring to *any* 'kingdom'.[4] "Whatever the nation and whatever its history, Yahweh applies but one test;
when by this test a nation is shewn wanting, Yahweh's eyes are against it
for destruction" (Edghill). None the less, though the Prophet does not
say so explicitly, it is clear from his *argument* that 'the children of Israel'
in particular are in his mind.

By 'sinful', Amos means *morally* guilty; *cf.* the note on 'sins', v. 12.

---

[1] Kittel, *Rel. of Israel*, p. 224.

[2] Such as appears, *e.g.*, in Ecclus. xlvii. 21, 'and out of Ephraim ruled a disobedient kingdom' (Hebrew *mamlekheth ḥāmās*).

[3] So Gressmann, *Ält. Proph.* edn 2, p. 358. Nowack is not of this opinion.
Holding that Amos never addressed an accusation against Judah, he thinks that
the designation 'sinful kingdom' is quite comprehensible as referring to the
Northern Kingdom upon which alone he pronounces judgment.

[4] As is said, '*the* righteous', '*the* wicked', '*the* fugitive'. See Dav. *Syn.*
§ 22 (*b*); *cf.* note on iii. 12, p. 161.

earth; saving that I will not utterly destroy the house of
Jacob, saith the LORD. 9 For, lo, I will command, and I will
sift the house of Israel among all the nations, like as *corn* is

For the last time in the book (*cf.* also *v.* 10) and very strikingly Amos,
declaring that his God punishes sin, asserts the doctrine of the Divine
righteousness. Jehovah and Jehovah-religion are essentially ethical.

and I will destroy it from off the face of the earth: Hebrew 'ground',
so Gen. vii. 4 *b.* Amos announces, and more unequivocally than ever, the
complete destruction of Israel; *cf.* v. 27, vi. 14 and, especially, vii. 9 and
vv. 2 and 3 of the present chapter.

8 *c*. saving that I will not utterly destroy the house of Jacob.[1] (1) In
itself the expression, 'house of Jacob', can hardly exclude either North
Israel or Judah; so also in iii. 13. The meaning might well be the same as
that of 'house of Israel' in *v.* 9, and 'sons of Israel' in *v.* 7. (2) It has been
held, however, that the reference is to North Israel *only*; *cf.* the use of
'Jacob' in Isa. ix. 8 (in Heb. ix. 7). (3) If (as is almost certain) the clause is
a late addition, the expression could apply to *Judah* alone (*cf.* Jer. v. 20,
Obad. *v.* 17). On 'I will not utterly destroy', *cf.* Additional Note, p. 319.
It has been shewn in the Introduction (pp. 67–78) that there are strong
reasons for believing that the happy section, *vv.* 11–15, was written at a
period considerably after the composition of the book of Amos. Many
critics regard *vv.* 8–10 as a whole as having been added at the same time
to form a connecting link or bridge between *vv.* 11–15 and genuine Amos;
cf. Cheyne in Robertson Smith, *Prophets*, edn 2, p. xv, and Duhm.
V. 9 (perhaps) and, also, as it stands, *v.* 8 (certainly) contain both threat
and hope. Whatever be the true interpretation and date of *vv.* 9 and 10,
at least *v.* 8 *c* is a late connecting link.

9. For, lo, I will command. For the expression, *cf. v.* 4. (1) If the
clause has to be connected with the end of *v.* 8, the sense is happy: 'Many
will be saved, *for* . . .'. (2) If 'for' follows up *v.* 8 *a, b* (' . . . earth') the sense
is, 'See what evil is coming, *for*'. . . . *V.* 10 also is a threat.

and I will sift the house of Israel among all the nations: *lit.*
'move to and fro', 'shake'. Earlier in the prophecy one nation only, *viz.*
Assyria, has been concerned—though König would add *Syria* (2 Ki. x. 32).
Clearly such an allusion to '*all* the nations' seems more appropriate at a
later period of Israelite history; see Jer. xliii. 5, Ezek. xxxvi. 21, and
especially 'Isa.' xi. 11, 12.[2] And the reference in the present passage, 'among
all the nations', is of a wider scope than even any of the above. (In
Hos. ix. 17 occurs the phrase, 'wanderers among the nations', but there are

---

[1] For other instances of the partial or entire reversal of a preceding statement
by means of '*ephes kî*, 'saving that', 'howbeit' (not, however, the work as here
of a *corrector*), see Deut. xv. 4, and *cf.* Numb. xiii. 28.

[2] To these references may be added the (fourth century) passage, Joel iii. 2:
'whom they have scattered *among the nations*'.

sifted in a sieve, yet shall not the least grain fall upon the

reasons against holding the verse to be by Hosea: Nowack.) Considerations
of metre would suggest that the words 'among all the nations' are a later
addition to the text of the passage, whatever its date; with the omission
the verse becomes a quatrain of perfect trimeters. This conclusion receives
a certain amount of support from MSS. of the LXX.[1]

like as corn is sifted in a sieve: *lit.* 'like as there may be shaking' (or,
'sifting'), or, 'as though it (*viz.* 'the house of Israel') were shaken, in the
sieve'. The word for 'sieve' (*keᵇbhārāh*) occurs here, only, in the Bible, though
it is employed in Mishnaic and later Hebrew for both a (basket) corn-sieve,
and a (stone) ash-sieve. (1) It has frequently been supposed[2] that the
purpose of such sifting, whether on the threshing-floor or in the home,
would be to shake out or to allow to fall through, dust, chaff[3] (and, possibly,
light grain). The best corn would remain. A fine-meshed sieve, called
ghirbāl,[4] is actually so used to-day and is, conceivably, the type referred to
in Isa. xxx. 28 under the name of *nāphāh*.[5] Thus the Prophet's metaphor
here, as applied to Israel, would mean that no righteous person among them
will be lost. (2) It is extremely doubtful, however, whether the comparison
is to such sifting. Is not the allusion, rather, to the sifting process[6] by
which the corn is made to pass through a *larger*-meshed sieve? In this
latter receptacle are retained stones and earth taken up from the threshing-
floor,[7] rubbish, pieces of straw cut by the threshing-instrument (*cf.* note

---

[1] The words 'among all the nations' do not occur in MSS. 87, 91, 97, 153, 310.
In some MSS. they occur in a different position.

[2] As, *e.g.*, by Marti, Harper, Mitchell, Canney, Köhler.

[3] The LXX translators seem to have thought not of the sieve but of the
common practice of *winnowing*, as having the same application. 'I will winnow
the house of Israel among all the nations as (anything) is winnowed with the
winnowing-fan' (λικμός = λίκνον) 'and not a fragment (σύντριμμα) will fall
upon the earth'. In Ps. i. 4 the wicked are likened to 'the chaff which the wind
driveth away'. Winnowing was done with either a fork (prong) or a fan (shovel)
(*cf.* Jer. xv. 7, Isa. xxx. 24), and it takes place *before* any sifting with a sieve.

[4] *Cf.* the word '*arbālā* which occurs in the Targum and Peshiṭta Versions
here.

[5] Through this sieve the nations are to be sifted until they are lost for ever.
Cf. Skinner, *ad loc.* But perhaps the term *nāphāh* stands for a *winnowing*-fan
(Cheyne).

[6] According to Preuschen after *winnowing*; but (so Nowack) before cleaning
with the *ghirbāl*.

[7] So Wetzstein; *cf.* below, note on 'the least grain'. In the LXX of 2 Sam. iv. 6
there appears to be a reference to such a sifting. The M.T. reads, 'And they
came thither into the midst of the house, as though they would have fetched
wheat...and Rechab and Baanah escaped'. The LXX yields the following
reconstruction of the Hebrew: 'and, behold the portress of the house *was
cleaning wheat* (from stones), and she slumbered and slept, and Rechab and
Baanah slipt in' (so Wellhausen, followed by Driver). This act being carried
on in the heat of the day, and apparently in the house itself, is, at all events,

on i. 3), and, in some cases, large unbruised corn to be returned to be threshed again. The process is described by Wetzstein in *Z.P.V.* xiv. 1891, pp. 2, 7.[1] This sieve like the *ghirbāl* is constructed of a hoop of wood, with a mesh-work of strips of camel-hide (*E.B.*, and *Jew. Encyc.* art. "Agriculture"). Such, probably, is the true meaning of *kebhārāh*, whether or not the word is etymologically connected with the modern Arabic *kirbāl*. The Greek equivalent is κόσκινον, which Aquila and Symmachus employ here. This interpretation seems to be the much more probable one.[2] Such a sieve is referred to in Ecclus. xxvii. 4 (Greek, 5), 'In the shaking of a sieve (κόσκινον) the refuse remaineth; so the filth of a man in his reasoning'.[3]

yet shall not the least grain. (1) Peculiar as renderings of the Hebrew *ṣerôr* is the expression, 'the least grain' (*Kornlein*, H. Schmidt), or even 'the good corn', 'the solid heavy grain'—as distinct from the poor or worthless; *cf.* Marti. *Ṣerôr* is never used in this metaphorical sense, nor does any ancient version so render it. (2) In the only other passage in the O.T. in which this particular word[4] is found it signifies a 'stone', a 'pebble' (2 Sam. xvii. 13, LXX λίθος), and this is in fact the only meaning really possible. The meaning of the Hebrew *ṣerôr* is fundamental to a true exegesis of the whole saying. The Targum in this verse actually renders it *'ebhen*, 'stone'; Aquila has 'pebble' (ψηφίον), and the Vulgate *lapillus*.[5] (*a*) Although no word in the context definitely suggests sifting of *corn*, it must be admitted that such an everyday, and indeed domestic, act would supply a good metaphor. (*b*) Gressmann believes that the reference is to a *sand*-sieve, *ṣerôr* so bearing its proper meaning of 'stone' (*Ält. Proph.*[2] p. 358, referring to a note by Kraus on *sand*-sifting, *Talmud. Archäol.* i. p. 455). Gressmann's idea is that useful sand passes through to the ground, whereas worthless stones remain in the sieve and are thrown away. Thus the application to the 'house of Israel' would be as (2) in preceding and following notes. (*c*) Van Hoonacker proposes to render: 'and it ("the house of Israel") will not

---

quite a different process from that of winnowing. The Greek for 'was cleaning' (ἐκάθαιρεν) suggests Hebrew *sôqelāh*; *cf.* Isa. lvii. 14 (LXX). The *kirbāl* to-day may be used either on the threshing-floor, or as a domestic implement in the house.

[1] In this article, *Über die Siebe*, Wetzstein describes also the *ghirbāl* (p. 3), but he quite definitely holds that the reference in Amos is to the *kirbāl*.

[2] It has the support of G. Hoffmann, *Z.A.W.* 1883, p. 125; Preuschen, *Z.A.W.* xv. 1895, pp. 24, 25; S. Kraus, *Talmud. Archäol.* i. pp. 98, 288, "note" 156 (last line); Volz; Nowack (edn 3); and Sellin.

[3] *Cf.* Oesterley's note, *ad loc.*, in Charles' *Apocrypha*, i.

[4] Connected with *ṣôr*, 'flint'. The root signifies 'to be sharp'. It should be distinguished from *ṣerôr*, 'bundle'.

[5] Though Jerome so translates *ṣerôr*, yet in his commentary he interprets the Hebrew, in the sense of 'pure wheat' (*purum frumentum*). The Douai version has rendered the Vulgate literally, 'there shall not a little stone fall to the ground'.

fall (*in*) *a mass*[1] upon the earth', *i.e.* there will be a separation between the elements by means of God's sieve. **yet**: may equally well be 'and'.

shall...fall upon the earth. (1) If the sieve is the fine variety, this phrase means, 'the whole house of Israel will not pass through the sieve and be lost'. In support of this (happy) sense, might be cited the identical Hebrew phrase occurring in 1 Sam. iii. 19, 'Jehovah...let none of his (Samuel's) words fall to the ground', *i.e.* fail to materialise. (2) If, however, as seems much more probable, the metaphor is supplied by the *big* corn-sieve, the expression has at least in the main a sinister significance, *viz.* that the stones will not escape through the meshes. This is capable of two applications. (i) 'Israel' represented by the 'stones' is kept in the hands of God for Him to punish as He wills. *If* 'among all the nations' is part of the genuine text, the nations form Jehovah's sieve which holds Israel fast. The whole passage is thus not a promise at all, but a threat of judgment.[2] Israel is entirely 'stones'. There is no wheat to pass through the sieve; at least, that question does not arise in the Prophet's mind. Therefore *vv.* 9 and 10 could be by Amos. (ii) But to some[3] it seems unlikely that the metaphor of a sieve of any kind (rather than of a solid receptacle) would be employed, unless the Prophet believed that there were at least *a few* righteous in Israel and that God would make a distinction in His judgment accordingly. If this is so, the verse implies that the good Israelites, like the corn, pass safely to the ground: the evil (the 'stones') are punished. Such was the outlook of the period succeeding the return from exile (Mal. iii. 17–iv. 3 (in Heb. iii. 17–21)). Even so the passage is cast in the form of a threat of punishment, and not of a promise of hope.   The metaphor of the sieve is used even more drastically for *absolute destruction* in Isa. xxx. 28; and in St Lu. xxii. 31, 32 the hope consists not in the words 'asked to have you that he might sift you as wheat', but in our Lord's prayer for St Peter which is placed in contrast. It will be seen that Am. ix. 9 does not refer to the descendants of Israel retaining their identity as such—which indeed they have not done, only the one tribe of Judah. *If* the verse contains any hope at all, it is that the few good will remain in exile whereas the evil will be slain there. It is very difficult to believe that *v.* 9, if it implies that any Israelites are to escape, is from the same hand as *vv.* 1–4. If the passage is intended to point to a differentiation, it is legitimate to suspect that *Amos*, at any rate, would have found a much clearer way of stating that the golden age (of *vv.* 11–15) is entirely dependent on the existence of righteousness in the nation (which, as a matter of fact, he has repeatedly declared to be wholly sinful).

---

[1] Apparently identifying *se̱rór* here with the commoner term meaning 'bundle', 'pouch' (from *ṣārar*, 'to bind'), which occurs in 1 Sam. xxv. 29, Gen. xlii. 35, *etc.*

[2] So Prof. Volz in an exhaustive article upon Am. ix. 9 in *Z.A.W.* 1919–20, pp. 105–111. He is followed closely by Nowack who, of course, holds (like the present writer) that *v.* 8 *c*, 'saving that I will not utterly destroy the house of Jacob, saith the LORD', cannot be part of the original text.

[3] *E.g.* G. Hoffmann and Riedel.

earth. **10** All the sinners of my people shall die by the sword,
which say, The evil shall not overtake nor prevent us.

10. All the sinners of my people. The word 'sinners' looks back to
'sinful kingdom' in *v.* 8. (1) Most scholars regard *v.* 10 as an addition to
the text of Amos, explaining the supposed metaphor of *v.* 9—the differentiation of the wicked and the just in Israel. Translate, 'all the sinners from
among my people'. (2) It would seem possible, however, to take the verse
as containing essentially the same thought as that to which Amos himself
has given expression elsewhere, notably in *v.* 8 *a, b* ('Behold the eyes...of
the earth'). He does not differentiate more than is maintained above to be
the case in *v.* 9. Previously in iii. 12 *b* he has pronounced the fall of the idle,
and in viii. 14 and *vv.* 1–4 of this chapter that of the shrine worshippers,
meaning all the while the fall of the *nation*. So here, by the destruction
of the *sinners*, he means that of 'the house of Israel' (*v.* 9) *as a whole.*
Moreover, the use of the expression 'all the sinners of my people' is perhaps
a way of saying in Hebrew, 'all my sinful nation'.[1]

Most critics hold that the book of Amos originally closed just before
v. 8 *c.* See pp. 67–69 on the Epilogue. It is true that the words, 'and I will
destroy it from off the face of the earth', would furnish an impressive
ending to the book of doom. *V.* 10, however, with its mock quotation of
impenitent Israel's response, representative of how by its actions it received
the Preacher's message, would seem to provide a *finale* not unworthy of
the original writer.

my people. By the same expression Amos refers to Israel in vii. 8, 15,
viii. 2. See also *v.* 14, below.

by the sword. There is no necessary allusion here to a 'mythological'
sword; *cf.* notes on *v.* 4 and vii. 9.

which say. (1) The Prophet does not of necessity imply (though he
may do so) that he is about to quote the people's very words. (2) Probably
he means, '*who act as if* evil shall not overtake them'; *cf.* 2 Chron. xxviii. 13,
'for ye *are-acting-in-such-a-way* (R.V. 'ye purpose') that guilt will come
upon us'; in vi. 3 *a* the idle nobles 'put far the evil day'. (3) Or this mode
of expression in Amos may be an instance of such *irony* as is alluded to in
the notes on iv. 4 and iv. 5.

The evil shall not overtake nor prevent us. 'The evil' may be either
(1) 'the evil' threatened by Amos, or (2) 'evil' in general, as in Eccl. xii. 1
(Hebrew, 'days of the evil'); *cf.* on iii. 12, '*the* shepherd'. The word translated 'overtake' means properly '*cause to* draw near'. It is preferable,
therefore, to read the *qal* voice, 'draw near'.[2] Instead of 'prevent', say
simply, 'befall'.[3] The Hebrew verb, *lit.* 'come in front', not seldom is to

---

[1] *Cf.* Torrey. For 'sinners from among my people' (as above) we should expect
a phrase like *ḥaṭṭā'îm mittôkh 'ammî.*

[2] Followed by 'unto' (Hebrew *'adh*, not *bᵉ'adh*) as in the construction of
Gen. xxxiii. 3 (*cf.* also Mic. i. 9).

[3] In German, *begegnen*: so Sellin.

11 In that day will I raise up the tabernacle of David that

be rendered 'meet' (with a person as *object*); *cf.* 2 Sam. xxii. 6, 19 (R.V. 'come upon'). The Targum translates, 'Evil will neither come nor hurry upon us'. For other examples of careless scoffing hearers of a prophet, and defiers of the Divine warning, *cf.* Isa. ix. 10, xxviii. 14, 15.

IX. 11–15. THE EPILOGUE PROPER

According to *v.* 8 c and possibly *v.* 9 there was to be a separation between the evil and the good in the Israelitish nation, the wicked being destroyed. Now it is predicted that those who survive, or their descendants (of Israel, or only of Judah), will, under David's dynasty (*v.* 11), re-conquer their possessions (*v.* 12). A condition of perhaps *Edenic* fertility in nature will characterise that age (*v.* 13). Israel's fortunes will be restored, and they will give themselves undisturbed to the cultivation of the soil (*v.* 14), without fear of being again carried captive (*v.* 15). That certain short additions to the book of Amos probably were made by early editors has been stated in this commentary in the notes upon the various passages concerned (*cf.* Introd. p. 66). *Vv.* 11–15 (or *vv.* 8 c–15) of this chapter present the largest consecutive portion of the book the connection of which with the prophet Amos has been seriously doubted. For a somewhat full discussion of the question the reader is referred to the Introduction, pp. 67 ff.

11, 12. The restoration, or 're-building', of the line of David, and the recovery of possession of foreign lands previously under the dominion of Israel.

11. In that day. The expression is used not uncommonly in O.T. prophecy when the connection of events is of the loosest character; *cf.* viii. 9 (following upon viii. 8). Indeed not seldom, as here, there is *no* connection and it suggests the hand of an editor rather than of the original author. There is a definite break from the thought of *vv.* 1–7. The phrases, 'in that day' and 'at that time', while by no means confined in usage to a supposed coming era of bliss, yet are frequently so used in the prophets, *e.g.* Isa. xi. 10, 11, xii. 1, xxvii. 2, Zeph. iii. 19; so also with 'those days', Jer. xxxiii. 15, l. 4, Joel iii. 1 (in Heb. iv. 1). *Cf.* Gressmann, *Eschatologie*, pp. 142, 143. For the use of 'in that day' by one and the same writer, see Zech. xii. 8, 9, 11, xiii. 1.

tabernacle of David. The Hebrew term (*sukkāh*) means, literally, ' booth ', or 'hut', made of intertwined branches,[1] *e.g.* as erected in a vineyard (Isa. i. 8), by Jonah during the heat (Jon. iv. 5), or by Israelites at the festival of Booths (Lev. xxiii. 40, 42, Deut. xvi. 13). Rarely, it is used poetically of a dwelling more substantial (2 Sam. xxii. 12 = Ps. xviii. 12). Here the expression stands for the *dynasty* of David,[2] usually in the O.T. styled a

---

[1] From the root *sākhakh*, 'to weave together' (Ps. cxxxix. 13). It is unlikely that, as some expositors have interpreted the present passage, the 'tent' (as from the common root *sākhakh*, 'to cover') is pictured as 'protecting' Israel.

[2] *Cf.* some MSS. of the Targum, 'the kingdom of the house of David'.

is fallen, and close up the breaches thereof; and I will raise up

'house' (2 Sam. vii. 5, 11), but in the present circumstances described as
something less firm. *Cf.* the note upon v. 26, *Sikkûth*, p. 302 *ad init.* For
an Additional Note, see p. 320.

that is fallen. Apparently the picture is that of a structure as not only
flimsy but as (1) collapsed, 'fallen'; or (2) at least, in the process of becoming
so—'falling'.[1] 'Fallen' is certainly the most natural rendering,[2] and this is
confirmed by the reference to 'breaches' and 'ruins'. The historical event
or condition here alluded to is either (1) the cessation of monarchy on the
capture of Jerusalem (586 B.C.), or after Zerubbabel's possible attempt to
assume royalty, or, far less likely, (2) some blow to the sovereignty or
prestige of David's dynasty, (*a*) the division of the realm upon the death
of Solomon (so Köhler), or (*b*) the defeat of Amaziah by Joash of Ephraim,
2 Ki. xiv. 13, 14 (so van Hoonacker), or (*c*) generally, to losses which
occurred subsequently to the Disruption. Interpretation (1) goes with a
late date for the passage, (2) with an early one. In any case the Prophet
here adopts the distinctive point of view of Judah, not that of North Israel.
It is not surprising that later Judaism should apply Am. ix. 11, 12 Mes-
sianically. Rabbi Naḥman (*d.* 320 A.D.) said to Rabbi Isaac, "Hast thou
heard when cometh the *son of the fallen?*"[3] He said to him, "Who is the
son of the fallen?" He (Rabbi Naḥman) said, "The Messiah". (Rabbi
Isaac asked), "Is the Messiah called son of the fallen?" (Rabbi Naḥman)
said to him, "Yea, as it is written, In that day will I raise up the tabernacle
of David that is fallen". T.B. *Sanhedrin*, 96 *b ad fin.*, 97 *a ad init.*

and close up. The expression is used elsewhere of the repairing of a
wall. The verb (*gādhar*) occurs together with 'breach' (*singular* number)
in the late passage, Isa. lviii. 12.

the breaches thereof. In M.T. 'thereof' is masculine *plural*, while in
the next clause the text reads, '*his* ruins'. Probably both should be singular.[4]
For *pereṣ*, 'breach' of a *broken part* of a wall, *cf.* Am. iv. 3, 1 Ki. xi. 27,
Neh. vi. 1. Riessler and others see in the walling up of 'breaches' a prophecy

---

[1] (1) For the Hebrew active participle with the meaning of the *perfect* tense, *cf.*
what is almost uniformly the usage with *mēth*, 'dead'. So also with this very
word (*nôphēl*) in 1 Sam. v. 3 (R.V. 'fallen'), and nearly without exception
elsewhere: *cf. Oxf. Heb. Lex.* (2) The participle with *present* meaning, 'falling',
would be entirely grammatical: *cf. v.* 10, 'who are saying'. (3) For the participle
with *future* meaning, *cf.* Jon. i. 3, 'a ship *about to go*'; Isa. xxx. 13, *pereṣ*
nôphēl, 'a broken wall *about to fall*'. Context alone can decide. See Ges.-K.
§ 116 *d*.

[2] So LXX τὴν πεπτωκυῖαν, Vulgate *quod cecidit*, Targum, Pesh.

[3] If this be the meaning. In Aram. *bar niphlê* might = 'son of untimely
births' (*n^e phîl* = Heb. *nēphel*). A little further on R. Naḥman lays down
the principle (citing Jer. xxx. 21) that if someone living in his day were to
become the Messiah, he would be even as himself (R. Naḥman), 98 *b ad fin.*

[4] *Feminine* singular, agreeing with the gender of *sukkāh*, 'booth', 'tabernacle',
as is the case in the succeeding clause, 'and I will build *it*'.

his ruins, and I will build it as in the days of old; **12 that they**

of the healing of the division in the kingdom between the north and south. In the Exile Ezekiel cherished such an ideal, Ezek. xxxvii. 15–28; nor is it demonstrable that Amos did not in the 8th cent. B.C.[1]

I will raise up his ruins. (1) If the text is correct, 'his' refers, rather awkwardly, to David, not to the 'booth' or 'dynasty'! (2) The 'ruins', like the 'breaches', are those of the dynasty, not of the land or nation.[2]

and I will build it. The Hebrew verb 'to build' is frequently employed in the sense of 'to re-build' (or, 'to repair'). See v. 14, 1 Ki. xvi. 34, Isa. xlv. 13 (of a city), Mic. vii. 11, Neh. ii. 17, etc. (of a wall), 2 Chron. xxxiii. 16 (of an altar). The expression 'to build a house' is used of building, i.e. establishing at the beginning, David's dynasty (Ps. lxxxix. 4), and, also, it is in keeping with Hebrew usage that it should mean, as here, either (1) strengthen (cf. Prov. xiv. 1) the dynasty, or (2) restore it.

as in the days of old. (1) This phrase (y⁰mē 'ōlām) represents more than merely 'formerly' (van Hoonacker), 'as aforetime' (Orelli). (2) Its use seems to imply an appeal to a remote, and perhaps semi-ideal, past as in Mic. vii. 14, Mal. iii. 4, and as the similar expression y⁰mē qedhem in such passages as Ps. lxxvii. 5, Isa. li. 9, Jer. xlvi. 26, Lam. v. 21. Certainly the lapse of time involved is greater than in the various expressions in Isa. i. 26, cited by Sellin in his note here. David himself lived but two and a half centuries before Amos; and the 'tent' or dynasty of David was, as a matter of history,[3] probably never more prosperous politically than during the reign of his lineal descendant Azariah, Amos' own king. Undoubtedly the appeal to 'the days of old' is a sign that the writer belonged to an age subsequent to the period of Amos.[4]

---

[1] To the picture of the union of the two kingdoms under one sovereign which is perhaps suggested in this verse, somewhat of a parallel might be found in the above-quoted oracle referring to the reunion of Upper and Lower Egypt under Ameny, or Amenemhet I: "There is a King shall come from the South, whose name is Ameny....He shall receive the White Crown; he shall assume the Red Crown; he shall unite the Two Powerful Ones" (or, "diadems"). See Introd. p. 45. The Egyptian oracle, however, differs from the present passage in being far too detailed for us to be able to regard it as a prediction.

[2] The word translated 'ruin' (hărîsāh) is, according to its form, much too late for Amos (Ehrlich). Cf. Isa. xlix. 19, hărîsûth (R.V. 'thy land that hath been destroyed'). It is interesting to note that for 'ruins' LXX MS. B has τὰ κατεσκαμμένα, 'the parts dug down'. Mss. A and Q adapting, doubtless, to the text of Acts xv. 16, read τὰ κατεστραμμένα, lit. 'the parts overturned'. Both are equally good renderings of the Hebrew.

[3] Unless the book of Chronicles is entirely unreliable in a matter of this sort.

[4] We do not agree with Gressmann's view (Eschatologie, p. 255) that the phrase, 'as in the days of old' "is as incomprehensible in or after the Exile as at the time of Amos. It is comprehensible only in court style, in which such exaggerations are common, which is fond of stating the dynasty to be of primitive times though it may have reached dominion" only quite recently. Nor does his later conjecture convince us that, with regard to Mic. v. 2 at least, the reference to David's being 'from of old, from everlasting' goes back to a belief in an

may possess the remnant of Edom, and all the nations, which are called by my name, saith the LORD that doeth this.

12. The revival of the dynasty of David is to issue in the national acquisition of the former dominion over Edom, and indeed over all peoples who have earlier been under Israelite suzerainty.

that they may possess. The 'they' has no direct antecedent in the previous verse. The construction is probably 'impersonal'; and the reference should not be taken as being only to 'the dynasty of David', but as including Israel as a people. For 'possess' in the sense of *subduing* surrounding nations, *cf.* Obad. *vv.* 17 and 19.

the remnant of Edom. Probably the Edomites are singled out because of their specially unbrotherly behaviour when Judah was in distress before the final fall of Jerusalem in 586 B.C. (Obad. *vv.* 10–14). See, upon this passage, the Additional Note on p. 321.

and all the nations, which...my name: means, probably, all the nations which had ever been possessed by Jehovah, *i.e.*, in effect, by *Israel*. The paraphrase of E.VV., 'which are called by my name', is sometimes, as here, misleading. *Lit.* the Hebrew is, 'all the nations *over whom* my name was (or, 'has been') called'. This idiom, denoting ownership, is best illustrated from the story of the subjugation of one of the very peoples to whom, doubtless, the Prophet is here referring. When Joab's campaign against the Ammonites led him to within sight of the fall of their capital, the general urged David to capture the city in person, 'lest *I*' (said Joab), 'take the city and *my name* be called over it' (2 Sam. xii. 28, *cf.* R.V. marg.). Thus the present reference is to the peoples who had at one time. been owned by Israel, and so (in a sense) by Israel's God. When a conqueror subdued lands he made the populations submissive in theory, if not in practice, to his national deity. See, further, the note, p. 322.

The phrase 'called by my name' is also used of Jehovah's claiming or owning *Israel* (*e.g.* Deut. xxviii. 9, 10, Jer. xiv. 9)[1] and even the *Temple* (*e.g.* 1 Ki. viii. 43).

that doeth this. Jehovah is represented as both the predicter and the accomplisher of these events. *Cf.* Mal. iii. 17, 'in the day wherein I do (this)', and iv. 3 (in Heb. iii. 21). The LXX translation is correct, λέγει

---

original ideal monarchy *in Paradise* such as is found in Egyptian folklore (*J.T.S.* Ap. 1926, pp. 248, 249). In this connection, however, it is interesting to note that in the present passage Paradise conditions (ix. 13) actually are associated with the ideal *king* (ix. 11, 12).

[1] And so Ehrlich seeks to interpret here, 'in order that those *over whom my name is named* (*i.e.* Israel) may inherit the remnant of Edom and of all other peoples'. It is, however, quite unnatural to take the relative clause which *follows* 'nations' as the subject to the *preceding* verb. König, *A.T. Rel.* p. 344, who argues against Ehrlich, nevertheless agrees with him to the extent of supposing that 'those over whom my name has been called' means Israel (the remnants of North Israel) to be possessed by Judah.

13 Behold, the days come, saith the LORD, that the plowman shall overtake the reaper, and the treader of grapes him that

Κύριος ὁ ποιῶν ταῦτα. In the citation in Ac. xv. 18 this becomes, ... ποιῶν ταῦτα γνωστὰ ἀπ' αἰῶνος, 'making this *known from of old*'.[1]

13: states a promise of extraordinary fertility of the soil of Palestine.

Behold, the days come. For the phrase in genuine Amos, see iv. 2 and viii. 11. Elsewhere it occurs in the canonical prophets only in the Babylonian period (Jer. and 'Isa.' xxxix. 6). Here the expression, like 'in that day' in *v.* 11, may be a sign of a further deposit upon the text of the book. It is not impossible that, as has been said above, the volume of Amos originally closed at *v.* 8 *b* ('earth'), or even at *v.* 7 ('Kir'). So also by successive[2] additions the remainder of the present book may have been added, in at least three sections: (*a*) *vv.* 8 *c*–10, beginning at 'saving that'; (*b*) *vv.* 11 and 12; (*c*) *vv.* 13, 14, 15. *Cf.* Robinson, *Heb. Text*; Gressmann, *Alt. Proph.* edn 2.

saith the LORD. So *vv.* 7, 8, 12. For the prophetic expression *nᵉ'ûm Yahweh*, see on ii. 11.

the plowman shall overtake the reaper. 'Overtake': in Hebrew *niggash*, 'approach', 'draw near to'. A rather fanciful hyperbole, of which there might be two explanations:

(1) The harvest, which should be ripe by April–May, is so *abundant* that the cutting of it is not finished until October when ploughing begins. Gressmann paraphrases the verse: "Behind the reapers, who cannot master the harvest quickly enough, the ploughmen already press on, and the wine-presser follows on the heels of the sower; thus do the seasons overlap one another as in the garden of God".[3] For the thought of such super-abundant harvest, *cf.* Lev. xxvi. 5, 'your threshing shall reach (Hebrew *nāsag*) unto the vintage and the vintage shall reach unto (or, 'overtake') the sowing time'. The promise there, however, is strictly conditional as in Deut. vii. 12–15, xxviii. 1–12. The present passage is more 'eschatological' in character; it is a reversal of the threat uttered in Paradise, Gen. iii. 18, 19.

(2) Less likely seems the exegesis of Driver[4] (which takes account of the ploughman in connection with the harvest which is to ensue, not with the

---

[1] St James' words can hardly be translated 'that doeth these things (which were) known from of old' (R.V. marg.). He seems to be adding, loosely, from such a passage as Isa. xlv. 21. For further remarks on St James' citation, see p. 322 and footnote.

[2] Not necessarily in the *order* (*a*), (*b*), (*c*). Indeed *vv.* 11 and 12 might even be genuine Amos, *cf.* Introd. p. 72.

[3] This view has the support of Duhm and Lukyn Williams. *Cf.* G. A. Smith, Marti, Sellin.

[4] So Mitchell, Harper, and *cf.* Nowack. See also Thomson, *Land and Book*, p. 219.

soweth seed; and the mountains shall drop sweet wine, and all the hills shall melt. **14** And I will bring again the captivity

harvest which is just over). "So rapid will be the growth of the crops, that the ploughman will hardly have finished breaking up the ground for seed, when the corn will be ready for the reaper". The farm must be presumed to be a large one: the first-sown seed is ripe for the reaping before all the ploughing is finished. This interpretation means in effect that the reaper approaches or 'overtakes' the *ploughman*.[1] The significance of the promise lies not in the quantity of the crops but in a miraculous *speeding of the ripening*, which in the ordinary course of nature would have extended over five months. The implication might be that there would be time for more than one harvest in the year, as in Rev. xxii. 2; *cf.* Schmidt, p. 105.—But the next clause, with reference to the vintage, is acknowledged by all commentators to concern abundance, not speed, and it is reasonable to interpret the "reaper" clause in the same way.

and the treader of grapes him that soweth seed. So abundant will be the vintage in the new age that the treading (normally over by October, having followed immediately upon the ingathering) will not be completed before it is time for cereal sowing (November). The grapes were crushed in a wine-press (Hebrew *gath*) by the 'treading' of feet, the juice passing into the wine-vat. For other allusions to such a 'treading' of grapes, see Judg. ix. 27, Isa. lxiii. 2, 3 (metaphorical for slaughter of enemies).

him that soweth seed. The Hebrew verb (*māshakh*) means *lit.* 'to draw out', hence, perhaps with reference to the action of the arm of the sower, to 'trail' or 'strew' seed.[2]

and the mountains shall drop sweet wine. Vineyards were, of course, chiefly upon mountain slopes.

sweet wine: Hebrew *'āsîs*, *lit.* 'that which is crushed' by treading. *Cf.* the verb, 'tread down', in Mal. iv. 3 (in Heb. iii. 21). Probably such drink was comparatively unfermented. The word occurs elsewhere in the O.T. only in Joel i. 5, iii. 18 (in Heb. iv. 18), Isa. xlix. 26, Cant. viii. 2. It appears to be a later synonym for *tîrôsh*.

and all the hills shall melt: or, 'dissolve themselves'[3] in the streams of wine issuing from their vintage. For an Additional Note on this passage, see p. 323.

14, 15. A promise of the restoration of the political fortunes of 'Israel'. Back in their own land they will devote themselves to agriculture; they will not *again* be taken away.

14. And I will bring again the captivity of my people. (1) Probably

---

[1] Gunkel actually alters the Hebrew text to secure this meaning (*qôṣēr baḥôrēsh*).

[2] Ps. cxxvi. 6 speaks of carrying a 'trail (*meshekh*) of seed', but the verb is used in this sense here only in O.T.

[3] For a very different use of this verb (and in the same voice) in connection with mountains, see Nah. i. 5; and *cf.* Ps. cvii. 26.

of my people Israel, and they shall build the waste cities, and inhabit them; and they shall plant vineyards, and drink the wine thereof; they shall also make gardens, and eat the fruit of them. **15** And I will plant them upon their land, and they

the reference in the phrase[1] in this context, as indeed usually, is specifically to a return from exile. The expression belongs *almost* exclusively to the post-exilic vocabulary. (2) In itself, however, it may mean only, in a general sense, 'restore the fortunes of', or, 'bring in the great change', and so be consistent with a pre-exilic date of the passage (Sellin). *Cf.* Ezek. xvi. 53, Job xlii. 10, Hos. vi. 11 (see Harper). In any case, there is no essential difficulty in supposing that a prophet who announces punishment of exile could foretell also a return from exile. Thus did Jeremiah (xxx. 1–3) and perhaps Hosea (xi. 11). But would *Amos?* (*Cf.* Introd. pp. 69–71.)

my people Israel. (1) If the passage is by Amos, the term 'Israel' would mean either the Northern Kingdom, or, more probably, Israel as a whole as in *v.* 7. König paraphrases the passage: "At the day of the judgment upon (N.) Israel (*v.* 10) Judah nevertheless, governed by the descendants of David, shall attain to its ancient extent (*vv.* 11, 12), and to it shall belong also those that have remained over from the kingdom of (N.) Israel (*vv.* 14, 15)". (2) If the Epilogue is post-exilic, 'Israel' might be used of the descendants of Judah who came to consider themselves the heirs to this title; Ezra iv. 3 *a*, *b*, Mal. i. 1.

they shall build the waste cities. For the thought, *cf.* Isa. liv. 3, Jer. xxxii. 43, xxxiii. 10. The view is held by some that we do not know sufficient about the history of Jeroboam's reign to be able to affirm confidently that the expression 'waste cities' would not be appropriate in the mouth of Amos; six plagues have come on Israel (Am. iv. 6–11).

they shall plant vineyards, and drink the wine thereof. This reverses the threat contained in v. 11 *b*. *Cf.* Isa. lxv. 21, Jer. xxxi. 5, 12, 24, Ezek. xxviii. 25, 26. It seems almost as if the writer of these verses had set himself to declare the revocation of various judgments contained in the book of Amos as he found it.

15. And I will plant them upon their land. The metaphor of 'planting' is applied in the O.T. to the re-settlement of Israel by Jehovah after captivity, but never to any improvement of their *pre*-captivity condition: Isa. lx. 21 *b*, Jer. xxxi. 28, xxxii. 41. The metaphor, however, goes back to the early idea of Jehovah planting Israel as a vine (Isa. v. 1–3, xxvii. 3).

and they shall no more be plucked up. The expression 'no more'

---

[1] *Shûbh sh^ebhûth, lit.* 'turn' (a transitive verb in this expression) 'a turning' (occurring some nineteen times in the O.T.). *Sh^ebhûth* is *probably* from this verb, not from *shâbhâh*, 'to carry captive', from which comes *sh^ebhî*, the term for 'captivity' in ix. 4. Or perhaps the roots, in usage, became confused. In Jer. xxxii. 44, and five times elsewhere, the phrase is *hêshîbh* (*Hiph'il*, not *Qal*) *sh^ebhûth*, in which cases there may be a more specific reference to the Exile. E.

shall no more be plucked up out of their land which I have given them, saith the LORD thy God.

is easily understood if uttered after Israel had been once removed from Palestine. It would be hardly intelligible if spoken to the Israelites of 760–740 B.C. Similarly the promise in Deut. xxx. 9, 'Jehovah will *again* rejoice over thee for good *as he rejoiced over thy fathers*', would be more intelligible if made in the later period of Israel's history, rather than by Moses.

which I have given them. If these words were omitted, the verse would almost become poetry. As it stands the verse is bare prose.

thy God: in consolatory sense. Contrast its only other occurrence in the book of Amos (iv. 12). For this happy use of the phrase, *cf.* Isa. lii. 7, '...good tidings of good, that publisheth salvation; that saith unto Zion, *thy God* reigneth!' So Isa. xli. 10, liv. 6, lxvi. 9, Hos. xii. 6, 9. For another explanation, see the Additional Note on p. 323.

The words of the Epilogue addressed to a later generation than the audience of Amos possess an authenticity of their own. We may say that the addition was in general accordance with the Divine mind if we could assume that, in the course of time, trials had wrought some degree of national amendment. God's message to men of one period may be predominantly one of Repentance: to those of another, in different circumstances, one of Hope. And the sentiment nobly expressed in Jer. xxix. 11[1] must be eternally true: 'I know the thoughts I cherish towards you—thoughts of weal and not of woe—to bestow upon you a future and a hope'.

Baumann (in *Z.A.W.* 1929, pp. 17–44), while deriving *sheᵇbhûth* from *shābhāh*, contends that the idea of deportation, where found, is entirely "accidental" and that the term *sheᵇbhûth* belongs essentially to the religious sphere.

[1] McFadyen's translation.

ADDITIONAL NOTES

₊ These further Notes may be used in connection with,
or independently of, the main commentary

CHAPTER I

5. the valley of Aven. Taking this as 'the Plain', situated between the Lebanons, it is noteworthy that from ancient times the sun was worshipped at Heliopolis (the modern *Baalbek*) in this plain; and it is not impossible that Amos, in using the expression 'valley of *Aven*', is alluding to this fact. No proper name 'Aven' is known, but the noun *'āwen* in Hebrew is used with reference to 'idolatry': in Isa. lxvi. 3 the E.VV. render 'an idol' (*cf.* Vulgate here, 'de campo *idoli*'). Similarly, Beth-aven is written instead of the geographical name Beth-el in Hos. iv. 15, v. 8. See Am. v. 5, note.

An ingenious suggestion is to point the consonants of Aven to read as On (so LXX, *'Ων*, and *cf.* R.V. marg.); and, having regard to the fact that the great Heliopolis in *Egypt* bears the name of Aûnû, or *On* (Gen. xli. 45), to make the conjecture that this *Aramaean* Heliopolis (Baalbek) also was known by the name of On. 'Valley of *On*' would then be a definite proper name for the same site as otherwise would be alluded to only obscurely as 'the valley of *'āwen* or idolatry'. It is interesting to note that not improbably this district, though possessing a petty prince who owed some kind of allegiance to Damascus, was already paying tribute to Israel at the time of Amos. *Cf.* note on vi. 14, 'Hamath'; and art. "Riblah" by Driver in *H.D.B.* iv. p. 269.

9. For three transgressions of Tyre. Before the discovery of inscriptions in the various Phoenician dialects, some idea of the language of the Phoenician colony Carthage was obtainable from the transliterated words occurring in Plautus' *Poenulus*. Until 1923 the oldest monuments of any importance found in Phoenicia (at Gebal) were of the 4th or 5th cent. B.C.; but since then inscriptions in Phoenician script have been discovered belonging to the 10th, and even to the 13th cent. B.C. (reign of Ramses II). *Cf.* Gressmann in *Z.A.W.* 1924, pp. 349–351; 1925, pp. 239, 291–294; and p. 136 of this commentary. All the Phoenician dialects exhibit a language differing comparatively little from Hebrew itself. A Phoenician inscription found in the colony of Carthage (in Cyprus), dating from the same century as Amos, is referred to in the note on vi. 6. Upon a bowl dedicated to Baal the words occur: "...The governor of Carthage, servant of Hiram, king of Sidonians, gave this to Baal of Lebanon, his Lord (*'ădōnêy*), of the best (*rē'shîth*) of bronze". This Hiram is probably one who paid tribute to Tiglath-pileser III in 738 B.C.[1] Phoenician writings have been discovered as distant from Phoenicia as *e.g.* the Piraeus, Malta and Marseilles.

To the Phoenicians has been assigned the credit of supplying the Greeks with an alphabetic form of writing. The discovery of Phoenician writing (to which reference is made above) of so early a period as perhaps 1250 B.C. has at least confirmed the tradition of the extreme antiquity of this alphabet of twenty-two letters, which was used alike by Phoenicia, Moab and Israel.

---

[1] G. A. Cooke, *N.S.I.* p. 52.

It is not in the least probable, however, that this trading people were the *originators* of any script.[1]

9, 10. Whether the oracle in Am. i. 9, 10 was actually uttered by Amos was questioned by Wellhausen on the grounds that (1) the charge against Tyre, except for the clause, 'not remembering the covenant of brothers', is the same as that against Gaza in *v.* 6. (2) The usual formulae of the Prophet, 'I will cut off...' and 'saith the LORD' (concluding), are wanting. (3) In contrast to the other prophecies, only one town, Tyre, is mentioned. However, with regard to the two last points, is rigid consistency of treatment really natural? As Principal Lofthouse says (in another connection), "It is not probable that any Hebrew prophet wrote with the fear of the standards of German literary criticism before his eyes" (*Ezekiel*, p. 46). On the whole question, Sir G. A. Smith shrewdly remarks (*XII Prophets*, p. 128), "It would have been strange if from a list of states threatened by the Assyrian doom... (Amos) had missed Tyre, Tyre which lay in the avenger's very path" (*i.e.* the route of the Assyrian army).

11, 12. For three transgressions of Edom.... (1) That the prophecy against Edom came from Amos has been doubted. The reasons suggested, unlike the difficulties with the oracle against Tyre, are historical rather than literary. It is claimed that, except for Numb. xx. 14–21 ('JE'), no pre-exilic Israelite authority speaks of unkindness on the part of Edom. Rather, it had been the victim of cruelty if 18,000 men had been wiped out by king David (2 Sam. viii. 13); or if Amaziah's treatment of 10,000 captives was at all like the description given in Chronicles. It would be easy to understand the charge in Am. i. 11, 12 if the verses were a later addition to the text, in (or after) the period of the destruction of Jerusalem—when Obadiah, also, pronounced doom upon Edom for vile behaviour at the time of Judah's misfortune ('the violence done to thy brother Jacob', Obad. *v.* 10).

(2) Against these arguments it may, surely, be urged that not sufficient is known of the actual history of the relationship between the two states during the monarchy for it to be said categorically that up to Amos' time

---

[1] Of the various attempts to solve the problem of the ultimate origin of the proto-Semitic alphabetic script, that of Dr Alan Gardiner seems to be of pre-eminent significance. He derives it from such an alphabet as is employed in the *Serâbît* (Sinaitic) inscriptions. These must be dated as early as 1500—if not the 17th cent.—B.C. The signs as a whole are not Egyptian, though many of them are borrowed from the hieroglyphics. "The common parent of the Phoenician, the Greek and the Sabaean may have been one out of several more or less plastic local varieties of alphabet" (see *J.E.A.* III. pp. 1–16 for Dr Gardiner's argument and for reproductions of the inscriptions). Prof. Sethe holds that the (Semitic) *Hyksos* were largely responsible for the copying of Egyptian models in the Sinai script; but the inscriptions may well be too early for this to be so. Prof. Butin has built upon the theory of Gardiner, and sees a greater (ultimately) Egyptian element than he in the Sinaitic alphabet (*Harvard Theol. Rev.* Jan. 1928, pp. 1–67). Dr Gardiner conjectures that the home of the Sinaitic alphabet was Midian, *P. E. F. Qrly St*, Jan. 1929, p. 55. Quite another view is that the earliest Semitic writing owes its origin to Minoan scripts of Crete (Sir Arthur Evans, *Scripta Minoa*, I; R. Dussaud, *Les Arabes en Syrie avant l'Islam*).

Edom had done nothing corresponding to what is said in Am. i. 11. Hadad the Edomite was 'an adversary to Solomon' (1 Ki. xi. 14–25). The circumstances which *led to* Amaziah's war (alluded to above) are unknown. It is proverbial that there is no hatred like that which shews itself from time to time between brother tribes. These facts concern the past. Further, it may not be without significance that the Edomites were involved in a wholesale trafficking in Judaean slaves at a recent date (*v.* 6).

To these considerations, the following conjectural evidence from the centuries previous to the fall of Jerusalem may be added—being in line with the character of Edom given in Am. i. 11, 12—in support of the authenticity of the verses. (1) The suggestion has much to commend it, that Balaam, who was hired to utter an oracle against the Israelites, and who, at least according to Numb. xxxi. 8, 16 ('P'), perished fighting against them in battle, was an *Edomite*.[1] Moab's southern neighbour was *Edom*, which may well be the true reading lying behind the 'Aram' of Numb. xxiii. 7.[2] Indeed the Targum understood the *Edomite* king Bela, son of Beor, of Gen. xxxvi. 32, to be identical with Balaam, son of Beor. (2) The oppression of Cushan-rishathaim, king of Aram(-naharaim), alluded to in Judg. iii. 7–11, was *Edomite*, if we accept the emendation of the passage suggested by Klostermann.[3] He even reads, "Cushan, *head of the Temanites, king of Edom*"; comparing *Husham...* of Gen. xxxvi. 34. In the words of C. F. Burney, "Granted that [this and other] emendations based upon the proper name are highly precarious, it is at any rate possible that an encroachment upon Southern Palestine by the Edomites may have occurred at this period" (*Judges*, p. 65). These two would be early instances of the ill-treatment of Israel by Edom. *Cf.* the Hebrew of Am. i. 11, 'He kept crushing down all pity, and his anger he cherished perpetually'. (3) Coming now to the time nearer to Amos, it is more than likely that the ships of Jehoshaphat were 'broken' at *Ezion-Geber* on the Red Sea (1 Ki. xxii. 48) with the assistance of the *Edomites*, cf. *C.A.H.* iii. p. 366.

Thus the oracles upon Tyre, Edom, and, also, if the view of Marti and Duhm is to be accepted, Philistia (Am. i. 6–8), would be regarded as interpolations. This would leave to Amos only the prophecies against Aram, Ammon and Moab. It is true that as the text of Amos i and ii stands, except that 'Aram' appropriately comes first, and 'Israel' last as the climax, the various peoples are enumerated with no clearly intelligible arrangement. If, however, in reality Amos uttered "oracles" against Aram, Ammon and Moab *only*, an obvious order is discernible, *viz.* from

---

[1] See Nöldeke, *Untersuchungen*, p. 87 (*cf.* his art. on "Edom", § 4, in *E.B.*); also Hommel, *Ancient Heb. Tradition*, S.P.C.K. p. 153; and W. W. Cannon, in a suggestive article on "Israel and Edom", in *Theology*, Sept. 1927. Mr Cannon rightly doubts the identification of Balaam with king Bela (*cf.* Driver on Gen. xxxvi. 32).

[2] According to the Peshiṭta and Vulgate of Numb. xxii. 5, Balaam lived on 'the river of the land of the sons of *Ammon*'. This fact again points to locating Balaam's home in Edom rather than in Mesopotamia.

[3] *Geschichte des Volkes Israel*, pp. 119 *ad fin.*, 122.

north to south upon the map. But it would seem truly remarkable that the list should have been so short as this.

CHAPTER II

4. the law of the Lord. The Hebrew word 'law', *tôrāh*, originally meant no more than 'direction' or 'instruction' as, *e.g.*, in Isa. viii. 16. Four usages of the word developed: (1) The moral and religious *teaching* of Jehovah given through His prophets; *cf.* 'Hear the word of the Lord, ye rulers of Sodom; give ear unto the law of our God, ye people of Gomorrah' ʹIsa. i. 10, where R.V. marg. has 'or teaching'). The same meaning appears also in Jer. vi. 19, where 'my law' is parallel to 'my words'; and the following verse shews that, whatever it is that the people have 'rejected', it certainly is not 'law' in the sense of *legal* ceremonial. (2) The summary of Jehovah's will in Deuteronomy (*e.g.* Deut. i. 5, iv. 8), or indeed the written law itself as contained in that book (*e.g.* Deut. iv. 44, xvii. 18, xxx. 10). (3) On the other hand, an earlier meaning of 'law' (although unsuitable in Am. ii. 4) was the oral 'direction' of the *priest* on points of ritual observance; *cf.* Hag. ii. 11, 'Ask now of the priests *direction*'. Similarly in Jer. xviii. 18 such *law* from the 'priest' is parallel to *counsel* from 'the wise' man, and *word* or *utterance* from the 'prophet'. In neither of these passages is there any question of *the* (written) law as E.VV. In the Hebrew the article is absent. Jer. ii. 8, however, *may*, and viii. 8 probably *does*, refer to some written code in use. There must have been much in existence, not only by the time of Jeremiah, but before that of Amos. (4) The clear-cut use of the term for a written legal code, *e.g.* Neh. viii. 1, 3, 'to bring the book of the law of Moses...', 'and he read therein'.

Of these meanings the most appropriate in the present passage are (1) and (2). Usage (1) would be that more natural in an early prophet like Amos, but the coupling of 'statutes' with 'law' makes the later meaning (2) more probable—the law of Jehovah, as taught by the school of Deuteronomy.

4, 5. With regard to the authenticity of the oracle against Judah, the difficulties in the way of attributing *vv.* 4 and 5 to Amos are greater than in the case of the oracles upon Philistia, Phoenicia and Edom, above.

(1) The charges against Judah are serious enough, but compared with those against the nations in i. 3–ii. 3 and against 'Israel' in ii. 6–16 they are insipid and lack detail. It would seem an inadequate answer to this, and one which surely would imply some unfairness in Amos' character, to maintain that he "may have desired to reserve the more pointed and definite charges in order to lay them against Israel" (Driver, p. 121). Moreover, the indictment stands apart from all those throughout the book of Amos (with the exception of v. 26, and possibly of iv. 5 *a*) in being connected with religion and the cultus, and not directly touching on morals. Conspicuously elsewhere in chs. i and ii does the Prophet seem to confine his denunciation to various sins of outrageous behaviour between man and man. (2) The general impression of the *language* of *vv.* 4 and 5 is that of the period of the teachers of the age succeeding Josiah's reformation.

(i) The term 'reject' (with reference to God's requirements), though it does occur about the time of Amos (Isa. v. 24), is more common in a period considerably later (*e.g.* in the Deuteronomic passages, 1 Sam. xv. 23, 26 and 2 Ki. xvii. 15, in Jer. vi. 19, Job v. 17, Prov. iii. 11). (ii) The word 'law' in itself may be early in the sense of 'teaching', yet with 'statutes' as a parallel it occurs (outside Exod. xviii. 16) only in literature influenced by Deuteronomic movement (that is, not earlier than the period of Josiah's reform). (iii) The word translated 'statutes' (*ḥuqqîm*) is used with overwhelming frequency in O.T. of the later codes of the Pentateuch (Deuteronomic or Priestly). (iv) The Hebrew verb, 'cause them to err', is found about the time of Amos (Mic. iii. 5), but its other occurrences are clearly later (2 Ki. xxi. 9, E.VV. 'seduced' and Jer. xxiii. 13 and 32). (v) The phrase, 'to walk after', with a religious meaning does, indeed, come in the contemporary passage, Hos. xi. 10, but otherwise almost only in Deuteronomy, and in writings generally after Josiah. Though no word of *vv.* 4, 5 is without some case of contemporary parallel, the association in one sentence of several terms which become familiar only later seems to suggest authorship after the time of Amos, and more particularly, it appears, proceeding from the Deuteronomic school. (3) The oracle against Judah differs from those by Amos in making no elaboration of the punishment predicted. In this respect it is to be compared with i. 9, 10 only—another suspected oracle. The poetic *strophe* is thus, as Duhm points out, not complete. Contrast the length of the preceding passage on Moab. Moreover, the words, 'and their lies have caused them to err, after which their fathers did walk', unless they are conceded in any case as an interpolation, would alone militate against the Amos authorship. In the Hebrew, they are heavy prose standing in the midst of verse. (4) If Amos, like Elijah (1 Ki. xviii. 31) and the prophets generally, conceived Israel as theoretically a single nation, he might well have composed no oracle against Judah especially. On the other hand a later editor, after the age of Josiah, might make bold to supply what seemed to him a deficiency. In the verses against 'Israel', ii. 6 ff., there is no hint that only North Israel is under consideration. See, also, the notes on ii. 6 ff. (p. 139), and iii. 1 (p. 150). *Cf.* Buttenwieser, *Prophets of Israel*, pp. 232, 233, and Welch, *Relig. of Isr.* p. 64. In these circumstances, *vv.* 4 and 5 as from Amos himself become wholly redundant. (5) To these arguments it should perhaps be added that if an oracle definitely against Judah and Jerusalem had recently been uttered by Amos, it is difficult to understand how the prophet Isaiah could ignore it and pronounce the message of absolute deliverance from Assyria in 2 Ki. xix. 32–34.

The strongest points urged for the Amos authorship seem to be: (1) At least one parallel in contemporary or older Hebrew literature can be found for each word taken by itself separately (see above). *Tôrāh* (without 'statute') in particular is used by Isaiah of prophetic *teaching*. (2) Taking the popular (as distinct from the prophetic) outlook that the two nations were so distinct as to be almost foreigners to each other, it is thought unlikely that Amos, while denouncing by name the countries around, would have omitted Judah from express mention. That Judah should not be contemplated at all in the Prophet's mind is inconceivable. Driver, Mitchell and van Hoonacker defend the authenticity of the oracle, following the older critics, Robertson Smith and Kuenen.—Otherwise, most scholars either reject, or strongly suspect, it. It is the one oracle which Gressmann denies to the prophet Amos.

6. because they have sold the righteous for silver. In Egyptian literature there are interesting examples of exalted teaching upon justice.

(1) In the story of the *Eloquent Peasant*, the king's high steward in the ninth Egyptian dynasty (3rd millennium B.C.) is urged by a petitioner to be "a ruler void of rapacity, a magnate void of baseness, a destroyer of falsehood, a fosterer of justice, one who comes at the voice of the caller. I speak; mayst thou hear. Do justice".[1]

(2) In the *Instruction* which a king of Egypt made for his son Merikerē, of a date not later than the above, the teacher enforces his lesson upon justice by a reference to the *eternal* judgment: "Do justice, that thou mayst endure upon earth. Calm the weeper. Oppress not the widow. Expel no man from the possessions of his father....

"...A man remains over after (reaching) the haven (of) death. His deeds are laid beside him for (all) treasure. Eternal is the existence yonder. A fool is he who has made light of (?) it. But he who has reached it without wrong doing, shall continue yonder like a God, stepping forward boldly like the Lords of Eternity".[2]

(3) The interest of the Deity in the administration of justice to the poor man is illustrated in the great *Hymn to Amun*, where that god is described as: "He who rescueth the fearful from the oppressor, who judgeth between the miserable and the strong".[3]

(4) This idea is more fully expressed in a later poem:

"Amun, lend thine ear to one that standeth alone in the court (of justice),
That is poor, and his (adversary) is rich.
The court oppresseth him:
'Silver and gold for the scribes!
Clothes for the attendants!'
But it is found that Amun changeth himself into the vizier,
In order to cause the poor man to overcome.
So it is found that the poor man is justified,
And that the poor (passeth) by the rich".[4]

---

[1] Transl. Gardiner in *J.E.A.* IX. p. 9. The rendering in Erman-Blackman, p. 120, represents these attributes as being already *possessed* by the judge in question. The MSS. date from the Middle Kingdom.

[2] Papyrus Petersburg 1116 A *recto*, transl. Gardiner in *J.E.A.* I. pp. 26, 27. Erman-Blackman, pp. 77, 78.

[3] Second Canto, transl. Erman-Blackman, p. 285. This well-known hymn is preserved on a papyrus in Cairo, written in or near the reign of Amenophis II (1447–1420 B.C.).

[4] *The Psalmists*, p. 184; *cf.* Erman-Blackman, p. 308.

(5) Also: "Amunrē...The vizier of the poor! He taketh not unrighteous reward, and he speaketh not to him that bringeth testimony....Amunrē judgeth the earth with his finger....He assigneth the sinner to hell, but the righteous to the West".[1]

(6) The duty of fair behaviour towards the poor man is urged in *The Teaching of Amenophis* (*i.e.* the sage Amen-em-ope), ch. II. iv. 4, 5: "Beware of robbing a poor wretch, of being valorous against the man of broken arm" (*i.e.* helpless, afflicted). Again, in XX. xx. 21, 22, xxi. 1–4:

"Bring no man into misfortune in a court of justice,
And wrest not justice.
Have no respect for fine clothes;
And turn him not aside because he is in rags.
Take no gift from the powerful,
And oppress not the weak one in his favour".[2]

(7) In Babylonia, a poet writes concerning the interest of the god Shamash in civic justice:

"Thou causest the unjust judge to see fetters,
Him who takes a bribe and perverts justice, thou dost punish.
He who takes no bribe, who befriends the poor,
Is acceptable unto Shamash; he will live long".[3]

11. of your young men for Nazirites. The features of Naziriteship were: (*a*) Probably the Nazirite *abstained from wine* (*cf. v.* 12, Judg. xiii. 4, 14),—on account of its intemperate use being a common Canaanite vice prominent in the worship of Baal;[4] *cf. v.* 8, above. Very similarly, the *Rechabites*, the son of whose founder Jehonadab was a supporter of Jehu in destroying the Phoenician cult in Israel (2 Ki. x. 15), were akin to the Nazirites, in that they refused the products of the vine (Jer. xxxv. 6). The reversion of the Rechabite corporation to the kind of nomadic life which had been characteristic of Israel before the conquest of Canaan, made agriculture impossible particularly that of the vine (Jer. xxxv. 7, 9, 10). (*b*) The Nazirite preserved his *hair long* (Judg. xiii. 5, 1 Sam. i. 11). In Numb. vi. 19 his hair is called his 'consecration', *i.e.* the *token* of it (Hebrew *nēzer*). (*c*) In addition to the two elements above, the (almost certainly late) law regulating the conduct of the Nazirite directed that he should *avoid contact with the dead* (Numb. vi. 6 'P').

---

[1] Transl. Erman-Blackman, p. 308, *ad init.*

[2] D. G. Simpson, "The Book of Proverbs and the Teaching of Amenophis", in *J.E.A.* XII. p. 236; Griffith, "The Teaching of Amenophis", *ibid.* p. 218; and Oesterley, *Wisdom of Egypt and the O.T.* pp. 78, 79. Prof. Oesterley is inclined to assign its dependence upon the O.T. rather than *vice versâ*. The date of the composition of *The Teaching* is uncertain. Professor Griffith appears to allow that it may be as late as the 7th cent. B.C. See, further, Introd. p. 50, footnote 2.

[3] Ungnad, *Relig. der Bab. u. Assyr.*, cited by G. R. Driver in *Psalmists*, p. 169.

[4] A Palmyrene dedicatory inscription (of the date A.D. 132) is to a god whose worshippers drank no wine, "very likely as a protest against the Dionysiac cult of Dûshara" (G. A. Cooke, *N.S.I.* p. 305, and see, further, S. A. Cook's note in W. R. Smith, *Semites*[3], p. 575). It should be noted, however, that Am. ii. 12 and Numb. vi are the only clear evidence that Nazirites of O.T. abstained from wine.

The law of Numb. vi takes account of a temporary obligation only. The cases found in O.T., however, were for life; and so doubtless were the Nazirites of Am. ii. Though Samson and Samuel (like John the Baptist) seem to have been dedicated from before their birth, more usually the call to make the vow would come to 'young men'.

The present verse seems to shew that the ideal was primarily, and in its early history, not the accumulation of personal merit after the manner of an oriental ascetic, but for the spiritual and moral benefit of the nation. The Targum paraphrases the word 'teachers'. Unlike the 'sons of the prophets' (2 Ki. vi. 1, 2), the Nazirites continued to live amongst the people, and so could come into contact with temptation from them to drink wine, as in v. 12. For Nazirites, see further J. B. Gray on Numb. vi; the present writer, however, cannot accept the paraphrase of Am. ii. 12 there tentatively given, '*You stopped the activity of* the Nazirites by making them intoxicated'.

CHAPTER III

3. Shall two walk together, except they have agreed? The exact exegesis of this well-known verse is beset with no little difficulty. Four explanations may be mentioned. The last is that which seems to the present writer to have the most to commend it. (1) Any interpretation of the Hebrew text, which assigns to 'agree' a metaphorical meaning such as 'be in harmony' ('*be* agreed', A.V., Harper and *cf.* van Hoonacker), lacks foundation in etymology, and cannot stand. (2) The natural translation would be 'unless they have made an appointment' to do so (*cf.* R.V. marg. and the Targum); so exactly in Job ii. 11 (R.V.), 'they *made an appointment* together to come to bemoan him'. Similarly the Hebrew word = 'meet by appointment' in Neh. vi. 2 and 10, Josh. xi. 5, 1 Ki. viii. 5. Though the special idea of 'appoint' or 'decide' is not quite so clear in the last two passages just cited, the verb obviously means to meet by *arrangement*, and not by chance. If this is the meaning, Amos' desert life must originally have suggested to him the idea, as is the case with all the other questions in the series. *In the wilderness of Tekoa* two people would not be proceeding in the same direction unless they had made an appointment. "Two men will hardly meet except they have arranged to do so" (G. A. Smith, p. 89; *cf.* p. 82). As, however, the words are addressed by the Prophet to the pilgrim throngs and without mention of the desert, the interpretation seems pointless, not being true to the facts of the listeners' experience. If this exegesis had been possible, the verse might have borne the application that the people must make an appointment by 'seeking Jehovah' (*cf.* v. 5). (3) Some commentators, therefore, fall back upon a translation which is in accordance with etymology, but which lacks illustration in Hebrew usage, 'unless they have agreed'—agreed, *i.e.*, to walk together. The arrangement has not been made previously, but simply at the time of starting. Such a thought, however, would seem to be hardly striking enough for so vigorous an orator as Amos. Marti regards the whole verse as a later addition to the text; but this appears an unnecessary proceeding. (4) In all the circumstances, probably the simplest solution is to substitute for the Hebrew the

LXX reading, 'Will two walk together unless they know one another?'[1] (γνωρίσωσιν ἑαυτούς). So Nowack, Riessler and Gressmann. Thus, as with interpretations (2) and (3), Amos makes a statement of a general truth, the point being that for the observed event there is always a cause—in this case *the persons know each other*. An advantage of this interpretation is that it lends itself to a special application if desired. To make it refer to Jehovah and Amos (as some commentators did even with the present Hebrew text) would be unnatural; but it could perhaps apply to Jehovah and *Israel*. Jehovah has 'known' His people (*cf. v.* 2, the same verb), but they do not 'know' Him. Compare Hos. iv. 1, vi. 6, and contrast Jer. xxiv. 7, xxxi. 34. He and they must, therefore, part ways. "The people have broken with their God, and their God breaks with them" (van Hoonacker). The catastrophe is at hand (*cf.* the climax of the argument in *v.* 6). Thus the sense would come back nearly to that of A.V., and to the metaphorical meaning which those commentators who hold interpretation (1) strive to obtain from the M.T.

6. shall evil befall a city, and the Lord hath not done it? The ancient Hebrews had little or no conception of what are called to-day 'secondary causes'. God was supreme: therefore, whether an event was one of dread or desire, 'evil' or good, it came as His direct and personal act.[2] In Exod. iv. 11 God is represented as saying, 'Who maketh a man dumb, or deaf, or seeing, or blind? *is it not I* the Lord?' Again, because only Jehovah, and not Baal, had any existence, His prophet actually conceived of *Him* as putting a lying spirit in the mouth of Ahab's prophets (1 Ki. xxii. 21–23). Similarly the Lord was pictured as Himself 'hardening' Pharaoh's heart. See Exod. iv. 21, *etc.* (*ḥāzaq*), x. 1 (*kābhēdh*). In the Babylonian captivity, when the Jews in contact with Zoroastrian Dualism might have been tempted to attribute evil to a *God of Evil*, a great prophet was forced to make a statement even more dogmatic than that in Am. iii. 6: 'I form the light, and create darkness; I make peace, and create evil; I am the Lord, that doeth all these things' (Isa. xlv. 7).

Though the mystery of the origin of evil remains, Christianity, and Science as well, have helped us to obtain a truer view of God than was possible in Amos' day. The 'evil' of which Amos speaks as coming to nation or city might be war, or pestilence (*cf. v.* 17, note). Our Christian forefathers could, but we cannot, take Amos' words and apply them: does typhoid break out in the city, and God hath not done it? In actual fact, though we believe God to be the ultimate Source of, and to be responsible for, the world, yet in one sense He is probably the only One who we can be certain has *not* 'done it'—(it, or indeed any other disaster); who, on the

---

[1] That is, נוֹדְעוּ for נוֹעֲדוּ.

[2] This is particularly so in the case of a community, as in Am. iii. 6. This, however, is not to say that the common people may not frequently (as Mowinckel and others have shewn) have attributed the cause of adversities which fell upon individuals to the work of demons or evil spirits brought into operation through the action of the magician.

contrary, has given all the sanitary and medical skill existing in this modern age for the very purpose of preventing it. War, famine, beasts and plague may be *permitted* by God, but it is doubtful whether it should be the Christian view that He 'sends' them in particular cases (contrast Ezek. xiv. 21). May not the author of Wisdom present a side of the truth absent from Amos, when he wrote (Wisd. i. 13), 'God made not death'? In the older religions He was conceived of as personally working alike in the cruel, and in the kind, acts of nature: in Christianity His strength is apparent, rather, in an all-powerful love for each of His children. Am. iii. 6 *b* is hard to reconcile with our Lord's teaching in St Lu. xiii. 2, 4.

7, 8. Surely the Lord God will do nothing...who can but prophesy? These verses seem logically to belong to a discourse separate from the section *vv.* 1–6. It may be noted that it is quite possible that not a few of the different utterances of the prophets were carried in the memory of disciples by being strung together, somewhat arbitrarily, by catchwords. Thus grouped they were finally committed to writing. If *vv.* 7 and 8 are part of another discourse, they may have been brought in here because Amos used in *v.* 8 the form of question indicating a *cause*, as in *vv.* 3–6, and in particular on account of the simile of the *lion* common to *vv.* 8 and 4. Again, if Amos himself was not responsible for the writing down of his prophecies, *vv.* 3–6 may have been arranged to follow *v.* 2 only because of the common word 'know'—'you only have I known' (*v.* 2), 'except they know one another' (*v.* 3). See p. 192, footnote 3, note on vii. 10 ff., p. 311, *cf.* viii. 11, 12. In the same way, it is difficult to suppose that, originally, in a *single* exhortation the prophet Isaiah uttered *v.* 10 following immediately upon *v.* 9, as recorded in ch. i. Rather, 'Sodom and Gomorrah' provided the link for connecting two separate discourses. *Cf.* also Kennett, *Isaiah*, p. 21. The same phenomenon is found in the N.T., and by no means in St Matthew's Gospel alone.[1]

7. his secret. The writer of Jer. xxiii. 18–22 goes further than Amos, and maintains in connection with his own gift of prophecy that God's 'true' prophets—as distinct from 'false' ones (or, as Duhm supposes, the apocalyptists)—are present, possibly to assist, at His *council*.[2] The same Hebrew word, *sôdh*, is used in both senses, (1) 'council', Jer. vi. 11, Job xix. 19, and (2) 'counsel'. Micaiah, the son of Imlah, states that he was present at what amounts to God's council with the 'host of heaven' (1 Ki. xxii. 19).

---

[1] St Matt. (in xiii. 1–32) groups together three parables having the common theme, 'seed'. St Mk ix. 50 did not originally follow ix. 49. Of the various "Logia" collected in St Mk xi. 22–25 (26) it has been well said that not all this fruit grew from that fig tree. In St John x. 1–18 what are perhaps two quite distinct parables (of 'the door' and of 'the shepherd') seem to be run together owing to the word 'shepherd' being common to both (*vv.* 2 and 11).

[2] This development, like that of the conception of God's heavenly assistants in Dan. iv. 17, *may* be due to the Babylonian idea referred to below. *Cf.* Gressmann in *J.T.S.* April 1926, pp. 251, 254.

Furthermore, the very early use by the prophets of the formula, 'Thus saith (or, 'said') Jehovah', implies their belief that they had a unique knowledge of Jehovah's purpose or counsel; *cf.* the thought in Mic. iii. 8. With the idea of an Israelite prophet being in God's council may be compared the Babylonian conception of Marduk's *assembly* of the gods deciding the destinies of heaven and earth. At this conclave *Nebo* (of the same root as the Hebrew *nābhî*, 'prophet') acts as scribe; *cf.* Meissner, *Babylonien*, II. pp. 97, 124, 125. In view of the relationship between God and His *prophet* implied in the word *sôdh*, the LXX rendering of it in Am. iii. 7, 'instruction' (παιδεία), is weak.

8. who can but prophesy? The exegesis given in the commentary seems entirely preferable to the view (of Harper, expanded by Edghill) that the words have a wide reference, thus—when Jehovah speaks (through the tramp of the Assyrian armies) is there anyone so destitute of imagination as not to be able to *interpret*? Indeed, 'prophesying' in the best sense does contain the element of "pointing the lesson" of current events;[1] but there is no evidence that Amos thought at the time that anyone but himself was capable of doing this, nor does the verb *nibbā* ever occur in the O.T. with the meaning of 'interpret', 'point the moral'. Moreover, such an exegesis of the present verse is inconsistent with the conception of 'secret counsel' in *v.* 7. More in keeping with the common usage of the term 'prophesy' would be the translation, 'Who would not be in ecstasy?' On the history of the Hebrew term 'prophesy' see Introd. pp. 15, 16.

12. on the silken cushions of a bed. The following methods of dealing with this phrase may be noted. (1) The Heb. rendered by R.V. 'silken cushions of' is *dᵉmésheq*, occurring here only, and has been taken to correspond to an Arabic word for 'silk' (*dimaqs*). (2) Two slight alterations of the Heb. points make it identical with the form of the word for the Syrian capital, *Damméseq*. Improbable as it would seem that, by the time of Amos, Damascus had become famous for its 'damask', yet it is not wholly impossible; at least the Heb. word 'Damascus', or at any rate *dimaqs*, may have been used for silken ware. (3) A somewhat similar meaning is arrived at by reading *dabbesheth* ('camel's hump', Isa. xxx. 6), as an ironical term for 'cushion'. This conjectural emendation of Duhm's has found favour with Marti (*Höcker des Diwans*), Nowack and Gressmann. A merit of any of the renderings (1), (2), (3) is that some material object is provided parallel to the preceding words, '*the corner of* a couch'.[2] (4) Undesirable is the reading of the place-name as in LXX, Vulgate and Peshiṭta, with the rendering of the A.V., Pusey, and R.V. marg. '*in Damascus* in a couch'. According to this, the proper name 'Damascus' stands in effective

---

[1] In Job xxxiii. 23 it is the *prophet* probably who is referred to as the 'messenger' (R.V. marg.) and '*interpreter*'—'one among a thousand'.

[2] Ibn Ezra, arguing from the parallelism of clauses, takes the passage as, 'in the corner of a couch, and on the *corner* of a bed'!

parallelism with 'Samaria'. But the syntax is awkward;[1] and, moreover, the 'children of Israel' would *not* be resident 'in Damascus'; indeed *v.* 9 (like the present verse itself) shews that the Prophet is addressing the inhabitants of *Samaria*. Even the translators of the A.V. seem to have felt a difficulty; for, as an alternative to their text, 'in Damascus in a couch', they inserted in the margin (on what authority?) 'on the bed's *feet*'! The LXX translators could render easily, 'the sons of Israel who dwell in Samaria, and (priests)[2] in Damascus', for by their time a Hebrew colony in the Syrian capital would be a familiar fact. The Targum has, instead, the difficult words, '*and trust in* Damascus', as if the Prophet were speaking to the Samaritan politicians of the reign of Pekah (*cf.* Isa. vii. 1, 2).

14. I will also visit the altars of Beth-el. It is by no means necessary to suppose that these are the words of some later writer who looked upon Ephraimite worship as being heathen. *Cf.* Sellin, p. 179. The same destruction of Jehovah's sanctuary is threatened, even more forcibly, in *v.* 5, vii. 9, and ix. 1. Later, Jeremiah said, as being the words of Jehovah concerning His temple at Jerusalem itself, 'Therefore will I do unto the house, which is called by my name...as I have done to Shiloh' (Jer. vii. 12–14; *cf.* xxvi. 6, 9, 12). Jeremiah was delivered from losing his life for blasphemy, only because a precedent was remembered in the equally amazing words of the early prophet Micah, 'Zion shall be plowed as a field' (Jer. xxvi. 18, Mic. iii. 12). For various *literary* reasons, which do not seem very convincing, Wellhausen and Duhm regard *v.* 14 *b* as an interpolation.

the horns of the altar shall be cut off. A monument from Têma in N. Arabia (of the 5th cent. B.C.)[3] shews a Semitic altar with 'horns' of a sort; one such has been found also at Byblos. Altar-horns should probably be regarded as a relic of ancient bull-worship: in the case of the bull-cult altar erected by Jeroboam I this is clearly so. The expression in the present passage supplies the nearest approach of Amos to a distinct mention of the Beth-el Bull. Contrast the several allusions by his contemporary Hosea (Hos. viii. 5, 6, xiii. 2). As the Israelites made the bull an emblem of Jehovah (Exod. xxxii. 4–6), so also the Aramaeans represented their god

---

[1] The Hebrew lacks a preposition 'in' before the word rendered 'bed'. Thus the sentence runs, 'that sit in Samaria in the corner of a couch, and in Damascus *a bed*' (or, 'in Damascus *of* a bed'; not 'in Damascus *in*' or '*on*, a bed').

[2] In this verse they dealt strangely with the Hebrew for 'bed', though they translated it correctly in vi. 4. The Hebrew '*eres* appears to have been changed into Greek letters; and the word so formed then became *hiereis* (ἱερεῖς), 'priests'! Editions place it either as the last word of *v.* 12, or else as the first of *v.* 13, 'Priests, hear and testify'. For a theory that the LXX translators as a whole used not the Hebrew text but Hebrew already transliterated into Greek, see F. Wutz, *Die Transkriptionen von der Septuaginta bis zu Hieronymus*, Lieferung I, 1925; and, before him, Tychsen, *Tentamen de variis codicum Hebraicorum Vet. Test.* MSS. *generibus*, 1772. *Cf.* A. Lukyn Williams in *Victoria Institute Transactions*, March 29, 1926, pp. 6–9.

[3] The inscription is alluded to in the note on v. 26, p. 200 (*Ṣelem*).

Hadad. Ancient Hittite monuments shew the animal as a symbol of the deity. In Babylonia and Egypt a like association occurs. Doubtless not a few emblems and rites from an earlier forgotten worship survived not only in Beth-el but also in Jehovah's temple at Jerusalem. According to the Pentateuch the offering-altar of the tabernacle was furnished with horns, to which blood had to be applied ceremonially, Exod. xxvii. 2, Lev. iv. 30, *etc.* From 1 Ki. i. 50, 51 it is learned that by catching hold of altar-horns a man put himself in sanctuary. It is just possible that the wording of the present passage is intended, not only to convey the idea of the terrible seriousness of the ruin predicted, but to suggest the taking away of all possibility of refuge from Jehovah's design to do to death the offenders.

Beth-el. (*a*) The city of Beth-el was famous among the many 'high places' in which Jehovah was worshipped (see vii. 9, note, p. 308). Abraham, as well as Jacob, had erected an altar at Beth-el (Gen. xii. 8, xxxv. 7). It is alluded to as a recognised shrine in 1 Sam. x. 3. Possibly this fact contributed to its choice, along with Gilgal (*cf.* Am. iv. 4), as one of the circuit cities of the judge Samuel (1 Sam. vii. 16). It may be because of the famous golden bull erected there by Jeroboam I that Hosea terms *Beth-el,* ironically, *Beth-aven*—'House of trouble' (or, 'wickedness'), iv. 15, x. 8.

What was the ultimate fate of Beth-el is uncertain. The shrine was, no doubt, dismantled by order of Sargon in 722 B.C. (2 Ki. xvii. 24–41); but a priesthood was provided there again by the Assyrian king (xvii. 28). A century later (according to 2 Ki. xxiii. 15–20) the altar of Jeroboam, but not *necessarily* other altars, was destroyed by order of Josiah, king of Judah.[1] For the suggestive view of Professor Kennett's that the Beth-el priesthood was descended from Aaron, and supplied the line of priests at Jerusalem from the period of the Exile onwards, see *J.T.S.* Jan. 1925, pp. 161–186, and *Old Testament Essays,* p. 82. A merit of the theory of Dr Kennett is that it suggests a background in history for the origin, and for the welding into a single book, of the laws of 'J' and 'E'.

(*b*) Originally the term *bĕth-'ēl* was a common noun (meaning, literally, 'house of the deity') applied to stones wherein the god was supposed to be resident. *Cf.* the stories in Gen. xxviii (especially *vv.* 17, 22, 'and this stone which I have set up for a *maṣṣēbhāh* shall be God's house' (or, a *beth-el*), and ch. xxxv (especially *vv.* 7, 14, 15). Such 'animated stones' in Phoenicia were designated βαίτυλος or βαιτύλιον. See *E.B.* art. "Massebah", col. 2977. Gressmann understands *Beth-el* here in the sense of 'sacred stone'.

It is, indeed, not wholly impossible that it is against the worship of a *god* 'Beth-el' that Amos is here uttering his threat. From the Elephantine

---

[1] 2 Ki. xxiii. 15 seems to limit the destruction to the 'altar' and 'high place' of Jeroboam. In any case, however, it is probable that in more than one particular the account given in 2 Ki. xxiii of Josiah's action at Beth-el is not historical—at least it is to be hoped so with regard to *v.* 20 a.

Papyri (No. 18, col. vii. ll. 4–6)[1], it appears that Jews in Egypt in the
5th cent. B.C. worshipped not only 'Yahu' (Jehovah) but deities 'Anath-
beth-el and Ashem-*beth-el* (see on viii. 14, p. 317). This may be evidence for
a worship by Israel of a (?) Canaanite deity Beth-el at the time of Amos;
cf. Jer. xlviii. 13, 'And Moab shall be ashamed of Chemosh, as the house
of Israel was ashamed of Beth-el their confidence'. If so, whether or not
such a deity, when worshipped by Israel, was regarded as really distinct
from Jehovah may be open to question. The fact that, in the Elephantine Papyri the female deity '*Anath* is associated with the name both of
'Yahu' and of 'Beth-el', suggests some sort of identification, at least in
the popular mind, of Beth-el and Yahweh. For the problem of idolatry in
the book of Amos, see notes on v. 26, viii. 14.

CHAPTER IV

2. The Lord God hath sworn by his holiness. For other instances of
the assigning to the Deity of actions and feelings characteristic of *men*
("anthropomorphism" or "anthropopathy"), see v. 21 ('I will not smell'),
vii. 6 (where Jehovah is represented as changing His purpose), ix. 8 ('the
eyes of the LORD'), and ix. 1 (where He is spoken of as being 'seen'). It
is not impossible that in some of these cases the Prophet does not betray
a lower conception of God than that held by the modern Christian, who also
experiences difficulty in speaking of God except in the language of men.
However, the attributing to God, in Scripture, of an *oath* exhibits a crude
idea of the Deity and is one which the Christian Church has outgrown.
Contrast the present verse (and *e.g.* Heb. vi. 17, 18) with the direct teaching
of our Saviour recorded in St Matt. v. 34, not to mention St James' words
in Jas. v. 12, 'But *above all things*, swear not'.

The anthropomorphism of the O.T., however, is not without its permanent value;[2] *cf.* Abrahams, *Judaism*, pp. 7, 8. Certainly it preserved
the *lovable* side of God's nature. Christians would be sorry to lose the
teaching conveyed in such a passage as Isa. lxii. 4, 5. After the Christian
era two tendencies are observable in Judaism: (1) the excessive and almost
absurd attempt of the Targums to *remove* anthropomorphic language from
the O.T. Scriptures, and (2) the anthropomorphism of the Talmud, at times
approaching to what appears to be actual irreverence.

4. Come to Beth-el, and transgress. The question naturally arises,
What is the cause of the Prophet's outburst in *vv.* 4 and 5? Why, precisely,
does he represent Jehovah as scorning the worship of the people? (1) It is
probably not because they, or some of them, worshipped other gods also,
though this may have been a fact. Throughout the book, it is the service

---

[1] In Ungnad's small edition of Sachau (1911) it is p. 34. In Cowley's edn
(Oxf. Press) and in his English translation (S.P.C.K.) it is No. 22, ll. 123–125.
[2] It would even appear that the anthropomorphic and anthropopathic conception of God, suggesting as it does real personality, is more true and useful
than that expressed in the First Article of Religion in the Church of England:
"Unus est vivus et verus Deus, aeternus, incorporeus, impartibilis, impassi-
bilis...."

of *Jehovah* of which Amos is speaking. There appears to be a reference to foreign gods in viii. 14, '*Ashîmâ* and *Dôdh*, but the allusion to Sakkûth and Kaiwān in v. 26 is but incidental. (2) Nor is it likely that he was rebuking the *idolatry*[1] which at that time certainly was a characteristic of the worship of Jehovah, even as it was of native cults. For, in that case, would not some clear charge be made? Apart from the interpolation ii. 4, 5, there is, in the whole book, not an allusion to the idolatrous worship of Jehovah. 'The guilt of Samaria' mentioned in viii. 14 is not an image of Israel's national God. (3) Still less is it because the services were conducted in other spots besides on mount Zion. The law against the 'high places' was unknown at the time (see note on vii. 9, pp. 208, 209). (4) Many feel that the language used by Amos suggests a definite polemic against *sacrifice* as an institution; *cf.* v. 22–25. Already in iii. 14, the Prophet apparently had contemplated with equanimity the fall of the principal altars erected to Jehovah in Northern Israel—those of Beth-el. In this connection the fact should be noted that the author of Mic. vi. 6–8 appears to advocate a non-sacrificial service. (Note the words in *v.* 8, '*What* doth the LORD require?' following the query about sacrifice in *vv.* 6, 7.) So Jer. vii. 22, 23, and possibly Isa. lxvi. 1–3,[2] not to mention Am. v. 25. Not dissimilar is the attitude of the writers of Pss. l. 7–15, li. 16, 17, lxix. 31. On such evidence, many scholars of great eminence hold that some, nay most, of the prophets desired the abolition of sacrifice. In the words of Marti, *Geschichte isr. Religion*, edn 5, p. 182, "The prophets never place in contrast to the practice of the cultus of their contemporaries another regulation of sacrifice or a better conception of sacrifice, but the practice of love and the knowledge of God.... Hence their opposition to it we must understand to be fundamental; and their language signifies in effect: No sacrifices, but love and a right knowledge of God". See, further, v. 25, note, p. 198, and Excursus III. p. 338. (5) It may, or it may not, be a fact that, in the words of Hölscher, "Amos desired to see an end of the local cult". If he did, could it not have been for more general reasons than any of the foregoing? Is he not upbraiding his hearers for sacrificing at the sanctuaries in *such a manner* as to be displeasing to Jehovah? For, the service was being performed mechanically as an act of empty ritual. It was unspiritual. And more than

---

[1] By the time of the Targum translation reasons (1) and (2) had become the conventional explanation of Amos' attitude towards the cultus. Ch. v. 5 *b* is rendered, 'Because they who worship (at) the altars (*bāmāsayyā* = Greek βωμός, and *cf.* Hebrew *bāmāh*, 'high place') of Gilgal will certainly go into exile, and they who serve the idols in Beth-el will become nought'.

[2] It is difficult to find any passages in the prophets approving of sacrifice except in Ezek. xl–xlvi, and the probably later passage, Jer. xvii. 26. Hos. iii. 4 is an *argumentum ad homines*; *cf.* the reference to 'image'. Isa. liii. 10 is perhaps an exception, but the allusion to the 'guilt offering' is only incidental, and the Hebrew text presents difficulties. The conception of the whole chapter is not that of animal sacrifice, but of the redemption wrought by the suffering of the innocent Israelite(s). If Isa. xliii. 22–26 favours sacrifice, it is phrased very ambiguously (*cf. vv.* 23 *b*, 25). The writer of Isa. lx. 7 has some very noble thoughts but he cannot free himself from a certain tendency to reaction (*vv.* 10, 12).

this: the daily life[1] of the worshippers outside of the sanctuary was not in correspondence with their implied profession of regard for their God.[2] It seems reasonable that when Isaiah (in Isa. i. 10–17) says, 'Who hath required this?' he can hardly be advocating the abolition henceforth for all time from the city of Jerusalem of 'sacrifice', 'incense', the observance of 'new moons', 'sabbaths', etc. Rather, by a strong contrast, he desires to recommend the practice of morality (vv. 16, 17). Hos. vi. 6 probably implies no more than 'If I declare my choice, it is mercy above sacrifice'. In Hos. iii. 4 the prophet seems to regard the loss of 'sacrifice' and of the maṣṣēbhāh as a catastrophe. Such an interpretation of the present passage would surely account sufficiently for the boldness of Amos in characterising Israel's worship as itself 'transgression'.

Whatever may be Amos' meaning, it is clear that the Prophet represents an ideal of religion altogether different from that of the peoples around Israel, or, indeed, from that of the mass of the nation itself. So far as evidence has survived, Amos marks a clear stage in the aggressive forward movement against Canaanitish ways and thought. However, upon the whole, he does not seem to be advocating ideals altogether above the heads of his audience. He is appealing to some good tradition—probably to that of Moses himself. From the abundant evidence of the O.T. alone this much may be said: hitherto in Israel common religious life had again and again approximated to paganism; Amos shews an advance upon such Semitic religion; and in his teaching we begin to see on the horizon the principles of Christianity itself. Yet it has been a fact that even "in the Christian church creed and sacrament have often thrown character into the shade; and against any such tendency the teaching of the prophets can even to-day serve not only as a protest, but as a protection" (Garvie, O.T. in the Sunday School, p. 79).

12. prepare to meet thy God, O Israel. Interpretation (1) given on p. 176 is that generally held in both modern and ancient times. So the Targum (quoted on p. 176, footnote 1); and cf. the LXX, 'prepare to call upon thy God'. On the other hand, may not just possibly the emphasis of the sentence be upon the clause 'to meet thy God' rather than upon the verb 'prepare'? In that case, the words do not constitute an offer, but they almost amount to the meaning (to use an English phrase), 'be prepared for (i.e. await) the worst'. Thus Mitchell calls it not an exhortation to repentance, but a challenge, 'ye have resisted my love and mercy;[3] now prepare to endure my anger'. More exact, however, is van Hoonacker's suggestion:

---

[1] The Targum of v. 5, reading ḥāmās for ḥāmēṣ, suggests this idea well, 'They exact by oppression the thank offering and they bring it with singing and they say: This is for acceptance'.

[2] This is finely put by G. A. Smith in ch. ix of his commentary. See also W. Robertson Smith, Prophets[2], pp. 138–140.

[3] After all, the chastisements in the preceding verses were each in turn removed; also they were but partial (v. 7, 'one' city'; v. 10 a, 'among you'; v. 11, 'some among you'...'as a brand plucked out').

'et puisque je te traiterai ainsi, *tiens-toi prêt* au-devant de ton Dieu, Israël'.

A fair paraphrase of the passage would then be, 'Hitherto you have had disasters, of a minor character (*vv.* 6–11); these have been sent in vain; therefore *thus* will I do. And, because I intend to do something terrific this time, expect forthwith to meet me'. The judgments so far have been for the most part *physical*; now they will be political, even the annihilation of the state at the hands of Assyria. As G. A. Smith points out (*XII Prophets*, pp. 69, 70) the same climax is observable in the Four Visions. Locusts and drought (vii. 1–6) are to give place to the 'desolation' of the sanctuaries and the 'end' of Jehovah's people Israel. And this nothing can avert, 'I will not pass by them any more' (vii. 8, viii. 2). Thus it is doubtful whether Am. iv. 12 *b* sounds the gospel trumpet. There is no evidence that the Prophet expected that 'a remnant would be saved'. (*Cf.* note on v. 15, p. 190.)

CHAPTER V

9. that bringeth sudden destruction upon the strong, so that destruction cometh upon the fortress. As an alternative to the treatment of this passage given on p. 187 and footnote, another line of conjectural emendation seems to be worthy of consideration. In 1883 G. Hoffmann proposed the text and rendering, 'Yahweh, who causes Taurus to arise after Capella, and causes Taurus to set after Vindemiator'.[1] Duhm accepted this, with the modification that he suggested that a *fourth* stellar name, Gemma,[2] lay behind the second occurrence of the Hebrew common noun, 'destruction'. Further, he substituted the translation 'with' for Hoffmann's

---

[1] *Z.A.W.* III. pp. 110, 111. Vindemiator is in the constellation Virgo. Capella's morning rising comes at the end of April during the early rains, that of Taurus in May (in corn-harvest). The morning setting of Taurus is in Nov. and could mark the beginning of the rainy season; the morning rising of Vindemiator (or, as it is now called, Vindemiatrix) takes place in Sept. Hoffmann interprets his text that Taurus sets after the morning *rising* of Vindemiator. But surely this is forcing the sense. Moreover, reference to a morning, is less common than to an evening, *setting* among the ancients.

[2] Gemma is identical with Alphecca. The argument of Duhm is in *Z.A.W.* 1911, pp. 9, 10, or *Anmerkungen zu den XII Proph.* pp. 9, 10. (*a*) The LXX represents the two occurrences of *shôdh*, 'destruction', by different words. Where the second *shôdh* stands, the Greek is ταλαιπωρίαν, which sometimes represents the Hebrew *shebher* (*e.g.* in Isa. li. 19, lix. 7, lx. 18, Jer. xlviii. 3). Hence Duhm believes that the LXX read *shebher* which, he supposes, was a corruption of an original Hebrew reading, *sh^ebhô*. The term *sh^ebhô* occurs in Exod. xxviii. 19 as representing a precious stone (LXX and Vulgate, 'agate'); *cf.* Assyrian word, *shubû*. This might stand for the star *Gemma*. (*b*) This scholar dropped the 'after' of Hoffmann as a rendering of the Hebrew *'al* (R.V. 'upon'), and on linguistic grounds rightly; though Hoffmann's rendering corresponds to astronomical facts. Still, if 'after' had been meant by the writer, he would probably have employed the unambiguous word *'aḥărē*. The Hebrew *'al* can mean 'with' (Duhm, *samt, mit*); *cf.* Am. iii. 15 ('the winter house *with* the summer house'), Job xxxviii. 32 ('*with* her train'), 1 Ki. xv. 20 ('*with* all the land of Naphthali'), Gen. xxxii. 12 ('the mother *with* the children'), *etc.* This use does not always involve the idea of *simultaneity*; *'al* can be employed in the sense of the modern English, 'as well as'.

'after'. Thus his rendering was, as indeed he had given it in his *Zwölf Propheten* (1910),

> (*v.* 8 *a*) 'Who created Sirius and Orion,
> (*v.* 9)   Who bids Taurus and Capella rise,
>   Who bids Gemma with Arcturus set'.[1]

The two halves of *v.* 8 Duhm transposed so as to bring together *six* stellar names. Duhm's adaptation of Hoffmann's original theory has been accepted by Nowack and by Gressmann.[2]

It might be well to shew rather more fully how such a text and translation were arrived at. The actual changes from the difficult and suspicious M.T. are really negligible, being almost entirely matters of vocalisation. (*a*) The word *mabhlíg* in the M.T., rendered by R.V. 'that bringeth suddenly upon', or 'causeth to flash forth' (R.V. marg.), receives a meaning in point of fact more in accordance with its proper force. In Ps. xxxix. 14 (13), Job ix. 27, x. 20, it is applied to a man's face *breaking into radiance* (R.V. marg. 'brighten up'). (*b*) The Hebrew for 'destruction' (*shôdh*) is read as *shôr*, 'ox', *Taurus*. (*c*) The Hebrew 'strong', *'az*, is pointed as *'ēz*, 'goat', *Capella*. (*d*) The Hebrew for 'cometh upon', *yābhô*, is changed to the *Hiph'il* voice, with the support of the Versions. For the meaning, *cf.* Am. viii. 9 ('I will cause the sun to go down'). (*e*) The word rendered 'fortress', *mibhṣār*, is vocalised as the participle, *mabhṣír*, 'grape-gatherer' (*cf.* Jer. vi. 9, *etc.*). In Greek there is a star called προτρυγητήρ, 'the bringer of grape-harvest'. By the Romans it was styled Vindemitor (Vindemiator), Provindemiator (Provindemia).

(1) Criticisms of any such emendations are obvious. (*a*) To assign a suitable date for the verse is difficult. There is no evidence of the stars in question being known to the ancient Hebrews by these names. The elaborate reference to the heavenly bodies might suggest a date for the doxology when Israel was in danger through Babylonian influence of *worshipping* 'the host of heaven' (*cf.* v. 26); yet these names do not appear to be Babylonian.[3] It would be necessary to postulate that the writer lived in the Greek period—or even the Roman. (*b*) Further, there is the objection, that if these star names were well known to the Hebrew doxologist interpolator, why were they unfamiliar to his Septuagint translator?

(2) On the other hand, (*a*) the treatment seems to solve the difficulty of giving a correct meaning to the word *bālag* of the M.T. (*b*) The occurrence of star names in Scripture is very rare indeed. *V.* 8 undoubtedly is one such passage, and it is a fact that, where 'Pleiades' and 'Orion' are referred to elsewhere in the O.T., it is along with at least one other star. (*c*) There is no need to suppose that the stars would not be mentioned unless they

---

[1] For Sirius, instead of Pleiades, as a translation of the Hebrew *kímáh*, *cf.* note, p. 185. 'Arcturus', in the constellation Bootes, is the vintage-star of Hesiod; Hoffmann gave it as an alternative to Vindemiator.

[2] *Alt. Proph.* edn 2, p. 347.

[3] Except indeed 'Bull', *Taurus*, and, if *'ēz*, 'Goat', be so interpreted, *Capricorn*.

possessed some *special* astrological or mythological significance. The movements of heavenly bodies were noticed in connection with seasons of the agricultural year (*cf.* also Driver[2], p. 183). The one point of the hymnwriter seems to be that Jehovah causes the 'rising' and the 'setting'.

Of the different changes, the introduction of *Gemma* seems the most precarious. There is no evidence of its use as a stellar name until postclassical times. The Hebrew reconstruction of Hoffmann is, therefore, more secure than Duhm's; but, for linguistic reasons, Duhm's translation ('with', rather than 'after') should be adopted. If so, the verse would run:

'Who bids Taurus with (= *and*) Capella rise,
Who bids Taurus with (= *and*) Vindemiatrix set'.

Obviously, any such reconstruction cannot go beyond the realm of the hypothetical; but if by more evidence it could become established, the description of God given in this verse, coupled with that in the preceding *v.* 8, would be a very dignified and striking one.

'He made *Pleiades* and *Orion*' (*v.* 8 *a*).
'He is the Lord of stars in their *rising* and *setting*' (*v.* 9),
'He causes *darkness* and *light*' (*v.* 8 *b*).
'*Wind* and *storm*' (*v.* 8 *c*):
'Jehovah of hosts is his name' (*v.* 8 *c*).

18. Woe unto you that desire the day of the LORD! The various uses of the expression 'Day of Jehovah' subsequent to the time of Amos are instructive, shewing, in the main at least, that the teaching of the Prophet never died. Approximately, they group themselves thus: (1) Jehovah's visitation upon His own people, or the wicked among them, (2) upon all nations, including Israel, (3) upon nations other than Israel.

(1) In Isaiah (ii. 10–22), the idea of God's judgment upon the Prophet's contemporaries is the dominant theme. The theophany in Jehovah's 'day' (*v.* 12) will be accompanied by earthquake. In Malachi (ch. iv), 'the great and terrible day of the LORD' is against sinners amongst the returned exiles, the 'day' when the righteous and not the proud will be happy (iii. 15–18). Ch. iii clearly limits the judgment to Jehovah's own people.

(2) Zephaniah (i. 14–18) means by the expression, 'the great day of the LORD', God's judgment upon the sinners of Judah. In addition, however, just as Amos in chs. i and ii had prophesied the punishment of the sins of the peoples around Israel, so does Zephaniah, making such visitation a part of Jehovah's 'day' (ii. 1–15).

(3) In and after the Exile, the tendency is to emphasise the advent of the 'day' upon nations outside Israel. (*a*) Ezekiel once uses the phrase 'day of Jehovah' for the 'day' on which Jehovah calls His people to protect His land (xiii. 5). Not dissimilarly, in the great apocalyptic passage, chs. xxxviii and xxxix, the same prophet states that there will be a 'day' when Jehovah will exterminate His nation's foes, the barbaric hordes ('Gog'). The nearest equivalent to the expression 'day of Jehovah' occurs in xxxix. 8, 'This is the day whereof I have spoken'; and *cf. v.* 22, 'Israel

shall know that I am the LORD their God, *from that day* and forward'.[1]
The Gog prophecy taken as a unit in itself appears to lack all ethical
connection. It seems to embody the kind of eschatology which might be
expected from false prophets. Micklem[2] makes the suggestion that it has
suffered from an editor who accepted Ezekiel's doctrine that God's judgment
would fall on the nations round about, but missed Ezekiel's ethical principle. It is a fact, however, that already in the book Israel's repentance has
been assumed. (*b*) The writer of Isa. xiii. 3–22 foretold the 'day of Jehovah'
as imminent especially in the fall of the Jews' oppressor Babylon. (*c*) In
Obadiah (*v.* 15), 'the day of Jehovah is near upon all the nations', and not
only upon Edom. But Zion, if it is not exempted, at least survives and
defeats Esau. (*d*) Joel, in ii. 1, 2 and 11 *b*, is in the true succession of Amos,
Isaiah and Malachi. He announces, 'The day of the LORD is great and
very terrible' upon the Jews of his time. Nevertheless, possibly in different
circumstances, he (or is it another prophet?[3]) seeks to comfort the people
by a prediction of a 'day of Jehovah' somewhat of the old kind such as
was dear to the hearts of Amos' hearers. The nations (not Israel), having
been judged (Joel iii. 12–14), will suffer (iii. 9, 10, 19), but Jehovah will be
'a refuge unto his people, and...Israel and Judah shall abide for ever'
(iii. 16, 17, 20). It is stated that God's spirit will have been poured out
upon Israel before He intervenes in their political and material affairs
(ii. 28–32).[4]

Passing to the N.T. it is noteworthy that in 1 Cor. iv. 3, ἡμέρα ('day')
occurs as a synonym for 'judgment', even human arbitrament; so definitely
had the term 'day' by this time come to be associated with a moral judgment. In the Fourth Gospel our Saviour is represented as speaking of a
present process[5] of 'judgment'; otherwise, the dominant conception in the
N.T. is that of a 'day' of judgment, called 'the day of the Lord' in such a
passage as 2 Pet. iii. 10. The idea of 'the day of the Lord' inspired the
mediaeval hymn, *Dies irae, dies illa*. It is interesting to trace how the
Christian ethical and eschatological use of the term 'day' had its origin in
O.T. prophecy, and possibly in a *pre*-prophetic eschatology.

26. Yea, ye have borne Siccuth...to yourselves. There are two obstacles
in the way of accepting *v.* 26 as a part of the original prophecy: (1) *V.* 26
seems not only difficult in itself, but it comes abruptly as a sequel to any
preceding thought of the Prophet, as expressed either in *v.* 25 or in *vv.* 21–23.
Moreover, (2) that there could have been the worship of Assyrian (or, to
be more correct, Babylonian) deities in Israel in the time of Amos would

---

[1] '*That* day' occurs frequently in the two chapters.
[2] *Prophecy and Eschatology*, p. 235.
[3] The division in the book would come at ii. 28 (English, *i.e.* ch. iii in the
M.T.). So Nowack and Sellin.
[4] For a careful discussion of the problem of "The Day of the LORD in Joel",
see W. W. Cannon, *Church Quarterly Review*, Oct. 1926, pp. 32–63. Mr Cannon
emphasises the *ethical conditions* of the future bliss of Judah, pp. 59–62.
[5] κρίσις, without the article, St John xii. 31, xvi. 11.

appear, upon such information as is available, to be very unlikely. This second point requires careful consideration. The only opportunity for a nation to adopt Assyrian deities would arise when Assyrian influence had become a political fact with that nation. Thus, as a result of such contact, the moon-god *Sin* of Ḥarran was worshipped in two northern Aramaean states, Sham'al and Nerab, later than the time of Amos, 727 B.C. (G. A. Cooke, *N.S.I.* pp. 182, 186). If Assyrian star-worship was a comparatively recent introduction into the Northern Kingdom, it might be connected with the payment of tribute by Jehu to Shalmaneser III a century before the time of Amos, when, not improbably, the Israelite monarch was confirmed upon the throne through Assyrian influence. Against this, however, must be set the fact that there is no hint of such idolatry in the Biblical account of Jehu's reign; nor indeed is there any allusion to this kind of worship in Israel at any period before the date of the present passage. This same absence of evidence also renders it doubtful that such worship should have existed throughout Israel's religious history from the time of the contact with Babylonia before the Amarna age, when, as a matter of fact, a city of Palestine bearing the name of Beth(house of) -ninib (Ninurta), the deity referred to in Am. v. 26 as *Sakkuth*) is mentioned. (i) Accordingly, it might seem best to follow Wellhausen and Duhm in taking Am. v. 26 as an addition to the text inserted after the date of Amos. Nowack suggests that the present verse is "the later addition of a reader who, in reference to the idolatry of his time, felt the want of the mention of it here".[1] Further, it is expressly mentioned in 2 Ki. xvii. 30 and 31 that the Babylonian immigrants into North Israelite territory introduced the worship of Adrammelech (*Adar-melech*)[2] and *Succoth-* (= ? *Sakkuth*) benoth. (ii) Nevertheless, in view of any possible evidence which may yet be forthcoming, it might be wise to suspend final judgment. In the opinion even of Gressmann, the situation is not out of the question in Amos' own time (*Alt. Proph.* 1921, p. 349). Moreover, the possible reference to another Babylonian deity in viii. 14 must be compared (*cf.* '*Ashîmâ*, 2 Ki. xvii. 30).[3] And of course it would have to be admitted that if *v.* 26 be not part of the true text, some clause or clauses have been irrecoverably lost. Loose as is the present connection between *v.* 26 and *v.* 25, the speech could not have *ended* at *v.* 25: and if *v.* 27 is the conclusion of the discourse, some further denunciation or threat is needed between *vv.* 25 and 27.

It remains to refer to the suggestion of Sellin (to some extent based on an emendation of Klostermann), though it does not appear to the present writer to be a very cogent one. The verb he points as a passive(w^e*nissē'them*), and, omitting the three consecutive words translated, 'Kaiwan your images,

---

[1] If so, may it not possibly have been by the same hand as that which inserted *vv.* 8 and 9 with their references to stars?

[2] *Cf.* note on 'Siccuth your *king*', pp. 199, 200.

[3] That the text of Am. v. 26 would supply, along with viii. 14, the only reference by Amos to the existence of general *polytheistic* and *idolatrous* tendencies should not be regarded as an objection to Amos authorship.

the star of', he obtains the rendering: 'And you will be carried captive
with the tabernacle of your king and *with* your god whom you have made
for yourselves'. The 'god' is, of course, the image of Jehovah at Beth-el.
The 'tabernacle' this scholar interprets as the weakened *dynasty* (of Jeroboam II) as in ix. 11 ('*tabernacle* of David'). But it seems difficult to believe
that anyone at the time could have spoken of the reigning dynasty as a
mere 'thicket' or 'booth'; and, in any case, a *line*, or succession, cannot be
'taken into exile'. Moreover, the grammatical implications of Sellin's thesis
raise serious questions.[1] However, so far as it goes, it would help in preserving the verse to the prophet Amos: for it removes entirely the problem
of the existence of Palestinian astral worship in his age.

27. Therefore will I cause you to go into captivity. This statement of
Amos, like that in iii. 6 *b*, raises a question of considerable theological
importance to men to-day. In what sense was it a fact that *God* brought the
Assyrians upon Israel? The same problem presents itself in the case of
Jeremiah's predictions of the victories of the Scythians (or the Babylonians)
over Judah. We have to remember that the idea, to us so familiar, of natural
law, and of the movements of tribes and nations in accordance therewith,
was wholly unknown to the ancient world. The Hebrews were a simple
people, dwelling in the midst of simple peoples. The only law known was
not '*natural* law' but the impulse, as they supposed, of the various *national*
gods. It was believed that, when one tribe prevailed against another, the
sole explanation was that the god of the attacking army was the stronger,
or else the god of the defending force, being for some reason angry with
his own people, allowed, or rather caused, their defeat. *Cf.* Rab-shakeh's
taunt in 2 Ki. xviii. 33–35, and Mesha's theory for Moab's defeat in Omri's
reign, Moabite Stone, l. 5, and see 1 Ki. xxii. 23, 2 Ki. v. 1. Now, it is a
specious supposition that Amos could see Assyria coming, and coming
to conquer. To him, of course, it was out of the question that his God was
not so strong as the gods of Assyria. Jehovah was about to use the great
empire of the East for His purposes. If it was Jehovah who was to bring
about Israel's overthrow, there must be a reason, and a good one. In the
case of Jehovah, who was above all things a just God and a righteous, this
could be neither (as *e.g.* with the deities Chemosh or Asshur) from an
unaccountable anger—nor owing to failure on the nation's part to offer
sacrifice, for this they did in abundance. It was because of ethical faults
in Jehovah's people.[2] Amos and the great prophets generally (who were
all monotheists) extended the application of the principle to the nations
outside Israel. This is to be observed in Am. i. 3–ii. 3. A remarkable feature
of Israel's seers was their realisation, we believe, that the enemy was coming,
whereas their contemporaries seemed to be blind to the trend of events.
Another point was that they conceived the punishment as being for *moral*

---

[1] Which are further increased by his proposed transposition of *vv.* 24 and
25.

[2] Similarly, as we know, the Prophet read a moral retribution in natural
phenomena—plague, earthquake and eclipse, *e.g.* in iv. 6–11.

offences rather than for ritual ones. In both these ideas there was, surely, more than human genius.

As, however, owing to the knowledge of science which God has given us, we no longer think that all the forces at work in the world are the direct and special actions even of the only true God, few would feel that the interpretation of history given by the prophets to their contemporaries was the ultimate one. It was the best—the *only* moral—one for the *time in which they taught.* Moreover, God has been revealed in Jesus Christ as a God who would be scrupulously fair in His judgments; and no wielding of Assyrian armies, entailing unimaginable suffering upon the good as well as upon the evil, could be really *just.* The origin of evil is a problem insoluble; but of this much we may be sure, the God of Christianity does not, for any purpose, bring one nation against another.[1] *Cf.*, further, the note on iii. 6, pp. 289, 290.

For the opposite view, *viz.* that it was the contemplation of Israel's sin that drove Amos to think of (amongst other punishments) an Assyrian captivity, see Introd. p. 28, footnote 3.

CHAPTER VI

2. then go down to Gath of the Philistines: be they better than these kingdoms? What was the situation with regard to Gath?

(1) 2 Chron. xxvi. 6 affords sufficient evidence of some defeat of Gath by king Uzziah. Just possibly this took place after the time of Amos; but if a short while before, the fact that Gath (though indeed still existing) had recently suffered[2] may have suggested to the Prophet the present allusion. The state had just proved itself to be not greater than 'these kingdoms', *viz.* 'Samaria' and 'Zion'. The words, 'Tell it not in Gath', in Mic. i. 10 as the text stands, provides some evidence, slight indeed, for the existence of Gath until a short time before it was taken by Sargon in 711 B.C. It may be that Gath is the city referred to as *Gimtu asdudim* in connection with the fall of Ashdod at that time. *C.O.T. (W.)*, II. p. 91.

(2) On the other hand, those scholars who regard *v.* 2 as referring to conspicuous examples of the complete downfall of once flourishing countries, maintain that Gath, whose name with great frequency recurs in the earlier history of the monarchy, had perhaps already disappeared when Amos wrote. This would be the simplest—though not the sole—explanation of the fact that Gath is the only city of the Philistine Pentapolis whose fall

---

[1] *Cf.* the criticism of Marcion, "Malorum factorem, et bellorum concupiscentem", cited in the note on Am. vii. 3, p. 307, footnote 1.

[2] Upon so late, and really ambiguous, evidence as the Chronicler affords, it would seem at the least precarious to speak, as some critics do, of 'the *destruction* of Gath by Uzziah'. After all, it is improbable that that monarch did more damage than Hazael of Syria (2 Ki. xii. 17). Jerusalem itself once and again had its 'wall broken down', but survived in strength, 2 Ki. xiv. 13 (and see also 1 Ki. xiv. 25, 26).

is not the subject of the prophecy in i. 6–8.[1] Without doubt its non-existence is the cause of the absence of allusion to Gath from lists of Philistine cities occurring later, in Jer. xlvii. 1–7, Zeph. ii. 2–7, Zech. ix. 5–7.— The reference, however, to Gath in the present passage of Amos (M.T.) does not, by its nature, prove that already Gath was wiped out.

13. ye which rejoice in a thing of nought, which say, Have we not taken to us horns by our own strength? *Cf.* the notes under this verse in the commentary. Ehrlich finds only one town-name, *viz.* Karnaim. Over this, Israel 'rejoices', whereas it is really but an insignificant capture, 'a thing of nought'. Some scholars, who translate 'Lo-debar' and 'Karnaim', claim that the Prophet is making intentional word-plays. This is not impossible, especially as regards the former word. Nowack follows Duhm in uniting *v.* 13 to *v.* 6.

Whatever the interpretation, the verse refers obviously to something of fairly recent occurrence. (1) If the period of Amos' preaching was about 760 B.C., the event could be the capture of two such cities when Jeroboam followed up his father's successes against Syria. These towns, situated as they were in the northern part of East Jordanland, would be among Jeroboam's last victories, and therefore might well have caused special exultation. (2) If, however, 742 or 741 B.C. be the date of Amos, the king's magnificent conquests were by then almost a generation old, and we must conclude from the present verse that something fresh had occurred to make it necessary for Lo-debar and Karnaim to be rescued *again* from the Syrians. (Ch. iv. 10 may supply evidence that there had been some fighting by Israel very shortly before Amos preached, and presumably *since* Jeroboam's victories.)

Whether Am. vi. 13 contains place-names or not, the words indicate a buoyant spirit in North Israel connected in some way with victory over Syria. The reader may be interested in the fact that it is this exuberant joyfulness in Israel and Judah at the time (*cf.* also *vv.* 3–6) that led the critic Eissfeldt (1922) to assign his presumed "optimistic" source 'J' (of the Pentateuch) to this period, in contrast to his less cheerful earlier "Lay" source, 'L'. For the spirit of the nobles in Judah somewhat later in the century, see Isa. ix. 10.

14. from the entering in of Hamath. What precisely is meant by 'the entering in of' is not clear. (1) Skinner, commenting on 2 Ki. xiv. 25, accepts the view of Buhl that the expression refers to the southern part of the extremely long valley, "the pass between *Hermon* and Lebanon, through which Coele-Syria is entered from the south".[2] That would be not so very far beyond Dan. (2) With much greater probability Driver, on the other hand, inclines to place the 'approach to Hamath' nearly a hundred miles

---

[1] *Cf.* G. A. Smith, *Hist. Geog.* p. 194, where an *Assyrian* destruction by the date 750 B.C. is presumed.

[2] So, apparently, G. A. Smith, *XII Prophets*, p. 177. The use of the word "pass" by Skinner does not, of course, characterise the valley as a *narrow* one.

farther on, at "the *north* end of the broad vale between Lebanon and *Anti-Libanus*, where, as the traveller from the south approaches Riblah, he finds himself entering a new district, and sees the country towards Hamath open out before him" (art. "Riblah", in *H.D.B.* p. 269, and *cf.* map in extra vol. at p. 368). So Burney on Judg. iii. 3, following Robinson, *B.R.*[3] III. p. 568. This might well be the normal southern frontier of the Hamath *state*: so Cheyne. To Hamath itself there would still be a distance of fifty miles. In fact in the present passage it is not impossible that there is, indirectly, an allusion to something like victory over Hamath. 2 Ki. xiv. 28 reads, 'how he (Jeroboam II) recovered Damascus *and Hamath*'.[1] Montgomery (*J. Bib. Lit.* xxviii. 1909, Pt 1, p. 63) makes the suggestion that Jeroboam, in alliance with other states, had actually brought about the fall of the dynasty of Zakir of Hamath; *cf.* on .i. 4, footnote 4. This would have been not long before the preaching of Amos. Köhler would omit 'the entering in of'. The fact that the entire expression occurs elsewhere six times in O.T. suggests that it was a stock phrase. But Amos may have wished to say 'from Hamath' as much as did the writers of 2 Ki. xvii. 24, Isa. xi. 11; moreover in the succeeding clause he does not seem to be afraid of changing a current phrase.

The vagueness geographically of the Hebrew expression *mill^e bhô' Hamâth* is reflected in the modern translations, 'Hamath highway' (Duhm), 'the region towards Hamath' (Nowack). Usually the northern limit of Israelite territory was at Dan (Judg. xx. 1, 2 Sam. iii. 10), *midway* between Beer-sheba and Hamath.

unto the brook of the Arabah. The '*Arābāh* was the deep depression both north and south of the Dead Sea, and, indeed, including this sea. This latter is called the '*sea* of the Arabah' in Deut. iv. 49, Josh. iii. 16, xii. 3, and 2 Ki. xiv. 25—in which last passage a phrase occurs strikingly similar to that in the present verse. 2 Ki. xiv implies that the southern boundary of the territory of Jeroboam II would be at a line stretching more or less eastward of the *northern* extremity of the Dead Sea, or perhaps as far south as the river Arnon, the sometime boundary between Reuben and Moab.

The problem in the present verse of Amos is: what is meant by the '*brook* (Hebrew *nahal*) of the 'Arābāh'? (1) Does it refer to one of the torrents which flow into the *northern* end of the Dead Sea? It would seem unlikely that such a name could have been given to any particular one out of the several streams which, as a matter of fact, enter at that point.

(2) A stronger case, it appears to the present writer, might be made out for its being at the *south* of the Dead Sea. If referring to some point on the south of the inland lake, the phrase in Amos would imply a recent conquest of the entire Moabite territory, as seems to be demanded by the exalted description of Jeroboam's military success given by the writer of

---

[1] Though the verse has certainly not come down in its correct text, the clause so far as it is quoted above seems to be sound.

2 Ki. xiv. 25, 28.[1] Moreover, if the author of Am. vi. 14 *meant* 'sea' (*i.e.* the northern extremity), why should he not have used the same phrase as the writer of 2 Ki. xiv, 'the *sea* of the Arabah'? (*a*) Some would identify 'the brook' with the present-day *Wady el-Aḥsa*. This has been conjectured to be the ancient boundary between Moab and *Edom*, referred to in Isa. xv. 7 as the 'brook of the willows' (or, 'poplars'), *naḥal hā-'ărābîm*. (*b*) Or, may not the *naḥal hā-'Arābāh* of Am. vi. 14 be the well-known *Wady el-'Arābah* itself, the wide valley stretching due south of the Dead Sea? That this valley is not watered does not constitute an insuperable difficulty. The term *naḥal* in Hebrew seems to correspond fairly exactly to the modern *wady*, and it is frequently used without any reference to water, *e.g.* in Job xxi. 33, xxii. 24, xxx. 6, Isa. lvii. 5, and 2 Sam. xvii. 13. In Gen. xxvi. 17, 18 the *naḥal* of Gerar is waterless. It might be possible further to identify the present-day *Wady el-'Arābah* with the *naḥal hā-'ărābîm* of Isa. xv. 7, if the latter passage could be rendered 'Wady of the Wastes' (*cf.* Skinner, *ad loc.*). Or, it would seem a simple emendation of it to read the singular, 'Wady of the Arabah', and so to bring the reference in Isa. xv into line both with the modern name and with Am. vi. 14.[2] In interpretation either (*a*) or (*b*), 'unto the brook of the Arabah' signifies geographically as far south as the southern end of the Dead Sea.

As the southern extremity of *Judah*,[3] 'the brook of Egypt' is frequently mentioned in the O.T. (*e.g.* in Numb. xxxiv. 5, Josh. xv. 4, and 1 Ki. viii. 65). This expression was read here by Wellhausen, who held that the M.T. *'Arābāh* was a later substitution by one who would exclude Judah from the Prophet's threat.

CHAPTER VII

3. The LORD repented concerning this. The use of the word *niḥam* in Hebrew, which has no modern equivalent, is interesting. (1) It is employed to describe the attitude of Jehovah[4] after Moses' intercession in Exod.

---

[1] Moab annoyed Israel even in the reign of Jeroboam's predecessor (2 Ki. xiii. 20). If Jeroboam was unable to reclaim Moab for Israel, then, except for the not very clear reference to Hamath in 2 Ki. xiv. 28, we know of no victory of his over any state but Syria (including perhaps Coele-Syria). Jeroboam's illustrious predecessor Omri had also made it his duty to conquer Moab.

[2] As an alternative it is possible (though in the opinion of the present writer it is less likely) that Am. vi. 14 should be rendered *Wady of the Willow*. (The name of the tree does not occur elsewhere in the singular; it may have been *'arabah* as much as the *'arabh* of the dictionaries.) Or, the text of Amos might be adapted to that of Isa. xv. So Marti (who points out that the LXX translators of Amos read a noun in the plural (δυσμῶν)). *Cf.* Duhm, van Hoonacker, Gressmann. That the same *wady*, or two closely neighbouring ones, could have borne names so similar in Hebrew as 'Willows' and 'Waste' would seem to be an unlikely coincidence.

[3] *Cf.* the reference to 'Zion' in *v.* 1 of Amos vi.

[4] The word *niḥam* (*lit.* 'console oneself') in the general sense of 'change one's purpose', occurs in the O.T. with a *human* subject only in Exod. xiii. 17, Judg.

xxxii. 12–14 ('J'), and is with great frequency applied, as here, to the relaxation of a chastisement which God had determined, or which at least was anticipated by the people (*e.g.* in Exod. xxxii. 14 and 2 Sam. xxiv. 16). The idea of the Deity changing His plans or purpose in response to a prayer, such as that of Amos, is amongst the ultimate problems of religion; it is not simply an outcome of the fact that with all ancient peoples primitive conceptions of the Deity pictured Him as liable to alter His mind or to cease from the fierceness of His anger, as a result of supplication or sacrifice. (2) In one passage (Jer. xviii. 10) God is represented as, upon occasion, likely to 'repent' of a *happy* intention. (3) In Gen. vi. 6, 7, and 1 Sam. xv. 11 Jehovah is supposed to 'repent of' (? = 'regret') His action (past) upon perceiving its consequence. It was doubtless with reference to such passages especially that (according to Irenaeus) Marcion said of the God of the O.T. that He was not only 'a maker of evil things, a lover of wars', but '*inconstant also* in His purpose'.[1]

In Numb. xxiii. 19, 1 Sam. xv. 29, the possibility of 'repentance' by Jehovah is actually denied, as being essentially characteristic of *man*.[2]

Notwithstanding the anthropomorphism (*cf.* Introd. p. 26) in these verses of Amos, a good and permanent element in *the Divine character* is conspicuously presented, which is not always to the fore in O.T. religion. He is the God, not only of judgment and, even, anger, but of mercy, as also in such passages as v. 15, Joel ii. 13, 14 ('repenteth him of the evil'), Pss. lxxxvi. 15, 16 *a*, cxvi. 5. In Rabbinical literature a favourite title for God is 'the Merciful'- or 'Loving-One' (*Raḥāmānā*). Also 'Merciful-One' occurs as the name of a deity in the Palmyrene Inscriptions in the 1st– 3rd cent. A.D. (G. A. Cooke, *N.S.I.* p. 276), and the quality of mercy is claimed especially by the Mohammedans as belonging to Allah. 'The Merciful-One' is a frequently recurring title in the Psalms of ancient Egypt. In the O.T., however, this attribute of Jehovah seldom carries with it the idea either of indulgence or of favouritism. There can be no question of such if *His* 'repentance' is preceded by man's moral repentance (*cf.* Jon. iii. 9, 10, 'they turned from their evil way'). On the contrary, *conditional* relaxation of punishment seems actually to imply that the great principles governing God's actions are righteousness and justice (Exod. xxxiii. 19, xxxiv. 6, 7, and, especially, Jer. xxvi. 13). Why, however, His course of action should

---

xxi. 6, 15, Job xlii. 6, Jer. viii. 6, xxxi. 19. The verb *niḥam* is used of repentance from *sin* in Jer. viii. 6 and Job xlii. 6 only. For this *moral* repentance the appropriate term is *shûbh* ('to turn'= Aram. *tûbh*, Gk μετανοέω).

[1] The Latin of Irenaeus is: "Malorum factorem, et bellorum concupiscentem et *inconstantem quoque sententiâ* et contrarium sibi ipsum dicens" (*adv. Haer.* I. 27). And the story of the chance sparing of Zoar against God's first intention and for no moral reason whatsoever, recorded in Gen. xix. 17–22, 30 *a*, can hardly be an accurate account of the mode of action of the God whom now Christians worship.

[2] In Hos. xiii. 14 (where the *noun* occurs), *nôḥam* implies that not seldom Jehovah does 'repent' of His threatenings.

be changed (as here) by the prayer of a righteous man, apart from people's repentance, must present a difficulty to many modern minds.

A good instance of the belief in *Divine mercy* occurs in a poem of thanksgiving of the period of Ramses II (1292–1225 B.C.). It contains the words of a father (Nebrê) with reference to his son (Nekhtamun), who, having confessed his sin against the god, was forgiven and restored to health.

> "He [the father] made hymns to his name [Amun's],
> Because of the greatness of his power:
> He made humble entreaties before him,
> In the presence of the whole land,
> For the draughtsman Nekhtamun, justified,
> Who lay sick unto death,
> Who was under the might of Amun, through his sin.
> He said [the father]:
> Though the servant [the son] was disposed to do evil,
> Yet is the Lord disposed to be merciful.
> The Lord of Thebes passes not a whole day wroth:
> His wrath is finished in a moment, and nought is left".

Transl. B. Gunn in *J.E.A.* III. 1916, pp. 84, 85; and *cf.* Blackman's edition of Erman, p. 311. Another illustration (out of many possible ones) is supplied in the poem to the goddess "the Peak of the West"; Gunn, *ibid.* pp. 86, 87. (The reference is to the Peak personified, or else to Hathor.)

> "I wrought the transgression against the Peak,
> And she chastised me.
>
> .　.　.　.　.　.　.
>
> I called upon my Mistress:
> I found that she came to me with sweet airs;
> She was merciful to me,
>
> .　.　.　.　.　.　.
>
> She turned again to me in mercy,
> She caused me to forget the sickness that had been (upon) me".

9. the high places of Isaac shall be desolate. It is probable that the worship and rites at the 'high places' were as a rule not so spiritual as at the Jerusalem shrine.[1] Many of these high places had been taken over from Canaanite use and were centres of religious prostitution. In any case they were under no central control. In all, however, at least by the time of Amos, it was *Jehovah* who was invoked. At the Beth-el 'high place', and perhaps at Dan, He was worshipped as a bull. Samuel had sacrificed at a 'high place' (1 Sam. ix. 12–14); likewise Solomon at Gibeon, 'for that was the great high place' (1 Ki. iii. 4). Until after the building of the Temple

---

[1] The words "as a rule" are used because of what is told of the 'house of the LORD' at Jerusalem in 2 Ki. xxiii. 7.

at Jerusalem there was a recognised 'temple' at Shiloh[1] (1 Sam. i. 9);
and Elijah in the Northern Kingdom had offered on mount Carmel, where,
so it appears, from before his time an altar of Jehovah had existed (1 Ki.
xviii. 30). The writer of Isa. xix. 19 saw no harm in the high place pillar
(*maṣṣēbhāh*), and similarly Hosea (Hos. iii. 4). In order to raise the level of
worship, and more especially, perhaps, to abolish idolatry, Hezekiah made
an attempt to dismantle the high places within his jurisdiction (2 Ki.
xviii. 22). At this period, even in the Judaean kingdom alone, there are
said (poetically, to be sure) to have existed an almost infinite number of
these local shrines (1 Ki. xiv. 23, Jer. ii. 20). Josiah, c. 620 B.C., set himself
the task of sweeping them away. He brought their priests to Jerusalem,
allowing them to fulfil only subordinate sacred offices in his Temple there
(2 Ki. xxiii. 9; cf. Ezek. xliv. 10–14). From this time onwards the cen-
tralisation of worship in one sanctuary became an all-important principle
in Judaean religion. It underlay the teaching of Deuteronomy (e.g. Deut.
xii. 5);[2] and the books of Kings were compiled from the same standpoint—
that the 'high places' even in Judah were in themselves (as, so to speak,
rivals of the Temple at Jerusalem) evil. (Cf. the phrase, '*but* the high places
were not taken away', e.g. 1 Ki. xv. 14, 2 Ki. xii. 3). On the other hand,
Amos did not hold this clear-cut legal view, any more than Elijah or Samuel
did. It is the opinion of some scholars that because the great prophets from
Amos onwards felt that the deadening effect upon the religious sense caused
by the indulgence in mechanical rites of sacrifice at the high places was so
great, therefore for this reason alone they wanted them destroyed. But the
emphasis in the present passage, and in iii. 14, does not seem to be upon
the mention of sacred places for any religious or moral reason at all. Rather,
their destruction is but an element in a terrible national catastrophe,
exactly as in the case of e.g. the Egyptian oracle of the Lamb (see p. 46).
Indeed, it is not impossible that in the present verse the use of the expressions
'high places' and 'sanctuaries' is only a poetic method of referring to the
country of Israel and its inhabitants.

It is sometimes said that the principal high places were spots hallowed
by traditions concerning Jehovah's relations with the *Patriarchs*. This is
true actually only in the case of Beth-el and Beër-sheba (both alluded to
by name in Amos; cf. the next verse, v. 5, viii. 14 b). No such stories,
however, are noticed in the O.T. in connection with the sites of Gilgal
(iv. 4) or Dan (viii. 14 a). Moreover, on the other hand, neither Mamre
(Gen. xviii. 1), Penuel (Gen. xxxii. 31), nor Mahanaim (Gen. xxxii. 2 ff.)
ever appear as religious centres. (Cf. Welch, *Relig.* p. 12.)

The demolition of what were obviously Israelite high places (Ataroth
and Nebo) is recorded by Mesha (ll. 11–18). Mesha erected the monument

---

[1] Though the term 'high place' is not actually found in connection with Shiloh
there can be little doubt that it *was* styled by this designation.

[2] For a discussion of the bearing of this reform upon the literary analysis of
the Pentateuch, see Chapman, *An Introduction to the Pentateuch*, pp. 131–145
(1911).

at what he expressly styles a (Moabite) 'high place' (l. 3). *Cf.* Isa. xv. 2, xvi. 12.

with the sword. See Introd. p. 63. It might be said by scholars, who hold that the primary factor in the call of Amos proceeded from Israel's sinfulness rather than from an Assyrian menace, that 'the sword' here, taken in conjunction with the phrase, '*I* will rise against', does not of necessity refer to Assyria[1] as God's instrument. There might be quoted the use of the expression 'the sword' in the analogous passage iv. 10 and in ix. 4, and the reference to the slaughter in v. 2. It has been argued with regard to ix. 4 (*cf.* note on that passage) that the expression 'with the sword' is used in a semi-abstract, semi-mythological sense, as *e.g.* in Isa. xxxiv. 5, 6, '*My sword* hath drunk its fill in heaven....*The sword of Jehovah* is filled with blood'.[2] *Cf.* Ezek. xxi. 3 (in Heb. *v.* 8), xxxii. 10. But, even so, it is open to question whether 'the sword of Jehovah' is ever seriously contemplated in the O.T. as acting except through a definite (though not necessarily expressed) human agency; *cf.* Judg. vii. 20 (in M.T.). In Zeph. ii. 12, '*My* sword' is that of the Scythians. In Isa. x. 5, 15 there is laid down the principle that the arms of Assyria are Jehovah's instrument. In the present passage it is natural to understand an allusion to some definite wielding of the sword by a foe acting on Jehovah's behalf; *cf.* the expression, 'I will avenge the blood of Jezreel', in Hos. i. 4 (also referring to Jeroboam's dynasty). In that case, it is probably the same enemy as is alluded to in Am. iii. 11, v. 5, 27, vi. 7, 14. However interpreted, the phrase, 'I will rise against', is anthropomorphic. After all, 'the sword' can be referred to without, in the context, *anyone* to wield it: 'the sword devoureth one as well as another' (2 Sam. xi. 25); and the phrase, 'with the sword', is common enough in the O.T. Supposing that these four visions constituted the 'call' of Amos, or accompanied that event, it may be that at this point, if never before, there flashed upon the shepherd's mind the significance of Assyria.

10. Then Amaziah the priest of Beth-el sent to Jeroboam. Does the record of this historical incident (*vv.* 10–17) come in its true position in the life of Amos? The narrative of vii. 10–17, abruptly introduced indeed, would fit in sufficiently well with the context. Amos in *v.* 9 has just foretold the destruction of the high places, and the end of Jeroboam's line. The court priest sends information to the king, and, moreover, challenges the Prophet to continue his (supposedly) seditious words. That he should be described as misrepresenting Amos (*vv.* 10, 11, contrast *v.* 9 *b*) only adds probability to the incident. However, it seems legitimate to ask whether the story, real though it be, in point of fact *is* set in the right place in the

---

[1] *Cf.* what is said by Micklem, *Prophecy and Eschat.* p. 114; Sellin, *Zwölf-prophetenbuch*, p. 149 and *ad loc.*

[2] See Gressmann, *Eschatologie*, pp. 77–80. He cites Isa. xxvii. 1, Jer. xlvii. 6, Gen. iii. 24 as evidence that there must have existed many myths concerning Jehovah's sword. If such a myth held a prominent position in Israelite thought, it seems strange that it does not appear to have existed in Babylon or Egypt also.

book. It is impossible for the English reader to appreciate fully how abruptly v. 10 follows upon vv. 1–9, especially upon vv. 8 *b*, 9, 'Then (Hebrew 'and') *said the Lord*, Behold,... and I will rise against the house of Jeroboam *with the sword.* (v. 10) *Then* (Hebrew 'and') *Amaziah...sent* to Jeroboam...'.[1] So far as an argument from *form* is of value, it may also be pointed out that the historical passage breaks into an intimately cohering quartet of visions; *cf.* on viii. 1–3, p. 239. The section in the third person probably existed at one time as a document in itself, and without heading. If so it may have been inserted in the position which it at present occupies only because the editor of Amos, or an early redactor, could think of no better place for it.[2] Furthermore, the piecing together of a prophet's utterances by 'catchwords' is not uncommon (*cf.* on iii. 7, 8, p. 290). In the present instance the mention of 'Jeroboam' and 'sword' in v. 9 may be the only reason that the section was placed here (*cf.* v. 11). Moreover, no mention of 'captivity' (v. 11) occurs in the present account of the visions, and the term 'Israel' appears to be used quite differently in vv. 10 and 11 compared with v. 8 *b*. It may be added that apart from this historical passage, there is nothing to shew that the four visions of chs. vii and viii were recounted at Beth-el. Quite different towns are mentioned in viii. 14.

If another position in the book is to be sought for the historical section, the close of ch. iii surely has a claim. In iii. 14 alone in Amos is 'Beth-el' mentioned by itself; and vv. 11–15 of that chapter predict havoc by 'an adversary' who is to encompass the land, demolishing (Amaziah's) 'altars' (vii. 10, 11, 17). Or the incident may have followed upon the recounting of the vision of ix. 1–4, which almost certainly took place at Beth-el, and wherein allusion is made to 'captivity' (ix. 4; *cf.* vii. 11, 17). Van Hoonacker would place the section at the close of ch. vi; L. Rost brings it into connection with ii. 6. (H. Schmidt and Gressmann *print* it before i. 3.)

14. I am no prophet (R.V. marg.). What is the significance of this utterance? (1) Perhaps the shepherd of Tekoa, not unlike him of the Midianite desert in Exod. iii. 11, laboured under an exceptional sense of humility. He does not profess to be a prophet; he is a shepherd. And when he says that he can prophesy, "modest, and at the same time proud, is his claim".[3] Amos' contemporary Hosea uses the term 'prophet' in one passage with considerable respect (Hos. xii. 10, 13), and so also, probably,

---

[1] If the narrative were truly continuous we should expect some phrase to introduce v. 10, such as, 'and it came to pass when Amaziah heard these words that he sent...'; *cf.* Jer. xxxvi. 16 or 22, 23.

[2] It would seem improbable that such a piece of biography should have been committed to writing until after interest in the man himself had been created by knowledge of his message through oral tradition or a written document of his "logia". Whatever be the literary history of Hos. i–iii, as a whole or in part, it is instructive to note that a section of the prose biography (Hos. i. 2–9) is in the third person and that either it or the passage in the first person (iii. 1–5) must be later than the book as a whole.

[3] Hölscher, *Profeten*, p. 196: "If Amos declines to be called a prophet, it is hardly because he sees in this title anything dishonourable".

does Isaiah (Isa. iii. 2). At first sight, there might appear to be some point in this explanation.

(2) It is generally held, on the other hand, that Amos (so far from hesitating to admit his right to an honourable title) by his words here repudiates association with the prophets and seers before and of his day as men with whom he has little in common.[1] Hos. iv. 5 may possibly point to a similar kind of attitude in Hosea. This exegesis appears to be somewhere near right.

(3) Amos could hardly have denied connection (even if he had wished to do so) with great and courageous men of God who occasionally had been raised up in Israel—especially the prophets Elijah and Nathan. Amos' own happy allusion to 'prophets' in ii. 11 suggests that in the present passage he is in reality not objecting to being considered in *any* sense a prophet.[2]

(4) Some understand by Amos' refusal to admit the title 'seer' or 'prophet' that he meant that he was under a *temporary commission*. 'I am for the moment acting as a prophet; but I am not one, for I have my own occupation and means of livelihood. Real prophets are so for life. I on my part received a special call to discharge a duty: when my task is over—in a week, in a year—I return to my sheep. I am a sheep-dealer'. It is difficult, however, to reconcile this interpretation with the statement of *v.* 15.

Even more to the point seems the reference in Am. iii. 7, 8, 'The Lord GOD will do nothing, but he revealeth...his servants the prophets...who can but prophesy?' This implies that God has made him a prophet. If the former of the two verses be an unhistorical gloss, certainly *v.* 8 is not. After all, the difference (great as it is) which existed between the order of prophecy of which, as far as we know, Amos was the forerunner, and that older one out of which it grew, can be exaggerated. The significance of the denial of Amos seems, therefore, to be in fact that hitherto much prophesying had been fanatical ranting and a means of livelihood—good prophets had been few and far between;[3] hence Amos draws a distinction between himself as a prophet and prophets who were less inspired. In other words, he is probably thinking of unworthy, as well as crude, past and contemporary seers or prophets, and, as he goes on to say, the '*sons of* the prophets'.[4]

Not dissimilarly Micah speaks of unworthy prophets and seers of his own day, contrasting himself thus: 'But I on the contrary am full of

---

[1] Some scholars interpret Amos' words as signifying in effect, 'I do not need to earn money as a prophet, as you can see when I tell you that I have a calling still', *viz.* that of shepherd, *etc.*

[2] Though in basing any conclusions upon ii. 11 it must be borne in mind that in that passage the reference to 'prophets' (and 'Nazirites') may be somewhat of the nature of an *argumentum ad homines*.

[3] Not to mention the actual spuriousness of the 'messages' alleged to have been received from Jehovah by many such men.

[4] *Cf.* McFadyen, *A Cry for Justice*, p. 103: "Of course he is a prophet, and he is not ashamed to call himself a prophet—in the deeper sense of the word".

power (even the spirit of Jehovah)', Mic. iii. 8. Jeremiah distinguishes himself from his contemporaries in Jer. xiv. 13–16 and especially in xxiii. 9–40. And the whole passage, Zech. xiii. 3–5, written when even the new order of prophecy was failing to produce men of true inspiration and vision, is based upon this very passage, Am. vii. 14.

At all events Amos, whatever title he may or may not reject, goes on to describe himself as a man who had been 'taken' by God and told to 'prophesy'.

the sons of the prophets (R.V. marg.). Some scholars hold that Elijah and Elisha were themselves outstanding examples of the 'sons of the prophets';[1] but it would seem that the 'sons of the prophets' normally belonged to a lower level of prophetic gift than did the 'prophet' more strictly so called; cf. Introd. p. 16. The expression at one time commonly used by expositors, '*schools* of the prophets', does not occur in the Bible. It represents the Hebrew 'sons of the prophets' only in the sense of 'school' = 'shoal' (*e.g.* as used of fish, or geese).[2]

The early history of the movement is obscure. (1) It is frequently supposed that an organised grouping of such prophets was inaugurated by *Samuel*. "It is an obvious, constantly recurring and fondly cherished supposition that this association of the unorganized bands into regular fellowship..., was the work of Samuel" (Kittel, *Religion*, transl. Micklem, p. 128). It is, however, mainly by no more than a process of exhaustion that any such part has come to be attributed to this particular prophet; the only direct evidence being feeble in the extreme.[3] (2) From 2 Ki. ii. 3, 5, 7, iv. 1, 38,

---

[1] Prior to Amos the terms 'prophets' and 'sons of the prophets' being often to all intents and purposes synonymous, this is by no means an impossible supposition. Similarly, the expressions 'son of man', 'sons of men' (*lit.* 'individual member(s) of the class, *man*') may be used virtually as synonyms for 'man' and 'men' respectively (Ps. viii. 4, Ezek. ii. 1, *etc.*; and Pss. iv. 2, xxxi. 19, xxxiii. 13, *etc.*).

[2] Even Ewald held that 'Naioth', Samuel's supposed colony of 'sons of the prophets', meant etymologically a place of *study*; hence it would be a 'college' or 'school' in the more usual meaning of the English word. See Driver, *Samuel*, edn 2, p. 159 (on 1 Sam. xix. 18). Thus in the early edition of *Church Hymns* the first verse of a hymn "For Theological Colleges" contains the words (obviously based on the phrase, the 'schools of the prophets'),

"Lord of life, prophetic Spirit,
Bless Thy family adoring,
As in Israel's *schools* of yore".

[3] (1) In 1 Sam. xix. 20 the R.V. has 'the company of the prophets prophesying and Samuel standing *as head* over them'. 'As head' is a very uncertain equivalent of the Hebrew (*niṣṣābh* = 'stationed'), which has the appearance of being a marginal gloss to the word 'standing' immediately preceding. It is absent from the Vulgate and Syriac. Probably the clause should run merely, 'and Samuel *standing by* them'. (For '*al* = 'by', *cf.* 1 Sam. iv. 20, xxii. 7, 17, *etc.*) In any event, the passage comes not from the early, but from the late and far less trustworthy, source of the book of Samuel; and any conclusions based upon it must stand or fall with the special view of prophets and kings constantly exhibited in this source. With reference to the 'band of prophets coming down

vi. 1, ix. 1, it may be legitimate to infer, but only with considerable reserve, that *Elijah* was the recognised head of these groups in his own day. But it must not be asserted too hastily that there was at any time any considerable degree of organisation, certainly not of central organisation. Elijah was accorded a position of importance among 'the sons of the prophets'; none the less he assumed little responsibility for them, sojourning as he did in time of drought to the east of Jordan or even in Phoenicia; and, when their lives were threatened by the king, it was the latter's chamberlain and not Elijah who tended them (1 Ki. xviii). (3) Later on *Elisha's* connection with 'the sons of the prophets' seems to have been much closer; *cf.* 2 Ki. iv. 1, 38, v. 22, vi. 1, ix. 1. From the first of these passages it is clear that, whatever community life the 'sons of the prophets' (or many of them) lived, these men were not necessarily unmarried.

17. Thy wife shall be an harlot in the city. The precise meaning of the term translated 'shall be an harlot',[1] and the exact point of 'in the city',[2] are not clear. The *circumstances* do not suggest, as in E.VV., that Amaziah's wife would become a common prostitute. Perhaps the point is, 'in *this* very city' (where at present she is honoured), or 'in the city', *i.e.* in public, Deut. xxii. 23; *cf.* Lam. v. 11 ('in Zion...in the cities of Judah').

It is regrettable that the E.VV. so often render the second and third persons of the Hebrew imperfect tense (when it represents only a simple *future*) by the peculiar Teutonic word 'shall'. Such a translation must have contributed not a little to create a misleading notion of the character of the God of love whom Christians worship. Similarly, the common English rendering of the Greek of St Mk x. 39 *b*, 'the cup that I drink ye *shall* drink' is unfortunate. In the present passage, to translate 'thy wife *will* be' tones down some of the harshness on the part of God, and lessens the possible element of vindictiveness in Amos personally. The clause, however, still remains an unlikely statement of what the 'LORD' would have 'said'. See Introd. p. 80 (v).

---

from the high place' (1 Sam. x. 5) there is no evidence to shew that they were under Samuel's leadership. (2) The argument from the etymology of the word 'Naioth' in 1 Sam. xix. 18 is of little value.

[1] The verb is *zānāh* in *Qal*, which (strictly speaking) should mean 'will be an harlot'. So the Targum probably understood, employing the softer equivalent expression 'will wander'—as in its version of Exod. xxxiv. 15, Lev. xix. 29 (Onkelos). Van Hoonacker is inclined to point the M.T. of Amos as a *Hoph'al*, *i.e.* 'will be *made* an harlot'; *cf.* the *Hiph'il* occurring in Lev. xix. 29, Hos. iv. 10, *etc.* The verb in the *Qal* is really not at all appropriate for expressing the soldiers' treatment of a captive, the word for which elsewhere in the O.T. is *shāgal*; Isa. xiii. 16, Zech. xiv. 2. The *Hoph'al*, if it could be paralleled in O.T., undoubtedly would read much easier than does the *Qal*. Hoffmann's suggestion to read the *Pu'al* is no improvement on the M.T.; see its one occurrence in the O.T. (Ezek. xvi. 34). Sellin is inclined to retain the vocalisation of the M.T., and to explain the significance of the prediction to be that Amaziah's wife, for a livelihood, will have to become a prostitute *after her husband's exile.*

[2] *Cf.* St Lu. vii. 37, 'a woman which was a sinner *in the city*' (Westcott and Hort's text and punctuation).

CHAPTER VIII

5. and the sabbath, that we may set forth wheat? (1) Sabbath observance was almost the only quasi-ritual precept which could claim prophetic support. The reason for this may lie to some extent in the *humane* purpose[1] with which it was early associated—the refreshment of a man's *cattle* and *dependents* (Exod. xxiii. 12; *cf.*, later, Deut. v. 14 *b*, 'that thy manservant and thy maidservant may rest as well as thou').

Thus in the present passage Amos, the champion of the poor, seems to be alluding with favour to the sabbath because it was regarded as one of the rights of the employed class. Perhaps also it is from love of the cause of the oppressed that the great prophet of Isa. lviii, who would substitute humanitarianism for the practice of ritual fasting (*vv.* 6, 7), is none the less the strongest of sabbatarians (*vv.* 13, 14). "The interests of the Sabbath are the interests of the poor: the enemies of the Sabbath are the enemies of the poor.... The Sabbath was made for man".[2] Neh. xiii. 15–22 furnishes a commentary upon the present passage. In contrast to such a grudging observance of the sabbath as Amos describes, Isa. lviii. 13 urges Jehovah's worshippers to 'call the sabbath a *delight*'.

(2) The ultimate origin and purpose of the Hebrew sabbath, and the philological meaning of the term, still present a problem. There seems no sufficient reason against holding the view that the sabbath as a religious institution in Israel goes back to the time of Moses. Gressmann conjectures —and it is *only* a conjecture—that the sabbath came to Israel from Midian.[3] But, as he admits, the name and the observance may owe their origin eventually to Babylon. It is essentially non-Canaanite (Neh. xiii. 17 ff.).

As to a Babylonian source for the sabbath, however, not all scholars are agreed as to whether the Babylonian *shabattum* (or *shapattum*) was either a *rest* day, or of *weekly* occurrence. Further, the Babylonians used a five-day

---

[1] *Cf.* Isa. lvi. 2, Jer. xvii. 21–24, Ezek. xx. 12. This purpose is obscured in the familiar Decalogue of Exod. xx by the reference in it (hardly as early as the precept itself) to the *Divine example* at the Creation (*v.* 11 *b*).

[2] G. A. Smith on Am. viii. 5. It may not be entirely out of place to refer here to the following weighty remarks of Archbishop Davidson which seem to have a bearing upon this point: "...I have no hesitation in reiterating my conviction that members of the Church of Christ ought everywhere to make their voices heard in support of our duty to safeguard for dear life the splendid traditions which are ours as to the sacred heritage of the Lord's Day....A strange selfishness leads many people, some of whom have leisure all the week through, to spoil the Sundays of other men by a carelessness which leads a man to think only of himself....Those on whom the sacrifice would be enforced belong chiefly to the class which has greatest need of the advantages of Sunday and is least able effectively to secure them...." (Letter to the Imp. Alliance for the Defence of Sunday, dated June 1, 1923.) It may perhaps be added' that the weekly day of cessation from all but essential work may be regarded as a boon to man and to all men, designed by their Creator, His gift to His children, howsoever it came into vogue and by whatsoever particular religious sanctions it has been preserved. *Cf.* also Prof. D. C. Simpson, *Development of Sabb. Ideal*, esp. pp. 18, 19.

[3] Eerdmans would say from the (smith) Kenites; and see Budde, *J.T.S.* Oct. 1928, pp. 1 ff.

week. Just possibly the sabbath was primarily the full-moon day. This theory is held by some scholars who reject the hypothesis of a connection with Babylon (*cf.* Meinhold, *Sabbat und Woche im A.T.*). The present passage in Amos is one of four in the O.T. in which 'sabbath' and '*new*-moon' festivals are mentioned together (*cf.* 2 Ki. iv. 23, Hos. ii. 11, Isa. i. 13). On the other hand, that the Hebrew sabbath was in some way derived from Babylon would seem difficult to doubt.

9. I will cause the sun to go down at noon. An Assyrian tablet about contemporary with the time of Amos records that 'in the month Siwan an eclipse of the sun took place'. This has been identified with the total solar eclipse of June 15, 763 B.C. (*C.A.H.* I. p. 149). As Am. viii. 9 supplies the clearest reference to an eclipse contained in the O.T. it would seem not unreasonable to suppose that the substance of the verse was suggested by this eclipse of 763 B.C. (1) The view that Am. viii. 9 is a *vaticinium post eventum* is held by many; but it is difficult to imagine a man of the stamp of Amos, at least, having this verse so written down in the hope that it would be understood as a record of an actual verbal prediction uttered before 763 B.C. Further, the wording, 'I will cause the sun to go down' (*i.e.* to set, in Hebrew *lit.* 'to go in'), appears to be not very appropriate to that particular eclipse which was observable in the latitude of Jerusalem as, at the most, "a fairly large partial eclipse" (Driver). (2) It is equally improbable (while, of course, not impossible) that God Himself would communicate miraculously to His prophet a definite prediction of the eclipse of 763 B.C. Moreover, it must be borne in mind that the time of the preaching of Amos was almost certainly subsequent to 763 B.C. (3) Probably the eclipse of 763 B.C. led Amos to prophesy yet another and greater one.

For attempts of earlier commentators to identify the event alluded to in viii. 9, *cf.* Pusey, *ad loc.* Such work had to labour under the disadvantage of the old chronology of the Israelite reigns. Another eclipse, on February 9, 784 B.C., which reached its height but thirty-six minutes before 'mid-day', seems just too far back to be in the Prophet's mind. What amount of accurate prediction is to be looked for in such threats as are made in this and the previous verse is a matter for legitimate difference of opinion. The moral truth underlying them is expressed in Prov. xi. 21.

14. by the sin of Samaria. The Hebrew is '*ash⁶math Shôm⁶rôn*, *i.e.* either (1) taking the text as it stands, Samaria's *guilt* in going to the Golden Bull at Beth-el; or (2) much more probably (with very slight textual emendation), '*Ashîmā*[1] (a god or goddess) in the city of 'Samaria'.

Suggestion (1). The Hebrew translated 'the sin' is not the *ḥaṭṭāth* of v. 12 but '*ash⁶māh*, 'guilt'.[2] Doubtless a reference would be intended to

---

[1] For a suggestive article upon the deity '*Ashîmā*, see König in *Z.A.W.* 1914, Heft 1, pp. 16–30.

[2] The LXX rendered '*ash⁶māh*, 'who swear by the *propitiation* (ἱλασμός) of Samaria'. In Lev. v. 24 (EVV. vi. 5), xxii. 16, the Hebrew term is applied to a 'guilt offering'.

apparatus (*e.g.* an idol, or an *'ashērāh*) in the worship of Jehovah. In the same way, in Hos. x. 8, the 'high places' of Beth-el are described as 'the sin of Israel' (and *cf.* Hos. viii. 6, xiii. 2); and the writer of Kings means by the 'sins of Jeroboam' the bull images used in Jehovah-worship (*e.g.* in 1 Ki. xvi. 31, 2 Ki. x. 31, xvii. 22). Amos may, indeed, here be inveighing against this calf-worship at Beth-el.

Suggestion (2). A deity *'Ashīmā*[1] is mentioned in 2 Ki. xvii. 30 as being in fact worshipped by the Hamath immigrants into the Northern Israelite territory, somewhat later than the time of Amos. Apparently, they brought the deity with them. Even more significant is the discovery of the remarkable fact that the Jewish colony—or some of it—in Elephantine, in Egypt, in the 5th cent. B.C., were still worshipping in addition to, or in some relationship with, 'Yahu', certain gods, *'Ashem*-Beth-el and *'Anath*-Beth-el.[2] In the compound name *'Ashem*-Beth-el, the element 'Beth-el' may be either (i) an ancient Canaanite *deity*,[3] the worship referred to perhaps being that of a male-female (or, rather, female-male) pair like the *'Ashtar-Chemosh* of the Moabite Stone;[4] or (ii) the *place-name* (*'Ashem* of) 'Beth-el', in the same way as in the present passage the deity is linked with a locality (*'Ashima* of) 'Samaria'. In either case, *'Ashīmā*, in Amos, is a god distinct (at least in the eyes of the Prophet) from Jehovah; and probably the reference is to an image. Jer. v. 7 may be compared: 'Thy children have forsaken me and *sworn* by them that are *no gods*'. Before the discovery of the Elephantine Papyri, W. R. Smith's emendation (accepted by Duhm), *'Asherah* of Samaria', was in the right direction, in suggesting some cult—in the city of Samaria itself (*Prophets*, p. 140); and *cf.* 2 Ki. xiii. 6.

As the way of Beer-sheba liveth. (1) Beer-sheba was another shrine (*cf.* the note on v. 5), and it is possible that 'the way' should be understood almost literally, as by the Vulgate, *vivit via Bersabee*. So, the Mohammedans swear by the pilgrimage to Mecca.[5] But, as Canney remarks, "there is no other instance of this kind of oath in O.T." Further, it may be added, it

---

[1] The form *'Ashīmā* may be (i) 'emphatic' *masculine*, and the deity might further be identified with the Phoenician *'Eshmun*; or, more likely, (ii) *feminine*. The LXX rather supports the feminine gender by its τὴν Ἀσειμάθ (not -μα). Not too much importance, however, must be attached to the Greek article being *feminine*, as the translator has prefixed the feminine article to every one of the deities in the list in *vv.* 30, 31 except the last. The simplest emendation of the M.T. of Amos, *viz.* *'Ashīmath*, is consistent with the deity being female.

The existing Hebrew text, 'guilt', may have arisen intentionally, rather than by a chance corruption. Similarly, *bôsheth* ('shame') was deliberately put into the text in place of 'Baal' in Hos. ix. 10, Jer. iii. 24, xi. 13, and in two proper names, 2 Sam. ii. 8 and xi. 21.

[2] Eleph. Papyri, No. 18, col. vii, ll. 4–6; see above, p. 294, footnote 1.

[3] *Cf.* the note on Beth-el, Am. iii. 14, pp. 293 *ad fin.*, 294.

[4] l. 17. And indeed *cf.* the combination Baal-Ashtarte of Phoenicia.

[5] So Orelli, and *cf.* Sellin. Mitchell quotes Rückert's *Hariri*, I. 189:

"By the pilgrimage and the height of Mina
Where the pious host stone Satan".

would seem rather bold to say in Hebrew,[1] 'as surely as the *pilgrimage*
lives' whereas the word 'liveth' is appropriate in an oath by a *deity*, as
'in thy God, O Dan'. (2) By 'way' some commentators, following the
Targum, understand 'way of worship',[2] 'ritual', A.V. 'manner', but this
is equally difficult to parallel in usage. (3) The LXX, 'thy God', seems to
give the right clue. For *derekh* ('the way of'), by a slight change in the
Hebrew consonants, Winckler and G. Hoffmann read *dôdhᵉkhâ*.[3] This
emendation has been generally accepted. The translation would be, either,
(i) 'thy darling' (*lit.* 'thy loved one, thy kinsman'; in Am. vi. 10, 'uncle'),
'O Beer-sheba', so Köhler; (ii) 'thy patron- (or, 'tutelary-') Deity,[4] O
Beer-sheba', so Nowack, Marti, van Hoonacker and Sellin; or (iii) 'thy
Dôdh' (a proper name), 'O Beer-sheba', so Gressmann. (i) and (ii) make
dôdh a description of Jehovah, (iii) introduces another deity.

The emendation *dôdh* was suggested by the occurrence of the word on
l. 12 of the Moabite Stone, in connection with Israelite worship on the east
of Jordan. Mesha says, 'I brought (or, 'carried captive') thence (*i.e.* from
Ataroth, mentioned in the previous line) the altar-hearth of *Dawdhôh*'
or *Dôdhô*—or else 'his tutelary-Deity', *i.e.* Yahweh of Ataroth.[5]

The present verse raises again the question already presented in v. 26.
Does Amos charge Israel with worshipping other deities in addition to
Jehovah? With regard to v. 26, though certainty is far from assured,
many authorities consider the passage to be a later gloss (mainly for the
reason that the (?) Babylonian deities, *Sakkûth* and *Kaiwân*, mentioned
therein can have been worshipped within Israel hardly so early as the time
of Amos). Some scholars would assign a late date to the present verse also,
for the following two reasons: (1) The earliest direct evidence for the
worship by Israel of '*Ashîmâ* occurs, like that for *Sakkûth*, after the fall of
Samariâ, 2 Ki. xvii. 30. (2) The text of Am. viii. 14, as it stands, is not
smooth; nor can the verse entire be connected easily with anything preceding. The difficulties would be removed with the *omission*, as a later
gloss, of the whole passage, 'they that swear by...Beer-sheba liveth'.
On the other hand, on behalf of taking the whole verse as a genuine part
of Amos, it may be urged that: (1) It would seem a reasonable hypothesis
that the Jewish colonists, who three centuries after Amos were worshipping
'*Ashem*-Beth-el in Elephantine, were but continuing a common practice
which they had brought with them *from Palestine*, and which may have
dated from before the time of Amos. (2) While the textual difficulty must

---

[1] Though Doughty, *Arabia Deserta*, I. 269 (cited by G. A. Smith, *Prophets*,
p. 186), states that Arabs to-day "swear 'by the life of', even of things inanimate;
'By the life of this fire, or of this coffee'".

[2] Connected especially with the Seven Wells of the sanctuary. *Cf.* Robertson
Smith, *Rel. of Semites*, edn 3, pp. 181, 182; and see Dr S. A. Cook's footnote to
p. 182; also *E.B.* art. "Beersheba", § 3.

[3] דֹּדְךְ for דַּרְךְ. Wellhausen and Elhorst had read, 'בָּאְרֵךְ, thy well'.

[4] *Cf.* the name *Dôdhâwâhû* in 2 Chron. xx. 37, 'Jehovah is my patron-deity'.

[5] So Marti. Sayce held that the name 'David' is to be traced ultimately to a
title of the sun god. *Cf.* also 'Dodo' in Judg. x. 1.

be admitted, it does not seem very serious; moreover, it is to some extent overcome by making *v.* 14 follow directly upon *v.* 12.

It has been generally held that it is a characteristic of Amos that he does not charge Israel with polytheism. The reading, however, of '*Ashímā* and *Dôdh* in the present verse, if the verse may be attributed to Amos' time, makes the proposition less secure. Whilst *dôdh* may not be a proper name but a common noun—a title in fact of Jehovah Himself—'*Ashímā* was a deity separate, or at least separable, from Jehovah. This is not to deny that '*Ashímā*-worship may have been closely connected with Jehovah-worship.[1]   After all, it still holds good that Amos' reference to the worship of other gods is, as it were, by the way, and that the whole stress of his message is upon the importance of *ethical* religion;[2] even as moral faults constitute the sole indictment which he brings against the nation when formally arraigning it in ii. 6–12.

CHAPTER IX

8. saving that I will not utterly destroy the house of Jacob. The force of the Hebrew is not perfectly clear: either (1) 'I will not *completely* (*i.e.* 'entirely,' van Hoonacker) destroy' (= 'I will destroy only the wicked'); or (2) 'I will not *certainly*, or at all, destroy'. The construction is that of the verb being preceded by an *infinitive absolute*, *lit.* 'I will not *destroying* destroy'. (1) There seem to be other instances (but only in affirmative utterances) of this idiom implying 'completeness of an occurrence' (Ges.-K. § 113 *n*). In Gen. xx. 18, 'The LORD had *fast* closed'; Job xiii. 5, 'Oh that ye would *altogether* hold your peace'; Joel i. 7, 'he hath made it *clean* bare'; and *cf.* perhaps Gen. xliii. 3, 7. But is this meaning naturally suggested by the Hebrew idiom? (2) Usually such a construction with the *infinitive absolute* would imply *certainty* in an affirmative sentence, and, in a negative one, emphatic *exclusion*; *e.g.* 1 Ki. iii. 26, 27, '*in no wise* slay it!' So Am. iii. 5 does not imply 'will not catch anything completely', but 'will not catch anything *at all*'. Deut. viii. 19 probably signifies 'if you *in the slightest degree* forget'. So in Am. ix. 8 we should expect the Hebrew to mean 'Nevertheless (Judg. iv. 9), I will *on no account* destroy the...'. Possibly the rather exceptional position of the negative particle, before and not after the *infinitive*, is intended by the writer to make all the difference to the force of the expression, but there is no support in O.T.; in Gen. iii. 4 the meaning is not 'you will not *completely* die', nor in Ps. xlix. 7, 'a man will not *completely* redeem his brother'.

In any case, it is hardly possible to conceive of a more direct contradiction to the statement made in the preceding part of the verse; *cf.* G. A. Smith, *Prophets*, p. 191. The verb translated 'destroy' is exactly

---

[1] Even as in Elephantine the pair 'Ashem-Beth-el seems to have been worshipped together.

[2] *Cf.* Micklem, *Prophecy and Eschatology*, pp. 121, 122.

the same as that in the earlier part of the verse (*hishmîdh*). Furthermore, with the omission of the entire clause 'saving that...Jacob', the verse is poetically complete.[1] There seems to be no escape from the conclusion that the line, contradicting also, as it does, *vv.* 1–4, must be regarded as a correction or gloss by a later hand; so Nowack, Köhler, and even Sellin who considers that, with this slight exception, the whole passage (*vv.* 8–15) is genuine Amos. Some defenders of the Amos authorship of *vv.* 8–15 have urged that the Prophet had always had a doctrine of a remnant. *Cf.* Driver, *Joel and Amos*, on v. 15, and p. 225 (edn 2). Gressmann, in his first edn of *Die älteste...Propheten*, wrote (on p. 356), "a remnant shall yet remain which shall grow into a real people of God....How could he (Amos) possibly have borne the horror which overcame him during his visions if no ray of hope had brightened the gloom?" But such passages as iii. 12, v. 14, 15 are hardly capable of a really optimistic meaning (see notes).

11. In that day will I raise up the tabernacle of David that is fallen. This prediction concerning David's dynasty probably had its origin in one of two ways. (1) It may be of the nature of a *political* promise. If so, we know of one situation which might have produced it, *viz.* when Zerubbabel was governor, and possibly was hoping to be king (*cf.* Zech. vi. 12). (2) Or, the reference may be of a *general* kind to an ideal (or, rather, idealised) past. Notwithstanding the limitations of David's character, of his judicial system (2 Sam. xv. 3) and of the general civilisation of his age (2 Sam. xiii. 13 *b*), the rule of the son of Jesse seems to have stood in the popular mind throughout Hebrew history for good administration and prosperity. To strengthen David's house (before the Captivity), or, still more, to restore it (after the Captivity), would seem to be to bring back the glorious 'days of old'. Some prophets foretell the advent of a single king of David's line, Isa. ix. 7, xi. 1, Mic. v. 2, and (in general terms) Isa. lv. 3; and *cf.* Josephus, *Jewish War*, VI. v. 4.

After the various prophecies in Am. i–ix. 10 that the land should be in affliction, the prediction in the present verse of the ultimate reign of an ideal dynasty may perhaps be compared with a not altogether dissimilar phenomenon in Egyptian oracles. The conception is natural enough. In the *Prophecy of Neferrohu* of *c.* 2000 B.C. the prophet in a sketch of the immediate future says: "All good things are passed away....I shew thee the land upside down; happened that which never (yet) had happened. Men shall take weapons of warfare; the land lives in uproar,...I shew thee the land upside down...". Then the sage is represented as adding, with neither introduction nor explanatory comment: "There is a king shall come. ...The people of his time shall rejoice; (this) man of noble birth shall make his name for ever and ever....The Asiatics shall fall by his sword, the Libyans shall fall before his flame, and the rebels before his wrath.... And Right shall come into its place, and Iniquity be cast (?) forth. He will

---

[1] In Jer. v. 10 the restrictive clause, 'yet make not a full end', not only coheres with the context, but is essential to the metre (not so Jer. v. 18, which may be an interpolation).

rejoice who shall behold and who shall serve the King".[1] Gressmann, moreover, emphasising the fact that a feature of Egyptian oracles[2] is this combination of threat and promise, expresses the opinion: "We are forced to conclude that it represents an older, more original stage in the evolution" (*J.T.S.* April 1926, p. 248). "Doubtless the stress is laid on the promises whilst the threats ultimately serve only as a contrast.... In the genuine (Egyptian) oracles which usually foretell calamity, the prophet feels the need of applying a salve to the wound which he has inflicted; the promise cannot, it is true, annul the threat, but it may make it bearable, for it developes a hope in a coming happiness. Here the threat is the logical *prius*, which must of necessity be followed by the prómise, in so far as the prophet loves his country".[3] It was his belief in the essential unity of Hebrew and Egyptian prophecy that led Gressmann in 1910 to maintain the Amos authorship of the Epilogue. "On world catastrophe there must necessarily follow world renewal. *Unheil* and *Heil* are as inseparably connected as the two shells of a mussel" (*Alteste...Proph.* edn 1, p. 356). But it is impossible to estimate how much of genuine *prediction* exists in these Egyptian prophecies, though it may be that the general scheme was that out of adversity would issue prosperity under a good king. For the view advocated in this commentary, *cf.* Introd. pp. 52 and 69–71.

12. that they may possess the remnant of Edom. By 'remnant' might be meant 'what remains of Edom' (1) at the time of the statement, or (2) proleptically, at the time of the *fulfilment* of the utterance. This latter is not in itself an unreasonable exegesis; *cf.* the note on 'the remnant of the Philistines' in i. 8 (p. 126). According to the former interpretation, (*a*) if the words are by Amos the reference may be to "the part of Edomite territory which remained independent after the victories of Amaziah and Uzziah" (König); or (*b*) if later than Amos, to the time when Edom and all such states had been ravaged by successive Assyrian invasions. (In any interpretation, the attributive term 'remnant' applies to Edom only and not also (as Ehrlich) to 'all the nations'.) Why is Edom singled out? Not as being typically heathen—at least, no objection to its worship is raised in the O.T.—but because it was, or had been, a particularly troublesome, or hated, neighbour of Israel. See pp. 282, 283. *If* by the time of Amos the history of these two peoples had been such as to warrant his writing i. 11, 12, such a reference here also by him is intelligible enough. On the other hand, it is undeniable that the allusion is more easily to be accounted for if the section be an addition to the book subsequent to the peculiarly evil behaviour of Edom in 586 B.C.[4] and, moreover, at a time after the Assyrian

---

[1] Gardiner's translation of the Pap. Petersburg 1116 B, in *J.E.A.* I. p. 105. See Introd. p. 45.

[2] *Neferrohu* supplies a conspicuous case in point. So also *The Potter* and *The Lamb*, Introd. p. 46.

[3] *Op cit.* p. 244.

[4] Obad. *vv.* 10–14. Perhaps Am. ix. 12 was written when such unkindness was very fresh in the Jews' memory, even before the period of the Return.

conquests when the descendants of Esau must have been more of a 'remnant' than in the age of Amos. There is a reference to a war of subjugation in Isa. lxiii. 1–6, such as Obadiah predicted (Obad. *vv.* 18, 19 *a*). Is it not incredibly difficult to suppose that he who could rise to the thought expressed in Am. ix. 7 was capable of proclaiming also Am. ix. 12?

Edom, and all the nations, which are called by my name. Like him who wrote Ps. ii the writer of Am. ix. 12 is thinking of national conquest; there is no allusion to God claiming certain peoples in any *spiritual* sense. If so, who does the selecting, Jehovah or Israel? It would seem that the present prophecy of national victory belongs not to the outlook of such men as Amos and Micaiah, son of Imlah (1 Ki. xxii. 17), so much as to that of the Jonah of 2 Ki. xiv. 25, or indeed of Micaiah's adversary Zedekiah (1 Ki. xxii. 24).

By the grace of God there were not wanting from time to time in Israel noble spirits who could believe that one day there would be something better than a kingdom of David restored. The great Prophet of the Exile looked to Israel itself to bring all nations under the spiritual sway of God who for this very purpose had blessed them. No enforced acceptance of a foreign religion lies behind the conception of such passages as Isa. li. 5, 'On mine (Jehovah's) arm shall they trust'. The ideal Servant will be 'a light to the Gentiles' (Isa. xlix. 6). The conversion of the Gentiles was the theme of the book of Jonah, and is not overlooked in such passages as Tob. xiii. 11 *a*, Enoch xc. 33. The 'possessing' of the nations by Jesus Christ (through a Christian community in Judaea) was truly part of God's will. The early Church rightly believed that in the name of Jesus (of the seed of David) all nations should be claimed for the kingdom of God.

St James is said to have appealed in a high spiritual sense to the present passage. The quotation as given in Ac. xv. 17 is sufficiently identical with the LXX translation.[1] But in an important particular they both depend on a faulty reading (different from the M.T.), by which reading the grammatical object in the Hebrew became *subject* in the Greek translation,

---

[1] In Ac. xv. 15 the quotation is introduced by 'And to this agree *the words of the prophets*'. Swete considers that the citation is a conflate one, and so it may be, but it is difficult to trace in *any* prophet the introductory phrase 'After these things I will return' (*v.* 16). The vagueness of the phrase, 'the words of the prophets', cannot be due to doubts existing in N.T. times as to ultimate authorship of the particular verses taken from the book of Amos. What are now called "the Twelve Minor Prophets" were massed together by the Jews into one volume, styled in the colophon in the Hebrew Bible "The Book of the Twelve". *Cf.* also Ecclus. xlix. 10, and Jerome's "*Liber* duodecim prophetarum" in the *Prologus Galeatus*, and see his *Preface* on the Twelve Prophets. Stephen, in Ac. vii. 42, cites Am. v. 25–27 as '*the book* of the prophets'. That in ancient times so great a work as that of Amos could be cited without name supplies an illustration of how slightly was the individuality of each several prophet considered. Amos, man and prophet, is a discovery of the 19th cent. A.D. *Cf.* Introd. p. 9.

thus: 'and the remnant of *men* will *seek*',[1] *yidhrᵉshû shᵉʾērîth 'ādhām*, in place of *yᵢrᵉshû shᵉʾērîth 'Edhôm*. Even if St Luke (who presumably was not present at the assembly) was correct in stating that such a quotation was used in the argument, we need not think that the momentous decision reached concerning the admission of the Gentiles into the Jewish Church would have been any other if one of the many far more apposite passages had happened to have been chosen from the O.T.!

13. and all the hills shall melt. In this and the preceding clause there is an improvement upon the more prosaic promises of streams (of water) in the desert given in Isa. xxxv. 6 *b*, 7. The verse appears verbatim in Joel iii. 18 (in Heb. iv. 18), except that it there reads, 'go (*i.e.* flow) with milk' in place of the word 'dissolve-themselves'; this is a better text. Moreover, as with Am. i. 2 (Joel iii. 16, in Heb. iv. 16), it is in Joel rather than in Amos that the passage seems in the more original context. Did the same editor add ix. 11–15 and i. 2?

Gressmann calls attention to the correspondence of this verse with the Hebrew picture of Paradise. "The fruitfulness of the land of God returns.... The gardens are replanted. The people of God live in undisturbed happiness.... But with the longing for this golden age which animates every human heart are connected national hopes" (*Alt. Proph.* edn 1, p. 356). With *vv.* 13, 14 the Assyrian oracle cited in Introd. p. 43 (v) may in a general way be compared; and also the concluding portion of the Egyptian *Prophecy of the Potter*, quoted p. 47, "Thereupon will summer again take its proper course, and well-ordered will the winds be". But all such ideas would seem to be so obvious that there is no need to postulate any *dependence* of the Hebrew prophet upon a foreign source.

It will be gathered that it is reasonable to regard the happy prediction in *vv.* 11–15 (like several others in the O.T. of a similar nature) as having served its true purpose in the general encouragement which it afforded to the Jews of the period. Contrast the exposition of *v.* 13 by Charles Simeon. "It seems highly probable, that, agreeably to the promise given by Moses (Lev. xxvi. 5), there will be; as nearly as possible, a literal accomplishment of these things in Palestine, after the Jews shall have been restored to their own land" (*Horae Homileticae*, x. p. 242). Even if *vv.* 14 and 15 might seem to be 'fulfilled' by the present-day return of members of two or three of the Tribes, what of *vv.* 11–13?

15. thy God. *If* the final clause is by the same hand as *vv.* 14 and 15, it is somewhat difficult to know why the Prophet uses the *singular* number, 'thy'. Throughout these two verses the reference to the people has been in the plural, 'they'. Still more curious is the change to the *second person*. Sellin[2] believes that the entire section, *vv.* 11–15, contains genuine words of

---

[1] To supply an object for 'seek' in Ac. xv. 17 is added 'the Lord', which addition found its way into MS. A of the LXX. (In the older, and purer, MS. B there is no object.) And see Swete, *Introd. to O.T. in Greek*, p. 400.

[2] In *Das Zwölfprophetenbuch*, and also in *Introd. to O.T.* edn 3, 1920.

Amos addressed to *Amaziah*, priest of the Beth-el sanctuary; and that it
has been transposed by a redactor to the end of the book from a position
immediately following vii. 10–17. The passage ix. 11–15 is held to have been
originally a continuation of the *threat* to the priest who had (perhaps)
spoken slightingly of Judah (vii. 12). Amos says in effect: (1) Beth-el shall
fall, thy land of North Israel shall become depopulated (vii. 17); whereas
(2)—unwelcome thought to an Ephraimite—there will date from 'that
day' (ix. 11) the beginning of the restoration of the old glory of the Southern
Kingdom of Judah (ix. 11,12); and (3) eventually Amaziah's own people will
enter upon a happy time *after the judgment* (ix. 13–15). The bitterness of it,
however, is that such bliss is not for Amaziah and the wicked of his generation, who will perish in an unclean land (vii. 17). The happy reference to
'land' in ix. 15 is in contrast with the references in vii. 11 and 17 ('Israel
shall surely be carried captive out of his land', *etc.*). "A more effective
close to Amos' prophecy against Israel in Beth-el could not be imagined".
Sellin claims, moreover, that the metre of the closing verses assists their
association with vii. 10–17.

But there are difficulties in the way of accepting Sellin's daring thesis.
(1) It will be seen that it depends upon the theory, at least doubtful, that
Amos addressed Northern Israel *only*. (2) It takes no account of the fact
(*apparent* fact, at least) that Amos himself proclaimed, not a chastisement,
but doom, and that without any real hope of escape; (3) and, moreover,
doom of *Judah* and not of the Northern Kingdom only (see iii. 1, note).
(4) Nor does it seem to do justice to such classes of objection to the Amos
authorship of the closing verses as are referred to in the Introduction (IV,
V, VI,[1] pp. 72–75). (5) Abrupt as is the change from 'they' in *vv.* 14
and 15 *a* to 'thy', yet it can be paralleled: *e.g.* in *v.* 11, 'thy', after *v.* 10
of ch. iii.[2] Such a transition is extremely common in the exhortations of
Deuteronomy. Still, the conjecture is ingenious, and Sellin makes a definite
point when he provides one instance elsewhere of the expression 'thy God'
being addressed to a wicked man (Ahaz, Isa. vii. 11). The other examples
cited of its use in connection with an *individual* rather than with the nation
are of the prophet Samuel (1 Sam. xv. 21, 30) and king David (addressed by
one who wished him well, 2 Sam. xiv. 11).

---

[1] Connected respectively with the lack of an ethical element, the difficulties
of language, and indeed of historical background.

[2] And, after all, 'thy' occurs in Am. ix. 15 only at the very close, as a suffix
to the word 'God'. The clause, 'saith thy God', is probably nothing more than
a scribal addition—as it not infrequently is in the prophets. *Cf.* Robinson, *Amos*,
p. 47.

EXCURSUSES

EXCURSUS I. DIVINE NAMES IN THE BOOK OF AMOS

I. YHWH (E.VV. 'THE LORD')

(1)

The commonest designation of the Deity, in the book of Amos, is Yhwh.[1]

The origin, the significance, and even the pronunciation of the sacred Name of the God of the Hebrews, are wrapped in obscurity. The name is generally known, from the translation in certain passages of the English Bible, as 'Jehovah';[2] and, inasmuch as the form has the advantage of being familiar, it seems convenient to continue its use.[3] Manifestly, 'Jehovah' is a better equivalent of the Hebrew Tetragrammaton than is the rendering 'the LORD', which usually stands for it throughout the A.V. and the R.V. of the O.T. However, the employment of the expression 'Jehovah' of necessity obscures an exceedingly important point, viz. the variation in theological content and significance which the name underwent during the long progressive revelation of Himself which God was pleased to make through the name Yhwh.[4] In the loftier parts of the O.T., Jehovah is represented as being almost as majestic and lovable as when revealed in His Son, Jesus Christ. And this is, perhaps, the conception brought to the mind of many Christians by the term 'Jehovah'. On the other hand, in the more primitive portions of the O.T., He who is in reality the same God is recognised by His worshippers at the time only as a tribal- or nature-Deity. 'Jehovah' (i.e. 'Yahweh', 'Yaho', or howsoever the Tetragrammaton should be pronounced) is the sacred Name of the God of Israel. In the days when each nation, while it had its own god (or gods), yet believed in the real existence of the deities of other peoples,[5] it was felt to be necessary for every god to possess a personal name. How else could any god know that at any moment he in particular was being invoked or 'called upon'? Moab's deity went by the name of Chemosh; the Phoenicians 'called upon' Melkarth

---

[1] For convenience the sacred Name is sometimes referred to as 'the Tetragrammaton'. When the Name occurs as a separate word in the O.T. it consists of four letters. But see below, p. 330 (*Yāh*).

[2] *E.g.* Exod. vi. 2, 3, Isa. xxvi. 4.

[3] Just as, indeed, we say 'Isaiah', in spite of the fact that the original pronunciation was so different that the Evangelical Prophet would not be able to recognise his name if he heard it so pronounced. The convenience to English readers of the use of the word 'Jehovah' is so obvious that the present writer does not scruple to employ the rendering in this commentary. *Cf.* G. A. Smith, *XII Prophets*, 1896, p. xiii.

[4] In its various forms: see, below, pp. 328, 329, 330, footnote 1.

[5] Thus Mesha of Moab says that Chemosh saved him from his enemy Israel; but also he does not seem to doubt the existence of Israel's God Yhwh, whose sacred vessels he dragged before his own god. Incidentally it is of interest that in this inscription is the first occurrence in literature of the Tetragrammaton. (The translation of this line—l. 18—suggested by Cowley, is hardly likely to obtain support, "and I took from thence what *should be* for myself".)

and Ashtarte. It is possible that the personal name of some gods fell into disuse. For example, the Nabataeans' god was known merely as lord of Shara ('Dushara'); even as in the O.T. there is to be found the expression, 'Baal of Hermon'. Yet in such cases the deity still possessed *some* distinguishing title.[1]

(2)

What is known of the early history of the sacred Name of the God of Israel? It *may* be that the first occurrence of the Name is as that of a Babylonian deity YAU or YAO[2] (though the identification is, to say the least, precarious). If it should be proved that the Hebrews derived their God ultimately from Babylonia, we must suppose that the only God, in revealing Himself to mankind, allowed Himself to be named *Yau*. He might have made Himself known to His world through any of the numerous deities of early times. He refined the ideals of Godhead, and poured into the Name a pure conception of His own Person and attributes. The same sacred Name is, *perhaps*, to be found in the (Canaanite) Taanach letters.[3] It may be pointed out that if the Name occurs outside ancient Israel, in the pages of the O.T. itself Jehovah is described as the God of *Shem*, not of Israel alone (Gen. ix. 26); even in the days of Enosh, the son of Seth, so it is stated in Gen. iv. 26, men began to invoke the Name of YHWH. To quote the words of S. A. Cook, "The general tenour of the O.T. itself suggests that Israel introduced into Palestine, not a new God, Yahweh, but a new stage in the history of His development".[4]

(3)

The etymological meaning of the sacred Name of the God of Israel, like that of the Moabite name Chemosh, probably is lost. In Exod. iii. 14, 15,

---

·[1] 1 Chron. v. 25. W. L. Wardle suggests that 'Yahweh' (or its equivalent) was originally not a name but only an "epithet" (*Israel and Babylon*, p. 251). In this way he would explain the use of the term 'Yahweh' by more than one Semitic people with reference to the particular god worshipped.

[2] *Ya-u-um-ilu*, 'Yau is God', *etc.* The inscriptions belong to the First Dynasty of Babylon. The Assyrian language contains no letter corresponding to the Hebrew *Hē*; so the form *Yau* may well be the equivalent of a Hebrew *Yahu*. The readings of the Babylonian are not certain, for *yaûm* may be a *possessive pronoun*: hence *Ya-u-um-ilu* may signify merely, 'God is mine'. *Cf.* Landsberger, cited by G. R. Driver in *J.T.S.* July 1926, p. 413. For arguments in favour of the identification with 'Yahweh', see Fried. Delitzsch, *Babel and Bible*, pp. 71 ff., Burney, *Judges*, pp. 243–253. Perhaps the deity was originally Amorite (*C.A.H.* I. p. 232); or the name may have been mediated from Babylonia to Israel through the Aramaeans, the Midianites (descendants of Abraham), or the Canaanites.

[3] A man's name occurs, *Akhi-yawi* or *-yami*, a form which would suggest the Hebrew *Ahijah*. The date of this tablet is probably 1500–1300 B.C. The name *Azriya'u* in the inscription (p. 40, footnote 1) may be that of a king of Judah, and not of a king of a North Syrian state. Even if it be the latter, this king may have been of part Israelite stock; *cf.* G. R. Driver in *J.T.S.* July 1926, p. 413.

[4] *Cf.* Exod. vi. 3; *C.A.H.* II. pp. 403, 404.

a tradition is preserved which apparently connected YHWH with the verb *hāyāh*, 'to be', or 'to become'.[1] If, as seems likely, the word had a long history before the date of that passage, it may be that the term was conceived of as taking on a *new* meaning at the Exodus, *viz.* 'He who is', or 'He who will become' (*qal* voice), or 'He who will cause to be' (*causative* voice). On the other hand it seems perfectly possible to read the passage with the hypothesis that *'Ehyeh* ('I will be') itself "may be a kind of 'surrogate' (throwing no more light on the original word than does *Adonai*)".[2]

(4)

As to the pronunciation of the Name, since the days of Ewald it has been customary to represent the four Hebrew consonants as 'Yahweh', on the strength of references in Theodoret (*Iabai*), and in Epiphanius (*Iabe*, with variant reading *Iaue*). The question of the pronunciation has, however, been re-opened, notably by Canon Lukyn Williams.[3] The arguments are too detailed to be reproduced here, but this scholar points out that the sound of the Name 'Yahweh' is in itself unsuitable[4] for the very purpose for which, presumably, divine names were used, *viz.* invocation. In early Babylonian (possibly), in the Elephantine Papyri,[5] and in the Hebrew Bible itself (in compounding of proper names),[6] the sacred Name is spelled without the final letter *hē*. Within the Bible it occurs even as a *bi*-literal, either *Yāh*, or (in composition) *Yō* (*e.g.* in the name Johanan). The pronunciation which Dr Lukyn Williams suggests is YAHO[h].[7] The final *hē* was employed in writing the Name, only in order to represent "the explosion of breath after the loud and prolonged *O*". At least his detailed argument shews that the (generally employed) pronunciation 'Yahweh' rests on not so secure a foundation as it has generally been supposed, and he is probably correct when he says, "YAO or YAHO is

---

[1] In Aramaic *hᵉwā*. This may be the correct etymology, but it was far from uncommon for the Hebrews to found an explanation of a word upon a derivation which was not sound linguistically, *e.g.* 'Babel' (Gen. xi. 9), 'Samuel' (1 Sam. i. 20, 28).

[2] Lukyn Williams, "YAHO[h]", in *J.T.S.* April 1927, p. 277.

[3] *Op. cit.* pp. 276–283.

[4] Adam Welch, *The Psalter*, 1926, p. 6, describes the word Yahweh as "ugly and cacophonous".

[5] *E.g.* 'Yahu the God', 'Yahu the Lord of Heaven', *etc.*, *etc.* (Nos. 22, 30 and *passim*, Cowley's *Jewish Documents*, S.P.C.K.).

[6] *E.g.* in the form 'Yirmᵉyāhû' (Jeremiah), 'Yᵉhônāthān' = 'Yāhô-nāthān' (Jonathan). This short, and also shorter, forms of the Divine Name occur in names found, too, on Palestinian inscriptions from the 8th cent. B.C. onwards: as well as of course in the transcriptions of Israelite names occurring in Assyrian and Babylonian. The name of God is not to be regarded as merely *abbreviated* for the purposes of composition. The title *Yahu* has been found alone on a coin in Gaza (with a representation of a god like Zeus, on a winged wheel). *Cf.* A. B. Cook, *Zeus*, I. p. 232.

[7] Of course, this is setting aside any connection with *hāyāh*.

fundamentally the right pronunciation".[1] In the opinion of the present writer there can be little doubt that the final *hē*, whatever its origin and significance, is a later growth, and that, strictly speaking, the sacred Name is not a "*Tetra*grammaton" at all.

II. The use of the term 'HOSTS' ($S^eB\bar{A}$'$\hat{O}TH$) in connection with the Divine Name

(1)

(i) The word 'host' (in Hebrew *ṣābhā'*, plural *ṣ^ebā'ôth*) is commonly applied to an army of *men*, notably in the phrase 'captain of the host'; (ii) it is also used, in the *singular* number, of a company of *angels*, e.g. in 1 Ki. xxii. 19, and, much later, in the *plural*[2] (but masculine, *ṣ^ebā'îm*) in Pss. ciii. 20, 21, cxlviii. 2; and (iii) of the army (*singular*) of the *heavenly* bodies, in Deut. iv. 19, 2 Ki. xvii. 16, Isa. xl. 26, *etc.* It is impossible, in the present state of our knowledge, to define the sense in which the term was first associated with Jehovah's name.

Not sufficient is known of early Semitic mythological ideas to be sure that the solution of the problem does not lie in remote mythology. Wellhausen thought that the original reference was to 'armies of demons'. Such a passage as Josh. v. 13–15 may suggest that there existed a belief in a heavenly army, presumably either *angelic*[3] (Gen. xxxii. 2, 2 Ki. vi. 17) or *astral*[4] (Judg. v. 20, Jer. xxxi. 35). That there should be war-hosts in

---

[1] *Cf.* also F. C. Burkitt, in *J.T.S.* July 1927, on Jer. xxii. 18, *hôdhôh*. Mr G. R. Driver has developed a thesis that the primitive pronunciation was *Yâ*, but that at the time of the Exodus the Divine Name underwent alteration "from the now meaningless *Yâ* to the, whatever its precise meaning, significant *Yahweh*". This latter form, believed to be of Divine origin, "came to be accounted so sacred that presently it might not lightly be taken upon the lips nor be set in writing, except in the Scriptures. In this spirit...the old form *Yā—Yā(w)* or *Yā(h)*—was employed both in proper names...and in every kind of profane writing" ("Evidence for the Name 'Yahweh' outside the O.T." in *Old Test. Essays*, 1927, pp. 21, 23, 24: and *cf.* (more fully) *Z.A.W.* April 1928, esp. pp. 20–25). For further information upon general questions connected with the sacred Tetragrammaton, see *E.B.* III. cols. 3320–23; Luckenbill, *A.J.S.L.* XL. pp. 277–283; van Hoonacker, *Schweich Lectures*, pp. 67–73.

[2] *Cf.* also, in the N.T., St Lu. ii. 13.

[3] So Driver in *H.D.B.* III. p. 138 *b*. Does Isa. vi. 2, 3 supply a comparatively early instance of the title 'Jehovah of hosts' containing a direct allusion to heavenly beings?

[4] This view has not commanded much support beyond that of Kuenen and Cheyne. Smend was of opinion that the title has reference to the elements and forces of nature, and that it originated perhaps with Amos himself (*A.T.-liche Religiongeschichte*, pp. 185–188; edn 2, pp. 202 ff.).

An interesting but not convincing conjecture is made by Gressmann (*Eschatologie*, p. 76) that Jehovah was not essentially a tribal war-God: that the epithet 'God of *hosts*' was taken over from some other deity, and assigned to Him.

heaven did not seem impossible even to the Christian Apocalyptist (Rev. xii. 7). After all, it is no petty idea that Jehovah, no less than an earthly king, should be conceived of as possessing His armies.

(2)

Although the matter is very uncertain, it seems safer to suppose that the earliest use in Israel of the expression was in relation to the *human* armies of Jehovah. As a fact, by itself the *plural* word *ṣᵉbā'ôth* is used down to the late Ps. xliv. 9 exclusively for the war-hosts of Israel. The phrase, 'Jehovah, God of hosts', appears for the first time in the O.T. in the period of the Philistine and other wars (2 Sam. v. 10); perhaps especially in connection with the sacred ark.[1] The words of 1 Sam. xvii. 45 may be taken as typical, and significant of this tribal-military sense. 'In the name of Jehovah of hosts, the God of the armies (Heb. 'ranks') of Israel'. But with the growth of the higher and wider conception of Jehovah, the expression took on a new connotation; and in this fuller meaning it became a favourite title for God, in the mouths of the Great Prophets. "It remains... the most plausible supposition that now the hosts of angels and perhaps also (at least in later times) of stars came involuntarily to be substituted for the earthly hosts, so that, finally, the idea of Ruler of the Universe connected itself *per se* with the title".[2]

(3)

In the five (or four) occurrences of the phrase in the genuine utterances of Amos it has clearly lost any primitive signification of 'God on behalf of Israel's armies'—Am. iii. 13, v. 16, vi. 8, and especially vi. 14 and [v. 27].[3] Even more in the "doxologies" (Am. iv. 13, ix. 5) something sublime is meant. No longer in Canaan nor even upon the earth are Jehovah's 'hosts'. In the passage v. 14, 15, 'the God of hosts shall be with you *as ye say*', the older popular meaning is not impossible. It is to be observed that, except in ix. 5 and in ix. 6, LXX, the book of Amos everywhere employs that form of the expression which must be the earlier one, *viz.* 'Jehovah *God* of hosts'; rather than the popular (?) abbreviation 'Jehovah of hosts', so common in Isaiah, in Jeremiah, and in the post-exilic prophets. As to the

---

Jehovah was a war-God only in so far as He was a *nature-God*. He fought for Israel with storm, hail, tempest, earthquake, fire, pestilence. Natural phenomena were His 'hosts' and his 'weapons'.

[1] 1 Sam. i. 3, 11, iv. 4, 2 Sam. vi. 2. *Cf.* Kautzsch in *H.D.B.* v. p. 637 *a*.

[2] Kautzsch, *ibid.* p. 637 *b*. So, before him, Herder. G. A. Smith (p. 57) accepts it. It has been said above, however, that it must not be ruled out of consideration that the reference *from the first* was to the angelic beings (*cf.* Isa. vi. 2, 3) or even to the heavenly bodies: but even so, it would perhaps be only as Jehovah's means of assisting His people.

[3] And this though it is to be noted that Amos (iii. 13, vi. 14) and the writer of ix. 5 use a form of the expression with the *definite article*, 'God of *the* hosts'. This occurs elsewhere only in Hos. xii. 5, and must be a usage earlier than that without the article.

"doxologies" of the book of Amos, it is to be noted that with one exception (ix. 5) there is no difference in the form of the expression in these, from that used by the Prophet himself. 'Jehovah God of hosts' occurs in iv. 13; so also in iii. 13, v. 16, vi. 14. 'Jehovah of the hosts' comes in ix. 5, and also in iij. 13, vi. 14. For the phrase 'Jehovah of hosts is his name', see on v. 8.[1]

(4)

The usage after Amos varies. In Jeremiah the expression seems to lack some of the force which it had in the earlier prophets. Ezekiel never uses the title. In Haggai and Zechariah, on the other hand, it occurs frequently; but it has lost its old power, and is sometimes hardly more than a tedious repetition of a mere phrase. It occurs no less than twenty-eight times in Zech. i–viii.

(5)

(1) The Septuagint sometimes renders (especially in the Psalms) by Κύριος τῶν δυνάμεων ('Lord of powers', or 'armies') with the vagueness of the original.[2] (2) Often, however, as in Amos and in the Minor Prophets generally, it represents it by παντοκράτωρ, 'All-ruling'—an excellent paraphrase of the prophetic conception. Hence it passes into the book of the Revelation and finally into the Greek Creeds as a description of the Christian's God. The Latin translation, *Omnipotens*, is unfortunate.[3] Frequently the LXX simply transliterates σαβαώθ. In this latter form the title is to be found in the N.T. in St James v. 4 and in the quotation in Rom. ix. 29 (= Isa. i. 9, LXX). The transliteration has been used by Christians in the *Te Deum* and in the Roman *Missal*.

(6)

Christian Gnostics used *Sabaoth* as a Divine Name. The Jews, on the other hand, to whom the Hebrew presented no charm arising from mystery, have not as a rule used it in their liturgy. In one passage, however, of the

---

[1] G. A. Smith, *XII Prophets*, pp. 204–206, has a useful note in this connection, on the distribution in the book of Amos of the various titles for God.

[2] *E.g.* in Ps. xlvi. 11 (Heb. 12). Is the use like that of δύναμις in Herodotus and Xenophon in the sense of army of men or of angels? Or, is the reference to the hosts of stars, *cf.* 2 Ki. xvii. 16? In St Matt. xxiv. 29, *etc.* ('*the powers* of the heavens shall be shaken') δύναμις is employed of the heavenly bodies.

[3] The true meaning of παντοκράτωρ may be illustrated from the use of the kindred title αὐτοκράτωρ by Polybius with reference to the Roman dictator, and by Plutarch with reference to the Emperor. It would appear to be a disadvantage that, through the faulty translation of παντοκράτωρ into Latin, which confused the meaning with the supposed sense of the Hebrew *Shaddai*, it should have become so widely spread in Western prayers, and not least in the English Prayer Book, in the word 'Almighty'. The attribute 'almighty' has its own difficulties philosophically. Even the Greek παντοκράτωρ occurs in the N.T. only in the Apocalypse (eight ti s), and in 2 Cor. vi. 18 (in the closing phrase of a—mixed—quotation from   writings).

Jewish Prayer Book,[1] the 'hosts' seem definitely to be conceived of as angelic beings. "Holy, holy, holy, is the LORD of hosts: the whole earth is full of his glory. And the Ophanim[2] and the holy Chayyoth with a noise of great rushing, upraising themselves towards the Seraphim, thus over against them offer praise and say: Blessed be the glory of the LORD from this place".[3]

III. 'ĂDÔNAI

'Ădônai is a title for God which is used in the book of Amos with considerable frequency. It sometimes retains its original meaning of 'my Lord', e.g. in iii. 7, 8, vii. 2. The LXX renders Κύριος, exactly as it represents the Hebrew Yahweh. In the E.VV. it is 'Lord'. The expression is well suited to Amos' conception of his God as (a) Lord or Master of nations (e.g. i. 8, ix. 1)[4] and not of Israel only, and (b) the Ruler over nature (e.g. viii. 9, 11).

(1) There are three occurrences of the title standing alone, viz. in vii. 7, 8, ix. 1.[5] (2) Frequently the word 'Ădônai is prefixed to the sacred Name Yahweh: LXX κύριος Κύριος; E.VV. following the usage of the Targum, 'the Lord GOD'. There are altogether twenty such passages in the M.T. of the book of Amos. In at least seven of these, however, viz. i. 8, iv. 2, vi. 8, vii. 4 a, b, 5, 6 the Hebrew text used by LXX contained only one Divine Name, either 'Ădônai, or, most likely, Yahweh; 'Ădônai being added into the text as a gloss upon the Tetragrammaton.[6] The combination 'Ădônai Yahweh becomes frequent in later prophetic writings, more especially in Jeremiah, II Isaiah, and (particularly) in Ezekiel.

IV. 'ĔLÔHÎM

A fourth title for the Deity occurring in the book of Amos is 'Ĕlôhîm ('God'). It is found alone in iv. 11, and in the form 'thy God' in iv. 12, ix. 15 only. For the expression 'Ĕlôhē ṣᵉbhā'ôth, see above.

---

[1] Morning Service, p. 131, edn Singer.
[2] These are 'the wheels' of Ezek. i. 16, etc., spiritualised into heavenly beings. The Chayyoth are the 'living creatures' of Ezek. i. 5 (R.V.). The word 'hosts' does not occur in the book of Ezekiel at all.
[3] Cf. also p. 129: "All the host (Hebrew singular) on high render praise unto Him, the Seraphim, etc."
[4] Cf. Josh. iii. 11, 13 ('Ādhôn).
[5] In the M.T. of v. 16, 'Ădônai makes an impressive addition to a description of God, but the word is absent from the LXX.
[6] The two names stand together in both M.T. and LXX in the following passages: iii. 7, 8, 11, iv. 5, v. 3, vii. 1 (MS. B), viii. 1 and 3 (MS. B), 9, ix. 5, 8. And see note on vii. 1.

EXCURSUS II. JEHOVAH'S RELATION TO ISRAEL

I. A CRITICAL INTERPRETATION OF AMOS III. 2

('You only have I known of all the families of the earth')

This passage may be of the nature of an *argumentum ad hominem*. Even if it is not, however, it is important to consider it in connection with the belief of the people rather than with the Prophet's conceptions, which far transcended that belief. It is difficult for us to know for certain what were the ideas concerning their God held by Amos' contemporaries; but even if there were any among the Prophet's hearers who shared his lofty view of Jehovah as the Disposer of nations (chs. i and ii, ix. 7), yet it can be affirmed with some assurance that, to the bulk of Amos' audience, Jehovah was much less. It would seem that what they believed was that He and the nation were linked together by what was, as they supposed, an indissoluble bond. It was simple fact that Jehovah had had personal relations with Israel and Israel only.[1] It was the Israelites who were Jehovah's 'valued property'.[2] Similarly, Chemosh 'knew' Moab and only Moab. This, so it appears, would be the outlook of those who heard the Prophet. Amos, in iii. 2, is not clearly referring to any Divine 'covenant' (*i.e.* a conditional relationship upon a moral basis) though in some *elementary* form such an idea may have been as ancient as the time of Moses;[3] Exod. xxxiv. 27 ('J'), xxiv. 6–8 ('E'). Amos does not necessarily imply any such religious concept. Unquestionably the 'covenant' theory in any really developed shape dated from the Deuteronomic literature onwards; when, moreover, it did contain the conception of Jehovah having 'chosen' a nation (Deut. iv. 37, vii. 6, 7, x. 15, xiv. 2, 1 Ki. viii. 53). But that was after the age of Amos. It would appear that in iii. 2 Amos builds merely upon the simple Semitic principle that Jehovah and His people are one;[4] and then proceeds to draw from it a conclusion which the prophet of no other Semitic people would have conceived concerning his own nation. By those outside Israel, by the average man within Israel, the conclusion to be expected would be 'therefore will I always do you material good'. Instead of this, Amos says in effect: "Jehovah is *a priori* a righteous God. Because you have neglected to gain any spiritual blessing from the relationship of being His people, therefore you must suffer (and not be blessed) at His hands".

It is usually held that the phrase, 'You only have I known of all the families of the earth' (whether or not actually translated, 'You only have

---

[1] With one possible exception contemporary with Amos, suggested by the occurrence of the name 'AzarIAH' in the Hamath inscription of *c.* 738 B.C.

[2] Hebrew *S^egullāh*. The translation 'peculiar people' in Exod. xix. 5, *etc.* is misleading.

[3] *Cf.* Skinner, *Proph. and Rel.* pp. 322, 323, 326.

[4] And *cf.* vii. 8, 'my people Israel'. See the Introduction, § VI, pp. 23, 29 *ad init.* Not selection, but oneness of purpose and interest is implied in such expressions as 'So let all *thine* enemies perish, O Jehovah' (Judg. v. 31). *Cf.* also 2 Sam. v. 20, 24.

I *chosen*') implies a selection. And the authorities supporting this view are weighty. Thus, *e.g.*, Prof. Peake (in *People and Book*, p. 267) paraphrases, "Free to choose any people, He had chosen Israel". Of course it would be quite in accordance with the Prophet's personal belief in the all but universal sway of Jehovah (*cf.* chs. i and ii) if he had represented his God as "dividing the world and appointing to each people its seat, selecting Israel as His own property.... He who has the right to choose has also the right to reject".[1] But (*a*) is there not a difficulty in harmonising this with Amos' general spirit and outlook, and especially with his emphatically expressed opinion that Israel had never meant any more to Jehovah than had the Kushites, Philistines, and Aramaeans (ch. ix. 7)? Sellin endeavours to surmount this difficulty by translating *v.* 2 a as a rhetorical question expecting the answer "No". Or it might be said that no prophet should be deemed incapable of the error of inconsistency. (*b*) There is still to be taken into account the fact (alluded to above) of the limitations of the popular notions concerning the Deity. Undoubtedly the words 'You only have I known, *etc.*' (be they an echo of some common saying, 'Us only has Jehovah known', or the Prophet's own composition) involve a belief in a certain greatness in Jehovah, but do they necessarily contain the idea of *selection*? It would seem reasonable that the message of Amos to his countrymen should be interpreted by us in the light of our knowledge of their limited beliefs: and particularly is this the case if *v.* 2 is actually an *argumentum ad hominem*. Jehovah and Israel were together. The people may have thought that it was they who chose Jehovah.[2] There is no evidence that they conceived of their God as possessing rights generally over nations other than Israel itself, a conception which is necessary to the idea of the Divine choice; it was the prophets, and not the people, who claimed that Jehovah was the God above all the earth. One of the changes in theological belief brought about by the Babylonian captivity was that the people themselves learned that their God was the only God in the world; and so those beliefs which had belonged to the theory of a tribal Deity came to be readjusted. Only gradually arose the explanation of how the nation had, from the first, believed in Jehovah and been blessed by Him, *viz.* that He had *chosen* 'it from among all peoples.

One thing at least may be said. If it is doubtful whether Amos' words to the people implied or admitted the principle that his God—to their own good—had chosen Israel: it is certain that he does not rise to the lofty doctrine of Israel's selection *for service and witness to mankind*. Thus, Harper (in his commentary on this verse) would seem to be going further than the evidence permits when he says: "The doctrine that Israel has been chosen by Yahweh for a service to the world lies at the basis of every expression of Hebrew thought". The idea of selection for service is not found in pre-exilic prophecy. The passage Isa. ii. 2–4 (= Mic. iv. 1–3) expresses quite a different thought. See the section following, p. 336 (B).

---

[1] Gressmann, *ad loc.*, and *cf.* Kautzsch in *H.D.B.* v. p. 684 *b*.
[2] *Cf.* Judg. v. 8, Josh. xxiv. 15.

II. Israel as God's Chosen People, in post-exilic Judaism and later

Whensoever the theory took shape that the God of the world chose Israel from among all nations, without doubt it was destined to become deeply rooted in the religious consciousness of the Hebrew people, being tenaciously held until the present day. Ethical problems of considerable interest to Christians are involved.

There were two different developments of this doctrine. (A) The belief usually took the form of God's having chosen Israel for the benefit of their own (a) material happiness, (b) religious life, and (c) ultimate salvation. This view rests on the hypothesis of Divine *favour*, pure and simple. (B) A few great minds conceived the idea of Jehovah's having chosen Israel as witnesses, or servants, to the nations of the world. It *is* hardly a question of Divine favour at all. The principles underlying this view are (a) privilege, (b) opportunity, (c) responsibility. This is a theological conception of which the Amos who uttered ix. 7 would not have been ashamed.

(A) The former, or more selfish, aspect of choice is reflected within the O.T. canon in such passages as Isa. lxi. 5, Ps. cxlix. 6 b–9. It may be illustrated further from Jewish literature.

(1) The Targum of Am. iii. 2 renders, 'You only *have I taken pleasure in*'.

(2) The ancient Morning Benediction reads,[1] "Blessed art Thou, O Lord our God, King of the universe, who hast not made me a heathen" (Hebrew *nokhri, lit.* "stranger") or, in the earlier form, "a Gentile" (Hebrew *gôi*).

(3) In *The Sayings of the Fathers*[2] R. Akiba, quoting Deut. xiv. 1, claims, "Beloved are Israel that they are called *children of God*.... Beloved are Israel that there was given to them the instrument with which the world was created" (*viz.* the Law).

(4) The ancient *Amidah* in the Jewish service for the New Year contains these words:[3] "Thou hast chosen us from all peoples, thou hast loved us and taken pleasure in us, and *hast exalted us above all tongues*; thou hast sanctified us by thy commandments and brought us near unto thy service, our King, and called us by thy great and holy name".

(B) The theory that Jehovah's choice of Israel provided an opportunity of service to the world, occurs frequently in II Isaiah, *e.g.* in xli. 8, xlii. 19, xliii. 10, *etc.* It is also the ruling thought in the mind of the writer of the book of Jonah. Though Judaism has not always[4] been influenced by this conception, nor, confessedly, has it sought (in Christian days) to realise its vocation as a missionary church to pagans, yet there are not wanting in Jewish literature noble expressions, both of a belief in God's

---

[1] Singer, *Prayer Book*, p. 5.
[2] III. 22, 23, edn Taylor; in Singer, p. 193, par. 18. *Akiba* was born c. A.D. 50.
[3] Singer, p. 240.
[4] For missionary activity, *cf. e.g.* St Matt. xxiii. 15 a.

will for the salvation of men who are not of the Jewish race, and of a desire that all nations of the world shall worship and serve Him.

(1) The Jonah allegory of the turning to God of heathen Nineveh is publicly read every year on the Jewish *Day of Atonement*.[1]

(2) Judaism has declared that "the righteous of all nations will share in the world to come".[2] Indeed, it is admitted that neither the privilege of being God's chosen people, nor even the worshipping of Jehovah, is ultimately to be a condition of salvation. Only obedience to the seven primitive laws of morality is necessary. For the germ of this doctrine, see *e.g.* Joshua b. Hananiah (cents. i–ii A.D.) in T.B. *Sanhedrin* 105 *a*; which principle was developed by Maimonides (cent. xii), *cf. Yadh* Melakhim, viii. 11.

(3) That the Jews have not desired to keep the true God to their own nation is shewn in the opening words of the *Amidah* for the New Year: "Now, therefore, O Lord our God, impose thine awe upon all thy works, and thy dread upon all that thou hast created, that all works (*sic*) may fear thee and all creatures prostrate themselves before thee, that they may all form a single band to do thy will with a perfect heart, even as we know, O Lord our God,...that thy name is to be feared above all...created".[3]

(4) The same broad outlook is exhibited in the *Alenu* prayer which is probably of pre-Christian date.[4] "We therefore hope in thee, O Lord our God, that we may speedily behold the glory of thy might, when thou wilt remove the abominations from the earth, and the idols will be utterly cut off, when the world will be perfected under the kingdom of the Almighty, and *all the children of flesh will call upon thy name*, when thou wilt turn unto thyself all the wicked of the earth. Let *all the inhabitants of the world* perceive and know that unto thee every knee must bow, every tongue must swear...let them all accept the yoke of thy kingdom, and do thou reign over them speedily, and for ever and ever. For the kingdom is thine...".

(5) Even more catholic in spirit is the following prayer[5] used by certain modern Jews: "Thou whose infinite power and wisdom are reflected in the infinite varieties of Thy creation, we see Thy handiwork also in the differences that prevail in the minds of men. We pray to Thee for *all men, Thy children, our brethren*. Take them all under the sheltering wings of Thy love. And may we, recognising that divergencies of thought and belief are of Thine implanting, strive the more zealously to be one in charity and forbearance, one in the desire to know and do Thy will".

No nation has been more convinced of Divine election than has Israel. And it has been a principle taken for granted by the Christian Church until the rise of Deistic thought in the eighteenth century. It has profoundly

---

[1] And *cf.* Abrahams, *Pharisaism, etc.* I. p. 149.   [2] Tosephta, *Sabbath*, xiii.
[3] Singer, p. 239. The concluding paragraph of the same *Amidah* is quoted above in A (4), p. 336. But see also Singer, p. 241, "Our God...reign thou... over the whole universe", *etc.*
[4] *Ibid.* pp. 76, 77.
[5] Extracted from the prayer-book of *The Jewish Religious Union* (Prayer, No. 20, by S. Singer).

influenced Christian theology in many ways, not least in providing the supposed foundation in Holy Scripture for the doctrine of the election, or predestination to salvation, of certain individuals. For if there was in ancient times a chosen *people*, there seemed to Predestinarians no moral difficulty in the idea of a sovereign Deity having a congregation of chosen *individuals* in the Christian Dispensation. The truth appears to be that the theory of God's choosing of Israel, in the sense of His singling them out for their own good, being an un-ethical one can have had no basis in *fact*. Christians can, however, admit that God's relations with Israel were unique through the line of prophets, culminating in the human birth of the Divine Saviour from the Israelite race. But this belongs to the idea, not of favour or choice, but of responsibility and service. Not Am. iii. 2 but Am. ix. 8 is in the line which leads to the true Christian conception.

EXCURSUS III. ANIMAL SACRIFICE (1)

I. WHAT DOES AMOS V. 25 IMPLY AS REGARDS THE USE OF SACRIFICE IN THE MOSAIC AGE?

('Did ye bring unto me sacrifices and offerings in the wilderness forty years, O house of Israel?')

Only two interpretations of this famous verse seem possible. (1) One hypothesis is that Amos believed, and appealed confidently to his hearers to support his belief, that the early religion of Israel was of an entirely non-sacrificial type (see also p. 295 (4)). This explanation of Am. v. 25 is strongly supported by the words of a later prophet concerning sacrifice. In connection with such offerings, even at the Jerusalem Temple, Jeremiah[1] states in the name of Jehovah, 'I spake not unto your fathers, nor commanded them in the day that I brought them out of the land of Egypt, concerning burnt offerings or sacrifices' (Jer. vii. 22). It may be that, as Prof. Kennett suggests, Jeremiah is engaging in a polemic against those

---

[1] Of all the prophets, Jeremiah is the most unambiguous upon this question; but the utterances of others should be compared: (1) Isa. i. 11–14, especially *v.* 12, 'When ye come to appear before me, *who hath required this* at your hand, to trample my courts?' (2) Mic. vi. 4–8 almost implies that sacrifice has nothing to do with what Jehovah 'required', when He 'redeemed' Israel 'out of the house of bondage'; *cf.* especially *vv.* 6 *b*, 7 *b*, 8, 'Shall I come before him with burnt offerings, with calves of a year old?...shall I give my firstborn for my transgression...? What doth the LORD *require* of thee, but to do justly...?' In any case, in the words of Kennett, "No one can fail to notice that in this passage the prophet includes in one category, and in one condemnation, both those sacrifices which in the Pentateuch in its final form are prescribed as essential, and those which are absolutely prohibited" (*Sacrifice*, p. 28, footnote 1).

It is taken for granted that Jer. vii. 21–26 represents a genuine Jeremian doctrine, and is not (as xvii. 26, xxxiii. 18, where the opposite view is suggested) a post-exilic passage.

who at the time were promoting a document[1] which claimed that in the wilderness Jehovah *had* recognised sacrifice (Exod. xxxiv. 19–26). Whatever be the particular circumstances of Jeremiah's utterance, in any case, as Skinner says (*Prophecy and Rel.* p. 182), "The whole system (of sacrifice), and all laws prescribing or regulating it are declared (by Jeremiah) to be outside the revelation on which the national religion of Israel was based". In view of the widespread use of sacrifice in pre-Mosaic times and after, the simplest explanation of Jer. vii. 22 is that the prophet, if he means that there was no early law at all on the subject, is quite mistaken or, at least, that he is exaggerating.[2] Still, many scholars take it as a fact that sacrifice had no place in the Mosaic teaching. If this be indeed so, the passage under consideration, Am. v. 25, is not to be regarded as representing "original" doctrine, so much as the preserving, or recovering, of the true Mosaic tradition.

(2) Is there another possibility? While a century and a half later Jeremiah's outlook certainly was that Jehovah had not commanded sacrifice, the words of *Amos* (whatever may have been the history of the use of animal sacrifice in Israel) fall short of the implication of those of Jeremiah. For it would seem that the position of Amos is not clearly and unmistakably that the Hebrews once had a form of worship in which sacrifice was not an element. The principle or moral, of course, amounts to the same as under interpretation (1), *viz.* that animal sacrifice, or indeed any offering, was not essential to religion. The Divine presence and favour were independent of them. What Amos said, however, was the bare statement that, as a matter of fact and history, during *the forty years in the wilderness* the *people* did not offer sacrifice.[3] It may not have come into his mind to question (*a*) whether *Jehovah* had ordained (or regulated) the institution from the mount of Sinai, as the codes 'E' and 'J' had claimed; or (*b*) whether the great leader Moses (or a priest) had, especially at the same holy spot, offered sacrifice. The fact was that in the wilderness wanderings the Israelites had little *opportunity*.[4] Indeed, in a sense, they were not clean

---

[1] Kennett suggests the document 'J', which, in his opinion, was quite recent, and not as old as according to Wellhausen's theory (Kennett, *Deuteronomy and the Decalogue*, pp. 19, 55, 56). The point of the statement in Jer. vii. 22 is *a fortiori*. If sacrifice was not commanded 'in the day that Jehovah brought' Israel out of Egypt, it *never* can have been enjoined.
Deut. v. 6–21 is a Decalogue of *moral* laws, containing no mention of sacrifice; and the Deuteronomist closes the passage with, 'and he added no more' (*v.* 22). Kennett, *op. cit.* p. 70.

[2] If the significance of his utterance is that God never wished for sacrifice he may have been right; *cf.* what is said below, p. 340.

[3] This interpretation of Am. v. 25 seems to be more in keeping with the Prophet's *casual* reference to the subject in the context. At least it would be strange if the words 'Did ye offer unto me' introduced a teaching entirely new and revolutionary.

[4] The writer of Exod. xiii. 11–16 admits that at least the sacrifice of the first-born was not observed in the wilderness.

ritually.[1] Moreover, the law received at Sinai concerning sacrifice (like many others) had to wait for its observance until the people arrived in the land which possessed holy sites, *e.g.* Gilgal, Beth-el, Shechem. With the exception of mount Sinai and perhaps Kadesh-Barnea, the wilderness was not Jehovah's soil, any more than was that of Damascus (2 Ki. v. 17). So it came about that Amos said, 'ye did not offer sacrifices in the wilderness'.

If interpretation (1) or even (2) be correct, Am. v. 25 has a bearing upon the literary history of the Pentateuch. Had the "Five Books of Moses" been in existence complete with the "Priestly Code" when Amos said these words, his hearers within the priesthood could, by pointing to such a passage as Numb. vii,[2] have discredited any claim of his to be one of the true succession of prophets and teachers sent by Jehovah. It is, indeed, remarkable that Amos and Jeremiah claim to have had knowledge of an early non-use of sacrifice, in face of the facts that (*a*) all Semitic nations offered it, and (*b*) in Israel itself for centuries before the time of Amos, it seems to have provided the normal[3] method of approach to God, as the history of the sacrifices of Samuel and Elijah is sufficient to shew. Amos' allusion to Israel's religious experience in the wilderness proved that sacrifice was not *necessary*. Jeremiah's shewed that, whatever law might or might not have existed from the Sinai period onwards, sacrifice was not *God's command.*

II. Ultimate Problems connected with Sacrifice as an Institution

To the greater question, whether animal sacrifice was ever God's will, or not, it is difficult to attempt an answer. (1) On the one hand, modern humanitarian instinct alone would make us shrink from associating the Deity, whom Christians worship, with the sanctioning of the cruelty necessarily[4] accompanying all animal sacrifice; though it is true that a great deal of 'sacrifice' amounted to hardly more than the consecrating of an ordinary (but comparatively rarely indulged in) meat meal (*cf.* 1 Sam. xvi. 5, 11 *b*). The present writer would hesitate to believe that God in any sense really wished for, still less commanded, ritual slaughtering. It was a very widely spread ancient rite; and, at most, He allowed it. Sacrifice, so far as it partook of a piacular[5] aspect, may have proved in

---

[1] Not being circumcised, as is shewn by Josh. v. 2–12. *Cf.* Prof. F. C. Burkitt in *J.T.S.* xxii. pp. 64, 65. There is no evidence that Moses fulfilled his suggestion to Pharaoh (Exod. v. 3) to sacrifice after three days.

[2] Esp. *vv.* 10, 13–17.

[3] This is not to ignore the possibility of the existence within ancient Israel of *groups* (like the Rechabites) who worshipped Jehovah without sacrifice. *Cf.* p. 342.

[4] Though the slaughter of a beast was more in accordance with the Divine mind than the sacrifice of a human being. Contrast Exod. xxxiv. 19, 20 ('J') with xxii. 29 ('E'). *Cf.* Gen. xxii. 13, 14.

[5] This is almost entirely post-exilic; *cf.* on iv. 4, p. 170.

some way to be a preparation for Christian doctrine, as a recognition of the sovereignty of the moral law of justice.[1] It is another question whether the sacrifices of the O.T. had a *typical* significance. They may have had; but in this connection it is strange that there is no hint of the existence of any typology within the O.T. itself.[2]

(2) On the other hand, it would not be right to assert as a principle that there was no underlying truth, albeit crudely expressed, in the primitive practice of animal sacrifice. Amos may seem (in v. 5, 14) to equate religion with ethics: but really to have done so would have been tantamount to a denial by him of the theory of *religion*. For, before ever man was, God is; and Amos, as much as we, must have realised the fact that a right behaviour towards one's fellow man cannot in itself take the place of such duties towards *God*, as reverence, communion and public worship.[3] These latter were supposed to be inherent (indeed very imperfectly) in even the primitive use of sacrifice. Amos and Jeremiah both stated that religion could go on without ritual slaughterings; but, not impossibly, it was only the truly pagan situation in which they found their contemporaries that caused them to say such a thing. It is not certain that they would have expressed themselves in the same way had they been living some centuries later, when the Jews were practising a religion which embodied a very considerable ritual, in which sacrifices fostered a due consciousness of guilt; and when, at the same time, they were living (at least as compared with the heathen world) a moral life.[4] Still less, one may presume, would the great prophets (were

---

[1] Perhaps *cf.* W. R. Smith, *Semites*[3], p. 424. The main position taken above receives some support from so conservative a scholar as Westcott. *Cf. Hebrews*, p. 283: "There is no reason to think that Sacrifice was instituted in obedience to a direct revelation....In due time the popular practice of Sacrifice was regulated by revelation as disciplinary, and also used as a vehicle for typical teaching".

And in general it may be said that the great prophets, howsoever interpreted, were closer to God's truth than were the priests. The words of Hosea (vi. 6), 'I desire mercy, and not sacrifice', were quoted by our Saviour (St Matt. ix. 13, xii. 7). Moreover, our Lord blamed His contemporaries in respect of formalism based on legal religion (St Mk vii. 6–23, St Matt. xxiii. 16–31). It is not recorded that He ever was present at a sacrifice in the Temple; and of the sacred building He said, quoting Isa. lvi. 7, 'My house shall be called a house of *prayer*'. See also Excursus IV. pp. 344, 345.

[2] *Cf.* "The Place of Sacrifice in the Church of Israel", by R. H. Kennett, *Interpreter*, July 1920, p. 261. It seems to the present writer that facts stated above in regard to O.T. sacrifice do not affect adversely belief in the objective redemptive work wrought by Christ. Reference may be permitted to the writer's essay, "The Contribution of the Prophets of Israel", in the symposium volume edited by L. W. Grensted, *The Atonement in History and Life* (S.P.C.K.).

[3] Not to mention the corresponding grace which comes from the due performance of such.

[4] Moreover, as regards pre-exilic "placatory" sacrifices, and the post-exilic "piacular" ones, though with the average Israelite these may have been directed towards Jehovah as a supposedly irritated or angry Deity, yet who can say that down the centuries there was not in many hearts something of a true

they alive now) feel that they saw the fulfilment of their teaching in the opposite tendency (of the present day) towards the neglect of public worship and of the Rite which, like primitive sacrifice, expresses and promotes a common fellowship with God.

EXCURSUS IV. ANIMAL SACRIFICE (2)

BELIEFS OUTSIDE THE WRITINGS OF THE PROPHETS (AND THE LITERATURE RELATED THERETO), WHICH HAVE A BEARING UPON THE ATTITUDE OF THE PROPHETS TO THIS QUESTION

A. HEBREW
B. EARLY RABBINIC
C. CHRISTIAN
D. LATIN, GREEK, EGYPTIAN, INDIAN

Views on sacrifice held by Prophets and Psalmists in orthodox Israel are referred to in the Excursus preceding and in the extended note on Am. iv. 4 (pp. 295, 296). The following references represent ideas and opinions concerning sacrifice held by (a) sections of the ancient Israelite nation, (b) Rabbinical teachers, (c) N.T. and Christian writers and, especially, (d) writers outside these great streams of thought. If investigation has shewn that the Prophets of Israel considered animal sacrifice to be not of the essence of religion—or that they even looked askance at the whole sacrificial institution—it is possible that such an attitude is not more revolutionary than that of many other religiously minded thinkers of ancient times.

A. HEBREW

(i) The Rechabites (Jer. xxxv, cf. 2 Ki. x. 15, 16), who are known to have lived for some two centuries of the period between the time of Moses and that of Jeremiah, were of the nature of a *sect* within the Hebrew ecclesiastical system. For the members of this party Jeremiah had the highest praise. As they were cut off by the principles of their clan from the cultivation of the soil, it is difficult for us to suppose that they can have taken part in

---

feeling of sin? What has been called "the universality of the sacrificial instinct" has an interest for us to-day so far as it implies that in all religions there have been men, however few among their fellow-worshippers, who possessed a sense of the reality of God, of His demand upon their conscience, and of the true nature of sin. The barrier between God and man caused by guilt was bridged over by some "atonement". Significant, however, it is that the notable promises of Divine forgiveness which are the glory of the O.T. are found not in the Law but in the Prophets. Moreover these offers in the Prophets (with the doubtful exception of Isa. liii. 10) are never conditioned by, or even related to, the sacrificial system: see Isa. xxxviii. 17, lv. 7, Dan. ix. 9, Hos. xiv. 4, Jonah iii. 9, 10. Cf. also Pss. lxxxvi. 5, ciii. 3 a, 12. Were the Prophets right or wrong?

the sacrificial festivals of their fellow-countrymen, which were connected with the agricultural seasons. The inference may be drawn that the use of sacrifice was not held to be necessary for qualification as a good Israelite; indeed, perhaps, there was already in Israel a tradition against sacrifice. *Cf.* the note on v. 25, p. 339.

(ii) The Jewish party known as the Essenes arose *c.* 140 B.C. and held indeed a sufficiently unconventional set of views. According to Philo (or rather his interesting interpolator) 'in their devotion to the service of God, they did not sacrifice animals, but made their own minds reverent' (*Quod Omnis Probus Liber,* §§ 12, 13, ii. p. 457, Mangey). Josephus, in his full account of the Essenes contained in *Jewish War,* II. viii. 2–13, does not refer to their attitude towards the question of sacrifice; but in *Antiquities,* XVIII. i. 5, he makes the following statement: "When they send what they have dedicated to God into the temple, they do not[1] offer sacrifices, because they have more pure lustrations of their own; on which account they are excluded from the common court of the temple, but offer their sacrifices themselves; yet is their course of life better than that of other men".

(iii) Philo (*fl.* A.D. 39), the Jew of Alexandria, in *De Sacrificantibus* (v. § 272 C.-W., ii. p. 253 Mangey), declares "they who bring *themselves* are offering...the most excellent sacrifice".

(iv) According to Justin (A.D. 140), the Jews of the Dispersion (cut off from all but occasional sacrifices at Jerusalem) applied Mal. i. 11 to shew the efficacy of prayer apart from sacrifice (*Dial.* xxii, lxviii).

B. EARLY RABBINICAL TEACHERS

The attitude of Jewish thought towards sacrifices after they had become impossible through the destruction of the Jerusalem Temple in A.D. 70 is represented by the following extracts from the literature of the 1st and 2nd cent. A.D.

(i) Johanan ben Zakkai (who probably was only a few years junior to St Paul) maintained that "*works of benevolence*[2] have atoning powers as great as those of sacrifice", citing Hos. vi. 6, Prov. xvi. 6, Ps. lxxxix. 2 (M.T. *v.* 3).

---

[1] *I.e.*, presumably, their non-animal offerings. The text quoted (Whiston, *cf.* Niese) seems more likely than "...they offer their sacrifices, under special condition of purity that they observe, on which account they are excluded..." (edn Margoliouth).

[2] *gᵉmîlûth ḥãsãdhîm.* Abrahams gives as an equivalent, "'the rendering of loving services'—services of money and yet more of person (T.B. *Sukkah,* 49 *b*)", *Studies in Pharisaism and the Gospels,* II. p. 197. This scholar points out that Johanan's opinion was not improvised after A.D. 70. While the altar still stood, Johanan had said. 'Just as the sin-offering atones for Israel, so also almsgiving (*sᵉdhãqãh*) atones for the nations', T.B *Baba Bathra,* 10 *b ad fin.* (p. 198, and *cf.* vol. I of the same work, p. 128) With Johanan's position is to be compared that of the author of Ep. Hebrews (xiii. 16 *b*, cited below, p. 344).

(ii) R. Akiba (born c. A.D. 50), in words quoted in the closing lines of the Mishnah Tractate, *Yoma*[1] viii. 9 (T.B. 85 b), ignores the need for atoning sacrifices thus: "Happy are ye, O Israel. Before whom do ye cleanse yourselves, and who cleanseth you? Your Father who is in heaven, as it is said: 'And I will sprinkle clean water upon you, and ye shall be clean: from all your filthiness, and from all your idols, will I cleanse you. A new heart also will I give you, and a new spirit will I put within you' (Ezek. xxxvi. 26). Moreover, it says: 'The LORD is the Hope—*miqweh*—of Israel' (Jer. xiv. 8). As the gathering[2] (of water)—also *miqweh* in Hebrew—cleanseth the unclean, so does the Holy One, blessed be He, cleanse Israel".

(iii) In the second-century *P*sikta d* Rab. Kahana*, xxv. 158 b (Buber), occurs this passage (cf. Jer. Talm. *Makkoth*, ch. ii. 6 f, 31 d ad fin.):[3] "*Wisdom* (i.e. the Wisdom Literature) when asked, 'What shall be the punishment of the sinner?' replies, 'Evil pursueth sinners' (Prov. xiii. 21). *Prophecy*, when asked, 'What shall be the punishment of the sinner?' replies, 'The soul that sinneth, it shall die' (Ezek. xviii. 4). *The Law*, when asked, 'What shall be done with the sinner?' replies, 'Let him bring a guilt-offering and the priest shall atone for him' (Lev. i. 4). *God Himself*, when asked, 'What shall be done with the sinner?' replies, 'Let him repent, and he will be atoned for: is it not said, Good and upright is the Lord, therefore will He teach sinners in the way of repentance (Ps. xxv. 8)? For, my children, what do I require of you? Seek me and live'".

C. THE N.T. AND CHRISTIAN WRITERS

(i) According to St Matt. ix. 13, xii. 7, our Lord quoted Hos. vi. 6, 'I desire mercy, and not sacrifice'.

(ii) Rom. xii. 1: 'I beseech you...to present your bodies a living *sacrifice*, holy, acceptable to God, which is your reasonable (R.V. marg. 'spiritual') *service*' (θυσίαν...λογικὴν λατρείαν).

(iii) 1 Pet. ii. 5: 'to offer up *spiritual sacrifices*,[4] acceptable to God, through Jesus Christ' (πνευματικὰς θυσίας). Cf. also Heb. xiii. 15, 16.

---

[1] The Day of Atonement.

[2] As e.g. in Gen. i. 10. Such a word-play as R. Akiba here makes is very popular in Jewish literature.

[3] It should be said that the last clause (commencing "For, my children") is missing from the parallel passages in the Jerusalem Talmud and the *Yalkuṭ* on Tehillim, § 702. Buber prints it in the *Pesiḳta*, but with a note. A. Wünsche (p. 227) translates it complete. In any event, the clause occurs substantially at the beginning of the chapter in the *Pesiḳta*. In both the *Pesiḳta* and *Yalkuṭ* the contrast between God's "reply" and that of the Law is striking.

[4] The idea of a *bloodless* so-called 'sacrifice' *in heaven* occurs in *Test. Levi*, iii. 5, 6 (c. 120 B.C. unless addition): "...The archangels who minister and make propitiation to the Lord for all the sins of ignorance of the righteous, offering to the Lord a sweet smelling savour, a spiritual and non-bloody sacrifice" (λογικὴν καὶ ἀναίμακτον θυσίαν). So runs Charles' '*a*' text; '*β*' seems more original with its προσφοράν ('offering'). In the course of time certain Christian liturgies expressing 'sacrificial' doctrine took up this phrase and applied it to the Eucharist: Brightman, *Liturgies E. and W.* I. p. 163, l. 29 (cf. p. 329, l. 13); *Ap. Constitutions*, II. 25. 7; VIII. 5. 7; 46. 15.

(iv) In Heb. **x.** 4 it is boldly stated: 'It is impossible that the blood of bulls and goats should take away sins'.

Thus Hebrew and Christian teachers alike express the view that man can offer something to the Deity other, nay better, than sacrifices. Strictly speaking, however, none of the various alternatives suggested—good conduct, almsgiving, praise, prayer—should be given the name of 'sacrifice' (θυσία, Hebrew *zebhah*, which means 'ritual slaughtering').

(v) *The Odes of Solomon* are not in the main stream of orthodox Church tradition. Possibly some of them were adapted from non-Christian sources. Ode **xx** concerns sacrifice. Is the speaker an official of a congregation—Hebrew, pagan or Christian?

> "Priest of the Lord am I,
> Within His court I stand,
> To Him I offer sacrifice
> As He doth me command.
> Not as men serve the flesh
> Or in the world have part,
> His sacrifice is righteousness
> And purity of heart.
>
> Blameless present thy soul;
> Thy neighbour do not wrong;
> Deceive him not, nor take for thine
> What doth to him belong.
> His life is as thine own,
> Nor bought nor sold can be;
> His needs are thine, his weal and woe
> Entrusted are to thee".[1]

D. Writers, neither Hebrew nor Christian

(a) *Latin and Greek*

(i) *Persius Flaccus* (*ob. c.* A.D. 62), Sat. **II.** 73 (transl. G. G. Ramsay), says: "You slay an ox...nay, rather let us offer to the gods...a heart rightly attuned towards God and man; a mind pure in its inner depths, and a soul steeped in nobleness and honour. Give me these to offer in the temples, and a handful of corn shall win my prayer for me".

(ii) *Apollonius of Tyana.* According to Philostratus he claimed that he followed the example of Pythagoras, "who would not stain the altars with blood; nay, rather the honey-cake and frankincense and the hymn of praise, these they say were the offerings made to the gods by this man, who had come to know that they welcome such tribute more than they do the

---

[1] Poetical transl. of S. P. T. Prideaux (S.P.C.K.). H. Grimme believes (but without sufficient reason, so it would appear) that the present Syriac text of the Odes goes back to a *Hebrew* recension. This scholar actually suggests that in the original form of the above Ode, most of the ethical sentiments were lacking.

hecatombs and the knife laid on the sacrificial basket" (*Vita Apollonii*, I. 1). In the passage it is also said that Pythagoras refused either food or clothing of animal origin, as Apollonius also. Apollonius' words to Domitian are said by Philostratus to have been: "In all my actions I have at heart the salvation of mankind, yet I have never offered a sacrifice on their behalf, nor will I ever sacrifice anything, nor touch hallowed things in which there is blood, nor offer any prayer with my eyes fixed upon a knife or a sacrifice such as my accuser understands. It is no Scythian, my prince, that you have before you, nor a native of some savage and inhospitable land; nor did I ever mingle with Barbarians, for in that case I should have reformed even them and altered their sacrificial custom" (VIII. 7). One would suspect that the view of sacrifice presented is not uninfluenced by Apollonius' supposed contact with Indian religion; but in a work attributed to Apollonius, *Concerning Sacrifices*, quoted by Eusebius in *Praeparatio Evangelii*, IV. 13, objection is not confined to sacrifice of *animals*. To the One Supreme God (as distinct from the lesser deities) it is not fitting to offer even a cake or incense. "...But ever let a man approach Him only with that best of Words, that I mean which goeth not through the mouth, and so ask for benefits from the Best of Beings by means of the best thing within us; and this thing is Reason (νοῦς), a faculty needing no instrument. According to this, therefore, no sacrifices should be offered to the Great God Who is over All".[1]

On the other hand, the philosophic Marcus Aurelius made a great point of the sacrifice of bullocks.

(iii) *Hermetis Trismegisti Poemander* (? 2nd cent. A.D.), edn Parthey, cap. 13, par. 21: "To God I send spiritual sacrifices (λογικὰς θυσίας). O God, Thou art Father, Thou art Lord, Thou art Mind. Accept spiritual sacrifices which Thou desirest from me". It is not impossible that the theology and language of Hermes are at times influenced by Christianity, though it seems (to the present writer, at least) easier to prove his indebtedness to the LXX than to the N.T.

(b) Ancient Egyptian

(iv) In the *Instruction* for king Merikerē (who reigned in the second half of the 3rd millennium B.C.)[2] there is a sentence which expresses the same view as that of the Hebrew prophets, "More acceptable is the nature of one just of heart than the ox of him who doeth iniquity". The context of the saying is as follows. To begin with, the royal father makes a definite

---

[1] *Cf.* Prof. Burkitt (in *Eucharist and Sacrifice*, edn 1, 1921; edn 2, 1927) whose also are the above translations. On the general problems raised by the τὰ εἰς 'Απολλώνιον, see J. S. Phillimore, especially pp. i–lxxxvi.

[2] The translation given is that of Dr Alan Gardiner (*J.E.A.* I. pp. 20 ff.). The Golénischeff Petersburg Papyrus dates from the middle of the 15th cent. B.C. (the Eighteenth Dynasty), but Dr Gardiner holds that the composition (apart from considerable redactional alterations) was made about the time of the reign of the king whose utterances it purports to give. There is a translation in Erman-Blackman. See especially pp. 78, 79, 83.

appeal to his son to support the cult. "Make beautiful monuments for the God; that causeth to live the name of him who doeth it.... Frequent the shrine. Be discreet concerning the mysteries, enter into the sanctuary. Eat bread in the temple. Replenish the table of offerings, increase the loaves. Add to the daily sacrifices, for it is profitable to him who does so. Make firm thy monuments according as thou art rich. For a single day giveth for eternity, an hour makes beautiful for futurity". However, further on in the document, while the teacher leads up to a somewhat similar thought, the stress seems to be upon acts of "reverence" to the deity other than sacrificial offerings; and a statement is made, similar to those of the great Hebrew prophets, upon the comparative value of sacrifice and *righteousness*. "...Make stately thy castle in the West, adorn thy place in the Necropolis; *even as one who is just, as one who doeth Right. This is that whereon men's hearts repose. More acceptable is the nature of one just of heart than the ox of him who doeth iniquity.* Work unto God, that he may work for thee the like; with offerings to replenish the offering tables, and with carved inscription—it is what pointeth out thy name. God is cognizant of (the man) who worketh for him".

(c) *Indian*

(v) Animal sacrifices are still offered in India;[1] yet in general the Vaishnavites and many Saivites are against the institution. This aversion to animal sacrifice may be not unconnected with the belief in the transmigration of souls.

The following passages from the *Bhagavad-Gita* (? c. A.D. 100), though not a definite protest against animal sacrifice as is the philosophy of Apollonius, yet shew that Krishna is content with offerings of a trifling character, sacrifice of animals being by no means essential to acceptable worship. At least they supply a contrast to the teaching of Gen. iv. 3, 4. In *Gita* ix. 26, 27 Krishna says: "If one of earnest spirit set before Me with devotion a leaf, a flower, fruit or water, I enjoy this offering of devotion. Whatever be thy work, thine eating, thy sacrifice, thy gift, thy mortification, make thou of it an offering to Me, O son of Kunti". Again in xviii. 68-70, "He who in supreme devotion toward Me shall recite this supreme secret among my worshippers shall assuredly come to Me. None of men shall be more acceptable of works than he; none shall be dearer to Me on earth than he...I shall be worshipped with the offering of knowledge...". (Transl. Barnett.) *Cf.* Principal S. Cave, *Redemption, Hindu and Christian*, pp. 110, 111. To appreciate the significance of such views it is necessary only to bear in mind the extraordinary importance attaching to the scrupulous observance of sacrifice in the more ancient religion of the Vedas. "The sacrifices were more powerful than the gods. The gods could be pleased or displeased; if the sacrifices were duly performed the prayers were bound to be fulfilled. The utterance or chanting of the stanzas of the Vedic hymns

---

[1] Conspicuously in the worship of Durgā (=Kālī), which, in Bengal especially, forms a large part of popular religion.

with specially prescribed accents and modulations, the pouring of the
melted butter in the prescribed manner into the sacrificial fire, the husking
of rice in a particular way, the making and the exact placing of the cakes,
all the thousand details of rituals—often performed continuously for days,
months and years with rigorous exactness—was called a *yajna* (frequently
translated into English, 'sacrifice')....All the good things that the people
wanted...were believed to be secured through the performance of these
sacrifices". (S. N. Dasgupta, *Hindu Mysticism*, p. 6.) This writer points out
that Hindu mysticism came to hold that the same results might be
obtained through certain kinds of *meditation*. "Instead of the actual performance of a horse sacrifice,...one might as well think of the dawn as the
head of a horse, the sun as its eye, the wind as its life, *etc*...." (*ibid*. p. 19).

INDEXES

NOTE

n. = footnote.   nn. = footnotes.

An asterisk (*) refers the reader to that portion of a footnote
which is to be found upon the following page.

I. GENERAL INDEX

adamant, 225 n. 1
Adapa myth, 257
Adrammelech, 200, 301
agent, the Divine, 222, 255
Allah, 'Merciful', 307
alphabet, origin of, 281, 282 n. 1
altar, at high place, 7, 163, 164; of
    Jeroboam, 163; Moabite, 135; at
    Têma, 292; horns of altar, 164,
    292, 293
Amaziah, 227–30, 237–9, 310, 323,
    324
Ammon, 119, 129, 132–4
Amorites, Amurru, 143, 144 and n. 1
Amos, call of, 11, 12, 28 n. 3, 35–7, 93,
    98 n. 2, 101, 146, 147, 224, 235,
    236
character of, 9, 19, 167, 168, 172,
    220, 239, 307
date of the preaching of, 5, 34–41,
    113, 154, 155, 172, 271, 304, 316
disclaims being a prophet, 232, 233,
    311–14
fulfilment of the political predictions
    of, 102, 103, 123, 126, 128, 129,
    131, 132, 134, 137, 139, 227
home of, 9, 10, 113, 130, 224, 231
importance of, 9, 12, 14, 18–22, 26
intercessions of, 221, 224, 226
name of, 10 and n. 4, 113, 229
occupation of, 10, 113, 161, 232,
    234
prophetic office, his conception of,
    18, 153, 155–8, 232, 233
religion, his conception of, 178, 180,
    181, 189, 198
religious ideas opposed by, 8, 23, 24,
    27–9, 138, 143, 168 ff., 194 ff., 253,
    294–6
scene and scope of the preaching of,
    3, 9, 10, 12–14, 150, 151, 163, 227,
    228, 236, 237, 255, 263, 265, 285
teaching of, 22–32, 141, 167, 168
visions of, 11, 18, 83–7, 91, 93, 98–
    101, 217 ff., 225, 239, 255 ff.

Amos, book of, additions to, vii, 139,
    156, 174, 190, 191, 200, 242, 253,
    260 n. 3, 282, 283, 301. *See also*
    Amos, book of, 'doxologies' *and*
    'epilogue'; oracles
anthropomorphisms in, 26, 80, 166,
    177, 255, 294, 301, 307, 310
anthropopathic language in, 195,
    222, 294 and n. 2
Aramaisms in, 65 n. 3, 147
'doxologies' of, 23, 31, 66, 176, 177,
    184, 185, 260, 261, 331, 332
'epilogue' to, 51, 64, 66–77, 265,
    269, 270, 274, 277, 319, 323
eschatology of, 29 n. 4, 30 n. 1, 31
    n. 2, 59–64, 246, 274
later influence of, 103, 104
literary problems of, vii, 65, 77, 311.
    See also Amos, book of, additions
    and 'doxologies' *and* 'epilogue'
literary style of, 65, 168
poetry of, 32–4, 115
scriptiones plenae in, 73
synopsis of, xvii, xviii
'Anath, 'Anath-beth-el, 294
Angela of Foligno, 87 n. 2
annihilation of Israel, 29, 31, 32, 68,
    69, 100, 146–9, 162, 239, 240, 252,
    256, 264, 268, 269, 324
anthropomorphisms, *see* Amos, book
    of
Aphek, 4 nn. 1 and 5
apocalyptists, 85, 86
apposition, 3rd *person* used, 167,
    183 n. 1
Arabah, the, 216, 217, 305, 306
Aram, the history of, 3–5, 102, 103,
    122
inscriptions of, *see* Index II
judgment on, 117–23, 132, 133,
    144 n. 2
use of the name, 117, 118
Arcturus, 185, 298
Armenia, 167. *See also* Urarṭu
Artemisia, 183

26

II. INDEX OF ANCIENT WRITERS AND DOCUMENTS

III. INDEX OF HEBREW WORDS

IV. INDEX OF BIBLICAL PASSAGES OUTSIDE AMOS